RESEARCH AND EVALUATION

in Education and Psychology

3

EDITION

RESEARCH AND EVALUATION

in Education and Psychology

Integrating Diversity With Quantitative, Qualitative, and Mixed Methods

3
EDITION

Donna M. Mertens
Gallaudet University

SAGE

Los Angeles | London | New Delhi
Singapore | Washington DC

For information:

SAGE Publications, Inc.
2455 Teller Road
Thousand Oaks, California 91320
E-mail: order@sagepub.com

SAGE Publications India Pvt. Ltd.
B 1/I 1 Mohan Cooperative
Industrial Area
Mathura Road, New Delhi 110 044
India

SAGE Publications Ltd.
1 Oliver's Yard
55 City Road
London, EC1Y 1SP
United Kingdom

SAGE Publications Asia-Pacific
Pte. Ltd.
33 Pekin Street #02-01
Far East Square
Singapore 048763

Printed in the United States of America

Library of Congress Cataloging-in-Publication Data

Mertens, Donna M.
Research and evaluation in education and psychology : integrating diversity with quantitative, qualitative, and mixed methods / Donna M. Mertens. -- 3rd ed.
p. cm.
Includes bibliographical references and index.
ISBN 978-1-4129-7190-4 (pbk.)
1. Education--Research--Methodology. 2. Psychology--Research--Methodology.
I. Title.
LB1028.M3964 2010
370.7′2—dc22 2009010779

This book is printed on acid-free paper.

10 11 12 13 10 9 8 7 6 5 4 3

Acquisitions Editor: Vicki Knight
Associate Editor: Sean Connelly
Editorial Assistant: Lauren Habib
Production Editor: Astrid Virding
Copy Editor: Taryn Bigelow
Typesetter: C&M Digitals (P) Ltd.
Proofreader: Dennis Webb
Indexer: Molly Hall
Cover Designer: Gail Buschman
Marketing Manager: Christy Guilbault

Brief Contents

Detailed Contents

Preface

When I studied about research in my graduate classes many years ago, only one approach to research was taught—a quantitative approach that emphasized closed-ended surveys and experimental designs. My basic statistics courses were taught in the agriculture department, with no emphasis on the messiness that enters into research when you study people compared to animals or types of fertilizers.

As I began conducting research studies myself in the messier world of people and educational and psychological policies and practices, I found that a piece of the puzzle was missing. I felt compelled to study the principles of qualitative approaches to research to get a more complete understanding of the phenomenon that I was researching. Later in my career, I began teaching at Gallaudet University and doing research for the deaf community. At this time, I began to search for approaches to research that could more accurately capture the experiences of people who were not exactly in the mainstream of society.

The idea for a different way of looking at research actually emanated from my work as a teacher of educational psychology. I came across Carol Gilligan's (1982) book *In a Different Voice,* in which she made the point that Kohlberg's theory of moral development had been developed based on data collected only from boys and young men. To further our understanding of the process of moral development, Gilligan explored responses to moral dilemmas by a group of females. Thus, Gilligan's work planted the seed that research needed to include people of both genders and that perspectives might be different for males and females on important, fundamental developmental issues.

Reading Gilligan's work led me to seek out other researchers who approached their work from a feminist perspective (e.g., Reinharz, 1992). I was especially interested in exploring the question, what does it mean to conduct research from a feminist perspective? Having worked with deaf people for many years, I could immediately see many parallels between the feminists' statements concerning discrimination and oppression based on gender and the experiences of people with disabilities. Other important sources of information for me were the writings of racial and ethnic minorities on more culturally sensitive approaches to research (e.g., Stanfield & Dennis, 1993).

As I struggled to put the pieces of the puzzle together, I found the organizing framework that I was seeking in the work of Patti Lather (1992) and Guba and Lincoln (1994) in their discussion of paradigms of research. They make clear that researchers' views of the world (i.e., their chosen paradigms) underlie their choices of research approaches. It is not simply a choice of method: Should I use quantitative or qualitative approaches to research, or should I mix the methods? Researchers make methodological choices based on their assumptions about reality and the nature of knowledge that are either implicitly present or explicitly acknowledged.

I am gratified to see that in the period of time since the first edition and the third edition of this text that there has been an amazing growth in the recognition of and discussions about diverse paradigms, theories, methodologies, and voices represented in the research and evaluation communities. In Chapter 1, I address some of the developments in the field in terms of publications and actions taken by professional associations that have made issues of social justice and cultural relevance more visible.

The goal of this book is to guide researchers in identifying their own assumptions and examining for themselves the implications of choices about research methodology based on those assumptions. It is my position that the newer paradigms add to our understanding of how to conduct more valid research. They should not be viewed as replacements for the older approaches to research. As a research community (whether we create or use research), we should be constantly building on the information we have from the past. If we know some things about how to conduct surveys from past experience, it is not wise to throw that out just because those learnings came from the original paradigm of research. If we can learn about how to conduct better surveys from feminists, racial and ethnic minorities, people with disabilities, and their advocates, then we should listen to what they are saying. *I believe that knowledge is cumulative and we learn by listening.*

Organization of This Book

This book is organized according to the logic of conducting a research study. Researchers must first examine their underlying assumptions about the nature of reality and knowledge to make sensible decisions about all of the other steps in the research process. Chapter 1 contains an explanation of the major research paradigms and their associated assumptions. Students who understand the research paradigms and their assumptions will not only be prepared to make methodological decisions about their own research, they will also be prepared to engage meaningfully in the debates in the research community about the most appropriate ways to approach the business of research. In addition, the topic of ethics is discussed in Chapter 1 as a fundamental principle that researchers must keep in the front of their minds as they begin to walk down the research road. Ethical issues are integrated into all of the chapters because they are of central concern throughout the research process.

Chapter 2 provides an overview of program evaluation as a special context for systematic inquiry. Its placement here is meant to underscore the transferability of social science research methods in evaluation, while still recognizing the uniqueness of the context within which evaluation is conducted.

In Chapter 3, the nuts and bolts of conducting a literature review and formulating a research problem are explained. This chapter has value for all students of research, whether they are preparing to conduct their own research or if they view themselves as consumers of research. Even students whose current self-perceptions are that they will use only the research that others produce may find that in future years they will be involved in a research team. This text will prepare them to participate in a meaningful way on such a team.

A variety of approaches to systematic inquiry are explained in Chapters 4 through 10, including experimental and quasi-experimental research, causal comparative and correlational research, survey methods, single-case research, qualitative methods, history and narrative study of lives, and mixed methods research. Although the book is somewhat oriented to a step-by-step process of how to do research, each chapter also contains perspectives from the four major paradigms, along with a discussion of issues that are controversial, depending on one's worldview. The final three chapters help the student complete the research process.

In Chapter 11, issues of the definition and selection of samples are explained, along with specific ethical concerns when working with human beings in a research context. Quantitative, qualitative, and mixed methods for data collection strategies are discussed in Chapter 12, along with standards for judging the quality of the data collected from a variety of perspectives. In Chapter 13, quantitative, qualitative, and mixed methods choices for data analysis are presented, and issues related to data interpretation and reporting of research results are discussed. In that chapter, students are also instructed in how to write a research plan, including a management plan and a budget for research that they might propose for thesis or dissertation requirements or for external funding.

Pedagogical Features

Many pedagogical features are to be found in this text. First, at the beginning of each chapter, students are given a list of the main ideas contained in that chapter. This can be used as an advance organizer for the students, and as an outline for students to keep themselves situated as they move through the complex process of learning about research. There is a summary presented at the end of each chapter to recapitulate the major points.

Each chapter contains many electronic resources that are available for researchers and evaluators to use from the Internet. These are available at a Web site especially constructed for this text—http://www.sagepub.com/mertensstudy. In many chapters, specific research studies are summarized, providing a realistic context for the discussion of the points throughout the chapter. Readers can see examples of what they can access at the Web site by looking in the inside front cover of this book. There are both full-length research studies and Web-based resources that are mentioned in each chapter. In addition, many chapters contain step-by-step processes for conducting a specific part of the research process. In every chapter, perspectives from the major paradigms are included as they relate to that chapter's topic, along with discussion of controversies that exist within the broader research community.

Questions for critical analysis are included in each chapter that students can apply in the critical analysis of extant research studies, as well as in the critical evaluation of their own planned research processes. Each chapter contains opportunities for "Extending Your Thinking" through questions for discussion and activities for application, thus providing students with an opportunity to further their understandings of the concepts presented in that chapter.

Finally, an outline for the preparation of a research proposal is contained in the appendix and can be used by those students who will be preparing a research proposal to meet course requirements, for the purpose of completing a thesis or dissertation, or for requesting funds to support research.

Changes in the Third Edition

The changes in the third edition reflect a growth in understandings of doing research in culturally complex communities that has emerged over the last few years, as well as the flourishing of electronic resources available to researchers. One major change that occurred between the first and second editions is that the term *emancipatory* as a label for one of the major paradigms in the first edition was changed to *transformative*. When writing the first edition of this text, I struggled to find the appropriate term as an umbrella for the many approaches that address issues of cultural complexity specifically. The term *transformative* is closer conceptually to the purpose of research and evaluation conducted from this paradigmatic perspective, and therefore I have chosen to use it throughout the second and third editions of the text. I have also included more examples from other countries to enhance the reader's understandings of international applications of research and evaluation.

More examples are drawn from program evaluation as a way of enhancing the usefulness of the entire text for the purposes of planning and conducting evaluations. This edition also expands information about mixed methods approaches in the chapter on mixed methods research, as well as in the chapters on sampling, data collection, and data analysis. The addition of many new electronic resources in the chapters is supported by the Web page (http://www.sagepub.com/mertensstudy) that gives the readers access to full text versions of many studies that are mentioned in the book, as well as to Web-based resources that appear in each chapter.

This book is designed for the advanced undergraduate student, master's students, and beginning doctoral students in psychology, education, and educational psychology. It can be used by those who will plan and conduct research, as well as by those who see their main goal as learning to locate, read, and critically evaluate research. Students will use the book differently, depending on their ultimate goal—to be an independent producer of research, a member of a research team, or a consumer of research. For students in the latter two categories, this book is quite comprehensive and could be used as a stand-alone text.

For advanced students who are preparing to conduct independent research, additional course work and resources are necessary. This book provides the foundation for making decisions about what additional study would be necessary. For example, students may need additional course work in statistics or psychometrics, because these topics are discussed at a conceptual level rather than in terms of "how to do it."

References are cited throughout the text that would lead to more depth in specific methodologies, such as survey research or focus groups. Many researchers who teach qualitative approaches to research believe that students should have a mentor to teach them to conduct fieldwork. These are ideas for expanding a student's expertise in different aspects of research once they have acquired the foundational information to guide them in the most appropriate directions.

Acknowledgments

Many people helped me through the years that this book has been in process. I want to thank the members of my professional organizations, especially Pauline Ginsberg, Martin Sullivan, and Katrina Bledsoe, because they have inspired me through their own work in creating more inclusive and transformative models of research.

I also want to thank the faculty members and graduate students at Gallaudet University who helped me in so many ways, especially Kay Meadow-Orlans, Marilyn Sass-Lehrer, Heidi Holmes, Raychelle Harris, and Amy Wilson. My thanks go also to the many graduate students who attended my classes and challenged, encouraged, and inspired me to produce a textbook that contained representation of the voices of struggling groups. I also thank Katherine Breene, Glenda Mobley, Esther King, and Sarah Houge for clerical support.

For their careful and thorough reviews, I wish to thank the following: Dorothy Ettling, Christine Nagy, James Ward, and Edward W. Wolfe, as well as Tracie Costantino, University of Georgia; Geni Cowan, California State University, Sacramento; Eagle Desert Moon, California State University, Northridge; Diane McNally Forsyth; Winona State University – Rochester Center; Michael G. Gunzenhauser, University of Pittsburgh; Barbara J. Helms, Education Development Center, Inc., Newton, MA; Lê Xuân Hy, Seattle University; Ryan J. Kettler, Peabody College at Vanderbilt University; and Charles A. Maher, Rutgers University. I want to continue to thank Lisa Cuevas, the editor at Sage for the second edition, and her predecessor, C. Deborah Laughton at Sage, who guided me through the first edition with her belief in me as a professional and a friend. Special thanks to Vicki Knight, the Sage acquisitions editor, who worked with me through the preparation of the third edition, offering good humor—often at a good meal that we shared; Sean Connelly, Associate Editor; Lauren Habib, Editorial Assistant; Stephanie Adams, Books Marketing Manager; Tina Papatsos, Journals Marketing Manager; Laureen Gleason, Production Editor Supervisor; Astrid Virding, Senior Project Editor; and Taryn Bigelow, Copy Editor.

I want to save my warmest thanks for my sons, Nathan (age 20) and Jeffrey (age 17), for accepting the sacrifices a family inevitably experiences when "Mom" is writing a book. I am inspired to try to make the world a better place because of the magic I find in the faces of my children.

About the Author

Donna M. Mertens is Professor in the Department of Educational Foundations and Research at Gallaudet University. She teaches research methods and program evaluation to deaf and hearing students at the MA and PhD levels.

She conducts research and evaluation studies on such topics as improvement of special education services in international settings, planning for the inclusion of students with disabilities in neighborhood schools, enhancing the educational experiences of students with disabilities, preventing sexual abuse in residential schools for deaf students, improving access to the court systems for deaf and hard-of-hearing people, and improving the preparation of teachers of the deaf through appropriate use of instructional technology. Her research focuses on improving methods of inquiry by integrating the perspectives of those who have experienced oppression in our society. She draws on the writings of feminists, racial and ethnic minorities, people with disabilities, as well as indigenous peoples who have addressed the issues of power and oppression and their implications for research methodology.

Dr. Mertens has made numerous presentations at the meetings of the American Educational Research Association, American Evaluation Association, Association for College Educators of the Deaf and Hard of Hearing, International Sociological Association, International Mixed Methods Conference, American Psychological Association, African Evaluation Association, Canadian Evaluation Society, Visitors Studies Association, and other organizations that explore these themes. She served as president and board member of the American Evaluation Association from 1997 to 2002 and as a member of the Board of Trustees for the International Organization for Cooperation in Evaluation, 2002–2003. She is the editor for the *Journal of Mixed Methods Research* (with Max Bergman as coeditor).

Her publications include three edited volumes, *Handbook of Social Research Ethics* (coedited with Pauline Ginsberg, 2009), *Creative Ideas for Teaching Evaluation* (1989), and *Research and Inequality* (coedited with Carole Truman and Beth Humphries, 2000), and several authored books, including *Transformative Research and Evaluation* (2009), *Research and Evaluation Methods in Special Education* (coauthored with John McLaughlin, 2004), and *Parents and Their Deaf Children* (coauthored with Kay Meadow-Orlans and Marilyn Sass Lehrer, 2003). She also publishes many chapters and articles in edited volumes, encyclopedias, handbooks, and journals, such as *Journal of Mixed Methods Research, Qualitative Social Work, Eye on Psi Chi, Educational Researcher, International Journal of Mixed Methods Research, New Directions for Program Evaluation, American Journal of Evaluation, American Annals of the Deaf, Studies in Educational Evaluation*, and *Educational Evaluation and Policy Analysis.*

In the late 1800s, the prevailing myth held that men were more intelligent than women. Mary Calkins, a psychologist, conducted experiments at Wellesley College in 1887 that demonstrated that women are just as intelligent as men.

—Furumoto, 1980

Which is better instructional practice for teaching reading to second- or third-grade Hispanic students with learning disabilities: a traditional basal approach with a high level of drill and practice or an interactive, conversational approach that consists of dialogue between the student and teacher? Echevarria's (1995) comparison of these two approaches indicated that children in both conditions were equally able to answer comprehension questions about what they read; however, the level of concept development was higher with the interactive, conversational approach.

Nearly half of American Indian students who enter kindergarten do not graduate from high school. In an extensive study of American Indian women who do graduate, Bowker (1993) reports that the single most important factor as to whether a girl stayed in school and graduated was the link with a caring, competent adult who not only modeled appropriate behaviors, but also encouraged the adolescent and served as an advocate when necessary.

1

An Introduction to Research

Why Bother?

Life is complex; the world is not perfect. Many different kinds of people live on this planet, and educators and psychologists do not know the best ways to educate or counsel many people who have a history of poor achievement in school and who suffer a poor quality of life in terms of low pay, poor working conditions, high rates of unemployment, and other social and psychological disadvantages. The brief descriptions of research findings presented at the beginning of this chapter illustrate the complexity of educational and psychological challenges that confront researchers in our society, and they provide a glimpse into the role that research can play in providing insights into how to change the life experiences of those who suffer discrimination and oppression.

This is not meant to imply that research in and of itself can solve all the world's problems, nor is it meant to suggest that all research must be oriented toward social action. There are methods for designing research that make it more likely to be useful to educators, psychologists, administrators, policymakers, parents, and students. Such applied social research is the focus of this text. There are also research studies (termed *basic research*) that do not attempt to have immediate application in a social setting. Basic research is not the focus of this text despite its potential for contribution to social transformation.

What Is Research?

Research is one of many different ways of knowing or understanding. It is different from other ways of knowing, such as insight, divine inspiration, and acceptance of authoritative dictates, in that it is a process of *systematic inquiry* that is designed to collect, analyze, interpret, and use *data*. Research is conducted for a variety of reasons, including to understand, describe, predict, or control an educational or psychological phenomenon or to empower individuals in such contexts.

The exact nature of the definition of research is influenced by the researcher's theoretical framework and by the importance that the researcher places on distinguishing research from other activities or different types of research from each other. For example, many students go to the Internet or the library and look up facts from a variety of sources and say that they are doing a research paper. Some journalists follow a similar search strategy and often include interviews with people close to the action that is the focus of a news report. The focus of this text is NOT on that type of "research." Rather, this text focuses on empirical research that is characterized as building on existing knowledge about a phenomenon. This base of knowledge (whether derived from scholarly literature or community interaction) is used to develop a research focus and questions and/or hypotheses, as well as systematic collection of data from selected participants. The data are analyzed, interpreted, and reported. Such empirical research is found in scholarly journals, although this is not the only source where empirical research can be found.

Two parallel genres of inquiry in the educational and psychological communities have grown side by side: research and program evaluation. At times, these two genres intersect; at other times, they follow very separate trajectories. The relationship between research and evaluation is not simplistic. Much of evaluation can look remarkably like research and vice versa. Both make use of systematic inquiry methods to collect, analyze, interpret, and use data to understand, describe, predict, control, or empower. Evaluation is more typically associated with the need for information for decision making in a specific setting, and research is more typically associated with generating new knowledge that can be transferred to other settings. In practice, a large area of overlap exists between evaluation and research. Hence, what students learn in their study of research has application in their understanding of evaluation as well. The contextual factors and approaches unique to evaluation are described in the next chapter so that readers who are interested in evaluation can use the methodological guidance in subsequent chapters to plan an evaluation study.

Extending Your Thinking: Definition of Research

One definition of research is provided in this text. Think about your own understanding of what it means to do research. Explore other definitions of research in other texts or through the Internet. Modify the definition provided or create a new definition that reflects your understanding of the meaning of the term *research*.

Research Terminology

Like most disciplines, researchers have their own jargon that has meanings different from everyday uses of the same terms. If you have studied research before, you might be familiar with these terms. However, it is almost impossible to talk about research without having at least a rudimentary understanding of these terms. Therefore, if you are new to the researcher's world, you should stop and review the terms and definitions presented in Box 1.1.

Box 1.1 Research Terminology: Definitions and Examples

1. *Quantitative/qualitative/mixed methods:* The description of these methods is the heart of this entire text. In quite simplistic terms, quantitative researchers collect numerical data; qualitative researchers collect words, pictures, and artifacts. Mixed methods researchers collect both types of data.

2. *Subject or participant or stakeholder:* The individual you are studying is the *subject* or *participant;* this is the person from whom you collect data. The term *subject* was used more frequently in the past and can still be seen in some journals. More recently, the term *participant* is used in recognition of the active role that human beings play in the research process as contributing participants. Hence, this is the term that is generally used in this text. Often, the participant in educational and psychological research is a student, client, teacher, administrator, or psychologist, but it could also be an animal or a textbook. For example, in Borman et al.'s (2007) study of school literacy, they had a total sample of 35 schools with 2,108 students who started in kindergarten and stayed in the same school for three years. NOTE: Stakeholder is a term that is sometimes used (more frequently in program evaluation) to indicate members of the community who have a "stake in the outcomes of the research." Stakeholder is usually more inclusive than the terms subject or participant because it can include those from whom data are collected, as well as administrators, staff, and others in the community who will be affected by the results of the inquiry.

3. *Independent variable and predictor variable:* The independent and predictor variables are the variables on which the groups in your research study differ, either because you have exposed them to different treatments (independent variable) or because of some inherent characteristics of the groups (predictor variable). When the researcher deliberately manipulates a treatment (e.g., introduces literacy training for one group but not the other), the treatment is called the *independent variable*. Common independent variables in education and psychology include variations in methods of teaching or therapy. If the researcher is interested in the effect of differences of an inherent characteristic, the variable is more frequently called a *predictor variable*. For example, in studies of gender differences, gender is the predictor variable.

(Continued)

Box 1.1 (Continued)

4. *Dependent variable and criterion variable:* The dependent or criterion variable is the variable that the researcher is interested in measuring to determine how it is different for groups with different experiences (dependent) or characteristics (criterion). The *dependent variable* gets its name because it depends on what the researcher does with the independent variable. The researcher manipulates an independent variable (treatment) and exposes groups to differing amounts or types of it and then measures a dependent variable to see if it is different for the different groups. When working with a predictor variable (inherent characteristic or nonmanipulated variable), the measurement of "effect" is called a *criterion variable.* Common dependent or criterion variables in education and psychology include academic achievement, social skills, personality measures, and income after leaving school. For example, in the Borman et al. (2007) study, the dependent variable was literacy skills as measured by the Woodcock Reading Mastery Test-Revised.

5. *Experimental and control groups:* In certain types of research, the researcher can divide the participants into two or more groups to test the effect of a specific treatment (independent variable). For example, a researcher might want to test the effect of providing social skills training to students with disabilities by comparing outcomes for students who receive such training with those who do not. The group that receives the training is called the *experimental group.* The comparison group that does not receive the training is called the *control group.* In true experimental research, participants are randomly assigned to conditions—that is, they have an equal and independent chance of being assigned to either the experimental or the control group. Borman et al. (2007) randomly assigned schools to experimental groups that implemented the Success for All treatment and compared them to control schools that did not implement that treatment. A researcher can study the effect of a treatment without manipulating it or comparing groups who do and do not receive it. This is commonly done in qualitative and descriptive research studies (Maxwell, 2004).

6. *Population and sample:* The *population* is the group to whom you want to apply your results. The *sample* is the group that you have chosen from your population from which to collect data. For example, researchers might have access to 3,000 students. Rather than collect data from all 3,000 students, they might choose 300 students to include in their study (10% sample).

7. *Generalizability and transferability: Generalizability* refers to the researcher's ability to generalize the results from the sample to the population from which it was drawn. The ability to generalize results depends on how representative the sample is of the population. The degree of generalizability can be discussed in statistical terms, depending on the type of sampling strategy that the researcher uses. For example, the researchers who select the 300 students might want to generalize their results to the 3,000 students in the population. In qualitative research, the researcher emphasizes the total context in which the research takes place to enable readers to make judgments as to the *transferability* of the study's results to their own situations.

8. *Statistically significant:* Statistical significance is important in studies in which comparisons between groups or estimations of sizes of relationships between variables are made. If groups are compared on a dependent variable (e.g., social adjustment or literacy skills), a test of statistical significance can be used to determine if the observed difference between the groups is too large to occur plausibly as a result of chance alone. On the basis of the laws of probability, a difference that is too large to attribute to chance is called *statistically significant.* Researchers in education and psychology will sometimes say that their results are statistically significant at the 0.05 or 0.01 level. These levels refer to the researchers' confidence that similar results would probably be obtained if the study were repeated using other samples drawn from the same population.
9. *Extraneous/lurking variables (also known as moderating or intervening variables):* Researchers are typically very interested in the effect of their independent (or predictor) variables on the dependent (or criterion) variables. But social phenomena are complex and are influenced by many variables other than those of central interest to the researchers. These other variables that can influence the effect of the independent or predictor variables are called *extraneous variables.* For example, a researcher might be very interested in testing the effectiveness of a new therapeutic or teaching approach. However, the participants might have varying degrees of enthusiasm for the different treatments. The counselors or teachers might be strongly wedded to the traditional approach, or they might be intrigued by the new ideas represented in your experimental treatment. Thus, it may be the extraneous variable of their enthusiasm that determines which approach produces the more desirable outcome rather than the approach itself. Other common extraneous variables can be associated with culture, gender, disability, ability, and ethnicity differences between groups.

Approach Taken in This Book

The main focus of this text is to examine, from a variety of philosophical and theoretical perspectives, the process of systematic inquiry that constitutes research and evaluation in education and psychology. The typical process for planning and conducting a research or evaluation study is displayed in Box 1.2. This process is rarely as linear as this figure suggests; it can be very iterative in nature. Although these steps are used to organize the information in this text, in actual practice, the researcher may take one step forward, three steps back, and then jump to Step 4, only to find it necessary to revisit Step 2.

In fact, the nonlinearity of planning and conducting research suggests that readers may choose to use this book in a nonlinear fashion. The first three chapters do provide an overview of the nature of research and evaluation and how to begin identifying a research topic. It would seem prudent, therefore, to begin with those chapters (although a reader may choose to skip the chapter on evaluation if that is not included in their course syllabus). If readers have a goal of designing a research proposal, they might start in the appendix to read about how to develop a research proposal and use that as a guide to deciding how to navigate through the rest of the text.

After that, readers might choose to read any of the subsequent chapters on specific research approaches (e.g., experimental design) and then complete their understanding of the process for that approach by reading the last three chapters on sampling, data collection and analysis, and reporting. Readers could then return to earlier chapters to learn about other approaches to research and build on what they learned in the first go-round with the text. Alternatively, readers who have a strong feeling that a specific research strategy is of interest to them could start with the chapter on that approach (e.g., survey research) and then jump to the last three chapters of the book.

Some research methods textbooks address quantitative research methods (research that measures variables in a quantifiable way) *or* qualitative research methods (research that captures holistic pictures using words). (These definitions are overly simplistic; they are expanded in later chapters.) An increasing number of books and journals have begun to focus on mixed methods research. In this book, I make the assumption that a reader needs to understand both quantitative and qualitative approaches to research before they move to mixed methods. Hence, mixed methods strategies are presented later in the text.

Box 1.2 Steps in the Research/Evaluation Process

Step 1:	Identify your own worldview and situate your work as research or evaluation (Chapters 1 and 2)
Step 2:	Problem sensing (Chapters 1–3)
Step 3:	Literature review; research questions (Chapter 3)
Step 4:	Identify design—quantitative, qualitative, or mixed (Chapters 4–10)
Step 5:	Identify and select sources of data (Chapter 11)
Step 6:	Identify and select data collection methods and instruments (Chapter 12)
Step 7:	Data analysis, reporting, and utilization (Chapter 13)
Step 8:	Identify future directions (Chapter 13)

This text sets the research methods within four major paradigms (ways of viewing the world), along with their respective philosophical assumptions. Two of these paradigms—postpositivist and constructivist—are commonly included in research methods texts. The transformative paradigm is somewhat of a newcomer in the research community, but is being more frequently recognized in research methods texts (e.g., Creswell, 2009; J. C. Greene, 2007; Mertens, 2009).

The pragmatic paradigm has emerged as one of the underlying philosophical frameworks for some advocates of mixed methods research (Morgan, 2007; Teddlie & Tashakkori, 2009). These four paradigms are explained in the next section on the history of research.

Why get tangled up in philosophy, theories, and politics? Why not just explain the methods? *Because doing so is very important.* It is true that there are a variety of viewpoints as to the importance of linking methodological choices to philosophical paradigms, and leaders in the field do not agree as to the need to acknowledge an underlying paradigm, nor do they agree on the role that such paradigms serve in the research process. The contrasting viewpoints with regard to the place of paradigms in the research design community range from Michael Patton's (2002) position that they are unnecessary and possibly handicapping to Thomas Schwandt's (2000) position that they are inescapable. See their comments below:

> My practical (and controversial) view is that one can learn to be a good interviewer or observer, and learn to make sense of the resulting data, without first engaging in deep epistemological reflection and philosophical study. Such reflection and study can be so inclined, but it is not a prerequisite for fieldwork. Indeed, it can be a hindrance. (M. Q. Patton, 2002, p. 69)

> The practice of social inquiry cannot be adequately defined as an atheoretical making that requires only methodological prowess. . . . As one engages in the "practical" activities of generating and interpreting data to answer questions about the meaning of what others are doing and saying and then transforming that understanding into public knowledge, one inevitably takes up "theoretical" concerns about what constitutes knowledge and how it is to be justified, about the nature and aim of social theorizing, and so forth. In sum, acting and thinking, practice and theory, are linked in a continuous process of critical reflection and transformation. (Schwandt, 2000, pp. 190–191)

Ladson-Billings (2000) takes an even stronger stance than Schwandt in asserting that the choice of a paradigm (and its associated epistemology or systems of knowing) represents a choice between hegemony and liberation. She recommends that the academy go beyond transformation to reconstruction, meaning that teaching, service, research, and scholarship would be equally valued and used in the service of furthering intellectual enrichment, social justice, social betterment, and equity (Ladson-Billings & Donnor, 2005, p. 295).

In the spirit of full disclosure of values held by researchers, it is my position as author of this text that a researcher's philosophical orientation has implications for every decision made in the research process, including the choice of method. It is true that many researchers proceed without an understanding of their paradigm or its associated philosophical assumptions. However, working without an awareness of our underlying philosophical assumptions does not mean that we do not have such assumptions, only that we are conducting research that rests on unexamined and unrecognized assumptions. Therefore, to plan and conduct your own research, read and critique the research of others, and join in the philosophical, theoretical, and methodological debates in the research community, you need to understand the prevailing paradigms, with their underlying philosophical assumptions.

Major Paradigms in Research: A Brief History of Research

A *paradigm* is a way of looking at the world. It is composed of certain philosophical assumptions that guide and direct thinking and action. Trying to categorize all educational and psychological research into a few paradigms is a complex and, perhaps, impossible task. Table 1.1 displays four of the major paradigms, along with a list of the variety of

Table 1.1 Labels Commonly Associated With Different Paradigms

Postpositivism	*Constructivist*	*Transformative*	*Pragmatic*
Experimental	Naturalistic	Critical theory	Mixed methods
Quasi-experimental	Phenomenological	Neo-Marxist	Mixed models
Correlational	Hermeneutic	Feminist theories	Participatory
Causal comparative	Symbolic interaction	Critical race theory	
Quantitative	Ethnographic	Freirean	
Randomized control trials	Qualitative	Participatory	
	Participatory action research	Emancipatory	
		Postcolonial/indigenous	
		Queer theory	
		Disability theories	
		Action research	

SOURCE: Adapted from Lather (1992) and Guba and Lincoln (1989, 2005).

terms used to describe each. I provide you with the alternative labels listed in Table 1.1 because you will find different labels used in different texts. For example, some authors use the label qualitative rather than constructivist for that paradigm; however, qualitative is a type of methodology, not a paradigm.

The four paradigms that appear in this book are based on an adaptation and extension of paradigms discussed by Lather (1992) and Guba and Lincoln (as depicted in their writings that span from 1994 to 2005). I adopted their use of the postpositivist and constructivist for the first two paradigms. In contrast to Guba and Lincoln's (2005) choice of "critical theory et al." to label a third paradigm, I chose to label this transformative. Theories provide frameworks for thinking about the interrelationships of constructs and are more limited in scope than paradigms; hence, critical theory is one theory that is appropriately included under the umbrella of the transformative paradigm. In the first edition of this text, I labeled the third column "emancipatory" because Lather labeled her third paradigm as emancipatory. However, I changed it in the second edition of this book (Mertens, 2005) to transformative to emphasize that the agency for change rests in the persons in the community working side by side with the researcher toward the goal of social transformation. Lather placed poststructuralism and postmodernism in yet a fifth paradigm, which she labeled *deconstructivist.* (See Box 1.3 for a brief explanation of postmodernism, poststructuralism, and deconstructivism.) Neither Lather nor Lincoln and Guba included the pragmatic paradigm. I include the pragmatic paradigm because some scholars in the field of mixed methods research use it as a philosophical basis for their work (Creswell, 2009; Morgan, 2007; Tashakkori & Teddlie, 2003). Guba and Lincoln (2005) suggest another paradigm called participatory, but to me this is a methodology that can be applied in various paradigms depending on the beliefs that guide the researcher; hence, I do not include it in the taxonomy of major paradigms.

Box 1.3 Postmodernism, Poststructuralism, and Deconstructivism

There is good news and bad news about postmodernism, poststructuralism, and deconstructivism—and both the good and bad news emanate from the basic tenet of these philosophical orientations, movements, or paradigms, that is, that definitive definitions of social phenomenon are not possible and by extension, definitive definitions of these three concepts are also not possible—otherwise the definer would violate the basic tenet. That being said, many authors who write about these topics begin with an explanation that their definitions of these terms are only one of many possible definitions, but it is necessary to use some words to explain what they mean, so the authors provide what they think is a useful definition. For example, Clegg and Slife (2009) write,

> From the postmodern viewpoint, any definition of anything, including the definition of postmodernism itself, is a value judgment, with ethical and even political implications. Another problem in defining postmodernism is that postmodernists (whoever these undefined entities are) resist the closed "totalizing" conceptions of things. They view such conceptions as inappropriate reductions of the real—stereotypes of the rich experience of whatever is being conceived or defined. (p. 23)

Crotty's (1998) explanation echoes this discomfort in defining postmodernism:

> Postmodernism refuses all semblance of the totalizing and essentialist orientations of modernist systems of thought. Where modernism purports to base itself on generalized, indubitable truths about the way things really are, postmodernism abandons the entire epistemological basis for any such claim to truth. Instead of espousing clarity, certitude, wholeness, and continuity, postmodernism commits itself to ambiguity, relativity, fragmentation, particularity, and discontinuity. (p. 185)

Hassan provides the following explanation of the ontological and epistemological implications of these terms:

> Deconstruction, decentering, disappearance, dissemination, demystification, discontinuity. . . . Such terms express an ontological rejection of the traditional full subject. . . . They express, too, an epistemological obsession with fragments or fractures, and a corresponding ideological commitment to minorities in politics, sex and language. (Hassan, cited in Wolin, 1992, p. 206, in Crotty, 1998, p. 192)

Scholars have ongoing debates about the relationship between postmodernism and poststructuralism; Crotty (1998) resolves this dilemma by saying that each informs the other. Poststructuralism is commensurate with postmodernism in the sense that its adherents reject the possibility of definitive truth. Foucault (1980), as a poststructuralist, extends this idea to focus on the role of language and

(Continued)

Box 1.3 (Continued)

power in creating realities, rather than thinking of reality as something that is there to be discovered. Derrida (1981) pushes the poststructuralist position to the point of deconstructing text, or, in other words, the reader has a responsibility to engage in a critical reading of text as an intervention, wrestling with multiple layers of meaning. St. Pierre (2000, 2002) describes deconstructivism as a process of engaging with text that analyzes how a "structure has been constructed, what holds it together, and what it produces" (St. Pierre, 2000, p. 482). This process makes visible previously silenced voices and the concomitant influences of dominant power structures as an act of resistance by the reader.

Despite the difficulties in pinning down definitions of postmodernism, poststructuralism, and deconstructivism, scholars from these orientations contribute to the debates of rigor in research in a number of ways. Readers who wish to pursue a deeper understanding of this philosophical orientation are invited to read the historical and contemporary references cited in this box.

Guba and Lincoln (2005) identify four basic belief systems characterized by the following questions that help define a paradigm:

1. The axiological question asks, "What is the nature of ethics?"
2. The ontological question asks, "What is the nature of reality?"
3. The epistemological question asks, "What is the nature of knowledge and the relationship between the knower and the would-be known?"
4. The methodological question asks, "How can the knower go about obtaining the desired knowledge and understandings?"

Four of the major paradigms in the research community are described in the next section. The lines between them are not altogether clear in practice. However, to guide their thinking and practice, researchers should be able to identify the worldview that most closely approximates their own. Answers to the paradigm-defining questions are summarized for each paradigm in Table 1.2.

Postpositivism

The dominant paradigms that guided early educational and psychological research were *positivism* and its successor *postpositivism*. Positivism is based on the rationalistic, empiricist philosophy that originated with Aristotle, Francis Bacon, John Locke, Auguste Comte, and Immanuel Kant. The underlying assumptions of positivism include the belief that the social world can be studied in the same way as the natural world, that there is a method for studying the social world that is value-free, and that explanations of a causal nature can be provided. Positivists held that the use of the scientific method allowed experimentation and measurement of what could be observed, with the goal of discovering

Table 1.2 Basic Beliefs Associated With the Major Paradigms

Basic Beliefs	*Postpositivism*	*Constructivism*	*Transformative*	*Pragmatic*[1]
Axiology (nature of ethical behavior)	Respect privacy; informed consent; minimize harm (beneficence); justice/equal opportunity	Balanced representation of views; raise participants' awareness; community rapport	Respect for cultural norms; beneficence is defined in terms of the promotion of human rights and increase in social justice; reciprocity	Gain knowledge in pursuit of desired ends as influenced by the researcher's values and politics
Ontology (nature of reality)	One reality; knowable within a specified level of probability	Multiple, socially constructed realities	Rejects cultural relativism; recognizes that various versions of reality are based on social positioning; conscious recognition of consequences of privileging versions of reality	Asserts that there is single reality and that all individuals have their own unique interpretation of reality
Epistemology (nature of knowledge; relation between knower and would-be known)	Objectivity is important; the researcher manipulates and observes in a dispassionate, objective manner	Interactive link between researcher and participants; values are made explicit; created findings	Interactive link between researcher and participants; knowledge is socially and historically situated; need to address issues of power and trust	Relationships in research are determined by what the researcher deems as appropriate to that particular study
Methodology (approach to systematic inquiry)	Quantitative (primarily); interventionist; decontextualized	Qualitative (primarily); hermeneutical; dialectical; contextual factors are described	Qualitative (dialogic), but quantitative and mixed methods can be used; contextual and historical factors are described, especially as they relate to oppression	Match methods to specific questions and purposes of research; mixed methods can be used as researcher works back and forth between various approaches.

SOURCE: Adapted from Guba & Lincoln (1994, 2005) and Morgan (2007).

general laws to describe constant relationships between variables. Positivists made claims that "scientific knowledge is utterly objective and that only scientific knowledge is valid, certain and accurate" (Crotty, 1998, p. 29). While the focus on empirical, objective data has some appeal, it falls short when applied to human behavior.

Because there is much about the human experience that is not observable but is still important (e.g., feeling, thinking), postpositivist psychologists came to reject the positivists' narrow view that what could be studied was limited to what could be observed, as well as to question the ability of researchers to establish generalizable laws as they applied to human behavior. Postpositivists still hold beliefs about the importance of objectivity and generalizability, but they suggest that researchers modify their claims to understandings of truth based on probability, rather than certainty. Research methodologists such as D. T. Campbell and Stanley (1963, 1966), T. D. Cook and Campbell (1979), and Shadish, Cook, and Campbell (2002) embraced postpositivism's assumptions.

An example of research conducted within the postpositivist paradigm is summarized in Sample Study 1.1. The study is summarized according to the main categories typically included in a report of research situated in this paradigm—that is, research problem, question, methods/design, participants, instruments and procedures, results/discussion, and conclusions. The researchers in the sample study, conducted by Borman et al. (2007), explicitly chose to operate within the postpositivist paradigm, which led them to use an experimental design in order to measure the effectiveness of a literacy development program (Success for All) because they wanted to avoid contamination of the results from extraneous variables such as inherent differences between schools that agreed to implement the program and schools that did not agree to implement it.

The answers to the paradigm-defining questions for postpositivism are as follows.

Axiology

No matter what paradigm a researcher uses, ethics in research should be an integral part of the research planning and implementation process, not viewed as an afterthought or a burden. Increased consciousness of the need for strict ethical guidelines for researchers occurs each time another atrocity is discovered under the guise of research. The Nazi's medical experiments, the CIA's experimentation with LSD, the Tuskegee experiments on Black men with syphilis, and the U.S. government's administration of radioactive substances to uninformed pregnant women stand as examples of the worst that humankind can do to each other. Ethical guidelines in research are needed to guard against such obvious atrocities as these; however, they are also needed to guard against less obvious, yet still harmful, effects of research.

In the postpositivist's view, ethics is intertwined with methodology in that the researcher has an ethical obligation to conduct "good" research. Good research in this paradigm means, "Intellectual honesty, the suppression of personal bias, careful collection and accurate reporting of data, and candid admission of the limits of the scientific reliability of empirical studies—these were essentially the only questions that could arise" (Jennings & Callahan, 1983, p. 6, as cited in Christians, 2005, p. 159).

Postpositivists are guided by the work of the National Commission for the Protection of Human Subjects of Biomedical and Behavioral Research (1978), which identified three ethical principles and six norms that should guide scientific research in the landmark report, *The Belmont Report*. The three ethical principles are as follows:

1. *Beneficence:* Maximizing good outcomes for science, humanity, and the individual research participants and minimizing or avoiding unnecessary risk, harm, or wrong

2. *Respect:* Treating people with respect and courtesy, including those who are not autonomous (e.g., small children, people who have mental retardation or senility)

3. *Justice:* Ensuring that those who bear the risk in the research are the ones who benefit from it; ensuring that the procedures are reasonable, nonexploitative, carefully considered, and fairly administered

Sample Study 1.1

Summary of a Postpositivist Research Study

Research Problem: The United States uses the National Assessment of Educational Progress (NAEP) to track academic performance of its students. National disparities in NAEP scores are evidenced on the basis of race/ethnicity (13% of African American, 16% of Hispanic, and 41% of Whites score at the proficient level), as well as on the basis of economic status (16% of students eligible for free lunch are proficient compared to 42% of noneligible students).

Research Question: "Does Success for All [a literacy development program] produce achievement effects for schools and students targeted by and exposed to the model's 3-year developmental literacy treatment?" (p. 706).[2]

Method/Design: A cluster randomized control trial was used to compare students who used the Success for All program over a three-year period from kindergarten to second grade with control students who did not receive the treatment. The design is called a cluster randomized design because schools (rather than individual students) were randomly assigned to treatment and control groups.

Participants: Forty-one schools in the urban Midwest and rural South were included in the first year of the study. By the third year, 35 schools remained in the study (18 experimental and 17 control). The treatment and control schools were matched on baseline demographics. The majority of the students were economically disadvantaged (72% were eligible for free lunch). Overall 56% of the sample was African American, 10% Hispanic, and 30% White. The final sample at the end of the third year consisted of 1,085 students in 18 treatment schools and 1,023 students in 17 control schools.

Instruments and Procedures: The Peabody Picture Vocabulary Test was given as a pretest; children whose home language was Spanish were given the Spanish version of this test. The third-year posttests were three subtests of the Revised Woodcock-Johnson Mastery Tests: Word Identification, Word Attack, and Passage Comprehension.

Results/Discussion: Hierarchical linear model analyses allowed researchers to test school-level and student-level effects. The results indicated a school-level effect that favored the treatment group on the three Year 3 measures. Student-level effects ranged from one-fifth to one-third of a standard deviation, meaning that they demonstrated between two and three months of additional learning as compared to the control group on the subtests.

Conclusions: The findings support a statistically significant improvement in literacy skills for children in diverse school settings under naturalistic implementation conditions. Success for All is a school-level intervention that requires commitment from leaders and teachers, as well as external support in the form of professional development and ongoing consultation.

SOURCE: Borman et al. (2007).

The six norms of scientific research are

1. Use of a *valid research design:* Faulty research is not useful to anyone and is not only a waste of time and money, but also cannot be conceived of as being ethical in that it does not contribute to the well-being of the participants.

2. The *researcher must be competent* to conduct the research.

3. *Consequences of the research must be identified:* Procedures must respect privacy, ensure confidentiality, maximize benefits, and minimize risks.

4. *The sample selection must be appropriate* for the purposes of the study, representative of the population to benefit from the study, and sufficient in number.

5. The participants must agree to participate in the study through *voluntary informed consent*—that is, without threat or undue inducement (voluntary), knowing what a reasonable person in the same situation would want to know before giving consent (informed), and explicitly agreeing to participate (consent).

6. The researcher must inform the participants *whether harm will be compensated.*

The topic of informed consent is discussed further in Chapter 11 on sampling. Additional information is provided there, including Web site URLs that relate to professional associations' codes of ethics and the United States federal government's requirements for protection of human subjects in research.

With specific reference to axiological beliefs that guide researchers in the postpositivist paradigm, Mark and Gamble (2009) explain the claims that underlie the choice of randomized experiments as ethical methods. The first claim relates to a condition in which it is important to establish cause and effect and that there is uncertainty as to the effects of a particular treatment. The second claim is that randomized experiments provide greater value in terms of demonstrating the efficacy of a treatment than is possible by other methods. Mark and Gamble (2009, p. 204) cite Henry (2009, p. 36) to further justify the ethics of using this approach: "Henry further contends that to achieve findings about program consequences that are 'as conclusive as possible,' the 'most conclusive and widely regarded means for producing findings that have these attributes are random assignment experiments.'" Mark and Gamble conclude, "a case can be made that good ethics justifies the use of research methods that will give the best answer about program effectiveness, as this may increase the likelihood of good outcomes especially for those initially disadvantaged" (p. 205).

Ontology

The positivists hold that one reality exists and that it is the researcher's job to discover that reality (naive realism) (Guba & Lincoln, 1994). The postpositivists concur that a reality does exist, but argue that it can be known only imperfectly because of the researcher's human limitations (critical realism) (Maxwell, 2004). Therefore, researchers can discover "reality" within a certain realm of probability. They cannot "prove" a theory, but they can make a stronger case by eliminating alternative explanations.

The ontological assumption in the Borman et al. (2007) research study exemplifies the postpositivist paradigm in that the researchers chose reading literacy as their variable of interest and used a quantitative measure of that variable to determine the level of literacy for the students in their study. They were aware of the need to eliminate alternative explanations—which they controlled by their design of the study, but this takes us into the realm of methodology, discussed later in this chapter. They were also able to apply statistics to their data to support their claim that the change in literacy skills was real, within a certain level of probability.

Epistemology

In early positivist thinking, the researcher and the participants in the study were assumed to be independent; that is, they did not influence each other (Lincoln & Guba, 2000). Postpositivists modified this belief by recognizing that the theories, hypotheses, and background knowledge held by the investigator can strongly influence what is observed (Reichardt & Rallis, 1994). This paradigm holds that objectivity in the sense that researchers do not allow their personal biases to influence the outcomes is the standard to strive for in research; thus the researcher should remain neutral to prevent values or biases from influencing the work by following prescribed procedures rigorously.

The epistemological assumption of the postpositivist paradigm is exemplified in the Borman et al. (2007) study in that the researchers used trained testers who were "unaware of students' experimental or control assignments. Testers who were recruited for the study were primarily graduate students" (p. 716). The testers were expected to follow exactly the same procedures for asking questions of the respondents and for recording their responses. To standardize the responses, the goal was to ask exactly the same questions, in the same way, to each of the students. The tests used a fixed-response format for the questions. The researchers checked the testers' performance to ensure that they were following the same procedures.

Methodology

As mentioned previously, positivists borrowed their experimental methods from the natural sciences. Postpositivists recognized that many of the assumptions required for rigorous application of the scientific method were difficult, if not impossible, to achieve in many educational and psychological research studies with people; therefore, quasi-experimental methods (methods that are sort of experimental, but not exactly) were developed (D. T. Campbell & Stanley, 1966; T. D. Cook & Campbell, 1979; Shadish, Cook, & Campbell, 2002). In other words, many times it is not possible to randomly assign people to conditions (as one can with plots of land for a study of fertilizers, for example); therefore, researchers devised modifications to the experimental methods of the natural sciences in order to apply them to people. Although qualitative methods can be used within this paradigm, quantitative methods tend to be predominant in postpositivist research.

A postpositivist approach to methodology is evident in the Borman et al. (2007) study in that the researchers used a randomized control experimental design that is associated with this paradigm. The researchers could not randomly assign students to conditions; however, they could randomly assign schools to conditions (experimental or control). The researchers summarized complex variables such as literacy skills and economic status (eligible for free lunch or not) into numeric scales. As mentioned previously, the researchers acknowledged the limitations of their study in that they did not include qualitative, contextual information such as teachers' and students' experiences with the program (although they did use qualitative data to discuss the extent of implementation of the treatment). Nor did they describe the differential effects within the treatment group, such as on the basis of type of disability.

Extending Your Thinking: The Postpositivist Paradigm

Identify a research study that exemplifies the postpositivist paradigm. Explain why this study represents this paradigm. What are the distinguishing characteristics that lead you to conclude that this study belongs to this paradigm (e.g., what are the underlying characteristics that define a research study in this paradigm)?

Constructivist Paradigm

Despite the recognition by postpositivists that facts are theory laden, other researchers questioned the underlying assumptions and methodology of that paradigm. Many different labels have been used for the constructivist paradigm, which can be seen from the sample list in Table 1.1. The constructivist label was chosen for this paradigm because it reflects one of the basic tenets of this theoretical paradigm, that is, that reality is socially constructed.

The constructivist paradigm grew out of the philosophy of Edmund Husserl's phenomenology and Wilhelm Dilthey's and other German philosophers' study of interpretive understanding called *hermeneutics* (Eichelberger, 1989). Hermeneutics is the study of interpretive understanding or meaning. Historians use the concept of hermeneutics in their discussion of interpreting historical documents to try to understand what the author was attempting to communicate within the time period and culture in which the documents were written. Constructivist researchers use the term more generally, seeing hermeneutics as a way to interpret the meaning of something from a certain standpoint or situation.[3] Clegg and Slife (2009, p. 26) further explain the concept of hermeneutics by citing the work of "Martin Heidegger (1927/1962) [who] argued that all meaning, including the meanings of research findings, is fundamentally interpretive. All knowledge, in this sense, is developed within a preexisting social milieu, ever interpreting and reinterpreting itself. This perspective is usually called hermeneutics." An example of a constructivist research study is presented in Sample Study 1.2.

The basic assumptions guiding the constructivist paradigm are that knowledge is socially constructed by people active in the research process, and that researchers should attempt to understand the complex world of lived experience from the point of view of those who live it (Schwandt, 2000). The constructivist paradigm emphasizes that research is a product of the values of researchers and cannot be independent of them. The answers to the paradigm-defining questions for the constructivist approach are as follows.

Axiology

Constructivist researchers (indeed almost all U.S.-based researchers, as well as most researchers located throughout the world) are expected to adhere to the basic principles of ethics found in *The Belmont Report* and in their professional associations' codes of ethics. However, constructivists provide a different slant on the meaning of ethics as compared to the postpositivists' noncontextual, nonsituational model that assumes that "a morally neutral, objective observer will the get facts right" (Christians, 2005, p. 148).

Sample Study 1.2

Summary of a Constructivist Research Study

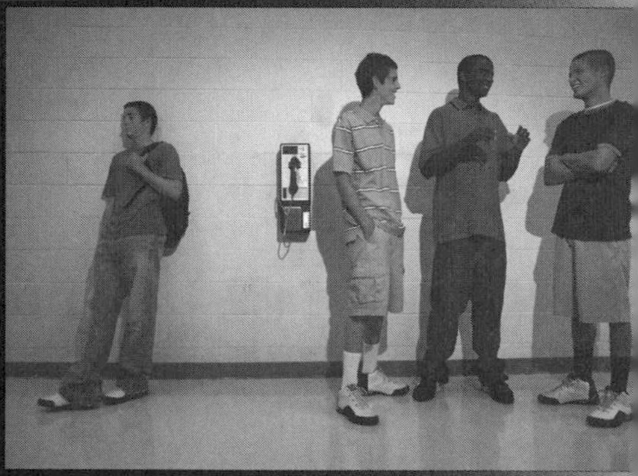

Research Problem: New pedagogical practices are needed to reach youth who are disengaged from learning because of challenges stemming from poverty, class, race, religion, linguistic and cultural heritage, or gender.

Research Questions: What do music teachers do to respond to and overcome challenges of re-engaging disaffected youth? "What is it that music teachers think they do in developing inclusive pedagogies in classroom contexts where young people are most at risk of exclusion?" (p. 63).

Method/Design: Burnard used a phenomenological case study approach that focused on ascertaining how teachers can affect student learning in a specific context with a specific group of people. The phenomenon under study was educational practices of teachers with disaffected students in three specific contexts (i.e., schools).

Participants: Schools that were performing poorly were selected based on national data on socioeconomic data and failing to meet national standards for achievement. Information from professional organizations and university partnerships was used to identify teachers within these schools who were known to work to engage disaffected learners through music education. Three secondary school music teachers participated in the study from three comprehensive schools in east and southeast regions of England.

Instruments and Procedures: Primary data collection consisted of two in-depth semistructured interviews with each teacher that lasted approximately two hours. Open-structured recall interviews made use of the school's music curriculum, students' work, and photographs as prompts during the interviews. The researcher spent one day observing each teacher in their music classes. However, the researcher limited her observations in the schools because all of the students were not willing to provide informed consent for videotaping in their classrooms.

Results: Demonstrating respect for students and recognition of the richness found in diverse backgrounds provided grounds for the teachers to relate to students who "have given up, who don't find school relevant let alone meaningful" (p. 67). One teacher engaged young people by designing creative performance projects that involved the students with musicians, composers, and performers from the community. "The visiting artists got us all talking in conversations about music, the arts, life . . . in which everyone feels safe to speak and all voices are respected" (p. 69). Another teacher used technology to engage learners through collaborative music making and sharing, as well as in media applications related to graphic art design.

Discussion: The three teachers demonstrated a deep commitment to meeting individual student's needs, holding their students to high standards of performance, and focusing on the development of feelings of self-worth and agency for the young people. The pedagogical activities ranged from "music participation, and ICT [Information and Communication Technology] based learning, to the high-status creative project or event-based activities that were believed to engender a redemptive self-respect in those who felt otherwise excluded from society" (p. 72).

SOURCE: Burnard (2008).

Early on, Guba and Lincoln (1989) developed a framework for ethical practice of qualitative research based on a revised understanding of the researcher-researched relationship. To this end, they put forth the criteria for rigor as trustworthiness and authenticity, including balance or fairness (inclusive representation of stakeholders in the process of the research), ontological authenticity (make respondents aware of their constructions of reality), educative authenticity (educate others of the realities experienced by all stakeholder groups), catalytic authenticity (enable stakeholders to take action on their own behalf), and tactical authenticity (training participants how to act on their own behalf). Lincoln (2009) reinforced these as appropriate criteria for constructivists and added reflexivity, rapport, and reciprocity as additional criteria that have emerged, and noted that along with their emergence have come additional ethical tensions. How can a researcher from a group imbued with unearned privileges by virtue of social class, language, race/ethnicity, gender, or other attributes establish rapport in an ethical manner with people who do not share such privileges? Constructivists also borrow notions of ethics from feminists in the form of combining theories of caring and justice as holding potential to address issues of social justice in ways that are both respectful of the human relations between researchers and participants, as well as to enhance the furtherance of social justice from the research (Christians, 2005; Denzin, 2003; Lincoln, 2009; Noddings, 2003). Hence, constructivists' writings on ethical principles are moving closer to alignment with those of transformative researchers.

Ontology

Reality is socially constructed. Therefore, multiple mental constructions can be apprehended, some of which may be in conflict with each other, and perceptions of reality may change throughout the process of the study. For example, the concepts of disability, feminism, and minority are socially constructed phenomena that mean different things to different people.

Schwandt (2000) describes what he calls "everyday" constructivist thinking in this way:

> In a fairly unremarkable sense, we are all constructivists if we believe that the mind is active in the construction of knowledge. Most of us would agree that knowing is not passive—a simple imprinting of sense data on the mind—but active; mind does something with those impressions, at the very least forms abstractions or concepts. In this sense, constructivism means that human beings do not find or discover knowledge so much as construct or make it. (p. 197)

But constructivist researchers go one step further by rejecting the notion that there is an objective reality that can be known and taking the stance that the researcher's goal is to understand the multiple social constructions of meaning and knowledge.

In terms of ontology, the Burnard (2008) study (Sample Study 1.2) exemplifies the constructivist paradigm in a number of ways. First, the researcher allowed the concepts of importance in the study to emerge as they had been constructed by the participants. Rather than studying the implementation of a defined curriculum or pedagogical approach, she studied pedagogical practices used to engage disaffected youth not as she conceptualized them but, rather, as they were constructed by the teachers in the study. She asked the question, "How [do] music teachers working with disengaged students—whose difficulties with learning in school are expressed through disruption, disengagement and withdrawal—promote inclusiveness through the development of particular pedagogic practices?...What is it that teachers think they do in developing inclusive pedagogies in classroom contexts where young people are most at risk of exclusion?" (pp. 62–63).

The author's ontological assumptions are also evidenced in her discussion of her decision to use the constructivist approach. Burnard acknowledges that her report of the three teachers' experiences does not result in a definitive capture of a reality that can be generalized to a larger population. Rather, she argues that these teachers' accounts shed light on teaching strategies that can be adapted by other teachers (whether of music or other subjects) in order to reach disaffected learners.

Epistemology

The inquirer and the inquired-into are interlocked in an interactive process; each influences the other. The constructivist therefore opts for a more personal, interactive mode of data collection. The concept of objectivity that is prominent in the postpositivist paradigm is replaced by confirmability in the constructivist paradigm (Lincoln & Guba, 2000). The assumption is made that data, interpretations, and outcomes are rooted in contexts and persons apart from the researchers and are not figments of their imagination. Data can be tracked to their sources, and the logic used to assemble interpretations can be made explicit in the narrative. For example, rather than having graduate students who were not personally familiar with the teachers collect data, Burnard (2008) visited the schools and spent a day with each teacher, observing them with their students prior to formal interviewing. Also, Burnard does not make a claim of objectivity in the sense of personal distance from the teachers in her study. Rather, she supported the validity of her claims by the multiple sources of data that she used and the multiple methods that she used to collect the data. She also provided multiple examples of direct quotations from the teachers to support the inferences that she drew from the data.

Methodology

Qualitative methods such as interviews, observations, and document reviews are predominant in this paradigm. These are applied in correspondence with the assumption about the social construction of reality in that research can be conducted only through interaction between and among investigator and respondents (Lincoln & Guba, 2000). This interactive approach is sometimes described as hermeneutical and dialectical in that efforts are made to obtain multiple perspectives that yield better interpretations of meanings (hermeneutics) that are compared and contrasted through a dialectical interchange involving the juxtaposition of conflicting ideas, forcing reconsideration of previous positions.

Eichelberger (1989) describes the methodological work of the constructivist (hermeneutical) researcher as follows:

> They want to know what meaning people attribute to activities...and how that related to their behavior. These researchers are much *clearer* about the fact that they are *constructing* the "reality" on the basis of the interpretations of data with the help of the participants who provided the data in the study. They often carry out their research much as anthropologists do in their studies of culture. They do a great deal of observation, read documents produced by members of the groups being studied, do extensive formal and informal interviewing, and develop classifications and descriptions that represent the beliefs of the various groups. (p. 9)

The methodological implication of having multiple realities is that the research questions cannot be definitively established before the study begins; rather, they will evolve and change as the study progresses. In addition, the perceptions of a variety of types of persons must be sought. For example, in special education research, the meaning of total inclusion needs to be explored as it has been constructed by regular and special education administrators and teachers, parents who have children with and without disabilities, and students with differing types and severity of disabilities (Mertens & McLaughlin, 2004). Finally, the constructivist researcher must provide information about the backgrounds of the participants and the contexts in which they are being studied.

Some of the methodological strategies that were used in the Burnard (2008) study of music teachers' pedagogical experiences that exemplify the constructivist paradigm include the following:

- Multiple data collection strategies were used, most of which resulted in qualitative data. The researcher made observations in the classrooms, conducted interviews, and reviewed documents such as the music curriculum, student work, and photographs.

- The researcher determined that videotaping in the classroom settings was not possible because some of the students would not sign informed consent forms. The researcher went on to explain that the students had learned to be guarded in their trust of observers. The students' historical disadvantages were understood as a wider contextual issue that influenced ethical methodological decisions.

- The teachers were not randomly chosen to represent a wider population. Rather, the sampling proceeded from identification of schools and then teachers within those schools. The schools were chosen purposefully because they served disadvantaged communities and had low achievement scores when compared to national performance. The teachers were then chosen (again purposefully) because they were recognized by their professional associations or university partnerships as leaders who actively pursued inclusion of disaffected students through music education.

- The interview questions evolved over time and were adjusted based on each previous interview to develop a transcript for each teacher that documents his/her experiences with the demands and opportunities in teaching music in their settings.

- The author included a detailed description of the context of the study in terms of the type of community, economic factors, and school characteristics.

- The focus of the study was to explain the teachers' pedagogical practices from their own point of view. The researcher shared her data, analysis, and interpretations with the teachers to allow them an opportunity to comment on their accuracy.

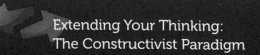

Extending Your Thinking: The Constructivist Paradigm

Identify a research study that exemplifies the constructivist paradigm. Explain why this study represents this paradigm. What are the distinguishing characteristics that lead you to conclude that this study belongs to this paradigm (e.g., what are the underlying characteristics that define a research study in this paradigm)?

Transformative Paradigm

The constructivist paradigm has been criticized not only by positivists and postpositivists, but also by another group of researchers who represent a third paradigm of research: the transformative paradigm. This group includes critical theorists, participatory action researchers, Marxists, feminists, racial and ethnic minorities, and persons with disabilities, among others. Transformative researchers acknowledge that the constructivist paradigm makes different claims with regard to reality, epistemology and methodology, and theories of causality than do postpositivists. As we saw in the description of the axiological assumptions of the constructivist paradigm, leaders in the field of qualitative methods are more and more citing the need to situate their work in social justice. This shift in the constructivist scholarship is an indicator of the permeability of the paradigmatic boundaries. However, the transformative paradigm directly addresses the politics in research by confronting social oppression at whatever levels it occurs (Oliver, 1992; Reason, 1994). Thus, transformative researchers consciously and explicitly position themselves side by side with the less powerful in a joint effort to bring about social transformation.

Although no unified body of literature is representative of the transformative paradigm, four characteristics are common to the diverse perspectives represented within it and serve to distinguish it from the postpositivist and constructivist paradigms (Mertens, Farley, Madison, & Singleton, 1994):

1. It places central importance on the lives and experiences of the diverse groups that, traditionally, have been marginalized (i.e., women, minorities, and persons with disabilities). L. Kelly, Burton, and Regan (1994) suggest that researchers not limit study to the lives and experiences of just one marginalized group, but to study the way oppression is structured and reproduced. Researchers must focus on how members of oppressed groups' lives are constrained by the actions of oppressors, individually and collectively, and on the strategies that oppressed groups use to resist, challenge, and subvert. Therefore, studying oppressed people's lives also means that a study of the oppressors' means of dominance must be included.

2. It analyzes how and why inequities based on gender, race or ethnicity, disability, sexual orientation, and socioeconomic classes are reflected in asymmetric power relationships.

3. It examines how results of social inquiry on inequities are linked to political and social action.

4. It uses a transformative theory to develop the program theory and the research approach. A program theory is a set of beliefs about the way a program works or why a problem occurs. Different types of program theories and their influence on the research process are explored in later chapters.

Researchers who were concerned about a number of different issues and events contributed to the development of the transformative paradigm. Some of these stimulating concerns and issues are discussed next.

Why Did the Transformative Paradigm Emerge?

The transformative paradigm arose partially because of dissatisfaction with the dominant research paradigms and practices and because of limitations in the research associated with these paradigms that were articulated by feminists, people of color, indigenous and postcolonial peoples, people with disabilities, members of the lesbian, gay, bisexual, transsexual, and queer communities, and others who have experienced discrimination and oppression, as well as other advocates for social justice. The need to reexamine our beliefs as researchers is exemplified in the following quotation from an indigenous African researcher, who wrote,

> The postcolonial condition remains pertinent and evident in educational research, where the application of mainstream research epistemologies, and their assumed universal validity, in assembling, analyzing, interpreting and producing knowledge today remains a highly foreign and a colonizing instrument that continues to define those from former colonies, and all the departments of their lives, as 'the other.'" (Chilisa, 2005, p. 662)

As these voices became more visible in the research community, professional organizations in education and psychology revised their standards of ethics and developed research agendas to be more responsive to transformative issues.

Feminist Perspectives. My first exposure to feminist psychology came from Gilligan's (1982) criticism of sociological and psychological theory because it was conducted from a male perspective using only male students as subjects. Theories formerly thought to be sexually neutral in their scientific objectivity have been found to reflect a consistent observational and evaluative bias. Gilligan cited many examples of dominant theories in psychology that were developed using the male as the norm, including Freud's theory of personality, McClelland's theory of motivation, and Kohlberg's theory of moral development. As these theories were reexamined from the feminist perspective, a new level of awareness developed as to the importance of giving credence to women's life experiences. Principles of feminist inquiry that are displayed in Box 1.4 illustrate the contribution of feminist scholars in terms of explicating the meaning of working from a feminist perspective. As will be discussed in later chapters, feminist theories are not univocal. There are many varieties of feminist theories, and they differ by regions of the world.

Box 1.4 Basic Principles Underlying Feminist Research and Evaluation

1. The central focus is on gender inequities that lead to social injustice. Every study should be conducted with an eye toward reversing gender inequities.
2. Discrimination or inequality based on gender is systemic and structural. Inequity based on gender is embedded in the major institutions and other shapers of societal norms such as schools, religion, media, pop culture, government, and corporations. This affects who has power and access.
3. Research and evaluation are political activities; the contexts in which the inquirer operates are politicized; and the personal experiences, perspectives, and characteristics researchers and evaluators bring to their work (and with which we interact) lead to a particular political stance. Acknowledging the political nature of such inquiry raises questions concerning the definition of objectivity within the traditional norms of science.

4. Knowledge is a powerful resource that serves an explicit or implicit purpose. Knowledge should be a resource of and for the people who create, hold, and share it. Consequently, the evaluation or research process can lead to significant negative or positive effects on the people involved in the evaluation/research.
5. Knowledge and values are culturally, socially, and temporally contingent. Knowledge is also filtered through the knower. The researcher/evaluator must recognize and explore the unique conditions and characteristics of the issue under study. The characteristics of the knower will influence the creation of knowledge; critical self-reflection is necessary.
6. There are multiple ways of knowing; some ways are privileged over others. Transformative knowledge is sought that emanates from an experiential base.

SOURCE: Sielbeck-Bowen, Brisolara, Seigart, Tischler, & Whitmore (2002).

Cultural Competency. Discussions at an American Psychological Association (APA) meeting in 1983 about cross-cultural counseling revealed that some ethnic minority psychologists believed that White researchers who study their communities do so without an understanding or caring for the people who live there (Mio & Iwamasa, 1993). Minority researchers expressed the view that their work had not been respected and that counseling and psychotherapy have failed to recognize the important contributions of minority authors. The Council of National Psychological Associations for the Advancement of Ethnic Minority Interests[4] (CNPAAEMI, 2000) published Guidelines for Research in Ethnic Minority Communities, and the APA's Joint Task Force of Divisions 17 and 45 published *Guidelines on Multicultural Education, Training, Research, Practice, and Organizational Change for Psychologists* in 2002.[5] The underlying principles and the guideline most directly relevant for cultural competency in research are displayed in Box 1.5.

Box 1.5 APA Guidelines on Multicultural Education, Training, Research, Practice, and Organizational Change for Psychologists: Principles & Research Guideline

The American Psychological Association Joint Task Force of Divisions 17 and 45 formulated their recent *Guidelines on Multicultural Education, Training, Research, Practice, and Organizational Change for Psychologists* (2002) based on these principles:

1. Recognition of the ways in which the intersection of racial and ethnic group membership with other dimensions of identity (e.g., gender, age, sexual orientation, disability, religion/spiritual orientation, educational attainment/experiences, and socioeconomic status) enhances the understanding and treatment of all people (Berberich, 1998; B. Greene, 2000; Jackson-Triche, Sullivan, Wells, Rogers, Camp, & Mazel, 2000; Wu, 2000).

(Continued)

Box 1.5 (Continued)

2. Knowledge of historically derived approaches that have viewed cultural differences as deficits and have not valued certain social identities helps psychologists to understand the underrepresentation of ethnic minorities in the profession and affirms and values the role of ethnicity and race in developing personal identity (Coll, Akerman, & Cicchetti, 2000; Medved et al., 2001; Mosley-Howard & Burgan, 2000; Sue, 1999; Witte & Morrison, 1995).

3. Psychologists are uniquely able to promote racial equity and social justice. This is aided by their awareness of their impact on others and the influence of their personal and professional roles in society (Comas-Diaz, 2000).

These principles led to the following guideline for research:

Guideline #4: "Culturally sensitive psychological researchers are encouraged to recognize the importance of conducting culture-centered and ethical psychological research among persons from ethnic, linguistic, and racial minority backgrounds" (p. 39).

Implications for Method: Related to the research question is choosing culturally appropriate theories and models on which to inform theory-driven inquiry (Quintana, Troyano, & Taylor, 2001). Psychological researchers are encouraged to be aware of and, if appropriate, to apply indigenous theories when conceptualizing research studies. They are encouraged to include members of cultural communities when conceptualizing research, with particular concern for the benefits of the research to the community (Fontes, 1998; LaFromboise, 1988). Applying this guideline to researchers and evaluators suggests that we must be wary of the deficit models that place the blame for social problems in the individual or culture, rather than in the societal response to the individual or cultural group.

Differential Achievement Patterns. Differences in school achievement by gender, race, class, and disability have been documented in educational research studies over many decades. In 1989, P. B. Campbell discounted the view that poor academic achievement is the result of genetic or biological factors. She suggested that the differences could be accounted for by the choice of test and test items, parental and teacher expectations, differential course taking, differential treatment in the same classes, and different experiences outside school.

The American Educational Research Association's Commission on Research in Black Education developed a Transformative Research and Action Agenda to address the issue of differential achievement on the basis of race, especially focused on African Americans and people of African descent globally (J. E. King, 2005). King asks this question: "How can research become one of the forms of struggle for Black education?" (p. 6). Her answer to this question reinforces the need for a transformative paradigm of research: "The ultimate object of a transformative research and action agenda is the universal problem of human freedom. That is, a goal of transformative education and research practice in Black education is the production of knowledge and understanding [that] people need to rehumanize the world by dismantling hegemonic structures that impede such knowledge" (p. 5).

Anyon (2005) suggests that educational research will only have an impact on equity in educational achievement if it is set in the larger context of the community and social forces. For example, researchers need to examine oppressive policies and practices that result in continued lack of access to resources in poor communities. The power structures and dynamics need to be studied to understand how the people in power make decisions. She contends that real change comes through organized social issue campaigns. Hence, important research questions center on examining the psychological process necessary to promote involvement in such campaigns. Effective interventions may need to go beyond curriculum and pedagogical practices to equitable access to resources, job creation, public transportation improvements, and affordable housing.

Philosophical and Theoretical Basis

The philosophical basis of the transformative paradigm is quite diverse, reflecting the multiple positions represented in that paradigm. The transformative paradigm provides a philosophical framework that explicitly addresses issues of power and justice and builds on a rich base of scholarly literature from mixed methods research (Tashakorri & Teddlie, 2003), qualitative research (Denzin & Lincoln, 2005), participatory action research (Reason & Bradbury, 2006), feminist researchers (M. Fine, Weis, Pruit, & Burns, 2004; Ramazanoglu & Holland, 2002), critical ethnography (Madison, 2005), culturally responsive research and evaluation (Hood, Hopson, & Frierson, 2005; Tillman, 2006), indigenous researchers (Battiste, 2000; Chilisa, 2005; Cram, Ormond, & Carter, 2004; McCreanor, Tipene-Leach & Abel, 2004; McCreanor, Watson, & Denny, 2006; L. T. Smith, 2005), disability researchers (Mertens & McLaughlin, 2004; M. Sullivan, 2009), and researchers in the international development community (Bamberger, Rugh, & Mabry, 2006). Framed from a historical perspective, the transformative paradigm is commensurate with the teachings of educator Paulo Freire and his "dialogical conscientization" model in Brazil; Habermas's communicative action theory; and Foucault, Lyotard, and Todorov on the academic rhetoric supportive of institutional forms of domination and control.

Based on S. Harding's (1987) typology of feminist thought, Olesen (2000) described the status of feminist theory as one of growing complexity and presented three broad approaches: standpoint theory, empiricists, and postmodern feminists. Interestingly, in Olesen's revised version of her chapter on feminist research in 2005, she deleted the empiricist approach and added two different approaches: globalization and postcolonial feminist thought as pathways to the major theories that are commensurate with the transformative paradigm from a feminist perspective. A summary of her approaches follows.

1. Standpoint theorists stress that all knowing substantively involves the standpoint or social and historical context of the particular knowers (Alcoff & Potter, 1993). Important standpoint theorists include S. Harding (1993), Hartsock (1983, 1985), and Dorothy Smith (1987). According to S. Harding (1993), standpoint theory is important in societies such as ours that are stratified by race, ethnicity, class, gender, sexuality, or other variables that shape the structure of society. She states,

> Knowledge claims are always socially situated, and the failure of dominant groups critically and systematically to interrogate their advantaged social situation and the effect of such advantages on their beliefs leaves their social situation a scientifically and epistemologically disadvantaged one for generating knowledge. (p. 54)

S. Harding (1993) continues, "Standpoint epistemology sets the relationship between knowledge and politics at the center of its account in the sense that it tries to provide causal accounts to explain the effects that different kinds of politics have on the production of knowledge" (pp. 55–56). S. Harding's portrayal of standpoint theory proceeds from a Marxist orientation, examining the researchers' role in the power structure (Olesen, 2000).

Patricia Hill Collins (2000) extended the idea of standpoint theory in her writings of Black feminist thought to question the myth of the essentialized, universalized woman. She emphasizes the importance of understanding what emanates from the specific social location of being a Black woman. Coming from the bottom of the social and economic hierarchies, Black women are better than others as starting points for seeking knowledge not only about their own experiences, but those of others as well. Thus it becomes important to look at the intersection of race, class, and gender within the context of issues of power.

2. Globalization and postcolonial feminist thought. In addition to criticisms from women of color in the United States, feminists were taken to task by scholars from postcolonial societies because of the oppression that was inflicted on people in these societies by White women. They write about the need to be cognizant of the contextual issues of power and culture when even using the word "feminist" in their countries (Chilisa, 2005). As globalization in labor markets and industry strengthens, this raises questions of its impact on women. Olesen (2005) identified two critical issues related to globalization for feminist researchers: "(a) the interplay of the dominance of the state and the economic forces in women's lives and women's enactment of or potential resistance, and (b) the production of new opportunities and/or the continuation of old oppressions" (p. 242).

3. Postmodern feminist thought is rooted in the philosophies of poststructuralism and postmodern thinkers such as the French feminists Cixous, Irigaray, and Kristeva and theorists Foucault, Lyotard, and Baudrillard (Olesen, 2000; Sands & Nuccio, 1992). Textual analysis and the role of text in sustaining the integration of power and oppression has been a central focus of postmodern feminist research. L. Richardson (2000) explores the idea of writing as a method of inquiry in itself in that researchers can learn things about themselves and their topics through the process of writing.

The transformative paradigm (as exemplified by the varieties of feminist thought) is broad and far from a unified body of work. Martusewicz and Reynolds (1994) describe the commonality of concern for feminist theories as "understanding and improving the lives and relations between women and men, economically, socially, culturally, and personally" (p. 13). Feminists generally agree that, historically, women have not enjoyed the same power and privileges as men, either in the public or private sphere. Women live their lives in an oppressive society; this concept of oppression links the voices of those who work in the transformative paradigm.

Similar themes emerge from the writings of African American scholars. Gordon (1995) writes,

> The Black challenge to Western ideological hegemony is older than both critical and feminist discourse and was born of the need for intellectual, ideological, and spiritual liberation of people who lived under both the racist domination and sexist patriarchal subordination to which both the critical and feminist discourse react and refer. (p. 190)

She criticizes the critical and feminist scholars as follows:

> The blind side of critical and feminist discourses is their inability, unwillingness, or complete lack of awareness of the need to focus on the conceptual systems that construct, legitimize, and normalize the issues of race and racism. This is demonstrated through the flagrant invisibility in their works of the critical and cultural model generated by the subjugated oppressed group from its own experiences within a dominant and hostile society. (pp. 189–190)

She does not see sufficient attention being given to the African American critical and liberatory pedagogy in most feminist discourse. A number of ethnic minorities have written that mainstream feminists are not representative of their views (e.g., P. H. Collins, 2000; James & Busia, 1993; Ladson-Billings, 2000; Stanfield, 1999), thus adding to the complexity of identifying *the* philosophical base of the transformative paradigm. Ladson-Billings (2000) explains the use of critical race theory (see Delgado, 1995; Tate, 1997) as a framework for researchers to uncover the racism that continues to oppress people of color, as well as to provide guidance for racial social justice.

Researchers who work in the lesbian, gay, bisexual, transgender, and queer (LGBTQ) communities express concern about the lack of critical reflection on how meaning making about gender and sexual identity is not only about the context, but also about the socially constructed identity of the individual in the setting. Queer theory has emerged as a way to challenge the hegemony inherent in the two-dimensional separation of male or female as a way of measuring gender and sexual identity. For the LGBTQ community, persistent internalized homophobia can conceal discrimination to the degree that persistent subtle degrading manipulation is not even acknowledged or those demeaned feel powerless to challenge the question (Dodd, 2009; Mertens, Foster, & Heimlich, 2008). By establishing a transformative approach and reaching out to concealed communities, researchers have the opportunity to engage voices that have been traditionally unrecognized or excluded.

More complexity is added by those who have written of a new paradigm for the disability community (Gill, 1999; Mertens & McLaughlin, 2004; Seelman, 2000; M. Sullivan, 2009). Persons with disabilities discuss a shift from a medical/deficit model to a social-cultural model as a framework for understanding this community's experiences. The social-cultural model of disability challenges the medical perspective by allowing people with disabilities to take control over their own lives by shifting the focus onto the social, rather than the biological factors, in understanding disability. Accompanying this shift in self-perceptions is a shift in research perspectives put forth by members of the disability community. Emancipatory research came from the disability community from the "nothing about us without us" political activism that was based on moving the control of research into the hands of persons with disabilities. However, M. Sullivan (2009) notes that maybe it is time for the disability community to walk side by side with nondisabled researchers using the transformative paradigm in the search for social justice.

These theoretical perspectives are discussed in great depth later in this text.

Extending Your Thinking: Oppression

Is it appropriate to use the "umbrella" term *oppression* to include the experiences of women, racial/ethnic minorities, immigrants, indigenous peoples, lesbian/gay/bisexual/transgender/ queer individuals, the elderly, members of minority religious groups, and persons with disabilities? Why or why not?

Are there fundamental differences between/among groups, or are these differences exaggerated? For example, between males and females? Persons of different ethnicities? Persons with disabilities and those without?

An example of a research study using a single method conducted within the transformative paradigm is summarized in Sample Study 1.3. A transformative mixed methods study is illustrated in Sample Study 1.4.

Sample Study 1.3

Summary of a Transformative Single-Method Research Study

Research Problem: People with mental illnesses often feel bewildered about the nature of their sickness and the effects and effectiveness of their treatment, even after they meet with a health care professional. Schizophrenia is a severe mental illness that is associated with isolation, difficulties in the everyday tasks of living, and sometimes suicide. Research is needed to determine ways interventions can be more effective with this population.

Research Questions: What topic is of importance to people with schizophrenia for research? What is the nature of experiences reported by people with schizophrenia with health care professionals? How can information about these experiences be used for personal transformation of the participants and transformation of the health care system?

Method: A transformative participatory design was used for this study. The research was initiated by a university researcher in conjunction with a member of a support group for people with schizophrenia. Once funding was obtained, the research team met with members of the support group over a three-month period to bring focus to the study. The group decided to use in-depth interviews with each other on their experiences with medical professionals.

Participants: The participants consisted of the members of the support group for people with schizophrenia.

Instruments and Procedures: The interview questions were developed by a group process with the participants and research team. The university researcher conducted training with group members on interviewing techniques. The members of the group interviewed each other in a group setting, allowing others who were present to ask questions or make comments. The interviews were tape recorded and transcribed. The group members conducted a thematic analysis of the data, aided by a graduate student. The group suggested content and quotations from the interviews to be used in a script that the university researcher wrote for a readers' theater performance.

Results: Two sides of a picture of experiences with health professionals emerged, one good and one bad, but both pictures centered on issues of communication. The issues that arose related to communications about their diagnosis (if it was clearly conveyed), medications (effectiveness and side effects), information about supports for people with schizophrenia, and being treated with dignity and respect.

Discussion: The research was conducted with a conscious attempt to engage the participants in transformative experiences. Through active involvement of persons with schizophrenia throughout the research process, individuals found a safe place to share their experiences and learn from each other. Group members described an increase in their ability to connect with others on an important topic, as well as solve problems that were broader than their individual stories. They conducted seven performances in a readers' theater format to audiences of professionals and people with mental illness. They also disseminated a list of recommendations to medical professionals that outlined how they wanted to be treated; they report receiving feedback from these professionals that indicate a change in the way they view and treat people in this marginalized group.

SOURCE: Based on Schneider et al. (2004).

Sample Study 1.4 **Summary of a Transformative Mixed Methods Evaluation Study**

Evaluation Problem: Gender violence affects millions of American women each year. While adolescents account for only 10% of the population, they are targets of an estimated 20% to 50% of all reported rapes. High rates of physical and psychological assault, sexual assault, and sexual harassment are other indicators of the problem.

Evaluation Question: Will the Mentors in Violence Prevention (MVP) program in the Massachusetts high school system lead to a reduction in adolescent gender violence? Did female abuse survivors in the program experience secondary trauma during the training? Is the bystander training an appropriate or helpful approach for girls?

Method: A feminist approach to evaluation was designed to incorporate both quantitative survey and qualitative case study research.

Participants: Participants include young women and men who are viewed as leaders in their schools. Every student who participated in the initial awareness-raising phase of MVP program at 10 school sites completed a pretest (n = 262) and 209 completed a posttest survey and filled out a satisfaction questionnaire. Two of the 10 schools served as case study sites where 21 student- and 6 key-informant interviews were conducted, as well as observations in 23 program training sessions.

Instruments and Procedures: The independent variable is the MVP program, which consists of a multiple-session training regimen of 12 to 14 hours of training over a two- to three-month period. The program focuses on empowering students to act as proactive bystanders in the face of abuse and violence.

Results: The case study data supported the argument that adolescent gender violence education and prevention programs, such as the MVP program, are sorely needed. Pre- and postsurvey data suggested that the program had the desired impact on students based on statistically significant changes in student knowledge, attitudes, and self-efficacy.

Discussion: Students knew more facts about gender violence, sexist attitudes diminished, and students' confidence to intervene in and prevent gender violence improved. As a feminist evaluation, this study investigated the emotional safety and well-being of young women who participate in programs like the MVP program. An agenda for social change to prevent violence against adolescent girls was presented to the school that commissioned the evaluation.

SOURCE: Based on Ward (2002).

With that lengthy introduction to the transformative paradigm, and in full recognition of its diverse and emerging character, the answers to the four defining questions follow.

Axiology

The transformative paradigm places priority on the axiological assumption as a guiding force for conceptualizing subsequent beliefs and research decisions. The starting point for transformative researchers is the territory that encompasses human rights and social justice. The transformative paradigm emerged because of dissatisfaction with research conducted within other paradigms that was perceived to be irrelevant to, or a misrepresentation of, the lives of people who experience oppression. Sieber (1992) writes, "Clearly, sound ethics and sound methodology go hand in hand" (p. 4). Greater concern about the rights and welfare of research participants generally leads to greater involvement of the participants themselves in the research process—one of the basic tenets of the transformative paradigm. Hence, the transformative axiological assumption is examined from a number of different perspectives:

- How transformative researchers critique and extend the principles of respect, beneficence, and justice on several fronts. Respect is critically examined in terms of the cultural norms of interaction in diverse communities and across cultural groups. Beneficence is defined in terms of the promotion of human rights and an increase in social justice. An explicit connection is made between the process and outcomes of research and evaluation studies and furtherance of a social justice agenda.

- Human rights initiatives through the United Nations reinforce the need to be aware of those whose rights are not respected worldwide.

- The code of ethics from relevant professional associations and organizations provide guidance for researchers and evaluators as to what constitutes ethical practice. As mentioned previously, those codes of ethics have been critically reviewed and revised to reflect a greater concern for principles that are reflective of the axiological assumptions of the transformative paradigm. The American Evaluation Association (AEA) modified its guiding principles to include an explicit principle related to the role of cultural competency in ethical evaluation practice. The American Psychological Association revised its ethics code in 2002, strengthening protection of people in research that involves deception (Fisher, 2003). Ethics in psychology have been extended by Brabeck's (2000) application of feminist principles in psychology.

- Interestingly, the APA's description of the role of the psychologist as an agent of prosocial change is reflective of the axiological assumption of the transformative paradigm that ethical research and evaluation are defined by their furtherance of social justice and human rights, all the while being cognizant of those characteristics associated with diverse populations that impede progress on these fronts. There are other ethical guidelines associated with various professional associations, government agencies, and donor agencies.

- Researcher guidelines are also available from indigenous communities that provide insights into ethical grounding of research and evaluation from that perspective. For example, Cram (2001, cited in L. T. Smith, 2005, p. 98) provided guidelines for researchers from the Maori people. These include:
    - Respect for people, meaning people are allowed to define their own space and meet on their own terms
    - Meet people face to face: Introduce yourself and the idea for the research before beginning the research or sending complicated letters or other materials
    - Look and listen: Begin by looking and listening and understanding in order to find a place from which to speak
    - Sharing, hosting, being generous: This forms the basis of a relationship in which researchers acknowledge their role as learners with a responsibility to give back to the community
    - Be cautious: Harm can come from a lack of political astuteness and cultural sensitivity, whether the researcher is an insider or an outsider
    - Do not trample on the dignity of a person (mana): Inform people without being patronizing or impatient. Be wary of Western ways of expression such as wit, sarcasm, and irony
    - Avoid arrogant flaunting of knowledge: Find ways to be generous with sharing your knowledge in a way that empowers the community.

Transparency and reciprocity are important values that are included in the transformative axiological position. An explicit connection is made between the process and outcomes of research and furtherance of a social justice agenda. In 1998, Sieber identified a number of benefits that may result from the conduct of research beyond adding to the knowledge base. She emphasized the importance of giving back to the community that provides the data. It is possible to provide incentives, such as money or materials (e.g., office supplies, or gift certificates for a book store, educational toys, or a fast food restaurant), but a transformative researcher would consider less tangible rewards and might offer additional training for community members, and provision of access to the results so they can be used to improve practice, obtain additional funds, or influence policy.

Pollard (1992) suggests that researchers adapt ethical guidelines that were based on developments for cross-cultural research when working with people from minority communities in the United States. Although the cross-cultural ethical standards were developed to guide researchers in other countries, they have applicability for research with Native Americans, Native Alaskans, Hispanics, African Americans, and other minority populations. Pollard provides an example of the application of cross-cultural ethical principles through his research with the American deaf community. Cross-cultural ethical principles require collaboration between the researcher and the host community. In the American deaf community, representatives of the host community could be identified through various national organizations, such as the National Association of the Deaf or Self-Help for Hard of Hearing People. Collaboration should not be limited to conversations with leaders, although building relationships with these initial contacts can be a way of learning how to appropriately access other members of the deaf community.

Other cross-cultural ethical principles require that the researcher communicate the intended research agenda, design, activity, and reports with members of the host community (LaFrance & Crazy Bull, 2009). The research should be designed in such a way as to bring benefit to the host community and to foster the skills and self-sufficiency of host community scientists. The visiting researcher should strive to conduct the research on an equal-status basis with the host community members. Errante (2001) provides good insights into the struggles faced by a researcher when the participants in the study question the benefit of their participation (see Box 1.6).

Box 1.6 Benefits of Participating in Research

Errante (2001) conducted an oral history of educational experiences in Mozambique. She found that some of the Mozambicans were cynical about the conduct of focus groups and interviews by internationals. They wanted to know why a rich foreigner could make her living by constantly asking them questions, yet nothing ever changed for them anyway. She commented,

> This lesson in humility reminded me once again of the importance of establishing mutual respect and trust with narrators. I now take more time just engaging in conversation. I explain what oral history work means to me more fully, and the value of the narrators' life experiences for the national patrimony. I ask narrators, particularly older ones, to think about what they would like their grandchildren to know about their life and their educational experiences. I ask them if they would like to know something about my life before we start. And I listen first and foremost to the story narrators want to tell me. All of this helps to construct an interpersonal bridge; it gives the narrator and me a chance to get to like each other. (p. 21)

Ontology

Truths are not relative. What are relative are opinions about truth.

—Nicolás Gómez Dávila, 2001

Like the constructivist paradigm, multiple versions of what is perceived to be real are recognized in the transformative paradigm. However, the transformative paradigm stresses that acceptance of such differences of perceptions as equally legitimate ignores the damage done by ignoring the factors that give privilege to one version of reality over another, such as the influence of social, political, cultural, economic, ethnic, gender, and disability lenses in the construction of reality. In addition, the transformative ontological belief emphasizes that that which seems "real" may instead be reified structures that are taken to be real because of historical situations. Thus, what is taken to be real needs to be critically examined via an ideological critique of its role in perpetuating oppressive social structures and policies.

Schneider et al. (2004) recognized that multiple perceptions of appropriate intervention for people with schizophrenia exist. Some of the ways of perceiving what is an effective intervention are harmful, that is, not sharing the diagnosis with the patients or not understanding the implications of severe side effects of some medications on the person's willingness to take their medications. The researchers deliberately set out to understand the perceived reality of an effective therapeutic relationship from the vantage point of people with schizophrenia.

Epistemology

The transformative paradigm's epistemological assumption centers on the meaning of knowledge as it is defined from a prism of cultural lenses and the power issues involved in the determination of what is considered legitimate knowledge. This means that not only is the relationship between the knower and the would-be known (i.e., the researcher and participants) interactive, it also involves a consciousness of cultural complexities in that relationship. In order to address issues of power in understanding what is valued as knowledge, S. Harding (1993) recommends that the researcher use a methodology that involves "'starting off thought' from the lives of marginalized people" (p. 56). This would reveal more of the unexamined assumptions influencing science and generate more critical questions. The relationship should be empowering to those without power. Thus, research should examine ways the research benefits or does not benefit the participants (L. Kelly et al., 1994).

Haraway (1988) describes feminist objectivity as "situated knowledge"—that is, recognizing the social and historical influences on that which we say we know. S. Harding (1993) argues that politically guided research projects have produced fewer partial and distorted results (as in sexist or racist) than those supposedly guided by the goal of value neutrality. Objectivity in this paradigm is achieved by reflectively examining the influence of the values and social position of the researcher on the problems identified as appropriate for research, hypotheses formulated, and key concepts defined.

In the Schneider et al. (2004) study, the epistemological assumptions of the transformative paradigm are evident in the participatory approach to constructing not only the research focus, but also in the collaboration that functioned throughout the entire two-year research period. The academic researcher (Schneider) approached the Schizophrenia Society of Alberta to determine interest in a collaborative research project based on transformative participatory research principles. The Schizophrenia Society runs a support group for people with schizophrenia, and the woman who runs that group agreed to work with Schneider on a grant proposal. Once funding was obtained, the research leaders met with the support group over a two-month period to determine the focus and methods of the research: experiences with mental health professionals. The research leaders and group members maintained a close relationship throughout the project, attending biweekly meetings for data collection. Schneider's comment illustrates the transformative epistemological assumption that underlies this research:

> As the interviews progressed, we realized that we had created a place in which members could talk freely about aspects of their lives that they normally have no opportunity to talk about....Hearing details of the life experiences of group members was often an emotional experience, both for those who were describing their experiences and for those who were listening. The structure of the interview process allowed even people who rarely speak at Unsung Heroes meetings to tell their stories. Through the interviewing, we became a caring and supportive community of friends. (p. 567)

Methodology

Scholars writing from the perspectives of feminists, ethnic minorities, poor people, and people with disabilities have commonly expressed dissatisfaction with both the postpositivist and constructivist paradigms of inquiry (Lather, 1992; Mertens et al., 1994; Oliver, 1992; Steady, 1993). Mertens (1995) identified three characteristics of the transformative paradigm with ethical implications for methodological choices:

1. Traditionally silenced voices must be included to ensure that groups marginalized in society are equally heard during the research process and the formation of the findings and recommendations.
2. An analysis of power inequities in terms of the social relationships involved in the planning, implementation, and reporting of the research is needed to ensure an equitable distribution of resources (conceptual and material).
3. A mechanism should be identified to enable the research results to be linked to social action; those who are most oppressed and least powerful should be at the center of the plans for action in order to empower them to change their own lives.

Transformative researchers are pluralistic and evolving in their methodologies. The empiricists who work within the transformative tradition tend to use quantitative methods; however, they emphasize a need for more care and rigor in following existing methods commonly associated with the postpositivist paradigm to avoid sexist, racist, or otherwise biased results (Eichler, 1991; S. Harding, 1993). Other transformative researchers use a wide diversity of methods; many make use of qualitative methods, such as interviews, observations, and document review, within a transformative framework (Reinharz, 1992). In transformative research that comes from the participatory action research tradition, it is viewed as essential to involve the people who are the research participants in the planning, conduct, analysis, interpretation, and use of the research. A common theme in the methodology is inclusion of diverse voices from the margin.

Schneider et al. (2004) exemplified the transformative methodology by focusing on methods that would allow opportunities for personal and systemic transformation, as well as by using a cyclical model for the research process. The cycle of research began with three months of group meetings to determine the focus of the research, the methods to be used for data collection (in-depth interviewing by members of the group of each other), and the specific interview questions. The results of that group process were used to frame the next cycle in the research: preparing for and conducting the interviews. The interviews were conducted in a group setting with an assigned interviewer and interviewee; however, anyone could make comments or ask questions during the interview.

The group members, with the assistance of a graduate student, analyzed the data to identify themes related to communication in the therapeutic relationship. The group members then recommended quotations for Schneider et al. to use in preparing a script for a readers' theater presentation based on the research study's findings. At the time the 2004 article was published, the group performed the presentation seven times to the public and health care providers. In addition, the participants/co-researchers developed a list of recommendations for professionals for how they would like to be treated.

Validity From a Transformative Perspective: A Methodological Issue

Validity is often thought of as related to the validity of a data collection instrument (see Chapter 12 on data collection), but validity has broader meanings. Kirkhart (1995, 2005) and Lincoln (2009) have been at the forefront of the discussion of the integral connection between the quality of the human relations in a research setting and the validity of the information that is assembled. Kirkhart (2005) proposes specific consideration of what she terms "multicultural validity,"[6] which she describes as referring to the "correctness or authenticity of understandings across multiple, intersecting cultural contexts" (p. 22). I argue that multicultural validity is a good candidate for considering transformative validity. She outlines five justifications for multicultural validity:

1. Theoretical: The cultural congruence of theoretical perspectives underlying the program, the evaluation, and assumptions about validity.

2. Experiential: Congruence with the lived experience of participants in the program and in the evaluation process.

3. Consequential: The social consequences of understandings and judgments and the actions taken based upon them.

4. Interpersonal: The quality of the interactions between and among participants in the evaluation process.

5. Methodological: The cultural appropriateness of measurement tools and cultural congruence of design configurations. (Kirkhart, 2005, p. 23)

Extending Your Thinking: The Transformative Paradigm

- Identify a research study that exemplifies the transformative paradigm. Explain why this study represents this paradigm. What are the distinguishing characteristics that lead you to conclude that this study belongs to this paradigm (e.g., what are the underlying characteristics that define a t research study in this paradigm)?

- How can the research community address the issues of oppression and group differences in access to power without engendering greater divisiveness?

- Who should and can do transformative research? S. Harding (1993) writes the following in answer to this question:

> But the subject of every other liberatory movement must also learn how gender, race, class, and sexuality are used to construct each other in order to accomplish their goals....It cannot be that women are the unique generators of feminist knowledge. Women cannot claim this ability to be uniquely theirs, and men must not be permitted to claim that because they are not women, they are not obligated to produce fully feminist analyses. Men, too, must contribute distinctive forms of specifically feminist knowledge from their particular social situation. (p. 67)

  Do you agree or disagree with Harding? State your reasons.

- How can a researcher from a dominant group (i.e., one with power) conduct meaningful research about those of differing race, class, gender, and disability? How can researchers conduct an inquiry on the same cultural group that they are a member of? How can those with less power "study up" the members of groups with more power?

- It is not clear whether the transformative paradigm is to replace existing paradigms or to be an alternative paradigm in conducting research. Do you see it as an alternative or preferred paradigm in conducting evaluations or research concerning marginalized groups? Or is it a paradigm to be integrated into the existing research methodologies, regardless of the research focus? Some researchers will argue that this paradigm is incompatible with scientific research methods. What is your response to this argument?

Pragmatic Paradigm

Tashakkori and Teddlie (2003) identify pragmatism as one of the paradigms that provides an underlying philosophical framework for mixed methods research.[7] It should be noted that mixed methods research can also be based in the transformative paradigm if the researcher adheres to the philosophical beliefs of that paradigm more strongly than to those of pragmatism (Mertens, 2009; Mertens & McLaughlin, 2004). As the transformative paradigm was extensively discussed in the previous section, the text here will focus on the pragmatic paradigm as described by Tashakkori and Teddlie (2003), Maxcy (2003), and M. Q. Patton (2002).

Historically, pragmatism can be divided into an early period from 1860–1930 and a neopragmatic period from 1960 to the current time (Maxcy, 2003). Early pragmatists included Charles Sanders Peirce (circa 1877), William James, John Dewey, George Herbert Mead, and Arthur F. Bentley. These philosophers rejected the scientific notion that social science inquiry was able to access the "truth" about the real world solely by virtue of a single scientific method. Thus their belief systems were closely aligned in this sense to constructionists. The neopragmatists, including Abraham Kaplan, Richard Rorty, and Cornel West, built on the work of the early pragmatists. However, they moved even further from the metaphysical and emphasized the importance of common sense and practical thinking. Crotty (1998, p. 212) writes that Rorty developed a postmodernist version of American pragmatism.

Understandings of pragmatism as a philosophical school have no doubt shifted throughout the centuries; the way this philosophy is interpreted in the current mixed methods research community has strayed somewhat from the earlier pragmatist philosophers. The current focus is related to earlier pragmatists in several ways: the focus is on "lines of action" (from William James and George Herbert Mead) and "warranted assertions" (from John Dewey), along with a general emphasis on "workability" (from James and Dewey) (Morgan, 2007, p. 66). Dewey would call inquiries what we do when we undertake to determine the workability of any potential line of action and the inquiry results would provide warrant for the assertions that we make about that line of action. In pragmatists' eyes, the lines of action are methods of research that are seen to be most appropriate for studying the phenomenon at hand. "The essential emphasis is on actual behavior ('lines of action'), the beliefs that stand behind those behaviors ('warranted assertions'), and the consequences that are likely to follow from different behaviors ('workability')" (Morgan, 2007, p. 67). The pragmatists' goal is to search for useful points of connection.

A pragmatic mixed methods study is illustrated as Sample Study 1.5. This is a study of student dropout and reenrollment in high school (Berliner, Barrat, Fong, & Shirk, 2008).

Axiology

Questions of ethics were very important to early pragmatists such as James, Dewey, and Mead. Dewey (and James) emphasized an ethics of care, particularly for the youngest members of society (Mottier, 2004). Contemporary researchers working within the pragmatic paradigm view the ethical goal of research to gain knowledge in the pursuit of desired ends (Morgan, 2007). This is somewhat akin to what Christians (2005) describes as the utilitarian theory of ethics in that "all that is worth valuing is a function of its consequences" (p. 144).

Ontology

Pragmatists have for the most part avoided the use of metaphysical concepts such as truth and reality that have caused (in their eyes) much endless and often useless discussion and debate (Teddlie & Tashakkori, 2003). In a pragmatic approach, there is no problem with asserting both that there is a single "real world" and that all individuals have their own unique interpretations of that world. Rather than treating incommensurability as an all-or-nothing barrier between mutual understanding, pragmatists treat issues of intersubjectivity as a key element of social life. In particular, the pragmatist emphasis on creating knowledge through lines of action points to the kinds of "joint actions" or "projects" that different people or groups can accomplish together (Morgan, 2007, p. 72).

Effectiveness is to be used as the criteria for judging value of research, rather than correspondence of findings to some "true" condition in the real world (Maxcy, 2003). Effectiveness is viewed as establishing that the results "work" with respect to the specific problem that the researcher seeks resolution of. "What is healthy about a pragmatic social science of mixed and multiple methods is...it allows a number of projects to be undertaken without the need to identify invariant prior knowledge, laws, or rules

Sample Study 1.5 Summary of a Pragmatic Mixed Methods Study

Research Problem: The United States has a very high dropout rate for high school students. Some of the students drop out and never come back; some reenroll and graduate. Students who do not graduate from high school have more challenges in terms of literacy necessary to succeed in the contemporary labor market.

Research Questions: How many students drop out of high school in this district? How many students who dropped out reenroll in high school? What are the reasons students drop out and reenroll?

Method: A pragmatic, sequential mixed methods design was used that included sequential collection of both quantitative and qualitative data to provide answers to the research questions. Researchers started with quantitative analysis of dropout and reenrollment data, followed by semistructured interviews with staff and students.

Participants: The study took place in one school district in California because it had a linked, longitudinal student-level data set that tracked dropouts and reenrollments in the district. This was a convenience sample of a large, urban, and racially diverse school district with a total of 3,856 students who were first-time ninth graders in 2000/01. Seven district administrators, seven principals, and six students were interviewed in 2007.

Instruments and Procedures: The quantitative portion of the study involved a statistical analysis of a longitudinal data set from 2000/01–2006/07. In addition, researchers had access to course information that the students took and demographic data about the students. The qualitative portion included interviews with 20 people from the school district, which lasted between 30 and 45 minutes each. The semistructured interviews were conducted by the researcher during a weeklong, in-person visit to the school district.

Results: About 45% of the students graduated in the allotted four years of high school with regular high school diplomas. About 35% had dropped out at least once during that time; 20% transferred to other schools and their whereabouts and status are unknown. Of the 35% who dropped out, 31% reenrolled at a school in that district and 18% of these graduated by 2005/06. The qualitative data from the reenrolled students revealed that they struggled academically, were bored, failed courses, or had other life circumstances like family crises, pregnancy, or gang pressure that led them to drop out and challenged their ability to complete their high school degrees.

Discussion: Dropping out is not a fixed outcome; students do reenroll and drop out and reenroll. Students returned to school for a variety of reasons, some because they could not get a job without a high school diploma, others because of urging from a significant person such as a counselor or coach. The administrators indicated that they needed additional resources to reach out to youth and to support them when they did reenroll for counseling and academic support.

SOURCE: Based on Berliner et al. (2008).

governing what is recognized as 'true' or 'valid.' Only results count!" (Maxcy, 2003, p. 85). This contrasts sharply with the other paradigms' emphasis on the nature of reality and possibility of objective truth. Instead, one of the defining features of pragmatism is an emphasis on "what difference it makes" to believe one thing versus another or to act one way rather than another (Morgan, 2007, p. 68).

In the Berliner et al. (2008) study, the researchers start by analyzing numbers of students who drop out and reenroll based on the assumption that it will be useful to know how many students drop out and reenroll and eventually graduate (or not) as it is ascertained from the longitudinal data kept by the school district. They want to add to their ability to interpret the numbers, so they also schedule interviews to get data that reflect administrators', principals', and students' perceptions of reasons for dropping out and reenrolling.

Epistemology

Rather than positioning oneself as a distanced observer, relational researcher, or socially and historically contextualized researcher, the pragmatist is free to "study what interests you and is of value to you, study it in the different ways that you deem appropriate, and utilize the results in ways that can bring about positive consequences within your value system" (Tashakkori & Teddlie, 1998, p. 30). The criterion for judging the appropriateness of a method, with its implied relationship between the researcher and the researched, is if it achieves its purpose (Maxcy, 2003).

The longitudinal data sets were available to the researchers without traveling to the district. Hence, this portion of the research was completed before the researchers visited the site. The researchers then made a weeklong site visit to the district, during which they interviewed district administrators, principals, and students. The researchers do not report the nature of the relationships they had with the individuals they interviewed.

Methodology

Qualitative and/or quantitative methods are compatible with the pragmatic paradigm. Method should be decided by the purpose of the research (M. Q. Patton, 2002). Neopragmatists wrote extensively of the importance of using mixed methods and avoiding being constrained by a single, monolithic method, as they perceived the "scientific method" to be according to the postpositivist thinkers (Maxcy, 2003). Rather, they see mixed methods as offering a practical solution to the tensions created in the research community concerning the use of quantitative or qualitative methods. Put simply, pragmatism allows the researchers to choose the methods (or combination of methods) that work best for answering their research questions (B. Johnson & Onwuegbuzie, 2004). Morgan (2007) asserts that research questions in and of themselves are not inherently important and methods are not automatically appropriate. Rather, the researcher makes a choice about what is important and what is appropriate, based on a general consensus in the community that serves as the researcher's reference group. He does encourage researchers to be reflexive about what they choose to study and how they choose to do so.

As mentioned under the epistemological assumption for this paradigm, Berliner et al. (2008) used a sequential mixed methods design, meaning that first they analyzed quantitative data from the district's longitudinal data set. They analyzed the data in terms of overall dropouts and reenrollments over a five-year period, as well as by subgroups by gender and race/ethnicity. They then scheduled a site visit to the district for one week to interview district administrators, principals, and students. Their results are contained in a report submitted to the U.S. Department of Education, which gave them the money to do the study.

Extending Your Thinking: The Pragmatic Paradigm

Identify a research study that exemplifies the pragmatic paradigm. Explain why this study represents this paradigm. What are the distinguishing characteristics that lead you to conclude that this study belongs to this paradigm (e.g., what are the underlying characteristics that define a research study in this paradigm)?

Extending Your Thinking: The Four Paradigms

Four paradigms that are currently guiding research in education and psychology are presented in this chapter. Write a short paper that reflects your own ideas regarding where you stand in terms of the options for paradigms of research. Do you find yourself intrigued by or more comfortable with one than another? Do you find yourself somewhat in the middle? Are you withholding judgment until you know more? What else do you want to know? Discuss your position in terms of the axiological, ontological, epistemological, and methodological assumptions of each paradigm.

Politics, Legislation, and the Paradigms

Why Is the Methodology of Research a Political Issue?

As stated in the history of research section of this chapter, the oldest paradigm for educational and psychological research is the postpositivist paradigm. The second paradigm to enter this research world was the constructivist paradigm, which was followed by the transformative paradigm. The pragmatic paradigm is the most recent addition as a philosophical base for some mixed methods research (although it should be noted that pragmatism as a philosophical school harkens back to the days of John Dewey, William James, and George Herbert Mead). In years past, the professional literature contained many attacks by postpositivists on constructivists (and vice versa). In fact, the debates between postpositivists and constructivists were at one time called the paradigm wars. As qualitative researchers became more accepted in the methodology community, less vitriolic rhetoric was seen in the literature. Examples of transformative research became more frequent in mainstream journals as more persons who had been pushed to margins were bringing their voices into the research community.

It seemed perhaps then an uneasy peace had sprung up among researchers, until the No Child Left Behind Act (NCLB), the reauthorized Elementary and Secondary Education Act, was passed by the United States Congress with the goal of supporting educational practice based on scientific evidence. To that end, the law mentions the use of scientifically based research (SBR) no less than 111 times. The definition of SBR in the legislation displayed in Box 1.7 is closely aligned with approaches to research that are at home in the postpositivist paradigm. Borman and his colleagues (2005) note that the law places a premium on "randomized experiments designed to develop and assess new and innovative practices" (p. 2). The intent of giving priority to this approach to research is the belief that reliable evidence of effectiveness is dependent on the use of "rigorous methodological designs and techniques, including control groups and random assignment" (No Child Left Behind Act, 2001). Very real consequences are attached to the use of this approach in terms of who will get grant funds from the federal government to study effectiveness of educational interventions. For example, the Reading Excellence Act, and its successor, Reading First, required that "grant funds be used to help schools adopt those programs that incorporate 'scientifically based principles' of reading instruction" (Borman et al., 2005, p. 2).

Professional Organizations' Response to NCLB

The prioritizing of experimental designs in research caused quite a stir in the wider research community. Many professional associations developed critiques based on the narrow definition of research that was found in the legislation. For example, the American Evaluation Association (AEA) takes the position that there is not one right way to evaluate the effectiveness of a program. In response to the U.S. Department of Education's requirement of the scientific method, the AEA (2003) stated, "While we agree with the intent of ensuring that federally sponsored programs be "evaluated using scientifically based research . . . to determine the effectiveness of a project intervention," we do not agree that "evaluation methods using an experimental design are best for determining project effectiveness" (http://www.eval.org/doestatement.htm).

The National Education Association (2003) communicated with U.S. Secretary of Education Rod Paige, cautioning that we need to use an approach other than the scientific method to demonstrate effectiveness of programs. Their position specifically states (1) that the "evaluation approach used be appropriate for the problem or question the program itself seeks to address; (2) that the evaluation definition and set of priorities used are not so narrow that they effectively preclude the funding of worthwhile programs; and (3) that the Department continue to recognize the importance of third party, independent evaluators" (http://www.eval.org/doe.nearesponse.pdf).

The American Educational Research Association (2003) also expressed a similar sentiment. They did commend the U.S. Department of Education for its focus on improving the quality of research in education; however, they were concerned about the narrowness of the methods suggested for achieving that goal. Their resolution for essential elements for scientifically based research reads in part:

> Council recognizes randomized trials among the sound methodologies to be used in the conduct of educational research and commends increased attention to their use as is particularly appropriate to intervention and evaluation studies. However, the Council of the Association expresses dismay that the Department of Education through its public statements and programs of funding is devoting singular attention to this one tool of science, jeopardizing a broader range of problems best addressed through other scientific methods. (p. 2)

The American Psychological Association took a different approach in their reaction to the NCLB. They did not criticize the narrowness of the research approach; rather, they emphasized the contribution that psychologists could make in the conduct of such research (Gaiber-Matlin & Haskell-Hoehl, 2007). They also made note of areas that are problematic in the legislation that should be addressed in reauthorization, such as violence in the schools, students with disabilities, and English Language Learners. Koretz (2008) addresses the issues of testing as it is currently mandated under the NCLB and suggests that it has resulted in teaching to the test that results in inflated state standardized test scores, except for those students (e.g., English Language Learners and students with disabilities) who often do not test well using such measures. Ironically, these are the students who were left behind prior to the legislation and continue to be left behind because of the nature of the law's mandates for testing.

Legislation can be amended; in the United States, it is expected that laws will be amended each time they are reauthorized. Hence, the discussion of politics and research does not simply rest on a specific piece of legislation at a specific point in time. Rather, the debate that ensued from the requirements of NCLB with regard to research resulted in deeper discussions about the meaning of quality in research, with specific reference to the concept of objectivity.

Box 1.7 Scientifically Based Research Definition in No Child Left Behind[a]

(Title IX, Part A, § 9101 [37])

(37) SCIENTIFICALLY BASED RESEARCH—The term scientifically based research -

A. means research that involved the application of rigorous, systematic, and objective procedures to obtain reliable and valid knowledge relevant to education activities and programs; and
B. includes research that—
   i. employs systematic, empirical methods that draw on observation or experiment;
   ii. involves rigorous data analyses that are adequate to test the stated hypotheses and justify the general conclusions drawn;
   iii. relies on measurements or observational methods that provide reliable and valid data across evaluators and observers, across multiple measurements and observations, and across studies by the same or different investigators;
   iv. is evaluated using experimental or quasi-experimental designs in which individuals, entities, programs, or activities are assigned to different conditions and with appropriate controls to evaluate the effects of the condition of interest, with a preference for random-assignment experiments, or across-condition controls;
   v. ensures that experimental studies are presented in sufficient detail and clarity to allow for replication or, at a minimum, offer the opportunity to build systematically on their findings; and
   vi. has been accepted by a peer-reviewed journal or approved by a panel of independent experts through a comparably rigorous, objective, and scientific review.

a. For additional information, see the U.S. Department of Education's Web site dedicated to No Child Left Behind (http://www.ed.gov/nclb/landing.jhtml).

Contested Territory: Quality, Causality, and Objectivity

The National Research Council (NRC, 2002) issued a report that contained a broad definition of Scientific Research in Education that includes both quantitative and qualitative methods. Despite this indication of a willingness to consider a variety of methods, the NRC's report contains the claim that experimental methods are the preferred strategy, the gold standard for causal investigations (Maxwell, 2004). The NRC model of causality rests on the premise that we cannot observe causality; we can observe regularities in the relationships between events that can be ascertained by randomized experiments and it dismisses qualitative approaches as a means to understanding causality.

The fundamental principle underlying the prioritizing of experimental research as outlined by the NRC is that greater quality is needed in educational (and psychological) research and that the randomized experiment is the pathway to achieve that quality based on the belief that this approach allows a researcher to determine causality by observing regularities between events in an objective manner. However, Bloch (2004) suggests that what constitutes quality in research, establishing causality, and acting in an objective way is not as simple as choosing an experimental design. She sees the determination of quality in research as contested territory and that acceptance of such a narrow way of reasoning excludes other possibilities that are important in educational and psychological research. She writes, "These exclusions would include the social, cultural, economic, and historical contexts in which the researched and the researchers are participating in research, the ways in which significant questions are defined and by whom, and the ways in which rigor and generalizability are established and by whom" (p. 101).

Bloch (2004) raises these questions for researchers to consider: "In what ways must this particular text be read as an historical and cultural/political document of its time that defines knowledge as high or low quality,...truth/nontruth of research, as based on the judgment of its being good or poor? What are the social and political consequences of this view of science?...Whose knowledge will be contested; whose will be accepted; whose will be left out of consideration (again)?" (p. 105).

As S. Harding (1993) argued in the early days of the emergence of transformative thinking in research, the socially situated basis for knowledge claims and feminist standpoint epistemologies (transformative) require and generate stronger standards for objectivity than do those that turn away from providing systematic methods for locating knowledge in history. She wrote,

> The starting point of standpoint theory—and its claim that is most often misread—is that in societies stratified by race, ethnicity, class, gender, sexuality, or some other politics shaping the very structure of society, the *activities* of those at the top both organize and set limits on what persons who perform such activities can understand about themselves and the world around them. . . . So one's social situation enables and sets limits on what one can know; some social situations—critically unexamined dominant ones—are more limiting in this respect, and what makes these situations more limiting is their inability to generate the most critical question about recorded beliefs. (p. 55)

Thus, she concludes that the researcher who "starts off thought" from marginalized lives is actually imposing a stronger objectivity by soliciting viewpoints that have been ignored in past research.

Extending Your Thinking: Objectivity and Relativism

One unresolved issue in the paradigm discussion relates to the tension between objectivity and relativism. Postpositivist scholars teach the student to value objectivity and the discovery of objective truth. But in the constructivist paradigm, multiple viewpoints are sought. The ontological assumption is not that there is one reality waiting to be discovered, but that there are multiple realities, depending on whose viewpoint you are soliciting. This ontological assumption has been labeled *radical relativism* by some who feel that constructivist research results only in "opinions" that cannot be substantiated. How do you respond to this dilemma for yourself?

Merging Paradigms

Throughout the chapters of this text, the strengths and challenges associated with various definitions of quality in research are examined. Educational and psychological phenomena are discussed from a variety of perspectives through the different lenses offered by the four major paradigms. What role do different paradigms play in research practice? Because many researchers combine the use of quantitative and qualitative methods, on the surface at least, it appears that a merger of paradigms is possible. Do depictions of paradigms, such as those in Table 1.2, emphasize differences more than similarities? In Kuhn's (1962/1996) early work on paradigms and scientific revolutions, he claimed that paradigms serve a purpose of providing a framework for discussion by researchers and that it is through that process that paradigms are changed, replaced, or modified. He did not hold the seeming incommensurability (i.e., paradigmatic belief systems do not share values or standards, hence communication across paradigms is difficult if not impossible) that is sometimes used to depict paradigmatic positions.

The permeability of paradigmatic positions is illustrated by Lincoln and Denzin's (2000) recognition that many scholars who use qualitative methods are becoming more cognizant of the perspectives of the gendered, historically situated, interacting individual. They described an ever-present, but shifting, center in the discourses of qualitative research that was previously situated primarily in the constructivist paradigm. The center shifts as new, previously oppressed or silenced voices enter the discourse. Thus, for example, feminists and critical race researchers have articulated their own relationship to the postpositivist, poststructuralist, and critical perspectives. These new articulations then refocus and redefine previous ontologies, epistemologies, and methodologies (Lincoln & Denzin, 2000, p. 1048). The lines between paradigms become more muddied when one examines Denzin and Lincoln's (2005) third edition of the *The SAGE Handbook of Qualitative Research* in which they explicitly solicited chapters that would connect qualitative inquiry to social justice and progressive political action.

Postmodernism, poststructuralism, and deconstructivism add to the discussion of the permeability of the lines around the major paradigms (see Table 1.2). While these philosophical orientations emerged as a reaction against the postpositivists' belief in a certain reality, they do share much in common with constructivists (recognizing multiple realities), transformative researchers (addressing issues of power), and pragmatists (noting that decisions about methods and findings are context dependent). In many ways, these positions give credence to the possibility for researchers' abilities to talk across paradigms. Koro-Ljungberg (2008) describes an increasing interest in postmodernism and poststructuralism by researchers who use qualitative methods. Is this a harbinger of a need for a fifth paradigm or an indicator of the permeability of the paradigmatic borders?

The field of research has not yet reached the point of full integration of paradigms. Therefore, this text presents the existing paradigms and their assumptions as starting points for thought with the hope that the framework will help clarify thinking and that the tensions will result in improved approaches to research and evaluation. Researchers should be aware of their basic beliefs, their view of the world (i.e., their functional paradigm), and the way these influence their approach to research.

In this book, quantitative, qualitative, and mixed methods are explained, and the viewpoints of the various research paradigms are incorporated into the descriptions of methods. The intent is to provide as full a picture as possible of what is considered to be "good" research methodology from a variety of perspectives. This text cannot provide an in-depth discussion of the philosophical underpinnings of each perspective, each approach to research, data analysis, or construction of measurement instruments. References are provided in appropriate chapters for more in-depth information on these topics.

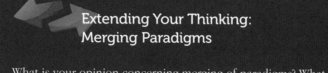

Extending Your Thinking: Merging Paradigms

What is your opinion concerning merging of paradigms? What do you envision as being required for a merger to occur (if you think it is possible)?

Summary of Chapter 1: An Introduction to Research

At this point, you should understand the importance of the philosophy of science for the conduct of research. You should be able to describe four major paradigms that are influencing researchers and evaluators by providing them with a philosophical framework to underlie their research decisions and actions. An inadequate but essentialist description of the four paradigms is as follows: Postpositivism emphasizes objectivity, experimentation, and generalizability. Constructivism emphasizes constructed realities, interaction with participants, and rich description. Transformative researchers focus on issues of social justice, human rights, and cultural complexity. Pragmatic researchers match the research questions with the choice of research methods, as indicated by each specific study's demands. Each of these paradigms has implications for methodological decisions that are explored in later chapters. Researchers operate in the real world, and therefore they are enmeshed in the politics of the real world that are visible in government policies and professional association standards. The field of research is an active, dynamic discipline that can be seen in the discussion of the permeability and possible merger of paradigms.

Notes

1. It should be noted that M. Q. Patton (2002) also uses pragmatism as the underlying paradigm for his methodological writings in qualitative research.

2. The researchers also investigated the effect of the treatment for students who entered the school during the three-year period of the study to determine the effects for all students with variable exposure to the treatment. This aspect of their study is not included in the interest of providing a simpler and clearer example of a postpositivist approach to research. The interested reader, however, can find the full details in the original source.

3. Schwandt (2000) provides detailed background on the philosophical base of the interpretive, hermeneutic, and constructivist paradigms, and Guba and Lincoln (1989) devoted an entire book to explaining the underlying assumptions of constructivism.

4. There are five national ethnic minority psychological associations: Asian American Psychological Association, Association of Black Psychologists, National Hispanic Psychological Association, Society for the Psychological Study of Ethnic Minority Issues (Division 45 of the APA), and the Society of Indian Psychologists. The presidents of these associations and the president (or his/her designee) of the APA constitute the CNPAAEMI.

5. Division 17 is Counseling Psychology, and Division 45 is Psychological Study of Ethnic Minority Issues.

6. Kirkhart first introduced the term multicultural validity in 1995; she has expanded the concept considerably in her 2005 chapter.

7. Morgan (2007) provides an excellent discussion of the basic beliefs of mixed methods researchers who work from a pragmatic philosophical base. He prefers not to use the term paradigm, preferring to describe the relevant belief systems as characterizing a pragmatic approach.

In This Chapter

- Evaluation is defined and distinguished from research in terms of purpose, method, and use.
- The history of evaluation and current theoretical models are explained, including the CIPP (Context, Input, Process, Product) model, responsive evaluation, theory-based evaluation, participatory evaluation, utilization-focused evaluation, Real World Evaluation, developmental evaluation, empowerment evaluation, inclusive evaluation, feminist evaluation, culturally responsive evaluation, and postcolonial and indigenous evaluation.
- Steps for planning an evaluation are described, including a description of what is to be evaluated, the purpose of the evaluation, the stakeholders in the evaluation, constraints affecting the evaluation, the evaluation questions, selection of an evaluation model, data collection specification, analysis and interpretation strategies, utilization, management of the evaluation, and meta-evaluation plans.
- Ethical guidelines from the American Evaluation Association (AEA) are also presented.
- Questions to guide critical analysis of evaluation studies are provided, with special reference to *The Program Evaluation Standards: How to Assess Evaluations of Educational Programs* (Joint Committee on Standards for Educational Evaluation, 2009).

In response to concerns about teenage pregnancies and escalating rates of sexually transmitted diseases and HIV/AIDS infection, the U.S. government enacted Title V, Section 510 of the Personal Responsibility and Work Opportunity Reconciliation Act of 1996 to promote an abstinence only educational program for school age youth. Because the federal funding for this program exceeded $1 billion, it seemed prudent to commission an evaluation to determine if abstinence only programs were effective (McClelland & Fine, 2008). Mathematica Policy Research Institute received funds from the federal government to conduct an evaluation of four selected abstinence only programs (Trenholm, et al. 2007). "Findings indicate that youth in the program group were no more likely than control group youth to have abstained from sex and, among those who reported having had sex, they had similar numbers of sexual partners and had initiated sex at the same mean age" (p. xvii). The programs also did not have an impact on the number of pregnancies, births, or STDs. A summary of this study is presented as Sample Study 2.1.

2

Evaluation

Defining Evaluation

Evaluators have not been immune to the generally pluralistic, and sometimes contentious, spirit prevailing in the research community. This is partially because evaluations are often (but certainly not exclusively) conducted on programs designed to help oppressed and troubled people. The direct relationship between the evaluation of social and educational programs and access to resources sets the stage for tensions that can sometimes result in conflicts. Ernie House (1993) captures this spirit in his description of the evolution of evaluation:

> Gradually, evaluators recognized that there were different interests to be served in an evaluation and that some of these interests might conflict with one another. The result was pluralist conceptions of evaluation in which multiple methods, measures, criteria, perspectives, audiences, and interests were recognized. Conceptually, evaluation moved from monolithic to pluralist conceptions, reflecting the pluralism that had emerged in the larger society. How to synthesize, resolve, and adjudicate all these multiple multiples remains a formidable question, as indeed it does for the larger society. Evaluation, which was invented to solve social problems, was ultimately afflicted with many of the problems it was meant to solve. (p. 11)

Sample Study 2.1

Summary of an Evaluation Study

Evaluation Problem: Teenage pregnancy and sexually transmitted diseases are associated with high personal and societal costs. A billion dollars of taxpayer money was used to implement abstinence only programs for school age youth.

Sample Evaluation Questions: What impacts do abstinence only programs have on behavioral outcomes (e.g., sexual abstinence, sexual activity, and risks of STDs and pregnancy)?

Method: The evaluation used an experimental design that involved random assignment of youth in four locations to either the abstinence education program or the control group that did not receive this program: two urban programs in Florida and Minnesota and two rural programs in Virginia and Mississippi.

Treatment: The programs in each setting were different in some respects, but they were all required to adhere to principles such as: exclusively teach that abstinence from sexual activity is the only certain way to avoid out-of-wedlock pregnancy, sexually transmitted diseases, and other health problems. The students participated in the programs over a three-year period (fall 1999 to fall 2001).

Participants: The final evaluation was based on 2,057 youth, 1,209 in the experimental group and 848 in the control group. The evaluation was conducted four to six years after the students began participating in the program. Two of the cases were in middle schools and the average age at the time of the final evaluation was 18 years old; two of the programs were implemented in upper elementary schools and their students averaged 15 years at the time of the final evaluation.

Data Collection: Evaluators used the Survey of Teen Activities and Attitudes; they administered it four times: baseline at the beginning of the program and three follow-up surveys either in school or by phone. During the implementation phase, survey data were supplemented by qualitative data collected during site visits. The final evaluation data were collected by a survey administered to youth in 2005 and 2006.

Results: The results are as stated at the beginning of this chapter: no differences in outcomes between experimental and control groups.

Discussion: Nationally, about half of all high school youth report having had sex, and more than one in five students report having had four or more sexual partners by the time they complete high school. In this study, 47 percent of sexually active youth had unprotected sex in the previous 12 months. One-quarter of sexually active adolescents nationwide have an STD, and many STDs are lifelong viral infections with no cure. "Findings from this study speak to the continued need for rigorous research on how to combat the high rate of teen sexual activity and its negative consequences" (p. 61).

SOURCE: Based on Trenholm et al., 2007.

Given the tone of House's words, it should come as no surprise that even the definition of evaluation has been contested. Many definitions of evaluation have been proposed. In the *Encyclopedia of Evaluation* (Mathison, 2005), Fournier (2005, p. 140) provided this as a general definition of evaluation:

> Evaluation is an applied inquiry process for collecting and synthesizing evidence that culminates in conclusions about the state of affairs, value, merit, worth, significance, or quality of a program, product, person, policy, proposal, or plan. Conclusions made in evaluations encompass both an empirical aspect (that something is the case) and a normative aspect (judgment about the value of something). It is the value feature that distinguishes evaluation from other types of inquiry, such as basic science research, clinical epidemiology, investigative journalism, or public polling.

The terms merit and worth used in this definition of evaluation also need clarification. In the same *Encyclopedia of Evaluation* (Mathison, 2005), we find these definitions:

- Merit is the absolute or relative quality of something, either overall or in regard to a particular criterion. To determine the merit of an evaluand in regard to a particular criterion, it is necessary to collect relevant performance data and to explicitly ascribe value to it; that is, to say how meritorious the evaluand is in that particular dimension. To determine the overall merit of the evaluand, a further step is required: synthesis of performances with multiple criteria. Merit determination and synthesis are two of the core methodological tasks that distinguish evaluation from the collection and reporting of descriptive data for interpretation by others. (Jane Davidson) (p. 247)

- Worth is an outcome of an evaluation and refers to the value of the evaluand in a particular context, as opposed to the evaluand's intrinsic value, which is its merit. Worth and merit are not dependent on each other, and an evaluand (e.g., a doctor) may have merit (she is a highly skilled cardiologist) but have little worth (the hospital needs an anesthesiologist). The opposite is also the case (the hospital has found an anesthesiologist but not a very good one). The worth of an evaluand requires a thorough understanding of the particular context as well as the qualities and attributes of the evaluand. (Mathison) (p. 452)

Scriven (2009) extends this distinction with this example: "Yes, it's a great (i.e., high quality/merit) car, but was it worth what it cost?," thus making the point that worth involves consideration of different types of costs, both monetary and nonmonetary. Michael Patton (2008) makes a further distinction of merit and worth: "Merit refers to the intrinsic value of a program, for example, how effective it is in meeting the needs of those it is intended to help. Worth refers to extrinsic value to those outside the program, for example, to the larger community or society. A welfare program that gets jobs for recipients has merit for those who move out of poverty and worth to society by reducing welfare costs" (p. 113). Box 2.1 contains an excerpt from the EvalTalk listserv in which an evaluator in Brazil, Robert Walker, queries Michael Patton about these concepts.

Box 2.1 EvalTalk Discussion of Merit and Worth

From: Robert Walker

To: EVALTALK@bama.ua.edu

Sent: Wednesday, January 7, 2009 3:46:58 PM

Subject: Re: Merit

Dear Michael Patton,

I'm a little confused by the following:

<Merit refers to the intrinsic value of a program, for example, how effective it is in meeting the needs of those it is intended to help.> [Patton, Utilization Focused Evaluation, 3rd ed.]

The example you give seems to refer to "internal" more than to "intrinsic." In fact, an evaluand that is of widespread value to many diverse parties (including future generations), with few if any "side effects," would seem to me to be of greater merit than something that is exclusively "effective in meeting the needs of those it is intended to help." Imagine an agricultural extension program to improve the productivity of tobacco farms, or of some other energy-intensive crop that destroys soil properties and has other environmental and social costs. If we take into account public health and environmental concerns, an "effective" program for the farmers involved may not be meritorious at all, given the big picture.

My Webster's unabridged defines intrinsic as "belonging to the real nature of the thing; not dependent on external circumstances; inherent."

Robert

Michael Patton replies:

Robert,

Your example moves from considerations of merit to considerations of worth. Indeed, a program judged to have merit may not be judged to have worth, as your example illustrates. That's the purpose of making the distinction.

An evaluand may have merit on one set of criteria and not on others. That's the reason the Encyclopedia of Evaluation definition of merit emphasizes the need for synthesis across multiple criteria of merit.

MQP

In international development communities, a distinction is made between monitoring and evaluation. The United Nations Development Programme (2002, p. 6) provides the following definitions that are relevant in evaluations undertaken in international development:

- Monitoring is defined as "a continuing function that aims primarily to provide the management and main stakeholders of an ongoing intervention with early indications of progress, or lack thereof, in the achievement of results. An ongoing intervention might be a project, programme or other kind of support to an outcome."

- Evaluation is defined as "selective exercise that attempts to systematically and objectively assess progress towards and the achievement of an outcome. Evaluation is not a one-time event, but an exercise involving assessments of differing scope and depth carried out at several points in time in response to evolving needs for evaluative knowledge and learning during the effort to achieve an outcome."

Alternative definitions tend to emphasize different aspects of the evaluation process. For example, Hadley and Mitchell (1995) define evaluation as "applied research carried out to make or support decisions regarding one or more service programs" (p. 48). Shadish (1994) calls for an expansion of the definition in terms of the purposes for which evaluations are done. His definition of evaluation included the "use of feasible practices to construct knowledge of the value of the evaluand that can be used to ameliorate the problems to which the evaluand is relevant" (p. 352). Even the part of the definition that refers to the purpose of the evaluation has been discussed and criticized. Sometimes, evaluations are done, but no big decisions are made based on the results. M. Q. Patton (2008) notes that evaluations can be used to reduce uncertainty about decisions that have to be made but that many other factors influence program decisions, such as availability of resources and the political climate. You can use the following list of questions to process the content of the various definitions and their implications for practice.

Extending Your Thinking: Definitions of Evaluation

1. What do the definitions of program evaluation mean to you? Explain in your own words.
2. How do the concepts of merit and worth figure into your understanding of the meaning of evaluation?
3. Search for alternative definitions of program evaluation by examining other texts of Web-based resources (see the American Evaluation Association's Web page (www.eval.org) for good sources). What similarities and differences do you see between/among the definitions? What distinguishes one definition from the others?
4. Why is it important which definition of evaluation you use? What kind of power rests in the definition to tell you what to do or how to do it?
5. What are the implications of the various definitions for working in culturally diverse communities? What are the advantages and disadvantages of adopting different definitions in a culturally complex setting?
6. What are your reflections on the power related to who gets to decide which definition of evaluation is used?

As already indicated, the definitions of evaluation contain some jargon from the evaluation community that requires explanation for you to really understand what evaluation is, such as the terms merit and worth. Additional terms are defined in Box 2.2. A more comprehensive listing of terms and their meanings can be found in the *Encyclopedia of Evaluation* (Mathison, 2005) and Scriven's *Evaluation Thesaurus* (1991).

Box 2.2 Definition of Terms in Evaluation Parlance

When evaluators talk about the evaluand or object of the evaluation, they are talking about what it is that will be evaluated. This can include a social or educational program, a product, a policy, or personnel. Examples of the kinds of programs that are evaluated include enrichment programs for deaf, gifted adolescents; drug and alcohol abuse programs for the homeless; and management programs for high-level radioactive waste.

Formative evaluations are conducted primarily for the purposes of program improvement. Typically, formative evaluations are conducted during the development and implementation of the program and are reported to in-house staff that can use the information to improve the program. A summative evaluation is an evaluation used to make decisions about the continuation, revision, elimination, or merger of a program. Typically, it is done on a program that has stabilized and is often reported to an external agency.

Internal evaluators work within the organization that operates the program; external evaluators are "experts" brought in from outside the organization for the express purpose of conducting or assisting with the evaluation.

Evaluators must respond to the concerns and interests of selected members of the setting being evaluated (often termed the stakeholders). These include the program funders, the administrators, staff members, and recipients of the services (and sometimes those who do not receive the services for various reasons). These are the audiences that the evaluators serve in the planning, conduct, and use of the evaluation study, compared with the scholarly, academic audience of the researcher.

Evaluations can be conducted on social and educational policies, programs, products, or personnel. For purposes of this chapter, I focus on the evaluation of social and educational programs. References for individuals interested in personnel evaluation are provided in Box 2.3.

Box 2.3 References for Personnel Evaluation

Books

Evers, A., Anderson, N., & Voskuijl, O. (Eds.). (2005). *The Blackwell handbook of personnel selection*. Oxford: Blackwell.

Joint Committee on Standards for Educational Evaluation. (2008). *The personnel evaluation standards* (2nd ed.). Thousand Oaks, CA: Sage.

Stronge, J. H., & Tucker, P. D. (Eds.). (2003). *Handbook on teacher evaluation: Assessing and improving performance*. Larchmont, NY: Eye on Education.

Wilkerson, J. R., & Lang, W. S. (2007). *Assessing teacher dispositions*. Thousand Oaks, CA: Corwin.

Journals

Counselor Education and Supervision

Educational Assessment, Evaluation and Accountability (formerly the *Journal of Personnel Evaluation in Education)*

Educational Leadership

Journal of Applied Psychology

Journal of Counseling Psychology

Journal of Occupational and Organizational Psychology

Personnel Psychology

Phi Delta Kappa

Professional School Counseling

Distinguishing Research and Evaluation

Given the definitions of evaluation already discussed, you may already have an inkling of how research and evaluation differ. While there is much overlap between the world of research and evaluation, evaluation occupies some unique territory (Mertens, 2009). J. C. Greene (2000) writes about the commonalities that demarcate evaluation contexts and distinguish program evaluation from other forms of social inquiry (such as research). She argues, based on the writings of M. Q. Patton (1987), Cronbach and associates (1980), and Weiss (1987), that what distinguishes evaluation from other forms of social inquiry is its political inherency; that is, in evaluation, politics and science are inherently intertwined. Evaluations are conducted on the merit and worth of programs in the public domain, which are themselves responses to prioritized individual and community needs that resulted from political decisions. Program evaluation "is thus intertwined with political power and decision making about societal priorities and directions" (J. C. Greene, 2000, p. 982).

Trochim (2006) argues that evaluation is unique because of the organizational and political contexts in which it is conducted, which require skills in management, group processes, and political maneuvering that are not always needed in research. Mathison (2008) makes a strong claim that evaluation needs to be considered as a distinct discipline because of its historical emergence in the 1960s as a mechanism to examine valuing as a component of systematic inquiry, as well as the ensuing development of methodological approaches that focus on stakeholder input and use of defined criteria (see the American Evaluation Association's *Guiding Principles for Evaluators* (2004) and the Joint Committee on Standards for Educational Evaluation [2009] discussed later in this chapter).

Scriven (2003) adds a thoughtful evolution of this train of thought by describing evaluation as a transdiscipline because it is used in so many other disciplines. He writes: "Evaluation is a discipline that serves other disciplines even as it is a discipline unto itself, thus its emergent transdisciplinary status" (p. 422). He says evaluation is like such disciplines as statistics and ethics that have unique ways of approaching issues but are also used in other areas of inquiry such as education, health, and social work.

Mertens (2009; Ginsberg & Mertens, 2009) recognizes the uniqueness of evaluation, as well as its overlap with applied research in education and the social sciences. While evaluation has contributed to our understanding of how to bring people together to address critical social issues, parallel developments have also been occurring in applied social research. Hence, "there is a place at which research and evaluation intersect—when research provides information about the need for, improvement of, or effects of programs or policies" (Mertens, 2009, p. 2). Thus, this provides additional rationale for including evaluation in this textbook as a major genre of systematic inquiry that borrows and enhances the methodologies developed in the research community.

This ties in (again) with the quotation that appeared earlier in this chapter. You might be wondering what time period is referenced in House's (1993) remark that "gradually, evaluators recognized..." (p. 11). When did evaluators think differently, and what did they think? I now present you with a brief history of evaluation that provides the context for understanding theories and methods in evaluation.

Extending Your Thinking: Research Versus Evaluation

Locate a published evaluation study. Explain why that study should or should not be classified as an evaluation study (as opposed to a research study) based on the definition of *evaluation*. What do you derive from this exercise in terms of the difference between evaluation and research?

History and Models of Evaluation

The origins of evaluation could be traced back to the 1800s, when the government first asked for external inspectors to evaluate public programs such as prisons, schools, hospitals, and orphanages (Stufflebeam, Madaus, & Kellaghan, 2000). However, most writers peg the beginning of the profession of evaluation, as it is now known, to the 1960s, with the passage of Great Society legislation (e.g., Head Start programs and the Elementary and Secondary Education Act) that mandated evaluations as a part of the programs. The history of evaluation is also complicated by its pluralistic disciplinary roots, with educational evaluators coming from a testing, assessment. and objectives-based evaluation background and psychologists more closely aligned with applied social research traditions (Mark, Greene, & Shaw, 2006).

Alkin (2004, 2007) attempted to depict the historical roots through a tree with three branches: use, methods, and valuing (see Figure 2.1). The tree is useful in some respects; however, it is limited in that it reflects the work of United States evaluation theorists and is not inclusive of evaluation theorists of color or those who represent indigenous groups. Hopson and Hood (2005) undertook the "Nobody Knows My Name" project in order to bring to light the contributions of African Americans to program evaluation. Hood and Hopson (2008) particularly note the work of African American scholars Asa Hilliard (1978, 1983, 1984, 1989, 1992, 1996, 1997, 2000, 2007), Aaron Brown (1944), Leander

Boykin (1950), and Reid E. Jackson (1940a, 1940b) that serve as a basis for their own work that extends responsive evaluation (Stake) to culturally responsive evaluation. This excerpt from Hood and Hopson's (2008, p. 414) discussion of Hilliard's work illustrates the potency of his contribution to evaluation from an Afrocentric perspective:

> In 1989, Hilliard combined his Afrocentric perspective with his observations about evaluation at the annual meeting of the American Evaluation Association in his keynote address entitled "Kemetic (Egyptian) Historical Revision: Implications for Cross-Cultural Evaluation and Research in Education." In particular, he reminded evaluators that they are engaged in the "manipulation of power and therefore politics in its truest sense. . . . Different approaches to evaluation can result in the painting of very different pictures of reality." (p. 8)

In a rough way, the three branches can be mapped on the major paradigms described in Chapter 1. The use branch equates to the pragmatic paradigm; the methods branch to the postpositivist paradigm and the valuing branch would need to be split to represent the constructivist and transformative paradigms. The transformative branch could then be extended to include culturally responsive, postcolonial, indigenous, and feminist evaluators.

Figure 2.1 Historical Roots of Evaluation (Alkin, 2004, 2007)

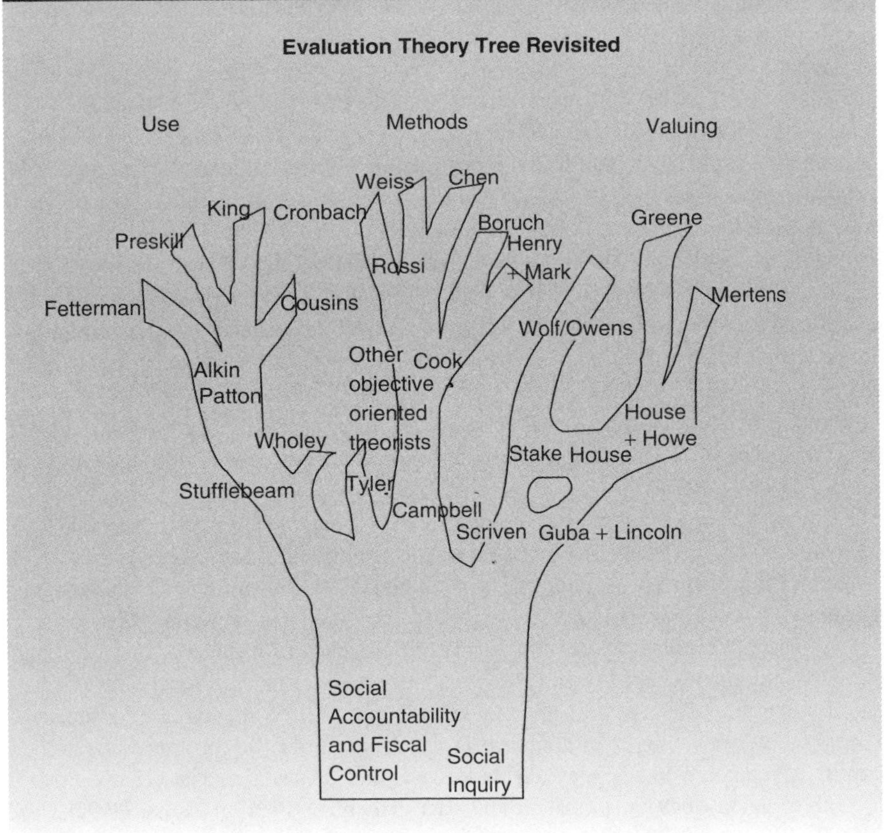

Postpositivist Paradigm

Evaluation in both education and psychology began in the postpositivist paradigm. In education, evaluation emerged from a tradition of testing to assess student outcomes and progressed through an era of specification of objectives and measurement to determine if the objectives had been met. Ralph Tyler (cited in Stufflebeam et al., 2000) developed the objectives-based model for evaluation, and Malcolm Provus (cited in Stufflebeam et al., 2000) developed the discrepancy evaluation model. In psychology, the early years of evaluation were dominated by the work of Donald Campbell (see Shadish, Cook, & Leviton, 1991) in quasi-experimental design (a topic that is discussed extensively in Chapter 4 of this book). Contemporary evaluators have not abandoned the use of testing, objectives, and quasi-experimental designs, but they have modified and extended these strategies and added new approaches in the ensuing years. Lest we think that the postpositivist paradigm is a thing of the past, consider this statement from the U.S. Department of Education's (2003) *Identifying and Implementing Educational Practices Supported by Rigorous Evidence: A User Friendly Guide*: "Well-designed and implemented randomized controlled trials are considered the 'gold standard' for evaluating an intervention's effectiveness, in fields such as medicine, welfare and employment policy, and psychology" (p. 1). The U.S. Department of Education also maintains a Web site called the What Works Clearinghouse (http://ies.ed.gov/ncee/wwc/) that lists educational programs that are deemed to have been rigorously evaluated because of the use of randomized experimental designs. Two of the sample studies described in this text provide examples of postpositivist approaches to evaluation—Sample Study 1.1 on the evaluation of the Success for All program (Borman et al., 2007) and Sample Study 2.1 on the evaluation of the abstinence only programs (Trenholm et al., 2007).

When evaluators discovered that using "objective social science methods" was not sufficient to ensure that their work would have an effect on public policy and social program decisions, they shifted their focus to more decision-based models of evaluation. As evaluators gained experience with trying to improve social programs, other models of evaluation were developed that tried to address some of the shortcomings of traditional educational assessment or experimental designs. Stufflebeam (1983) was instrumental in extending the definition of evaluation beyond the achievement of objectives to include the idea that it was a process of providing information for decision making. From his efforts with the Ohio State Evaluation Center and under the auspices of Phi Delta Kappa, Stufflebeam worked with other pioneers in the field of evaluation (including Egon Guba) to develop the CIPP (Context, Input, Process, Product) model of evaluation. Thus the CIPP model tries to incorporate many aspects of the program that were not considered under earlier models. The components of the model can be explained by the nature of the evaluation questions asked for each component (see Table 2.1).

The context and input phases represent a needs assessment function that evaluation sometimes plays to determine what is needed in terms of goals and resources for a program. For more extensive information about needs assessment, refer to Altschuld and Witkin's (2000) work on this topic.

Additional contributions to postpositivist approaches to evaluation can be found in the extensions of Donald Campbell's work explicated in the current writings of Chen and Rossi (Chen, 1990a, 1990b, 1994; Chen & Rossi, 1992) on theory-based evaluation. Theory-based evaluation is an approach in which the evaluator constructs a model of how the program works using stakeholders' theories, available social science theory, or both to guide question formation and data gathering. Chen and Rossi (1992) view

Table 2.1 CIPP Evaluation Questions

Component	*Evaluation Questions*
Context	What are the program's goals? Do they reflect the needs of the participants?
Input	What means are required to achieve a given set of goals, in terms of schedules, staffing, budget, and the like?
Process	How were the participants informed of the process? How were the resources allocated? How were the materials adapted?
Product	What is the evidence of outcomes? Should we terminate, continue, or revise this program? Should we decrease or increase funds? Should we merge it with another program?

theory-based evaluation as a way to mitigate the problems encountered in a more simplistic notion of quasi-experimental design when applied in an evaluation setting. The role of the evaluator is to bring a theoretical framework from existing social science theory to the evaluation setting. This would add insights to the structure of the program and its effectiveness that might not be available to the stakeholders in the setting. They warn against uncritically accepting the stakeholders' viewpoints as the basis for understanding the effectiveness of the program. They acknowledge that qualitative methods can be used during the program conceptualization and monitoring, but they advocate the use of randomized experiments for assessing program impact. Because theory-based evaluation, as it is conceptualized by Chen and Rossi (1992), is guided by a preference to use structural modeling methods, the kinds of question formulated for the evaluation are those that fit neatly into causal modeling (Shadish et al., 1991).

Donaldson (2007) expanded understandings about theory-driven evaluations, suggesting that the role of the evaluator is to come to a thorough understanding of the social problem, program, and implementation context (i.e., uncover the intended program theory) before deciding on the evaluation questions and methods. "Program theory-driven evaluation science is the systematic use of substantive knowledge about the phenomena under investigation and scientific methods to improve, to produce knowledge and feedback about, and to determine the merit, worth, and significance of evaluands such as social, educational, health, community, and organizational programs" (Donaldson & Lipsey, 2006, p. 67). Bledsoe and Graham's (2005; Fitzpatrick & Bledsoe, 2007) evaluation of the Fun With Books program is a multi-approach study that illustrates theory driven, empowerment, and inclusive practices; it is summarized as Sample Study 2.2.

Thus a theory-driven program evaluation must first develop the program theory that guides the program in its definition of a solution to a social problem. The evaluator obtains information about the program and its underlying theory by reviewing prior research, making public the implicit theories held by those closest to the program, and observing the program in operation. After the program theory has been made explicit, the evaluator can then work with the stakeholders to make decisions about evaluation questions and methods. Bledsoe and Graham (2005) synthesized the stakeholder's program logic with social science theory related to developmental psychology and emergent literacy to make visible the underlying causal assumptions of the program.

Sample Study 2.2

Multiple Evaluation Approaches: Theory Driven, Empowerment, Inclusive

Evaluation Focus: Research on early literacy emphasizes the importance of family involvement; lack of early literacy development has been cited as one of the major contributors to academic underachievement for children from families who face challenges of poverty. Fun With Books (FWB) is a program designed to promote interactive family literacy by in-home reading of children's literature and using related arts, crafts, and music to support the development of early literacy skills needed for success in school and later in life.

Sample Evaluation Questions: How was FWB implemented? How were cultural and socioeconomic status differences between the program staff and families addressed? What activities occurred and how were those activities tied to outcomes? Does FWB lead to an increase in (a) in-home reading between parent and child, (b) the child's motivation to learn, (c) the child's capacity to learn, and (d) the child's opportunity to learn?

Methods/Design: The evaluators describe their methods as reflecting multiple approaches: theory-driven, empowerment, and inclusive evaluation approaches. They worked closely with program staff and families to ensure that the methods were appropriate to the cultural groups and responsive to the agency's needs. The basic design was a pretest, posttest design with concentration of activity at the beginning on conceptualization of the program and emphasis on capturing process variables during its implementation.

Participants: The program was implemented in Trenton, New Jersey, a diverse community racially and ethnically (52% Black and 32% Latino, with large immigrant populations from Latin America, Caribbean, and Eastern Europe) and an economically distressed area. Participants included staff of the project as well as family members of those in the program (10 staff members and administrators; 17 families and 31 children.)

Instruments and Procedures: Evaluators used mixed methods: surveys, videotaped observations, interviews, and focus groups, as well as document reviews of the organization's history and practices. They also used established reliable measures that had been developed for Head Start programs such as a child social awareness assessment.

Results/Discussion: FWB did increase parents reading to their children; it improved access to books and provided time and encouragement for reading. The evaluators also had several recommendations for improving the program related to discussing the effects of cultural and socioeconomic differences between volunteers and the families, reaching out to current and former participants to benefit from their experiences, extending the length of the program, and including formal testing of outcomes.

SOURCE: Bledsoe & Graham, 2005.

Constructivist Paradigm

Theorists such as Guba and Lincoln (1989), M. Q. Patton (1991), Stake (1983), and House (1993) were influential in bringing the constructivist paradigm, along with qualitative methods, into evaluation. Stake's (1983) early work in responsive evaluation led the way to the introduction of the constructivist paradigm to the evaluation community. Guba and Lincoln (1989) acknowledge the foundation provided by Stake's work in responsive evaluation in their development of what they termed *fourth-generation evaluation*. They conceptualized the four generations this way:

First generation: Measurement—testing of students

Second generation: Description—objectives and tests (Tyler's work, cited in Stufflebeam et al., 2000)

Third generation: Judgment—the decision-based models, such as Stake (1983), Scriven (1967), and Stufflebeam (1983)

Fourth generation: Constructivist, heuristic evaluation

Guba and Lincoln (1989) depict the stages of evaluation as generations, with the more recent replacing those that came earlier. It is my perception that the evaluation community does not generally share this depiction, in that many of the methods and models that were developed in evaluation's earlier days continue to have influence on theory and practice.

Stake (2004, 2006) combined some of the elements of the CIPP model and discrepancy evaluation in his model of responsive evaluation. He includes the idea that evaluation involves comparing an observed value with some standard. The standard is to be defined by the expectations and criteria of different people for the program, and the observed values are to be based on those values actually held by the program. The evaluator's job is to make a comprehensive statement of what the observed program values are with useful references to the dissatisfaction and satisfaction of appropriately selected people. He extended his work in the direction of case study methodology, thus further strengthening the place of qualitative methods in evaluation inquiry. Other scholars have also extended the responsiveness evaluation approach, notably Abma (2006), J. C. Greene and Abma (2001), and Schwandt (2001).

Currently, the evaluation community seems to have reached a certain comfort level with a pluralistic approach to methodology. Qualitative methods for research with applicability to evaluation are discussed in Chapter 8.

Transformative Paradigm

Although constructivist qualitative evaluators recognize the importance that values play in the inquiry process, this paradigm does not justify any particular set of values. Many years ago, House (1993) and Sirotnik and Oakes (1990) raised the question of what social justice and fairness mean in program evaluation. Within the evaluation community, some evaluators have shifted the focus to prioritize social justice and fairness within evaluation, with the consequent opening of the door to the transformative paradigm of social inquiry for evaluators (J. C. Greene, 2000; Mathison, 2009; Mertens, 2009). Transformative approaches to evaluation parallel many of the transformative approaches in research discussed in Chapter 1 and elsewhere in this text; hence, I offer a brief listing of these approaches here as they have been developed in the evaluation community.

• Mertens (2003) developed an approach based on the transformative paradigm called inclusive evaluation, in which community members who would be affected by the results of the evaluation would be included in the methodological decisions. There is a deliberate attempt to include groups that have historically experienced oppression and discrimination on the basis of gender, culture, economic levels, ethnicities/race, sexual orientation, and disabilities, with a conscious effort to build a link between the results of the evaluation and social action. To this end, the inclusive evaluator attempts to redress power imbalances in society by involving all relevant stakeholders in a way that was authentic and that accurately represented the stakeholders' viewpoints. Inclusive evaluators are cognizant of issues of social justice that impact the definition of social problems. For example, they are aware that deficit models can place the blame for social problems on individuals or their culture, rather than on the societal response to the individual or cultural group.

Inclusive evaluation involves a systematic investigation of the merit or worth of a program or system for the purpose of reducing uncertainty in decision making and to facilitate positive social change for the least advantaged. Thus, inclusive evaluation is data based, but the data are generated from an inclusive list of stakeholders, with special efforts to include those who have been traditionally underrepresented. It does not exclude those who have been traditionally included in evaluations. Mertens (2009) expanded the notion of inclusive evaluation in her work on transformative evaluation, which is a broader philosophical framework for this type of evaluation.

• Deliberative democratic evaluation emerged from the early work of Hilliard (1984), House and Howe (2000), and B. MacDonald and Kushner (2005). House and Howe (1999) identified three foundational conditions of deliberation about the results with relevant parties, inclusion of all relevant interests, and dialogue so that the interests of various stakeholders can be accurately ascertained. These form the basis for a democratic deliberative evaluation with the capacity to equalize power relations in making evaluative judgments. A deliberative evaluation involves reflective reasoning about relevant issues, including preferences and values. An inclusive evaluation involves including all relevant interests, stakeholders, and other citizens in the process. A dialogical evaluation process entails stakeholders and evaluators engaging in dialogues allowing stakeholders' interests, opinions, and ideas to be portrayed more completely (see also J. C. Greene, 2006; Howe & MacGillivary, 2009; Lehtonen, 2006).

• Fetterman and Wandersman (2004) developed an approach called empowerment evaluation, defined as "the use of evaluation concepts, techniques, and findings to foster improvement and self-determination" (p. 10). Fetterman and Wandersman (2007) acknowledge that not all empowerment evaluations are meant to be transformative. Empowerment evaluation can be practical or transformative, much the same as Whitmore (1998) describes these two perspectives for participatory evaluation. Practical empowerment evaluation focuses on program decision making and problem solving. Transformative empowerment evaluation focuses on psychological transformation, as well as political transformation. An underlying principle of this approach is that program participants conduct their own evaluations with an outside evaluator who often serves as a coach or facilitator depending on internal program capacities. "Empowerment evaluation is an approach that aims to increase the probability of achieving program success by (1) providing program stakeholders with tools for assessing the planning, implementation, and self-evaluation of their program and (2) mainstreaming evaluation as part of the planning and management of the program/organization" (Wandersman et al., 2005, p. 28). Empowerment evaluation has been criticized on a number of bases and, to Fetterman's credit, he posts the criticisms and his responses to them on the empowerment evaluation Web site (http://homepage.mac.com/profdavidf/). Criticisms have come from evaluators such as Scriven (2005), who asserts that empowerment evaluation is not really evaluation. N. L. Smith (2007) argues that empowerment evaluation is not an evaluation approach; rather it is an ideology. And R. L. Miller and Campbell (2007) conducted a review of studies conducted using empowerment evaluation since 2005 to determine its effects and concluded that there is "little warrant for claims that the specific empowerment evaluation process used provides, of itself, any additional positive benefits beyond the general benefits of having conducted an evaluation" (p. 580). Finally, empowerment evaluation, as conceptualized by Fetterman (2001), does not explicitly address the issues of power related to sexism, racism, or oppression of people with disabilities (Whitmore, 1996). Fetterman's (2009) responses to his critics can be found at his Web site, indicated above.

• Developmental evaluation evolved from the work of Stockdill, Duhon-Sells, Olsen, and Patton (1992) and M. Q. Patton (1994), in which they explored ways to actively involve people of color in the evaluation process of a multicultural education project. Stockdill et al.'s reflections capture the impetus for the emergence of the developmental evaluation model:

> My training taught me that carefully developed data-collection instruments could obtain the needed information validly and reliably. Now I am learning that my white female culture got in the way, and that I was isolated from critical pieces of information. For example, it was only through visits to Cambodian families' homes that the Cambodian staff member could determine their concerns about their children's education. It was only through telephone calls by African American parents to other African American parents that we learned of the racism experienced by their children. It was only because of the cultural sensitivity of Saint Paul American Indians in Unity that eighteen of twenty Indian parents attended a meeting and shared the depth of their frustration about the failure of schools to educate their children. (Stockdill et al., 1992, p. 28)

Developmental evaluation is defined as evaluation that "supports program and organizational development to guide adaptation to emergent and dynamic realities from a complex systems perspective [and] it involves changing the program mode itself as part of innovation and response to changed conditions and understandings" (M. Q. Patton, 2008, p. 278). Patton recognizes that this conceptualization of evaluation might be problematic for others in the evaluation community who view evaluation as a process of rendering judgment about whether or not a program's goals have been met. He argues that this is one option for evaluators who wish to be valuable partners in the design process of programs for which the goals are emergent and changing and for which the purpose is learning, innovation, and change.

• Feminist evaluation includes judgments of merit and worth, application of social science methods to determine effectiveness, and achievement of program goals as well as tools related to social justice for the oppressed, especially, although not exclusively, women. Its central focus is on gender inequities that lead to social injustice. It uses a collaborative, inclusive process and captures multiple perspectives to bring about social change. In Seigart and Brisolara's (2002) *Feminist Evaluation: Explorations and Experiences,* they acknowledge that there is no single definition of feminism, nor a single definition of feminist evaluation. However, there are principles that have been identified across studies that claim to have a feminist orientation that are listed in Chapter 1 of this text. A summary of a feminist evaluation is presented as Sample Study 1.4. Box 2.4 offers a commentary on what makes the evaluation in that sample study feminist. The comments roughly parallel the principles for feminist inquiry found in Chapter 1.

Box 2.4 What Are the Characteristics of a Feminist Research/Evaluation Study?

1. Women's realities were placed at the center of the evaluation planning and analysis. The client was alerted to the attention to women's experiences, multiple observations were made of training sessions, and in-depth interviews were used. Analyses included gender differences. Centering means honoring the young women's realities and interpretations. Ward (2002) discusses the challenges involved personally when the women engaged in victim blaming (e.g., "she dressed provocatively"). She also mentions that centering on young women does not mean that the experiences of young men are excluded; it does mean that as the most vulnerable group, the young women and their experiences were given careful and considered attention.
2. The problem context was understood from a feminist perspective as it was revealed through literature review and discussion with advocates. This led to the perspective that gender violence affects girls more severely, consistently, and negatively than it does boys. Data collection instruments were constructed to reflect feminist analyses of adolescent gender violence, and interviews were conducted with the sensitivity that some of the participants might be survivors of gender violence themselves. This framework led to the two evaluation questions related to secondary trauma for survivors and the helpfulness of bystander training as a model.
3. Participant input was assured. Student participants contributed to the instrument development, interviews, observations, and questionnaires, as well as offered advice during the data analysis. The evaluator encountered resistance on the part of teachers who did not want to let students out of regular classes to participate in Mentors in Violence Prevention (MVP) program training or evaluation activities.
4. A willingness to challenge the status quo to achieve social change was explicit. The MVP program was originally designed for boys by men. The MVP program staff agreed to address the issue of how such a program would impact girls. Schools were given the results with the challenge that they need to make their environments less tolerant of sexism and violence that pervade students' everyday lives.
5. Mixed methods were used. Resources to support this approach were challenging, as the funder required the quantitative survey and the evaluator and MVP program staff were committed to hearing the voices of the students through a feminist approach.
6. Collaboration with advocates and activists can be done by using an expert panel if resources are available to do so. In Ward's study, she used a collaborative relationship with the MVP program staff to advise her on literature, instruments, crafting language for the survey, ways to best reach students, and interpretation of data.
7. Findings were actively disseminated and opportunities to use the results to advocate for change were highlighted. MVP program staff agreed to allow a second year of evaluation that included all-girl focus groups to continue the investigation in a safer environment for them, and the evaluator is assisting the staff in using the results to write proposals to obtain funds to continue the effort.

SOURCE: Based on Ward's (2002) evaluation of the MVP program.

• Transformative participatory evaluation (akin to participatory action research, described in Chapter 8) requires that the investigator be explicitly concerned with gender, class, race, ethnicity, sexual orientation, and different abilities and the consequent meaning of these characteristics for access to power. Participation can be built into a project in ways that reflect cultural competency (see commentary in Box 2.5).

While participatory evaluation means that evaluation is a participatory process that involves the stakeholders in the various tasks of the evaluation so that the results are fully comprehensible to project participants (Cousins & Earl, 1995; Mertens, Berkeley, & Lopez, 1995; Owano & Jones, 1995), not all participatory evaluations are transformative. The question of who is invited to participate in the process and the nature of their participation determines the extent to which participatory evaluation exemplifies the principles of the transformative paradigm. For example, Cousins and Earl (1995) explicitly acknowledge that participatory evaluation, as they conceptualize it, does not have as a goal the empowerment of individuals or groups or the rectification of societal inequities. Rather, they seek to enhance the use of evaluation data for practical problem solving within the contemporary organizational context.

Nevertheless, the basic processes involved in the conduct of participatory evaluation provide a first step toward a transformative perspective in evaluation in that the professional evaluator works as a facilitator of the evaluation process but shares control and involvement in all phases of the research act with practitioners. In participatory evaluation, the evaluator helps to train key organizational personnel in the technical skills vital to the successful completion of the evaluation project. These key organizational personnel—often administrators, counselors, or teachers—are taught sufficient technical knowledge and research skills to enable them to take on the coordinating role of continuing and new projects, with consultation with a professional evaluator as necessary.

The project participants are co-planners of the evaluation who complete the following tasks:

1. Discuss the evaluation questions that need to be addressed to determine if the project is making progress
2. Help define and identify sources of data required to answer evaluation questions
3. Are involved in the data collection and analysis and in report preparation

The main goal of participatory evaluation is to provide information for project decision makers and participants who will monitor the progress of, or improve, their project (Owano & Jones, 1995).

Box 2.5 Participatory Methods: What Approaches Reflect a Culturally Competent Evaluator With Different Groups?

Depth of understanding culture is not necessarily missing from participatory approaches, but it's not necessarily there. Participatory [evaluation] is more amenable to the manifestation of cultural competence in an evaluation setting, but I think that in and of itself it doesn't qualify. When people use the words "participatory" and

(Continued)

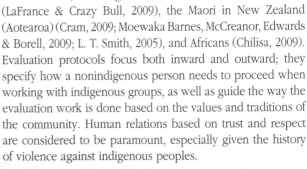

Box 2.5 (Continued)

"empowerment," not a lot of people get below the surface of talking about, well, what does that mean in terms of having a true understanding of the group you are working with? What does it mean in terms of appropriate ways that are considered to be culturally comfortable to establishing the questions for collection of data? What are the variations within that group? I do think there is danger in thinking I can take a strategy and just walk into a group and use a cookbook approach on how to do participatory or how to do empowerment without thinking about what does it mean that I am the researcher or evaluator in this process? There needs to be that sensitivity to the way you interact and how you engage people in a respectful way.

—Donna Mertens, quoted in Edno, Joh, & Yu, 2003

- Hood, Hopson, and Frierson (2005) developed the culturally responsive evaluation approach based on their experiences with evaluation in African American communities. They place priority on understanding the cultural and historical context in which programs are situated, as well as critiquing perspectives of community members that are based on deficit thinking. The culturally responsive approach to evaluation is well illustrated in the approach used to evaluate the Talent Development Model of School Reform (Thomas, 2004). These evaluators recognize the importance of matching salient characteristics of the evaluation team with the participants, establishing trusting relationships, and contributing to the overall progress of the educational enterprise in an ongoing manner (see also Mertens, 2009).

- Postcolonial and indigenous approaches were developed by members of postcolonial and indigenous communities, reflecting the cultural roots of American Indians (LaFrance & Crazy Bull, 2009), the Maori in New Zealand (Aotearoa) (Cram, 2009; Moewaka Barnes, McCreanor, Edwards & Borell, 2009; L. T. Smith, 2005), and Africans (Chilisa, 2009). Evaluation protocols focus both inward and outward; they specify how a nonindigenous person needs to proceed when working with indigenous groups, as well as guide the way the evaluation work is done based on the values and traditions of the community. Human relations based on trust and respect are considered to be paramount, especially given the history of violence against indigenous peoples.

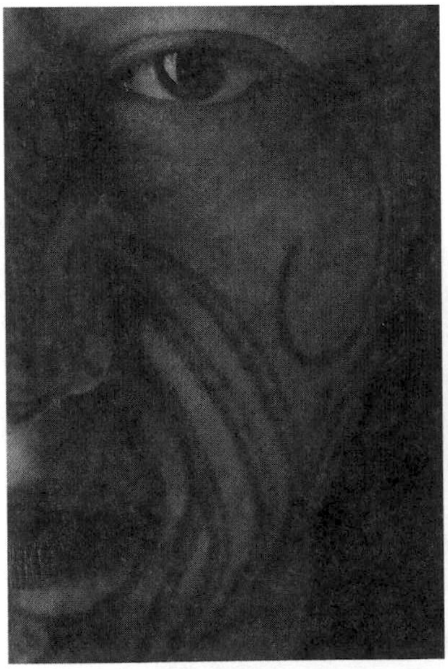

Proponents of a transformative approach to evaluation argue that working within this paradigm can lead to more appropriate interventions and more judicious distribution of resources. The transformative paradigm in evaluation follows the same principles outlined in Chapter 1 for research. Within the field of evaluation, these approaches explicitly address issues of power and representativeness of groups that have been traditionally pushed to the margins. Using the transformative paradigm as a base, the evaluator views each step in the evaluation process as an opportunity to raise questions about social justice, challenge the status quo, and bring in the voices of those who have been marginalized or inaccurately represented in previous evaluation studies.

Pragmatic Evaluation Approaches

This branch of the evaluation tree roughly parallels Alkin's (2007) use branch; the focus is on making the information from the evaluation useful to stakeholders. The major approaches include evaluations that focus on organizational culture (Preskill & Torres, 1999; Rogers & Williams, 2006), M. Q. Patton's utilization-focused evaluation, and the international development model of evaluation called Real World Evaluation (Bamberger, Rugh, & Mabry, 2006).

- Preskill and Torres (1999) provide this definition situated in organizational culture: "We envision evaluative inquiry as an ongoing process for investigating and understanding critical organization issues. It is an approach to learning that is fully integrated with an organization's work practices, and as such, it engenders (a) organization members' interest and ability in exploring critical issues using evaluation logic, (b) organization members' involvement in evaluative processes, and (c) the personal and professional growth of individuals within the organization" (pp. 1–2). Preskill (2008) expands this approach to evaluation by discussing methods for engaging organizational management in the cultivation of a culture that seeks and uses information for improvement. She emphasizes the need to build capacity in organizations to participate in and learn from evaluations through such mechanisms as training, technical assistance, written materials, establishing communities of practice, providing internships and apprenticeships, coaching and mentoring, engaging in appreciative inquiry activities, and using technology (Preskill & Boyle, 2007).

- M. Q. Patton (2008) developed an approach known as *utilization-focused program evaluation* (UFE), defined as "evaluation done for and with specific intended primary users for specific intended users for specific, intended uses" (p. 37). Patton first published the UFE book in 1978, and this approach has been widely used. He clearly states that utilization should be considered from the very beginning of an evaluation study and that the quality of the evaluation is dependent on the actual use made of its findings. This was considered to be a radical idea in 1978; however, it has been accepted as common sense by many in the evaluation community today. According to Patton, the evaluator has a responsibility to facilitate the planning and implementation of evaluations to enhance the use of the findings. This of course necessitates the identification of the intended users (stakeholders) with whom the evaluator negotiates the type of information that the client would find useful.

- *Real World Evaluation* is an approach that emerged from the world of international development evaluation in which, for better or worse, funding agencies often impose severe constraints in terms of time and money (e.g., an evaluator might be brought into a country for a short period of time to conduct an evaluation) (Bamberger et al., 2006). Bamberger et al. offer strategies to adapt evaluation designs to meet the constraints imposed by the funding agency while still trying to be responsive to the cultural complexities in the evaluation context. For example, they suggest that a local consultant can be engaged to collect background data and conduct exploratory studies prior to the arrival of the outside evaluator. This might include preparation of reports on the social and economic characteristics of the targeted community, describing key features of the program to be evaluated, and a list of potential key informants and potential participants in focus groups. Other design features are similar to those discussed in the methodological chapters of this text.

Extending Your Thinking: Evaluation Approaches

Review the historical and current models of evaluation presented in this chapter. Select four models (one from each paradigm, perhaps). For each model, determine the theorist's viewpoint regarding the following:

a. The purpose(s) of evaluation
b. The role of the evaluator in making valuing judgments
c. The role of the evaluator in making causal claims
d. The role of the evaluator in accommodating to the political setting
e. The role of the evaluator in providing information for decision making
f. The perception of the theorist as to who is the primary audience for the evaluation
g. The perception of the theorist as to the appropriate role of stakeholders in the evaluation
h. The perception of the theorist as to the role of other parties affected by or interested in the evaluation
i. The most appropriate way to train an evaluator based on that theoretical perspective

Resources and Processes for Conducting Evaluations

A general outline for steps in conducting evaluations is presented below. However, for the student who is seriously considering conducting an evaluation study, the following list of resources is provided.

Evaluation Resources

Books and Monographs

Donaldson, S. I. (2007). *Program theory-driven evaluation science.* Mahwah, NJ: Lawrence Erlbaum.

Fetterman, D. M., & Wandersman, A. (2004). *Empowerment evaluation principles in practice.* New York: Guilford.

Fitzpatrick, J. L., Sanders, J. R., & Worthen, B. R. (2004). *Program evaluation* (3rd ed.). Boston, MA: Pearson.

Guba, E. G., & Lincoln, Y. S. (1989). *Fourth generation evaluation*. Newbury Park, CA: Sage.
Hood, S., Hopson, R. K., & Frierson, H. T. (Eds.). (2005). *The role of culture and cultural context: A mandate for inclusion, the discovery of truth and understanding in evaluative theory and practice*. Charlotte, NC: Information Age.
Mathison, S. (Ed.). (2005). *Encyclopedia of evaluation*. Thousand Oaks, CA: Sage.
Mertens, D. M. (2009). *Transformative research and evaluation*. New York: Guilford.
Mertens, D. M., & McLaughlin, J. (2004). *Research and evaluation methods in special education*. Thousand Oaks, CA: Corwin.
Patton, M. Q. (2002). *Qualitative research & evaluation methods* (2nd ed.). Thousand Oaks, CA: Sage.
Patton, M. Q. (2008). *Utilization-focused evaluation* (4th ed.). Thousand Oaks, CA: Sage.
Rossi, P. H., Freeman, H. E., & Lipsey, M. W. (2003). *Evaluation: A systematic approach* (7th ed.). Thousand Oaks, CA: Sage.
Seigart, D., & Brisolara, S. (Eds.). (2002). *Feminist evaluation: Explorations and experiences* (New Directions for Evaluation, No. 96). San Francisco: Jossey-Bass.
Shadish, W. R., Jr., Cook, T. D., & Leviton, L. C. (1991). *Foundations of program evaluation*. Newbury Park, CA: Sage.
Shaw, I. F., Greene, J. C., & Mark, M. M. (Eds.). (2006). *The SAGE handbook of evaluation*. Thousand Oaks, CA: Sage.
Stake, R. E. (2004). *Standards-based & responsive evaluation*. Thousand Oaks, CA: Sage.
Stufflebeam, D. L. & Shinkfield, A. J. (2007). *Evaluation theory, models, and applications*. San Francisco: Jossey-Bass.
Thompson-Robinson, M., Hopson, R., & SenGupta, S. (Eds.). (2004). *In search of cultural competence in evaluation: Toward principles and practice*. (New Directions for Evaluation, No. 102). San Francisco: Jossey-Bass.
Whitmore, E. (Ed.). (1998). *Understanding and practicing participatory evaluation*. (New Directions for Evaluation, No. 80). San Francisco: Jossey-Bass.

Online Resources

• The Web site of the American Evaluation Association (AEA; www.eval.org) includes many links to evaluation resources that are available online.

• The *W. K. Kellogg Foundation Evaluation Handbook* (1998; www.wkkf.org) outlines a blueprint for designing and conducting evaluations, either independently or with the support of an external evaluator/consultant; W. K. Kellogg Foundation also publishes the Logic Model Development Guide (2004), also available on its Web site.

• The National Science Foundation's *User-Friendly Handbook for Mixed-Methods Evaluations* (2002; www.nsf.gov) discusses designing and conducting evaluations integrating quantitative and qualitative techniques for outcome evaluations that are "practical rather than technically sophisticated."

• William M. Trochim's (2006) The Research Methods Knowledge Base. The second edition is available at http://www.socialresearchmethods.net/kb/. Trochim developed an online course in research and evaluation methods that is accessible at this Web site; it contains many links to other resources relevant for evaluators.

• The U.S. General Accountability Office (GAO) has an online GAO Policy and Guidance Materials (2000; www.gao.gov), which offers documents that discuss evaluation synthesis, designing evaluations, case study evaluation, and prospective evaluation methods.

Evaluation Journals

American Journal of Evaluation

Educational Evaluation and Policy Analysis

Evaluation and Program Planning

Evaluation & the Health Professions

Evaluation Review

New Directions for Evaluation

Studies in Educational Evaluation

Professional Associations

The American Evaluation Association (AEA) is the primary professional organization for practicing evaluators in the United States and has a strong representation of evaluators from other countries. Other countries and nations also have professional organizations, such as the Canadian Evaluation Society, the African Evaluation Association (AfrEA), and the Australasian Evaluation Society. The AEA publishes two journals, *The American Journal of Evaluation* and *New Directions for Evaluation*.

The International Organization for Cooperation in Evaluation (IOCE) was established in 2003 through a worldwide collaboration of evaluation organization representatives (Mertens, 2005). The IOCE maintains a Web site that provides links to many evaluation organizations around the world (www.ioce.net). It now lists 75 different regional and national evaluation organizations, up from 5 organizations in 1995.

Steps in Planning an Evaluation

In some respects, the steps for conducting an evaluation parallel those used to conduct any research project. However, variations occur in terms of the process of inquiry because this is an *evaluation* study and because of such factors as the status of the program being evaluated and the model of evaluation chosen for use. The steps are listed in Box 2.6 and are further explained in the next section.

What follows is a general description of the steps for focusing and planning an evaluation. I have integrated ideas from all four paradigms, drawing on the work of Brinkerhoff, Brethower, Hluchyji, and Nowakowski (1983), Guba and Lincoln (1989), Mertens (2009), Mertens and McLaughlin (2004), Shadish et al. (1991), Stockdill et al. (1992), and Fitzpatrick et al. (2004).

Before launching into a discussion of the focusing stage, I want to acknowledge that all evaluators would not necessarily move through the process in exactly the same way. Nevertheless, if these steps are viewed as a nonlinear, iterative framework for planning an evaluation, they should provide a helpful guide to that end for all evaluators, no matter what their orientation. Furthermore, my remarks are probably biased toward the perspective of an external evaluator, because that has been my perspective for the last 30 years or so; however, I did work as an internal evaluator for about 8 years prior to assuming the external status. I attempt to write information that would be pertinent and helpful to both internal and external evaluators.

Box 2.6 Steps for Planning an Evaluation Study

Focusing the Evaluation

- Description of what is to be evaluated
- The purpose of the evaluation
- The stakeholders in the evaluation
- Constraints and opportunities associated with the evaluation
- The evaluation questions
- Selection of an evaluation model

Planning the Evaluation

- Data collection specification, analysis, interpretation, and use strategies
- Management of the evaluation
- Meta-evaluation plans

Implementing the Evaluation

- Completing the scope of work specified in the plan

Focusing Stage

During the focusing stage, the evaluator needs to determine what is being evaluated, the purpose of the evaluation, the stakeholders in the evaluation, and the constraints within which the evaluation will take place. In one sense, the evaluator is stuck with a "which came first, the chicken or the egg" dilemma, even in the first stage of the evaluation, in that just learning about what is to be evaluated implies contact with at least one group of stakeholders. Typically, the evaluator is contacted to perform an evaluation by some individual or agency representing one group of stakeholders in the program. Often, this first contact is initiated by a program director, policymaker, or funding group. When listening to the description of the evaluand, purpose, stakeholders, and constraints within this initial context, the evaluator can gain valuable information by asking the right kinds of questions. These questions can provide a sufficient knowledge base to direct further planning efforts and to alert the initial contact person of things that might not have been thought of, such as theoretical perspectives (Chen, 1990b) or groups that need to be included because they will be affected by the program (S. Harding, 1993; Mertens, 2009).

Description of the Evaluand. The evaluand, you will recall, is what is being evaluated (e.g., a substance abuse prevention program, a multicultural education program, or a state agency policy). The evaluator needs to determine the status of the evaluand: Is it a developing, new, or firmly established program? If it is developing, it is possible that the evaluator will be asked to play a role in the evolution of the evaluand. Thus an evaluator who is using the developmental evaluation model (M. Q. Patton, 2008) might find that a considerable amount of time is spent collaboratively designing the evaluand. If it is new or firmly established, the program is probably described in printed documents. It is always a good idea to ask for whatever printed documents are available about the program in advance of your meeting with the initial stakeholders, if possible. Reading documents such as an annual report, accreditation agency report, previous evaluation reports, or a proposal can give you a good background about the evaluand and the context within which it functions. Questions to start with include the following:

- Is there a written description of what is to be evaluated?
- What is the status of the evaluand? Relatively stable and mature? New? Developing? How long has the program been around?
- In what context will (or does) the evaluand function?
- Who is the evaluand designed to serve?
- How does the evaluand work? Or how is it supposed to work?
- What is the evaluand supposed to do?
- What resources are being put into the evaluand (e.g., financial, time, staff, materials, etc.)?
- What are the processes that make up the evaluand?
- What outputs are expected? Or occur?
- Why do you want to evaluate it?
- Whose description of the evaluand is available to you at the start of the evaluation?
- Whose description of the evaluand is needed to get a full understanding of the program to be evaluated?

You should read available documents and hold initial discussions with the conscious realization that things are not always being played out exactly as they are portrayed on paper or in conversation. Therefore, it would behoove you to alert the client to the fact that you will want to observe the program in action (e.g., in its development, implementation, etc.) to get a more accurate picture of what is being evaluated. You should also let the client know that you are aware that programs are generally not static (i.e., you will expect changes in the program throughout the duration of the evaluation) and that multisite programs will probably not be implemented in exactly the same way from site to site.

You should be aware that different individuals with different relationships with the program may view the program quite differently. Explain to your client that this often happens in evaluations and that you want to build in a mechanism to discover diverse views about the program and to explore these diversities within a public context. In this way, you can increase the chances that the program you think you are evaluating is the one that is actually functioning or developing. Without this assurance, you may find at the end of the evaluation that your results are challenged because you did not adequately represent different perceptions of the program.

Part of the description of the evaluand should include ascertaining diverse views of the program's purpose. For example, the evaluator can help program staff members, advisory committees, and partnership teams make "claims" statements regarding the program, that is, statements that represent the participants' perceptions of what would change as a result of the program activities. The evaluator leads the meeting by asking the stakeholders to comment on what they are committed to changing—and asks them to voice their real expectations for change. In this way, the evaluator hopes to increase the ownership by those responsible for the program activities for the intended changes. The following is an example of a claims statement that was generated by the group in the Stockdill et al. (1992) study of a multicultural education program:

> School staff interact with students, families, and communities with cultural awareness, warmth, and sensitivity—on the phone, in person, and in written communication. They use proper pronunciation of names, arrange children's seating to provide for integrated classroom environments, avoid racial jokes and innuendo, and confront prejudice when expressed by children or adults. (p. 30)

A common tool that evaluators use to depict the evaluand is called a logic model (McLaughlin & Jordan, 1999). A logic model is a graphic technique that allows the explicit depiction of the theory of change that underlies a program. It should reflect a model of how the program will work under certain conditions to solve an identified problem. Logic models can be quite simple, including three major components: the program that is delivered, the people who receive the program, and the results that are expected. Arrows connect the various elements of the logic model to indicate the logical flow from one element to the next. A good resource for developing logic models is the *W. K. Kellogg Foundation Logic Model Development Guide* (2004). Evaluators in international development also use graphics similar to logic models, but they call them logframes—a type of table-based logic model (Davies, 2004). Many evaluators find logic models or logframes useful; however, they also acknowledge the limitations in trying to depict a complex, dynamic program in terms of a linear, two-dimensional graphic. A sample logic model based on a program to improve early literacy skills for deaf youngsters can be found in Figure 2.2.

Purpose of the Evaluation. Evaluations can be conducted for multiple purposes. As you discuss the evaluand, the purpose of the evaluation may begin to emerge. However, it is important to directly address this issue, within the context of what stimulated the need for the evaluation and the intended use of the evaluation results. The purpose of the evaluation needs to be distinguished from the purpose of the program. The sample claims statement presented above exemplifies a partial statement of purpose for the program. As was mentioned earlier in this chapter, Scriven (1991) identified formative and summative as two types of evaluation purposes.

Formative evaluations are conducted during the operation of a program to provide information useful in improving the program. Summative evaluations are conducted at the end of a program to provide judgments about the program's worth or merit. Developmental evaluations are typically designed to provide systematic data in a fluid, dynamic, changing context of program development. Although summative evaluations tend to focus more on program impact, formative and developmental evaluations can include program impact data that is viewed as a barometer for program changes.

M. Q. Patton (2008; Stockdill et al., 1992) also distinguished a purpose for evaluation in terms of work that might occur prior to either a formative or summative evaluation. Formative evaluation typically assumes that ultimate goals are known and that the issue is how best to reach them. By contrast, developmental evaluation is preformative in the sense that it is part of the process of developing goals and implementation strategies. Developmental evaluation brings the logic and tools of evaluation into the early stages of community, organization, and program development.

Figure 2.2 Shared Reading Project Logic Model (Delk & Weidekamp, 2001)

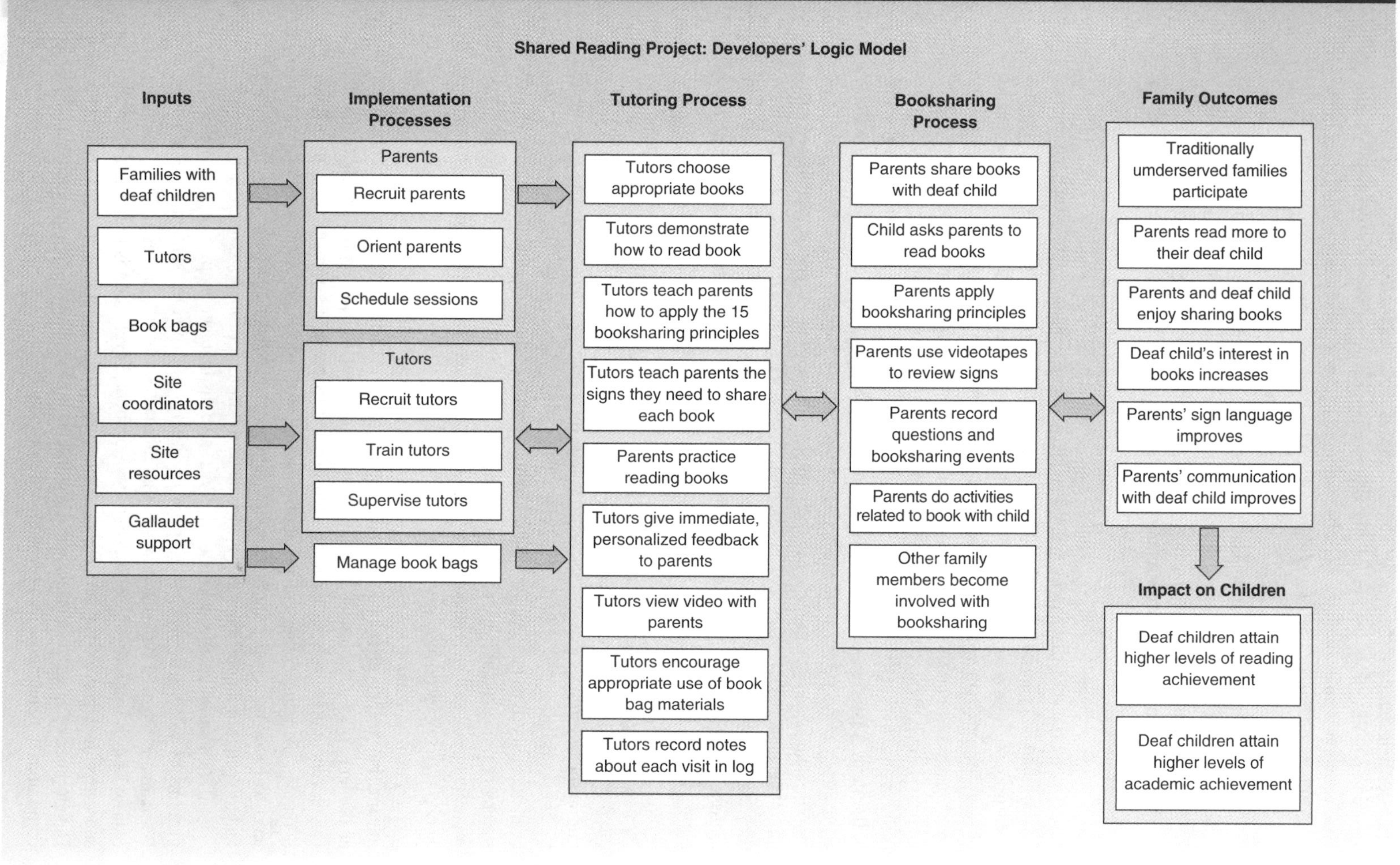

Shared Reading Project: Developers' Logic Model
Inputs
Families with deaf children
Tutors
Book bags
Site coordinators
Site resources
Gallaudet support
Implementation Processes
Parents
Recruit parents
Orient parents
Schedule sessions
Tutors
Recruit tutors
Train tutors
Supervise tutors
Manage book bags
Tutoring Process
Tutors choose appropriate books
Tutors demonstrate how to read book
Tutors teach parents how to apply the 15 booksharing principles
Tutors teach parents the signs they need to share each book
Parents practice reading books
Tutors give immediate, personalized feedback to parents
Tutors view video with parents
Tutors encourage appropriate use of book bag materials
Tutors record notes about each visit in log
Booksharing Process
Parents share books with deaf child
Child asks parents to read books
Parents apply booksharing principles
Parents use videotapes to review signs
Parents record questions and booksharing events
Parents do activities related to book with child
Other family members become involved with booksharing
Family Outcomes
Traditionally underserved families participate
Parents read more to their deaf child
Parents and deaf child enjoy sharing books
Deaf child's interest in books increases
Parents' sign language improves
Parents' communication with deaf child improves
Impact on Children
Deaf children attain higher levels of reading achievement
Deaf children attain higher levels of academic achievement

Questions can be asked to determine the purposes of the evaluation; the questions should be asked with an understanding of diversity of viewpoints and the necessity of representation of appropriate people in the discussions. Possible questions include these:

- What is the purpose of the evaluation?
- What events triggered the need for the evaluation?
- What is the intended use of the evaluation findings?
- Who will use the findings and for what purpose?
- Whose views should be represented in the statement of evaluation purpose?

Fitzpatrick et al. (2004) identify a number of possible purposes for evaluations:

- To decide whether to adopt a new program or product
- To determine whether to continue, modify, expand, or terminate an existing program
- To examine the extent to which the operation of an endeavor is congruent with its design
- To judge the overall value of a program and its relative value and cost compared with that of competing programs
- To help evaluation sponsors, clients, participants, and stakeholders determine whether identified problems are being solved

Fitzpatrick et al. (2004) also warn against a number of purposes for evaluation that are indicative of not conducting an evaluation. The evaluator should be on the alert for evaluations conducted without a clear commitment to use the results, for which decisions have already been made and the decision maker is looking for justification or cases in which the evaluation is looked at only as a public relations activity. Of course, decision makers are unlikely to characterize the purpose of the evaluation in such blunt terms, so the evaluator must be aware of establishing a clear purpose with intentions for use prior to commencing on the evaluation proper.

The purpose of the evaluation is also something that may change as the project evolves. For example, Wallerstein and Martinez (1994) developed an empowerment evaluation model to evaluate an adolescent substance abuse prevention program. In the initial stages of the evaluation, they viewed the purpose as documenting the processes and conditions necessary for a Freirean program to promote community change. (A Freirean program is one based on the teachings of Paulo Freire [1971], in which empowerment is viewed as establishing a connection with others to gain control over your own life in the context of improving the life of the community.) As the evaluation continued, the purpose shifted to focusing on analyzing how individual actors engaged in the larger change process. The areas of change included three that were predicted from the Freirean theory:

1. Changes in the youths' abilities to engage in dialogue
2. Changes in their critical thinking ability to perceive the social nature of the problems and their personal links to society
3. Changes in the youths' level of actions to promote changes

The evaluators also found that two other areas of change emerged from the study that had not been predicted from the theory:

4. Changes in the youths' emotions related to connectedness with others and self-disclosure
5. Changes in self-identity

Identification of Stakeholders. Of course, by now, you should know who the primary players in the program are. However, you should ask specific questions to ascertain whether all of the appropriate stakeholders have been identified. It is not uncommon in evaluations to address the concerns of the funding agency, the policymakers, or the program managers. However, this does not really cover all the people who are or will be affected by the program. Therefore, it is incumbent on you as the evaluator to raise questions about who should be involved in the evaluation process and to raise the consciousness of the powerful people to include those who have less power.

Possible questions at this stage include:

- Who is involved in the administration and implementation of the program?
- Who are the intended beneficiaries?
- Who has been excluded as being eligible for participation in the program?
- Who stands to gain or lose from the evaluation results?
- Which individuals and groups have power in this setting? Which do not?
- Did the program planning and evaluation planning involve those with marginalized lives?
- Who is representative of the people with the least power?
- What opportunities exist for mutual sharing between the evaluators and those without power?
- What opportunities exist for the people without power to criticize the evaluation and influence future directions?
- Is there appropriate representation on the basis of gender, ethnicity, disability, and income levels?
- Who controls what the evaluation is about and how it will be carried out?
- Who has access to the program resources?
- What are the dominant cultural values and assumptions in the program?
- Who are the supporters of the program? Who are its opponents?
- Possible stakeholders in evaluations include the following:
    - Sponsors and funders
    - Governing and advisory boards
    - State- and federal-level agency representatives
    - Policymakers
    - Administrators (at various levels)
    - Staff members (e.g., regular education teachers, special education teachers, resource personnel, psychologists)
    - Service recipients (clients, students, etc.)
    - Nonrecipients (who may or may not be eligible, but are not receiving services)
    - Parents of service recipients
    - Grassroots organization representatives in the community
    - Public community representatives

This list is not meant to be exhaustive but, rather, to give you an idea that the breadth of the impact of an evaluation can extend far beyond the individuals with whom you first discuss the evaluation project. Various strategies can be used to identify stakeholders. You might start with the people who invited you to do the evaluation and then ask them to nominate others. You might ask for people to become involved by some type of organizational or public announcement of the evaluation. You can often identify many stakeholders by reviewing the organizational chart of the program and asking questions of your early contacts about who is represented in the charts and who is not and why that is so.

Constraints of the Evaluation. Evaluations occur within specific constraints:

- Money: "We have budgeted so much money for the evaluation."
- Time: "We need the results of the evaluation before the board meets six months from now."
- Personnel: "The teachers will be given four hours per week release time to assist with data collection."
- Existing resources: "Data program records are on disk, and they contain information about all recipients and their characteristics."
- Politics: "If this program were reduced, it would free up additional funds to respond to other needs."

Politics are integrally involved in the evaluation process. Therefore, the evaluator must be aware at the start, and sensitive throughout the process, of who supports or opposes the program; who would gain or lose if the program was continued, modified, reduced, or eliminated; who sanctions the evaluation and who refuses to cooperate; who controls access to information; and who needs to be kept informed as the evaluation progresses. This would be a good time in the evaluation planning to bring up the issue of communication lines and mechanisms so that you are sure there is a formalized understanding of who needs to be informed of what and by what means.

Also, it is important to note that people move in and out of programs, so it is not safe to assume that the understandings engendered by your initial efforts will be shared by those who enter the program later (Mertens et al., 1995). You will need to orient those who enter the program later about the purpose, process, and so on of the evaluation. If you do not do it yourself, you might establish a mechanism to have other knowledgeable participants take on the task of orienting newcomers.

It is usually a good idea at this point to prepare a synthesis of your current understanding of a program, in terms of the evaluand, purpose of the evaluation, stakeholders, and constraints. You can then share this synthesis with the stakeholder groups, characterize it as your current understanding, and ask for their feedback.

Evaluation Questions

Evaluation questions can be derived from the statement of purpose for the evaluation, expanded on by holding brainstorming sessions with stakeholder groups, borrowed from previous evaluation studies, or generated by a theoretical framework that is relevant to the study. The GAO examined categories of evaluation questions that would provide useful information for Congress (Shipman, MacColl, Vaurio, & Chennareddy, 1995). I share these with you, as they seem to have generic relevance for evaluators in local settings as well.

Descriptive questions are those that tell what the program is and what it does:

- What activities does the program support?
- Toward what end or purpose?
- Who performs these activities?
- How extensive and costly are the activities, and whom do they reach?
- Are conditions, activities, purposes, and clients fairly similar throughout the program, or is there substantial variation across program components, providers, or subgroups of clients?

Implementation questions are those that tell about how and to what extent activities have been implemented as intended and whether they are targeted to appropriate populations or problems:

- Are mandated or authorized activities actually being carried out?
- Are the activities in accordance with the purpose of the law and implementing regulations?
- Do activities conform to the intended program model or to professional standards of practice, if applicable?
- Are program resources efficiently managed and expended?

Impact questions illuminate the program effects:

- Is the program achieving its intended purposes or outcomes? What is the aggregate impact of the program? How did impact or outcomes vary across participants and approaches? How did impact vary across providers? Specifically, did the program support providers whose performance was consistently weak?
- What other important effects relate to the program (side effects)? What unforeseen effects (either positive or negative) did the program have on the problems or clients it was designed to address? Did the program have an effect on other programs aimed at a similar problem or population?
- How does this program compare with an alternative strategy for achieving the same ends? Are the effects gained through the program worth its financial and other costs? Taking both costs and effects into account, is the current program superior to alternative strategies for achieving the same goals?

If evaluation questions are prepared within the transformative framework, they exemplify an understanding of the power relationships that need to be addressed (Mertens, 2009). Examples of evaluation questions from this perspective might include the following:

- How can we teach and counsel students and clients so that they do not continue to be oppressed?
- Are the resources equitably distributed?
- How has the institution or agency been unresponsive in meeting the needs of people with disabilities?

The focus of these questions is to place the problem in an unresponsive system with power inequities rather than in the individual without power.

No matter what the initial evaluation questions, the evaluator should always be sensitive to emerging issues that necessitate a revision of these questions. This might be especially important in responsive and transformative evaluations.

Selection of an Evaluation Model

Evaluators carry an inclination, based on their worldview, to use specific models in their evaluation work. However, the needs of the evaluation will determine the appropriateness and feasibility of using a specific model. At this point, evaluators must ask themselves, Can I conduct this evaluation using the model that seems most appropriate to me, given my view of the world? Can I modify, adjust, or adapt my way of thinking to be responsive to the needs of this client in this setting? Can I use my way of thinking to help the client think about the problem in ways that are new and different and, ideally, more constructive and productive? I suspect that older, more experienced evaluators can make choices based on compatibility with their worldviews more readily than newer, less-experienced evaluators. Perhaps newer evaluators would find it easier to adjust their model selection to the needs of the client. For example, M. Q. Patton (2008) declares himself to be a pragmatist in his choice of models and methods, asserting that sensible methods decisions should be based on the purpose of the inquiry, the questions being investigated, and the resources available.

The reader should review the major models of evaluation as they are presented earlier in this chapter. If one model seems to address the needs of the evaluation more than another, consider if that is a model that aligns with your worldview. If you think that you can "enlighten" a client to a different approach to evaluation, give it a try: One of the roles that evaluators fulfill is educating the client about evaluation. Just as the implicit or explicit model that you entered the situation with influenced your decisions up to this point, the model that you choose to operationalize influences your next steps in planning the evaluation.

Planning the Evaluation

Data Collection Decisions. Data collection decisions basically answer these questions:

- What data collection strategies will you use?
- Who will collect the data?
- From whom will you collect the information (sampling)?
- When and where will you collect the information?
- How will the information be returned to you?

Your basic choices for data collection strategies are the same as those outlined in Chapters 11 and 12 (on sampling and data collection, respectively) in this text, as well as those discussed in Chapter 6 on survey research and Chapter 8 on qualitative methods. Your major concern is choosing data collection strategies that provide answers to your evaluation questions within the constraints of the evaluation study and that satisfy the information needs of your stakeholders. The constraints of data collection in public institutions and agencies sometimes include specific policies about who can have access to information. When the data collection plan is being developed, the evaluator should inquire into such possible constraints. Stakeholders should participate in the development of the data collection plan and should reach agreement that the data collected using this plan will satisfy their information needs. Of course, you need to stay flexible and responsive to emerging data collection needs.

Analysis, Interpretation, and Use. Issues related to analysis, interpretation, and use planning are directly affected by your data collection choices. These topics are discussed in Chapter 12. Nevertheless, as a part of the evaluation plan, the steps that you will take for analysis, interpretation, and use of the evaluation data should be specified. Your model of evaluation will determine how interactive and iterative the analysis and interpretation phases are. For example, in transformative or constructivist evaluations, you would expect to have fairly constant interaction with the stakeholder groups. You would share preliminary results and consult on the use of the findings for the purpose of program modification, as well as for directions for further data collection and analysis. If you are functioning within a postpositivist model, you would be less likely to have such a high level of interaction with your stakeholder groups. Rather, you would attempt to maintain distance so that your presence did not unduly influence the effects of the program. In terms of interpretation, evaluators have emphasized the development of a standard for use in making judgments about a program's merit or worth. For example, if a program is designed to reduce the dropout rate of high school students, is a 50% reduction considered successful? How about a 25% reduction? Such standards are appropriate for studies that focus on impact evaluation, although process-oriented standards could be established in terms of number of clients served or number of participants at a workshop.

Management of the Evaluation

The management plan for the evaluation should include a personnel plan as well as a budget (see Chapter 13 for more on this topic). The personnel plan specifies the tasks that will be done, as well as how, when, and by whom they will be done. The cost plan specifies the costs of the evaluation in such categories as personnel, travel, supplies, and consultants. Together, these two parts of the management plan can be used as the basis of a formal contract between the evaluator and the sponsoring agency.

Meta-Evaluation Plan. The meta-evaluation plan specifies how the evaluation itself will be evaluated. Typically, the meta-evaluation specifies when reviews of the evaluation will be conducted, by whom, and with reference to what standards. In evaluation work, three time points often seem appropriate for meta-evaluation to occur: (a) after the preliminary planning is finished, (b) during the implementation of the evaluation, and (c) after the evaluation is completed. The meta-evaluation can be accomplished by asking a person outside of the setting to review the evaluation planning documents, the progress reports, and the final report. It can also involve feedback from the stakeholder groups. One source of standards that the evaluation can be measured against is *The Program Evaluation Standards: How to Assess Evaluations of Educational Programs* (Joint Committee on Standards for Educational Evaluation, 2009). These standards are discussed in the next section.

Extending Your Thinking: Evaluation Planning

Find a published evaluation study. On the basis of information given in the article, create an evaluation plan (in retrospect) using the guidelines for planning provided in this chapter. Your plan should include the following:

a. Description of what is to be evaluated
b. The purpose of the evaluation
c. The stakeholders in the evaluation
d. Constraints affecting the evaluation
e. The evaluation questions
f. Description of the evaluation model
g. Data collection specifications
h. Analysis, interpretation, and use strategies
i. Management plan
j. Meta-evaluation plans

If you are unable to locate information from the published article that would provide a complete retrospective plan, make a note of the missing elements. *Add* a section to your plan indicating what you think it would have been good to include to make a complete plan. This will require some creative thinking on your part.

Standards for Critically Evaluating Evaluations

The Program Evaluation Standards (referred to above and hereafter referred to as the *Standards)* were developed by a joint committee that was initiated by the efforts of three organizations: the American Educational Research Association (AERA), the American Psychological Association (APA), and the National Council on Measurement in Education. Representatives of these three organizations were joined by members of 12 other professional organizations (e.g., American Association of School Administrators, Association for Assessment in Counseling, and the National Education Association) to develop a set of standards that would guide the evaluation of educational and training programs, projects, and materials in a variety of settings. The *Standards* have not yet been adopted as the official standards for any of these organizations; however, they do provide one comprehensive (albeit not all-encompassing) framework for examining the quality of an evaluation.

The *Standards* are organized according to five main attributes of evaluations:

- Feasibility—the extent to which the evaluation can be implemented successfully in a specific setting
- Propriety—how humane, ethical, moral, proper, legal, and professional an evaluation is
- Accuracy—how dependable, precise, truthful, and trustworthy an evaluation is
- Utility—how useful and appropriately used an evaluation is
- Meta-evaluation—the extent to which the quality of the evaluation itself is assured and controlled

Each of the main attributes is defined by standards relevant to that attribute. Box 2.7 contains a summary of the standards organized by attribute. Guidelines and illustrative cases are included in *The Program Evaluation Standards* text itself. The illustrative cases are drawn from a variety of educational settings, including schools, universities, the medical and health care field, the military, business and industry, the government, and law.

Box 2.7 A Summary of the Program Evaluation Standards

Utility

U1 Evaluator Credibility

Evaluations should be conducted by qualified people who establish and maintain credibility in the evaluation context.

U2 Attention to Stakeholders

Evaluations should devote attention to the full range of individuals and groups invested in the program and affected by its evaluation.

U3 Negotiated Purposes

Evaluation purposes should be identified and continually negotiated based on the needs of stakeholders and intended users.

U4 Explicit Values

Evaluations should clarify and specify the individual and cultural values underpinning purposes, processes, and judgments.

U5 Relevant Information

Evaluation information should serve the identified and emergent needs of evaluation users.

U6 Meaningful Processes and Products

Evaluations should construct activities, descriptions, findings and judgments in ways that encourage participants to rediscover, reinterpret, or revise their understandings and behaviors.

U7 Timely and Appropriate Communication and Reporting

Evaluations should attend in a continuing way to the information needs of their multiple audiences.

U8 Concern for Influence and Consequences

Evaluations should promote responsible and adaptive use while guarding against unintended negative consequences and misuse.

Feasibility

F1 Practical Procedures

Evaluations should use practical procedures that are responsive to the customary way programs operate.

F2 Contextual Viability

Evaluations should recognize, monitor, and balance the cultural and political interests and needs of individuals and groups.

F3 Resource Use

Evaluations should use resources efficiently and effectively.

F4 Project Management

Evaluations should use effective project management strategies.

Propriety

P1 Responsive and Inclusive Orientation

Evaluations should include and be responsive to stakeholders and their communities.

P2 Formal Agreements

Evaluations should be based on negotiated and renegotiated formal agreements taking into account the contexts, needs, and expectations of clients and other parties.

P3 Human Rights and Respect

Evaluations should protect human and legal rights and respect the dignity and interactions of participants and other stakeholders.

P4 Clarity and Balance

Evaluations should be complete, understandable, and fair in addressing stakeholder needs and purposes.

P5 Transparency and Disclosure

Evaluations should make complete descriptions of findings, limitations, and any resulting conclusions available to all stakeholders, unless doing so would violate legal and propriety obligations.

P6 Conflicts of Interests

Evaluations should identify, limit, and if necessary play a mediating role in situations where conflicts of interest may compromise processes and results.

(Continued)

Box 2.7 (Continued)

P7 Fiscal Responsibility

Evaluations should account for all expended resources, comply with sound fiscal procedures and processes, and ensure that clients are knowledgeable about fiscal resources expended.

Accuracy

A1 Trustworthy Conclusions and Decisions

Evaluation conclusions and decisions should be trustworthy in the cultures and contexts where they have consequences.

A2 Valid Information

Evaluation information should have sufficient validity and scope for the evaluation purposes.

A3 Reliable Information

Evaluation information should be precise, dependable, and consistent.

A4 Explicit Evaluand and Context Descriptions

Evaluations should document evaluands and their contexts with appropriate detail and scope for the evaluation purposes.

A5 Sound Qualitative and Quantitative Methods

Evaluations should employ sound information selection, collection, and storage methods.

A6 Sound Designs and Analyses

Evaluations should employ technically adequate designs and analyses that are appropriate for the evaluation purposes.

A7 Explicit Evaluation Reasoning

Evaluation reasoning leading from information and analyses to findings, interpretations, conclusions, and judgments should be clearly documented without omissions or flaws.

A8 Valid Communication and Reporting

Evaluation communications should be truthful in detail and scope and as free as possible from misconceptions, distortions, and errors.

Metaevaluation

M1 Purposes

Metaevaluations should be responsive to the needs of their intended users.

M2 Standards of Quality

Metaevaluations should identify and apply appropriate standards of quality.

M3 Documentation

Metaevaluations should be based on adequate and accurate documentation.

Mertens (2009) and Kirkhart (2005) recognize that concerns about diversity and multiculturalism have pervasive implications for the quality of evaluation work. Kirkhart proposed specific consideration of what she terms "multicultural validity," which she defined as "the vehicle for organizing concerns about pluralism and diversity in evaluation, and as a way to reflect upon the cultural boundaries of our work" (1995, p. 1). She outlines three types of validity traditionally discussed in the inquiry process, but addresses them from the perspective of multicultural validity. She then identifies threats specifically relevant to multicultural validity. The traditional types of validity are defined and discussed below:

1. *Methodological validity* concerns the soundness or trustworthiness of understandings warranted by our methods of inquiry, particularly with reference to the measurement instruments, procedures, and logic of inquiry.

2. *Interpersonal validity* refers to the soundness or trustworthiness of understandings emanating from personal interactions.

3. *Consequential validity* refers to the soundness of change exerted on systems by evaluation and the extent to which those changes are just.

The specific threats to *multicultural validity* were identified as these:

1. It takes time to reflect multicultural perspectives soundly. Many evaluations are conducted in compressed time frames and on limited budgets, thus constraining the ability of the evaluator to be sensitive to the complexity of multicultural dimensions.

2. Cultural sophistication needs to be demonstrated on cognitive, affective, and skill dimensions. The evaluator needs to be able to have positive interpersonal connections, conceptualize and facilitate culturally congruent change, and make appropriate cultural assumptions in the design and implementation of the evaluation.

3. The evaluator must avoid cultural arrogance that is reflected in premature cognitive commitments to a particular cultural understanding as well as to any given model of evaluation.

Ethics and Evaluation: The Guiding Principles

Another important resource for designing high-quality evaluations is the AEA's *Guiding Principles for Evaluators* (2004; www.eval.org). There are five guiding principles:

- *Systematic Inquiry.* Evaluators should conduct systematic data-based inquiries about the program being evaluated.

- *Competence.* Evaluators provide competent performance in the design, implementation, and reporting of the evaluation, including demonstration of cultural competence.

- *Integrity/Honesty.* Evaluators need to display honesty and integrity in their own behavior and attempt to ensure the honesty and integrity of the entire evaluation process.

- *Respect for People.* Evaluators must respect the security, dignity, and self-worth of the respondents, program participants, clients, and other stakeholders with whom they interact.

- *Responsibilities for the General and Public Welfare.* Evaluators should articulate and take into account the diversity of interests and values that may be related to the general and public interests and values.

The *Program Evaluation Standards* and the *Guiding Principles for Evaluators* should be used by the evaluator in developing and implementing the evaluation study. Conducting the meta-evaluation at the design stage not only ensures that a worthwhile evaluation has been constructed that is likely to produce the information needed by users, but also will increase the confidence of those associated with the evaluation. Conducting the meta-evaluation across the life cycle of the evaluation will improve the evaluation.

Questions for Critically Analyzing Evaluation Studies

The following questions are designed to parallel the *Standards* and to address issues raised by the construct of multicultural validity as it was described by Kirkhart (1995, 2005).

Feasibility

1. Practical Procedures—What evidence is there that the evaluation used practical procedures that were responsive to the customary way programs operate?

2. Contextual Viability—How did the evaluation recognize, monitor, and balance the cultural and political interests and needs of individuals and groups?

3. Resource Use—How did the evaluation use resources efficiently and effectively?

4. Project Management—What evidence is there that the evaluation used effective project management strategies?

Propriety

1. Responsive and Inclusive Orientation—How did the evaluation include and be responsive to stakeholders and their communities?

2. Formal Agreements—What evidence is there that the evaluation was based on negotiated and renegotiated formal agreements taking into account the contexts, needs, and expectations of clients and other parties?

3. Human Rights and Respect—How did the evaluations protect human and legal rights and respect the dignity and interactions of participants and other stakeholders?

4. Clarity and Balance—Was the evaluation complete, understandable, and fair in addressing stakeholder needs and purposes?

5. Transparency and Disclosure—How did the evaluation make complete descriptions of findings, limitations, and any resulting conclusions available to all stakeholders, unless doing so would violate legal and propriety obligations?

6. Conflicts of Interests—What evidence is there that the evaluators identified and limited, and if necessary played a mediating role in, situations where conflicts of interest might compromise processes and results?

7. Fiscal Responsibility—How did the evaluations for all expended resources comply with sound fiscal procedures and processes and ensure that clients are knowledgeable about fiscal resources expended?

Accuracy

1. Trustworthy Conclusions and Decisions—What evidence is there of the trustworthiness of the conclusions and decisions in the cultures and contexts where they have consequences?

2. Valid Information—What evidence is there of the validity of the evaluation information and scope for the evaluation purposes?

3. Reliable Information—What evidence is there that the evaluation information is precise, dependable, and consistent?

4. Explicit Evaluand and Context Descriptions—How did the evaluation document evaluands and their contexts with appropriate detail and scope for the evaluation purposes?

5. Sound Qualitative and Quantitative Methods—How did the evaluation employ sound information selection, collection, and storage methods?

6. Sound Designs and Analyses—What evidence is there that the evaluation employed technically adequate designs and analyses that are appropriate for the evaluation purposes?

7. Explicit Evaluation Reasoning—How was the evaluation reasoning leading from information and analyses to findings, interpretations, conclusions, and judgments clearly documented without omissions or flaws?

8. Valid Communication and Reporting—What evidence is there that the evaluation communications are truthful in detail and scope and as free as possible from misconceptions, distortions, and errors?

Utility

1. Evaluator Credibility—What is the evidence that the evaluation was conducted by qualified people who establish and maintain credibility in the evaluation context?

2. Attention to Stakeholders—How did the evaluation devote attention to the full range of individuals and groups invested in the program and affected by its evaluation?

3. Negotiated Purposes—What were the evaluation purposes and how were they continually negotiated based on the needs of stakeholders and intended users?

4. Explicit Values—What were the individual and cultural values underpinning purposes, processes, and judgments and how did the evaluation address these?

5. Relevant Information—How did the evaluation information serve the identified and emergent needs of evaluation users?

6. Meaningful Processes and Products—What evaluation activities, descriptions, findings, and judgments encouraged participants to rediscover, reinterpret, or revise their understandings and behaviors?

7. Timely and Appropriate Communication and Reporting—How did the evaluation attend in a continuing way to the information needs of its multiple audiences?

8. Concern for Influence and Consequences—How did the evaluation promote responsible and adaptive use while guarding against unintended negative consequences and misuse?

Metaevaluation

1. Purposes—What evidence is there that the metaevaluation was responsive to the needs of its intended users?

2. Standards of Quality—How did the metaevaluation identify and apply appropriate standards of quality?

3. Documentation—What evidence is there that the metaevaluation was based on adequate and accurate documentation?

Interpersonal Validity

1. Personal Influences—What influences did personal characteristics or circumstances, such as social class, gender, race and ethnicity, language, disability, or sexual orientation, have in shaping interpersonal interactions, including interactions between and among evaluators, clients, program providers and consumers, and other stakeholders?

2. Beliefs and Values—What are the influences of the beliefs and values of the evaluator and other key players in filtering the information received and shaping interpretations?

Consequential Validity

1. Catalyst for Change—What evidence is there that the evaluation was conceptualized as a catalyst for change (e.g., shift the power relationships among cultural groups or subgroups)?

2. Unintended Effects—What evidence is there of sensitivity to unintended (positive or negative) effects on culturally different segments of the population?

Multicultural Validity

1. Time—Were the time and budget allocated to the evaluation sufficient to allow a culturally sensitive perspective to emerge?

2. Cultural Sophistication—Did the evaluator demonstrate cultural sophistication on the cognitive, affective, and skill dimensions? Was the evaluator able to have positive interpersonal connections, conceptualize and facilitate culturally congruent change, and make appropriate cultural assumptions in the design and implementation of the evaluation?

3. Avoidance of Arrogant Complacency—What evidence is there that the evaluator has been willing to relinquish premature cognitive commitments and to be reflexive?

Extending Your Thinking: Evaluation Standards

1. Find a published evaluation study. Critically analyze the study using the questions for critical evaluation of evaluation studies listed in this chapter. Summarize the strengths and weaknesses of the study. Suggest possible changes that might strengthen the study.

2. Find a second published evaluation study that exemplifies a different evaluation model or paradigm. Critically analyze it using the questions for critical evaluation of evaluation studies listed in this chapter. Suggest possible changes that might strengthen the study.

3. Contrast the types of strengths and weaknesses that emerge from the two studies that were conducted from a different evaluation model or paradigm. How did the differences in the studies affect your use of the evaluation standards that were presented in this chapter (the Joint Committee's *Standards* [2009], and Kirkhart's [1995, 2005] multicultural validity standards)?

4. Because the *Standards* were developed within the context of educational evaluations, there has been some discussion about their applicability to evaluations in other settings. Review an evaluation study based in another type of program (e.g., drug abuse, clinical services). Critically comment on the usefulness of the *Standards* within this context. Use the points presented in the previous question to structure your response.

5. Brainstorm ideas for an evaluation study. Working in a small group, design an evaluation plan following the steps outlined in this chapter. Include in your plan all the components listed in Chapter 2. Critique your plan using the questions for critical analysis listed in this chapter.

Summary of Chapter 2: Evaluation

Evaluation and research share many things; however, the differences between the two genres of systematic inquiry should be apparent to you after studying this chapter. Evaluation has its own jargon, including the evaluand (what is evaluated), stakeholders (people who have a stake in the outcomes of the evaluation), and other terms reviewed in this chapter. It also has a history of development from the early 1960s to the present; it is a dynamic field with new developments occurring in response to challenges and political factors. The four major paradigms can also be used to frame evaluation studies, just as they can be for research. The planning process of an evaluation is premised on ongoing involvement of stakeholder groups. Professional associations and standards for quality in evaluation are useful resources for anyone interested in pursuing an evaluation study.

In This Chapter

- Two major reasons for conducting a literature review are explained: as a basis for conducting your own research or as an end in itself.
- A nine-step process for conducting a literature review is outlined:
  1. Development of the focus of your research
  2. Review of secondary sources to get an overview of the topic
  3. Development of a search strategy, including identification of preliminary sources and primary research journals, and accessing personal networks
  4. Conduct the search
  5. Obtain full text resources (e.g., journal articles or books)
  6. Read and prepare bibliographic information and notes on each article
  7. Evaluate the research reports
  8. Synthesize your findings
  9. Use the literature review to develop a conceptual framework and formulate research questions, hypotheses, or both
- Issues and questions related to the critical analysis of literature reviews are presented.

Why would you be interested in doing or reading a literature review? Isn't it easier just to run down the hall and ask someone what they would do about a problem you encounter? Suppose you are a science teacher with students who are immigrants labeled in the school system as English Language Learners? How would you address that challenge? O. Lee (2005) decided to do more than ask the teacher down the hall. She began by conducting a literature review of science instruction practices, especially as they have been applied to culturally and linguistically diverse populations, including immigrants in the United States and multilingual communities in other countries, such as India and Africa. She used her literature review as a basis for recommending a blend of experience-based science instruction that employs code-switching between English and the student's home language. Additional research is needed to explore the intersection of literacy, science education, and linguistic and cultural complexity.

3 Literature Review and Focusing the Research

When asked, Why do a literature review?, a somewhat cynical answer may have popped into some of your minds: "Why do a literature review? It is required for my research class," or "I have to do a thesis or dissertation." Then, again, some of you may have more socially redeeming motivations, such as wanting to change the world or improve your practice of a profession.

Literature reviews are important as research tools, especially in emerging areas, with populations that typically yield small samples (e.g., special education research often does), or in areas that represent value-laden positions adopted by advocacy groups. Literature reviews are also valuable in light of the knowledge explosion and the consequent impossibility of reading everything. Therefore, it is good that someone does literature reviews.

A few definitions will make your progress through this chapter more enjoyable:

Preliminary sources: Databases that contain information about research articles that are published on the topic of interest to you.

Secondary sources: Literature reviews that are published on your topic of interest consisting of a synthesis and analysis of previous research published on that topic.

Primary empirical research: Reports of studies that are conducted by the researcher(s) that include a description of the methods, sampling and data collection strategies, and data analysis and results.

Reasons for Doing Literature Reviews

There are two major reasons for conducting a literature review: to conduct primary research oneself (or as a part of a team) or as an end in itself.

Literature Reviews for Planning Primary Research

Almost every primary research study begins with a review of the literature. The purpose of the literature review section of a research article is to provide the reader with an overall framework for where this piece of work fits in the "big picture" of what is known about a topic from previous research. Thus, the literature review serves to explain the topic of the research and to build a rationale for the problem that is studied and the need for additional research. Boote and Beile (2005) eloquently explain the purpose of a literature review in planning primary research:

> As the foundation of any research project, the literature review should accomplish several important objectives. It sets the broad context of the study, clearly demarcates what is and what is not within the scope of the investigation, and justifies those decisions. It also situates an existing literature in a broader scholarly and historical context. It should not only report the claims made in the existing literature but also examine critically the research methods used to better understand whether the claims are warranted. Such an examination of the literature enables the author to distinguish what has been learned and accomplished in the area of study and what still needs to be learned and accomplished. Moreover, this type of review allows the author not only to summarize the existing literature but also to synthesize it in a way that permits a new perspective. Thus a good literature review is the basis of both theoretical and methodological sophistication, thereby improving the quality and usefulness of subsequent research. (p. 4)

Researchers use the literature review to identify a rationale for the need for their own study. Some of the specific rationales for your research that might emerge from your literature review include the following:

1. You may find a lack of consistency in reported results across the studies you have chosen to review and undertake research to explore the basis of the inconsistency. For example, Berliner et al. (2008) noted inconsistencies in research on high school dropouts; they suggested that the problem might be that researchers were not differentiating between high school dropouts who reenrolled and those who did not.

2. You may have uncovered a flaw in previous research based on its design, data collection instruments, sampling, or interpretation. For example, Borman et al. (2007) reviewed research on the Success for All literacy program and found that no randomized control studies had been conducted on its effectiveness. The quasi-experimental designs from past research left the findings open to possible criticism based on uncontrolled extraneous variables.

3. Research may have been conducted on a different population than the one in which you are interested, thus justifying your work with the different population. For example, Schirmer and McGough (2005) reviewed research literature on reading development and reading instruction and found that there was a lack of research of this type on students who are deaf. Therefore, they proposed a need for research on reading instruction that

has been found to be effective with hearing students to be conducted with deaf students. Another justification for the conduct of research with deaf students when the previous research is based on hearing children might be to devise a very different innovative method of reading instruction that is based on sign language and deaf culture.

4. You may document an ongoing educational or psychological problem and propose studying the effect of an innovative intervention to try to correct that problem. For example, Burnard (2008) wanted to explore innovative pedagogical practices to engage students who were facing challenges stemming from poverty, class, race, religion, linguistic and cultural heritage, or gender. In particular, she was interested in how music teachers engaged students who were disaffected.

5. Uncertainty about the interpretation of previous studies' findings may justify further research. For example, prior research with people with schizophrenia indicated that participants sometimes continued to feel bewildered about their condition and treatment, even after meeting with a health care professional. Schneider et al. (2004) undertook a study from the perspective of people with mental illness to determine what contributed to their perceptions of effective and ineffective relations with professionals.

As mentioned previously, a literature review can be used at the beginning of the study to explain what is known about your topic and provide a rationale for the study you are planning. In addition, the literature review can be used to help in the design of the study by providing guidance as to appropriate sample size or identifying promising data collection practices or instruments that can be used in your study. Familiarity with the literature is useful for both quantitative and qualitative studies no matter what the researcher's paradigm. Everyone who prepares a literature review should do so with a critical eye: What are the strengths and weaknesses of the prior research? What is missing from the formal body of scholarly literature that might be necessary in order to formulate an appropriate research focus and method of investigation?

When your purpose is to plan your own research study, the number of studies that you actually cite in your literature review may be fairly limited because of space limitations (for authors who publish in journals) or because the review is considered a learning activity (in your own course work). Typically, primary research articles published in journals contain 20 to 30 references to primary research. The number of citations may be quite limited for a course activity or more extensive if you are preparing a proposal for a thesis or dissertation. The exact number varies, depending on the purpose of the literature review and the extant literature. The primary criterion for inclusion should be centrality to your topic, within whatever constraints are imposed by instructors, advisers, or publishers.

Use of the literature review to plan and conduct a study requires that you critically evaluate the research that you read. This critical analysis can form the basis for your rationale or for your choice of data collection procedures. Criteria for evaluating primary research studies are provided at the end of each chapter.

Review of Literature as an End in Itself

The review of literature can be seen as an end in itself, either to inform practice or to provide a comprehensive understanding about what is known about a topic. The process for conducting this type of literature review varies, depending on your purpose. If your purpose is to *improve your professional practice,* you will want to base your literature review on the problem you encountered in your profession. Therefore, when you look to the literature for a solution, you may rely on other people's literature reviews, or you may seek out primary research reports until you find one that seems to fit your situation. For example, Mayo (2007) reviewed literature from the LGBTQ community with a specific focus on the act of "coming out" as it is researched in schools from the perspective of obstacles that the youth encounter, as well as in terms of the agency and resiliency demonstrated by some youth. Mayo uses the literature review to suggest promising strategies for school leaders, youth, and researchers to make progress on this issue.

When a literature review is conducted to provide a *comprehensive understanding* of what is known about a topic, the process is much longer. For example, Mckinley et al. (2007) included over 300 references in their literature review of race as a construct in educational research, examining such topics as the meaning of equity, inequality, whiteness, and race as social constructs, and implications of desegregation and placement in special education for members of racial minority groups. Gadsden (2008) included almost 200 references in her review of arts education in order to examine the changing place of the arts in education through a lens of power, culture, and representation. She draws conclusions for researchers and educators in terms of future directions suggested by the current body of scholarly knowledge in this area.

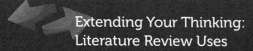

Extending Your Thinking: Literature Review Uses

- When writing a literature review for the purposes of planning a research study, what are some of the uses that the literature review can serve for you?
- Why is a literature review especially important in areas that (a) are emerging, (b) typically have small samples (e.g., special education research), or (c) represent value-laden positions adopted by advocacy groups (e.g., gender differences)?
- Students receive different kinds of advice as to how much literature to review and at what stage of the research process this should occur. What is your reaction to the following pieces of advice:

> When you have enough sense of the conversation to argue persuasively that the target for your proposed study is sound, and that the methods of inquiry are correct, you know enough for the purpose of the proposal. (Locke, Spirduso, & Silverman, 1993, p. 68)

J. M. Morse (1994) recommends reading in the general area of the inquiry once a topic has been selected:

> At this stage, the researcher should become familiar with the literature, with what has been done generally in the area, and with the "state of the art." He or she should develop a comfortable knowledge base without spending an extraordinary amount of time on minute details or chasing obscure references. (p. 221)

The Search Process

No matter what the reason for the literature review or the paradigm within which the researcher is working, many aspects of the literature review process are the same. A general outline for conducting a literature review is provided in Box 3.1. Some of the differences in the process that emanate from paradigm choice include the following:

1. With the postpositivist paradigm, the researcher who plans to conduct experimental research needs to be able to develop a hypothesis (a best guess as to the outcome of the planned research) based on previous research. Quantitative researchers examine research in order to build a knowledge base of a topic that is sufficient to develop a hypothesis that can be tested and to benefit from guidance in terms of methodology found in prior studies.

2. With a constructivist orientation, the researcher should have a good understanding of previous research but remain open to possible emerging hypotheses that would require examination of additional literature during the study (Marshall & Rossman, 2006). Qualitative researchers (Corbin & Strauss, 2008) note that a literature review can be useful in order to decide on a research topic, to formulate a research plan, and to enhance the researcher's awareness of subtleties uncovered in previous research. They do caution both novice and experienced researchers to be careful so that their perceptions of their findings emanate from their own data and not on expectations generated by reading extant literature.

3. In addition to review of scholarly literature, researchers working within the transformative paradigm should consult with persons who have experienced oppression and seek out literature that represents their viewpoints (Mertens, 2009). In order to do this, researchers need to develop an understanding of themselves as individuals with potential biases, as well as understand themselves in terms of their relationships with the community of interest. Hence, transformative researchers are more inclined to work with community members to develop the focus of the research, rather than rely solely on extant literature.

Extending Your Thinking: Literature Reviews and Qualitative Research

When conducting qualitative research, some texts advise against conducting a comprehensive literature review because it may bias the researcher to see "what others say they saw" instead of looking with fresh eyes. What do you think?

Box 3.1 Steps in the Literature Review Process

1. Identify a research topic.
2. Review secondary sources to get an overview of the topic: For example, look at the *Review of Educational Research, Harvard Educational Review, Psychological Bulletin, Review of Research in Education,* or the *Annual Review of Psychology.*
3. Develop a search strategy and use appropriate preliminary sources and primary research journals (see Boxes 3.2, 3.4, and 3.6), check the references at the end of relevant research publications, access personal networks, and/or build relationships with appropriate community representatives.
4. Conduct the search and select specific articles to review.
5. Obtain full text references (e.g., journal articles or books).
6. Read articles and prepare bibliographic information and notes on each article.
7. Evaluate the research reports.
8. Synthesize your findings.
9. Use the literature review to gain a conceptual framework and to formulate research questions, hypotheses, or both.

In the following sections that describe the steps in the literature review process, the commonalities in the search process are described, along with recognition of appropriate caveats that differentiate work within alternative paradigms.

Step 1: Identify Research Topic

A few pieces of advice should guide (novice) researchers as they begin their literature review process. They should be flexible in their conceptualization of the research problem being investigated, and they should begin with a broad idea and be prepared to narrow it down as they progress through the search. Sometimes, students choose topics for research that turn out to be not very researchable (in that no one else has conceptualized the problem quite that way), and as they begin reading and seeing what is available, their ideas change as to what they want to investigate. Also, if the topic definition is too narrow, it may not be possible to identify any previous research that addressed that specific topic. Therefore, be flexible and start broadly. In my experience with students who are beginning a literature review, their topics shift as they become more familiar with the topic. Some students write me desperate e-mails explaining that they want to change their topics and they hope that this is OK. In most cases, I write them back to assure them that this is a normal part of an evolutionary process of developing the topic. (Only rarely do I think, what in the world is that student thinking!)

Sources of Research Topics

A research topic can emerge from a wide variety of sources, including the researcher's interests, knowledge of social conditions, observations of educational and psychological problems, challenges that arise in one's professional practice, readings in other courses, talking to other researchers, and the availability of funds to conduct research on a specific topic (sponsored research). Any of these is appropriate as a source to help identify the primary research topic. For researchers interested in conducting a comprehensive review of literature for its own sake, another criterion must be met: They must study topics that appear in the literature.

For sponsored research, the researcher needs to clarify with the funding agency what the research problem is (Mertens, 2009). Often, students can apply for funding to support their own research, usually with a faculty sponsor. When applying for funds, it is important to know what the agency is interested in sponsoring and to tailor one's research interests to match those of the agency. Other students might work as research assistants to faculty members who have received financial support from an outside agency.

Scholars working in the transformative paradigm have been instrumental in stimulating research on a variety of topics that had previously received little attention, such as spousal abuse, sexual abuse, sexual harassment, homophobia, unpaid labor, and motherhood and child care. For transformative research, S. Harding (1993) recommends beginning with marginalized lives. To define the research problem, the researcher might want to involve persons affected by the research through informal or formal means such as focus groups (Mertens, 2009). The following quotation from Schneider et al.'s (2004) study of people with mental illness illustrates the transformative effect of engaging participants in the process of developing a research topic.

> There was also a real transformation in group members' sense of themselves as people who could accomplish something. They had all been subjects in many research projects and, at the beginning of the project, could not conceive of themselves as people who could do research. By the end of the project, they had taken on a sense of themselves as researchers. They saw that they could articulate problems, come up with ways to investigate the problems, and produce solutions. This experience increased their awareness of themselves as people with resources and strengths who could make a significant contribution to society. (p. 575)

Extending Your Thinking: Selecting Your Research Topic and Setting

Students of research are sometimes given conflicting advice about the topic and site for their own research. The following quotations exemplify such conflicts. Where do you stand on these two issues (i.e., choice of a research topic and setting) and why?

> The key to selecting a qualitative research topic is to identify something that will hold one's interest over time. New investigators can best identify such a topic by reflecting on what is a real personal interest to them. (J. M. Morse, 1994, p. 220)

> Using. . . personal experiences as the impetus for a research study is not wrong, but it is best if the researcher is aware of his or her possible

(Continued)

(Continued)

motives for conducting the study, as such experiences may give the study a particular bias. Of even more concern is the possibility that the researcher, when meeting and interviewing participants who have had the same experience, may have many unresolved feelings emerge and may be emotionally unable to continue with the study. (J. M. Morse, 1994, p. 221)

One common instance of the problem of investigator biography occurs when graduate students . . . design a study that requires them to return to the context of public education and play the role of unbiased spectator. . . . This particular problem is difficult to overcome and is precisely why it sometimes is best to select problems in a context with which the investigator has had little previous experience. (Locke et al., 1993, p. 114)

When injustice persists with no evidence of unhappiness, rebellion, or official grievance, we need to study the reasons why. . . . Faculty, staff, and students in the feminist and African-American communities have argued . . . that the *absence* of grievance substantiates the very depth of and terror imposed by harassment. Feminist research must get behind "evidence" that suggests all is well. (M. Fine, 1992, p. 23)

Step 2: Review Secondary Sources to Get an Overview

A good literature review written by someone else can provide you with an overview of what is known about your chosen topic. Specific places that you can look for literature reviews include journals that typically publish literature reviews, such as the *Review of Educational Research, Harvard Educational Review,* and the *Psychological Bulletin,* and books that contain literature reviews, such as the following:

- *Review of Research in Education:* This series is published annually by the American Educational Research Association. Each volume contains a series of chapters on various topics, such as implications for socially just education rooted in discipline-specific areas such as literacy and science for diverse groups of students (Vol. 31, Parker, 2007). What is counted as knowledge is examined in Volume 32 of this series from the perspective of discipline (arts, English, foreign languages, history, literacy, mathematics, and science) with specific focus on assessment of English Language Learners, and implications across cultural, linguistic, and social class lines (G. J. Kelly, Luke, & Green, 2008).

- *Yearbook of the National Society for the Study of Education:* The NSSE yearbook was published as both a book and a journal until 2005; since then, it has been available only as a journal subscription. Two volumes are published on a specific topic annually. Recent topics include examining the reasons for education in the contemporary world, with emphasis on democracy, globalization, and culture (Coulter, Weins, & Fenstermacher, 2008). The three yearbook volumes that preceded Coulter et al.'s are Moss (2007), an edited volume on evidence and decision making; Smolin, Lawless, and Burbules (2007), on information and communication technology; and Ball (2006), on achieving equity and excellence as a way to realize the potential of the *Brown v. Board of Education* decision.

- *The Annual Review of Psychology* contains literature reviews on topics of interest in psychology and education, such as counseling or learning theory.

- *Research in Race and Ethnic Relations* is published annually to address race relations and minority and ethnic group research.

- Other handbooks have been published on specific topics:

  Banks, J. A., & McGee-Banks, C. A. (Eds.). (2003). *Handbook of research on multicultural education* (2nd ed.). San Francisco: Jossey-Bass.

  Bursztyn, A. (2006). *Praeger handbook of special education.* Westport, CT: Greenwood.

  Kitayama, S., & Cohen, D. (Eds.). (2007). *Handbook of cultural psychology.* New York: Guilford.

  Klein, S. (2007). *Handbook for achieving gender equity through education* (2nd ed.). Mahwah, NJ: Lawrence Erlbaum.

  Ponterotto, J. G., Casas, J. M., Suzuki, L. A., & Alexander, C. M. (Eds.). (2001). *Handbook of racial/ethnic minority counseling research* (2nd ed.). Thousand Oaks, CA: Sage.

  Richardson, V. (Ed.). (2001). *Handbook of research on teaching.* Washington, DC: American Educational Research Association.

Step 3: Develop a Search Strategy

Four paths for search strategies are described in this section: (a) identify preliminary sources, (b) identify primary research journals, (c) access personal networks, and (d) involve community members. These are explained below. Decide which are the best strategies for you to follow in your search process, and remember, stay flexible.

Identify Preliminary Sources[1]

Preliminary sources include databases and indexes that contain a compilation of bibliographic information, abstracts, and sometimes full text articles for a wide range of topics and are accessible in print form, on compact disks (CD-ROM), or through online services. Examples of the most frequently used preliminary sources are listed in Box 3.2. Additional abstract and index services that specifically target marginalized groups include *African Urban and Regional Science Index, Women's Studies Abstracts,* and *Women's Studies Index.*

Box 3.2 Most Frequently Used Preliminary Sources

- ERIC: The Educational Resources Information Center (ERIC) contains more than 1.2 million abstracts of journal articles and research reports on education-related topics. The database can be searched by going to www.eric.ed.gov, or by using ERIC in commercial databases provided in many libraries. Most ERIC documents are available electronically, in print, or on microfiche in libraries. Many non-journal materials are available, at no charge, as PDF documents or via links to publisher Web sites. Check with your local library (academic, public, etc.) to find out if they can provide journal articles or documents that are not available online. If the library cannot do this for you, print copies of journal articles can be purchased through such article reprint services as Ingenta (www.ingentaconnect.com).

(Continued)

Box 3.2 (Continued)

- ProQuest® Education Journals: The database includes more than 750 journals in primary, secondary, and university-level education. More than 600 of these titles include full texts of the articles. This and similar ProQuest products are available at many libraries.

- JSTOR: This is a database of academic journals, monographs, and other academic papers from multiple disciplines, including the social sciences, humanities, and the sciences. It is available from libraries that subscribe to the service. Individuals in the United States can subscribe for a modest amount; JSTOR made special arrangements for individuals in Africa to have access to this database for free (www.jstor.org).

- PsycINFO: This is a product of the American Psychological Association (APA) that contains indexes and abstracts from 1,300 journals, as well as books and book chapters related to psychology. Both members and nonmembers can search the database and purchase articles. Information about that is at http://psycnet.apa.org/index.cfm?fa=main.landing. As with other databases, you can check on its availability at your local library.

- PsycARTICLES: This is another product of the APA, but it includes the full text articles of 42 journals related to psychology that APA publishes. Information about this database can be found at http://psycnet.apa.org/index.cfm?fa=main.landing. The database can be searched by APA members and by nonmembers (for a small fee).

World Wide Web (WWW) sites are easily and pervasively available to assist you in your literature searching. There are many search sites on the Web, and new ones appear with some regularity. In October 2008, the Consumer Search Web site (www.consumersearch.com) listed the top two choices for search engines as Yahoo! and Google.[2] These two search engines were recognized because of the size of their databases, ability to search HTML and PDF files, accuracy in results, and advanced searching power using Boolean logic. The search process on Web sites generally employs Boolean logic (explained later in this chapter) but can differ a bit from site to site. Because this is such a dynamic area, it is best to check *PC Magazine* or some other computer source to find out what sites are recommended and to determine appropriate search strategies for those sites. One word of caution: The WWW sites do not have a peer review system to screen what is accepted (as most professional journals do); therefore, scholars raise questions about the quality of information available from those sources. In addition, the Web sites are not designed to contain information specifically about research in education and psychology as are the other databases described in this chapter.

The computerized databases are a tremendous resource for the researcher in the literature review phase of a project. A researcher can identify thousands of references by only a few keystrokes on the computer. Because of the tremendous coverage provided by the databases, the researcher should plan to include a search of appropriate databases in the literature review process. Box 3.3 provides an example of how one researcher described his method of searching the literature.

Box 3.3 Description of Literature Review Search Method

The studies were gathered from a search completed in June of 2006 using the Educational Resources Information Center (ERIC), Academic Search, and Education Full Text databases, as well as the library book database at the University of Wisconsin, Madison. Initially, the search terms "high stakes testing" and "state-mandated testing" were used to identify potential studies for use in my qualitative meta-synthesis.

—Au, 2007, p. 259

One important limitation should be noted about the available databases. You can get out of them only what was put into them. In other words, the databases are selective about the journals they include. For example, many of the best-known feminist journals are not included in the databases. A survey of 17 feminist journals indicated that only 6 are included in ERIC[3] (see Box 3.4). Some of the feminist journals listed in Box 3.4 might not be considered appropriate for inclusion in ERIC because their content is not directly related to education or psychology. However, readers who are not familiar with feminist journals might find the list helpful as a way of broadening their resource base. For example, *Hypatia* publishes mainly philosophical work and thus would be of interest to those who want to delve more deeply into that aspect of feminist theory. *Camera Obscura* publishes work that could be of interest to scholars in educational media or social learning theory (e.g., the study of the power of media to shape cultural expectations by gender).

Box 3.4 Feminist Journals

Camera Obscura A journal of feminist perspectives in film, television, and visual media.

Feminist Studies The first feminist academic journal (started in 1972) is based at the University of Maryland. It publishes an interdisciplinary body of feminist knowledge and theory that makes visible assumptions about gender and sexual identity and the experiences and contributions of women across a wide range of difference.

Feminist Teacher[a] Since 1984, *Feminist Teacher* has published discussions about how to fight sexism, racism, homophobia, and other forms of oppression in classrooms and in educational institutions. A peer-reviewed journal, it provides a forum for interrogations of cultural assumptions and discussions of such topics as multiculturalism, interdisciplinarity, and distance education within a feminist context.

Gender and Education[a] Published in England, *Gender and Education* is an international forum for discussion of multidisciplinary educational research and ideas that focus on gender as a category of analysis.

(Continued)

Box 3.4 (Continued)

Gender & History An international journal for research and writing on the history of gender relations, sexuality, and the semiotics of gender in a wide geographical and chronological scope. *Gender & History* examines changing conceptions of gender and maps the dialogue between femininities, masculinities, and their historical contexts.

Gender & Society This journal emphasizes theory and research from micro- and macrostructural perspectives. It aims to advance both the study of gender and feminist scholarship.

Genders Based at the University of Colorado, *Genders* publishes innovative work about gender and sexuality in relation to social, political, artistic, and economic concerns.

Hypatia This journal publishes scholarly research at the intersection of philosophy and women's studies.

Initiatives[a] Published by the National Association for Women in Education, this journal covers topics of interest to women in all aspects of higher education since 1937.

Journal of Women's History An international journal that covers new research on women's history, it includes scholarship about women in all time periods that is broadly representative of national, racial, ethnic, religious, and sexual grouping.

Meridians A feminist, interdisciplinary journal with the goal of providing a forum for scholarship and creative work by and about women of color in U.S. and international contexts.

NWSA Journal An official publication of the National Women's Studies Association (NWSA), it publishes up-to-date interdisciplinary, multicultural feminist scholarship linking feminist theory with teaching and activism.

Psychology of Women Quarterly[a] A scientific journal that reports empirical research and critical reviews, theoretical articles, brief reports, and invited book reviews related to the psychology of women and gender.

Sex Roles: A Journal of Research[a] *Sex Roles* publishes original research articles and theoretical papers concerned with the underlying processes and consequences of gender role socialization, perceptions, and attitudes.

Signs: Journal of Women in Culture and Society[a] An international journal in women's studies that publishes articles from a wide range of disciplines in a variety of voices—articles engaging gender, race, culture, class, sexuality, and/or nation.

Women's Studies International Forum The goal of this journal is to aid the distribution and exchange of feminist research in the multidisciplinary, international area of women's studies and in feminist research in other disciplines.

Women's Studies Quarterly This journal focuses on teaching in women's studies. Thematic issues include such features as course syllabi, discussions of strategies for teaching, and bibliographies.

a. Journals are indexed in ERIC.

Identify Primary Research Journals

Additional primary research articles can be identified by examining the reference lists found at the end of relevant journal articles or books. You can also go directly to journals that you know publish articles related to your topic. This is especially important in light of the selectivity of the databases discussed in the previous section. Researchers who are working from a transformative paradigm should be aware of the journals that deal with issues specific to marginalized groups, such as those in Box 3.4 for feminists, as well as journals such as *Latin American Perspectives, Hispanic Journal of Behavioral Sciences, Journal of Multicultural Counseling and Development, Journal of Negro Education,* and *Journal of Black Studies*. *Disability, Handicap & Society* is a journal that frequently focuses on the transformative paradigm in research with people with disabilities, and *The Counseling Psychologist* (2008) devoted an entire issue to the topic of multicultural counseling for psychologists and educators (Vol. 36, No. 2). A more extensive list of special education journals can be found in Box 3.5.

Box 3.5 Selected Journals Containing Special Education Resource Information

American Annals of the Deaf

American Journal on Mental Retardation

Annals of Dyslexia

Australasian Journal of Special Education

Behavioral Disorders

British Journal of Special Education

Career Development for Exceptional Individuals

Education and Training in Mental Retardation

Exceptional Children

Exceptionality: A Research Journal

International Journal of Disability, Development and Education

Journal of Autism and Developmental Disorders

Journal of Deaf Studies and Deaf Education

Journal of Early Intervention

Journal of Learning Disabilities

Journal of Special Education

Journal of Speech and Hearing Research

Journal of the Association for Persons With Severe Handicaps

Learning Disability Quarterly

Mental Retardation

Remedial and Special Education

Research in Developmental Disabilities

Volta Review (deafness)

Personal Networking

Additional resources can be found by talking to people who are doing work in areas related to your interest. This can include people at your own institution or those you meet through professional associations, such as the American Educational Research Association, the American Evaluation Association, the American Psychological Association, the Council for Exceptional Children, or the National Association of the Deaf. Talking to people who have completed related work can reveal sources that you were unaware of, such as unpublished research reports, and provide you with leads from work that is in progress for that researcher.

Two examples of well planned and documented searches are provided in Boxes 3.6 and 3.7. As a researcher, it is always a good idea to carefully document your search strategy. In this way you can backtrack to helpful strategies if you need additional information and indicate to the reader how thorough you were in your search process.

Box 3.6 Method Used in Literature Review: Example 1

The primary purpose of the accommodations research conducted over the past 3 years has been to determine the effect of accommodations use on the large-scale test scores of students with disabilities.

Method

Four major databases were searched to identify research on test accommodations published from 1999 through 2001: ERIC, PsycINFO, Educational Abstracts, and Digital Dissertations. Research papers were also obtained at major conferences. Additional resources for identifying research included

- Behavioral Research and Teaching at the University of Oregon (brt.uoregon.edu/)
- Education Policy Analysis Archives (epaa.asu.edu)
- National Center for Research on Evaluation, Standards, and Student Testing (www.cse.ucla.edu/)
- Wisconsin Center for Educational Research (www.wcer.wisc.edu/testacc/)

Several search terms were used. The terms were varied systematically to ensure the identification of all research on changes in testing, published from 1999 through 2001. Search terms included

- accommodation
- test adaptation
- test changes
- test modifications
- test accommodations
- state testing accommodations
- standards-based testing accommodations
- large-scale testing accommodations

A decision was made to limit the selection of publications to empirical research. Included within this realm are studies with samples consisting of preschool, kindergarten through high school, and postsecondary students. The focus of the empirical research was not limited only to large-scale testing, but also included studies that incorporated intelligence tests and curriculum-based measures (CBM). We decided to focus on testing accommodations as opposed to instructional accommodations, although there is some overlap between these purposes in the literature. We did not include any conceptual or opinion pieces in this analysis.

SOURCE: S. Thompson, Blount, & Thurlow (2002, pp. 2–3).

Box 3.7 Literature Review in Science Education With English Language Learners (ELLs): Example 2

In selecting research studies for inclusion in this synthesis, a systematic review of the relevant literature was conducted according to the following parameters:

1. Studies with direct relevance to the topic, i.e., those involving ELLs in science education and those addressing the intersection between science education and English language acquisition. To the extent that language and culture are interrelated ("languaculture" according to Agar, 1996), this review includes studies examining cultural beliefs and practices that ELLs bring to the science classroom.

2. Studies published from 1982 through 2004. The landmark for science education reform was the release of the *Science for All Americans* document (American Association for the Advancement of Science, 1989). The period between 1982 and 2004 spans the years leading up to the release of this document (1982–1989) and more than a decade afterward (1990–2004).

3. Studies conducted within the United States and abroad, but limited to those published in English and focusing on settings where English is the main medium of science education.

4. Studies focusing on science education at the elementary and secondary levels, K–12. Studies involving postsecondary or adult learners are not included.

5. Empirical studies from different methodological traditions, including (a) experimental and quasi-experimental studies; (b) correlational studies; (c) surveys; (d) descriptive studies; (e) interpretative, ethnographic, qualitative, or case studies; (f) impact studies of large-scale intervention projects; and (g) demographics or large-scale achievement data.

6. Literature reviews and conceptual pieces.

Within these parameters, the process of gathering studies from the various sources was carried out as follows. First, a search of the ERIC database was conducted using

(Continued)

Box 3.7 (Continued)

the terms "science education" and "school" combined with the following keywords: "bilingual," "limited English proficient (LEP)," "English Language Learner (ELL)," "English to Speakers of Other Languages (ESOL)," "English as Second Language (ESL)," "equity," "diversity," "minority," "culture," "language," "multicultural," "at-risk," "race," "immigrant/immigration," and "urban education."

Second, selected journals were reviewed manually, including the journals supported by the American Educational Research Association (*American Educational Research Journal, Educational Researcher, Review of Educational Research,* and *Review of Research in Education),* as well as other well-known journals focusing on science education (*Journal of Research in Science Teaching* and *Science Education)* and bilingual/TESOL education (*TESOL Quarterly* and *Bilingual Research Journal).*

From the sources named above, only peer-reviewed journal articles were included. Among these, articles, empirical studies, literature reviews, and conceptual pieces were included. Empirical studies were used to report research results, whereas literature reviews and conceptual pieces were used to frame key issues.

Neither practitioner-oriented articles (e.g., teaching suggestions or descriptions of instructional programs, materials, or lesson plans), nor opinion or advocacy pieces unsupported by empirical evidence were included.

SOURCE: O. Lee, (2005, p. 495).

Involvement of Community Members

The combination of self-knowledge with cultural knowledge and skills in effective partnering facilitates the development of the research or evaluation focus and identification of questions, development of interventions, and making decisions about design, measures, samples, data collection, analysis, interpretation, and use that are in keeping with the philosophical assumptions of the transformative paradigm (Mertens, 2009). Following proper channels to enter a community is important, and strategies for doing this will vary by context. Some Native American Indian communities have developed specific protocols for anyone who wants to conduct research in their communities (LaFrance & Crazy Bull, 2009); Maori people from New Zealand have also developed similar protocols for research in their community (Cram, 2009). Deaf researchers have adapted the Maori Terms of Reference to suggest a protocol for research in that community (Harris, Holmes, & Mertens, 2009). These protocols will be discussed in more depth in the chapter on sampling. However, it is important for researchers to know how to enter a community with respect, to communicate their intentions to members of the community in the appropriate way, and to make clear what benefits will accrue to themselves and to the community. Schneider et al.'s (2004) method of involving people with mental illness is one example of how community members can be involved in the decision process about what topics to study in the research.

Step 4: Conduct the Search

In conducting the search, you should make a plan to search preliminary sources, check the table of contents, abstracts, and lists of references in primary research journals, access your personal network, and involve community members as appropriate. The remainder of this section focuses on the search strategy as it applies to accessing preliminary sources.

Prepare to Search Preliminary Sources

Select the preliminary sources that you think contain the best information on your topic (see Box 3.2). Then identify key terms that will help you locate the literature included in the database of choice. One way that researchers select key terms is to find one primary research article that is "exactly" on target and identify the terms used to describe that article.

A search strategy based on using the ERIC online system is used to illustrate this process. The search strategy is similar when using other databases and indexes, such as PsycARTICLES and PsycINFO. Most databases give you many choices for searching, such as title, author, abstract, subject, or full text. The title, author, and abstract choices are fairly self-explanatory. Author and title are not usually used in the beginning of a literature review because you usually are not seeking a specific article during the early stages of searching. The subject choice needs a bit of explanation. *Subject* words are those that were used by the people who work for the database to categorize that item. These words are contained in a thesaurus, usually available in the online system. Each item in the database has a field associated with it that contains subject words that an indexer selected, and that is the field that is searched when you choose a subject word strategy. Full text searchers, on the other hand, allow researchers to choose words that reflect their own vocabulary in the description of the topic. *Full Text* means the computer searches for these terms using a "free text" strategy; that is, it searches anywhere in the document for the words that you enter. Advantages and disadvantages accrue to whichever search strategy is chosen.

The easiest way to start is to use a key word strategy to determine if the words that you think are appropriate produce references that match your conceptualization of the problem. For example, for the topic of sexual abuse of deaf students, I started in ERIC using *sex abuse deaf* as key words. The computer said there were no articles available that combined those three terms. I took a few minutes to read the directions in ERIC and found that I could use a multifield search strategy, separating the terms. So I used sex? AND abuse AND deaf?. (There is a good reason, explained later, for the inclusion of the *?* and the word *and* in this search specification.) This resulted in 19 entries. One of the entries was Black and Glickman (2006), "Demographics, Psychiatric Diagnoses, and Other Characteristics of North American Deaf and Hard-of-Hearing Inpatients" (see Box 3.8).

If you have difficulty finding references using your own key word vocabulary, check a thesaurus of terms to determine how the indexers might have conceptualized your topic. Use of subject descriptors can be helpful in narrowing down a search, as long as the descriptors are defined in a way that is compatible with your topic. They can also be helpful in broadening a search by suggesting other terms that could prove fruitful in searching.

Box 3.8 Journal Citation Entry From ERIC

Black, Patricia A. Glickman, Neil S. Demographics, Psychiatric Diagnoses, and Other Characteristics of North American Deaf and Hard-of-Hearing Inpatients [Journal Articles. Reports—Research] Journal of Deaf Studies and Deaf Education. v11 n3 p303–321 2006 AN: EJ738331

Abstract: This study examined demographic and clinical data from a specialty deaf inpatient unit so as to better understand characteristics of severely and chronically mentally ill deaf people. The study compares deaf and hearing psychiatric inpatients on demographic variables, psychiatric discharge diagnoses, a language assessment measure, a cognitive ability measure, and a measure of psychosocial functioning and risk of harm to self and others. Overall, findings indicate a broader range of diagnoses than in past studies with posttraumatic stress disorder being the most common diagnosis. Compared with hearing patients in the same hospital, deaf patients were less likely to be diagnosed with a psychotic or substance abuse disorder and more likely to be diagnosed with a mood, anxiety, personality, or developmental disorder. Psychosocial functioning of the deaf patients was generally similar to hearing psychiatric patients. Deaf patients presented significantly higher risks than hearing patients in areas of self-harm and risk of sexual offending. Cognitive scores show that both the deaf and hearing inpatient population is skewed toward persons who are lower functioning. An additional surprising finding was that 75% of deaf individuals fell into the nonfluent range of communication in American Sign Language. (Author)

Now, why include a *?* in the search terms, and what is the importance of the *and* in the list? You can refine your search in the following ways:

1. Truncate the terms you use. This has the effect of broadening the search to include any terms that begin with the letters that you enter, no matter how they end. In ERIC (the Educational Resources Information Center), the truncating symbol is a *?* Therefore, entering *sex?* would include *sex, sexual, sexes,* and so on, and *deaf?* would include *deaf, deafness, deafened,* and so on.

2. Use Boolean or positional operators to combine terms. Boolean logic allows you to use the words *and, or, not,* and *nor* (one but not both words are in a record). Thus asking for *sex? and abuse and deaf?* yields references in which the three terms appear in the same record. The *or* operator yields references that have either or both words in the same record. So, I could have asked for *sex? abuse or child abuse and deaf?*. This would have given me all the records that contain *sex? abuse* or *child abuse* and *deafness*. In addition, I could have broadened my search by including *deaf? or hearing-imp?*. This would have resulted in all references that had either *deaf, hearing-impaired, hearing impaired,* or *hearing impairment* in their records.

Positional operators include *same, with, adj,* and *near,* and they limit retrieval by specifying how near key words must be to each other. *Same* means that both words must be in the same field of the same record; *with* means both words are in the same section of the same field of the same record; *adj* requires that the words must be next to one another (adjacent) in the order specified; and *near* finds references in which words are next to one another in any order (e.g., *sex abuse* or *abuse sex*).

3. There are other ways to limit the search, such as by year of publication or limiting the field that is searched (e.g., title only). Certain *stop* words are not allowed to be used as key words (e.g., *about, all, its),* but all of these things can be learned by reading the online instructions. As you get into using a database, it is always a good idea to read the online instructions to see what can be accomplished and how.

4. Obviously, the search process can be broadened by inclusion of additional databases or indexes. For example, when I searched PsycARTICLES using the same descriptors (i.e., *sex? and abuse and deaf?),* I identified 57 additional references that did not overlap with those found in ERIC.

A final word of advice: Cultivate a good relationship with your librarian. I invite the research librarian to my research classes to make a presentation on databases, search strategies, and documentation of findings from the search. Students report that visiting the research librarian is extremely helpful.

Interpret What You See

You can locate at least two types of documents in ERIC: journal articles and other references that are available through ERIC. Journals may be obvious because they have the name of the journal, but if you are not sure look for an EJ code in the ERIC citation. Other references are noted with the abbreviation ED (education document) and are typically presentations made at professional meetings, curriculum guides, research reports, or other similar materials. An example of an ERIC full text abstract for a journal article was presented in Box 3.8 and one for an ERIC document is in Box 3.9.

Box 3.9 ED Document Citation From ERIC

Accession Number	ED477969
Author	Karcher, Michael J.
Title	The Hemingway: Measure of Adolescent Connectedness—Validation Studies.
Page Count	59
Peer Reviewed	No
Date of Publication	2001
ERIC Subject Headings	*Adolescent Development Adolescents Age Differences Behavior Problems Delinquency *Interpersonal Relationship *Psychometrics *Social Environment Substance Abuse Test Validity

(Continued)

Box 3.9 (Continued)

Identifiers	*Social Connectedness.
Abstract	This investigation reports the development of a measure of adolescent connectedness and estimates of its psychometric properties. A measure was developed to assess the ecological and developmental dimensions of adolescent connectedness, defined as adolescents' caring for and involvement in specific relationships and contexts within their social ecology. Exploratory and confirmatory factor analyses in studies one and two yielded theoretically consistent factor solutions. These models were cross-validated in studies three and four with three geographically and ethnically diverse adolescent samples totaling 1454 adolescents. The measure of adolescent connectedness demonstrated satisfactory inter-item and test-retest reliability and convergent validity across samples. Consistent with social control and problem-behavior therapy, two higher order factors emerged across all of these samples: conventional vs. unconventional connectedness. These two dimensions of connectedness were found to differentially explain substance use for delinquent and non-delinquent adolescents. Using this ecological assessment, adolescent connectedness appears to differ as a function of age, sex, and problem-behavior status; varies across relationships and contexts; reflects either conventional or unconventional behaviors and attitudes; and can explain engagement in risk-taking behaviors. (Contains 62 references and 6 tables.) (Author)
Notes	Paper presented at the Annual Conference of the American Psychological Association (109th, San Francisco, CA, August 24–28, 2001).
Level of Availability	1
Publication Type	Information Analyses. Reports—Research. Speeches/Meeting Papers.
Language	English
Entry Month	200402

Select Titles

Most databases provide an abstract of the articles listed. By scanning these abstracts, you can make a decision as to the worth of obtaining the complete article. Advances in technology now also make it possible to view many full text articles while you are engaged in the search process. Hence, researchers are faced with a bit of a paradox concerning the amount of time it takes to do a literature review. If you only have the abstract, you read it quickly and make a determination if it is what you want. If you think it is and full text is not available, then you need to go to the library or order the article through interlibrary loan or some other mechanism. If the full text is available, you may find yourself (like me) reading many articles because they are interesting and then you wonder how the day is done and you have not made the progress that you expected. Intellectual curiosity is good; focus is also good.

Step 5: Obtain Full Text Resources

As mentioned previously, many journal articles and books are now available online in full text versions. If you cannot obtain the article in this manner, then it would be good to check the list of holdings at your library. If the journal you seek is held by your library, you are in luck: Go to the shelves (or the librarian at the help desk) and read the article. However, if your library does not have the item, you may avail yourself of an interlibrary loan service. If you provide complete bibliographic information, the librarian can determine which other library has the article and make a request to have it sent to you. There is often a small charge for this service. In some libraries, obtaining a copy of the article is available by an online request as you are doing your search. The computer may ask you if you want to order the document, and then it will tell you how much it costs to obtain. You have the option of agreeing to pay the cost, and, if you agree, the library that holds the reference is electronically contacted and asked to transmit the article to your library. Amazing! (The researcher's equivalent to Home Shopping Network.)

If you have chosen to review an ED document from an ERIC search, that document may also be available in full text online. However, if it is not, then the document should be available for your review on microfiche in the library. The microfiche are organized in ascending order according to their ED numbers, so they are usually easy to find.

Extending Your Thinking: Primary and Secondary Sources

What is the difference between a primary source and a secondary source? When and why would you choose to use one or the other? Have you been able to locate a secondary source on your topic of interest?

What search strategies have you found to be particularly effective in locating research on your topic of interest? Have you used networking? Professional associations? Why would these be important resources? What computerized databases have you used? Do you feel comfortable in using the computer to search for articles of interest for your research topic? Have you sought out journals or other sources of information (e.g., direct dialogue with individuals who are experiencing oppression) that represent the "transformative perspective" in research?

H. M. Cooper and Hedges (1994) recommend that researchers limit their literature review efforts to "mainstream" journals on the grounds that these represent the "cream of the crop" of research efforts. Transformative researchers might contend that this would result in a bias because the viewpoints of oppressed people might not be represented in those journals. Where do you stand on this issue?

Step 6: Read and Prepare Bibliographic Information and Notes

Once you have the article in hand, read the document to determine if it is really what you want. If you decide that it is relevant to your topic, you will want to record bibliographic information and notes on each article. This can be done electronically or manually, using old-fashioned note cards.

Bibliographic Information

If you are searching such databases as ERIC or PsycARTICLES, you can use a new digital resource called RefWorks to electronically save the bibliographic information about all the references that you select. When you are ready, RefWorks will print out a reference list in APA format (or the format that you select). That is not all: If the article is available in full text, you can save it in RefWorks with the bibliographic information. If you do not have access to this electronic resource, then you can save the bibliographic information on note cards or in a word processing document. The important thing is to make sure you get ALL the information you need when you are working with the document so you do not have to try to find it later when you are writing up your literature review. Words of wisdom—painfully learned.

The most important thing to remember in recording bibliographic information is to be complete and accurate. Some of the problems associated with recording bibliographic information have been reduced because of the ability to print such information directly from the computer screen. However, if you have hundreds of printouts, you may want to record the information on index cards or in some other easily retrievable electronic format. (I do not always have a computer with me when I want to record bibliographic information, so index cards are handy. My secret at the moment: I cut and paste from the full text documents and then type up the references later; next time I write a book, I plan to use RefWorks.)

Although several options are available for the format of recording bibliographic information, the most common style for education and psychology is based on the American Psychological Association's (2001) *Publication Manual* (5th ed.). This is the basic format for a journal citation:

Author's Last Name, Initials. (date). Title of journal article. *Title of Journal, volume number*(issue number), page numbers.

For example:

Sullivan, P. M. (1992). The effects of psychotherapy on behavior problems of sexually abused deaf children. *Child Abuse and Neglect: The International Journal, 16*(2), 297–307.

Book:

Author's Last Name, Initials. (date). *Title of book*. Place of publication: Publisher.

For example:

Mertens, D. M. (2009). *Transformative research and evaluation*. New York: Guilford.

Book chapter:

Author's Last Name, Initials. (date of publication). Title of chapter. In Name of Editor (Ed.), *Name of book* (page numbers of chapter). Place of publication: Publisher.

For example:

LaFrance, J., & Crazy Bull, C. (2009). Researching ourselves back to life: Taking control of the research agenda in Indian Country. In D. M. Mertens & P. Ginsberg (Eds.), *Handbook of social research ethics* (pp. 135–149). Thousand Oaks, CA: Sage.

There are differences in citation style associated with different types of documents (e.g., books, chapters in books, government reports, etc.), so you are advised to obtain a copy of the APA *Publication Manual* to guide the compilation of bibliographic information. In addition, APA has added a great deal of information about how to handle Web-based information. Some of that is reflected in the *Publication Manual,* but you can go to the APA's Web site (www.apa.org) for an update on changes that they recommend and click on their publications link.

Notes on Each Study

Exactly what notes to write for each study varies greatly and depends on the nature of the study, the purpose of the review, and the intended use of the data. If the researcher intends to conduct a comprehensive literature review of studies that report their results in statistical form, the use of coding forms and computerized databases is recommended.

For empirical research studies, the following outline can be helpful:

1. Area of interest; literature cited; need addressed; theoretical framework; research questions/hypothesis
2. Paradigm of researcher(s)
3. Design, including
   a. Specific research approach
   b. Sampling strategy
   c. Characteristics of participants
   d. Data collection instruments and procedures
4. Data analysis strategy
5. Results
6. Conclusions
7. Your own evaluation (including strengths and weaknesses and ideas for your own research, such as promising methodological or conceptual suggestions).

The evaluation of research reports is Step 7 (discussed below). Once you have evaluated the research report, you should return to your note cards or files and enter your own assessment of the strengths and weaknesses of the research.

Step 7: Evaluate the Research Reports

You will be learning how to evaluate research as you progress through this text. A listing of critical analysis questions for evaluating primary research is provided at the end of each chapter. The questions are organized according to the sections of the research report (e.g., introduction, method, etc.), with additional specific questions relevant to each approach to research (e.g., experimental, quasi-experimental, etc.).

Step 8: Synthesize the Studies

Before you actually begin the synthesis of the research, there are a few things to keep in mind. Organization is a plus. If you can develop a flexible framework for organizing the studies as you find them, it will be easier for you to approach the synthesis stage. I say flexible because the framework might add, delete, or redefine categories as you move through the review process. For example, for the revisions to the third edition of this book, I had categories for relevant studies I found in the early stages that related to each chapter title. As I found studies, I saved them into those files. As I began writing, I moved some of the files to more differentiated categories; for example, what started as the Chapter 1 introduction became paradigms, and paradigms became postpositivist, constructivist, transformative, and pragmatic. So, as I approached writing I had studies that were relevant to each part of the chapter. Of course, you sometimes run into problems in that one study may have applicability for more than one topic, but no one said this would be simple. Some of my students like to keep tables of the studies they find and then organize the studies in tables under headings that make sense for their writing; some like to keep note cards on their studies that they can rearrange manually. Other students like to use a qualitative software package to save the articles as "data files" that can be coded and searched when it is time to write. This approach has merit but demands technical skills with the software and diligence to do the coding. However, once you get to the search and retrieve part, it may all seem worth it.

An example of a thematic organizational approach can be seen in Billingsley's (2004, p. 39) study of teacher attrition and retention in special education. She addressed four major themes: teacher characteristics and personal factors, teacher qualifications, work environments, and teachers' affective reactions to work. She included a critical analysis of definitions, concepts, and methods used to study special education attrition. In another example, Au (2007) included the following themes in his literature review about high stakes testing: Subject matter content, pedagogy, and structure of knowledge. Au offers some important insights into the flexible and evolving nature of coding systems. He writes,

> The full elaboration of my coding template evolved during the course of the research. For instance, it has been widely asserted over the past 20-plus years that high-stakes tests cause a narrowing or contraction of nontested subject areas. I was aware of research substantiating this assertion prior to beginning the template analysis and thus assumed that I would need to code the studies that reported the theme of contraction of subject matter content. (p. 259)

Two main options exist for the synthesis of research studies: narrative and statistical methods. The choice of the type of synthesis depends on the type of extant research literature on a topic and on the purpose of the researcher. In this chapter, I focus on the narrative approach to synthesizing literature. The statistical approach (meta-analysis) is explained in Chapter 13.

Narrative Synthesis

The narrative approach to literature synthesis is most commonly used in primary research studies. It is appropriate for studies that use a qualitative design as well as for quantitative studies. In a narrative synthesis, the writer must organize the studies in a conceptually logical order and provide sufficient detail about the studies to support relevant critical analysis of them. The amount of detail provided (as well as the number of studies cited) will be influenced by the purpose of the literature review:

1. Typically, the literature review section of a journal article includes a limited number of references that are selected on the basis of relevancy to the problem at hand, presenting a balanced picture, and establishing a rationale for the reported research.

2. A literature review for a research proposal is usually more extensive. If the research proposal is for a thesis or dissertation, it is expected to be quite comprehensive in most universities.

If you organized your literature into meaningful categories as you collected it, then this makes your writing easier. Provide an overview of your topic and describe the methods you used to search the literature. Then provide an advance organizer for the reader of the subtopics that you will address. For each study make a determination if it is important to report details of its strengths and weaknesses in order to establish the overall picture of knowledge in the field or to provide support for your choice of methods. It is possible to explain several studies in detail and then cite other studies that agree or disagree with the findings of those studies, rather than a detailed critique of every study in your literature review. Sometimes literature reviews include a separate section on the proposed study's theoretical framework based on prior research. The literature review should lead to a statement of the need and purpose for the study, research questions, and hypotheses.

Step 9: Use the Literature Review

The narrative or statistical synthesis serves as a basis for the literature section of a research proposal or report. The Appendix contains an outline for a research proposal for a thesis or dissertation. It is important for the proposal writer to realize that each institution and sponsoring agency has its own requirements for proposal writing, so it is best to check with those sources before proceeding with writing. Proposal writers must also realize that in this synthesis of research they are "selling" their ideas to a research committee, institutional review board, or funding agency. So above all, make it clear why the research is important (based on what is known from the extant literature).

Conceptual Framework and Program Theory

In some ways, the conceptual framework is like the chicken-or-the-egg controversy. A researcher's original conceptual framework influences the planning and conducting of the literature review. However, if a researcher keeps an open mind throughout the literature review process, a more sophisticated and (often greatly) modified conceptual framework should emerge. Table 3.1 displays the influence of the theoretical framework on the choice of research questions and its implications for action. On the basis of work by Villegas (1991) on theoretical frameworks used to explain differential achievement by ethnic minority students, four different research questions are used to illustrate this point. The IQ deficit theory and the cultural deficit theory reflect a theoretical stance that suggests the problem is either "in the child" or "in the cultural group from which the child comes." The cultural difference theory reflects the constructivist paradigm, and the power inequity theory reflects the transformative paradigm.

These various explanations for poor academic achievement by ethnic minority children exemplify alternative theories that might be held by the researcher or by the research sponsor or participants. Researchers must be aware of their own personal theoretical base as well as that of the sponsors and the participants. For example, J. E. Davis (1992) noted that research on African American families often depicts them as deviant, pathological social organizations unable to fulfill the major responsibilities of socializing their members for productive roles in society (the *deficit model*). The conclusion based on this model, then, is that this undersocialization leads to negative outcomes, such as low academic

Table 3.1 Influences of Different Theoretical Frameworks on Research

Theory	*Sample Research Question*	*Recommendations for Action*
IQ deficit theory	Are minorities genetically inferior to White students?	Remedial education, but the problem is really "in" the child.
Cultural deficit theory (sociocultural deficits in home life)	Is there a higher rate of single-parent families among minorities? How do Black and White parents compare in discipline techniques?	Remedial education, but the problem is really "in" the family.
Cultural difference theory	What is the nature of language use at home and at school in terms of asking and answering questions or in seeking help?	Build on students' prior experiences; increase their language use structures.
Power inequities (school failure is rooted in a struggle for power; schools play a role in the preservation of the socioeconomic order)	How can we teach minority students so they do not continue to be oppressed?	Explicitly teach minority children the means to access power, including linguistic forms and ways of talking, writing, and interacting. Teach them to value ethnic characteristics and that the culture of the dominant group is not necessarily superior.

achievement, juvenile delinquency, drug abuse, and teenage pregnancy. This conclusion is reached by ignoring the data that "inform us of the unique and often precarious position of African Americans" (J. E. Davis, 1992, p. 59). More than one third of the African American population in the United States lives at or near the poverty level. It is the economic condition and its implications (e.g., inadequate housing and food, poor sanitation, overcrowding) that bring about negative consequences, such as poor health, family violence, and delinquency. Ladson-Billings (2006) presents data that suggest that conditions have not improved for African American students since Davis wrote her work in 1992. Ladson-Billings suggests that there is a more insidious reason that underlies both economic and education deprivation: racism. Thus, the use of a theoretical framework that starts with the marginalized lives allows researchers to understand the experiences of oppressed groups.

In the past, much of educational and psychological research on racial or ethnic minorities, women, people with disabilities, and other marginalized groups derived from a deficit perspective that located the problem in individuals and focused on the negative reasons that they did not achieve or perform certain functions or activities. More recently, researchers have shifted to a social-cultural perspective that focuses on the dynamic interaction between the individual and environment over the life span (Seelman, 2000; A. T. Wilson, 2001). This focus on strengths and modifications of contextual factors has emerged under a variety of names such as *positive psychology* (Aspinwall & Staudinger, 2003; S. J. Lopez & Snyder, 2003; Seligman & Csikszentmihalyi, 2000) and *resilience theory* (J. H. Brown, D'Emidio-Caston, & Benard, 2001; R. Cooper, 2000). Such a theoretical framework has led to reframing research questions to focus on strengths. For example,

> What are the positive aspects of parenting a deaf child? (Szarkowski, 2002)
>
> What are the variables that contribute to successful transition from high school to college for deaf African American students? (Williamson, 2002)

J. M. Morse (2003) also notes that the theoretical framework in qualitative research is used to focus the inquiry and give it boundaries rather than to serve as *the* guide for data collection analysis. Deductive analysis based on a static theoretical framework violates the assumption of constructivist qualitative inquiry. The theoretical framework should be viewed as a conceptual template with which to compare and contrast results, not seen as establishing a priori categories for data collection and analysis.

Research Questions and Hypotheses

The literature review serves as a foundation for forming research questions. Hedrick, Bickman, and Rog (1993) suggest that the research questions operationalize the objectives of the proposed research. They focus the research hypotheses and clarify what information needs to be collected from what sources under what conditions.

Framing the research questions can be a difficult task for beginning researchers. Hedrick et al. (1993) present a taxonomy for categorizing research questions that includes four categories of questions: descriptive, normative, correlational, and impact. Each is briefly discussed in the following paragraphs.

Descriptive research questions are designed to produce information about what is or has been happening in relation to the target of the research. For example, the researcher might want to describe certain characteristics of the participants in an intervention. Alternatively, the researcher might be interested in describing the prevalence of a particular disability within an identified domain (e.g., What is the prevalence of mental retardation in Black middle school children?).

Normative research questions go beyond description and require that the information generated in response to the descriptive research question be compared with some standard or expected observation. For example, in special education, there are minimum requirements regarding most aspects of the service delivery system. A normative research question might ask, Were individual education plans (IEPs) in place before the placement was made, in accordance with the minimal service delivery requirements?

Correlative research questions are used to identify relationships to enable the explanation of phenomena. As Hedrick et al. (1993) point out, data derived in response to such questions indicate the strength and direction of a relationship between two or more variables, not causality. For example, the special education researcher might ask, What is the relationship between the size of family and the presence of emotional disturbance in siblings? If a strong, positive relationship is found, this would not lead to the conclusion that large families cause emotional disturbance in siblings. Such a relational finding would suggest the need for further study to uncover the causal relationships.

Impact research questions represent the last category offered in the Hedrick et al. (1993) taxonomy. Here, the researcher's aim is to identify effects, to establish causal links between an independent variable (the intervention) and a dependent variable (the anticipated change). According to Hedrick et al.'s framework, the researcher might investigate two types of effects: simple and relative. Research on the impact of an intervention (literacy intervention) on a behavior (reading) is one example of an impact study. The research question might ask, do students who participate in the literacy intervention perform better on end-of-year assessments in reading than students who do not participate? If the researchers choose (and this is good practice) to explore the impact of the intervention on other related outcomes (e.g., math, self-confidence), additional questions could address relative effects.

Impact questions can then be reformulated and stated as hypotheses. A hypothesis is an "if . . . , then . . ." statement. For example, a hypothesis might state this: "If students are exposed to a particular intervention, they will behave in a certain, predictable manner." A sample hypothesis for the literacy study cited above might read this way: "If students participate in the literacy intervention, then their scores on the end-of-year reading assessments will be higher than the scores for students who do not participate." This is known as a *directional hypothesis* because it is stated in the direction of the expected outcome. A researcher could choose to state a *null hypothesis*—that is, a statement that did not specify the expected direction of the outcome. The previous hypothesis could be restated as a null hypothesis: "There will be no difference in end of year reading assessments for students who do participate in the literacy intervention as compared to those who do not."

In summary, the literature review serves many purposes. It establishes a historical perspective on the intended research, provides a vision of the need for additional research, and enables the researcher to develop a conceptual framework for the research. This framework allows the researcher to generate research questions and hypotheses to guide the design and conduct of the research. In qualitative research, typically, the researcher will refine, modify, add, and even discard questions throughout the progress of the study (J. M. Morse, 1994). Therefore, qualitative researchers are advised to begin with broader questions that can be modified in response to discoveries made during the study. No matter which research paradigm or approach is used, the literature review is an essential ingredient in the research process.

Critical Analysis of Literature Reviews

The criteria for critically analyzing literature reviews depends (again) on the nature of the review being analyzed. A literature review that serves as an introduction to a primary research study reported in a journal would be subject to a different type of scrutiny than would a comprehensive literature review on a topic. Nevertheless, a framework initiated by Hart (1999) and extended by Boote and Beile (2005) provides a way to assess the quality of a literature review. (Their rubric of these categories is included as Table 3.2.) Boote and Beile included five categories for their framework.

- Coverage refers to the adequacy of the coverage of the topic, as well as making explicit criteria for exclusion and inclusion of studies for the review. Does the reviewer include relevant works and exclude irrelevant ones? Writing a dissertation does not mean citing every study ever written on your topic. Coverage should be judged in terms of comprehensiveness, breadth, exclusion, relevance, currency, availability, and authority (Bruce, 2001). Researchers can bias the results of a literature review by excluding data that is methodologically questionable, based on their own personal, subjective judgment (Ogawa & Malen, 1991). Or they may present conclusions that are more firm and clear-cut than is justified because of the exclusion of studies with "murky" results. Without a clear specification of the method used to search for research and of the criteria used for inclusion or exclusion, it is difficult to judge the quality of a review. Au's (2007) review of high stakes testing literature provides an example of decision rules for inclusion/exclusion when a large pool of studies is initially identified. He narrowed the studies to those

    (a) based on original, scholarly research,

    (b) using qualitative methods,

    (c) taking place in the United States, and

    (d) specifically addressing the relationship between high-stakes tests and either curriculum or instruction or both (p. 259).

Table 3.2 Literature Review Scoring Rubric

Category	*Criterion*	*1*	*2*	*3*	*4*
1. Coverage	a. Justified criteria for inclusion and exclusion from review	Did not discuss the criteria inclusion or exclusion	Discussed the literature included and excluded	Justified inclusion and exclusion of literature	
2. Synthesis	b. Distinguished what has been done in the field from what needs to be done	Did not distinguish what has and has not been done	Discussed what has and has not been done	Critically examined the state of the field	
	c. Placed the topic or problem in the broader scholarly literature	Topic not placed in broader scholarly literature	Some discussion of broader scholarly literature	Topic clearly situated in broader scholarly literature	
	d. Placed the research in the historical context of the field	History of topic not discussed	Some mention of history of topic	Critically examined history of topic	
	e. Acquired and enhanced the subject vocabulary	Key vocabulary not discussed	Key vocabulary defined	Discussed and resolved ambiguities in definitions	
	f. Articulated important variables and phenomena relevant to the topic	Key variables and phenomena not discussed	Reviewed relationships among key variables and phenomena	Noted ambiguities in literature and proposed new relationships	
	g. Synthesized and gained a new perspective on the literature	Accepted literature at face value	Some critique of literature	Offered new perspective	
3. Methodology	h. Identified the main methodologies and research techniques that have been used in the field and their advantages and disadvantages	Research methods not discussed	Some discussion of research methods used to produce claims	Critiqued research methods	Introduced new methods to address problems with predominant methods
	i. Related ideas and theories in the field to research methodologies	Research methods not discussed	Some discussion of appropriateness of research methods to warrant claims	Critiqued appropriateness of research methods to warrant claims	
4. Significance	j. Rationalized the practical significance of the research problem	Practical significance of research not discussed	Practical significance discussed	Critiqued practical significance of research	
	k. Rationalized the scholarly significance of the research problem	Scholarly significance of research not discussed	Scholarly significance discussed	Critiqued scholarly significance of research	
5. Rhetoric	l. Was written with a coherent, clear structure that supported the review	Poorly conceptualized, haphazard	Some coherent structure	Well developed, coherent	

NOTE: The column-head numbers represent scores for rating dissertation literature reviews on 3-point and 4-point scales (endnote 4 explains our choice of the two types of scales). Adapted frome *Doing a Literature Review: Releasing the Social Science Research Imagination* (p. 27) by Christopher Hart. 1999, London, SAGE Publications. Copyright 1999 by SAGE Publications. Adapted with permission.

Au (2007) excluded studies that examined the

> relationship between high-stakes testing and retention, studies that focus on the role of high-stakes testing and access to teacher education programs (e.g., Praxis II), studies that focus on the tests themselves (e.g., discourse analyses of the actual test content), and policy studies that use qualitative methods to compare pressures between states. In addition, because of their ambiguous and complicated positions in school hierarchies, studies that focus on student teachers are also excluded. (p. 259)

- Synthesis is the second category, and it refers to how well the author summarized, analyzed, and synthesized the selected literature on a topic. The criteria include how well the author

  (a) distinguished what has been done in the field from what needs to be done,

  (b) placed the topic or problem in the broader scholarly literature,

  (c) placed the research in the historical context of the field,

  (d) acquired and enhanced the subject vocabulary,

  (e) articulated important variables and phenomena relevant to the topic, and

  (f) synthesized and gained a new perspective on the literature. (Boote & Beile, 2005, p. 7)

To satisfy these criteria, the writer needs to identify tensions and inconsistencies in the literature, provide clarity discussing the strengths and weaknesses of the individual studies as factors that influence the interpretation of their results, and use the extant knowledge base to suggest directions and topics for additional empirical investigations.

- Methodology as a criterion for judging a literature review refers to the author's accurate inclusion of details about method that have relevance for identification of methodologies and research techniques, and their strengths and weaknesses, and discussion of the relationship between theories and ideas in the field to the research methodologies (Boote & Beile, 2005).

Literature reviews should not be simple summaries of findings of previous research; they should be critical analyses of previous research. In order to critically analyze the strengths and weaknesses of prior research, several skills are necessary. One is the ability to accurately identify the methodologies; a second is the ability to identify strengths and weaknesses in the methodologies and how they impact the interpretation of results. Unless you have had prior experience critiquing research, you are probably wondering how you can do this type of critical analysis. You can continue through this book, and by the end you'll be able to critically analyze the major approaches to research in education and psychology. At the present moment, we will focus on your being able to critically analyze the literature review section of a research study, and then you can add to your skill set as you progress through subsequent chapters. What you can do for the moment is know that when you take notes about your studies, you want to include information about the methodology, not just the results.

- Significance is the fourth category and includes establishing both the practical and the scholarly significance of the research problem (Boote & Beile, 2005). While some research studies will focus more or less on one of these aspects, it is useful to provide implications for both the practical and scholarly significance of research.

- Rhetoric is the final category and it refers to the writers' ability to organize and write cogently about the literature in such a way that they can articulate and support their claims about the knowledge in the field (Boote & Beile, 2005).

Extending Your Thinking: Choices in Literature Reviews

How much and what kind of information should you include about each study in your literature review? About your literature review search method?

What are your rules for inclusion and exclusion of studies in your literature review?

Several caveats are in order at this point:

- The points made in this chapter are relevant to almost all types of educational and psychological research, whether it is a single empirical study, cyclical study, master's thesis, or doctoral dissertation.

- The act of reviewing the literature does not just occur in the beginning of a research study and is not completed once the introduction to the article or the proposal for the research is completed. Literature review should be an ongoing process, and the results of that review should be integrated into the body of the report at appropriate points, but especially in the discussion and conclusions sections.

- The researcher should be aware of potential biases in literature reviews. There is a greater tendency for research with statistically significant results (i.e., those showing group differences larger than chance) to be published. Research studies that show no differences either are not submitted by the authors or are rejected more frequently by journal editors (Begg, 1994; P. B. Campbell, 1989). Campbell suggested that this publication bias leads to an exaggerated concept of differences between males and females. Begg recommended tracking down (or determining if authors of literature reviews tracked down) unpublished studies on the topic to correct for this bias. However, Begg also cautioned that the quality of the unpublished data may be suspect because they have not been through a review process. For this reason, he recommended a conservative interpretation of literature review results (especially meta-analyses).

- Matt and Cook (1994) focus on threats to inference from research syntheses based on the quality (or lack thereof) of the primary research studies included in the review. They point out weaknesses commonly found in quantitative research studies that could be used in a statistical synthesis of previous research findings. In assessing the conclusions reached in any literature review, the reader should be cognizant of the quality of the studies included.

Questions for Critically Analyzing Literature Reviews

The following questions can be used to determine if a literature review is satisfactory. In preparing your answers to these questions, cite evidence in the article to support your answers.

1. The purpose of the literature review is to place the current research into the "big picture" of what is known and not known about a specific topic. What is the big picture into which this study fits? What is the central topic? How is the researcher conceptualizing the problem?

2. What is the nature of the literature cited?
   a. Is the review current, using research that is recent enough to have applicability to the proposed research?
   b. Is the review based predominately on primary research rather than on secondary or opinion pieces?
   c. Does the review provide a critical analysis of existing literature, recognizing the strengths and weaknesses of previous research? Or, is the review just a summary of prior research?
   d. Is the literature review well balanced, presenting evidence on both (or all) sides of the issue?

3. Is the review free from the biases of the reviewer? Is there any evidence in terms of emotional language, institutional affiliation, funding source, and so on to suggest that the reviewer might be biased?

4. To what extent does the review establish a need for the study? What is the author's rationale for why this study is needed? What do we know? What do we need to know? Why is this study important (practically and in terms of scholarship)?

5. What is the theoretical framework and what are the research questions? Does the review provide enough information to support the researcher's theoretical framework and research questions posed?

6. Does the review provide sufficient information to guide the research procedures, including the identification of subject participants, selection of data collection and analysis processes, and use of appropriate reporting strategies? After you read the review and you see what research questions and methods are used, do you think they are logically connected? Does what the researchers do in terms of method make sense in terms of what is presented in the literature review?

7. Are sources cited inclusive of "marginalized" voices? Are citations made that reference viewpoints of those with the least power?

To really have a basis for critically analyzing research, it is helpful to have broad experience with different types of research as well as with a number of studies that represent the same research approach. Of course, such breadth and depth takes time to achieve. Nevertheless, a long journey begins with a single step. Throughout this text, you will be encouraged to identify full text research articles that relate to your area of interest and to critically analyze those studies. The ability to critically analyze research is also a skill that becomes more holistic with experience.

When you are in the beginning stages of learning critical analysis, it is helpful to look at each section of the research study. So, in this chapter, we focus on the introductory section that includes the literature review and research problem, hypothesis, questions, or objectives. Later, you will be able to look at other aspects of the article, such as how the author handled certain aspects of data collection, analysis, credibility building, or ethics. You can then do comparisons across studies on these dimensions, analyzing how and why texts differ, how they relate to theoretical readings, whether the authors are justified in their methods or presentations, and how they can help you in your own decisions about research. With each research article that you review, you will increase your ability to determine the quality of the author's work and the validity of the findings.[4]

Extending Your Thinking: Critically Analyzing Literature Reviews

- Locate several empirical research studies. Identify the following features of the studies: (a) the paradigm that the researchers used, (b) the research problem, (c) the theoretical framework that underlies the study, and (d) the research questions or hypothesis.
- Using the questions at the end of Chapter 3 for critically analyzing literature reviews, critique literature reviews in several different literature studies, identifying their strengths and weaknesses and supporting your claims with evidence from the articles.

Summary of Chapter 3: Literature Review and Focusing the Research

A review of scholarly literature provides information that can be used to investigate a topic of importance to learn what is known about that topic for its own sake (i.e., to improve teaching or therapeutic practices) or as a basis for designing a research study. The formulation of a research topic is enabled by reading about research that has already been conducted because the reader can figure out what is already known as well as become acquainted with the strengths and weaknesses of methods used in prior research. Multiple sources exist for the conduct of literature reviews, including secondary sources that provide an overview of past research and primary sources that report original research. Primary sources can be identified through several different electronic means that are described in this chapter. Persons conducting literature reviews can summarize their results in narrative form or a quantitative form known as meta-analysis that is described in more detail in Chapter 13. A literature review is used to develop research questions of different types, such as descriptive, correlational, or interventionist. Researchers can also benefit by looking outside of published scholarly research to community members to provide a different perspective on what needs to be studied and how it should be studied. You are now ready to consider which specific research approach is appropriate to answer the research questions.

Notes

1. I want to acknowledge the contribution of Gallaudet's research librarian, Jane Rutherford, for her many years of support for the students in my courses and for keeping me up-to-date on resources available from the library.

2. *Search engine* is the term used in the technology literature for search sites.

3. This is twice as many as were included in the first edition of this book published in 1998.

4. I am indebted to the comments of an anonymous reviewer for this framing of critical analysis.

In This Chapter

- The importance of experimental design in the postpositivist paradigm is discussed.
- Independent and dependent variables, experimental and control groups, random assignment, and internal and external validity are defined and illustrated.
- Threats to internal and external validity, along with ways to minimize these threats, are explained.
- Research designs are diagrammed and explained for single-group, experimental, and quasi-experimental studies.
- Other design issues are discussed, such as the type of treatment variable, ordering effects, and matching subjects.
- Complex issues concerning experimental research in the transformative paradigm are discussed.

Quantitative research is rooted in the postpositivist paradigm, which holds that the purpose of research is to develop confidence that a particular knowledge claim about an educational or psychological phenomenon is true or false by collecting evidence in the form of objective observations of relevant phenomena (Gall, Gall, & Borg, 2007). Research design can be defined as a process of creating an empirical test to support or refute a knowledge claim. Two tests of knowledge claims exist in the postpositivist paradigm: (a) Is the knowledge claim true in this situation (does it have internal validity)? (b) Is the knowledge claim true in other situations (does it have external validity or generalizability)?

Knowledge claims concerning internal validity require some complex thinking. Suppose you have a first grader who generally refuses to sit in his seat and pushes so hard on the paper when he tries to write that the paper tears. When he does sit in his seat, he bangs his head on the desk. It does not matter whether you are the parent, teacher, counselor, or school administrator, you want to be able to identify the variables that cause the behavior and figure out a treatment that allows this child to learn and thrive. You might formulate a wide variety of hypotheses as to why these behaviors are occurring. You might speak with other staff members and find out that they have observed similar behaviors with other children. You might consult the literature and find that such behaviors could result from a lack of self-confidence in a school setting or from frustration associated with a learning disability or a developmental delay. The recommended courses of action could be to try to build the child's self-confidence, to change teaching strategies to address the learning disability, or to lessen the demands on the child until maturation occurs.

If you are operating in the postpositivist paradigm, you might design a research study in which you decide to administer a selected treatment (e.g., a program designed to build self-confidence) to one group of children, and another similar group of children would not get the treatment. Suppose that the group of children who received the treatment improved their behavior more than the other group. How can you claim that it was your "treatment" that caused the observed change in behavior? For the researcher to make a knowledge claim that this treatment caused this effect, certain tests of internal validity must be met. These tests of internal validity are the subject of a major portion of this chapter.

Most quantitative research is of two types: studies aimed at discovering causal (or correlational) relationships and descriptive studies that use quantitative data to describe a phenomenon. Six approaches to undertaking quantitative research are explained in this text: single-group, experimental, and quasi-experimental designs (Chapter 4); causal comparative and correlational research (Chapter 5); survey methods (Chapter 6); and single-case research (Chapter 7).

4

Experimental and Quasi-Experimental Research

Importance of Experimental Design

The importance of experimental research within the postpositivist paradigm is evident in the following quotations:

> The best method—indeed the only fully compelling method—of establishing causation is to conduct a carefully designed *experiment* in which the effects of possible lurking variables are controlled. To experiment means to actively change x and observe the response y. (D. Moore & McCabe, 1993, p. 202)

> When well-specified causal hypotheses can be formulated and randomization to treatment and control conditions is ethical and feasible, a randomized experiment is the best method for estimating effects. (Feuer, Towne, & Shavelson, 2002, p. 8)

> The experiment is the design of choice for studies that seek to make causal conclusions, and particularly evaluations of education innovations. (Slavin, 2002, p. 18)

These authors maintain that experimental research is the only type of research that can truly establish cause-and-effect relationships, although they do recognize that there are many educational problems for which the experimental method is inappropriate. Feminists have interpreted such statements as evidence of an inappropriate hierarchy of prestige in research methods (Reinharz, 1992). Some issues are not amenable to experimental research; thus certain types of reform become extremely difficult to achieve if scientifically based research (SBR) in the form of experimental studies is accorded this exclusive position in the "truth hierarchy." Maxwell (2004) argued against experimental design as the "gold standard" of educational and psychological research because it is based "on a restrictive and problematic model of causality" (p. 3). He challenges the "privileged position that SBR gives to randomized experiments in educational research, and the concomitant dismissal of qualitative research as a rigorous means of investigating causality. I argue that a realist understanding of causality is compatible with the key characteristics of qualitative research, and supports a view of qualitative research as a legitimately scientific approach to casual explanation" (Maxwell, 2004, p. 3). Ways to consider the ability of qualitative research to make causal statements are addressed in later chapters. For now, it is sufficient to make visible that this issue has been raised as a critique of sole reliance on randomized control designs as those that can lead to cause and effect statements.

Nevertheless, both educators and psychologists have been criticized for employing practices that are not evidence based (Bickman, 1999; Feuer et al., 2002). The use of experimental designs received increased attention with the passage of the No Child Left Behind legislation as discussed here and in Chapter 1. The act calls for evaluating the effectiveness of school-based practices using "scientifically based research" that uses "rigorous, systematic, and objective procedures to obtain valid knowledge" (No Child Left Behind Act of 2001, Pub. L. No. 107-110, Title IX, Part A, A7 9101[37]). This created a political climate that supports the use of experimental or quasi-experimental designs, preferably with random assignment to groups. A related implication is that the probability of obtaining funding for innovative programs will be increased if this method is chosen.

As was discussed in Chapter 1, researchers in the postpositivist paradigm recognized the complexity of establishing a definitive cause-and-effect relationship with social phenomena. The underlying logic calls for controlling as many variables as possible and then systematically manipulating one (or a few) treatment variables to test the effect. The control of many variables (such as differences in background characteristics of the participants) can result in an oversimplification that distorts how the phenomenon occurs in the real world. Yet it is the controlling of many variables that allows the researcher to claim that one variable had a specific effect. Thus the researcher in this paradigm works within a tension between control and manipulation (changing one or a few variables at a time) and representation of a phenomenon in the real world. The fundamental assumption of this paradigm is that a researcher needs to eliminate possible alternative explanations to make a knowledge claim that one variable caused a change in another. Even with the careful control of variables and the systematic manipulation of the treatment variable, researchers within this paradigm are careful to acknowledge that their results are "true" at a certain level of probability and only within the conditions that existed during the experiment. The knowledge claim is strengthened when the results can be demonstrated repeatedly under similar conditions.

Research Designs and Threats to Validity

Any parent, teacher, counselor, or administrator who encounters students who are not reading as well as one thinks they should experiences a complex challenge to figure out how to improve performance. Is the poor performance due to a skill deficit, inappropriate instruction, lack of home support, resistance to pressure to perform, insufficient reinforcement for efforts made, a lack of maturity or "readiness to read," or what? Educators and psychologists have wrestled with this question and, through the use of systematic explanatory designs, attempted to find ways to improve reading performance.

Borman et al. (2007) tackled the problem of improving reading comprehension in schools where achievement was historically low. In this example, the *independent variable* (i.e., the variable that is manipulated) is the approach to teaching reading. It had two levels: Success for All and conventional teaching. The *dependent variable* (i.e., the variable that will be affected by, that "depends on," the independent variable) is reading comprehension. (See Box 4.1 for an example of how dependent variables were identified for family research.) The group that gets the new teaching strategy (Success for All) is the *experimental group* (sometimes called *treatment group*), and the group that gets the conventional instruction is the *control group*. If the participants are randomly assigned to the experimental and control groups, you have a true experimental design. Random assignment means that every person has an equal chance of being in either the experimental or control group. This can be done by pulling names out of a hat, flipping a coin, throwing dice, using a table of random numbers, or having a computer generate a random list of names.

Box 4.1 Development of Dependent Variables for Family Research

The U.S. Office of Special Education funded the Early Childhood Outcomes (ECO) Center to develop appropriate outcomes (dependent variables) for children with disabilities and their families (Bailey et al., 2006). They focused on family outcomes as opposed to outcomes specific to the child. They defined family outcome as "a benefit experienced by families as a result of services received" (p. 228). The ECO went through a yearlong, multistep process to develop the family outcomes, including use of an Advisory Board that included professionals and parents with children with disabilities, a literature review, convening of an expert technical working group of family research experts, and an open review process based on a Web posting of the draft outcomes for comment. As a result of this stakeholder-driven process, Bailey et al. identified five outcomes that could be used as dependent variables in research to determine if early intervention programs were effective for the children and their families:

1. families understand their child's strengths, abilities, and special needs,
2. families know their rights and advocate effectively for their child,
3. families help their child develop and learn,
4. families have support systems, and
5. families are able to gain access to desired services and activities in their community. (Bailey et al., 2006, p. 227)

Experimental research is fundamentally defined by the direct manipulation of an independent variable. Thus, the Borman et al. (2007) study exemplifies experimental research in that the researchers themselves decided how to operationalize the experimental treatment. They operationally defined the Success for All condition to teaching based on the program developed at Johns Hopkins University. They hypothesized that children who participated in the Success for All would score better on the reading tests than children who did not participate in the program.

In the next sections, I discuss internal and external validity, ways to minimize threats to internal and external validity by using various research designs with examples from education and psychology, and challenges associated with the application of these designs in educational and psychological research.

Internal Validity

Internal validity means that the changes observed in the dependent variable are due to the effect of the independent variable, not to some other unintended variables (known as *extraneous* or *lurking variables, alternative explanations,* or *rival hypotheses*). If extraneous variables are controlled, the results can be said to be due to the treatment, and therefore the study is internally valid. D. T. Campbell and Stanley (1963) identified eight extraneous variables that can threaten internal validity.

1. *History.* History refers to events that happen during the course of the study that can influence the results. For example, suppose you are investigating the effectiveness of various reading strategies. During your study, the president of the United States announces that he (or she) will give a certificate for a free ice-cream cone for every book that the school children read. This *event* could have an impact on the children's ability to comprehend what they read; however, it is *not* the treatment that you have in mind. History can be controlled by having a control group that is exposed to the same events during the study as an experimental group, with the exception of the treatment. If this magnanimous president had made such an offer to the students during the Borman et al. (2007) study, *all* of the students (in both the experimental and control groups) would have "read for ice cream," and thus its effect would be assumed to balance out and leave only the effect of the experimental treatment.

2. *Maturation.* Maturation refers to biological or psychological changes in the participants during the course of the study. This might refer to changes such as becoming stronger, more coordinated, or tired as the study progresses. For example, the children in a reading study might become tired after reading the first passage. This fatigue might cause them to perform more poorly on the second passage. However, the children in the control group should also experience a similar maturational change, and thus its effect should balance out. Maturation is controlled by having a control group that experiences the same kinds of maturational changes—the only difference being that they do not receive the experimental treatment.

3. *Testing.* Testing is a threat to validity that arises in studies that use both pre- and posttests and refers to becoming "test-wise" by having taken a pretest that is similar to the posttest. That is, the participants know what to expect, learn something from the pretest, or become sensitized to what kind of information to "tune into" during the study because of their experience with the pretest. Testing is a potential threat to validity only in research studies that include both pre- and posttests. Borman et al. (2007) had a pretest but it was different from the posttest, so testing would not be a threat. And, all the children in the study took both pre- and posttests, so the effect of pretesting should balance out.

4. *Instrumentation.* Instrumentation is another threat to validity in studies that use both pre- and posttests, and it arises when there is a change in the instrument between the pre- and posttests. It is possible that one test might be easier than the other test, and then changes observed on the dependent variable are due to the nature of the instrument, not to the independent variable. Instrumentation is a potential threat to validity only when the difficulty of the instrument used for data collection changes from one observation time period to the next. Examples of such situations include using a different test for pre- and posttesting, or collecting qualitative data by observation, which can be associated with changes in the researcher as instrument. Borman et al. (2007) did give a pretest, but they did not use it to measure amount of change on a posttest. Rather, they used the pretest to document the similarities of the comparison groups prior to the intervention.

5. *Statistical Regression.* Statistical regression is a threat to validity that occurs when the researcher uses extreme groups as the participants (i.e., students at the high or low end of the normal curve). For example, if you select students who score at the 10th percentile on an achievement measure and test them again on a similar measure at the conclusion of the study, their scores could increase simply because of statistical regression rather than because of your treatment. This is due to the role that chance plays in test scores. We cannot measure achievement with 100% precision. Therefore, there is always an element of error in any measurement. If the researcher selected students from the bottom of the normal curve, then it is most likely that their scores will go up (because they are already at the bottom, it is unlikely that they will go down). This threat to validity is a problem only in studies that use a pretest to select participants who are at the lowest or highest ends of the normal curve and then test them again using that instrument for the dependent measure. Borman et al. (2007) did not use extreme groups; the students in the classrooms represented the full range of abilities in reading.

6. *Differential Selection.* If participants with different characteristics are in the experimental and control groups, the results of the study may be due to group differences, not necessarily to the treatment or the independent variable. For example, in your hypothetical study of reading instruction, the experimental group might include children who are older than the students in the control group. If the experimental group scores higher than the control group on your outcome measure (dependent variable), how would you know if it was due to your treatment or to their age difference (which is confounded with variables such as maturity, length of time exposed to reading, or opportunity to learn)? Borman et al. (2007) controlled for differential selection effects by randomly assigning schools to the two conditions. Because they could not assign individual students to conditions, they did extra work to show the similarity of the control and experimental groups. They compared the two groups of schools on pretest scores and demographic characteristics. They did this to ensure that the students were equally distributed by initial literacy levels, race/ethnicity, and economic disadvantage within the conditions. Differential selection is theoretically controlled by the random assignment of participants to conditions because differences should balance out between and among groups.

7. *Experimental Mortality.* Experimental mortality refers to participants who drop out during the course of the study. It becomes a threat to validity if participants differentially drop out of the experimental and control groups. For example, suppose you have a new strategy for teaching reading to learning disabled students during a special summer program. The experimental group gets the new strategy and the control group gets the traditional approach. During the study, many of the higher-ability students drop out of the experimental group. At the end, the scores for the lower-ability students who complete the experimental treatment are higher than scores for all of the students in the control

group. Can you say that your program was successful? Maybe, maybe not. It could be that the program is successful for the lower-ability students but is dreadfully boring for the higher-ability students. This threat is theoretically controlled by the random assignment to conditions under the assumption that randomization will lead to the same level of dropouts in both experimental and control groups. Researchers can test this assumption by having pretest measures that allow them to determine if people who drop out of the study are systematically different from those who complete it. Testing for experimental mortality effects, Borman et al. (2007) compared the pretest scores for students who completed the three-year program with those who dropped out. This revealed that students who stayed with the program had higher pretest scores than students with missing data or who left the school (mobile students). Thus, this limits the generalizability of the results to nonmobile students who remained in the school for three years and had complete data.

8. *Selection-Maturation Interaction.* Selection-maturation interaction combines the threats to validity described previously under differential selection and maturation; however, maturation is the differential characteristic that causes the groups to differ. For example, suppose that the students with learning disabilities in the experimental group are older than those in the control group. The difference in their reading achievement might be due to this maturational characteristic rather than to the educational treatment.

T. D. Cook and Campbell (1979) extended this list of potential extraneous variables by adding the following additional items.

1. *Experimental Treatment Diffusion.* People will talk, and if the ideas they hear sound interesting, they might just try to use them themselves. If the treatment group is in proximity to the control group, it is possible that the control group participants may learn about the independent variable and begin using some of the ideas themselves. This would cloud the effect of the treatment. The researcher should conduct observations of selected classes to determine if the control group has become contaminated and should also conduct interviews with the participants to determine their perceptions of what they are doing. In order to address this threat to validity, the researchers in the Borman et al. (2007) study did quarterly observations in the schools to document if contamination occurred between experimental and control classes in the same schools. They found two control classrooms in which Success for All strategies were used and three that had Success for All materials in them. They reminded the teachers of the need for discrete conditions, and the materials were returned to the experimental classrooms.

2. *Compensatory Rivalry by the Control Group.* This threat is also known as the John Henry effect after the folktale of the railroad worker who was pitted against a machine. John Henry wanted to prove that man was superior to the machine, so he tried extra hard. He did beat the machine and then he died. (Let this be a warning to the control group.) Some individuals who think that their traditional way of doing things is being threatened by a new approach may try extra hard to prove that their way of doing things is best.

3. *Compensatory Equalization of Treatments.* Members of a control group may become disgruntled if they think that the experimental group is receiving extra resources. To keep everybody happy, a principal may decide to give extra resources to the control group. This could cloud the effect of the treatment. Borman et al. (2007) ran into a situation where none of the schools wanted to be in the control group, so they compromised by allowing the "control" schools to use the Success for All in Grades 4–7 (the experiment was in K–3).

4. *Resentful Demoralization of the Control Group.* This is the opposite of the John Henry effect. The control group may feel demoralized because they are not part of the "chosen" group, and thus their performance might be lower than normal because of their psychological response to being in the control group. Members of a control group could become quite angry if they find out that they are not going to receive an experimental treatment. If that happened, the control group in that setting could not be considered to be "unbiased."

External Validity or Generalizability

External validity is the extent to which findings in one study can be applied to another situation (Gall, Gall, & Borg, 2007). If the findings from one study are observed in another situation, the results are said to be generalizable or externally valid. The concept of population validity (i.e., to whom you can generalize the results based on sampling strategies) is described in Chapter 11. Bracht and Glass (1968) describe another type of external validity, termed *ecological validity,* which concerns the extent to which the results of an experiment can be generalized from the set of environmental conditions created by the researcher to other environmental conditions. They identified 10 factors that influence ecological validity.

1. *Explicit Description of the Experimental Treatment.* The independent variable must be sufficiently described so that the reader could reproduce it. This is a common criticism in educational and psychological research, particularly as it applies to instructional or therapeutic interventions. Asking questions such as, "Is mainstreaming effective?" or "Does behavior modification work?" is absurd because there are so many ways that such interventions can be implemented.

2. *Multiple-Treatment Interference.* If participants receive more than one treatment, it is not possible to say which of the treatments, or which combinations of the treatments, is necessary to bring about the desired result. For example, Success for All is an intervention that is purchased as a comprehensive package, which includes materials, training, ongoing professional development, and plans for delivering and sustaining the model (Borman et al., 2007). Because all of the treatments were applied simultaneously, it would not be possible to isolate the effects of the different components.

3. *The Hawthorne Effect.* The Hawthorne effect derives from a study at the Western Electric Company of changes in light intensity and other working conditions on the workers' productivity (Roethlisberger & Dickson, 1939). The researchers found that it did not matter if they increased or decreased the light intensity: The workers' productivity increased under both conditions. Seemingly, the idea of receiving special attention, of being singled out to participate in the study, was enough motivation to increase productivity.

4. *Novelty and Disruption Effects.* A new treatment may produce positive results simply because it is novel. Or the opposite may be true: A new treatment may not be effective initially because it causes a disruption in normal activities, but once it is assimilated into the system, it could become quite effective.

5. *Experimenter Effect.* The effectiveness of a treatment may depend on the specific individual who administers it (e.g., the researcher, psychologist, or teacher). The effect would not generalize to other situations because that individual would not be there.

6. *Pretest Sensitization.* Participants who take a pretest may be more sensitized to the treatment than individuals who experience the treatment without taking a pretest. This is especially true for pretests that ask the participants to reflect on and express their attitudes toward a phenomenon.

7. *Posttest Sensitization.* This is similar to pretest sensitization in that simply taking a posttest can influence a participant's response to the treatment. Taking a test can help the participant bring the information into focus in a way that participants who do not take the test will not experience.

8. *Interaction of History and Treatment Effects.* An experiment is conducted in a particular time replete with contextual factors that cannot be exactly duplicated in another setting. If specific historical influences are present in a situation (e.g., unusually low morale because of budget cuts), the treatment may not generalize to another situation.

9. *Measurement of the Dependent Variable.* The effectiveness of the program may depend on the type of measurement used in the study. For example, one study of the effects of mainstreaming might use multiple-choice tests and conclude that mainstreaming does not work; another study that uses teachers' perceptions of behavior change might conclude that it is effective.

10. *Interaction of Time of Measurement and Treatment Effects.* The timing of the administration of the posttest may influence the results. For example, different results may be obtained if the posttest is given immediately after the treatment as opposed to a week or a month afterward.

Borman et al. (2005) summarize the quality of their study as follows:

> The sample selection process and randomization procedure appear to have produced a baseline sample of schools with good internal validity, in that there are no large, statistically significant treatment-control differences, and good external validity, in that the sample's demographic characteristics resemble those of the overall population of Success for All schools and a range of regional contexts are included, representing the national reach of the program. (Borman et al., 2005, p. 8)

As briefly mentioned at the beginning of this chapter, a tension always exists between internal and external validity. To achieve perfect internal validity (e.g., the control of all extraneous variables), the laboratory is the perfect setting—a nice, clean, sterile environment in which no variables operate except those that you, as the researcher, introduce. To achieve perfect external validity, the research should be conducted in the "outside" world, in the clinic, classroom, or other messy, complex, often noisy environment in which the practitioner will attempt to apply the research results. Of course, all the "noise" in the outside world plays havoc with the idea of testing the effects of single variables while eliminating the influence of other variables.

For example, some research in memory processes is conducted in laboratories (usually with college students enrolled in beginning psychology courses). A researcher conducting basic research to determine the optimal number of items a person can recall might be pleased to report (and publish) that participants can remember 7 items better than 10 when they are presented in black letters on white background and flashed individually on a wall for a specified period of time. A teacher might view those results as minimally applicable to helping her students remember that different schedules of reinforcement yield different expectations for maintaining and extinguishing behaviors—her students' memory tasks are more complex than the researcher's laboratory ones. As researchers move to increase the external validity of their work, they sacrifice internal validity. Nevertheless, there is room for both types of research, as well as a need to build bridges between them. Some of the cooperative inquiry approaches to research have been developed with this in mind—for example, making the intended users of the research part of the research team. (See Chapter 8 in this text and also the Kemmis and McTaggart [2000] chapter in the second edition of Denzin and Lincoln's *Handbook of Qualitative Research* [2000] for further discussion of cooperative inquiry.)

Researchers who work in a laboratory setting need to acknowledge the limitations of their work, especially as it applies to external validity. In addition, they need to strive to make explicit the context within which the research was conducted so that practitioners can better judge its applicability to their own setting.

Other Threats to Validity

Two other threats to validity deserve mention here because of their importance in educational and psychological research. The first is *treatment fidelity,* in which the implementer of the independent variable (e.g., a teacher, counselor, psychologist, or administrator) fails to follow the exact procedures specified by the investigator for administering the treatments (Gall, Gall, & Borg, 2007). Researchers should try to maximize treatment fidelity by providing proper training and supervision and developing strategies to determine the degree and accuracy of the treatment as implemented. There are a variety of ways for researchers to both increase the probability of treatment fidelity and to check to see how successful they are in that endeavor. First, researchers can train the implementers of the treatments very carefully. Second, they can collect data as to the integrity of the implementation in a number of ways. F. Erickson and Gutierrez (2002) suggest that a considerable portion of the research budget should be devoted to documenting the treatment as delivered. In order to provide an answer to the question, "What was the treatment, specifically?" qualitative research methods will need to be employed (see Chapter 8). Observation and teacher logs are common ways to gather evidence on the integrity of the treatment. Finally, researchers can analyze the data within groups to determine if there are patterns of differential impact in the experimental group. They would then need to determine what contextual factors other than the treatment might account for the differences in performance.

Before researchers can establish the impact of an experimental treatment, they must provide evidence of what treatment was actually implemented. As Erickson and Gutierrez (2002) state, "A logically and empirically prior question to 'Did it work?' is 'What was the "it"?'—What was the 'treatment' as actually delivered?" (p. 21). At first blush, this may seem like a simple matter of providing sufficient description of the treatment as outlined by the researcher. However, treatments are often implemented by people other than the researcher, and sometimes in many locations simultaneously, thereby making it very difficult for the researcher to verify that the treatment was implemented as intended.

Borman et al. (2007) used several strategies to ensure treatment fidelity: Teachers received 3 days of training and 16 days of on-site follow-up each year. Success for All trainers visited the classrooms quarterly, met with teachers, and monitored students' progress. There were some problems with treatment implementation. Several schools took a full year to implement the program, while others got started immediately. Last-minute recruitment meant several of the schools had insufficient time to plan before implementation and few of the schools were able to implement all the features of the program such as tutoring and having full-time facilitators.

The second threat to validity (other than treatment fidelity) concerns the *strength of the experimental treatment*. An experiment to determine the effectiveness of an innovative teaching or counseling strategy can last for a few hours or for days, weeks, months, or years. It may not be reasonable to expect that clients' or students' learning, attitudes, self-concepts, or personalities can be affected by an experiment of short duration. If the study results do not show evidence that the treatment was successful, this may not mean that the approach is ineffective, but simply that it was not tried long enough. Interventions designed to change behaviors, attitudes, and knowledge often require more time than would be possible in a short experiment of one or two sessions. Borman et al. (2007) continued their study over a three-year period, certainly sufficient time to effect change in literacy skills.

Single-Group, Experimental, and Quasi-Experimental Designs

Research design can be thought of as answering the question, Who gets what when? It involves decisions about how many groups to have and how many times to administer the dependent variable with an eye to controlling threats to validity.

Three types of research designs are explained: single-group, experimental, and quasi-experimental. For each of these designs, a coding system is used with the following symbols:

R = Random assignment of subjects to conditions

X = Experimental treatment

O = Observation of the dependent variable (e.g., pretest, posttest, or interim measures)

Generally, internal threats to validity are controlled by means of the research design. For example, history and maturation can be controlled by having a control group, and differential selection can be controlled by random assignment to conditions.

Single-Group Designs

Three single-group designs are briefly described here. For a more in-depth discussion of research design options, see Shadish, Cook, and Campbell (2002).

One-Shot Case Study

In the one-shot case study, the researcher administers a treatment and then a posttest to determine the effect of the treatment. The one-shot case study is depicted as follows:

X O

For example, a researcher could study the effects of providing peer tutors for students with learning disabilities to increase ability on math performance. Here, the experimental treatment (X) is the use of peer tutors, and the dependent variable is math performance (O). This design is subject to the threats of history, maturation, and mortality (if subjects drop out) because there is no control group and no pretest. If the students score well on the math test, you would not know if it was the result of having a peer tutor because you did not pretest their math knowledge. Even if you think the students are performing better in math, you could not be sure it was your experimental treatment that caused their enhanced performance. Other events (such as having the opportunity to play math-based computer games) might have been the cause, thus constituting a threat to validity based on history. Maturation is an uncontrolled threat to validity in this design because the students could have matured in their ability to understand numerical concepts. This design is very weak and does not allow for a reasonable inference as to the effect of the experimental treatment.

One-Group Pretest-Posttest Design

Mark and Gamble (2009) discuss the relatively simple quasi-experiment, the one-group, pretest-posttest design, as a study in which participants are measured on an outcome variable both before and after the treatment of interest. The researcher's hope is that if the treatment is effective, outcome scores should improve, while scores will hold steady if the treatment has no effect. However, a variety of validity threats exist, including maturation and statistical regression. This design is represented as follows:

O X O

For example, the researcher could administer a pretest of math problems (O), then provide peer tutoring to students with learning disabilities (X), and measure math ability again after the intervention (O). This design is stronger than the one-shot case study because you can document a change in math scores from before the treatment to after its application. However, this design is open to the threats of history, in that the children could have experienced an event (e.g., math-based computer games), or a maturational change (e.g., maturing in their ability to understand numerical concepts) that could result in a change in their math scores. Without a control group who might have had the same experiences except for exposure to the experimental treatment, you are limited in your ability to claim the effectiveness of your treatment (i.e., peer tutoring). This design can also be open to the threats of testing (if the students do better on the posttest simply because it is the second time they are taking the test) or instrumentation (if the pre- and posttests were different). Mortality is not a threat because you have pretest data on the students at the beginning of the experiment, and thus you could determine if those who dropped out were different from those who completed the study.

Although this design does have many weaknesses, it may be necessary to use it in a situation in which it is not possible to have a control group because the school would not allow differential provision of services. This design is justified under circumstances in which you are attempting to change attitudes, behavior, or knowledge that are unlikely to change without the introduction of an experimental treatment (e.g., few students learn research design "incidentally," without direct instruction).

Time Series Design

The time series design involves measurement of the dependent variable at periodic intervals. The experimental treatment is administered between two of the time intervals. This design is depicted as follows:

O O O O X O O O O

For example, the researcher could give weekly math tests (O O O O), then institute a peer-tutoring program for students with learning disabilities (X), and follow up with weekly math tests after the intervention (O O O O). This design is based on the logic that if the behavior is stable before the introduction of the experimental treatment and it changes after the treatment is introduced, then the change can be attributed to the treatment. The biggest threat to this design is history, because the experiment continues over a period of time and there is no control group who might experience the "historical event" but not the treatment. In this example, you might find that performance in math prior to the peer tutoring is consistently low. If you found improved performance after peer tutoring, you would need to be sensitive to other historical events that might have led to the improvement, such as math-based computer games, distribution of free calculators, or exposure to a new, fun-filled math television program.

The time series design does provide for control of several threats to validity. For example, it is unlikely that maturation would be a threat if the scores were found to be consistently low before treatment and consistently high after treatment. If maturation was having an effect, it is likely that it would be reflected in a more erratic pattern in the pretest scores. The same logic can be applied to ruling out testing as a threat to internal validity in this study. If repeated testing, in and of itself, was having an effect, it would be evident in an erratic (or gradually increasing) pattern during the pretesting period. Differential selection is not a problem in studies in which the same persons are involved in all of the measurements and treatments.

Experimental Designs

Six experimental designs that use control groups and random assignment of participants are briefly described here:

Pretest-Posttest Control Group Design

In pretest-posttest control group design, participants are randomly assigned to either the experimental group or the control group. It is depicted as follows:

R O X O

R O   O

The experimental group receives the treatment and the control group receives either no treatment or an alternative treatment (to avoid such threats to validity as the John Henry effect or compensatory equalization). This design controls for the effects of history, maturation, testing, instrumentation, and experimental mortality by the use of control groups and for differential selection by the use of random assignment to conditions.

If we focus only on the two groups of schools (trained vs. traditional) in Borman et al. (2007), this study can be used to illustrate this design. Borman and associates used a pretest-posttest control group design to study the impact of their experimental treatment on reading comprehension. The group who received the training is the experimental group and this group is depicted in the top line of the design, where

R = Indicates they were randomly chosen to participate in the training

O = Indicates the students were pretested on their vocabulary knowledge prior to training

X = Indicates they received the training

O = Indicates the students were posttested on their reading comprehension

The control group is depicted in the second line of the design. They were also randomly assigned to their condition (R), were pretested on their vocabulary (O), and then participated in traditional reading instruction. The blank space in the second line between the two O's is used to indicate that this group did not receive the experimental treatment. They were also posttested at the end of the study to determine their reading comprehension levels.

Thus the design would look like this:

R O X O

R O   O

Borman et al. (2007) were able to conclude that students of the teachers who participated in the training had higher reading comprehension scores as compared to the control group at greater than a chance level. They attributed the increase to their experimental treatment because students who were in the control group and had not been exposed to the treatment did not score as high on the reading comprehension test. They ruled out the possibility of threats to validity such as history, maturation, and testing because the control group would have shared all of these same experiences. Thus, even if the students had been exposed to "Reading Is Wonderful Week" during the experiment, all of the students would have experienced that. Theoretically, the only difference in the students' experience during the experiment was exposure to the experimental treatment.

Instrumentation was ruled out as a threat to validity because the dependent measure was recorded as student responses to a reading comprehension test that was different from the vocabulary test taken prior to the treatment implementation (Borman et al., 2007). They also ruled out experimental mortality because they had a pretest and they could determine if there were systematic differences in the characteristics of students who completed the study and those who dropped out. Finally, they were not concerned about differential selection because the schools were randomly assigned to the experimental and control groups. Thus they assumed that any differences in background characteristics in the two groups would be balanced out by the random assignment. If the researchers had chosen the participants on the basis of extreme pretest scores, the use of random assignment to experimental and control groups would also control the effect of regression. It would be assumed that the control group would regress as much as the experimental group, and thus the effect of this threat to validity would be balanced out by the design.

Posttest-Only Control Group Design

The posttest-only control group design is similar to the pretest-posttest control group design except that no pretest is given. It is depicted as follows:

RXO

R O

It controls for the threats to validity in the same way as the previously discussed design, except that mortality can be a problem if people drop out of the study.

Again, if Borman et al. (2007) had not administered a pretest, then their study of reading comprehension would exemplify the posttest-only control group design. The R indicates the random assignment of schools to experimental or control conditions. The X indicates the treatment that the experimental group received—that is, the training in Success for All. The O indicates the measure of the students' reading comprehension scores. The blank space between R and O on the second line of the design indicates that the control group did not receive the experimental treatment.

D. T. Campbell and Stanley (1966) state that a pretest is not necessary, because "the most adequate all-purpose assurance of lack of initial biases between groups is randomization" (p. 25). Thus differential selection is not a problem in studies that use this design. It would be assumed that randomization would also result in the equalization of mortality effects, although the astute researcher would want to monitor the pattern of dropouts from the study. Finally, without the use of a pretest, the threats of testing and instrumentation disappear.

Single-Factor Multiple-Treatment Designs

Single-factor multiple-treatment designs are an extension of the randomized control group designs presented previously, but here the sample is randomly assigned to one of several conditions (usually three or four groups are used). If Borman et al. (2007) had included a third group that had received a different intervention (e.g., phonics-based instruction), this would exemplify the single-factor multiple-treatment design. Then the students could have been randomly assigned to one of three conditions:

X1 = Success for All

X2 = Phonics-based instruction

Control group = Traditional reading comprehension instruction

Thus their design could be depicted as follows:

R O X1 O

R O X2 O

R O   O

The O's represent the pre- and post-questionnaire on strategy use that was administered before training and after all other posttesting. Internal threats to validity are controlled by randomly assigning students to conditions and by having comparison groups (two experimental groups and one control group).

Solomon 4-Group Design

The Solomon 4-group design was developed for the researcher who is worried about the effect of pretesting on the validity of the results. The design looks like this:

R O X O

R O   O

R   X O

R   O

As you can see, the researcher combines the pretest-posttest control group design with the posttest-only control group design. Because half the participants receive the pretest and half do not, the researcher can test the effect of taking the pretest and thus eliminate that threat to validity without sacrificing the valuable information that can be obtained from a pretest. The disadvantage of this design is that it necessitates having four groups and thus increases the number of participants that one would need to test.

Factorial Design

Researchers who choose the experimental approach grapple with the issue of the complexity of reality and how to represent that complexity while still reducing their choice of variables in their studies to a manageable number. One way to include more than one variable is to include multiple *independent* variables. Such designs are known as *factorial designs,* and each independent variable is called a *factor.*

For example, returning to the Borman et al. (2007) study of reading comprehension, I have already introduced you to their first independent variable: instructional strategy (*A*), which had two levels. If they also had a second independent variable: gender, which had two levels, then as a factorial design, their study could be depicted as a 2×2 design (two independent variables, each with two levels). The factors and their levels are as follows:

A = Instructional strategy

A_1 = Success for All

A_3 = Traditional reading comprehension instruction

B = Gender

B_1 = Female

B_2 = Male

In conducting the analysis for a factorial design, the researcher tests the effects of the main variables, as well as their possible interaction:

A

B

A × B

A × B refers to the interaction between A and B. In the Borman et al. (2007) study, this would take the form of testing for the main effect for instructional strategy (A), the main effect for gender (B), and the interaction effect (A × B) to see if the treatment was differentially effective by gender, depending on the condition. Often, a graphic presentation of interaction effects is useful to interpretation. This discussion foreshadows the information on how to analyze and present data from these experimental designs presented in Chapter 13 on data analysis.

Factorial designs are quite common in experimental research because they allow researchers to test for effects of different kinds of variables that might be expected to influence outcomes, such as grade level, age, gender, ethnicity or race, or disability type. As you can see, there are multiple variations on the number of variables and how they can be put together into a design for research. The main limitation in the number of variables arises from the number of participants needed for each condition (a topic addressed in Chapter 11) and the resulting complexity in interpretation of the results (see Chapter 13). If your head was swimming a bit at trying to "see" the A × B interaction, the level of complexity is greatly enhanced by adding a third variable (C), such that effects would be tested for the following:

A

B

C

A × B

A × C

B × C

A × B × C

Let your mind wander around the thought of adding yet a fourth variable and reach your own conclusions as to why researchers tend to limit their factorial designs to two or three factors.

Cluster Randomization Design

Borman et al. (2007) used a cluster randomized design, meaning that schools, not students, were randomly assigned to conditions. However, data were collected on individual students and not at a school level. Because schools were the unit of assignment, the researchers needed to conduct statistical analyses that allowed for the test of school-level effects first. Then students could be compared once the school-level effects were controlled. This statistical technique is called hierarchical linear regression and is discussed further in Chapter 13.

Quasi-Experimental Designs

Quasi-experimental designs are those that are "almost" true experimental designs, except that the participants are not randomly assigned to groups. In quasi-experimental research, the researcher studies the effect of the treatment on intact groups rather than being able to randomly assign participants to the experimental or control groups. Borman et al. (2007) noted that prior studies on the Success for All program used quasi-experimental designs and therefore were open to numerous threats to internal validity. For example, if 80% of a school's staff had to agree to participate in Success for All, then the schools that agreed to participate and constituted the "experimental group" in the quasi-experimental studies might have had better leaders or more solidarity on the part of the teachers. Other competing explanations that could not be controlled in quasi-experimental designs might be the level of funding that a school has (e.g., do schools that agree to use Success for All have more funding than schools that do not?), or whether schools with greater challenges seek a program such as Success for All as opposed to schools with students who achieve above average already? Also, previous studies of Success for All had all been conducted by developers of the program, which could raise concerns about the effects of the experimenters as a threat to validity. To minimize this threat, Borman et al. (2007) enlisted colleagues from other universities to collect the data in their experimental study.

A sample quasi-experimental study evaluating the impact of two delivery systems for mental health services is displayed in Sample Study 4.1. I use selective variables from their study to exemplify the quasi-experimental designs. Their main independent variable was the provision of mental health services for children and adolescents. There were two levels:

X = Mental health services as part of a continuum of care

Control = Referral for mental health services

Sample Study 4.1

Evaluation Study Using Quasi-Experimental Design

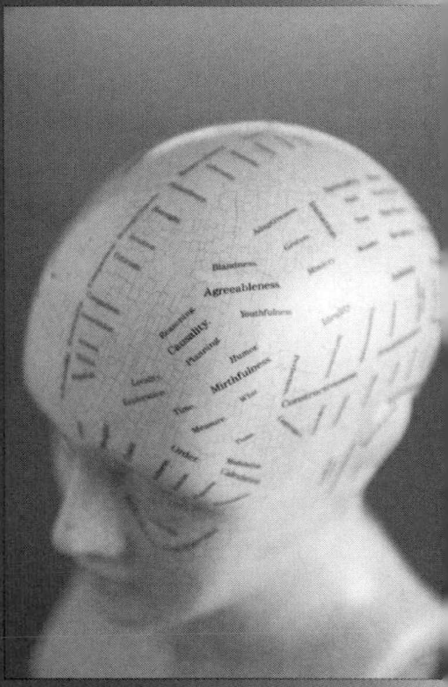

Research Problem: The continuum model was at the heart of current government policy for reforming mental health services for children and adolescents in the United States. There were high expectations that a continuum of care would produce better clinical outcomes at lower cost.

Research/Evaluation Questions: How did the mental health outcomes for children and adolescents who were referred for mental health treatment compare when that treatment was offered as part of a continuum of care versus when families arranged and coordinated their own care program? Was the demonstration program implemented as planned?

Method: A quasi-experimental design was used to compare the effectiveness of the services for children who participated in the demonstration site at Fort Bragg and the children who received their services at two comparable army posts.

Participants: Participants consisted of 984 children between the ages of 5 and 17, with 574 in the experimental group and 410 in the comparison condition. Eighteen characteristics were collected on each child; comparisons indicated that the children in the two groups were not statistically significantly different on 13 of the 18 characteristics.

Procedures: This study examined the follow-up outcomes of a demonstration project designed to improve mental health outcomes for children and adolescents who were referred for mental health treatment. The demonstration provided a broad continuum of mental health services, including outpatient therapy, day treatment, in-home counseling, therapeutic foster homes, specialized group homes, 24-hour crisis management services, and acute hospitalization. Individual case managers and interdisciplinary treatment teams worked with children assigned to more intensive services to integrate and fit services to the needs of each child. Treatment plans used the least restrictive service options, and services were community based. At the comparison sites, families arranged and coordinated their own care and included outpatient therapy and residential care in psychiatric hospitals or residential treatment centers. Over a five-year period, Bickman, Lambert, Andrade, and Penaloza (2000) used 10 different dependent measures related to mental health, such as the Child Behavior Checklist (Achenbach, 1991) and the parent- and child-reported Vanderbilt Functioning Index (Bickman, Lambert, Karver, & Andrade, 1998).

Results: A random regression longitudinal model was used to analyze data collected over a five-year period at seven different points in the study. The results indicated that at both short-term and long-term points in the five-year period that continuum-treated children were no better than those of comparison children based on 10 key outcome variables.

Discussion: The researchers discussed their results in terms of national policy, suggesting that large investments in systems of care infrastructure are unlikely to affect children in the manner intended. They emphasized the need to focus on the quality of services or treatments to improve outcomes.

SOURCE: Bickman et al. (2000).

Because the experimental treatment was located at a particular army base, the researchers were unable to randomly assign youth to conditions. Therefore, their design is quasi-experimental because they were working with intact groups. There were multiple dependent measures of the children's mental health; however, for the purposes of this illustration, I focus on the Child Behavior Checklist.

Three quasi-experimental designs are briefly described here.

Static-Group Comparison Design

Static-group comparison design involves administering the treatment to the experimental group and comparing its performance on a posttest with that of a control group. It is depicted as follows:

X O

....

O

The dotted line is used to indicate that the participants were not randomly assigned to conditions.

The two main threats to this design are (a) differential selection, because the groups might differ initially on an important characteristic, and (b) experimental mortality if participants drop out of the study. It is very important with this design to collect as much background information as possible about the two groups to determine how they differ. *If* Bickman et al. (2000) had used only one dependent measure and had only administered it once and had NOT used a pretest (which they did), then their design would look like this:

X O

....

O

where X is the continuum of care treatment and the blank space on the next line under X indicates the control group that received referrals for mental health services. The O's here represent the posttest of mental health functioning, which in this example is assumed to have been given only at the end of the study.

As mentioned before, the two main threats to internal validity for this design are differential selection and experimental mortality (or attrition). Bickman et al. (2000) compared demographic characteristics between the experimental and control group to demonstrate that the two groups were similar on many dimensions. They presented data that indicated that the two groups were similar in terms of age, gender, race, and percentage that had previous mental health treatment. The groups differed in that the parents of the children in the experimental group were more highly educated and had a higher family income. The researchers acknowledged that the groups were not perfectly matched, but were similar enough to allay serious concerns about differential selection as a threat to validity. Experimental mortality was a serious issue because about half the participants dropped out over the five-year period (not surprising for military families who move a lot). Bickman et al. calculated a statistical correction for attrition and entered that as a variable in their analyses to control for the experimental mortality threat to validity.

In actuality, Bickman et al. (2000) did use a pretest, and that leads us to the next quasi-experimental design.

Nonequivalent Control Group Design

The nonequivalent control group design is similar to the static-group comparison design except for the addition of a pretest. It is depicted as follows:

O X O

……………..

O   O

This design controls for differential selection and mortality somewhat by the use of the pretest. The researcher would be able to determine if the two groups differed initially on the dependent variable.

Because Bickman et al. (2000) actually did ask the youth and their parents in their study to provide data on their mental health functioning *before* the study started, the design could be depicted as follows:

O X O

……………..

O   O

with the O's representing the mental health functioning pre- and postmeasures. Thus, they were able to establish that there was no statistically significant difference on the Child Behavior Checklist for youth in the treatment and control groups prior to the intervention.

Regression-Discontinuity (R-D) Design

Mark and Gamble (2009) propose a regression-discontinuity design for situations where an experimental design is not possible but there is a demonstrated great need for services. This is a bit complicated, but here is how Mark and Gamble describe it:

> In the R-D design, the treatment that participants receive depends on their scores on a prior measure called the quantitative assignment variable, or QAV. People who score above a specific cutoff value on the QAV receive one treatment, and those below the cutoff receive the other treatment. In a study of a compensatory afterschool reading program, for example, prestudy reading scores might be the QAV, with students scoring below the cutoff assigned to the compensatory reading program and students above the cutoff to a comparison group. Later, after the program, students would be assessed on the outcome measure, say, postprogram reading scores. For a merit-based intervention, such as merit scholarships, the treatment group would consist of participants scoring above the cutoff, and the comparison group those below. The basic logic of the R-D design is that if the program is effective, there should be a detectable jump in scores at the cutoff. Moreover, generally there are no plausible validity threats that could account for a discontinuity in scores occurring precisely at the cutoff. (p. 208)

For an accessible presentation on the logic and analysis of the regression-discontinuity design, see Mark and Reichardt (2009). Historically, the R-D design has been implemented only rarely (Shadish et al., 2002), but it has received increased attention in recent years, including investigation of alternative analysis approaches (e.g., Hann, Todd, & Van der Klaauw, 2001). Thus, continued enhancements of the quasi-experimental regression-discontinuity design may increase its acceptability as an alternative to the randomized experiment. "Stronger" quasi-experimental designs, such as the regression-discontinuity design and complex interrupted time series designs, generally tend to rule out more validity threats than do "weaker" quasi-experiments such as the one-group pretest-posttest design. This design offers promise of avoiding ethical criticisms of the randomized experiment, with little, if any, loss of internal validity.

Other Design Issues

Type of Treatment Variables

In this chapter, I have focused almost exclusively on *manipulable* variables—the type of variable that is under the control of the researcher, such as counseling or instructional strategies. Such variables are at the heart of experimental design research. Other types of variables are more difficult to manipulate because of logistical, ethical, or genetic factors. For example, people cannot be randomly assigned to be males or females, or to be Caucasian, African American, or Latino. The effects of such variables might be very important to investigate, but because they cannot be manipulated, different approaches to research have been developed, such as causal comparative and correlational research, which are described in the next chapter. Nevertheless, these nonmanipulable variables can be combined with manipulable variables in experimental studies that use factorial designs.

Ordering Effects

In some research studies, a researcher might be concerned that exposure to one treatment before another would have different effects than if the treatments had been administered in reverse order. Researchers who are concerned about the ordering effects of treatments can choose to use a counterbalanced design in which some of the participants receive one treatment first and some receive the other treatment first. After measuring the dependent variable once, the administration of treatments can be reversed for the two groups.

For example, suppose a team of researchers had developed a strategy for teaching science using either "virtual reality" technology for animal dissection or the traditional approach. They might divide their sample in half and teach one half a unit using the virtual reality first, followed by a unit taught in the traditional mode. The other half of the participants would participate in the traditional mode first and then the virtual reality condition.

Matching

In research in which randomization is not possible (e.g., in this chapter, quasi-experimental designs), a researcher might choose to try to match participants on variables of importance—for example, gender, age, type of disability, level of hearing loss, or ethnicity. By matching pairs between the treatment and control groups, the researcher can control for some extraneous variables (e.g., older children tend to be more mature). Problems always arise in matching in trying to find a "perfect" match. Participants for whom no match can be found must be eliminated from the study. Matching on more than one variable can be quite problematic.

A researcher who uses matching has several important questions to answer: On which variables should the participants be matched? What is the theoretical rationale for the choice of matching variables? On how many variables should the groups be matched? How close does the match have to be? Is the matching based on a one-to-one match or on group similarities (Breaugh & Arnold, 2007)? Matching is problematic in that it is not possible to match on all variables that differentiate people in the two groups. Researchers need to be cautious in interpreting results from studies that use matched groups.

Denscombe (2008) conducted a study in which he compared responses to open-ended questions using either a computer-based or paper questionnaire. Because he used intact groups (classes in schools in England), he matched the groups on the basis of sex, age, ethnicity, academic ability, computer experience, and area of residence. These variables were chosen because they have been shown in prior to research to be related to competence in computer use. He used statistical tests to compare the groups on the basis of these matching characteristics and reported no significant differences. His results indicated no difference in the length of answers under the two administration modes of the questionnaire. However, he acknowledges that important differences might exist between the groups that were not matched (e.g., is it possible that the paper group included more people who are verbally fluent and if this characteristic had been controlled, would the outcome be different?).

Elbaum (2007) used a counter-balanced design to test the effects of administration mode of math tests for students with and without learning disabilities. The two administration modes included a standard administration in which introductory instructions were given to the students, who then completed the test without further teacher comment; in the experimental condition, the teacher read each item aloud to the students and allowed them time to complete the items before reading the next question. Half the students had the standard administration followed by the read-aloud administration; this order was reversed for the other half of the students.

Challenges to Using Experimental Designs in Educational and Psychological Research

Many challenges face the researcher who would like to use experimental designs to investigate educational and psychological phenomena. Several of these factors include school policies restricting differential treatment, difficulty in identifying appropriate comparison groups, small sample sizes, sampling bias, and ethical considerations. Because of these problems, some researchers have turned to single-subject designs (described in Chapter 7) and qualitative designs (see Chapter 8).

Transformative Perspectives Regarding Experimental Research

Transformative researchers are divided as to the appropriateness of using single-group, experimental, and quasi-experimental designs for educational, psychological, and sociological research. Feminists, such as Reinharz (1992), Lather (2004), and St. Pierre (2006), raise questions about research methods rooted in postpositivist assumptions such as the rigidity needed to control extraneous variables, the manipulative nature of the researcher in making decisions about treatments, lack of consultation with participants who would be affected by the treatment (or lack thereof), and the maintenance of distance from the members of the community that could result in inaccuracies of understandings that might be corrected by having a closer, personal relationship with members of that group. Involving members of the targeted group in the study planning, conduct, and interpretation of results might lead to very different understandings. Also, feminists expressed concern about sex bias in research at all stages of the process as evidenced by major educational and psychological theories that were based on male subjects only or were constructed with a male bias (see discussion in Chapter 1 on this topic). Equally common is that research done with all-White populations has been generalized to minority populations.

The laboratory setting of some research studies is viewed as "unnatural" and not capable of reflecting the complexity of human experience. Phenomenologists and cultural theorists argue that the detached "objectivity" of experimental research cannot adequately explain the complexity of social life (M. Fine & Gordon, 1992). This decontextualizing of the research setting occurs not only in laboratory research, but in experimental research that tries to control the settings in order to eliminate rival hypotheses. However, the controlled variables may limit the validity of the findings in other settings. Researchers who focus on the reduction of a complex social phenomenon to one or more numbers that can be statistically analyzed run the risk of overlooking important variations in terms of implementation of treatment and characteristics of study participants that may have explanatory power for the results (F. Erickson & Gutierrez, 2002).

One of the most serious criticisms raised by many feminists and other ethicists concerns the use of randomized assignment to experimental and control groups. Randomization means that each person has an equal chance of being in the control or the experimental group and their designation to their group is random. However, ethical arguments could be made on several bases, such as the importance of providing a service to someone who truly needs them because they need them, not because of random assignment. Another basis of argument is the difficulty logistically and ethically to randomly assign people to treatment or control groups in the real world. Borman et al. (2007) provide insights into how difficult it is to use random assignment in research conducted in schools. The schools and the districts in their study had many demands put on them. They had to agree to be designated as experimental or control schools by random assignment, participate in training, administer individual and group testing for the students, allow observers in their school, participate in interviews, and provide access to their school records for a three-year period. The researchers tried to recruit schools under the terms that Success for All had required of other schools: The schools had to pay $75,000 the first year, $35,000 the second year, and $25,000 the third year. No schools were willing to participate under these conditions. The researchers offered discounts to the schools, but still an insufficient number of schools agreed. Finally, the researchers ended up giving all the schools (experimental and control) $30,000 as a one-time payment; still, only six schools agreed. Part of the schools' resistance was based on their unwillingness to serve as control groups that received no treatment. Therefore, the researchers allowed the schools to use Success for All either in Grades K–2 or in Grades 3–5, so that at least a portion of their students would get the experimental treatment. The schools with the Grades 3–5 Success for All constituted the control group because the comparisons were made in the Grade K–2 school years.

An ethical problem emerges with the use of control groups in that the experimental group receives the treatment, but the control group does not. Feminists raise the question, Is it ethical to deny "treatment" to one group on a random basis? The Helsinki Declaration

(Okie, 2000), an international accord for research ethics, includes in its 32 principles the statement that "the benefits, risks, burdens and effectiveness of a new method should be tested against those of the best current prophylactic, diagnostic, and therapeutic methods" (p. A3). This has been interpreted to mean that the control group should receive the best available alternative. Denial of treatment (as in the provision of no treatment) is only permissible if there is no known alternative treatment.

Postpositivist Rejoinder

In addition to offering the best available treatment rather than no treatment, Mark and Gamble (2009) list several ways that the concern about denial of treatment could be addressed, including offering the "the more effective treatment to those in the other group after the study is over, when this is practical; providing participants with benefits that leave them better off than they would have been without participating in the study (e.g., payment for participation; health services in a study of job training), even if these are unrelated to the primary outcome variable" (p. 205). In assessing the benefit-risk ratio for study participants, Mark and Gamble argue that it is appropriate to consider opportunities that would not have been present if the study had not been conducted. They use the Congressionally mandated experimental trial of an Early Head Start program that created preschool opportunities as an example of a situation in which those in the treatment group would not have had access to the services in the absence of the experiment. Transformative researchers might ask: Is it true that this society would not provide services to enhance the development of children who are born into poverty unless an experimental study was underway?

Stop rules are another technique that can help attenuate risk. A stop rule is an explicit protocol to cease an experiment after a significant treatment effect of a specific magnitude is observed in preliminary analyses. Without stop rules, an experiment typically would continue until a specified number of participants or point in time was reached. Stop rules can reduce risk to participants by reducing the number of participants exposed to the less effective treatment, or by reducing the length of time they received the less effective treatment, or both. Especially in cases in which these participants can then receive the more effective treatment, stop rules can reduce risk and thus contribute to more ethical experimentation. Mark and Gamble (2009) contend that with stop rules and other procedures "such as informed consent to random assignment, experiments may in some cases raise fewer ethical concerns than alternatives, at least if one considers the relative fairness of the implicit rules that otherwise govern assignment to condition. These implicit rules may include the happenstance of location, first come first served, cronyism, and so on" (p. 205).

Final Thoughts

Reinharz (1992) notes that those feminists who do not oppose the use of experimental methods have used them to expose myths about the inferiority of women as well as to raise consciousness on a number of other issues. These feminists recognize that experiments have utility as a powerful tool for achieving feminist goals through policy formation.

For example, Fidell (1970) reported that attaching a woman's name or a man's name to a fictional set of application materials for a psychology professorship yielded higher ratings for the male. Thus, experimental methods were used to support the hypotheses of discrimination based on sex.

Although Reinharz (1992) acknowledges the usefulness of experimental methods for feminists, she also warns those interested in social change not to rely solely on the results of such research:

> We should also recognize that society is unlikely to be willing to change *even if* experimental research does provide information suggesting that change is needed. . . . Putting one's eggs in the basket of so-called definitive research is a very risky strategy to use to achieve social change. (p. 108)

Scott-Jones (1993) discusses problems faced by members of ethnic minority communities related to the use of experimental designs that deny treatment to one group (the control group) to test the effect of an intervention. She cited as an example the Tuskegee experiments that were conducted by the U.S. Public Health Service from 1932 to 1972. In these experiments, African American men with syphilis were not given treatment so that researchers could study the disease's progress. The participants were poor and illiterate, and did not know they had syphilis (J. H. Jones, 1992). When the U.S. Senate learned of this project, it passed the National Research Act, which established institutional review boards charged with the responsibility of overseeing ethical issues in research (see Chapters 1 and 10 for further discussion).

Nevertheless, Scott-Jones (1993) maintains that many low-income minority children participate in no-treatment control groups by the *de facto* requirements of experimental research designs. Thus, children who need the treatment most do not receive it. She discussed the following possible resolutions for the ethical dilemmas associated with experimental designs:

1. Give the potentially beneficial treatment to the control group at some time point after the experimental group received it. (This is not acceptable in situations in which children need specific interventions at specific times in their development. Delay in receiving the intervention may result in prolonging the undesirable conditions and, possibly, irreversible delays in development.)

2. Have two (or more) potentially beneficial treatments so all participants receive some intervention.

3. Compare the treatment group outcome to some carefully chosen standard.

4. Conduct intra-individual comparisons rather than cross-group comparisons.

5. Use individual baselines as comparison standards.

6. Include minority researchers as part of the research team.

These criticisms of and reflections on the experimental approach to research are meant to elucidate the thinking that has emerged from scholars in the transformative paradigm. The strength of the research world at this historical moment is the debate and dialogue that is occurring across paradigms.

Questions for Critically Analyzing Single-Group, Experimental, and Quasi-Experimental Designs

Internal Validity

1. *History*. Could events (other than the independent variable) have influenced the results?

2. *Maturation*. Could biological or psychological changes in study participants (other than those associated with the independent variable) have influenced the results?

3. *Testing*. Could the participants have become "test-wise" because of the pretest?

4. *Instrumentation*. Was there a difference between the pre- and posttests?

5. *Statistical regression*. Were extreme groups used?

6. *Differential selection*. Did the experimental and control groups differ in ways other than exposure to the independent variable?

7. *Experimental mortality*. Did participants drop out during the study?

8. *Selection-maturation*. Was differential selection a problem based on the biological or psychological characteristics of the sample?

9. *Experimental treatment diffusion*. Were the treatment and control groups close enough to share ideas?

10. *Compensatory rivalry by the control group*. Did the control group try extra hard?

11. *Compensatory equalization of treatments*. Were extra resources given to the control group?

12. *Resentful demoralization of the control group*. Was the control group demoralized because of being "left out"?

External Validity (Ecological Validity)

(See Chapter 11 on *population validity*)

1. Was the experimental treatment described in sufficient detail?
2. Were multiple treatments used? Did they interfere with each other?
3. Was the Hawthorne effect operating?
4. Was the treatment influenced by being novel or disruptive?
5. What was the influence of the individual experimenter?
6. Were the participants sensitized by taking a pretest?
7. Were the participants sensitized by taking a posttest?
8. Was there an interaction of history and treatment effects?
9. What was the influence of the type of measurement used for the dependent variable?
10. What was the influence of the time period that elapsed between the treatment and the administration of the dependent variable?

Other Threats to Validity

1. Were steps taken to ensure the treatment was implemented as planned?
2. What was the influence of the strength of the treatment?
3. Was it ethical to deny treatment to the control group?

Extending Your Thinking: Experimental and Quasi-Experimental Research

1. Through a computerized literature search or by going directly to the main journals that publish empirical, quantitative research studies, identify five research studies, each of which uses a slightly different design. Be sure to include both experimental and quasi-experimental studies. For each study, do the following:
    a. Identify the research problem.
    b. Identify the independent and dependent variables.
    c. Categorize the study as experimental or quasi-experimental.
    d. Explain the basis for your categorization.
    e. Draw the design that depicts the administration of treatment and dependent measures.
    f. Critique the studies using the questions for critical analysis at the end of this chapter.
2. Brainstorm a number of different problems that would be appropriate for experimental or quasi-experimental research.
3. Select one research problem and do the following:
    a. Identify the independent and dependent variables.
    b. Sketch a design that could be used to study your research problem.
    c. Explain how your design would satisfy the questions for critical analysis for experimental and quasi-experimental research.
4. Under what circumstances would you *not* recommend using experimental or quasi-experimental approaches to research? What kind of alternative approach would you suggest?

Summary of Chapter 4: Experimental and Quasi-Experimental Research

Experimental and quasi-experimental designs are the hallmark methodologies of the postpositivist paradigm. These designs are intended to determine if an independent variable caused a change in a dependent variable by controlling the effects of extraneous variables as much as possible. The experimental designs require random assignment of participants to conditions, a demand that is not always possible in educational and psychological research. Hence, the quasi-experimental designs maintain much of the rigor of the experimental designs, but allow for the use of intact groups in conditions. Internal validity considerations are used to determine the extent to which the researcher can make the claim that it is the independent variable that caused the change in the dependent variable. External validity is related to sampling (Chapter 11), but it is also related to how the independent variable was implemented. Researchers from the constructivist and transformative paradigms have questioned the claims of postpositivist researchers that experimental designs are the only way to establish causality, as well as criticized the lack of information about context in such studies that limit the ability of researchers to know why an intervention worked or did not work.

Where to From Here?

In keeping with my earlier suggestion that readers can use this text in a nonlinear fashion: If you are interested in completing your understanding of this approach to research, I strongly encourage you to go to Chapters 11, 12, and 13 and study the sections on quantitative sampling, data collection, and data analysis. You can then return to Chapter 5 to investigate causal comparative and correlational research approaches.

In This Chapter

- The types of variables appropriate for causal comparative and correlational research are explored.
- Challenging issues in this type of research are discussed that relate to focusing on group differences, group identification, the fallacy of homogeneity, and the post hoc fallacy.
- Steps for conducting causal comparative research are explained and illustrated, focusing on strategies for strengthening this approach.
- Correlational research is described in terms of challenges and steps for conducting both relationship and prediction studies, with special attention given to statistical decisions for analysis of data.
- Questions for critically analyzing causal comparative and correlational research are presented.

The school psychologist announced to the faculty that the school would participate in a research study to compare the effect of a new strategy for improving students' self-concepts. To control for the differential selection effects, all the names of the students in the school would be put in a hat and then randomly assigned to the high- and low-self-concept groups. Of course, this example is absurd. You can't assign people to different self-concept levels at random. Many characteristics of individuals are not manipulable or should not be manipulated for ethical reasons—for example, disabilities, gender, ethnicity, age, cognitive abilities, and personality traits, such as aggression or anxiety. Causal comparative and correlational research strategies represent two approaches that are appropriate for studying such nonmanipulable variables.

Causal Comparative and Correlational Research

A variety of types of variables are appropriate for causal comparative and correlational research:

1. Inherent characteristics (organismic)—for example, gender, ethnicity, age, disability, socioeconomic class, ability, and personality traits.

2. Characteristics that should not be manipulated for ethical reasons—for example, illegal drug use, cigarette smoking, or alcohol consumption.

3. Characteristics that could be manipulated but that are not—for example, school placement, social promotion to the next grade, or participation in psychotherapy.

When studying such characteristics, a researcher can use either a causal comparative or a correlational approach. These types of research are quite common in education and psychology because of the frequency of comparisons of persons with different characteristics (such as gender, race, and disabilities). Although both approaches explore cause-and-effect relationships between variables, neither involves the experimental manipulation of treatment variables, and therefore the results should not be used as proof of a cause-and-effect relationship.

For example, Gudiño, Lau, Yeh, McCabe, and Hough (2009) investigated racial disparities in the use of mental health services for youth ages 6 to 18 from Southern

California who had active cases in the mental health system in such programs as alcohol/drug treatment, child welfare, juvenile justice, mental health, and public school services for youth with serious emotional disturbance. The racial/ethnic groups were based on self-report in the following categories: non-Hispanic Whites (NHW), Hispanic Americans (HA), African Americans (AA), and Asian American/Pacific Islanders (AAPI). They established the need for their study based on prior research that suggested that members of ethnic/racial minority groups had lower rates of use of mental health services. This group of researchers wanted to go beyond simple comparisons of racial/ethnic groups to examine the complexities associated with use of services on the basis of the type of presenting problem. They examined four types: no clinically significant problems, internalizing (e.g., depression or anxiety), externalizing (e.g., ADHD, conduct disorder), and comorbid (e.g., both internal and external symptoms).

Gudiño et al. (2009) reported that NHW youth were more likely to receive services when only internalizing need was present; HA and AA youth were more likely to receive services when purely externalizing and/or comorbid problems were present. African Americans were least likely to receive mental health services outside of the school setting. However, they were likely to receive services from a school counselor if their problems were external; they did not differ from other groups in this respect. The researchers did not conclude that racial disparities in and of themselves account for the evidence of racial disparities in use of mental health services. Rather, they examined the meaning of the type of presenting symptoms as an indicator that minority youth are put at risk by lack of responsiveness to internalizing problems. As a corollary, African American youth particularly may be identified and referred for external problems because of bias or stereotypes. As Gudiño and colleagues explain,

> Stereotypic beliefs about minority child behavioral patterns may make the recognition of internalizing symptoms by other adult gatekeepers (e.g., teachers and social workers) less likely. Conversely, problems of an externalizing nature are more easily identifiable and are perceived as troublesome by parents and adult gatekeepers outside the family. Growing evidence suggests that social and institutional factors result in AA youth being more closely scrutinized for disruptive behavior, resulting in disproportionate rates of referral for services in various sections of care. (p. 12)

Gudiño et al. recommend additional research to understand the basis for referrals and for provision of services for members of minority groups who experience internalized problems.

Although both causal comparative and correlational research are used to study phenomena involving the inherent characteristics of participants, there is an important difference between the two approaches: Causal comparative research focuses on making group comparisons (e.g., comparing academic achievement in groups with high vs. low self-concepts). Although correlational research can also be used to make group comparisons, its main focus is on providing an estimate of the *magnitude* of the relationship between two variables (e.g., examining the relationship between the level of self-concept and academic achievement). The difference in focus of the two types of studies leads to a difference in the kinds of conclusions that can be drawn. In the causal comparative study, the researcher might conclude that a group of students with high self-concepts differed significantly on academic achievement compared with a group with low self-concepts. In a correlational study, a researcher might conclude that there is a strong, positive relationship between self-concept and academic achievement. With advances in statistical analysis tools, the difference between causal comparative and correlational research has become murky. In many of the studies that I reviewed in writing this chapter, I found that researchers may have started with a causal comparative question (e.g., what is the difference between these two groups?), but they moved on to examine competing explanations beyond the initial categorization by the use of more complex correlational analyses. I take this to be an indicator of progress in the research world.

Inherent Characteristics: Challenging Issues

By their very nature of comparing individuals who differ based on such inherent characteristics as ethnicity, gender, socioeconomic class, or disabling conditions, these approaches to research have serious implications for researchers in terms of how the research questions are framed and the basis that is used for group definition. In Chapter 11, issues are examined around the complexity of defining who fits into a particular racial/ethnic, gender, or disability category. These issues have relevance in causal comparative and correlational research because these approaches to research commonly attempt to examine differences based on these types of characteristics. In Chapter 11, the discussion focuses on the myth of homogeneity (e.g., all African Americans are the same; all deaf people are the same). Even a variable that might be naively thought to be fairly straight forward (e.g., gender) is problematized and viewed from a culturally diverse perspective. In this chapter, the focus is on reasons that such categorizations can be misleading and strategies for sensibly researching such important topics related to differences and similarities.

Focusing on Group Differences

In 1979, Unger set off a sea change in the way researchers used language in terms of sex and gender (Zurbriggen & Sherman, 2007). Unger's paper, published in the *American Psychologist* and entitled "Toward a Redefinition of Sex and Gender," described sex as a biological variable and gender as a socially constructed concept. Since that time, the research community has moved from using the term sex differences to gender differences; however, many researchers do not make clear how they are operationalizing the two concepts (Glasser & Smith, 2008). The increase in the use of the term *gender* in place of the term *sex* may be traced back to Unger's early work and to the American Psychological Association's inclusion of this same distinction in the fourth and fifth editions of their publication manual. The fifth edition (2001) includes a guideline that explicitly states that sex refers to biological entities while gender "is cultural" (p. 62). APA recommends that writers in psychology should be clear about using the terms appropriately.[1]

In large part, researchers agree that sex is determined by biology, while gender is a socially constructed concept. Glasser and Smith (2008) offer evidence from published studies that many researchers tend to use the terms gender and sex as if they are synonymous. They state that this evidence "is sufficient to show that the lack of conceptual clarity is a problem . . . for all who seek to understand how students engage, participate, and perform in our schools. If gender means something different from sex . . . then the difference must be articulated. For research on gender to be meaningful, efforts at explicitness and clarity are necessary" (p. 345). While it is convenient to have two categories (males/females, boys/girls), this binary characterization of sex or gender is problematic in that it obscures important aspects of heterogeneity in the population.

Early feminists such as P. B. Campbell (1988, 1989), M. Fine and Gordon (1992), and others (Shakeshaft, Campbell, & Karp, 1992) pointed out that the focus of much sex- or gender-related research has been on differences. P. B. Campbell (1988) noted, "Even the sound of 'sex similarities' sounds new and strange" (p. 5). These researchers point out that focusing on sex differences obscures the many areas in which males and females overlap. Yet, researchers have noted that gender differences in academic abilities have been exaggerated and that girls and boys are actually quite similar in their academic skills and aptitude. Hyde and Lindberg (2007) report that there is a significant overlap between the distributions for males and females and that within-gender variability is substantial. With few exceptions, the capacity for learning is essentially the same for both boys and girls.

Although Hyde and Lindberg (2007) positioned their work in the frame of gender differences, many of the issues that they describe have relevance for explaining misperceptions of differences between racial/ethnic groups and people with disabilities. This section examines reasons that differences among groups may be exaggerated, including several methodological issues and researchers' beliefs that account for the misperceptions regarding differences in both academic achievement and psychosocial characteristics.

1. Researchers typically report the results of their studies in terms of statistical significance (the term is defined in Chapter 1 and discussed more fully in Chapter 13). If very large sample sizes are used, it is easier to get statistical significance. Hence, studies of gender, race/ethnicity, or disability differences report that the difference between groups is statistically significant. However, there is a difference between statistical and practical significance and there is a statistic that allows a researcher to report the practical significance of the differences. That statistic is called an effect size. Reliance on statistical significance, particularly with large data sets, without examination of the associated effect size, leads to misinterpretations.

2. Reviews of literature are more powerful than the results of a single study as a basis for determining if a difference or similarity is sustainable across people and situations. Hyde and Lindberg (2007) recommend the use of meta-analysis (a quantitative approach to research synthesis which is also described in Chapter 13). They do caution that publishers tend to be more likely to publish articles that show statistically significant differences rather than those with no significant differences. Hence, there is a built-in bias in publications that favors studies that obtain statistically significant results.

3. Bias in measurement is also a consideration in determining differences between sex or gender groups. If girls score less than boys on a test, it might mean that they have less of that characteristic, or it could mean that the test is biased in favor of boys. The same applies to other groups who are not in the privileged mainstream of society.

4. One of the major mistakes associated with causal comparative or correlational research is assuming causality between the variables in the study (e.g., gender causes math performance; hearing status causes reading ability). When this happens in research, it is called the *post hoc fallacy* (P. B. Campbell, 1989). The types of studies discussed in this chapter (e.g., comparisons of males and females, Non-Hispanic Whites and African Americans) are particularly susceptible to the post hoc fallacy, and therefore competing explanations for the results should be carefully examined.

C. D. Lee (2008) severely criticizes studies that reveal inequities in education based on racial or ethnic variables and then offer such competing explanations as:

- If parents do not read books to their children before they come to school, the children are not likely to become competent readers.

- If parents do not engage in the kind of talk that we imaginatively think goes on in middle-class homes, the children's vocabulary will be so limited that they can never catch up.

- If children have not learned the alphabetic principles and how to count to 10 before they reach kindergarten, they will be behind forever.

- If children do not speak "the King's English," they cannot be taught.

- If parents do not come to school, they are not interested in their children's education.

At best, such pronouncements are based on studies of White middle-class samples. At worst, they reflect our stereotypes about poor people and their children. Moreover, these "folk beliefs" presume a monolithic approach to teaching that does not create multiple pathways for reaching common goals (C. D. Lee, 2008, p. 273).

5. Researchers' beliefs influence what questions they choose to investigate, how they investigate those questions, and their interpretation of the findings. For example, in regard to the choice of research question, researchers have devoted themselves to investigating gender differences in mathematics performance—what Caplan and Caplan (2005) have called the *preservative search of sex differences in mathematics ability*. Very, very few researchers have investigated gender similarities in mathematics performance and their implications for education" (Hyde & Lindberg, 2007, p. 21). Hence, it is not surprising that differences rather than similarities are reported in the published literature.

C. D. Lee (2008) adds to concerns about the blinding effects when researchers' adopt a deficit perspective in their work comparing racial/ethnic groups.

> Research focusing on ethnicity and learning or ethnicity and psychosocial development typically tries to address some set of negative outcomes for marginalized youth: learning outcomes explained by stereotype threat, family practices posited as noncanonical (e.g., practices of parents who do not read books to their young children at home), lack of mastery of academic English as a constraint on learning, and so forth. . . . The domains of everyday knowledge and disciplinary knowledge are worlds apart. . . . If there are connections (such as in the cognitive research on the role of prior knowledge, naive concepts, and misconceptions), the everyday side of the equation is typically the deficit calculation. (p. 271)

M. Fine and Gordon (1992) present an extension of the arguments that criticize gender difference research. They write that "this almost exclusive construction of gender-as-difference functions inside psychology as a political and scientific diversion away from questions of power, social context, meaning, and braided subjectivities" (p. 8). They suggest that what is needed is a new language, because the issues are less about sex as biology or even gender as social construction and more about the politics of sex-gender relations that can transform oppressive social arrangements. Although sex and gender may feel biological or psychological, the more important focus is on the political implications. Zurbriggen and Sherman (2007) note that a focus on sex differences is used to construct women as inferior and to justify social inequities (to wit, the 2005 statement by the former president of Harvard University about men's supposed superiority in mathematics). Hence, this highlights the importance of being cognizant of the heterogeneity within communities when characterized in terms of sex or gender or sexuality, as well as when supposed differences in sex, gender, and sexuality are used as tools of oppression.

Group Identification

Another area of challenge for the researcher in the causal comparative and correlational approaches to research is the definition of who belongs in which group. This may seem to be more a problem with race, class, and disability-related research rather than with gender-related research; however, the oversimplification of gender as a variable is being interrogated by advances in the field of LGBTQ studies (Dodd, 2009). Definitions of race and ethnicity somewhat parallel those of sex and gender; that is, one is considered to have a biological basis and the other a socially constructed basis. However, Stanfield (1993a) identifies the difficulties in answering such questions as "What is a White person?" or "What is a Black person?" as stemming from the "extensiveness of ethnic mixing that has occurred in the United States in reciprocal acculturation and cultural assimilation processes, if not in miscegenation experiences" (p. 21).

Problems arise in terms of which basis for categorization to use. Stanfield (1993a) recognizes that most classifications of racial identity are based on skin color and other phenotypic characteristics: For example, a person who has dark skin, woolly hair, and a broad nose is readily identified as an African American. The problems for a researcher arise when the skin color of the African American person becomes lighter so that he or she might "pass" for European American or with people of mixed-race descent who do not readily identify with any of the standard racial categories.

Qualitative researchers tend to construct the meaning of a person's racial identity based on the respondents' self-perceptions of race and ethnicity and their influence on one's life experiences. Quantitative researchers, on the other hand, have tended to rely on statistical categories derived from government documents and survey coding. Stanfield (1993a), however, warns both groups of researchers that they have no way of knowing "whether an informant's expressed racial identification is a response to the objectified categorization derived from learning experiences in a race-saturated society or merely a subjective admission" (p. 18).

Bias can result when the method of determining racial or ethnic identity does not adequately represent the complexities of the situation. For example, if research is done on Latino populations and the respondents are selected based on a Spanish surname, children of Latino fathers who use the names of their fathers would be included but not the children of Latino mothers (Shakeshaft et al., 1992). Problems also arise when differences by country of origin are ignored. Also, experiences of recent immigrants are different from those of people who have lived in another country longer, perhaps for generations. The practice of lumping together biological and social definitions of race under a common racial label results in a biased sample. This is the situation that results when children of a Black and a White parent are identified as African American.

Stanfield (1993a) raises some important questions for researchers who choose to work in the causal comparative or correlational mode with respect to race and ethnicity:

- How do we conceptualize identity issues in race and ethnicity research that go beyond reified, simplistic stereotyping?

• How do we use official data sources with care in exploring racial identity questions, realizing the problematic aspects of aggregate data and ill-defined circumstances of self-reporting versus actual self-identity?

• If we have to categorize people to understand who they are and how they define themselves, how do we do so in this area of research more in terms of self-definitions than in terms of what popular cultural folk wisdom dictates?

• How do we incorporate understanding in research designs regarding the interactional aspects of identity formation in dominant and subordinate populations that would make such considerations much more sociological? (p. 24)

The U.S. Census Bureau (2001) modified the way it asked about a person's race/ethnicity in the 2000 census by giving respondents the opportunity (for the first time) to identify themselves in more than one racial category. As you will recall from Chapter 1, the census findings revealed that 98% of respondents chose only one category. The frequency of responses by group was as follows: White only (75%), Black or African American only (12%), Asian only (4%), and American Indian or Alaska Native only (less than 1%). Hispanics, who could put themselves in any racial category in the census, represented about 13% of the population. Forty-eight percent of those who identified themselves as Hispanic also identified as White only, while about 42% chose "some other race."

The whole debate over racial or ethnic identity is further complicated by the conflict between the reality of social oppression based on such phenotypic characteristics as skin color and the realization that no single gene can be used to define a race. The American Anthropological Association passed a resolution saying that differentiating species into biologically defined "races" is arbitrary and subjective and has led to countless errors in research (American Anthropological Association, 1998). Anthropologists have replaced the concept of race with a focus on how people identify themselves, by geographic origins or by other means.

Some ideas for how to address the issue of race/ethnicity as categorical variables include

• Identification by geographic origins

• Use of a multiracial category

• Use of an "other" category, allowing the respondent to write in a response

• The addition of categories related to Native American tribal heritage, Native Hawaiians, Middle Eastern heritage, and so forth, which are used by people in the group you are researching.

Anthropologists recognize the need to study race as a "social/cultural reality that exists in a realm independent of biological or genetic variations" (Smedley, 2007, p. 1) because they believe that discrimination and other realities of racism cannot be explained by reference to human biological differences. Despite all the problems associated with categorizing people according to race or ethnicity, disabling conditions, and gender, researchers need to be aware of the benefits that have accrued from cross-group comparisons. Causal comparative and correlational research studies have been used to document oppression based on skin color and other phenotypic characteristics. Discontinuing such research based on the rationale that our understanding of race, gender, and disability is limited needs to be weighed against the benefit associated with revealing inequities in resources and outcomes in education, psychology, and the broader society. As C. D. Lee (2008) reminds us, "to ignore race is to take our vision away from the ways in which our society institutionalizes challenges to particular groups of people" (p. 272).

The Myth of Homogeneity

Stanfield (1993a) discussed the myth of homogeneity—that is, assuming similarities within racial and ethnic groups on other characteristics, such as socioeconomic class. Much of the research done in cross-race comparisons ignores the generally higher socioeconomic class associated with people of European American descent. Teasing out the effects of race and poverty is a complex and difficult (if not impossible) task.

Problems similar to those associated with race can be found in Mertens and McLaughlin's (2004) discussion of the identification of persons with disabilities. One example of the heterogeneity in the deaf community is explored in Box 5.1, which contains a description of a sampling strategy used in a study of court accessibility for deaf and hard-of-hearing people in the United States.

Box 5.1 Sampling for Focus Groups: Heterogeneity in the Deaf and Hard-of-Hearing Community

In preparing a sample design for focus groups that were conducted as part of a study of court accessibility for deaf and hard-of-hearing people in the United States, Mertens (2000) worked with an advisory board that included people who preferred a variety of communication modes and represented different aspects of the judicial system. The sample design was constructed to represent the diversity of communication modes in the deaf and hard-of-hearing communities, including highly educated deaf users of American Sign Language (ASL); deaf adults with limited education and reading skills, some of whom communicated with sign language, gestures, and pantomime; deaf/blind adults who used interpreters at close range; highly educated hard-of-hearing adults who used personal assistive listening devices; deaf adults who used Mexican Sign Language (MSL); and deaf adults who relied on oral communication (reading lips) and print English. In addition to the diversity in terms of communication preference, the groups were selected to be diverse in terms of gender, race/ethnicity, and status with the court (e.g., juror, witness, victim).

Extending Your Thinking: Dimensions of Diversity

Review the sampling strategy included in Box 5.1. Answer the following questions:

a. What are the dimensions of diversity that are illustrated in this example?

b. What are the dimensions of diversity that you would need to consider to avoid the myth of homogeneity in a cultural group that you intend to study?

Causal Comparative Research

The steps for conducting causal comparative research are similar to those outlined in Chapter 1 for any research undertaking:

1. Identify a research problem.

2. Select a defined group and a comparison group.

3. Collect data on relevant independent and dependent variables and on relevant background characteristics.

4. Analyze and interpret the data, with special focus on competing explanations.

First, a research problem is identified. Zhang and Katsiyannis (2002) examined differences in special education placement by race and ethnicity (see Sample Study 5.1). This is a long-standing problem that has implications for many students in terms of the quality of their education and potential social stigma.

The second step in conducting causal comparative research is to select a defined group and a comparison group. The researcher has a number of options for creating the groups that yield more or less control over the differential selection threat to internal validity. Because causal comparative research compares the performance of two (or more) intact groups, the threat of differential selection must be addressed. If the two groups differ significantly on characteristics other than the explanatory variable (e.g., economic status), those other (extraneous) characteristics might explain the difference between the groups.

Some strategies that researchers can use to control the threat of differential selection include the following:

1. Matching on particular characteristics of relevance (discussed further in Chapter 10)
2. Using a statistical technique such as analysis of covariance to control for preexisting differences (discussed further in Chapter 13)
3. Eliminating subjects with specific characteristics (e.g., those with multiple disabilities)
4. Analysis of subgroups

The creation of homogeneity by elimination of people with specific characteristics comes at a cost, in restricting the generalizability of the findings to that "homogeneous" population.

In the Zhang and Katsiyannis (2002) study, the groups of interest were people who had been identified as having some kind of disability, as well as those whose disabilities were mental retardation, learning disabilities, or emotional or behavioral disorders. They also defined groups by race or ethnicity based on self-report.

The third step in a causal comparative study involves collecting data on the independent and dependent variables as well as on relevant background characteristics. The data Zhang and Katsiyannis (2002) used were taken from nationally available data sets. Their independent variables included race/ethnicity and region of the country; their dependent variable was identification of a disability or a specific type of disability. They used poverty rate as a covariate.

Sample Study 5.1

Summary of a Causal Comparative Study

Research Problem: Compared with Whites, racial and ethnic minorities are overrepresented in special education.

Research Questions: What is the extent of minority representation (by minority group) across states and regions for all disabilities, along with high-incidence disability (i.e., learning disabilities, mental retardation, and emotional-behavioral disorders)? What is the difference in special education placement when minorities are compared to representation in the total student population? What happens when state poverty rates are considered?

Method: The researchers used a causal comparative approach to examine the number of students in each racial group for students with learning disabilities, mental retardation, emotional-behavioral disorders, and all disabilities by state.

Participants: The racial groups included American Indian/Alaska Native (AI/Alaskan), Asian/Pacific Islander (Asian/PI), African American, Hispanic, and White. Participants were from all 50 states and the District of Columbia and ranged in age from 6 to 21 years.

Instruments and Procedures: The researchers used extant data sources from the U.S. Department of Education, the National Center for Educational Statistics, and the U.S. Census Bureau.

Results: "White representation ranks third of all five racial groups; more African American and AI/Alaskan students are represented, and fewer Asian/PI and Hispanic students are represented. . . . White representation in EBD ranks third of all five groups; African American and AI/Alaskan students are more heavily represented; Asian/PI and Hispanic students are less represented. In the LD category, African American representation is the highest among all racial groups. The second most represented group is AI/Alaskan, followed by White and Hispanic; Asian/PI representation is the lowest. In the MR category, the most represented group is also African American, followed by AI/Alaskan, White, Hispanic, and Asian/PI" (p. 182).

Discussion: The researchers raise concerns related to the overrepresentation of African Americans and AI/Alaskans as a civil rights issue possibly related to misclassification or inappropriate placement. At the same time, educators need to be cognizant of the importance of providing appropriate support services for students who really need them.

SOURCE: Based on Zhang & Katsiyannis (2002).

The fourth step involves analyzing and interpreting the data. For Zhang and Katsiyannis (2002), analysis of the data included several steps: First, the researchers graphed the data and calculated descriptive statistics in order to reveal overall trends in over- or underrepresentation. Second, they calculated correlations to examine the relationship between racial representation and state poverty data. (Technically, this part of their study belongs in the next section under correlational research). Then, they conducted analyses of variance (ANOVA) to look at regional differences and analysis of covariance (ANCOVA) to control for the effects of poverty.

Researchers need to avoid overly simplistic explanations for results that are based on causal comparative studies. A person's race or ethnicity is not a causal factor in their identification as having a disability. Zhang and Katsiyannis (2002) avoided this mistake by discussing the possibility of misclassification or inappropriate placement of African American and American Indian/Alaskan students. They framed their discussion through a civil rights lens, acknowledging the possibility that youth were being denied access to education in the mainstream possibly as a result of discrimination and oppression. Blanchett (2006) and O'Connor, Lewis, and Mueller (2007) discussed Zhang and Katsiyannis's findings in terms of White privilege and racism in American society as a whole. They argue that the overrepresentation of minority youth (particularly African American youth) in special education is the result of inequitable resource allocation, inappropriate curricula, and inadequate teacher preparation. Thus, Zhang and Katsiyannis's (2002) study demonstrates that a comparison of racial or ethnic groups without consideration of relevant contextual characteristics would oversimplify interpretations of subgroup analyses.

Correlational Research

Correlational studies can be either *prediction* studies or *relationship* studies. In prediction studies, the researcher is interested in using one or more variables (the predictor variables) to project performance on one or more other variables (the criterion variables). For example, kindergarten test scores can be used to predict first-grade test scores, if there is a strong relationship between the two sets of scores. In prediction studies, it is important to be aware of any other variables related to performance on the criterion variable. Relationship studies usually explore the relationships between measures of different variables obtained from the same individuals at approximately the same time to gain a better understanding of factors that contribute to a more complex characteristic.

It is important to realize that the correlation coefficient can range between 0 and +/–1.00. The closer the correlation coefficient is to +/–1.00, the stronger the relationship. A positive correlation means that the two variables increase or decrease together. For example, a positive correlation might exist between age and reading skills for deaf children, meaning that older children tend to exhibit higher reading skills. A negative correlation means that the two variables differ inversely; that is, as one goes up, the other goes down. For example, reading skills may be higher for children with less severe hearing losses—for example, as hearing loss goes up, reading skills go down. If the correlation coefficient is near zero, no relationship exists. For example, lip-reading ability might be unrelated to reading skills in deaf children.

A word of caution should be entered here regarding the inadvisability of assuming cause and effect from correlational data. It is possible to calculate a correlation coefficient between any two sets of numbers:

- The number of PhDs in a state and the number of mules (it is strongly negative)
- The number of ice-cream cones sold and the number of deaths by drowning (it is strongly positive)
- The number of churches and bars in the same vicinity (it is strongly positive) (Beins, 1993)

There are obvious explanations other than causality for these correlations. Such high correlations that are due to some third variable (such as rural areas, hot weather, urban crowding) are called *spurious*. Nevertheless, it should be remembered that a high correlation does not in and of itself negate the possibility of a causal relationship (to wit, smoking and lung cancer).

An extension of this word of caution is necessary about assumptions of causality that center on the finding by researchers that the sum is somehow larger than the parts. In other words, even though a strong relationship may be found between a set of variables and an outcome measure, it is not always possible to achieve the desired outcomes by manipulating the set of prediction variables. Many years ago, Wittrock (1986) used the failure of the input-output model for effective teaching to make this point. He notes that researchers were able to find strong correlations between various teacher behaviors, such as use of positive reinforcement and student achievement. However, when teachers were trained to increase their use of such behaviors, corresponding increases in student achievement did not occur. He attributes the failure of the correlational approach to inappropriate theoretical assumptions that did not recognize teachers' and students' cognitive variables and to contextual variables outside the teacher-student dyad.

Steps in Conducting Correlational Research: Relationship Studies

The steps for conducting correlational research are as follow:

1. Identify an appropriate problem.
2. Identify variables to be included in the study.
3. Identify the appropriate research participants.
4. Collect quantifiable data.
5. Analyze the data and interpret the results.

The first step in correlational research, as in all other approaches, is to identify an appropriate problem. Remember, correlational research can be either for prediction purposes or to explain relationships between variables. Steps for conducting a relationship study are explained here, and the following section contains information specific to prediction studies.

One example of a relationship study is Fetner and Kush's (2008) investigation of variables related to the presence or absence of gay-straight alliances (GSAs) as extracurricular activities in high schools that serve to support and advocate for the rights of lesbian, gay, bisexual, transgender, and queer students (see Sample Study 5.2 for a summary of this study). The research problem arose from the observation that some areas of the country seem to have more GSAs than others, and that LGBTQ youth experience a higher amount of harassment and abuse than straight youth.

The second step in a relationship study is to identify the variables to be included in the study. The variables in correlational research are sometimes called *explanatory* or *predictor* variables instead of independent variables because they are not experimentally manipulated. The dependent variable is then termed the *outcome* or *criterion* variable.

Sample Study 5.2

Summary of a Correlational Study of Relationship

Research Problem: Lesbian, gay, bisexual, transgender, and queer (LGBTQ) people can have a difficult time in high school. In some schools, gay-straight alliances have emerged as student-led groups to support and advocate for the rights of LGBTQ students, yet they are absent in a large number of schools.

Research Question: What is the relationship between various school characteristics and the formation of a gay-straight alliance?

Method: The researchers used a correlational approach, collecting quantitative data on explanatory variables (school-level variables such as school size, location in terms of urban/rural, region of the country; state-level variables such as antidiscriminatory laws or adult-led gay-straight alliances), and examining their relationship to the presence/absence of an alliance in the high school.

Participants: 17,900 schools were chosen for the sample from national databases.

Instruments and Procedures: School- and state-level data came from *Common Core of Data, Public Elementary/Secondary School Universe Survey,* a data set of all public schools for the 2001–2002 school year, from the National Center for Education Statistics (NCES, 2001–2002). Information about GSAs came from several sources, each of them private, nonprofit, LGBTQ organizations: GLSEN, GSA Network, Out Proud, and Project 10 East (GLSEN, 2003; GSA Network, 2003; OutProud, 2003; Project 10 East, 2003).

Results: Simple descriptive statistics indicated that urban and suburban locations had the most GSAs as compared to rural areas or small towns. Logistic regression analysis was used because the dependent variable was dichotomous and this statistical tool allows for testing relationships between a number of independent (or predictor) variables and the dependent variable.[2] A significant relationship was found between presence of a GSA and the region of the country (more in the Northeast and West), whether the school was in a rural or urban area (with more GSAs in urban/suburban areas), size of the student body (larger schools are more likely to have GSAs), and financial resources (schools with more resources have more GSAs.) The state-level variables also had a statistically significant positive relationship with GSA presence; states with antidiscrimination laws and adults who supported GSAs were more likely to have GSAs in the high schools.

Conclusions: The researchers hypothesize that a critical mass of LGBTQ students may be necessary for a GSA to be supported. In addition, the absence of school resources tends to cut into all extracurricular activities, and thus GSAs would be less likely to receive support in poorer areas. The researchers were surprised by the large number of GSAs in suburban areas and speculated that it may represent a generational cultural shift of openness. They still caution that having a GSA does not ensure safety for LGBTQ students in schools. And they express concern about the students in small schools, poor neighborhoods, rural areas, or in the South or Midwest, who are least likely to have a GSA available to them.

SOURCE: Based on Fetner & Kush (2008).

One advantage of correlational research is that several variables can be included in one study (more easily than in experimental or causal comparative designs). (Of course, the number of variables is moderated by sample size. The recommended number of participants per variable is 15, at a minimum.) However, the choice of variables should be done using a theoretical framework rather than a shotgun approach (Gall, Gall, & Borg, 2003).[3] A researcher should give considerable thought to the variables chosen for inclusion for explanatory purposes. It is possible to "pour" many variables into the computer and then focus on those that come out as statistically significant. Because statistics work on the theory of probability, with enough variables, it is probable that some will appear to be significant. It is more important that researchers include those variables that they have reason to believe are related to the outcome variable, based on previous research and theory.

In the Fetner and Kush (2008) study, the authors wanted to examine the relationship between school-level and state-level variables with the establishment of GSAs in high schools. They hypothesized that size, location, resources, and political climate would be related to their outcome variable. Thus, the researchers used this theoretical model to select their independent (predictor or explanatory) variables. Their dependent (criterion) variable was presence or absence of a GSA.

The third step in a correlational study is to identify appropriate participants. Borg and Gall (1989) suggest that the groups be homogeneous or that subgroup analyses be done, because variance in the criterion variable may be explained by different sets of variables for different subgroups. For example, in explaining high school dropout behavior for females, early pregnancy is an important variable; for males, economic need is a stronger predictor.

Fetner and Kush (2008) chose to use a very large national sample so they could test regional effects. Rather than do subgroup analyses, they controlled for differences through the use of logistic regression analysis.

The fourth step is to collect quantifiable data. For example, all the independent (predictor) variables in Fetner and Kush (2008) were quantifiable. The dependent variable was dichotomous (0 or 1).

The fifth step is to analyze the data and interpret the results. The researcher has a number of options for correlational analysis, including simple correlation, regression analysis, multiple regression analysis, discriminant function analysis, canonical correlation, path analysis, and factor analysis. These analytic techniques are described in Chapter 13. In this chapter, I explain some of the issues related to the use of statistical techniques for correlational research studies.

Graphs and Curvilinear Relationships

No matter what statistic is chosen, the researcher should always start with a graphic display of the relationships between the variables. One reason for this is that it gives you a commonsense base for interpreting the correlation coefficients that are subsequently calculated. Another very important reason is that simple correlation analysis is based on the assumption of a linear relationship between the variables. For example, as one's number of years in a job increases, one's salary increases. However, if a curvilinear relationship is depicted in the graph, simple correlation is an inappropriate statistical choice. For example, if a sample's ability to increase its earnings was restricted (e.g., because it had reached a "ceiling" within the organization), the relationship would be represented as shown in Figure 5.1. The correlation coefficient would be low, suggesting a lack of relationship, when in actuality, a curvilinear relationship exists.

Figure 5.1 Nonlinear Relationship Between Years Working and Salary

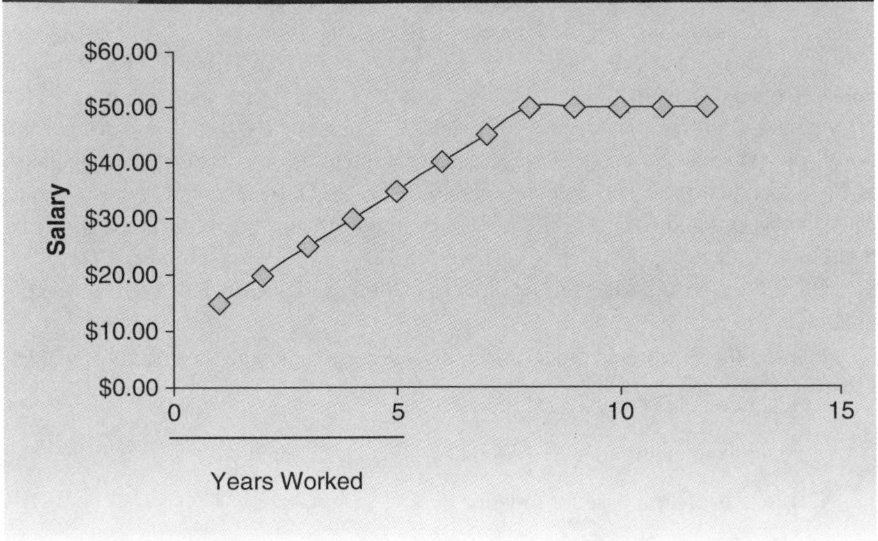

Choice of a Correlation Coefficient

The choice of a correlation coefficient depends on the scale of measurement. For variables with a continuous scale, the Pearson product-moment coefficient is typically used. For rank-level data, Spearman's Rho can be used. For nominal (dichotomous) data, a biserial correlation coefficient can be used. (These coefficients are explained in more depth in Chapter 13.)

Size and Interpretation

The interpretation of the size of the correlation depends on the purpose of the study. For relationship studies, a test of statistical significance can be applied to a correlation coefficient (see Chapter 13 for further discussion of this concept). For prediction studies, generally, a correlation above 0.60 is considered to be adequate for group predictions and above 0.80 for individual predictions (e.g., school placement decisions).

Common or Explained Variance or r^2

Interpretation of correlation coefficients is often based on the amount of *common* or *explained variance* found by squaring the correlation coefficient (r^2). The explained or common variance refers to the difference in one variable that is attributable to its tendency to vary with the other (Airasian & Gay, 2003). For example, Gonzalez and Uhing (2008) studied the relationship between familial variables and oral English skills for children in an early intervention program from families who spoke Spanish but lived in the United States. They obtained a correlation coefficient of .39 between library use and oral English scores. Thus, library use accounts for 15% of the variance in oral English scores. If library use were perfectly correlated with oral English performance, the two variables would have 100% common variance (and a correlation coefficient of –1.00). Because many variables other than library use influences oral English scores, the two variables have 15% shared or common variance.

Multiple Regression and Ordering Variables

The order of entry for variables in multiple regression equations is important. When the predictor variables are correlated (a situation called collinearity), the amount of variance that each independent variable accounts for can change drastically with different orders of entry of the variables. Although there is no "correct" method for determining the order of variables (Gay, Mills, & Airasian, 2009), the researcher must decide on a rationale for entry.[4] If the researcher is interested in controlling for the effects of background characteristics before testing the effects of a treatment, it makes sense to enter the background characteristics first. Then, the treatment variable will explain what is left of the variance.

Other possible rationales for the order of entering variables include the following:

1. Enter the variables in order of their highest correlation with the criterion variable.
2. Enter them in chronological order.
3. Enter them in an order established by previous research.
4. Use a theoretical base for ordering.

Sample Study 5.3 provides an example of choices that researchers made with regard to ordering variables:

> The regression was done in two steps to evaluate the incremental validity associated with adding the set of Minnesota Kindergarten Assessment (MKA) subtests from the cross-domain to predicting second-grade outcomes. The second-grade reading scores were first regressed onto the literacy subtests, and then the set of numeracy subtests was added to evaluate the incremental increase in validity. Likewise, second-grade math scores were regressed on the set of early numeracy subtests first, and then the set of literacy subtests were added. Standardized regression coefficients were computed to evaluate the relative importance in predicting second-grade achievement scores when all MKA subtests were entered into the model. (Betts, Pickart, & Heistad, 2008, p. 6)

In hierarchical regression, R^2 is generated as the amount of explained variance accounted for by the entry of variables in the equation. For example, Smalls, White, Chavous, and Sellers (2007) conducted a study of the relationship between experiencing discrimination and self-reported negative behaviors in school. They used three blocks of predictor variables: background (e.g., gender), racial identity variables, and racial discrimination. They reported that experiencing more racial discrimination related to more self-reported negative behaviors at school (beta = .13, SE = .01, $p < .01$; $F(14, 390) = 2.18$, $p < .008$).

Discriminant Function Analysis

The statistical technique of discriminant function analysis is used to predict group membership on the basis of a variety of predictor variables. For example, a number of different test scores could be used to see if they discriminate between individuals who have mental retardation, learning disabilities, or no educational disability. Or discriminant function analysis could also be used to see if measures of self-esteem, social skills, and participation in recreational activities can discriminate between people who are lonely or not lonely.

Canonical Correlation

Canonical correlation is also used to determine group membership; however, it can be used with multiple independent (explanatory or predictor) *and* multiple dependent (criterion) variables. For example, explanatory variables, such as sex, socioeconomic status, and educational level, can be combined with criterion variables, such as income, employment, and prestige, to determine if any discernible patterns emerge that could be used to separate people into groups.

Path Analysis

Path analysis is used when a researcher wants to test a causal theoretical model. For example, based on previous research, a causal model of academic achievement could be developed that included various student background characteristics (e.g., sex, ethnic status, presence or degree of disability) and instructional process variables (e.g., teacher expectation, degree of sensitivity to cultural differences). The researcher must specify the model in advance and then test to estimate the strength and direction of the relationships.

Factor Analysis

Factor analysis is an empirical way to reduce the number of variables by grouping those that correlate highly with each other. Betts et al. (2009) used a test of early literacy and math that had numerous subscales. The literacy subtests used rhyming, alliteration, letter naming, and letter sounds subtests; and number sense, patterning/functions, and spatial sense/measurement subtests for the early numeracy subtests. They wanted to confirm that the literacy and math tests did indeed measure different sets of skills. Therefore, they conducted a factor analysis using data on all the subtests. The results revealed two factors: one for literacy and one for math.

Cross-Validation

Perhaps all research seemingly could merit from replication to substantiate that the results are not a fluke. However, because of the lack of control and manipulation in correlational research, it is advisable to *cross-validate* the results of correlational analysis with a separate, independent sample. For example, would a positive correlation between an early literacy measure and second-grade reading scores that appears for one sample of students in Minnesota also hold for a separately drawn sample of students from the same population?

Correlational Studies: Prediction

An example of a correlational study for predictive purposes is summarized in Sample Study 5.3. In predictive correlational studies, the procedures are very similar to relationship studies. However, a few differences should be noted.

Sample Study 5.3

Summary of a Predictive Correlational Study

Research Problem: Early skills in literacy and numeracy are needed in order for students to progress in school. Kindergarten is the beginning of academic instruction and it is important to know how the development of literacy and numeracy in this first year of school can predict later achievement.

Research Question: How well do the Minneapolis Kindergarten Assessment (MKA; Minneapolis Public Schools, 2004) scores at the end of kindergarten predict later outcomes in reading and mathematics measured at the end of second grade?

Method: The independent (predictor) variable is the MKA. The predictive part of this research investigated the external validity of the MKA battery measured in kindergarten with measures of reading and mathematics measured at the end of second grade. Correlations between MKA subtests and second-grade outcomes were computed.

Participants: The participants in this study were kindergarten students in a large, urban, Midwestern school district. Originally, all 3,174 kindergarten students were assessed. However, because of attrition, 2,180 students (69%) were evaluated at the end of second grade on both math and reading outcomes. Ethnicity of participants was as follows: 39% African American, 30% European American, 16% Hispanic American, 11% Asian American, and 4% American Indian. Twenty-eight percent of the students were identified as limited English proficient with the following primary home languages: 48% Spanish, 26% Hmong, and 15% Somali; the other 11% consisted of more than 70 different languages. About 60% of the students were eligible for free or reduced-price lunch. Seven percent of the children had Individual Education Plans.

Instruments and Procedures: The MKA was the instrument used to measure the predictor variables. Second-grade outcomes were reading and math achievement scores from the Northwest Achievement Levels Test (NALT). The NALT (Northwest Evaluation Association, 2003) has specific academic achievement tests of reading and mathematics.

Results: Correlations between the MKA subtests and all achievement tests were significant ($p < .01$). The MKA numeracy subtests accounted for 33% of the variance in the second-grade math tests. When both MKA numeracy and literacy subtests were used as predictors, the amount of explained variance increased to 46%. MKA literacy subtests explained 48% of the variance for second-grade literacy measures; this increased to 52% when MKA numeracy scores were added as predictor variables.

Discussion: "Predictive validity with respect to both reading and mathematics outcomes at the end of second grade was strong" (p. 9). The researchers note the support for both literacy and numeracy in early grades as being necessary for progress in math and literacy in later grades. They also recognize the limitation of their study in terms of external validity, that is, in being able to generalize the results to other populations in other places.

SOURCE: Betts et al. (2008).

The first step is to identify the research problem. Betts et al. (2008) wanted to know if an early literacy and numeracy measure had predictive validity for later academic achievement in school. The second step is to identify the variables to include in the study. Betts et al. focused on the scores of the students on the numeracy and literacy subtests of the MKA; they also included literacy and math scores for the same students in the second grade.

In prediction studies, the researcher who focuses on one predictor variable (e.g., score on the Graduate Record Exam [GRE]) needs to be aware of the multiple criteria used to select people for admission to graduate school. A simple correlation between

GRE scores and graduate school grade point average (GPA) would probably be low for a number of reasons:

1. Many criteria are used to select people for graduate school, including their undergraduate GPA, letters of reference, and personal position statement.

2. The range of scores for those accepted is restricted on a predictor variable such as the GPA.

3. The range of scores in the graduate school GPA (the criterion variable) is very restricted. (In many graduate schools, only A's and B's are acceptable for continuation in the program. If a student gets a C, he or she can be put on probation or dismissed.)

Thus, a high correlation between GRE and graduate school GPA could be obtained if a random sample of people took the GRE, all were accepted into graduate school, and all were allowed to remain in the program, no matter what grades they got. Not a likely scenario. Researchers who conduct predictive correlational studies must be concerned not only with the number of predictor variables but also with the reliability and range of the criterion variable.

The third step in a predictive study is to identify appropriate participants for the study. Betts et al. (2009) collected data from all kindergarten students who stayed in the same school district through the completion of the second grade in an urban setting in Minnesota where poverty is prevalent. The students represented a high level of diversity in terms of race/ethnicity and home language.

The fourth step is to collect quantitative data. One big difference that should be noted about prediction studies is that a time period must be allowed to elapse between the predictive variables and the criterion variables. In a prediction study, there is a need for an appropriate time delay between the measurement of your explanatory (predictor) variable(s) and your criterion variable. For example, suppose you wanted to use children's scores on a reading readiness measure to predict their ability to read at the end of first grade. You would need to administer the reading readiness measure at the beginning of the school year and then wait until the end of the school year to measure their reading abilities. This is similar to the situation that Betts et al. (2008) studied, although they waited three years between the original data collection time and data collection at the end of second grade.

The fifth step is to analyze the data and interpret the results. The statistical choices for prediction studies are similar to those for relationship studies. One difference in predictive studies concerns the amount of variance that can be explained in the criterion variable. If predictor variables are to be useful, they should (in combination) explain about 64% of the variance in the criterion variable. This would translate into about 0.8 correlation between one predictor and one criterion variable. In the Betts et al. (2008) study, they did conduct a regression analysis (as described earlier in this chapter) and they reported the percentage of variance that was accounted for by the predictor variables.

Questions for Critically Analyzing Causal Comparative and Correlational Research

1. Is a causal relationship assumed between the independent (predictor) variables and the dependent (response) variable? What unexpected or uncontrollable factors might have influenced the results? What competing explanations are explored?

2. How comparable are the groups in causal comparative studies?

3. Did the authors address group similarities and differences?

4. How did the authors operationally define who belonged in each group—for example, based on ethnicity or race or on disability? How did they address the issue of self-reporting versus actual self-identity? How were issues related to multiracial people addressed?

5. How did the authors address the fallacy of homogeneity?

6. How did the authors avoid the post hoc fallacy?

7. After the initial groups were defined, were subgroup analyses conducted, based on age, race/ethnicity, disability, grade level, sex, socioeconomic status, or similar variables?

8. Could a third variable cause both the independent (predictor) and dependent (criterion) variables?

9. For correlational studies, what was the rationale for choosing and entering explanatory or predictor variables? What was the percentage of variance explained by the explanatory or predictor variables?

10. If a predictive relationship was studied, was the predictor variable the only criteria used to select participants in the study? Would combining the predictor variable with other screening criteria improve its predictive validity? (A predictive validity coefficient of about 0.8 is needed for an accurate prediction.)

11. What is the reliability of the criterion variable (compared with the test used to make the prediction)? Is there a restricted range for the criterion variable?

12. Were the results cross-validated with a separate, independent sample?

Extending Your Thinking: Causal Comparative and Correlational Research

1. Through a computerized literature search or by going directly to the main journals that publish empirical, quantitative research studies, identify four research studies—two that use a causal comparative approach and two that use a correlational approach. For each study do the following:

   a. Identify the research problem.
   b. Identify the independent or predictor and dependent or criterion variables.
   c. Categorize the study as causal comparative or correlational.
   d. Explain the basis for your categorization.
   e. Critique the studies using the questions for critical analysis at the end of this chapter.
   f. For each study, note how the authors addressed the challenges of focusing on group differences, group identification, the fallacy of homogeneity, and the post hoc fallacy.

2. Brainstorm a number of different problems that would be appropriate for causal comparative or correlational research.

3. Select one research problem and explain how you would approach it using a causal comparative approach:
   a. Identify the independent and dependent variables.
   b. Explain how your approach to the study would satisfy the questions for critical analysis for causal comparative research.
4. Select one research problem and explain how you would approach it using a correlational approach:
   a. Identify the independent or predictor and dependent or criterion variables.
   b. Explain how your approach to the study would satisfy the questions for critical analysis for correlational research.
5. Under what circumstances would you *not* recommend using causal comparative or correlational approaches to research? What kind of alternative approach would you suggest?

Summary of Chapter 5: Causal Comparative and Correlational Research

Causal comparative and correlational research both focus on the study of inherent or nonmanipulable variables. Causal comparative research compares groups on various characteristics such as sex and race. The reader should now be aware of the complexities involved in accepting "taken for granted" definitions of such seemingly simple variables. Correlational research looks at the strength and direction of relationships between or among variables. In both of these research approaches, the researcher needs to avoid making causal inferences between the predictor variables and the criterion variable. As in any approach to research, careful consideration is needed in defining variables, as well as in interpreting the results.

Notes

1. "This is exactly the point Unger made throughout her paper, but she is not cited in the APA *Publication Manual,* nor in many other publications that continue to make this same point" (Zurbriggen & Sherman, 2007, p. 476).

2. For people who want a more sophisticated explanation of this statistical tool, I provide the following: "Logistic regression applies maximum likelihood estimation after transforming the dependent variable into a logit variable (the natural log of the odds of the dependent occurring or not). In this way, logistic regression estimates the odds of a certain event occurring" (North Carolina State University, Stat Notes, Public Administration Department, 2008; http://faculty.chass.ncsu.edu/garson/PA765/logistic.htm).

3. A shotgun scatters the "shot" in a broad area; it does not hit a precise area. Thus, the likelihood of hitting something is increased with a shotgun, but it may not be the precise thing that you intended to hit.

4. A sophisticated understanding of statistical practices is necessary to actually conduct multiple regression and make decisions about ordering variables. Nevertheless, you should be aware of the potential problems associated with inappropriate ordering of variables in research that uses this type of analysis.

In This Chapter

- Steps for conducting a survey research study are outlined, including the design phase, the sampling plan, designing the questionnaire, and conducting the survey.
- Construction of different types of questions, such as demographic, sensitive and nonthreatening behavioral, knowledge, and attitude questions, is considered.
- Response rate considerations are described.
- Notes specific to phone interviews, as well as to Web-based surveys, address specific issues related to those approaches.
- Issues related to the transformative perspective are discussed: feminist, disabilities, racial/ethnic minorities, and children.
- Questions for critical analysis of survey research are presented.

Surveys can be thought of as methods used for descriptive research or as data collection methods used within other research designs. For example, a survey used to collect data about attitudes toward affirmative action can be used to compare effects of levels of race-based prejudice on such attitudes; hence, the study takes on characteristics of causal comparative and correlational studies (Steinbugler, Press, & Dias, 2006). I have chosen to devote an entire chapter to this approach to research because surveys are used pervasively in educational and psychological research and because many design issues are an integral part of the planning and conduct of surveys.

6

Survey Methods

Surveys are a familiar part of most peoples' lives in the sense that survey results are often cited in the popular media, such as newspapers, magazines, and television programs. You should be aware of the strengths and limitations of survey research compared with other research strategies. Surveys are good because they allow collection of data from a larger number of people than is generally possible when using a quasi-experimental or experimental design. However, unlike many quantitative and qualitative research approaches that involve direct observation of behavior, surveys rely on individuals' *self-reports* of their knowledge, attitudes, or behaviors. Thus the validity of the information is contingent on the honesty of the respondent. You might assume that people who do not give an honest answer have something to hide. However, as can be seen in the following quotation from George Burns (1984), a comedian from a bygone era, people might not know the answer, or they might not know that they do not know the honest answer:

> If you were to go around asking people what would make them happier, you'd get answers like a new car, a bigger house, a raise in pay, winning a lottery, a face-lift, more kids, fewer kids, a new restaurant to go to—probably not one in a hundred would say a chance to help people. And yet that may bring the most happiness of all. (p. 141)

The American Association for Public Opinion Research has provided a summary of the steps in planning and conducting a survey with supplemental information available at their Web site (see Box 6.1). As they note, the first step is to define the purpose or goals of the survey. The following section illustrates examples of the many purposes for surveys that are determined during the design phase of a survey study.

Box 6.1 Best Practices for Survey and Public Opinion Research

1. Have specific goals for the survey.
2. Consider alternatives to using a survey to collect information.
3. Select samples that well represent the population to be studied.
4. Use designs that balance costs with errors.
5. Take great care in matching question wording to the concepts being measured and the population being studied.
6. Pretest questionnaires and procedures to identify problems prior to the survey.
7. Train interviewers carefully on interviewing techniques and the subject matter of the survey.
8. Construct quality checks for each stage of the survey.
9. Maximize cooperation or response rates within the limits of ethical treatment of human subjects.
10. Use statistical analytic and reporting techniques appropriate to the data collected.
11. Carefully develop and fulfill pledges of confidentiality given to respondents.
12. Disclose all methods of the survey to permit evaluation and replication.

SOURCE: American Association for Public Opinion Research (2008).

Design Phase

During the design phase, the researcher should begin to articulate the purpose(s) of the survey, state specific objectives, consider the types of information needed, and evaluate design options. Sample Study 1.4 summarized an example of a mixed methods transformative study that examined the effect of a gender violence prevention program using both quantitative surveys and qualitative surveys based on interviews. A second study that used the survey approach is presented in Sample Study 6.1.

Purposes of Surveys

Surveys can be used for a wide variety of purposes:

- The American Association of University Women's (AAUW) Educational Foundation analyzed survey data collected by the Baccalaureate and Beyond Longitudinal Studies, conducted by the U. S. Department of Education National Center for Education Statistics on education and pay equity for men and women. They reported that one-year-out-of-college women earned 80% of what men earned; by 10 years after graduation, women earned only 69% as much as men earned (Goldberg-Dey & Hill, 2007).

- In Kansas, the Fairfax County Youth Survey was conducted in 2001, 2003, 2005, and 2008 to examine both positive and negative youth behaviors, experiences, and other factors that influence the health and well-being of the county's youth for students in Grades 6 to 12 (Southeast Kansas Education Service Center, 2008).

- The National Gay and Lesbian Task Force Policy Institute conducted a survey to examine the experiences of discrimination for lesbian, gay, bisexual, and transgender Asian and Pacific Islander Americans (Dang & Vianney, 2007).

Sample Study 6.1

Survey Research and Arts Education

Research Problem: The arts represent a potential avenue to reach diverse students and to enhance academic performance. Teachers may benefit by having appropriately designed professional development opportunities focused on the integration of arts education into their regular classroom instruction. "How can teachers be encouraged to attend professional development workshops and make use of the methods they learn there in a time of increased pressure for test score results and standardized curriculum?" (p. 56). Evidence is needed to design appropriate professional development in arts education.

Research Question: "To what extent can variance in teachers' self-reported frequency of use of the arts in their teaching be explained by demographic characteristics (i.e., gender, ethnicity, years of teaching experience, grade level taught), personal experience with the arts (i.e., past and current involvement in the arts, attendance at arts-based professional development), and their scores on attitude measures on the Teaching with the Arts Survey?" (p. 57). "What do teachers consider to be the primary issues related to the use of the arts in their teaching?" (p. 58).

Methods/Design: A mixed methods descriptive survey design was used to collect the data.

Participants: Data were collected from 423 urban, suburban, and rural K–12 teachers.

Instruments and Procedures: The 48-item Teaching with the Arts Survey measures teacher demographics (15 items), frequency of use of the arts in the classroom (8 items), and attitudes toward the arts that may be related to arts use in teaching (25 items). The Teaching with the Arts Survey was distributed to all teachers in the participating schools but were completed and returned voluntarily.

Results/Discussion: The response rate was 43%. Teachers of younger students reported using arts-based instruction more frequently than those in middle or high school. Teachers who participated in arts workshops reported using arts more frequently in their instruction than nonparticipants. Age and years of teaching were not related to the use of the arts. Teachers mentioned the need to gain skills and self-confidence in using the arts, especially as they related to making connections with other areas of the academic curriculum. Teachers reported seeing increased ability to reach diverse learners through integrating the arts into their teaching.

SOURCE: Oreck (2004).

- The U.S. Census Bureau conducts the American Community Survey that asks about a variety of topics, including the status of people with disabilities in the United States (W. Erickson & Lee, 2008).

- The U.S. Department of Education is supporting two important surveys focused on the experiences of students with disabilities. The National Longitudinal Transition Study-2 (NLTS2) began in 2000 with students aged 13 to 16 and is a 10-year project; hence current data from the survey focus on the postsecondary experiences of people with disabilities (L. Newman, 2008). The experiences of younger students with disabilities are being studied in a 10-year project called the Special Education Elementary Longitudinal Survey (SEELS; Blackorby et al., 2007) that focuses on their transition from elementary to middle to high school.

- Based on feminist standpoint theory and other critical theories, a combined closed-ended and open-ended survey was used to give members of marginalized groups an opportunity to share their experiences of discrimination and their ideas about the meaning of cultural competence in service providers (Gentlewarrior, Martin-Jearld, Skok, & Sweetser, 2008).

• Children who receive mental health services are sometimes also involved in the juvenile justice system. Graves, Frabutt, and Shelton (2007) conducted a survey to determine the factors associated with children's involvement in both these systems, including demographic, person-level, family-level, and school-level factors.

A number of national surveys are conducted in the United States on a regular basis that yield useful information; such as the labor market statistics generated by the Bureau of Labor Statistics and the Bureau of the Census, and basic data about health conditions, use of health service, and behaviors that affect the risk of illness from the National Health Interview Survey carried out by the Bureau of the Census for the Public Health Service. Also, the Center for Assessment and Demographic Studies at Gallaudet University conducts the Annual Survey of Hearing Impaired Children and Youth, which includes demographic, audiological, and educationally related information about the students and program information about the schools they attend. Information about these surveys is generally available on the Internet. Box 6.2 contains a listing of a variety of resources that are available related to survey research, as well as the results of national survey projects.

Box 6.2 Survey Resources Available on the Web

- Cultural Policy and the Arts National Data Archive (CPANDA)
  - Interactive digital archive of policy-relevant data on the arts and cultural policy in the United States.
- Gallup Research Center (University of Nebraska, Lincoln)
  - Conducts national and international surveys on social and behavioral issues.
- National Opinion Research Center (NORC)
  - Conducts research on a national level on issues of race, education, health, environment, and other policy issues.
- Pew Research Center for the People and the Press
  - The center's purpose is to serve as a forum for ideas on the media and public policy through public opinion research.

Statistical Data on the United States

U.S. Census Bureau
www.census.gov

U.S. Bureau of Labor Statistics
www.bls.gov

U.S. National Center for Health Statistics
www.cdc.gov/nchs

A good first step in starting a survey is to write the purpose of the survey in 25 words or less. This purpose can then be expanded in terms of specific objectives that the survey will strive to address. The following examples illustrate purpose statements and specific objectives taken from a study of professional development needs for school psychologists and a study of youth behavior in a school system:

• "The purpose of this study was to conduct a comprehensive and systematic survey of practicing school psychologists throughout the United States to examine their perceptions of two global issues: (a) the extent to which advances in specific areas of practice were perceived to have improved the services provided by the respondent and (b) the areas in which the respondent believed he or she would like additional professional development training." (Wnek, Klein, & Bracken, 2008, p. 151)

- "The survey is designed to provide information about youth behaviors—those that are positive as well as those that are harmful. These data provide insight into the prevalence and frequency of substance abuse, violence and delinquency, health and health risk behaviors, and positive behaviors. Information from this survey allows the county to monitor trends in substance abuse, health, mental health, and delinquency, in order to support county efforts to plan, evaluate, and improve community and school programs designed to prevent health problems and promote healthy behaviors. The 2008 survey included questions in several new areas, including sexual health, physical activity, nutrition, weight perceptions, weight loss behaviors, and dating violence. . . . The major [objectives include gathering information about]:
    - Substance Use
    - Sexual Activity
    - Delinquent Behaviors
    - Bullying and Aggression
    - Health, Mental Health, and Safety
    - Physical Activity and Health and Nutrition
    - Risk and Protective Factors" (Southeast Kansas Education Service Center, 2008, p. 12)

Specification of such objectives can then be used as a basis for further methodological decisions.

Design Considerations

In survey research, the researcher has a choice between simple descriptive, cross-sectional, and longitudinal approaches. The *simple descriptive* approach is a one-shot survey for the purpose of describing the characteristics of a sample at one point in time. The *cross-sectional* design involves examining the characteristics of several groups at one point in time (e.g., first-, third-, and fifth-grade students). *Longitudinal* designs survey one group or cohort of subjects at different points in time (e.g., 1 year, 2 years, and 3 years after leaving school). Cross-sectional designs have the advantage of collecting information in a shorter time frame. The disadvantage is that the experience of the students who are now in the fifth grade may have been different in the first grade, compared with students who are now in first grade. The advantage of longitudinal research is that it follows the same (or highly similar) subjects over a period of time. The disadvantage is that it takes a long time to do it, and conditions may not be the same for students who are graduating three years later. Short of a time warp, there is no easy solution to these problems other than acknowledging the limitations of individual studies.

The descriptive design is exemplified in the previously cited studies of school psychologists' needs for professional development (Wnek et al., 2008), integration of arts into academic teaching (Oreck, 2004), and discrimination experiences of members of the Asian and Pacific Islander LGBTQ community (Dang & Vianney, 2007) and of members of several marginalized groups (Gentlewarrior et al., 2008). The survey of dual involvement of youth in the mental health and juvenile justice systems that includes the age of the child as a variable (Graves et al., 2007) and the study of obesity at three grade levels by Mellor, Rapoport, and Maliniak (2008) represent the cross-sectional approach. Longitudinal designs were used in the surveys of academic pay differentials for men and women (Goldberg-Dey & Hill, 2007), Fairfax County Youth Survey of risk and resilience factors (Southeast Kansas Education Service Center, 2008), and the surveys of the experiences of students who have disabilities (Blackorby et al., 2008; L. Newman, 2008; Wagner, Newman, Cameto, Levine, & Marder, 2007).

Particularly with special education students, the researcher must be aware that progression from one grade to another may not be the most appropriate way to measure passage of time. The students' Individual Education Plans (IEPs) often define goals for individual growth rather than for progression from grade to grade; thus longitudinal research with these populations would more appropriately focus on age rather than grade.

Extending Your Thinking: Survey Design

Select a topic for a survey research study. Use that topic to exemplify how you could design a descriptive, cross-sectional, and longitudinal survey research study.

Data Collection Choices

In the past, survey researchers had a choice of mail, telephone, and personal interviews. Technological advances have added options for the conduct of survey research, including e-mail, Web-based surveys, video-based surveys, or a combination of these as methods of data collection. The method selected depends on the purpose of the survey, the nature of the data to be collected, cost factors, and the size and characteristics of the sample. Advantages and disadvantages are associated with each approach. For example, mail surveys are good for collecting detailed information in a closed-ended format, the cost is relatively low, and they can allow a respondent to consult records before responding (e.g., checking on the level of expenditure within specific categories). The disadvantages of mail surveys are that the surveyor does not have an opportunity to probe for more in-depth answers or to determine if the respondent understood the questions appropriately. Phone interviews are good for collecting open-ended responses; however, they are more costly than mail surveys. In phone interviews, the surveyor does have the opportunity to probe for additional information; however, one cannot observe the interviewees' body language and their contextual surroundings as a part of the interview. The most costly type of interviewing is the personal interview. (This topic is covered in Chapter 8). With this type of interview, the advantages are that the interviewer can use a less structured approach, conduct the interview in a more conversational style, and probe more easily for understanding and additional information.

Converse, Wolfe, Huang, and Oswald (2008) identified the following advantages of using Web-based surveys: convenient access to samples, reduced costs, faster responses, more interactive or tailored formats, quick troubleshooting, automated data collection, scoring, reporting, and access to larger samples. However, research has also suggested that Web-based surveys are associated with lower response rates than for smaller scale, more targeted surveys (Dillman, 2007; Shih & Fan, 2008). Converse et al. conducted a study to compare the response rates for mixed-mode survey design that included a survey sent

> (a) via mail with a follow-up contact via e-mail that directed them to a Web-based questionnaire or (b) via e-mail that directed them to a Web-based questionnaire with a follow-up contact via mail. Results indicate that these mixed-mode procedures produce moderately high response rates. However, the mail survey tended to be more effective than the e-mail/Web survey, when serving either as the initial contact or as the follow-up contact. These results suggest that survey implementation involving mail followed by e-mail/Web, or even mail-only approaches, may result in larger samples than implementation involving e-mail/Web followed by mail. (p. 99)

For additional methodological issues regarding Web surveys, see the WebSM (Web Survey Methodology) Web site, a nonprofit Web site dedicated to such issues (www.websm.org).

De Leeuw (2005, p. 241) summarized the increasing use of multi-modes of data collection in survey research:

> In recent years various studies have used sequential mixed-mode strategies and showed that switching to a second, and even third, mode is an effective means of improving response rates, even for newer data collection methods such as IVR and the Internet (Dillman, Phelps, Tortora, Swift, Kohrell, & Berck, 2005). Sequential mixed mode surveys will increase response both for the general population (Brambilla & McKinlay, 1987; Fowler et al., 2002; Jackson & Boyle, 1991), for different racial and ethnic groupings (Beebe et al., 2005), for special groups like mothers with Medicaid eligible children of different ethnic/racial background (Grembowski & Phillips, 2005).

Box 6.3 provides an example of a multi-mode design that is used to track television watching behaviors in the United States. Additional discussion of response rate considerations appears later in this chapter.

Box 6.3 Multi-Mode Survey Data Collection Strategies

A very good example of a mixed-mode system is the Nielsen media research methodology (see Bennett and Trussell, 2001; Trussell and Lavrakas, 2004). This mixed-mode system uses an RDD-selected [Radom Digit Dialing] sample of households to which addresses are matched. The mixed-mode system consists of seven steps: first a pre-recruitment postcard is mailed to all homes for which addresses are available; this is followed by a recruitment phone call; the third contact attempt is again by mail and is an advance postcard announcing the diary; next the diary survey package is mailed to all homes for which an address is now available (regardless of the result of the recruitment call). This diary survey package includes a cover letter, diaries, a cash incentive, a return envelope, and a brochure. A reminder postcard in Step 5, a reminder phone call in Step 6, and again a reminder postcard in Step 7 follow the survey package. Although the actual data collection is unimode (diaries), the data collection system is multi-mode with mail and telephone advance notifications and reminders.

—de Leeuw, 2005, p. 237

Extending Your Thinking: Developing a Survey

Select a topic for a survey research study.

a. Write a statement of purpose for the study.

b. Write specific objectives that relate to your purpose.

c. Decide if you would conduct your survey by mail, phone, or personal interviews.

d. Justify your choice of data collection method.

Response Rate Considerations

Many different factors have been investigated as to what influences people to return mail survey forms, or to agree to participate in phone or personal interviews and Web-based surveys. The American Association for Public Opinion Research offers a definition of response rate and various methods to calculate them at their Web site (www.aapor.org/). The definition, one formula, and the URL to their electronic spreadsheet for calculating response rates are displayed in Box 6.4.

Box 6.4 Response Rate: Definition and Calculation

Response rates—The number of complete interviews with reporting units divided by the number of eligible reporting units in the sample. The American Association for Public Opinion Research report provides six definitions of response rates, ranging from the definition that yields the lowest rate to the definition that yields the highest rate, depending on how partial interviews are considered and how cases of unknown eligibility are handled.

To calculate:

I = Complete interview

P = Partial interview

R = Refusal and break-off

NC = Noncontact

O = Other

UH = Unknown if household/occupied housing unit

UO = Unknown, other

Response Rates

$$RR1 = \frac{I}{(I + P) + (R + NC + O) + (UH + UO)}$$

Response Rate 1 (RR1), or the minimum response rate, is the number of complete interviews divided by the number of interviews (complete plus partial) plus the number of noninterviews (refusal and break-off plus noncontacts plus others) plus all cases of unknown eligibility (unknown if housing unit, plus unknown, other).

The American Association for Public Opinion Research offers an online Excel spreadsheet that you can use to calculate your response rate: http://www.aapor.org/responseratesanoverview?s=response%20rate

SOURCE: American Association for Public Opinion Research (2008b).

Research on response rates reveals a continuing trend for lower response rates, especially in phone surveys (Kolar & Kolar, 2008). Researchers in survey research have consistently reported that topic salience and use of incentives have a positive effect on response rates (Groves et al., 2006). Kolar and Kolar examined variables that influence a decision to respond to phone surveys, including having the time to respond, interest in the interview topic, and perceived benefit to society or self. This implies that the interviewer communicates how the gathered data will be used. In addition, they state that "respondents would also like to feel important and competent, suggesting that a kind of 'gratification assurance' might also be used for increasing the perceived value of the survey at the introductory stage. . . . Hence, informed prearrangement of the survey appointment and tailoring introductory assurances to relevant respondent motives seems a logical if not unavoidable alternative to the current practice of 'cold calls'" (p. 379). De Leeuw's (2005) recommendations to achieve higher response rates, while keeping the overall costs low, include the use of mixed-mode strategies, starting with the less costly method first. For example, the American Community Survey is a mail survey with follow-up telephone interviews for nonrespondents, followed by face-to-face interviews for a subsample of the remaining nonrespondents. Beebe, Davern, McAlpine, Call, and Rockwood (2005) devised a strategy to contact ethnic groups whose first language was not English. In their mail survey, which was in English only, they had an explicit statement on the cover in several languages, urging respondents interested in completing a telephone survey to contact the survey center, where bilingual interviewers were available.

Shih and Fan (2008) conducted a meta-analysis of 39 studies published within the last decade that compared mail and Web survey response rates. They reported that mail surveys seemed to have higher response rates for medical doctors, schoolteachers, and general consumers, while Web surveys had higher response rates for college students. They also reported that follow-up reminders had less effect with Web surveys than for mail surveys. (Based on my personal experience, follow-ups on Web surveys result in a surge of responses immediately following the reminder.)

C. Cook, Heath, and Thompson (2000) conducted a meta-analysis of factors influencing response rates in Internet-based surveys. They found three factors that increased response rates. Follow-up contacts with nonrespondents, personalized contacts, and contacting sampled people prior to sending out the survey were the three dominant factors in higher response rates. Other suggestions for increasing response rates include these:

- Personal interviews generally yield higher response rates than do mail surveys; phone interview response rates have been dropping steadily over the last decade (Kolar & Kolar, 2008).

- Questionnaire length sometimes has an effect on response rates. Short questionnaires will be returned at a higher rate than long ones unless the respondent endorses the importance of the topic.

- Monetary and nonmonetary incentives can increase response rates.

- Sponsorship (through a respected organization or signature by a high-ranking administrator) can yield higher response rates.

- Good timing is *very* important, especially with populations that organize their time around a school calendar. Avoid sending the questionnaires at the very beginning or end of a school year or around a holiday period.

- Be sure to make it easy to return the questionnaire by providing a stamped, self-addressed envelope (and maybe a pencil). Even your choice of stamps versus metered mail can influence response rates, especially if you are able to locate a stamp that has salience for your population. For example, the U.S. Postal Service has printed stamps that depict a deaf mother signing "I love you" to her child.

- Consider using an attention-getting delivery mode, such as express mail, special delivery, or airmail, and, possibly, printing your questionnaire on brightly colored paper.
- Handwritten envelopes seem to attract more attention now than computer-generated address labels.
- Your follow-ups could be delivered via humorous postcards or telephone calls.

Nonresponse is a serious issue for survey researchers, as illustrated by another observation from George Burns (1984):

> I've always suspected that people who have hobbies were happier than people who didn't. A few days ago to find out if I was right, I took my own private poll. I stood on the corner of Wilshire and Rodeo Drive, stopped ten people passing by and asked them if they had a hobby. Seven told me to mind my own business, and the other three didn't speak English. I guess Dr. Gallup must use a different corner. (p. 91)

A response rate of around 70% has generally been recommended as acceptable (B. Johnson & Christensen, 2008). However, this recommendation is based on the assumption that respondents and nonrespondents are fairly similar. Researchers should take measures to determine how representative the sample is of the target population by one of the strategies recommended in this chapter, for example, follow-up with selected nonrespondents or comparison with known characteristics of the population. Kolar and Kolar (2008) suggest that increasing response rates rests on the researchers' abilities to cultivate cooperative relationships with respondents, a theme echoed throughout this book as a key to validity in research.

Theoretical Lenses and Diverse Populations

Feminist Theories. Feminists have expressed different views in terms of survey research; some view it as a rigorous and scientifically sound method that has credibility with many people in the social science community and with the public at large (Reinharz, 1992). However, other feminists express deep distrust of survey research and other statistically based forms of research. Feminists' criticisms of quantitative, closed-ended survey research are based on the problem of oversimplifying complex issues by reducing them to a limited number of questions and response options. Some researchers try to address these concerns by asking many questions that attempt to get at some of the details of the events and by including participants' verbatim comments in the text. Hodgkin (2008) situates her work in the transformative paradigm (Mertens, 2009) because it highlights the strengths inherent in mixed methods and focuses on issues of power and discrimination. Hence, Hodgkin recommends that feminist researchers consider mixing quantitative and qualitative approaches in survey research in order to give visibility to the breadth of issues related to girls and women, as well as to give voice to the rich complexity of experiences that provide context for understanding those experiences. She applied this approach by conducting a broad quantitative survey and asking respondents if they were willing to be interviewed in more depth. She then selected a smaller sample of women to interview using open-ended questions.

Literacy Levels. If the population of interest has documented low literacy levels, then researchers need to be aware that the use of a self-completed print survey is not an appropriate strategy. In such circumstances, they could consider face-to-face interviews. The International Social

Survey Programme uses self-completion of print surveys; however, they also have a flexible policy that surveys methods should be adapted to the specific needs of the target population. Therefore, they allow the use of face-to-face interviews for populations with low literacy levels (Skjak & Harkness, 2003, cited in de Leeuw, 2005, p. 242).

Children. Surveys conducted with children must follow the same ethical guidelines discussed in Chapter 11 on sampling that all research with children follows. In a review of active parental consent for their children to participate in surveys that dealt with sensitive behaviors (e.g., alcohol use, smoking), Mellor, Rapoport, and Maliniak's (2008) review of possible biases associated with differential rates of parental consent noted that parents were more likely to give consent for their children to participate if the parents did not believe that their children engaged in the behavior. In school-based surveys, researchers can use strategies for parents to either actively or passively give their consent. Mellor et al.'s study of obesity in school-age children revealed the bias that can be associated with lack of active consent. For passive consent, the school sent home letters to inform parents that school personnel would collect data on the height and weight of all third-sixth-, and seventh-grade students. If parents did not want their child included, then they had to contact the school to opt out of the study. This resulted in data collection from 90% of the students. The researchers also sought active consent from the parents for the students to complete a researcher-administered survey. For this part of the study, consent form packets were mailed to parents and legal guardians for the same group of students. Active parental consent for the survey was obtained from 26% of the parents. The researchers were then able to compare an obesity index for children for parents who gave active consent with those who did not. They reported that parents whose children were overweight or at-risk of being so were less likely to give active consent for participation in the survey. This is consistent with prior studies suggesting that the requirement of active parental consent can result in a positive bias in a study's results.

Teenagers.[1] Researchers experience different challenges when collecting data from teenagers than when working with adults or children. Bassett, Beagan, Ristovski-Slijepcevic, and Chapman (2008) describe their frustrations when conducting a survey of families from three racial/ethnic groups in Canada (European Canadian, African Canadian, and Punjabi Canadian). They struggled with strategies to engage the teenagers when the young people had been "volunteered" by their parents, as well as how to get the teens to express themselves beyond a monosyllabic response. (Think of the answers to the perennial questions that parents ask: How was school today? Fine. Where are you going? Out. Who with? Friends.) Bassett et al. included the following example that illustrates their frustration in asking the teenagers about their food choices:

I: So you had mentioned that you're all vegetarian in the house?

Sharon: Yeah.

I: And then you said you tried to be a vegan?

Sharon: Yeah.

I: But that didn't work?

Sharon: No.

The interviewers tried different strategies and reported more success when they were able to visit the families several times because they were able to ask the teenagers about their interests as they got to know them better. They also found that disclosing their own food choices seemed to help build rapport with the youth. The European Canadians responded to references to mainstream culture, such as *Super Size Me*, a movie about excessive fat and portions offered by fast food restaurants in the United States. The African Canadians and Punjabi Canadians were not similarly responsive to this reference; however, they did open up more when the discussion centered on traditional gender roles and food preparation.

Disability Perspectives. Combinations of methods can result in better response rates. For example, the NLTS2 survey of youth with disabilities used three different methods (Wagner et al., 2007). If parents said their children could respond to questions, the interviews were conducted by telephone (Computer Assisted Telephone Interviewing—CATI). If the parents said their children could answer for themselves but not by telephone, then the data were collected by a mailed questionnaire. If parents indicated their children could not answer questions either through telephone or printed questionnaire, then the interviewer asked the parents to answer those questions. Additional data about the youths' academic experiences were collected though in-person interviews.

Computer technology offers another tool to provide supportive accommodations for collection of data in the deaf community (Gerich & Lehner, 2006). The purpose of the Gerich and Lehner survey was to gather data about different strategies for therapies and medical or psychological attention in the clinic for hearing-impaired persons in a local hospital. The majority of the deaf people in the sample used sign language; therefore, the researchers designed a multimedia computer assisted survey instrument (CASI) to use with deaf people as a standardized, self-administered questionnaire that included sign language. The respondent could see a window for video as well as text and features of responding and navigating through the survey. The video sequences showed the question and answer categories in sign language, while corresponding print text in another screen showed one item at a time.

Sampling Plan

Identification of the Respondents

When you conduct a survey, you should inquire as to who has access to the kind of information you need. You might choose to collect the information from the person who experienced an event, from another person (such as a parent or responsible adult), or by examining records (such as a student's file). Your choice of the source of information will depend on the following factors:

1. Who has access to the information? You may need to inquire to find out who would have access to the kind of information that you need.

2. The characteristics of the people who have experienced the event in terms of age or disabling conditions. If the child is very young or has moderate to severe disabilities that would prevent meaningful participation, it may be necessary to ask the parent or responsible adult for the information. Freeman and Mathison (2008) provide specific strategies for interviewing children, including using drawing, photography, the Internet, and games. Researchers should be aware that federal legislation requires parents' permission before asking children questions for research purposes.

3. The type of information needed can help determine the best source of that information. For example, a parent would most likely be aware of whether or not the child is employed, the type of job he or she has, and how much the child is being paid. Thus they could serve as a proxy to be interviewed if the child was unavailable. However, parents might be a less reliable source for attitudinal information, such as the child's satisfaction with the job. School records are valuable as sources of information regarding courses taken and graduation status.

In longitudinal studies, the researcher must also decide which type of group will be followed over the years. Here are three possible choices:

1. Trend analysis involves studying the same general population but not the same individuals.

2. Cohort analysis involves studying the same specific population but not necessarily the exact same individuals.

3. Panel analysis involves following the exact same individuals over the time period of the study.

Population Definition

Once the general nature of the respondents has been identified, it is time for the researcher to become more specific about the information sources. Thus the conceptual definition of the population must be translated into operational terms.

Sampling Decisions

Sampling procedures are described in Chapter 11. These include *probability sampling* (simple random sampling, systematic sampling, clustered sampling, and stratified random sampling) and *purposeful sampling* (e.g., a "snowball" strategy that involves asking each person who is interviewed to suggest names of additional people who should be interviewed, usually with some guidance as to the nature of the characteristics being sought).

If a probability sampling procedure is used, researchers need to specify to whom the results will be generalized. If a purposeful sampling procedure is used, the researcher needs to provide sufficient details about the people in the study to communicate to the reader their important characteristics. Serious bias can occur in the interpretation of results from a survey that does not make explicit its sampling strategy and the characteristics of the respondents. For example, parents' satisfaction with a drug and alcohol prevention program might appear to be artificially high if a researcher surveys only parents of children who completed the program. To get a more balanced view, parents of children who dropped out of the program should also be surveyed. It is very important to make explicit the sampling strategy and the characteristics of the sample.

When using a probability sampling approach, the researcher needs to specify a *sampling frame*—that is, a list of the people who have a chance to be selected. A sample can be representative only of the population included in the sampling frame; therefore, it is important to provide evidence concerning how well the sampling frame corresponds to the population (Fowler, 2008).

Braverman (1996) lists the following sources of error in sampling for surveys: coverage, nonresponse, and sampling. *Coverage errors* arise in two circumstances: (a) people who should be in the sampling frame are *not* there, or (b) people who are truly ineligible (i.e., they are not members of the target population) are in the sampling frame. A coverage error could occur if you are surveying parents of deaf children and a parent's name is omitted from the sampling frame because the school has not updated its records. Or you might be interested in surveying only hearing parents with deaf children. If the school does not identify parents' hearing status, you may have deaf parents with deaf children inappropriately included in your sampling frame.

A *nonresponse error* occurs when someone refuses to be interviewed or to complete the questionnaire or cannot be reached (e.g., because of an incorrect address or phone number). Response rate considerations are discussed later in this chapter. A *sampling error* occurs because each sample drawn from a population is somewhat different from any other sample that could be drawn. The probability-based sampling strategies discussed in Chapter 11 are designed to statistically control for sampling error.

Sampling Minority Populations

A few ideas about sampling strategies with minority populations can guide the researcher in decisions about survey research with this population. The National Opinion Research Center (NORC) recommends using a soundly constructed national, cross-sectional survey to address potential underrepresentation of Black and Latino respondents (C. Cohen, 2006). For more than 20 years, they have used an oversampling strategy in order to obtain a sufficient number of Black and Latino participants in their survey to enable them to do group comparisons. C. Cohen applied a mixed sampling strategy in NORC's Black Youth Project. She used a standard national sampling strategy and a supplemental sample in areas that are 15% or higher Hispanic or non-Hispanic African American as a percentage of the total population. This resulted in sufficient numbers of these racial/ethnic groups to allow comparisons among the groups.

Yancey et al. (2003) noted that national research programs have challenged researchers to develop research designs and recruitment strategies that are more effective in attracting individuals from underrepresented populations. "The policies stipulate that researchers cultivate understandings and partnerships with understudied populations that encourage consent to participate and continued study protocol adherence and long-term study retention to meet conventional standards of validity" (p. 181). Yancey et al. cite numerous strategies that have been used to recruit participants of color such as ethnically tailed recruitment messages, project teams with substantive representation of members of the targeted racial/ethnic groups, and logistical support services: "Perhaps the most consistent theme in the literature on recruiting people of color is the importance of forging connections in the community where the research or intervention is to be conducted and gaining the trust and support of community leaders" (p. 181). Several researchers have recommended going through churches in Black communities to reach this population (James & Busia, 1993; Margaret Neily, January 1995, personal communication on researching the use of smoke detectors in Black communities; Jane Reisman, August 1994, personal communication on researching the homeless population in Seattle). Yancey et al. (2003) used a variety of community sites, including schools, churches, community centers, and libraries, to recruit African American participants to complete a survey about demographics, health status, physical activity, and eating habits. They concluded that word-of-mouth was an effective recruitment method for lower-SES African American participants. The use of the social networks was also successful in reaching African Americans; it was not as successful with those who had a lower SES.

Random Digit Dialing

Random digit dialing (RDD) is a technique that researchers use in selecting samples for telephone surveys (Fowler, 2008). It involves identifying areas to be sampled (at random) and their corresponding area codes and exchanges (the first three digits of the phone number). Then the last four digits of the number to be dialed could be generated at random according to the number of units needed in the sample. It is possible to identify which exchanges are used primarily for residential telephones and to focus the sampling on that subgroup.

C. Cohen (2006) applied the RDD technique in NORC's Black Youth Project by oversampling from exchanges in the geographic areas with 15% or more density of Black or Hispanic populations. Unfortunately, response rates to telephone surveys have fallen off precipitously over the last 10 years, making RDD a less-effective strategy to collect this type of data (Fowler, 2008).

Designing the Survey Instrument

Before undertaking the task of designing a survey instrument, researchers should do what they should always do before making data collection decisions: Review the literature! Check to see what else has been done from which you might be able to borrow (with appropriate citations and permissions, of course). Many of the national survey organizations publish their questionnaires, and these are available in databases such as ERIC or Psychological Abstracts or from the organizations themselves.

If you decide that you need to develop your own survey instrument, some general directions are in order, along with specific suggestions related to different types of questions.

- Outline the various topics you want to include in your survey. One important alternative to devising the topics yourself for your survey is to use a strategy called the Delphi Technique, which was developed by the Rand Corporation in the 1950s (Sieber, 1998). It is a method of allowing experts to contribute ideas concerning the important issues that should be included in a survey on a particular topic, and then following up with collection of data with a larger sample of experts. The experts are asked to anonymously suggest ideas, which the researcher then formats into a survey that can be distributed to the study's respondents. The steps for using the Delphi Technique appear in Box 6.5. (The disadvantage of using this technique is that it may take months to complete; so if time is a factor, choose another strategy.)

Box 6.5 Steps in Using the Delphi Technique

1. Assemble a pool of specialists and highly invested potential consumers of information about the topic in question.

2. Using an open-ended questionnaire, ask respondents to propose a few essential statements that represent the critical needs or issues in the topic area. This may require defining such terms as critical, needs, and the field.

3. Gather the responses and eliminate overlap or redundancies in the topics suggested. Reformat the topics into a clear and consistent survey form.

(Continued)

Box 6.5 (Continued)

4. Return the reformatted list to each expert participant for review. Ask participants to rate each topic on a seven-point scale ranging from *very critical* to *of little importance*. Panelists should also be given the opportunity to add more topics if they wish.

5. Calculate the mean and standard deviation for each item; report these summary statistics back to the respondents. Ask members of the panel if they wish to re-rank any of their items after seeing how others ranked them. Invite them to write a brief statement if they disagree greatly with the group position.

6. Use their responses to develop a final survey form that is sent to the intended target population.

SOURCE: Adapted from Sieber (1998) and Sulzer-Azaroff, Fleming, Tupa, Bass, & Hamad (2008).

- Explain to yourself why you are asking each question. Sometimes researchers are tempted to make a very lengthy survey because they are going to be sending out a questionnaire and may as well get as much data as possible. However, this "everything but the kitchen sink" approach can backfire in that participants may be unwilling to respond to an overly long questionnaire or to questions that do not seem directly relevant to the topic as it is described by the researcher. Therefore, examine each question with regard to your intended purpose of this particular research study and eliminate any just "nice to know" questions.

- Decide on the degree of structure that is most appropriate (e.g., closed- vs. open-ended formats or some combination of these). Closed formats include questions in which the respondent chooses from a list of possible options (e.g., multiple-choice questions, true-false questions, scalar questions (e.g., 1—strongly agree to 5—strongly disagree), or a checklist that asks the respondent to mark all that apply or to select from a long list of response options). Open formats are questions that allow respondents to answer in their own words. Here are examples of each format:

Closed-Ended Format

What are your child's preferred activities during a free play period (check all that apply)?

_____ Fantasy play with action figures
_____ Coloring or painting
_____ Fantasy play with dolls
_____ Physically active outdoor play (e.g., swinging, climbing)
_____ Playing board games

Open-Ended Format

What are your child's preferred activities during a free play period?

____

____

____

If you plan to use a closed format, such as a multiple-choice question, be sure that you ask the questions in an open format to a pilot group first. You can then use their answers to develop the response options. This will help ensure that you have included all reasonable response alternatives. Did you include the right options? Are they all-inclusive, or do you allow for the respondent to enter additional options, if necessary?

• Generally, avoid psychologically sensitive questions. Of course, you cannot avoid psychologically sensitive questions if your topic of interest is a sensitive area; however, you should be aware that this type of question should be handled carefully. I advise you to read the section later in this chapter on sensitive behavioral questions before attempting this type of survey question. Many people react defensively when asked about topics such as citizenship (Did you vote?), morality (Did you attend church on Sunday?), social responsibility (Did you help the homeless?), illnesses (Have you been treated for a mental illness?), illegal activities (Have you used illegal drugs?), sexuality (Have you ever had a homosexual experience?), and finances (How much money do you make?). In many cases, psychologically threatening questions have "socially desirable" answers, and to appear socially appropriate, people may misrepresent their actual attitudes, behaviors, or knowledge. Parents of children with disabilities can find questions about their child's disability threatening, especially if the diagnosis is recent or they have not fully accepted their child's condition.

• *Clarity* is paramount. Make sure that all the items mean the same thing to all the respondents. This may or may not be possible to do (especially recognizing the social construction of reality). If you are using terms that are commonly open to multiple meanings, you can improve clarity by providing a definition of the terms as you intend them to be understood in your survey. For example, *mainstreaming* is a term commonly used in surveys about the placement of students with disabilities, and it is open to many different interpretations. In such cases, the researcher should provide a definition of the term for the respondent to be sure that everyone is interpreting it in a similar manner.

• Short items are generally preferable to long items.

• Negative wording should be avoided (e.g., "Which of these are not contributors to violence against women?").

• Avoid items that ask about more than one idea. Ask about only one idea in each question (e.g., do not ask a question such as, do you believe that services provided to teenage mothers should include supplements for child care, psychological services, and training?).

• Avoid jargon and big words. You should know the approximate reading level of your intended respondents and design your questionnaire accordingly. Also, you should assume that the respondent needs any acronyms spelled out (at least the first time they appear in the questionnaire). This is a problem that can be reduced by pilot testing the questionnaire.

• Avoid biased or leading questions. I used to have a congressional representative who had very well-known views on military spending. For some reason, he used to send surveys to his constituents to ask their views about this topic. (The reason I am not clear as to why he asked is that I am sure that he would not change his views no matter what I said.) The questions were asked in a way that suggested the answers he was looking for (e.g., do you think that we should increase military spending in view of the threat to national security that is posed by America's enemies who could attack us at any time?).

• Emphasize *critical* words by using italics or underlining or bold letters. This is much easier to do now with fancy font options in word processing programs.

Formatting the Questionnaire

Here are a few hints about the physical appearance of your questionnaire:

a. Make it attractive: For example, use colored ink, colored paper, different type styles.

b. Organize and lay out the questions so that they are easy to answer.

c. Be sure to number the items and the pages.

d. Put the name and address of the person to whom the questionnaire is to be returned at the beginning and end of the questionnaire, even if a self-addressed envelope is included. You would be surprised at how many times the questionnaire and the envelope become separated, and a well-intentioned respondent is unable to return your survey because she does not know where to send it. (Does this sound like personal experience?)

e. Include brief, clear instructions. Specify what to do with the completed questionnaire.

f. Use examples before any item that might be confusing (especially important if the item involves *ranking* responses). Show respondents exactly what you want them to do.

g. Organize the questions in a logical sequence (i.e., group related items together).

h. Begin with a few interesting and nonthreatening items.

i. Do *not* put the most important items at the end of a long questionnaire.

j Avoid using the words *questionnaire* or *checklist* on your forms. (I have found the title "Response Form" to be useful, because it suggests what I want the respondent to do.)

Give sufficient thought to the format of the survey instrument in terms of visual layout because even small variations in the visual presentation can change how people respond to items. (Dillman, 2007). Christian and Dillman (2004) compared response patterns for items that only gave the anchors (1 = completely satisfied; 5 = not at all satisfied) with responses that required the respondent to use the same scale but to write the number in a box. Response patterns suggested that participants became confused about the direction of the scale when it was not provided as part of the response option and they had to write it in the box. Stern (2008) extended this research to a Web-based survey in which he compared three different visual formats for display of an attitude question that asked, "How do you consider Washington State University as a place to go to school?" The visual formats included three types of response items: (a) numbers were displayed, but only end-points of the options were labeled: 1 = very desirable; 5 = not at all desirable; (b) numbers were displayed along with labels for all options (1 = very desirable; 2 = somewhat desirable; 3 = neither desirable nor undesirable; 4 = somewhat undesirable; and 5 = very undesirable); and (c) no numbers were displayed; only end-point labels (very desirable and very undesirable). Stern found that the fully labeled condition resulted in less time to reply and fewer changes in responses. Response patterns for individuals with only the end-points labeled were somewhat similar, although those with only the words made fewer changes than those with numbers and words. So, it seems, participants clearly prefer labeled options.

Pilot Testing the Questionnaire

Pilot testing your questionnaire means that you try it out with a small sample similar to your intended group of respondents. You can follow these steps in the pilot test:

1. Select a pilot sample that is similar to your population.

2. In formatting the questionnaire, you may want to modify it a bit if necessary to allow room for comments to be written on the pilot version.

3. Instruct your pilot respondents that you are interested in their reactions to the process and questions and encourage them to note any ambiguities or response options that are not included.

4. Follow the procedures for administration that you plan to use in your study (i.e., if it is a mail survey, ask the pilot group to read the survey and answer it first without asking you any questions). Desimone (2006) suggests using a number of strategies during the pilot testing phase to enhance the quality of the questions.

For example, researchers can conduct cognitive interviews, hold focus groups, and ask individuals to record their thoughts as they complete the pilot survey instrument. Cognitive interviews ask the pilot participants to complete the questionnaire in the presence of the researcher, who asks questions about what they are thinking and what the questions mean to them and can include asking for suggestions for rewriting questions that are unclear or too complex. Researchers can also include a section at the end of every questionnaire where participants can record any additional questions they think should have been asked.

5. When the data from the pilot survey are collected,
   a. Read the comments.
   b. Check the responses item by item. Look for blanks, unexpected answers, and clusters of responses that suggest misinterpretation of questions, and so on.
   c. Do a brief analysis. Do you have the information that you need?
   d. Add, change, or delete any questions as needed.
   e. Follow instructions regarding establishing reliability and validity as found in Chapter 12. Desimone (2006) and Fowler (2008) both address additional strategies for establishing reliability and validity in survey research.

Dillman and Christian (2005) remind researchers of response patterns that have been associated with bias in responses, such as social desirability (answering according to cultural expectations), acquiescence (a tendency to agree when interacting with another person), recency (the tendency to chose the most recently offered options), or primacy (the tendency to select the first-offered option).

Language Differences Between the Researcher and the Respondent

When the language of the researcher is different from the respondents', the usual method of constructing the instrument is to rely heavily on collaboration with native-speaking colleagues. A process of back translation is often used in which the native speaker is asked to translate the instrument (either alone or in a committee), and the instrument is then retranslated into the language of the source document to ensure that the original intent was preserved.

McKay et al. (1996) suggest that the process of back translation can result in an instrument that is stilted, awkwardly worded, or even incomprehensible. They recommend extending the back translation with a strategy called *decentering,* which entails modifications to the source document wording to accommodate concepts that are not directly translatable. Thus the language in *both* the source document *and* the translated documents are subject to change until comparable questions are achieved in both languages. McKay and her colleagues reported that their experiences with national surveys with Hispanic populations in the United States had underscored the importance of language adaptations based on country of origin, geographic region in the United States, and educational level of the respondents.

McKay et al. (1996) conducted a statewide study of alcohol and drug prevalence in which they translated the survey into six languages other than English. They described their lessons learned in this process as follows:

> First, avoid literal translations. While these are grammatically correct and follow the wording of the original text, they may be too formal for the average speaker, convoluting the language to borderline comprehensibility. Next, when creating the source language instrument, avoid the use of slang and technical terms, which may not translate well into other languages. Also, keep modifiers and examples to a minimum. Modifiers and examples used to increase comprehension in the source instrument added to the difficulty of translating the instrument. Some examples simply did not translate while others were foreign to the different cultures. The examples also tended to get very long in translation, exacerbating an already existing problem of length. Next, try to use questions, phrases, and examples that are culturally sensitive and that fit the life experiences of the persons to be interviewed. To be sensitive to the linguistic style of the target community, ask the translators to indicate which questions might be offensive or missing important polite phrases necessary for good form in an interview. Finally, as with any survey instrument, thorough pretesting of all aspects is the best way to discover potential pitfalls in a translated questionnaire. (McKay et al., 1996, pp. 102–103)

As de Leeuw (2005) notes, literal translation is not the goal; the translation of concepts is the key. The problem of translation is equally relevant whether the survey involves two different languages (French and German) or the same language used in different countries (e.g., American English and British English).

McKee (1992) cautioned that survey researchers may fail in their research despite precautions related to the translation of the instruments, essentially for reasons that go beyond the actual language used. McKee conducted an interview-based survey in a small town on the Mexican border. Her results illuminate the need to integrate a sociolinguistic, contextual perspective in this type of research. She used the following question to explore the people's notion of "fate": "Does it seem to you that things happen because they are destined (*son cosas del destinos*) or because people struggle to bring them about?" (p. 357). Based on a linguistic and semantic analysis of their responses, McKee was able to refute the stereotypical perception of fatalism and passivity that has been attributed to Mexican Americans in other research studies. Although 22% of respondents did state that they believed things happen because they are fated to do so, the majority of the respondents used the term *destino* to distinguish between circumstances they were powerless to control and those they believed they had a chance to affect. In addition, she noted nearly everything about the way the people live indicates that they consistently struggle, plan, and adapt to changing circumstances to gain a measure of control over the forces that affect their lives.

She cautioned researchers in cross-cultural studies to be careful in their interpretations of data and to base them on a thorough understanding of the culture that produced them. Because survey research decontextualizes words through its very nature, the researcher must be careful to interpret the words in light of particular cultural circumstances.

As a segue from cultural issues to question types, I offer this bit of advice about the influence of theoretical lenses on the development of survey questions. As survey questions are developed, researchers should be aware of the contrast in questions that represent a "blame-the-victim" theory versus a "transformative" theory in the communities they plan to survey. Blame-the-victim questions place the responsibility for a problem on those who suffer from the problem and not on the social conditions that underlie the problem (McDermott, 2007). For example, Oliver (1992) used sample questions from the Office of Population Census and Surveys (OPCS) in Great Britain as examples that locate the problem of disability within the individual, such as "Are your difficulties in understanding people mainly due to a hearing problem?" The question could have been worded: "Are your difficulties in understanding people mainly due to their inabilities to communicate with you?" Thus, researchers indicate their theoretical perspective in the framing of the survey questions themselves.

Special Types of Questions

Many different organizational frameworks could be used to describe different types of questions. In this chapter, I discuss the following types: demographic, nonthreatening behavioral, sensitive behavioral, knowledge, and attitudinal questions.

Demographic

The demographic part of the questionnaire is commonly labeled "Background Information" and asks about the personal characteristics of the respondents. Although the design of demographic questions might seem relatively simple in light of the many standardized questionnaires that have asked such questions, they are not entirely unproblematic. Some questions seem to serve researchers fairly well, such as the ones shown in Box 6.6. However, other background characteristics are a bit more controversial or difficult to identify precisely. As mentioned in Chapter 5 on causal comparative and correlational research, race, class, sexual identity/orientation, and disability represent complex identifications.

The suggestions for handling race identification (found in Chapter 5) include the following:

1. Add a "multiracial" category (and leave a blank line with the instructions "Please explain.")

2. Add an "other" category (and leave a blank line with the instructions to "Please specify.")

3. Provide an open-ended question to probe for information on race and ethnicity.

4. Add some categories not traditionally included, such as Native American, Native Hawaiian, and Middle Easterner.

Box 6.6 Demographic Questions

1. Which of the following categories best describes where you live?
   a. City of 100,000+
   b. Suburb of a city
   c. Town of 50,000 to 100,000
   d. Town of 10,000 to 50,000
   e. Town of 5,000 to 10,000
   f. Town of 1,000 to 5,000
   g. Town of less than 1,000
   h. Rural area
2. What is the month, day, year of your birth?
   Month ______ Day ______ Year ______
3. How old were you on your last birthday? ________
4. What is the highest level of formal education you have obtained?
   a. Elementary school or less
   b. Some high school
   c. High school graduate
   d. Some college
   e. Associate, two-year college degree
   f. Four-year college degree
   g. Postgraduate degree started
   h. Postgraduate degree finished

Macias (1993) explored distinctions related to language and ethnic classification of language minority students in relation to Chicano and Latino students.[2] He noted that federal surveys do not systematically collect comparable English language proficiency data across states and school districts for describing the English proficiency of language minorities or Latinos. He suggested that researchers explore ways to more consistently identify language use, language proficiency, and ethnicity. He identified several important constructs for researchers to consider, including non-English language background, non- or limited-English proficiency, English difficulty, and linguistically isolated households.

The collection of demographic data about disabilities can be aided by knowledge of the categories as they are defined in the federal Individuals With Disabilities Education Act (IDEA):

- Specific learning disabilities
- Speech or language impairments
- Mental retardation
- Serious emotional disturbance
- Multiple disabilities
- Hearing impairments

- Orthopedic impairments
- Other health impairments
- Visual impairments
- Deaf-blindness
- Autism
- Traumatic brain injury

In addition to reviewing IDEA itself, a useful source of information is a data dictionary maintained online by the Free Appropriate Public Education (2008) Web site (www.ideadata.org/docs/bdatadictionary.pdf), which includes definitions of key terms in special education legislation.

The reader should be aware that the terms used in the IDEA legislation are not without controversy (Mertens & McLaughlin, 2004). For example, heterogeneity exists within all categories, such that "other health impairments" includes people with heart conditions that interfere with their educational performance as well as those with the more recently recognized disability labeled attention deficit hyperactivity disorder (ADHD).

Nonthreatening Behavioral Questions

Nonthreatening behavioral questions ask people about behaviors that are typically performed and easily talked about. The closed and open-ended format questions about children's play behavior presented earlier in this chapter exemplify this type of question. Here are a few thoughts to keep in mind:

1. Aided recall may help. This means that you might ask a general question and provide the respondent with a list of potential behaviors or put examples of the kinds of behaviors that you mean in the question.

2. Especially with behavioral questions, it might be helpful to put a time period in the question. This is called "bounded recall" and could be worded "In the last year . . ." or "In the last week . . ." It is best to avoid asking about "usual" behavior, because this is ambiguous.

3. If you want detailed information about low-salience behavior, a diary approach might be useful. For example, the major survey firms that investigate people's television watching habits have found that a daily diary is useful for people to record what they are watching.

4. Specify whose behavior you are interested in. Is it the individual, the entire household, the staff of the school, the oldest sibling, or someone else?

Sensitive Behavioral Questions

The notion of sensitive behavioral questions was introduced earlier in this chapter. Any questions that potentially elicit a defensive reaction in the respondent fit this category. For example, most people feel a bit uncomfortable talking about how much alcohol they drink (especially if they feel they drink a bit too much). The following are a few hints about asking such questions:

1. Open-ended questions are usually better than closed-ended questions on frequency of socially undesirable behaviors. Respondents tend to avoid extremes and so might choose a midlevel response to a closed-ended question in terms of frequency just to appear "not too deviant."

2. In contrast to the general rule that was presented earlier about length of questions, *longer* sensitive questions are generally better than shorter ones. It seems to give people some time to recover from their initial shock that the researcher would ask about such a topic, and they can begin to formulate their response in whatever carefully selected words they choose. Here is an example of a *long* "sensitive" question:

> We know that some kids drink alcohol and some kids don't. Some might drink alcohol a little bit and some a lot. Some might have a few drinks now and then, whereas others drink to get drunk. Some kids drink alone and others drink with their friends. Some kids drink wine or beer, and others drink the harder stuff like whiskey and gin. How about you? Have you drunk any alcohol in your life?

3. Use words that are familiar to respondents. This can be accomplished by asking respondents what words they use for certain people, things, or activities. For example, the researcher might say, "There are a lot of different ways to talk about buying illegal drugs. Some people say they 'scored,' others use other terms. What words do you use when you talk about someone buying illegal drugs?" The researcher can then use the words that are most communicative with that respondent.

4. Other ways of allowing respondents to indicate their answers can increase their honesty. For example, people may insert their answers into sealed envelopes, use a card-sorting procedure, write their responses on a confidential form, or enter their responses into a computer without the interviewer seeing what they are typing. For example, the U.S. National Survey on Drug Use and Health (NSDUH) now uses computer-assisted self-interviewing (CASI), where respondents answer most questions privately by directly entering the answers in the computer, and only a few nonthreatening questions are asked by an interviewer (NSDUH, 2005).

5. The wording of the question can suggest to the respondent that it is all right for him or her to reveal some aspect of his or her behavior that might not be socially desirable. Possible phrasing might include the following:

> "Many people have taken a drink . . ."
>
> "Such behaviors occur with different frequencies . . ."
>
> "Some doctors recommend drinking a glass of wine . . ."
>
> "Did you ever happen to . . ."
>
> "Many people complain that the tax forms are just too complicated . . ."

These phrases suggest that even if respondents have engaged in socially undesirable behavior, they are not alone and are free to focus on the frequency of their own behaviors.

6. Survey researchers who are asking about sensitive topics may find that using multiple measures will enhance the reliability and validity of their results. Again, referencing M. Smith's (1994) work on surveys of violence against women, he notes that respondents sometimes do not mention being victimized when the interviewer first broaches the subject. Rather, this information surfaces toward the end of the interview, usually in answer to another, related question. He suggested that this may happen because the respondents either remember a previously forgotten incident or have second thoughts about their initial decision not to disclose. Thus, providing them with a second or third opportunity to disclose may reveal the true extent of victimization.

Knowledge Questions

Knowledge questions are typified by those found on tests in school. These questions ask how much a person knows about a particular subject. Henry (1996) recommends using knowledge questions in surveys to understand people's knowledge and sentiments about public policies and programs. He contends that researchers could obtain information through the use of this strategy that would be useful in interpreting the meaning of respondents' expressed opinions. If the public's knowledge of social conditions and policy is limited, that affects the interpretation of their expressed opinions.

For example, the Applied Research Center at Georgia State University conducted a survey of a nationwide sample of U.S. residents to ascertain their knowledge of public issues such as the economy, health insurance, social welfare, education, and the federal budget (Henry, 1996). At the time the survey was conducted, only 21% of the public knew that the average stay on welfare was 2 to 5 years, and fewer than half of the respondents knew that more children than seniors live in poverty. The public had inaccurate information about the social conditions related to this issue and the size of the problem. As the country's elected officials struggled with welfare reform, the public was expressing opinions on this very important policy issue without much factual data.

A few suggestions for writing and using knowledge questions in surveys follow:

1. Use a knowledge question as a screen before you ask an attitude question. For example, you might ask someone if he or she approves or disapproves of the U.S. policy concerning provision of educational benefits to individuals with disabilities. The interpretation of responses should be different for those who actually know what that policy is compared with those who have an opinion about many things about which they know very little.

2. Use an appropriate level of difficulty. (Just another reminder: Know your population and its general reading level and presumed knowledge levels about various topics.)

3. When possible, reduce the level of threat of knowledge questions by asking, "Do you happen to know . . . ?" No one likes to look stupid.

4. One technique that political scientists have used is the name recognition list—just to see if people are reporting opinions about someone they really know or someone they are pretending to know. For example, a list of candidates for office could also include the researcher's spouse and brother-in-law. If people claim to know these people as well as the presidential candidates, their responses should be considered suspect.

5. Usually, mail surveys are not appropriate for knowledge questions, because the person could go look up the answer.

Attitude Questions

In attitude questions, make sure that the attitude object is clearly specified. For example, asking people's opinions about mainstreaming is not very sensible if the people don't know the meaning of the term. The researcher could probe with such comments as "Explain to me what you think the question is asking . . ." Or the respondent can be given a definition of the concept. See Box 6.7 for differences in results that can be associated with differences in the wording of a question.

Box 6.7 Impact of Different Wording of Questions on Response Results

In a national survey by *The Chronicle of Higher Education,* only 8% of Hispanic respondents strongly supported the use of racial preferences in college admissions, compared with 3% of White respondents and 24% of Black respondents (Potter, 2003b).

Yet, when asked if colleges and universities should admit students from racial minority groups even if they have lower high school grade point averages and standardized-test scores than other students, 61% of Hispanic respondents agreed, compared with 25% of White respondents, and 56% of Black respondents.

A few suggestions for writing and using attitudinal questions include the following:

1. Consider asking about the three components of attitudes—for example, affective (like vs. dislike: How does the person *feel* about this?), cognitive (knowledge: What does the person *know* about this?), and action (What is the person willing *to do* about this?).

2. Assess attitude strength (e.g., How much do you like or dislike . . . ?).

3. Avoid questions that include more than one concept (e.g., Would you vote for me and peace or my opponent and war?).

4. Generally, use bipolar questions rather than unipolar ones (e.g., Are you in favor of or opposed to . . . ? Are you satisfied or dissatisfied with . . . ?).

5. Start with the answer to the bipolar question, then move on to measure the degree of positive or negative attitude. For example,

Question 1: Are you in favor of, opposed to, or don't you care?
If in favor:
Are you strongly in favor or moderately in favor . . . ?
If opposed:
Are you strongly opposed or moderately opposed . . . ?

6. Do not use more than five points on the rating scale, unless you can give the person a visual aid with the options presented on it.

7. Ranking should be limited to no more than five alternatives and should be done only when the individual can see or remember all the alternatives.

8. More complex ratings can be achieved by employing card-sorting procedures.

Extending Your Thinking: Developing Survey Questions

Using the topic you chose for a survey research study, draft a set of questions appropriate for use in a mail survey that exemplify the following types of questions: demographic, knowledge, behavioral (sensitive *and* nonthreatening), and attitudinal.

Letter of Transmittal

A letter of transmittal can be used as a cover letter for mail surveys or as an introductory letter for a phone, Web-based, e-mail, or personal interview survey. In addition to specifying the purpose of the survey, the most important function that a letter of transmittal can serve is to give the respondent a good reason to respond to your survey.

Here are some hints related to establishing motivation for responding to a questionnaire:

1. Appeal to authority: Send the letter out under the most well-known and respected person's signature (with his or her permission, of course); make the letter "look" official.

2. Appeal to self-interest: "You are one with the experience and expertise (information, background, etc.) to be able to help us with this problem."

3. Appeal to professional interests: "This is a very important question in our profession (our society, our state, etc.)."

4. Appeal to altruism: "The results of this survey will be used to help solve one of our nation's most pressing problems."

5. Appeal to curiosity: Offer to send a copy of the results.

6. Appeal to greed: Offer to send a monetary incentive.

7. Appeal to a sense of connection with you: Enclose a tea bag and ask them to have a cup of tea with you while they jot down their thoughts; enclose a pencil to make it easier to sit down and start writing.

Other things to keep in mind when writing a transmittal letter should be to specify the time frame in which the study is taking place. If it is a mail survey, specify the date by which the form should be returned and to whom (and to which address) it should be sent. (Mail surveys should always enclose a stamped, self-addressed envelope.) If it is an introductory letter for a phone, Web-based, e-mail, or personal interview, be sure to indicate the date(s) on which the person can expect to hear from you, and then be sure that they are contacted at that time.

Whatever your intended purpose for the letter, be sure that you use professional production techniques for it. A letter signed in a different color ink is more impressive than one that appears to have a copied signature.

Extending Your Thinking: Letter of Transmittal

Prepare a cover letter that you could use as part of your mail survey.

Using your cover letter, administer your questions for the mail survey to a small sample (in your class).

Conducting the Survey

The following steps summarize the process of conducting the survey itself:

1. Be sure to send out an advance letter. (This can be the cover letter for a mail survey.) People who receive many phone calls (especially from solicitors) may choose not to talk with you without an official letter that arrives in advance of your call.
2. Enclose the questionnaire with the transmittal letter for mail surveys.
3. Supervise the data collection. Watch the calendar. If the time specified for returns was 2 weeks, be sure that you have gone through your mail a few days after the 2-week time period. If you coded your questionnaires, you can check to see who has responded during the "first wave."
4. Send a follow-up to nonrespondents. You could follow this process:
   - Send another letter and questionnaire a few days after the time limit to nonrespondents.
   - Send a second follow-up (a postcard reminder).
   - Call a select sample of nonrespondents (if it is possible to identify who did not return the survey and obtain a telephone number for them).
5. Control processing errors. Be sure to monitor questionnaires as they are returned and the data are entered. You should develop a checklist or matrix of some kind to keep track of which questionnaires come from which "wave" (i.e., the original mailing is the first wave; the first follow-up is the second wave, etc.). Be sure that you keep the returned questionnaires in some kind of organized fashion so that they are not misplaced when it is time to enter the data for analysis.
6. Enter the data into the database of your choice.
7. Clean up the data before you begin analysis.

The number of questions you ask in the telephone follow-up depends on the length of your initial questionnaire. Because the people you are contacting by telephone chose not to respond to your initial invitation to participate, it is unlikely that they would be willing to answer all of the original questions in a telephone interview. However, they might be willing to answer two or three questions, and you could then compare their responses to those of your original respondents. If you choose the items judiciously, you could determine whether nonrespondents have any pattern of difference with the respondents that could affect generalizability of the results. This approach can be used even when return rates are fairly high. It cannot be used when your sample was chosen through an organization (such as a school or clinic) in such a way that you do not have access to names and phone numbers of nonrespondents. In that case, you could do an analysis on whatever information the school or clinic might be willing to release in aggregate form about the nonrespondents (if they can be identified) or about the population as a whole.

For example, one school system allowed a survey to be conducted of parents of children with disabilities. However, they would not approve the release of the parents' names and phone numbers. Therefore, the researcher requested that the schools provide a frequency distribution of types of disability. Although this was not ideal, at least respondents could be compared against the population on this key variable.

Notes Specific to Phone Interviews

The following ideas should help you plan and conduct phone interviews:

1. It is usually a good idea to send an advance letter (unless you are using an RDD strategy, in which case you would not necessarily know the names and addresses of respondents).

2. Provide a brief explanation of your purpose, who you are, and what your expectations are.

3. Make sure that you are talking to the right person! You may find that your initial contact would prefer to refer you to someone else who would be more appropriate for your purposes.

4. Once you are sure that you are talking to the right person, make sure that this is a good time to talk. If not, schedule an appointment for a follow-up call—and be sure to return the call at the appointed time.

5. Try to keep the phone time to a short duration. (What is short? Who knows? But based on pilot testing, you should be able to give the respondent a rough estimate of the amount of time that the survey will take.)

6. On the telephone, it is sometimes best to use somewhat structured questions.

7. Establish rapport and move quickly. Be organized. Don't be shuffling papers trying to find out what to ask next.

8. Make your first questions fairly simple and nonthreatening.

9. Allow "don't know" as an option because of lack of knowledge.

10. Use an appropriate tone of voice (friendly and conversational). Sound enthusiastic, fresh, and upbeat. If you get tired, take a break. (No one wants to continue in a survey if you are asking questions with your head down on the desk from fatigue.)

11. Speak at an appropriate speed (sometimes, matching the respondents' speed will increase their comfort level).

12. Keep a log of calls made and their outcomes (e.g., busy, no answer, completed, follow-up appointment made) and date and time your notes.

13. *Before* conducting the survey, be sure to rehearse.

14. Set hour-by-hour goals (e.g., "I want to make 5, 10, or 20 phone calls each hour."). With a large telephone survey, it is easy to start feeling that you are not getting anywhere, so set your goals and you will see that you are making progress if you keep with it.

15. You can tape-record a phone call, but you must inform the respondent that you are doing so.

Couper (2005) notes that changes in telephone technologies have implications for survey research and nonresponse. In particular, many phones allow for screening calls by means of caller ID, answering machines, and voice mail. Also, mobile phones might not necessarily be kept on at all times (think of the many times you are asked to silence your phone), meaning that researchers might not necessarily reach a live person when they call. Because mobile phones are with the person while they go about many everyday activities, they may not be willing to interrupt what they are doing to answer a survey.

Extending Your Thinking: Phone Surveys

1. Take the questions generated on your topic for a survey research study by mail and transform them into a set of questions that an interviewer could ask in a phone interview. Write some brief introductory comments.

2. In groups of four, role-play a phone interview, using the questions generated by responding to the first bullet in this extending your thinking about phone surveys. One person should play the respondent and one the interviewer. The other two should act as evaluators and provide feedback concerning the following:

a. Making a statement of purpose, credentials, expectations, and anonymity
b. Asking "Is this a good time to talk?"
c. Asking highly structured questions
d. Establishing rapport
e. Using an appropriate tone of voice
f. Being assured that this is the right person to interview
g. Being enthusiastic, fresh, and upbeat

After the Interview

Allow at least twice as much time as you spent interviewing to go over the notes as soon as possible. Fill in gaps in your notes before you move on to the next task. Follow instructions on analyzing data found in Chapter 13.

Notes Specific to Web-Based Surveys

Internet access is growing. In the United States, 73% of the population have access to the net; however, in Africa the percentage is below 6% (Internet World Stats, 2008).

Those covered differ from those not covered, with the elderly, lower-educated, lower-income, and minorities less well represented online (de Leeuw, 2005, p. 236). Dillman (2007) suggests that researchers use a mixed method survey approach to address the problem of coverage—using mail and telephone surveys and personal interviews along with Web surveys.

As mentioned previously, Web-based surveys offer advantages because of their ability to accommodate such strategies as branching, editing, tailoring, and randomization, as well as avoiding interviewer effects and reducing costs (Couper, 2005). Format options are increased because of the possibility of using color and graphics, video, handwriting recognition, increased storage capacity, and touch-screen tools. In addition, recorded voices can be used to present questions and the technology can accurately record answers in formats that facilitate analysis. Also, technological advances offer the possibilities of moving from fixed-place survey administration to mobile administration via handheld devices such as Internet-capable telephones. One example is the use of portable global positioning systems (GPS), permitting the collection of location and spatial data as part of the survey process. A variety of other portable devices and add-ons to handheld computers—digital cameras (video and still), bar code readers, and so on—are further expanding the view of what constitutes survey "data."

Another concern with Web-based surveys lies in the observation that people often respond quickly to questions as they move from screen to screen (Stern, 2008).

> This quickness in answering is likely to produce errors, which, by extension, leads to changes. Additionally, the use of the mouse to answer questions on a screen involves a certain level of hand-eye coordination that could lead to errors and changes. . . . Web surveys make it much easier for respondents to check one answer then change to another in that there is no erasing involved; thus, entering and changing one's answers is not labor intensive. (Stern, 2008, p. 390)

Web-based surveys have been used successfully to investigate several sensitive topics and to engage communities that might wish to maintain confidentiality about their identities. For example, Broad and Joos (2004) and R. Harding and Peel (2007) describe how they used online surveying to maintain a safe space for members of the LGBTQ. As mentioned previously, Gerich and Lehner (2006) described how they used video-based technology to survey deaf people. The capacity to creatively design the survey may provide useful ways to adapt the survey to meet the restrictions that might be encountered in surveying a person with specific disabilities. Persons with low-incidence disabilities—blindness, severe physical disabilities, and hearing impairment—may be able to respond more effectively to the Web survey. On the other hand, the technical sophistication of the survey may prevent some from participating. Again, the mixed-mode process suggested by Dillman (2007) may be the best answer for acquiring the amount and quality of information needed to answer the research questions.

Fortunately, along with the increased trend toward self-administered, Web-based surveys, there has been an increase in the number of resources available for constructing, administering, and analyzing the surveys. All one has to do is conduct an Internet search to find resources for Web surveys. One such search in 2008 resulted in 6.6 million hits, compared to just over 10,000 hits for a similar search conducted in 2004. I recommend that the researcher consult Dillman's (2007) principles for designing and conducting Web surveys to help the researcher navigate these resources. There is a growing number of software development systems designed specifically for Web-based surveying. Examples include Perseus's Survey Solutions for the Web, which is fairly expensive but can handle quite complex survey needs, and Survey Monkey, which can be used on a limited basis for free and for a modest fee if you want to conduct a bit more complicated survey. These packages tend to offer features specific to survey research. Examples include managing the distribution of cover letters, built-in statistical analysis and reporting capabilities, and automatic tracking of people who have responded coupled with the ability to send out follow-up reminders to those who have yet to respond. They also have HTML editors that allow you to simplify and streamline the process of developing and formatting the question response fields. The American Evaluation Association maintains a link to resources related to survey software at www.eval.org/Resources/surveylinks.asp.

Data Analysis With Survey Research

Data analysis techniques in general are discussed in Chapter 13. However, a few issues related to data analysis are specific to survey research:

1. If you have conducted a follow-up of nonrespondents (which you should do!), you can do a comparison between respondents and nonrespondents.
2. You can also do comparisons between those who responded on the first wave, second wave, and so on.
3. You do need to make decisions about how to handle missing data. If someone answered some, but not all, of the questions, can his or her responses be used anyway? Be sure to instruct data entry people and the computer as to how to represent and treat missing data.
4. Sometimes it is helpful, with quantitative data particularly, to take a clean copy of the questionnaire and fill in raw numbers for frequency counts, percentages, and measures of central tendency where appropriate.
5. Look for interesting findings that suggest extremes, trends, or patterns in the data.
6. Do cross-tabulations for subgroup analyses where possible.
7. Display the data using tables and graphs.

Questions for Critically Analyzing Survey Research

1. Examine the wording of the questions. Could the way questions are worded lead to bias because they are leading?
2. Because surveys are based on self-reports, be aware that bias can result from omissions or distortions. This can occur because of a lack of sufficient information or because the questions are sensitive. Could self-report result in bias in this study?
3. Were any other response-pattern biases evident, such as question-order effects, response-order effects, acquiescence, no-opinion filter effects, or status quo alternative effects?
4. What was the response rate? Was a follow-up done with nonrespondents? How did the respondents compare with the nonrespondents?
5. Who answered the questions? Was it the person who experienced the phenomenon in question? Was it a proxy? How adequate were the proxies?
6. If interviews were used, were interviewers trained? What method was used to record the answers? Was it possible or desirable to "blind" the interviewers to an "experimental" condition?

7. How did the surveyors handle differences between themselves and respondents in terms of gender, race or ethnicity, socioeconomic status, or disability? What consideration was given to interviewer effects?

8. If the survey instrument was translated into another language, what type of translation process was used? What kind of assurance do you have that the two forms were conceptually equivalent and culturally appropriate? How was accommodation made for language differences based on country of origin, geographic region, and education level of the respondents?

9. What sampling strategy was used? Was it appropriate to reach adequate numbers of underrepresented groups (such as ethnic minorities or low-incidence disability groups)?

10. Was the survey descriptive, cross-sectional, or longitudinal? How did this design feature influence the interpretation of the results?

Extending Your Thinking: Critically Analyzing Survey Research

Find several examples of survey-based studies. Critique them using the criteria found at the end of this chapter.

Summary of Chapter 6: Survey Methods

Surveys are commonly used in educational and psychological research. The quality of a survey is tied to the effort put into design, including specification of purpose and mode of data collection. Pilot testing a survey is a critical part of ensuring quality that researchers can use to determine the quality of the questions as well as the need for modifications in the implementation of the survey. Two other critical criteria for quality in survey research include the response rate and follow-up of nonrespondents. Surveys can be administered by mail, phone, or electronic means, as well as in person. Researchers need to be aware of the implications of each type of data collection in order to enhance the quality of their results. In-person interviewing is discussed further in Chapters 8 and 9.

Notes

1. As a mother of two teenagers, I feel compelled to include a section on people in this age group because they are quite different from "children."

2. "Chicana and Chicano are cultural and political identities that were popularized during the Chicano movement of the 1960s. They are composed of multiple layers and are identities of resistance that are often consciously adopted later in life. The term *Chicana/Chicano* is gender inclusive and is used to discuss both women and men of Mexican origin and/or other Latinas/Latinos who share a similar political consciousness." (Delgado Bernal, 2002, p. 121)

"Latino is a term used in the United States to identify persons of Spanish speaking origin or descent who designate themselves as Mexican American, Chicano, Puerto Rican, Cuban, or of some other Hispanic Origin. This ethnic group is comprised of individuals from diverse racial backgrounds and diverse countries of origin, including South America, Central America, and the Caribbean." (Torres Campos, 2008, p. 2)

In This Chapter

- Possible uses for single-case research are explored.
- Characteristics of single-case research are identified that enhance experimental validity, reliability, generalizability, and social validity.
- Five design options are explained: phase change (withdrawal, reversal, ABAB), changing criterion, alternating-treatment, multiple-baseline (across people, situations, and behaviors), and factorial designs.
- Data analysis options are discussed: visual and statistical.
- Questions for critical analysis of single-case research are presented.

Washington, D.C., Chancellor Michelle A. Rhee has "dispatched a team of administrators and extra security to an Anacostia middle school where three teachers have been assaulted, a 14-year-old was charged with carrying a shotgun and students have run the hallways discharging fire extinguishers" (Turque, 2008, p. C01). Such measures might be necessary when a school is in a state of crisis; however, single-case research offers another avenue for addressing disruptive and sometimes life-threatening behaviors in schools as is exemplified in Lannie and McCurdy's (2007) study of an intervention with a teacher who was ill-prepared to deal with these types of behaviors (see Sample Study 7.1 later in this chapter).

7

Single-Case Research

Single-case research is a type of research that closely follows the logic laid out in Chapter 4 for experimental and quasi-experimental research, with the exception that you are using an *N* of 1 (i.e., you have only one person—or a small number of persons—in your study). This type of research used to be called single-subject research, but the terminology has been changed to single-case research because of what Levin (1992) calls a humanitarian spirit that discourages using the term subjects for human beings who participate in research studies. It is also important to note that single-case research differs from case study research, which is discussed in Chapter 8 on qualitative methods.

Single-case research is particularly appealing to researchers and practitioners in education and psychology because it is based on an interest in the effectiveness of an intervention for a single, particular individual. Thus, teachers in classrooms or psychologists in clinics can use this approach to conduct research in their own setting with particular students or clients who have presented them with a challenging problem. The single-case design can be used to test the effectiveness of a specific instructional strategy or a therapeutic technique on behaviors, such as learning word definitions, academic achievement, social behaviors, self-injurious behaviors, aggression, property destruction, and disruptive behaviors. The recommendations found in the President's Commission on Excellence in Special Education (U.S. Department of Education, Office of Special Education and Rehabilitation Services [OSERS], 2002) served as a significant stimulus in the special education committee to engage in single-case research studies. (See Box 7.1 for additional explanation of response to intervention in special education.)

Box 7.1 Response to Intervention in Special Education

The President's Commission on Excellence in Special Education (U.S. Department of Education, Office of Special Education and Rehabilitation Services [OSERS], 2002) recommended that diagnosis, determination of services, and program monitoring for students with learning disabilities and other high-incidence disabilities be made on the basis of "response to intervention," rather than on the basis of test scores. According to Barnett, Daly, Jones, and Lentz (2004, p. 66),

> Response to intervention builds on concepts found in the Individuals with Disabilities Education Act (IDEA) as well as the No Child Left Behind Act, which, among many science-based program components, requires that students undergo effective instruction and progress monitoring before entering special education, to provide a starting place for educational accountability. . . . Although the issues are complex and multifaceted, a key aspect of the development of any response-to-intervention model is the need for high-quality evaluation designs for decision making. The core features of single-case design may prove especially useful for evaluating interventions along a continuum of intensity that underlies response to intervention.

Hawken, Vincent, and Schumann (2008, p. 214) note that the National Association of State Directors of Special Education (Batsche et al., 2005) recently published a manual outlining the core components that should be in place to effectively implement an RtI [response to intervention] model: "These core components include (a) use of a multi-tier model of service delivery; (b) use of a problem-solving method to make decisions about appropriate levels of intervention; (c) use of evidence-based interventions; (d) student progress monitoring to inform instruction and intervention; (e) use of data to make decisions regarding student response to intervention; and (f) use of assessment for three different reasons—screening, diagnostic, and progress monitoring."

Many examples of single-case research studies from a variety of disciplines are published in journals such as *Behavior Modification, Behavior Therapy, Behaviour Research and Therapy, Exceptional Children, Journal of Applied Behavior Analysis, Journal of Behavior Therapy and Experimental Psychiatry, Journal of Learning Disabilities, Journal of Special Education,* and *Journal of the Association for Persons With Severe Handicaps.* Two examples of single-case research include the work of (a) Wood, Murdock, and Cronin (2002), who studied the effect of teaching students with chronic disciplinary problems to self-monitor their performance, and (b) Matson and LoVullo (2008) and Bock (2007), who designed single-case studies to increase the social functioning for students with Asperger syndrome, a form of high-functioning autism. An edited volume on behavior psychology in the schools provides a broader look at such topics as disciplinary practices, academic remediation, and reduction of violence in the schools (Luiselli & Diament, 2002). Morgan and Morgan (2009) authored a text that describes and illustrates single-case research methods in the behavioral and health sciences.

As in experimental research with multiple subjects, single-case researchers are concerned with ways to increase the validity, reliability, and generalizability of their findings. These and other related issues are discussed in the next section.

Quality Issues in Single-Case Research

Validity and Reliability

Kratochwill (1992) provided a comprehensive discussion of the single-case research approach that has been updated, but not substantially changed, by other scholars. Morgan and Morgan's (2009) book *Single-Case Research Methods for the Behavioral and Health Sciences* is a comprehensive guide for professionals in health and social sciences. The following section is a reflection of the work of single-case researchers that integrates the work of Kratochwill and Morgan and Morgan. Research strategies that promote improved reliability and validity of inferences from single-case research are summarized and illustrated.

- Typically, single-case research is based on observational data, such as counting the number of words spelled correctly or disruptive behaviors that occur in a specific period of time. The validity of the inferences that can be drawn is enhanced by the use of *objective data;* that is, data that can be counted with a high degree of accuracy and reliability should be used to measure the dependent variable(s). For example, Lannie and McCurdy (2007) included three dependent measures: student on-task and disruptive behaviors and teacher response statements. The researchers needed to define these variables in a way that could be counted reliably. They defined student on-task behavior as

> the student attending to the assigned work or teacher (i.e., having eyes oriented to work or teacher). On-task behavior included both active and passive forms (e.g., looking at teacher during lecture, writing answer to math worksheet). Student disruptive behavior was defined as any behavior that is not included in the on-task category such as academically unrelated verbal (e.g., call outs, talk to other students) or motoric (e.g., out-of-seat, throwing objects) behaviors. A broad category of disruptive behavior was chosen, so as to represent the host of behaviors that would typically elicit reprimands by a teacher during instruction or independent seatwork (e.g., staring around room, out-of-seat, tapping pencil, talking to a peer). . . . Teacher response rate was defined along 3 categories: (1) positive, consisting of a praise statement following a student behavior (behavior-specific praise was not required); (2) neutral, consisting of statements that do not have a positive, negative, or instructional connotation; and (3) negative, consisting of a warning or negative response to a student behavior. (p. 88)

Technological advances have contributed to the ability of researchers to count behaviors more accurately (Conroy, Stichter, Daunic, & Haydon, 2008). Use of computer-based measurement systems adds considerably to the researcher's ability to not only measure multiple behaviors, but to do so over a longer period of time without exhaustion. In addition, it increases the probability that researchers can measure sequential relations between teacher and student (or therapist and client) behaviors. Conroy et al. describe the advantages of technology-enhanced observations in this way:

> Researchers can thus examine the sequence of (a) specific teacher behaviors (e.g., OTR [Opportunities to Respond]) and (b) target student behaviors (e.g., compliance and engagement) in the presence of (c) different types of classroom-setting factors (e.g. academic tasks, large-group activities) and evaluate the outcomes of those sequences (e.g., escaping tasks or activities). With this type of sophisticated data collection, the relations among a larger number of variables can be captured with precision and accuracy. (p. 216)

• The validity of inferences from single-case research can also be enhanced by providing *repeated measurements* across all phases of the experiment—that is, not just one measurement of behavior before and after the intervention is applied (Kratochwill, 1992), The number of measurements needed in order to claim that an accurate picture of pre- and post-intervention behaviors has been captured is not determined by a simple rule. Morgan and Morgan (2009) suggest that baseline (pre-intervention) observations should be continued long enough to assure that no substantial upward or downward trend in the targeted behavior is observed. They call this a "steady state" (p. 102). They note that the length of time during this phase of a study is not unproblematic: "Among the practical concerns that researchers face in this regard is the length of time during which baseline observations should be made and, correspondingly, the amount of data that contribute to a steady state. This issue often pits the demands of scientific rigor against the ethical and practical concerns of the clinical practitioner" (p. 102). For example, in the Lannie and McCurdy (2007) study of on-task and disruptive behaviors, they completed only four observation periods in baseline that lasted for 30 minutes each. They felt that this was sufficient because there were no significant upward or downward trends in the data and because outside documentation supported the critical need for intervention (the teacher was ready to quit; the parents were asking to transfer their children out of the classroom).

• As in experimental research, greater credibility is given to studies based on *direct interventions* that are designed as part of the study rather than on ex post facto variables that are not part of the planned study (Kratochwill, 1992). Morgan and Morgan (2009) raise questions similar to those found in Chapter 4 related to sufficient description of the treatment or intervention, as well as to treatment fidelity, that is, documentation that the treatment was implemented as planned. Lechago and Carr (2008) point out that this is a critical problem and provide examples of the level of detail needed from early and intensive behavioral interventions for children with autism, such as demographics of families and their level of involvement, sequencing of curricular targets (e.g., receptive language taught before expressive language), specific treatment procedures used (e.g., prompting, error correction, reinforcement), intensity and duration of treatment (e.g., how many hours of therapy each child receives over what period of time), how many therapists are used, level of therapists' education and training, and how they are supervised. Lannie and McCurdy (2007) provide the following description of how their research team checked on the integrity of their treatment:

> The primary investigator developed scripted protocols to measure adherence to the Game procedures. The protocols listed the primary steps of the Game (e.g., post recording sheet, identify occurrences of disruptive behavior, record occurrences on sheet, determine and announce winning teams). During 29% of the sessions, the primary investigator recorded whether the teacher followed the procedures of Game implementation according to the Game integrity checklist. Across all sessions sampled, treatment integrity was assessed to be at 88%. (Lannie & McCurdy, 2007, p. 92)

• Kratochwill (1992) notes that the validity of inferences is enhanced when the target behaviors represent *problems of a long duration* and are unlikely to change without intervention. If the problems are of short duration, the behavior might change without any treatment. As Morgan and Morgan (2009) note, single-case research is most appropriate for behavior that can be continuously measured. For example, most children who cannot read on Monday do not wake up without any intervention and are able to read on Tuesday. This type of complex behavioral change occurs over a period of time and is supposed to be influenced by thoughtful interventions.

• Kratochwill (1992) states that *large and immediate impacts* should be evidenced when considering trend and level of change in the data. Morgan and Morgan (2009) take issue with Kratochwill on this point and state that this criterion may not be applicable to all single-case research studies. Some studies may be designed to elicit a large and immediate impact; however, others may involve an intervention designed to produce small, delayed but genuine improvement (e.g., increasing homework time will improve performance; however, the impact may not be large and immediate). Therefore, Morgan and Morgan (2009) suggest that consideration be given to the practical and clinical significance attached to the size and immediacy of the effects.

• The treatment should be *applied to several people* who differ on a variety of characteristics (Kratochwill, 1992; Morgan & Morgan, 2009). For example, Sansosti and Powell-Smith (2006) tested the effectiveness of using social stories to improve the social behavior of three children with Asperger syndrome. Easterbrooks and Stoner (2006) used a visual tool to improve writing as measured by number of adjectives and improvements in grammar for three deaf students.

• The procedures for the treatment should be *standardized,* formalized in written form, and monitored to ensure that they are implemented according to the plan (Kratochwill, 1992; Lechago and Carr, 2008). This is a point of contention among single-case researchers, some of whom believe that an approach known as *response-guided experimentation* is needed in some cases; that is, the experimental conditions are adjusted on the basis of the responses each person makes during the experiment. Response-guided experimentation prohibits the use of randomization, a technique required for the use of statistical analysis of data. Therefore, researchers who place greater importance on the ability of the researcher to statistically analyze the data also place greater importance on randomization than on response-guided experimentation.

• *Multiple-outcome measures* that demonstrate a similar strong effect can be used to strengthen evidence of the effectiveness of the experimental treatment (Kratochwill, 1992; Morgan & Morgan, 2009). As mentioned previously, Lannie and McCurdy (2007) measured three outcomes of their intervention. The researcher can also measure nontargeted behaviors to demonstrate a discriminative effect of the treatment.

• Generalization of effect can be demonstrated by measurement of targeted and nontargeted responses, in conjunction with a *multiple baseline* across behaviors, persons, or settings. (These design options are explained in the next section of this chapter.) Levin (1992) cautions that the researcher should look for *discriminant validity* rather than generalizability across participants, behaviors, and settings. The experimental treatment should be judged to be successful only when applied to those behaviors or situations to which they are conceptually tied. He uses as an example different types of training to address different types of deviant behaviors. For example, discipline training in a biology class should be expected to affect disruptive behavior in that class, not necessarily a student's fear of snakes. He suggests that researchers also examine *transfer-appropriate processing* in that Treatment A might be more effective in modifying Behavior X, and Treatment B more effective for Behavior Y. For example, assertive discipline strategies might be more effective in reducing disruptive behaviors, and imagery desensitization therapy might be more effective for reducing fear of snakes.

- Single-case research studies often involve more than one component in the experimental treatment (Morgan & Morgan, 2009). For example, in educational settings an experimental treatment might combine a number of instructional strategies, such as directed instruction, reinforcement, and feedback. The researcher can attempt to *dismantle the joint effects* by using reversal on each treatment component, using a series of simultaneous treatment designs or by using a series of multiple-baseline designs. None of these solutions is a perfect solution, both for theoretical and logistical reasons. It might be logistically impossible to formulate enough conditions to test the individual component effects; whatever results were achieved would depend on the exact ordering of the components as they were delivered in the various conditions, and the sum of the parts simply might not add up to the whole. Educators and psychologists design experimental treatments that they believe have integrity and for which all of the components are necessary to achieve the desired goal. If one component is removed, the experimental treatment might fail because of the lost integrity.

- *Social validation* is a criterion used to judge the quality of the research from the perspective of its social importance, the social significance of the goals, and the appropriateness of the procedures (Conroy et al., 2008). For the research to have treatment integrity and fidelity, it has to have social validity, that is, it has to be viewed by those implementing it as applicable, feasible, and useful. Social validity also increases the probability of sustainability of the intervention and its associated change in targeted behaviors. Common ways to measure social validity include asking teachers or psychologists to complete a Likert-type scale to rate the costliness, intrusiveness, usefulness, effectiveness, and/or probability of continuing the intervention (Morgan & Morgan, 2009). Although it is not specifically associated with the transformative paradigm, social validation is an important concept that fits well within that paradigm's basic philosophy if the people asked to do the ratings are those with the least power but who will be affected by the treatment. Typically, social validation procedures have included people other than the researcher, educator, or therapist in the process. Questionnaires or interviews can be used to ask whether the goal is valuable, whether the outcome is valued, whether the process is acceptable, and what the optimal levels of performance might be. Storey and Horner (1991) reviewed the special education literature regarding social validation and raised a number of methodological questions that the researcher should consider:

    - Who should do the rating for the social validity part of the research? (Options include staff, parents, experts, employers, students, clients, and people with disabilities.) How many people should be involved in the rating?
    - Should the same people be involved in rating all aspects of the social validity of the study (i.e., social importance, social significance of the goals, and appropriateness of the procedures)?
    - Should the raters be trained? If so, how and by whom?
    - Were reliability and validity established for social validation instruments?

Reliability of observations needs to be established. This can be done by having two or more observers view the same behavioral segment (often on videotape) and comparing their behavioral counts. In Lannie and McCurdy's (2007) study, the primary investigator and two graduate students served as observers. The primary investigator trained the graduate students in the observation system until they achieved proficiency in terms of inter-observer agreement. During the study, they calculated interobserver agreement (IOA) in 29% of the observations. "Percentage of agreement for student on-task and disruptive behaviors was calculated on an interval by interval basis by dividing the number of agreements by the number of agreements plus disagreements and multiplying by 100%. Mean IOA for on-task behavior was 81.4% (range = 71 to 93%) and 82.8% (range = 73 to 90%) for disruptive behavior" (p. 91).

Extending Your Thinking: Single-Case Research Problem Formulation

- Brainstorm a number of different problems that would be appropriate for single-case research.
- Choose a somewhat ambiguous concept, such as self-concept or social skills, and describe how you could operationalize it in an "objective, countable" way.

Design Options

Five basic types of design options can be used in single-case research: phase change designs (sometimes called withdrawal, reversal, or ABAB(+) designs), changing criterion designs, alternating-treatment designs, multiple-baseline designs (across people, situations, and behaviors), and factorial designs. These different types of designs are described with examples in this section.

Phase Change Designs: Withdrawal, Reversal, or ABAB(+)

Phase change designs are based on the logic that if you can establish consistency in behavior *before* an intervention (the period *prior* to the intervention is labeled Phase A), then any change in behavior after the intervention is probably due to the treatment (the treatment period is labeled Phase B). The first observation period before the intervention is applied is also called the *baseline* period. A withdrawal component can be added to the design to determine if the behavior changes in the direction of the original baseline in the absence of the treatment. (This would again be labeled Phase A.) Assuming that the researcher wishes to see the desired behavior that was elicited by the treatment continue, he or she would then reinstate the treatment. (This would be labeled Phase B.) Thus, if the researcher included these four phases in the study, the design would be called a withdrawal, reversal, or ABAB design. In some cases, researchers add a second intervention or treatment after demonstrating the effectiveness using an ABAB design, hence the depiction in the heading for this section as ABAB(+).

Lannie and McCurdy (2007) measured the number of on-task and disruptive behaviors before the intervention period to establish baseline (A = 4 sessions). Then they trained the teacher in the Good Behavior Game, which had these rules: Raise your hand and wait to be called on; keep hands, feet, and objects to self; remain in seat; follow directions the first time given. The teacher played the game with the students every day for 5 days during her 30-minute math class and the researchers counted the two target behaviors at that time. During initial baseline, student on-task behavior was stable (*M* = 53.25%) while disruptive behavior showed an increasing trend (*M* = 36.5%). During the first implementation phase (B), on-task behavior showed an increasing trend (*M* = 68%), with the exception of Session 7, and a decreasing trend for student disruptive behavior (*M* = 22.33%). During the withdrawal phase (A), change was evident for both on-task and disruptive behaviors (*M* = 47% and 43%, respectively). With the reimplementation of the game (B), some initial variability preceded an increasing trend for on-task behavior and a concomitant decreasing trend for disruptive behavior (*M* = 75.6% and 25%, respectively).

Sample Study 7.1

Summary of a Single-Case Research Study

Research Problem: Teachers sometimes find themselves overwhelmed by challenging student behaviors in their classrooms, such as being off-task or being disruptive. Lack of preparation can leave a teacher frustrated and parents demanding that their children be moved to a different classroom.

Research Question: How can a teacher use a Good Behavior Game to increase on-task behaviors and decrease disruptive behaviors?

Method: Lannie and McCurdy (2007) used a withdrawal design to test the effects of using the Good Behavior Game on decreasing disruptive behaviors and increasing on-task behaviors.

Participant: One teacher in a first-grade classroom with 22 children was used in this study.

Instruments and Procedures: The researchers first established a baseline (Phase A) of the frequency of on-task behaviors and disruptive behaviors. They then applied the intervention treatment (the game) and counted the frequency of the two dependent variables (Phase B). Following the introduction of the experimental treatment, they noted trends of increasing on-task behavior and decreasing disruptive behaviors. They then removed the experimental treatment (Phase A) and counted the number of the two variables. In the final phase, they reintroduced the experimental treatment (Phase B). Again, they observed the increase in on-task behaviors and decrease in off-task behaviors.

Results: The results of the study suggest that the game was effective in increasing student on-task behavior and reducing disruptive behavior.

Discussion: The experimenters demonstrated the effectiveness of their treatment by tracking the change in two behaviors during periods of implementation of the game. The authors acknowledge the limitation of their study because they focus only on the game and these two behaviors. They do not include any data about the nature of instructional practices in their study, although these are known to be important predictors of student behaviors.

SOURCE: Based on Lannie & McCurdy (2007).

A researcher might choose to use a simpler version of the ABAB design, such as AB, or a more complex version of the ABAB design can be used. Barnett et al. (2004) describe more complex designs such as ABC, which indicates baseline, one treatment, followed by a second treatment (e.g., B = reinforcement; C = feedback). Such flexibility in adding treatments gives researchers control in increasing the intensity of the treatment and possibly determining the minimal treatment necessary to see an effect.

The AB design is weaker in terms of inference of causality than the ABAB design; however, such a choice would be justified if it is not possible to withdraw a treatment because of ethical reasons or because a skill has been learned or an attitude changed that cannot be unlearned by removing a treatment. Under these conditions, researchers may use changing criterion designs, alternating-treatment designs, or multiple-baseline designs.

Changing Criterion Design

Sometimes researchers select behaviors for their dependent measures that are expected to improve in increments, rather than show dramatic improvement all at once (Morgan & Morgan, 2009). This is especially true for skill building such as exercising, writing, and reading. In such cases, researchers establish a criterion for improvement that is appropriate given the participant's baseline. The research will then progress through various phases so that the criterion can be adjusted based on the participant's change in performance during each phase. For example, Easterbrooks and Stoner (2006) used a changing criterion design to increase the use of adjectives by deaf students in their writing. The criterion for number of adjectives was established for each of three students for phase one based on their performance during baseline. The first phase intervention consisted of a modeled writing experience using a visual tool and list of questions in generating a paragraph response to a picture; they were then asked to complete this task independently. When each student met the established criterion with this intervention, it was increased and the second intervention was introduced (a shared writing experience with the teacher). The researchers continued to monitor behavior change and as the students achieved the set criterion, the researchers increased the criterion through five phases of intervention that ended with fading out the direct modeling and support of the teacher to encourage independent writing. The specific goals for each student were to increase one student's total number of adjectives from 14 to 21, another student's from 11 to 17, and the third student's from 8 to 12.

A second changing criterion example is Larwin and Larwin's (2008) study of how to increase physical activity and decrease use of media such as television, computers, Internet, video games, and phones by children. The single case was a 14-year old girl who enjoyed electronic entertainment but did not relish physical activity. The study was set up so she had to earn her time with electronic gadgets by walking on a treadmill that recorded distance and speed of travel. Following the baseline period, the participant was asked to walk as far as she was interested/able to walk for that session; she then stopped the treadmill and recorded the final reading of distance.

The criterion for the first phase was set at a relatively modest level: She received one hour of daily Internet time for every mile walked on the treadmill. (If she walked additional miles, she could earn extra Internet time.) During the second phase, she earned 1.5 hours on the Internet or phone usage time for 1.5 miles walked. She could increase her phone usage time by walking increments of .5 miles above the 1.5-mile criterion. If she did not walk at least 5 of 7 days in a row, she did not earn any phone or Internet time. The researchers chose the changing criterion design for physical reasons (building up to being physically active) as well motivational reasons (positive reinforcement early in the process with more being asked as she grew stronger.) They reported that the girl continued to exercise, even at a one-year follow-up.

Alternating-Treatment Designs

An alternating-treatment design involves two (or more) treatments that can be delivered in an alternating pattern, such as in the morning and afternoon, every other day, or every other week (Morgan & Morgan, 2009). This design is useful when more than one treatment comes to mind for a particular condition and the researcher wants to determine which treatment is more effective for an individual.

For example, Conroy, Asmus, Sellers, and Ladwig (2005) used an alternating-treatment design with one boy who was autistic to determine an effective intervention to decrease his stereotypic behavior, such as hand flapping. They had two treatments that both involved the use a visual cue card that alerted the boy to when it was appropriate or not appropriate to engage in such behaviors. The researchers wanted to show a decrease in stereotypic behavior when the inappropriate visual cue card was shown as compared to the appropriate condition. The inappropriate condition was 10 minutes in math class during which the teacher gave whole group instruction. The appropriate condition was 10 minutes in math class when the students engaged in seatwork. Thus the treatment conditions were alternated every 10 minutes. You can see that the difference between alternating treatments and the ABAB design is that in the alternating treatments both A and B are given throughout the experimental period. In contrast, in the ABAB design, only one treatment is applied during each phase of the experiment.

Multiple-Baseline Designs

Multiple-baseline designs involve repetition of the treatment across behaviors, people, or settings. Comparisons can then be made both between and within a data series (Kratochwill, 1992; Morgan & Morgan, 2009).

Multiple-Baseline-Across-Behaviors Design

In the multiple-baseline-across-behaviors design, the researcher chooses two different behaviors (e.g., requesting cereal and requesting milk) to target for change. A baseline is then established for both behaviors and an intervention is implemented for the first behavior. If a change is observed in that behavior, the intervention is applied to the second behavior. For example, an experimenter could implement a training program to modify a child's mode of requesting cereal at snack time. When that behavior changes in the desired direction, she could then apply the same treatment to the requesting-of-milk behavior. If the child showed an increase in the second behavior following treatment, added credibility is given to the effectiveness of the treatment. J. W. Johnson, McDonnell, Holzwarth, and Hunter (2008) conducted a multiple-baseline-across-behaviors study with three students with developmental disabilities. The behaviors included answering questions from the science curriculum, identifying sight words from the reading curriculum, and making requests using an electronic communication device. The results indicated that the instruction was effective across all three behaviors.

Multiple-Baseline-Across-People Design

In the multiple-baseline-across-people design, the researchers use one behavior and try to establish a change using the same independent variable (treatment) with more than one person. Several of the studies discussed so far in this chapter have included more than one participant in them. In addition, Sansosti and Powell-Smith (2006) used such a design for their study of improving social stories to improve social behavior for three children with Asperger syndrome. They conducted another study (2008) that combined computer-presented social stories and video models to increase the social communication skills of three similar students. They found that the treatment package was effective, although modifications were needed to allow access to social reinforcement in two cases. Only one participant was able to demonstrate generalization of the skills. Gaynor and Harris (2008) also used a multiple-baseline-across-people design in their study of interventions to address depression in adolescents. They studied four depressed adolescents who demonstrated remission following a behavioral activation intervention. For two of the four participants, increased activation appeared to have a positive effect.

Multiple-Baseline-Across-Settings Design

In the multiple-baseline-across-settings design, the researcher chooses one behavior, one independent variable, and one person and attempts to change that person's behavior in two or more situations. For example, if you have a student who is not interacting effectively in social situations, you could start by trying to modify his or her behavior in physical education class. You could focus on an operational, countable definition of effective social interaction and design an intervention for reinforcement of that behavior. Then, you would identify two settings in which you desire to see an improvement in social interaction (e.g., homeroom and physical education class). You would then establish a baseline for effective social interactions in both settings. The treatment (reinforcement) would be introduced into the first setting (e.g., homeroom), and you would count the number of effective social interactions observed for a specified period of time. After observing an improvement to the desired level in the homeroom setting, you would then apply your treatment in the physical education setting. If the student's behavior improved in both settings, this would provide evidence of the effectiveness of your independent variable. For example, Bock (2007) trained a student with Asperger syndrome in a social interaction skill that was first applied in English, then lunch, and finally in activity periods. The student was able to demonstrate increased appropriate social interactions in each of the three settings.

Randomization in Multiple-Baseline Designs

To statistically analyze the results of multiple-baseline designs, Edgington (1992) reminds researchers of the need to incorporate randomization into the design. For multiple-baseline designs, he suggests that researchers randomly choose as follows:

Multiple Baseline Design Randomization Strategy	
Across Behaviors	Randomly determine which behavior will be subjected to the treatment first
Across People	Randomly determine which person will take the earliest intervention
Across Settings	Randomly determine in which setting the treatment will be applied first

Factorial Designs

Factorial designs are not commonly used in single-case research; however, it is possible to test the effect of two (or more) independent variables within a single-case study. For example, a researcher could investigate the differential effects of reinforcement treatments by identifying the independent variables as follows:

A Type of reinforcement
  A1 Consumable
  A2 Nonconsumable

B Timing of reinforcement
  B1 Immediate
  B2 Delayed

A factorial design in a single-case study would look like this:

	Consumable Reinforcement	*Nonconsumable Reinforcement*
Immediate Reinforcement		
Delayed Reinforcement		

Multiple observations would then be made within each of the four cells created by the design.

Extending Your Thinking: Designing a Single-Case Study

- Select one research problem and
  1. Identify the independent and dependent variables.
  2. Sketch a design for a single-case research study using:
     a. A phase change design
     b. A changing criteria study
     c. An alternating-treatment design
     d. A multiple-baseline-across-behaviors design
     e. A multiple-baseline-across-people design
     f. A multiple-baseline-across-settings design

Discuss the appropriateness, advantages, and disadvantages of each design for your chosen problem. Under what circumstances would you *not* recommend the use of a reversal design? Give an example of such an instance.

- For the following example
  1. Identify the research design
  2. Critique the study using the appropriate criteria

Researchers investigated the effectiveness of high-probability requests and timeout as treatments for noncompliance that appeared to be maintained by contingent attention in two developmentally normal children. The introduction of high-probability requests increased compliance for one child but not the other. Timeout was effective with both children.

Data Analysis in Single-Case Research

Traditionally, data analysis of single-case research results has consisted of a visual display of the data in graph form and the researcher's skilled personal judgment to decide what the experiment shows. Figure 7.1 offers an example of a graphic display of data from a fictitious single-case study with an ABAB withdrawal design. Visual analysis usually depends on the viewer's sense of a trend in the data, changes in mean performance, and the shifts in the trend line at the point of intercept with the intervention. Which of these elements is selected as a standard for visually judging the results can differentially affect the researcher's conclusions.

Figure 7.1 The ABAB Design: Percentage of Ariel's Imitative Behaviors in Small Group Activity

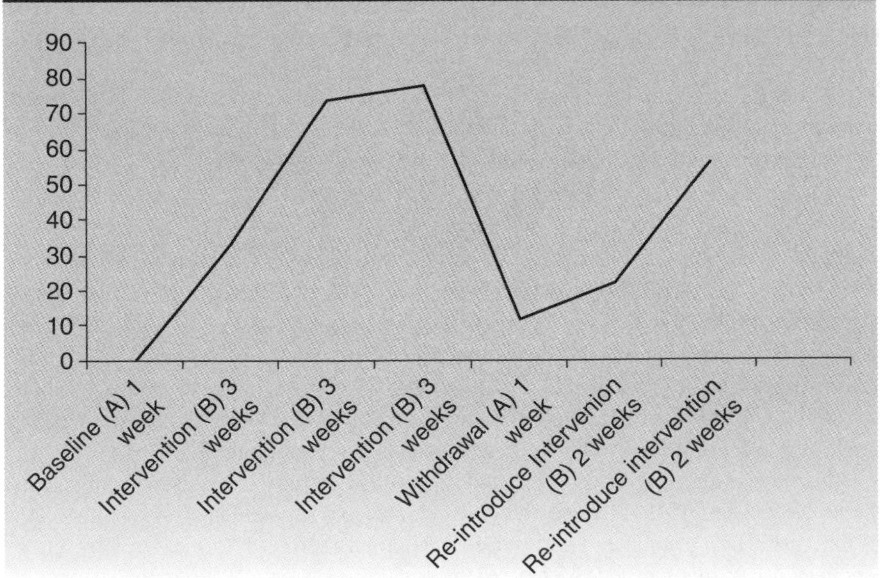

Brossart, Parker, Olson, and Mahadevan (2006, p. 536) offered the following recommendations for design and measurement in single-case studies in order to improve visual data analysis:

1. Graphs should be fully contextualized, describing a particular client, target behavior(s), time frame, and data collection instrument.

2. Judges should not be asked to predict the size or significance of a particular statistic, but rather should be asked to judge graphs according to their own criteria of practical importance, effect, or impact.

3. Judges should not be asked to make dichotomous yes/no decisions, but rather to judge degree or amount of intervention effectiveness.

4. No single statistical test should be selected as "the valid criterion"; rather, several optional statistical tests should be tentatively compared to the visual analyst's judgments.

Brossart et al. (2006) conducted a study in which they compared researchers' interpretations of visual graphs and statistical analyses for single-case designs. They noted the increase of the use of effect sizes as a statistical tool to report data in single-case studies and they wanted to explore how such statistical test results would compare with judgments of intervention analysis based on visual analysis. (See Chapter 13 for more about effect sizes.) They do note that the use of effect sizes is not a panacea in that it is possible to calculate an effect size for a simple AB design, but not for a three- or four-phase design. There is no consensus on how to analyze these more complex designs because the third phase and all subsequent phases are influenced by prior phases. Faculty and doctoral students served as judges in their study; each was given 35 graphs that depicted an intervention for a student with temper tantrums. They used a 5-point scale to indicate how convinced they were by the visual data that the treatment was effective. Interestingly, the visual portion of the ratings yielded a .89 inter-observer agreement. The researchers then calculated effect sizes for each graph and reported that they could use the effect sizes to sort the graphs according to their judged effectiveness. "However, the range of effect size values for each technique was large, suggesting that interpretational guidelines need to be specific to the technique used to calculate the effect size. Use of the effect size has a few advantages over tests of statistical significance in that it is not based on a dichotomous decision (significant or not significant) and it is not affected by sample size; however, it needs to be interpreted in light of the recent advances in the use of this statistical tool.

Brossart et al.'s (2006) study highlights a few of the complexities associated with the use of statistical analysis in single-case studies. Another problem relates to the difficulty of meeting the assumptions associated with the use of parametric assumptions (discussed in Chapter 13). In particular, parametric statistics make assumptions about the normal distribution of residual errors that cannot be met when data are time series from one individual, which results in autocorrelation because of the inherent relationship when data are taken from the same person over a period of time. Assumptions about randomization are also associated with parametric statistics (see Chapter 4). When a single case is involved, it is difficult to make claims about randomization.

Many years ago, Edgington (1992) and Busk and Marscuilo (1992) both recommended the use of statistical tests for single-case research data as a supplement to visual inspection of the data. They recommended the use of randomization tests to measures of central tendency for changes in levels of behavior and to measures of slopes for changes in trends of behavior. As mentioned in the multiple-baseline design section of this chapter, the use of randomization statistical tests requires incorporation of randomization in the design of the study. This may be possible in some circumstances; however, it may be in conflict with the response-guided principle discussed earlier in this chapter.

Hence, researchers using single-case designs tend to place emphasis on the practical and clinical implications of the change in behavior. This involves a judgment made by a clinician or teacher. Brossart et al. (2006) contend that because client improvement is the aim of most single-case research, practical significance should be based on a favorable change for the client, as judged by the clinician or teacher. If, as an educator or psychologist, you are primarily concerned with achieving a predetermined level of behavior, you make the determination of what constitutes clinical or practical success. In that case, statistical analysis is unnecessary. However, if you are interested in assessing the likelihood of a particular intervention-based outcome, statistical analysis would be appropriate.

A researcher's decision as to the use of statistical or visual analysis has implications for the type of conclusions that can be made. Recommendations for improving the impact of single-case designs are offered by Conroy et al. (2008) that include broadening applications outside typical classroom or therapy settings. Also, researchers can add relevant dimensions of diversity to their studies by examining effects within cultural contexts appropriately. Such thinking can be extended to consider replication with members of diverse groups, as well as scaling up single-case studies for possible application in "group design studies, multifaceted assessment protocols, and collaborative efforts that continue to enhance how researchers work with one another and with schools to 'go to scale'" (Conroy et al., 2008, p. 218).

As mentioned previously in Chapter 4 and in this chapter, researchers need to give attention to treatment integrity, "especially if an intervention is implemented over time with repeated measures of dependent variables, monitoring treatment integrity is critical (R. H. Horner et al., 2004, as cited in Conroy et al., 2008, p. 218). Conroy et al. point out that sufficient attention is not typically given to measuring the fidelity of the independent variable as implemented. It is possible that teachers or therapists are trained in a particular technique for the intervention and that they have good intentions of implementing the intervention as specified by the researcher. However, when they get into their classrooms or into their therapeutic settings, their intentions to implement may be overcome by other demands. Conroy et al. (2008) claim that

> treatment integrity is currently under-measured or underreported and should be a high priority and integral component of classroom-based research. As in measuring dependent variables of interest, researchers may want to consider using multiple measures. In comparison to indirect measures such as teacher reports of implementation procedures, direct observation provides a more accurate measure . . . although preferable, direct observation (including reports of interobserver agreement) is often not used because of practical considerations. Treatment fidelity measurement needs as much emphasis as do other aspects of research rigor. In sum, to describe intervention effects accurately at any stage of the scaling up process, all aspects of the independent variable, including teacher training and treatment fidelity and implementation, require accurate measurement. Researchers should use the same stringent criteria to evaluate implementation of the independent variables, including reliability measures, as they use to measure the dependent variables. It is important to measure initial skill acquisition following training, ongoing implementation, and ultimately whether the intervention is maintained. (p. 218)

Researchers can include those who do not follow through with the intervention by incorporating an intent-to-treat model in which treatment group participants are included in study outcomes regardless of how much exposure (dosage) they receive. In order to include this aspect in their study, researchers need to carefully measure the degree of exposure to the intervention, as well as other variables that might moderate or confound treatment effects.

In research in which the independent and dependent variables overlap, such as interactions between teachers and students, researchers can analyze a sequence of teacher and student behaviors. According to Conroy et al. (2008),

> The dependent variable might be teacher use of praise statements following training, for example, but once the teacher learns to use praise in response to the target student's appropriate behavior, these statements take on the role of an intervention (independent variable), and the dependent variable becomes the student's behavior. Measures of treatment integrity are thus critical in both phases. (p. 216)

Questions for Critically Analyzing Single-Case Research

1. What was (were) the dependent variable(s)? How was (were) it (they) operationally defined? Was (were) the dependent variable(s) operationally defined in terms of measures of objective data that could be counted with a high degree of accuracy and reliability?

2. How many observations were made in each phase of the experiment? Were they sufficient to establish a stable pattern of responding?

3. What was the independent variable? Was it a direct intervention specifically designed as part of the study?

4. Were the target behaviors representative of problems of long duration that were unlikely to change without direct intervention?

5. Were immediate and large effects of the interventions visible in the data following intervention? If not, was the behavior one that might justify small, delayed results?

6. Was a multiple-baseline design used, in that the treatment was applied to several behaviors, people, and settings? How diverse was the population to which the treatments were applied? Could the effect be attributable to the uniqueness of the individual in the study?

7. Were treatment procedures standardized, formalized in written form, and monitored to ensure that they were implemented according to plan? Could an argument be made that the experimental procedures needed to be modified to meet the needs of the individuals in the study (response-guided experimentation)?

8. What dependent measures were used? Were multiple dependent measures or a single dependent measure used?

9. Were targeted and nontargeted responses measured in the study? Could discriminant validity be established in that the treatment was successful in appropriate situations but not in others? Was transfer-appropriate processing evidenced?

10. If the treatment consisted of more than one component, did the researcher attempt to dismantle the joint effects? How would dismantling the joint effects affect the integrity of the intervention?

11. Was social validation established for the quality of the research from the perspective of its social importance, the social significance of the goals, and the appropriateness of the procedures? Who was involved in rating the social validity? Were the people with the least power involved in the rating? Were all the same people involved in rating all aspects of the social validity? Were the raters trained? Were reliability and validity established for social validation instruments?

12. Were the people doing the behavioral observations trained? What was the level of reliability for the various behaviors? Was the level of reliability tested within all the phases of the experiment?

13. Was a baseline for behaviors established prior to intervention? Was the baseline period sufficient to indicate a stable level of responding?

14. If a reversal design was used, was the intervention discontinued for a sufficient period of time? Was the intervention then reinstated with the same desired results?

15. Were ethical issues considered in the choice of the design? Would ethical concerns preclude the use of a reversal design?

16. Was randomization used as a part of the design? Would response-guided experimentation preclude the use of randomization in the design?

17. Were the data visually or statistically analyzed or both? What was done in visual analysis to reduce the effect of subjectivity and bias? Were the appropriate statistics used?

Extending Your Thinking: Critically Analyzing Single-Case Research

- Through a computerized literature search or by going directly to the main journals cited in this chapter, identify five research studies—one for each of the main design types. For each study, use the Questions for Critically Analyzing Single-Case Research presented at the end of this chapter to analyze its strengths and weaknesses.
- Identify three studies that investigated their social validity. Compare the methods and results of the three studies.

Summary of Chapter 7: Single-Case Research

Single-case research is designed to determine the conditions necessary to change an identified behavior of a single person (or a small number of people). This research requires that the targeted behavior be quantifiable and countable in a reliable manner. The designs for single-case research all begin with a baseline measure to determine the frequency of the behavior before intervention. Design choices include an ABAB approach in which an intervention is introduced, removed, and reintroduced to demonstrate its effectiveness. Other designs include multiple baselines in which the intervention is applied to additional persons, in different situations, and on different behaviors. These designs are intended to demonstrate that the intervention is the cause of the observed behavior changes. Analysis of single-case research is typically done with graphing the frequency of behaviors; descriptive statistics can also be used when appropriate.

In This Chapter

- Reasons for choosing qualitative methods are explored.
- Strategies for qualitative inquiry and their methodological implications are discussed, including ethnographic research, case studies, phenomenology, grounded theory, participatory research, clinical research, and focus groups.
- General methodological guidelines are presented for qualitative research.
- Criteria for critically analyzing qualitative research are provided.

Two studies summarized in Chapter 1 of this text exemplify qualitative approaches to research. In one study, the researcher noted that little is known about how teachers respond to challenges involved in engaging disaffected youth (Burnard, 2008; Sample Study 1.2). Burnard conducted a qualitative study with three music teachers to document how they used pedagogical strategies to reengage these young people. In the second study (Sample Study 1.3), Schneider et al. (2004) used a transformative qualitative approach to determine a research focus with a group of people with schizophrenia. Subsequently, they conducted a participatory qualitative study to investigate communication issues between people with schizophrenia and medical professionals.

8 Qualitative Methods

Qualitative methods are used in research that is designed to provide an in-depth description of a specific program, practice, or setting. Here is a "generic" definition of a qualitative study:

> Qualitative research is a situated activity that locates the observer in the world. It consists of a set of interpretive, material practices that make the world visible. These practices transform the world. They turn the world into a series of representations, including field notes, interviews, conversations, photographs, recordings, and memos to the self. At this level, qualitative research involves an interpretive, naturalistic approach to the world. This means that qualitative researchers study things in their natural settings, attempting to make sense of, or to interpret, phenomena in terms of the meanings people bring to them.
>
> Qualitative research involves the studied use and collection of a variety of empirical materials—case study; personal experience; introspection; life story; interview; artifacts; cultural texts and productions; observational, historical, interactional, and visual texts—that describe routine and problematic moments and meanings in individuals' lives. (Denzin & Lincoln, 2000, p. 3)

Key words associated with qualitative methods include *complexity, contextual, exploration, discovery,* and *inductive logic*. By using an inductive approach, the researcher can attempt to make sense of a situation without imposing preexisting expectations on the phenomena under study. Thus the researcher begins with specific observations and allows the categories of analysis to emerge from the data as the study progresses.

For example, Schneider et al. (2004) knew that schizophrenia is a medical condition that is characterized by social isolation, and treatment for this condition requires interaction with medical professionals. The researchers placed themselves within a participatory transformative framework because of their belief that the experts on this topic are members of the community who live the experiences being studied. Rather than make assumptions about what needed to be researched based solely on scholarly literature, the researcher from the university (Schneider) contacted a support group for people with schizophrenia and began a process of determining their interest in working with her, outlining parameters for working together, and brainstorming topics that the community members valued for research purposes. They chose the topic of communicating with medical professionals. The results indicated negative and positive experiences in communicating with medical professionals centering on diagnosis, medication, getting information about the disease, needing support, and issues of respect and dignity in treatment settings. For example, concerns about medication included being overmedicated or suffering from side effects that were debilitating. One man commented, "I feel weighted down by the medication. It's hard to move, walk, do things. It's like walking in slavery, like lifting heavy bricks all the time, weighed down by the illness" (p. 570). In the end, the group made a list of recommendations for professionals when they interact with people with schizophrenia and they developed a readers theater script based on the data collected during the study to perform for professionals and people with schizophrenia to share their results.

Basis for Selection of Qualitative Methods

Possible reasons for choosing qualitative methods are explored in this chapter: the researcher's view of the world (paradigm) and practical reasons associated with the nature of qualitative methods.

The Researcher's View of the World

Constructivist View

Guba and Lincoln (2005) note that many changes have occurred in the status of paradigms and choice of methods over the years, such that various paradigms are beginning to "interbreed." They note that their own work within the constructivist paradigm is influenced by facets of the transformative paradigm, such as action research, critical theory, participatory research, and feminist theory. While recognizing the influence of other paradigms on their work, they continue to identify themselves as social constructionists who accept the ontological assumption associated with constructivism that reality is not absolute, but is socially constructed and that multiple realities exist that are time and context dependent. Consequently, they choose to carry out studies using qualitative methods so that they can gain an understanding of the constructions held by people in that context. Lincoln and Guba identify qualitative methods as the preferred methods for researchers working in the constructivist paradigm; however, they also recognize that quantitative methods can be used within this paradigm when it is appropriate to do so.[1]

Transformative Views

People With Disabilities. As exemplified in the Schneider et al. (2004) study, transformative researchers who work with communities with disabilities place high priority on developing relationships with members of the community, building trust, and recognizing the expertise that community members have. McDuffie and Scruggs (2008) add that qualitative research is useful because of the need to individualize education for students with disabilities—hence the need for research approaches that can capture the nature of those experiences. Qualitative approaches also allow for the study of accommodations needed for individual students that are specifically developed to address that student's learning needs and how they are implemented, whether in instruction or assessment. Special educators have also championed the idea of social validity (i.e., the perceptions of participants and relevant stakeholders as well as logistical considerations that influence desire, ability, and comfort associated with implementing an intervention). "Qualitative data would also be necessary (e.g., interviews with teachers, students, and administrators; observations of classrooms) to uncover the myriad issues that might influence the social validity of the approach and, correspondingly, the degree to which it is implemented in schools" (McDuffie & Scruggs, 2008, p. 96).

Many of the criteria that establish the appropriateness of choosing qualitative methods parallel the conditions in special education. In special education, low-incidence conditions, such as deaf-blindness, cause sample sizes to be restricted or small. Students with disabilities are unique with diversity across categories of disabilities as well as within them. In special education, each student's program, by definition, is deliberately designed to be unique to satisfy that student's needs. This is reflected in the requirements of the Individuals With Disabilities Education Act (IDEA), including an individualized education plan (IEP) for school-age students; an individual family service plan (IFSP) for children, birth through 3 years old; and an individual transition plan (ITP) required for all individuals by their 16th birthday. By definition, if not by legal mandate, the programs for special education students are diverse and idiosyncratic.

Racial/Ethnic Minorities. Stanfield's (1994) reflections on how to best study the experience of African Americans and other people of color include a proposal to reject the postpositivist paradigm and the accompanying quantitative methods. Peters (2007) asserts an important role for qualitative research in uncovering the systemic presence of racism reflected in student selection and placement processes, ethnocentric curricula, and racist attitudes and discriminatory behaviors that impact school achievement.

Feminists Perspectives. Reinharz (1992) describes the diversity of viewpoints held by feminists regarding the use of qualitative methods in research. Some feminists reject postpositivism and quantitative methods as representations of patriarchal thinking that result in a separation between the scientist and the persons under study. They believe that qualitative methods are the only truly "feminist" choice because they include the use of open-ended interviewing and ethnographic data collection to focus on interpretation, allow the immersion of the researcher in the social setting, and facilitate intersubjective understanding between the researcher and the participants. Reinharz acknowledges that fieldwork is important for correcting the patriarchal bias in social science research. However, she cautions that conducting research using qualitative methods is not inherently feminist. Furthermore, she states that qualitative methods such as fieldwork are not the only research methods that feminists can use. Olesen (2005) expands on the diversity of viewpoints held by feminists who conduct qualitative research that allow for increased understanding of the complexities of women's lives and the associated power dynamics across the globe. Dodson, Piatelli, and Schmalzbauer (2007) suggest that the role of feminist qualitative research is to challenge "the myth of neutrality to seek out subordinated perspectives and to provoke critical analyses of the standing distribution of power" (p. 823).

Immigrant Groups. Dodson et al. (2007) also address concerns regarding the conduct of qualitative research with recent immigrants, undocumented workers, and wage-poor people. They acknowledge that a trusting relationship in such contexts is more likely to reveal valid information; however, the trust also implies particular attention to how researchers use the findings. Dodson reflected on her work in low-income neighborhoods: "I understood a common code that divulging accurate accounts of everyday life was generally considered foolhardy, probably a disservice to one's immediate material interests, and in some cases dangerous" (p. 827). The researchers thought they were asking neutral questions that would not pose a threat to the families such as, "With whom do you live? What child care do you use when you go to school?" (p. 827). However, these questions are fraught with danger because of rules about cohabitation in public housing, which might mean that a woman would lose her home if it were discovered that she shared her living situation with another person. Or, mothers in poverty may not make enough money to pay for child care and basic living expenses, thus putting them in a difficult position. If they reveal that they leave the children alone or with a sibling, that could result in having their children taken away from them. This also presents an ethical dilemma for the researcher with regard to child safety and reporting accurate information.

Practical Reasons (Pragmatism)

The nature of the research question itself can lead a researcher to choose qualitative methods. M. Q. Patton (2002) identifies the following types of research questions for which qualitative methods would be appropriate:

1. The focus of the research is on the process, implementation, or development of a program.

2. The program emphasizes individualized outcomes.

3. Detailed, in-depth information is needed about certain clients or programs.

4. The focus is on diversity among, idiosyncrasies of, and unique qualities exhibited by individuals.

5. The intent is to understand the program theory—that is, the staff members' (and participants') beliefs as to the nature of the problem they are addressing and how their actions will lead to desired outcomes.

M. Q. Patton (2002) describes a basis for choosing qualitative methods that is rooted in pragmatics associated with these methods, in addition to the nature of the research questions themselves. He notes that the choice of qualitative methods might be appropriate in three conditions. First, because many educational and psychological programs are based on humanistic values, the intended users of the research may prefer the type of personal contact and data that emerge from a qualitative study. Intended users should be involved in the decisions about choice of methods so that they will find the results credible and useful.

Second, qualitative methods may also be chosen when no acceptable, valid, reliable, appropriate quantitative measure is available for the desired outcomes of a program. See Box 8.1 for an example in which qualitative methods were chosen for this reason In addition, the example comes from a cross-cultural context in which similar concepts related to people with disabilities did not exist between the two cultures.

A third reason for choosing qualitative methods might be to add depth to a quantitative study. M. Q. Patton (2002) notes that the use of mixed methods can provide breadth, depth, and numerical data that can give a more complete picture of the phenomena under study. For example, in survey research, respondents commonly indicate their answers by circling a number on a Likert-type, 5-point scale. Follow-up interviews can be used to determine the meaning attached to their numerical ratings (S. Lopez & Mertens, 1993).

Box 8.1 No Standardized Measurements Exist Cross-Culturally

I served as the evaluator for a study of the impact of professional development on teaching students who were deaf, blind, or mentally retarded in Egypt. One of the interesting impacts of this study was the effect of the training on Egyptian administrators' and teachers' attitudes toward people with disabilities. At the time of the study, no standardized measures for attitude change were available that were appropriate within the Egyptian culture. Therefore, data collected from observations and interviews were used to document the kinds of language used to describe people with disabilities throughout the project. The evolution of the participants' comments regarding the use of sign language and the role of the deaf community in the education of deaf children illustrate how qualitative methods cans be used to document changes in attitude.[2]

Behavioral indicators at the beginning of the project suggested that the Egyptian participants held beliefs that sign language use was not beneficial and could even be seen as a distraction:

- The participants said: "We don't use sign language in our schools for the deaf because we know that it will interfere with the deaf child's learning to speak and use their residual hearing." This is a myth that was overturned by early research on deafness in the United States by Meadow (1967) that revealed that deaf children with deaf parents who used sign language with their children excelled in educational, social, and linguistic measures (including speaking) when compared to deaf children with hearing parents who did not sign with their parents. This finding might be seen as a surprise—deaf children of deaf parents are superior to deaf children of hearing parents—until one reflects on the role of early language acquisition for cognitive and linguistic development. The deaf children with deaf parents had access to a language in their early formative years.

- At Gallaudet University, both hearing and deaf faculty sign when they give presentations. When the Egyptian participants saw the faculty signing during the professional development sessions, they asked the faculty to stop using sign language during their presentations, because they found it "distracting."

Contrast these behavioral indicators with what was observed in the middle of the project:

- After reading research about the value of sign language and reflecting on the professional credentials of the deaf faculty who led parts of the training, some of the participants asked to be taught sign language.

(Continued)

Box 8.1 (Continued)

- They were told that they would need to learn sign language from Egyptian deaf people so that they would learn the signs appropriate for their deaf school children.

- The faculty said that they could provide training in how to teach sign language to the deaf Egyptians whom the administrators and teachers identified in their country.

By the end of the project, five deaf Egyptians had been trained how to teach sign language and had begun teaching Egyptian sign language to the teachers and administrators.

In the final evaluation, the participants commented that they had not had enough training in sign language yet and that more deaf people needed to be trained to teach sign language in their communities. Thus, Mertens et al. (1995) were able to document changes in attitudes that were manifest in changes of behavior without the use of quantitative measures.

SOURCE: Mertens et al. 1995.

Extending Your Thinking: Reasons for Using Qualitative Research

1. In your opinion, for what types of settings and problems are qualitative research methods appropriate and not appropriate?
2. What are the philosophical assumptions of the constructivist paradigm, and what are the methodological implications of those assumptions? How do they reflect the decision to use qualitative methods?

Types of Qualitative Research

Many different types of qualitative research are practiced in educational and psychological research. I chose to focus on seven strategies in this chapter:

1. Ethnographic research
2. Case study
3. Phenomenological research
4. Grounded theory
5. Participatory research
6. Clinical research
7. Focus groups

These seven approaches are included in *The SAGE Handbook of Qualitative Research* (Denzin & Lincoln, 2005) and M.Q. Patton's (2002) *Qualitative Research & Evaluation Methods,* and thus their inclusion is based on the rationale that they represent important approaches for educational and psychological qualitative research. (Two other qualitative strategies, historical and biographical/narrative, are addressed in Chapter 9.)

Ethnographic Research

Buch and Staller (2007) describe ethnography as a form of research that "asks questions about the social and cultural practices of groups of people. . . . Thus, ethnographers study the lived experiences, daily activities, and social context of everyday life from the perspectives of those beings studied to gain an understanding of their life world. Ethnographers provide holistic understandings of people's everyday lives, which means that ethnographers strive to describe and analyze systematic connections between domains of social life such as religion, economy, and kinship" (pp. 187–188). A key assumption is that by entering into firsthand interaction with people in their everyday lives, ethnographers can reach a better understanding of the beliefs, motivations, and behaviors of the people in the study than they could by using other methods (Tedlock, 2005). For example, Harry, Klingner, and Hart (2005) conducted a three-year ethnographic study of the process of school placement for African American and Hispanic students to investigate the overrepresentation of minority students in special education. They conducted this study using an ethnographic approach that examined data ranging from the broadest information available at the district level to the most specific information available on each particular student to gain insight into the quality of early instruction, the referral and psychological evaluation process, and the quality of special education placements for students of minority ethnicity.

Hammersley (2006, cited in Lillis, 2008, p. 358) identifies the following features of ethnography:

- Ethnography is concerned with the collection and analysis of empirical data drawn from "real world" contexts rather than being produced under experimental conditions created by the researcher.
- The research involves sustained engagement in a particular site.
- A key aim is for the researcher to attempt to make sense of events from the perspectives of participants.
- Data are gathered from a range of sources, but observation and/or relatively informal conversations are often key tools.
- The focus is a single setting or group of relatively small scale; or a small number of these. In life-history research, the focus may even be a single individual.
- The analysis of the data involves interpretation of the meanings and functions of human actions and mainly takes the form of verbal descriptions and explanations, with quantification and statistical analysis playing a subordinate role at most.

Atkinson and Hammersley (1994) portray traditional ethnographic work as the researcher making the decisions about what to study, how to study it, and whose voice to represent in the written ethnography with the goal of ethnographic research as the production of knowledge. In contrast to this description of traditional ethnography, several other approaches have emerged that reflect responsiveness to race, gender, sexual identity, postcolonial, and indigenous social movements including critical ethnography, feminist ethnography, autoethnography, performance ethnography, portraiture, and photo-ethnography with a goal of social change.

- *Critical ethnography* was initially rooted in Marxist theory and primarily reflected concerns about social class; however, it has more recently embraced many dimensions of diversity related to those in power and those who suffer oppression (Foley & Valenzuela, 2005). Critical race theory (CRT) is a theoretical framework that allows scholars to interrogate social, educational, and political issues by prioritizing the voices of participants and respecting the multiple roles held by scholars of color when conducting research (Chapman, 2007). Data are collected, analyzed, and interpreted through a race-based epistemological lens rather than through critical or feminist methodologies or theories that first privilege class and/or gender. CRT focuses on how people of color transcend structural barriers and create successful moments for themselves and others (Delgado & Stefancic, 2001).

- *Feminist ethnography* is characterized by focusing on women's lives, activities, and experiences, use of feminist theories and ethics to inform methods and writing styles, and uses a feminist theoretical lens to analyze power differences related to gender (Buch & Staller, 2007; Lather, 2007).

- Spry (2007) describes *autoethnography* as a mean to achieving personal transformation when the researchers place their experiences within the larger context of society by means of critical self-reflection and subverting an oppressive dominant discourse. According to L. Anderson (2006), the researcher is a very visible social actor in the written text, including his or her feelings and experiences and how they changed to vital data that contribute to understanding the social world being described. "When the focus is turned completely inward, personal essay becomes autoethnographical writing that displays multiple layers of consciousness, connecting the personal to the cultural . . . usually written in first person voice, autoethnographic texts appear in a variety of forms—short stories, poetry, fiction, novels, photographic essays, personal essays, journals, fragmented and layered writing, and social science prose" (Ellis & Bochner, 2000, p. 739). Autoethnography focuses specifically on reflexivity and self-consciousness; hence, it makes sense to use criteria for judging quality that reflect both rigor in terms of method and understandability to a lay reader.

- *Performance ethnography* (also known as ethnodrama) is yet another permutation of developments in the world of qualitative research (Leavy, 2009; Madison, 2005) that involves the development of a script and often a staged reenactment of ethnographically derived data. The power of performance combined with ethnography serves to bring the results of the study to life in a way that is engaging and informative for the purpose of raising consciousness and stimulating action. This is discussed further in the final chapter of this book in the section related to reporting research.

- *Portraiture* is a research methodology that blends the aesthetics of various art forms (music, literature, visual art) with the rigor of science to "document and illuminate the complexity and detail of a unique experience or place" (Lawrence-Lightfoot, 2005, p. 13). Portraiture captures the voices, relationships, and meaning making of participants, as individuals and community members, in one fluid vision that is constructed by researchers and participants. Moreover, in portraiture, "the person of the researcher—even when vigorously controlled—is more evident and more visible than in any other research form" (Lawrence-Lightfoot, 2005, p. 11). Portraiture and CRT allow the researcher to evoke the personal, the professional, and the political to illuminate issues of race, class, and gender in education research. The combination of CRT and portraiture is unique in that portraiture uses events and societal contexts to build a composite of an individual and group, whereas CRT uses the individual or group to highlight broader issues of society (Chapman, 2007).

- In *photoethnography,* researchers give a camera to individuals to document some aspect of their lives (C. S. Davis & Ellis, 2008). The researcher develops the photos and conducts follow-up interviews with the participants. The participants then describe what the pictures symbolize to them with a goal of working for social change. Dockett and Perry (2003, cited in Darbyshire, MacDougall, & Schiller, 2005) used photoethnography in a study of children's experiences in their school. The researchers started with focus groups, followed by asking the children to map their local social and recreational spaces and by photographing those spaces and activities. The researchers suggested that the children take pictures of what they thought a new student to the school would need to know. The children used their photos to create a book that could be shared with new children at the school. Farough (2006) conducted a photoethnographic study of White masculinities through the use of pictures taken by 26 men in their communities, followed by three photoethnographic interviews to explore ways the White men visually interpret race and gender within particular social contexts.

Case Study

McDuffie and Scruggs (2008) describe case study as an approach that involves an in-depth exploration of a single case, or example, of the phenomenon under study. A case may be based on any number of units of analysis: an individual, a group of individuals, a classroom, a school, or even an event. For example, Mastropieri et al. (2005) conducted four case studies of co-teaching that examined the experiences of four pairs of co-teachers, each consisting of a general and a special education teacher. The data were collected through extensive observations of class activities, interviews with general and special education teachers and students, field notes, videotapes of classes, and other artifacts. According to Mastropieri et al., "The purpose of this study was to thoroughly examine the co-teaching practices of these particular co-teaching cases to gain insight into the nature of co-teaching and the important and sometimes subtle ways it might vary across contexts" (p. 92). Using the aforementioned multiple data sources, these researchers provided a rich description of co-teaching, including perceived benefits and challenges as well as essential components of effective co-teaching from the perspective of participating teachers and students.

Stake (2005) recognizes the somewhat problematic situation that emerges in trying to define a case study as a unique form of research. To solve the problem, he uses the criterion that case study research is not defined by a specific methodology but by the object of study. He writes, "The more the object of study is a specific, unique, bounded system" (p. 436), the greater the rationale for calling it a case study. Case studies focus on a particular instance (object or case) and reaching an understanding within a complex context. Differences of opinion exist as to whether case study is a method or a research design. In that a variety of methods are used to collect data within case study research, I opt to discuss case studies as one option in qualitative research strategy choices.

To study a case, Stake (2005) recommends data collection of the following types of information:

- The nature of the case
- Its historical background
- The physical setting
- Other contexts, such as economic, political, legal, and aesthetic
- Other cases through which this case is recognized
- Those informants through whom the case can be known

The process of making comparisons with other cases is often left to the reader of the case study who comes to the report with preexisting knowledge of similar and different cases. Stake (2005) warns readers not to lose that which is unique about a given case in an effort to find similarities with other cases. Some people view case study methods as leading to scientific generalizations, but Stake emphasizes the intrinsic interest in each case as being important.

Yin (2009) recommends starting a case study by developing a research design (as has been the prevailing logic in this book all along). He identifies the following steps in the development of the case study design:

1. *Develop the research questions* (first discussed in Chapter 3). Yin suggests that "how" and "why" questions are especially appropriate for case study research. Youm (2007) conducted a case study in arts-based education that had the following research questions:

   a. What are the steps in developing and planning a curriculum that integrates regular classroom content with music, visual arts and media?

   b. What are the roles of the teachers in different subject areas in the development and implementation of an (arts) integrated curriculum? (p. 43)

2. *Identify the propositions (if any) for the study.* Propositions are statements akin to hypotheses that state why you think you might observe a specific behavior or relationship. All case studies may not lend themselves to the statement of propositions, especially if they are exploratory. However, Yin (2009) says the researcher should be able to state the purpose (in lieu of propositions) of the study and the criteria by which an explanation will be judged successful. Propositions help narrow the focus of the study—for example, integration of arts into the curriculum. The purpose of the Youm's (2007) study was to contribute to understanding the process involved in integrating arts-based curriculum in the first grade.

3. *Specify the unit of analysis.* Specification of the case involves the identification of the unit of analysis—for example, an exemplary student or a challenging psychotherapeutic client. Some cases can be more complex and harder to define than an individual—for example, a program, an organization, a classroom, a clinic, or a neighborhood. Researchers need to base the design on either a single case or multiple cases and establish the boundaries as clearly as possible in terms of who is included, the geographic area, and time for beginning and ending the case. Once the case has been identified, the unit of analysis can then be described within the context of the case. One unit of analysis may be selected, or several. A holistic unit of analysis might be an individual's relationship with his or her parents. Other units of analysis might be added, such as individual projects within a program or process units, such as meetings, roles, or locations. Yin (2009) labels single-unit case studies that examine the global nature of an organization or program as *holistic* designs and multiple-unit studies as *embedded* designs. Youm (2007) chose three first-grade classroom teachers and three arts team teachers in one school.

4. *Establish the logic linking the data to the propositions.* Yin (2009) suggests that researchers attempt to describe how the data will be used to illuminate the propositions. He recommends use of a type of time-series pattern-matching strategy developed by D. T. Campbell (1975) in which patterns of data are related to the theoretical propositions. Youm (2007) collected data through observations during planning meetings and classroom teaching, interviews with individual teachers, document reviews that centered on their lesson plans, and artifacts such as compact discs, books, and photographs.

5. *The criteria for interpretation of the findings should be explained.* No statistical tests are typically appropriate for use as a criterion for case study decisions. Yin (2009) suggests that researchers use judgment to identify "different patterns [that] are sufficiently contrasting" (p. 27) to compare rival propositions. Youm (2007) used a systems-based framework to analyze the processes that were necessary for the integration of regular classroom curricula with the arts by looking at the support that the teachers needed from the administration in terms of substitute teachers and planning time. He looked at the dynamics of interactions among the teachers themselves to document the types of collaboration that facilitated the integration. He then examined the effects of the integration on the students and reported, "The teachers stated that integration made connections for learning concepts and enhanced student creativity and higher-level thinking" (p. 50).

In case study research, theory development is one essential part of the design phase. Yin (2009) defines theory as an understanding (or theory) of what is being studied. As noted in Chapter 3, the literature review is an excellent source for the identification of appropriate theories to guide the case study design.

Phenomenological Research

Phenomenological research emphasizes the individual's subjective experience (Bogdan & Biklen, 2003). It seeks the individual's perceptions and meaning of a phenomenon or experience. M. Q. Patton (2002) framed the typical phenomenological research question as, "What is the meaning, structure, and essence of the lived experience of this phenomenon for this person or group of people?" (p. 104). The intent is to understand and describe an event from the point of view of the participant. The feature that distinguishes phenomenological research from other qualitative research approaches is that the subjective experience is at the center of the inquiry.

Researchers using the phenomenological approach in special education could study what the experience of being in a total-inclusion classroom is like or what the experience of being a student with a disability (or one without a disability) in an integrated classroom is like. In contrast, an ethnographic approach to special education research could include investigation of the impact of a program designed to facilitate integration of students with disabilities, studying the culture of the total-inclusion classroom, or studying interactions between children with or without disabilities. Sample Study 1.2 provides a summary of a phenomenological study of how teachers use music education to engage disaffected youth (Burnard, 2008).

Readers interested in the philosophical basis of phenomenology from a historical perspective are referred to Gubrium and Holstein (2000). The key characteristic of phenomenology is the study of the way in which members of a group or community themselves interpret the world and life around them. The researcher does not make assumptions about an objective reality that exists apart from the individual. Rather, the focus is on understanding how individuals create and understand their own life spaces.

Gubrium and Holstein (2000) identify phenomenology as the philosophical base for interpretive research strategies, such as ethnomethodology and conversational analysis, which have at their core the qualitative study of reality-constituting practices. Within this realm, the scientist's job is to discover the meaning of the world as it is experienced by the individual. In *ethnomethodology,* the analyst focuses on describing how individuals recognize, describe, explain, and account for their everyday lives. *Conversational analysis* is one example of ethnomethodological research that examines the sequential organization of topics, management of turn taking, and practices related to opening, sustaining, and closing a conversation.

Feminists have used ethnomethodological strategies to highlight the oppressing effect of language use in describing women's experiences: for example, describing families as "intact" only if they reflect the (somewhat) mythical model of father and mother married to each other and living in the same home with their children. This social construction of the family tends to convey a negative value to the many families represented by patterns other than that described. Many households are headed by single women who struggle against great odds (including those psychological stresses imposed by the socially constructed language) to raise their children in a positive manner.

Extending Your Thinking: Types of Qualitative Research

Identify the characteristics of two of the types of qualitative research: ethnography and phenomenology. How are they similar to and different from each other? Using specific research studies, give an example in your discipline of an application of each of these approaches. What are the defining characteristics that determine that these studies are ethnographic or phenomenological?

Grounded Theory

Grounded theory has a dual identity as both method of inquiry and a product of inquiry (Charmaz, 2006). Grounded theory was developed by Glaser and Strauss and can be described as "a general methodology for developing theory that is grounded in data systematically gathered and analyzed" (Strauss & Corbin, 1994, p. 273). The defining characteristic of grounded theory is that the theoretical propositions are not stated at the outset of the study. Rather, generalizations (theory) emerge out of the data themselves and not prior to data collection. Thus, the emergent theory is grounded in the current data collection and analysis efforts.

Because the initial or emerging theory is always tested against data that are systematically collected, this approach to research has been called the *constant comparative method.* It was created explicitly for the purpose of developing theory based on empirical data. On the basis of the viewpoints expressed by participants in the research, researchers accept the responsibility to interpret the data and use them as a basis for theory generation. The constant comparative method calls on the researcher to seek verification for hypotheses that emerge throughout the study (in contrast to other qualitative approaches that might see this as the role of follow-up quantitative research). They explicate the processes and techniques associated with grounded theory in their book titled *Basics of Qualitative Research* (Corbin & Strauss, 2008).

The key methodological features include the following:

1. The researcher needs to constantly interact with the data; ask questions designed to generate theory and relate concepts. Make comparisons, think about what you see, make hypotheses, and sketch out mini-frameworks to test ideas.

2. Use theoretical sampling—that is, select incidents for data collection that are guided by the emerging theory; as you ask questions of your data, you will begin collecting data that will help you fill in gaps in your theoretical formulation.

3. Use theoretical, systematic coding procedures and conceptualize how the substantive codes relate to each other as hypotheses to be integrated into a theory. Corbin and Strauss (2008) identify different types of coding decisions—open coding and axial coding—explained in Chapter 13 on data analysis.

4. Ask questions of your data that allow you to depict the complexity, variation, and nature of the relationships between variables in your study. Corbin and Strauss (2008) provide guidelines for increasing theoretical sensitivity, such as sitting with your data and asking questions—Who? When? Where? What? How? How much? Why? Also, be sensitive to red flag words such as *never, always,* and *everyone*. Provide sufficient details so the reader can see the progression in your conceptual development and induction of relationships.

Charmaz (2006) suggests that researchers using the grounded theory approach need to be aware that rigid adherence to these steps may create a false sense of confidence in the results. She recommends adopting more of a constructivist approach to grounded theory that recognizes that the categories and concepts are not inherent in the data, awaiting the researcher's discovery. Rather, the researcher creates the categories and concepts as the result of interaction with the field and the questions that are asked. The narrowing of research questions, creation of concepts and categories, and integration of the constructed theoretical framework reflect what and how the researcher thinks and does about shaping and collecting the data. Szarkowski (2002) conducted a transformative grounded theory study of the positive aspects of parenting a deaf child. She took a situation that has been described as tragic and associated with mourning—the loss of the dream of the perfect child—and studied how parents made the most of the situation. Based on interviews with parents, observations in their homes, and review of journals that the parents kept during the study, she built a theory that encompasses the challenges and resilience of parents with deaf children. She reported that parents come to cherish their child and the experience of raising a deaf child, indicating that it changed their lives for the better. Such a theoretical framework offers the potential to share resilience factors with parents who learn that their child is deaf in a way that reframes deafness from a deficit to a dimension of diversity that provides opportunity for growth in many ways.

Participatory Research

Reason and Bradbury (2006) discuss the emergence of a worldview that emphasizes participation as a core strategy in inquiry. Two approaches to participatory research differ in their fundamental assumptions of the role of the researchers and the influence of power on the researcher-participant relationships: cooperative inquiry and participatory action research (PAR).

Cooperative Participatory Research

Cooperative inquiry involves participation of all people in the research process but does not explicitly address power relations and the potential transformative effects of the research. In the context of program evaluation, Whitmore (1996) termed this *practical participatory evaluation*. In education, cooperative inquiry is closer to the concept of classroom action research, in which teachers (sometimes with help from academics) conduct research into their own practice and ways to improve it (Kemmis & McTaggart, 2005). Cho and Trent (2006) give the example of classroom research that is collaborative and undertaken by practitioners in order to make better-informed decisions about daily operations.

Cooperative inquiry is based on the importance of self-determination, and thus all people are involved in the research as co-researchers. They contribute to the decision making through generating ideas, designing and managing the project, and drawing conclusions from the experience, and *also* as co-subjects, participating in the activity being researched (Reason & Bradbury, 2006). The methodological implications of cooperative inquiry include the following:

1. Co-researchers identify a research problem and procedures that they want to work on together.

2. They implement their research procedures in everyday life and work.

3. They review and interpret the data and draw conclusions for change in practice or need for additional research.

Transformative Participatory Action Research

Transformative participatory action research (PAR) also involves members of the community in the research process in varying roles, but does so with explicit recognition of power issues and a goal of transforming society. PAR is associated with inquiries that are based on social transformation, often in developing countries. In the program evaluation context, Whitmore (1996) termed this *transformative participatory evaluation*. Kemmis and McTaggart (2005) also discuss critical action research as being similar to PAR, with mixed groups of participants, including researchers and community members. Cho and Trent (2006) discuss the importance of the theoretical constructs of race, class, and gender and power because of the desire to change the status quo of schooling or some other aspect of society in which inequality and injustice exist.

PAR emphasizes the role of the researcher as a change agent who establishes conditions for liberating dialogue with impoverished or oppressed groups and the political production of knowledge (Kemmis & McTaggart, 2005). The methodological implications arise from the need for dialogue between the more formally educated researcher and the cultural knowledge of the people. As in cooperative inquiry, the focus is on the people's participation in setting the agenda, participating in the data collection and analysis, and controlling use of the results. However, PAR emphasizes the use of methods that allow the voices of those most oppressed to be heard.

Thus, such research might take the form of community meetings and events that allow the oppressed people to tell their own stories, to reflect on their communities, and to generate ideas for change. The components of participation and dialogue can center on identification of needs, evaluation of services, or design of interventions (See Sample Study 1.3 in Chapter 1). Specific methodologies that are commonly used in PAR are discussed in the chapter on data collection. PAR can also make use of other more orthodox research methods, both quantitative and qualitative, as long as the sense making comes from the community.

Box 8.2 provides a list of questions researchers can ask themselves to determine to what extent they are doing PAR. The questions were prepared by Tanis Doe (1996) of the World Institute on Disability in Oakland, California. For additional readings on PAR, the reader is referred to Kemmis and McTaggart (2005), and Reason and Bradbury (2006). Also, Flores (2007) provides a detailed guide to involvement of youth in participatory action research.

Box 8.2 Questions Related to Participatory Action Research

1. Was the problem addressed by the research originally identified by the community who experienced the problem?
2. Was the goal of the research to fundamentally change and improve the lives of people with disabilities (or other marginalized, oppressed groups)?
3. Did the research process give power to participants?
4. Did the research participants belong to the group—usually a marginalized or oppressed population—who experience the problem being studied?
5. Will the participants experience increased consciousness, skill development, and resources?
6. Do researchers and participants share a peer relationship?
7. Can the results be used by and benefit the participants?

SOURCE: Adapted from Doe (1996).

Farough (2006) noted that photoethnography is often used in participatory action research, where individuals are given cameras to document the needs of the community. The researcher develops the photos and sets up a follow-up interview with the respondent. The participants then describe what the pictures symbolize to them. The goal of this technique is to work for social change. As mentioned previously, Farough used this approach to study a group located in the context of privilege: White men. Upon completion of an intensive interview, he asked the respondent if he would be willing to take pictures of phenomena that reminded him of race relations and/or whiteness and things that reminded him of gender relations and/or masculinity.

Clinical Research

Clinical research actually comes from the application of qualitative methods to biomedical problems (W. L. Miller & Crabtree, 2005). I include it primarily because of the close parallels between investigating the physician-patient relationship and the therapist-client relationship. Clinical research design was developed to adapt to the peculiarities of trying to understand a problem within a clinical context. Miller and Crabtree suggest that clinical qualitative research should investigate the physical, behavioral, cultural, historical, social, emotional, and spiritual ramifications of the following questions:

- What is going on with our *bodies?*
- What is happening with our *lives?*
- Who has what *power?*
- What are the complex *relationships* among our bodies, our lives, and our power? (p. 614)

Through the use of in-depth interviews and participant observation, the researcher can come to understand the multiple forces that influence the effectiveness of different types of therapy.

Clinical research methods were developed to provide an additional avenue for understanding the efficacy (or nonefficacy) of prescribed treatments based on inclusion of the variables in the patient's everyday life. Much medical research is conducted using randomized designs that try to control or eliminate extraneous effects of everyday life. However, the physician who treats patients needs to prescribe treatments that take these variables into account. Clinical research uses qualitative methods to account for the effect of such variables as having young children to care for, restrictive insurance policies, or workers' compensation laws.

Focus Groups

Focus groups can be viewed as a data collection method or as a strategy for research. I introduce here only a brief description of focus groups as a strategy for research and elaborate on them as a data collection method in Chapter 12. Focus groups, in essence, are group interviews that rely, not on a question-and-answer format of interview, but on the interaction within the group (Krueger & Casey, 2000). This reliance on interaction between participants is designed to elicit more of the participants' points of view than would be evidenced in more researcher-dominated interviewing.

Using focus groups as a research strategy would be appropriate when the researcher is interested in how individuals form a schema or perspective of a problem. The focus group interaction allows the exhibition of a struggle for understanding of how others interpret key terms and their agreement or disagreements with the issues raised. They can provide evidence of ways that differences are resolved and consensus is built.

Systematic variation across groups is the key to research design with focus groups. Examples include composing groups that vary on different dimensions:

1. Variation in terms of characteristics, such as age, ethnicity, gender, or disability
2. Using homogeneous groups versus heterogeneous groups (Warning: Hostility can result from bringing together two groups whose lifestyles do not normally lead them to discuss a topic together.)
3. Comparing responses of individuals who are brought back for more than one group (i.e., the same group meets several times together)

The determining criteria for group composition vary with the purpose of the research. In a study of court system access for deaf and hard-of-hearing people in the United States, an advisory group recommended that the most salient characteristic that needed to be used to compose the groups was the preferred mode of communication (Balch & Mertens, 1999; Mertens, 2000). Box 5.1 contains information on how the groups were constructed.

The group is considered the unit of analysis; therefore, the researcher must decide how many groups to have. This is the determinant of the degree of variability that will be possible. Krueger and Casey (2000) use four to six groups as a "rule of thumb" that is adjusted to meet specific research questions.

Madriz (2000) makes the argument that focus groups provide a potential mechanism suited to the advancement of an agenda for social justice for women because they can serve to validate women's everyday experiences of subjugation and their individual and collective survival and resistance strategies. Madriz provides many useful examples of uses of focus groups to elicit and affirm the voices of women from minority ethnic/racial groups, as well as women of lower socioeconomic status. In addition, researchers have used focus groups with deaf populations to both gather information about their understandings about HIV/AIDS, as well as a venue to share information about the disease (Crowe, 2003). Another researcher used focus groups to develop a culturally appropriate survey for deaf people in Brazil about HIV/AIDS (Bisol, Sperb, & Moreno-Black, 2008).

Extending Your Thinking: Different Approaches in Qualitative Research

1. Brainstorm ideas for a qualitative research study. Choose one idea and briefly explain how you could use each of the qualitative strategies to investigate that topic:
   a. Ethnographic research
   b. Case study
   c. Phenomenological research
   d. Grounded theory
   e. Participatory research
   f. Clinical research
   g. Focus groups
2. Which of these strategies do you think would be most appropriate for your research topic? Why?
3. Identify one research study for each qualitative research strategy listed in Question 1. Explain your basis for categorizing each study. For each study, do the following:
   a. Identify the research problem.
   b. Identify the unit of analysis.
   c. Describe the data collection methods that were used.
   d. Identify the organizing framework for the findings.
   e. Summarize the main findings.
   f. Use the questions for critical analysis at the end of this chapter to critically analyze each study.

Data Collection

Typically, qualitative researchers use three main methods for collecting data: participant observation, interviews, and document and records review. Interviewing is discussed in this chapter; the other methods are discussed in Chapter 12 on data collection. I list them here to provide context for my remarks about methodological guidelines.

Personal Interviews

Personal interviews are often associated with qualitative research. The following ideas can guide you through the planning and conducting of personal interviews.

Preparing for the Interview

1. Hold an introductory meeting to share the purpose, discuss confidentiality issues, and get assurance that the person does want to participate. Then, schedule the interview at the respondent's convenience.

2. Learn the local language. This is a reiteration of the advice given in the section on sensitive questions in Chapter 6; that is, the researcher should use terms familiar to the respondent: "What name do you use for . . . (your school, your parents, your group of friends, your educational program, etc.)?"

3. Make an interview schedule as best you can at the beginning of the study. This may include names, positions, or characteristics of the individuals you think you should interview. If it is important to talk with some people before others, this should be reflected in the schedule. How many people is it reasonable to interview in a day? That will depend on the nature of your survey, but bear in mind that this is hard work and you do need time to process what was said to you.

4. Make an interview guide. This can be very general (these are the types of issues that I think I should ask about) to very specific (I want to be sure I ask all these questions of everyone). Often, personal interviews raise issues that you had not previously considered and want to follow up with additional participants. So stay flexible as far as the interview guide goes.

5. Don't structure the interview guide around yes-or-no questions. This would defeat the purpose of having the person there to converse with. Plan to ask open-ended questions:

"How do you feel about the program?"

"What is your opinion about the program?"

"What do you think about the program?"

"What is your role here?"

"What are you trying to do in this program?"

6. Definitely pretest your interview procedures.

7. Plan to conclude with open-ended questions: for example, "Is there anything that I didn't ask about that you think I should know?" "What didn't I ask about that I should have?" or "Is there anything else that you wanted to tell me that hasn't come up so far?"

8. If you are training interviewers, do the following:
    - First, have the interviewers study the interview guide and learn about the interviewing conditions and logistics.
    - Second, have the interviewers practice interviews and receive feedback until performance reaches a desired level. (Videotaping can help with this.)

Starting and Conducting the Interview

1. Start by establishing rapport: Briefly review the purpose of the interview, your credentials, and the information needed. Provide assurances of confidentiality.

2. Focus your attention on what the person is saying. Use your "extra mind" time to evaluate what they are saying. This would allow you to formulate more than one possible hypothesis about what is happening. Test your various hypotheses. Ask for clarification: for example, "You mentioned several things. Let me be sure I have this straight . . ."

3. Sequence the questions from general to specific. People need time to think about a question. Summarize what you have heard, then ask for specifics.

4. When asking for criticisms of a program, be sure to use a constructive framework to structure the questions: for example, "Are there any special factors about this problem that I should understand?"

5. Put answers in perspective: Ask for specific examples. Ask what opinions others might hold: for example, "How do administrators and teachers see this issue? The same way? Or differently?" Ask for definitions for words that a respondent might use, such as *impact, urgent, critical,* and *blunders*. Be wary of generalizations (e.g., "the problem is staff incompetence"), convoluted answers, or answers that fit preconceived notions too well. If respondents say that they want to talk "off the record," then put your pencil down and listen to what they have to say. Be sure to get their permission to continue taking notes when they are ready to go back "on the record."

6. A variety of different kinds of questions can be asked in interviews. (This is a slightly different conceptualization than that presented previously in the discussion of demographic, behavioral, knowledge, and attitude questions.) An interviewer might ask about these things:

Experiences or Behaviors: It is possible to elicit descriptions of experiences by asking questions such as the following:

"What do you do?"

"If I were in this program, what kinds of things would I be doing?"

"Imagine that I am a new participant in this program, what kind of advice would you give me to help me get adjusted?"

"Imagine that I'm a new kid here. I just arrived today. What would you tell me so that I would know what to do and expect?"

Opinion or Value Questions:

"What do you believe is the problem here?"

"What do you think are the strengths of this approach?"

"What do you think about that?"

"What would you like to see happen?"

"What is your opinion about that?"

Feeling Questions:

"How do you feel about that?"

"How would you describe your feelings? Happy, anxious, afraid, intimidated, confident . . . ?"

Knowledge Questions:

"What services are available?"

"Who is eligible?"

"What are the characteristics of the clients?"

Sensory Questions:

"What do you see? hear? touch? taste? smell?"

"What is said to you?"

Background Questions:

"In what field are you trained/educated?"

"What positions did you hold prior to this one?"

"How long have you been in this program?"

Ask only one question at a time.

Avoid asking "why" questions. Some people view these as sensitive. To avoid a possible defensive reaction, try wording the questions in one of these ways:

"What was it that attracted you to the program?"

"What other people played a role in your choice to participate?"

Try using role play or simulation questions: for example, "Suppose I was a student in your classroom, what kinds of activities would I be involved in to learn to read?"

Avoid disagreements, sarcasm, playing "Can you top this?," and correcting facts and dates. Admit an error if you make one.

Record the interview if possible and always take notes even when recording the interview in case of a technological failure with the equipment.

Concluding the Interview

1. Ease into the conclusion by summarizing what you have just heard.
2. Explain what you plan to do with the data.
3. Thank the person for participating.
4. Probe gently ("Did I miss anything?").
5. Follow up with a phone call or letter thanking the person again and clarifying any confusion.

Extending Your Thinking: Face-to-Face Interviews

1. Take the questions generated for a phone interview in Chapter 6 and transform them into a set of questions (or into an interview guide) that an interviewer could ask in a face-to-face interview. Write some brief introductory comments.

2. In groups of four, role play a face-to-face interview, using the questions generated for the previous activity. One person should play the respondent and one the interviewer. The other two should act as evaluators and provide feedback concerning the following:

   a. Making a statement of purpose, credentials, expectations, and anonymity
   b. Using open-ended questions
   c. Using probes on unclear responses
   d. Asking only one question at a time
   e. Avoiding "why" questions
   f. Avoiding disagreements

Transformative Perspectives on Interviewing

Feminists have explored a wide range of methodological issues related to interviewing as a data collection method in research. What feminist researchers have in common in their consideration of social science methods is a strong concern with reflexivity, research relationships, and the protection of the researched (Sampson, Bloor, & Fincham, 2008). This emphasis on reflexivity, on the consideration of power within research relationships, and on the potential for researchers to harm participants, is not exclusive to feminist researchers, but it has been emphasized and brought to the fore in their writing. Based on the early writings of Reinharz (1992) and more recently by Naples (2003), feminists raise the following issues:

- Desirability of repeat interviews with the same respondent
- Number, sequencing, and type (closed, open, or both) of questions
- Ability of the interviewee to question the interviewer
- Standardization of the process or questions
- The location of the interview
- The method of recording the data
- Conducting the interview yourself or using trained interviewers
- Doing face-to-face or phone interviews
- Determining who will be present during the interview
- Doing interviews individually or in a group
- Whether or not the interviewer and interviewee know each other in advance
- Having the interviewee read the interview transcript and interpretation and modify the data and interpretations in the study

Feminists have reported that multiple, in-depth interviews build bonds and provide an opportunity to share transcripts and interpretations. The goal of multiple interviews is to increase the accuracy of the results.

Who Can Interview Whom?

Is it necessary for women to interview women? For deaf people to interview deaf people? For African Americans to interview African Americans (Mertens, 2009)? These are not simple questions, nor do they have simple answers. Researchers struggle with the tensions created by the need to have interviewers who understand the cultural experiences of their respondents and potentially contributing to further marginalization associated with taking a position that only members of a group can interview each other. This is sometimes seen as an insider-outsider issue. Bassett et al. (2008) make the argument for insider status as follows:

> With richer knowledge of their own group, an interviewer's lived experience of the culture means categories and behaviors that apply to one group are not used to understand another group. Any member of a "minority group" experiences not only their own culture but also that of the dominant group since they must live seamlessly in both cultures. This may afford minority group members a dual understanding, allowing them to see the positive and negative aspects of membership in both minority and dominant groups (Caldwell, Guthrie, & Jackson, 2006). The advantage when interviewing minority group members is that both types of cultural values can be understood when they are invoked by participants. (p. 129)

A contrasting view is presented by anthropologists, who provide some insights into benefits of having "outsiders" conduct interviews:

> As one of the founding feminist anthropologists I never objected to men studying women or women studying men. Indeed, my resistance to the concept of male

> dominance in the early 1970s (Sanday, 1981) was based on the conviction that because men did not study women they were blind to local realities, which made it easy to project ethnocentric ideas about power and dominance. (Sanday, 2008, p. 207)

> I consistently bring to the discussion an understanding of gender as a relation of dominance and subordination. Accordingly, I believe that interrogation of how *gender privilege* influences male anthropologists' work is the key to productive anthropological research by men, *qua* men, about women. (Hackett, 2008, p. 211)

Foster (1993a, 1993b) reflected on her own position as a hearing person conducting research in the deaf community. She contends that she does not have to be deaf to conduct research in deafness because what is important is a willingness to enter into meaningful dialogue with deaf people and to place control of the research agenda in their hands. She suggested several strategies that she used to improve the quality of her work: (a) choosing qualitative methods, (b) seeking advice from an advisory group with deaf representatives, (c) having her work reviewed by deaf colleagues, (d) conducting research in collaboration with deaf researchers, (e) using an interpreter who is fluent in the many varieties of sign language (e.g., American Sign Language, Total Communication, Signed English), and (f) acknowledging that we are all multi-positional. Thus, although she might not share the characteristic of deafness with her respondents, commonalities can be found on other grounds, such as both being women, mothers, and so on.

The concept of cultural competence brings added insight into the insider-outsider complexity. Gentlewarrior et al. (2008) conducted a study to determine the views of cultural complexity from the perspectives of members of marginalized groups. Their respondents described the following strategies as means to meet their needs: "to recognize the diversity within diverse groups, experience diverse communities and relationships, become trained in cross-cultural knowledge, be aware and respectful of beliefs that differ from our own, and listen to diverse people for information to help us understand both their problems and possible solutions" (p. 220).

Should the Interviewer and Interviewee Be Friends or Strangers?

Somewhat related to the insider-outsider dilemma, researchers have also concerned themselves with the issue of the status of interviewer as friend or stranger. Many ethical review boards want to know if the researcher has a relationship with the participants, and if so, what the nature of that relationship is. Reinharz (1992) suggests that if the interviewer and interviewee were friends prior to the interview, the interviewee may feel greater rapport and be more willing to disclose information. However, there could be a feeling of greater safety with a stranger in that the respondent can say what he or she thinks and not see the interviewer again.

For many participants taking part in research on sensitive topics, it is the first time that they have told someone their story, and this can raise difficulties not only for them, but also for the researcher who is listening to the story. This sharing of hidden or unexplored aspects of people's lives can change the expectations of the participants. The fact that qualitative research often requires supportive listening may make researchers ultimately more vulnerable to crossing the boundaries from research into friendship (Dickson-Swift, James, Kippen, & Liamputtong, 2007).

This characterization of researcher-as-friend is contentious. Fowler (2008) recommends a role as a standardized interviewer because he values trying to "neutralize" the effect of the interviewer so that differences in answers can be attributed to differences in the respondents themselves. Fowler argues that if interviewers ask each question in the same way for each respondent, biasing effects of the interviewer will be avoided. However, in qualitative research, the goal is to explore the unexpected and follow the lead of the interviewee, so this type of standardization is not seen as desirable in qualitative research.

Reciprocity

The issue of reciprocity is related to the role of the researcher in terms of feeling that they want to give something back to the participant during the interview process. Sampson et al. (2008) describe this tension as follows:

> Researchers spoke of a desire not to exploit the people they researched; they expressed an acute awareness of the power relationships pervading research settings; they sought to limit harm to participants and often to offer something in "return" for research participation in the form of emotional support, or the conduct of a personal service. Such sensitivities and the emotional investment and pain associated with them link strongly to the discourse of feminist research methods. (p. 928)

Feminists have written about ways to structure interviews to try to raise the consciousness of the interviewee who is experiencing abuse or some other form of trauma. For example, L. Kelly et al. (1994) said that when women were blaming themselves for abuse, the interviewers tried to help them explore their reasoning in more depth and to link this to the intention and behavior of the perpetrator, thereby opening up different ways of understanding. They concluded as follows:

> If we accept that conducting and participating in research is an interactive process, what participants get or take from it should concern us. Whilst we are not claiming that researchers have the "power" to change individuals' attitudes, behavior, or perceptions, we do have the power to construct research which involves questioning dominant/oppressive discourses; this can occur within the process of "doing" research, and need not be limited to the analysis and writing up stages. (pp. 39–40)

How self-disclosive should the interviewer be? How much information should an interviewer share about himself or herself during the interview? Reinharz (1992) recognizes a tension between engaging in a true dialogue with the respondent and possibly biasing responses by triggering "expected" responses. She recommended that interviewers be sensitive to possibly biasing the interviewee by the information that they choose to disclose about themselves.

Extending Your Thinking: Interviewing in Qualitative Research

1. What is your opinion about the following:
   a. Standardizing the interview process
   b. The duration of interviews
   c. The desirability of repeat interviews with the same respondent

(Continued)

(Continued)

d. Number, sequencing, and type (closed-ended, open-ended, both) questions
e. Interviewees questioning the interviewer
f. Standardizing the process or questions
g. Where the interview takes place
h. How the interview is recorded
i. Doing the interviewing yourself or having an assistant do it
j. Face-to-face or phone interviews
k. Who is present during the interview
l. Doing the interviewing individually or in a group
m. The interviewer and interviewee knowing each other in advance
n. The interviewee reading the interview transcript (and interpretation) and modifying the data and interpretations in the study

2. Who can interview whom?
   a. Can women interview men? Can men interview women? Can women interview other women? Can men interview other men?
   b. Can White people interview racial/ethnic minorities? Can racial/ethnic minorities interview White people?
   c. Can people with disabilities interview people without disabilities? Can people without disabilities interview people with disabilities?
3. How do you address the following?
   a. Dominant groups using negative labels for nondominant group experiences
   b. Connection and empathy
   c. Interviewee-guided interviews
   d. Putting the interviewee at ease
   e. Doing reliability checks

General Methodological Guidelines

Because there is no one correct method for conducting qualitative research, Bogdan and Biklen (2003) recommend that researchers describe their methodology in detail. There are multiple ways to structure and conduct a qualitative research study. Therefore, I discuss the process of designing and conducting such a study in terms of typical actions that occur in qualitative research and decisions that need to occur. This should not be interpreted as a lockstep approach to qualitative research. In a qualitative research proposal, the researcher needs to present a plan that includes a description of methods yet makes clear that changes will occur as the study progresses. The reader who intends to conduct a qualitative research study is referred to other texts that explore this topic in more depth (Bogdan & Biklen, 2003; Charmaz, 2006; Denzin & Lincoln, 2005; M. Q. Patton, 2002; Yin, 2009).

The Researcher Is the Instrument

Unlike a printed questionnaire or test that might be used in a quantitative study, in a qualitative study the researcher is the instrument for collecting data. The qualitative researcher decides which questions to ask and in what order, what to observe, what to write down. Therefore, considerable interest has been focused on who the researcher is and what values, assumptions, beliefs, or biases he or she brings to the study. In general, qualitative research texts recognize the importance of researchers' reflecting on their own values, assumptions, beliefs, and biases and monitoring those as they progress through the study (perhaps through journaling or peer debriefing) to determine their impact on the study's data and interpretations.

In transformative research in particular, the issue has been raised as to the ability of men to study women, members of a dominant ethnic group to study minority ethnic groups, or people without disabilities to study persons with disabilities. This issue was touched on in Chapter 6 (on survey research) under the topic of interviewing people who are similar to or different from yourself. In this context, the issue is more broadly addressed. What can a person who is not a member of the group do to try to enhance the validity of the information collected from that group, especially if the researcher represents a dominant group? Some researchers choose to do volunteer work in the community to build rapport and increase their understandings before they conduct their research. For example, M. L. Anderson (1993) is a White woman who wanted to conduct a study of race relations in a community that was racially divided with a history of paternalism. She spent many hours doing volunteer work at the senior center. She also did not pose herself as an "expert" on their lives. Rather, she presented herself as someone who was interested in learning about their lives. Foster (1993b)—a hearing researcher—also reported assuming this stance in conducting ethnographic work with deaf people.

M. L. Anderson (1993) reports sharing information about herself and her own feelings with the women. She describes her experiences as follows:

> In my project, despite my trepidations about crossing class, race, and age lines, I was surprised by the openness and hospitality with which I was greeted. I am convinced that the sincerity of these women's stories emanated not only from their dignity and honor, but also from my willingness to express how I felt, to share my own race and gender experiences, and to deconstruct the role of expert as I proceeded through this research. (p. 50)

She was an active volunteer in the senior center that these women regularly attended. Her participation in the everyday activities of the women's culture, both in the center and in their homes, resulted in conversations that were filled with emotional details of their lives.

Speaking for the Other

Going beyond the question of whether or not a member of a dominant group can legitimately study the experiences of an oppressed group lays the ethical issue of who can speak for another. The problem inherent in the role of the researcher speaking for the other was captured by bell hooks (1990, quoted by M. Fine, 1994, p. 70) in the following passage that depicts a hypothetical conversation between a researcher and a participant:

> No need to hear your voice when I can talk about you better than you can speak about yourself. No need to hear your voice. Only tell about your pain. I want to know your story. And then I will tell it back to you in a new way. Tell it back to

> you in such a way that it has become mine, my own. Re-writing you, I write myself anew. I am still author, authority. I am still the colonizer, the speak subject, and you now at the center of my talk.

M. Fine, Weis, Weseen, and Wong (2000) warn that researchers can unwittingly or deliberately contribute to the continuation of oppression by presuming to speak for the groups in our research. Through collaborative construction of text, researchers can enable resistance to continued oppression. This topic is explored further in Chapter 13 in the section on writing research reports.

Focus on an Area of Inquiry

As discussed in Chapter 3, the qualitative researcher starts with a literature review that leads to the formulation of research questions. The important caveat, repeated here, is that the area of inquiry, as defined by the initial literature review and the research questions, should be viewed as tentative and evolving. The researcher must be open to a change of focus if that is dictated by the data emerging from the field experience.

Explore Research Sites

You can use information gathered from preliminary visits to potential research sites to convince a funding agency or a research committee that you are capable of conducting a qualitative study and to determine the site's accessibility and suitability (Bogdan & Biklen, 2003). During your visits, you can conduct pilot work (with permission of the gatekeepers at the site) that will allow you to suggest possible activities, locations, and people (possibly defined in terms of positions within the organization) that you want to include in your study. Because of the ontological assumption of multiple realities, be sure to include in your list of people those with diverse viewpoints about the phenomenon of interest. Sampling procedures are discussed in Chapter 11. The researcher should be aware that data provided by participants may vary based on the place, activity engaged in, or social variables at the time of the data collection (M. Q. Patton, 2002). The researcher should provide a description of the setting, research site, and the conditions operating at the time the data were gathered and report exactly how the participants were selected along with their characteristics.

Your initial pilot work may also give you an idea about the length of time needed to complete your study, in addition to the number of site visits that you will need to make. In some ethnographic texts, the length of a study is recommended to be between 6 months and 1 year; however, the time frame will be dictated by a number of factors. In some cases, the length of the program may be limited to a few months, and thus the length of the study may correspond to the length of the program. In other cases, a funding agency will impose a limit of the amount of funds available and thus constrain the amount of time that the study can continue. The one guiding principle in the decision should be that the researcher avoids premature closure—that is, reaching inaccurate conclusions based on insufficient observations.

Gaining Permission

Before data are collected, the researcher must follow appropriate procedures to gain permission from the gatekeepers (typically defined as those with power in the organization or agency) of the organization or community. In organizational settings, such as schools, clinics, or community agencies, formal procedures are established that define how permission is to be obtained. Issues surrounding such procedures are discussed further in Chapter 11, on sampling; however, the researcher should contact the organization or agency to determine their specific procedures.

The notion of entry into a setting by means of access granted by gatekeepers is problematic for researchers who work from a transformative perspective. Recall Sandra Harding's (1993) direction to start your research from marginalized lives and the key questions raised in the section of this chapter on PAR. The focus is on addressing problems that were originally identified by the community that experiences the problem (Doe, 1996). Thus, researchers operating within the transformative paradigm must consider strategies for entry into the community with respect to those who have the least power.

Dickson-Swift et al. (2007) reported the words of one of their participants who reflected on the responsibility:

> It is so much more than just signing a form to say that they are willing to offer you information, they are actually allowing you into their lives, they are telling you personal information that might be quite hard, so you need to demonstrate a certain degree of discretion, of respect, of appreciation for what they are doing 'cause the reality is that it is more than just words, it's more than just what you are going to analyze, it's their life, their experience and you need to make sure that you are aware of that. (p. 330)

Negotiating Entry

J. M. Morse (1994) provides practical advice for negotiating entry into sites for research. She suggests that the researcher visit a number of sites and "tentatively sound out administrators to determine if the proposed project would be welcomed and if researchers would be tolerated on site" (p. 222). She warned that administrators might be wary of research that was aimed at evaluating their personnel or institution or that might reflect badly on their organization. Administrators usually look for some assurances about the amount of control they will have over the research process and the use of the findings. The researcher needs to consider the nature of assurances that can be made without compromising the integrity of the research. The researcher also needs to learn about and adhere to the organization's review process in terms of protection of human beings and identification of costs to the organization. Talking with other researchers who have conducted research in similar settings can be quite helpful.

Entering the Field

The researcher needs to make plans to enter the field in the least disruptive manner possible, taking care to establish good rapport with the participants. As mentioned previously, this can be facilitated by accommodating yourself to the routines of the informants, establishing what you have in common, helping people out, displaying an interest in them, and acting like a person who belongs (and *being yourself*).

Warren (1988) identifies a number of variables that influence the researcher's entry into the field:

> The fieldworker's initial reception by the host society is a reflection of cultural contextualization of the fieldworker's characteristics, which include marital status, age, physical appearance, presence and number of children, and ethnic, racial, class, or national differences as well as gender. (p. 13)

Although Warren speaks primarily within the context of conducting research in other countries, all contexts have their own cultural norms and expectations based on various biological and socially defined characteristics of the people in them. The researcher should be sensitive to what these norms are and how they might affect the research work.

Role of the Researcher

In M. L. Anderson's (1993) examination of the role of the researcher within the context of being a White woman studying the experiences of African American women, she suggests that White researchers doing research on race and ethnicity "should examine self-consciously the influence of institutional racism and the way it shapes the formulation and development of their research, rather than assume a color-blind stance" (p. 43). Thus, she rejects the "unbiased, objective" scientific research stance in favor of one that recognizes the influences of the researcher's own status (e.g., race, gender, etc.) on the shaping of knowledge. This requires that researchers build more inclusive ways to discover the multiple views of their participants and adopt more personally interactive roles with them. Whereas M. L. Anderson (1993) addresses issues related to a member of the dominant culture studying other adults who have less power, how the researcher positions her/himself and how the researcher adopts a definition of being "an adult" has a major impact on the research context and the involvement of children (Dickson-Swift et al., 2007). Christensen (2004) described the importance of negotiating a position that recognizes researchers as adults, albeit an unusual type of adult, one who is seriously interested in understanding how the social world looks from children's perspectives but without making a dubious attempt to be a child. Through this the researcher emerges first and foremost as a social person and secondly as a professional with a distinctive and genuine purpose.

G. Fine and Sandstrom (1988) discuss the following issues in regard to developing the friend role when conducting research with children. First, researchers must provide the children with their reasons for being there. The researchers can be explicit and explain the complete and detailed purposes and hypotheses for the research. This could bias the research in that the kids may act in a way that could deliberately try to confirm or deny the researcher's hypotheses. The researchers could try for a "shallow cover"; that is, admitting that they are doing research on children's behaviors but not providing details. The problem with this role is that the children will develop their own ideas as to what the researcher is studying, and they may feel betrayed when they find out what the "real" reasons were. A third option would be to maintain "deep cover"; that is, not to tell the children that they are being observed. However, the researcher runs the risk of arousing suspicion and creating bad feelings after being "discovered."

A second issue related to the role of the researcher as friend is associated with the settings in which an adult would be viewed comfortably as a friend. For example, kids may feel comfortable with an adult present during many of their behaviors, but not at a party where sexual behaviors could be observed.

A third issue in the researcher's role as friend is that of giving gifts or rewards. As a friend, the researcher might give companionship, praise, help with schoolwork, food, monetary loans, rides to activities, or movie tickets. G. Fine and Sandstrom (1988) warn researchers to be wary about using such gifts to manipulate their respondents or to allow the children to manipulate them by excessive demands for rewards (or loans and the like).

The age of the child is important in deciding which role to adopt. With very young children (preschoolers), the researcher could choose to act childlike or to just hang around and wait for gradual acceptance. The childlike behavior may thrill the children but "turn off" supervisors. With older children (preadolescent), the researcher could choose to assume the role of older sibling (big brother, big sister), student, journalist, or protector. With adolescents, the researchers can treat the children as people that they sincerely wish to get to know.

Warren (1988) discusses the role of the researcher as it has emerged in sociological and anthropological research. She notes that many times the role of the researcher is assigned by the respondents in terms of what they see as his or her proper place in the social order. Young, unmarried women are often assigned the role of adoptive daughter or child (i.e., one who has to learn from the older community members). Reinharz (1992) notes that the role of daughter might be useful to gain entry but be in conflict with the competent researcher role. She suggests that the researcher ask herself, "Can I function effectively within this role?"

Other roles include sister or brother, spy, androgynous person, honorary male, or invisible woman. In her work in a drug rehabilitation clinic, Warren (1988) overheard one respondent say, "Aah, what harm can she do, she's only a broad" (p. 18).

Gender Issues

Sexual harassment is another issue that surfaces in fieldwork. This may take the form of sexual hustling, as well as assignment to traditional female roles and tasks in the field, such as "go-fer," or being the butt of sexual or gender jokes (Warren, 1988). The researcher's response to sexist treatment creates a tension in terms of "harmonious research relations in the field (based on the pursuit of knowledge and of career advancement) and the typically feminist politics of fieldworkers in academia (based on the struggle to overcome sexism)" (p. 38).

Reinharz (1992) suggests that the woman ethnographer who experiences sexual harassment might choose to avoid her harasser and thus accept the resulting alteration of her study. Or she might choose to overlook the harassment to avoid losing that informant. Reinharz also notes that women in field settings must be cognizant of the physical risks to which they are vulnerable, especially if working alone. At the same time, women researchers must be sensitive to the threat they may pose to men and the need to modify their behavior to gain access in a primarily male setting. Warren (1988) suggests that this is an area in which additional research is needed in terms of how best to respond to sexist situations.

Translation Issues in Multilingual Contexts

G. I. Lopez, Figueroa, Connor, and Maliski (2008) discuss the difficulties in qualitative research of collecting reliable and valid information when conducting research in a language other than the researcher's primary language. Although standards of rigor exist for the data collection, analysis, interpretation, and reporting of qualitative data, no such standards exist for translation in qualitative research. The researchers conducted interviews in Spanish and transcribed them verbatim. Translator were hired who were bilingual and bicultural, having spoken both English and Spanish all their lives; they also had seven years of experience each doing translations in a research context. These research staff translated the interviews into English. If questions arose in the translation process, the staff made a note of it and then discussed it with the research team. They kept a log of all questions and how they were resolved in order to build knowledge about the process of translation. All translated transcripts were reviewed by a third translator and then by the researchers. If necessary, additional team meetings were held to resolve questions.

Qualitative Data Collection Methods

Interviewing as data collection in qualitative research was discussed extensively in this chapter. Many other types of data collection methods can be used in qualitative studies. Examples of other specific methods are discussed in Chapter 12. I want to acknowledge that data analysis is generally considered to be an ongoing task during a qualitative study. However, for purposes of teaching you about how to do research, I discuss the techniques of qualitative data analysis in Chapter 13.

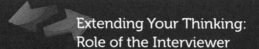

Extending Your Thinking: Role of the Interviewer

1. Should the interviewer be a friend or a stranger? Should the interviewer take action to help empower the interviewee (e.g., by raising consciousness of oppression)?

2. How much should you as the interviewer disclose about yourself during an interview?

3. In qualitative research, the problem of trust between the researcher and participant is very important. Describe strategies that you can use to build trust. Select several combinations from the 8-cell table that follows and role play strategies for building trust within that context.

	Gender			
	Researcher		Participant	
Race/Ethnicity	**Male**	**Female**	**Male**	**Female**
Dominant culture				
Minority culture				

4. Add other dimensions to the role play, such as sexual harassment; passive-aggressive behavior; seductive, flirtatious behavior; expectation of deferential behavior; and so on.

5. Create other contexts with other variables, such as presence or absence of a disability, type of disability, and severity of disability, and role play strategies for gaining trust.

6. Can you empathize with some respondents and not with others?

7. In feminist writing about ethnography research, Reinharz (1992) notes that many feminists encourage the development of a close, nurturing relationship between researcher and participants in field settings. What is your opinion of the advantages and disadvantages of such a relationship?

8. What should researchers reveal about their role as the researcher? Should they be complete participants? Should they perform other work in the setting (such as volunteer work)?

9. Judith Stacey (1988, cited in Reinharz, 1992) remarks that fieldwork relations are inherently deceptive and instrumental and feminists ought not relate to women in this way. Reinharz says that the manipulative nature of the relationship can be reduced by reminding informants of your research intentions, being reciprocally nurturing rather than manipulative, and being motivated by concern for women, not by their exploitation. Where do you stand on this issue?

10. Some ethnographic researchers have reported a dilemma in their fieldwork in that the women they are studying do not seem to be aware of their subordinate position. Is it the researcher's responsibility to raise their level of consciousness? To raise questions about their oppression? Or would this reflect an inappropriate imposition of the values of the researcher as a feminist?

Critically Analyzing Qualitative Research

Quality indicators for qualitative research are dependent on the approach and purpose of the study. Standards for evidence and quality in qualitative inquiries requires careful documentation of how the research was conducted and the associated data analysis and interpretation processes, as well as the thinking processes of the researcher. Freeman, deMarrais, Preissle, Roulston, and St. Pierre, 2007 discussed the issue of validity (sometimes called credibility) in qualitative research as a process of using "data as evidence to warrant claims within different theoretical frameworks and specific communities of practice" (p. 28). (Note: This is in keeping with the points made in Chapter 1 about use of evidence to support claims of strengths and weaknesses in the critical analysis of all types of research.)

Criteria for judging the quality of qualitative research that parallel the criteria for judging positivist, quantitative research have been outlined by a number of writers (Guba & Lincoln, 1989). Guba and Lincoln equate credibility with internal validity, transferability with external validity, dependability with reliability, and confirmability with objectivity. They added the additional category of authenticity for qualitative research. In Lincoln's 1995 address to the American Educational Research Association, she listed a number of criteria for quality that have emerged from the transformative paradigm. In this section, each criterion is explained along with ways to enhance quality in research that uses qualitative methods. (See Box 8.3 for a listing of these criteria.)

Box 8.3 Listing of Criteria for Judging Quality in Qualitative Research

Credibility (parallels internal validity)

- Prolonged and persistent engagement
- Peer debriefing
- Member checks
- Progressive subjectivity
- Negative case analysis
- Triangulation

Transferability (parallels external validity)

- Thick description
- Multiple cases

Dependability (parallels reliability)

- Dependability audit

Confirmability (parallels objectivity)

- Confirmability audit/chain of evidence

Transformative

- Fairness
- Ontological authenticity
- Community
- Attention to voice
- Critical reflexivity/Positionality or standpoint
- Reciprocity/Sharing perquisites of privilege
- Catalytic authenticity/Praxis or social change

Credibility

Prolonged and Persistent Engagement. Lincoln and Guba (1985) and Lincoln (2009) proposed criteria for quality in qualitative research that include the deep and close involvement of researchers in the community of interest combined with sufficient distance from the phenomenon under study to record accurately observed actions. Claims should be made based on sufficient data to support them and processes of analysis and interpretation should be made visible. Implications that derive from these criteria include spending sufficient time in the field to be able to avoid premature closure (i.e., reaching conclusions that are erroneous based on limited exposure to the phenomenon; the conclusions might well be quite different with additional time spent in the field). Prolonged and persistent observation in simplistic terms means how long did the researcher stay on site and how many observations were made in what types of settings? The more complicated version of the criteria asks that researchers stay long enough to get it right and observe in sufficiently diverse situations to get a full and accurate picture. For example, conducting observations in a classroom the week before winter holidays is probably not going to give the researcher an accurate picture of typical student and teacher behaviors. There is no hard-and-fast rule that says how long a researcher must stay at a site. When the researcher has confidence that themes and examples are repeating instead of extending, it may be time to leave the field.

Member Checks and Peer Debriefing. In addition, checking with stakeholders (participants) in the research (member checks) and working with other researchers (peer debriefers) are recommended practices. Member checks involve the researcher seeking verification with the respondent groups about the constructions that are developing as a result of data collected and analyzed. Cho and Trent (2006) discuss this concept of "validity in qualitative research as an interactive process between the researcher, the researched, and the collected data that is aimed at achieving a relatively higher level of accuracy and consensus by means of revisiting facts, feelings, experiences, and values or beliefs collected and interpreted" (p. 324). Member checks can be formal and informal. For example, at the end of an interview, the researcher can summarize what has been said and ask if the notes accurately reflect the person's position. Drafts of the research report can be shared with the members for comment. Cho and Trent (2006) offer several different types of member checks: "'technical (focus on accuracy, truth),' 'ongoing (sustained over time, multiple researcher/informant contacts),' and 'reflexive (collaborative, open-ended, reflective, critical),' all of which are meaningfully compatible with particular research purposes, questions, and processes" (pp. 334–335).

Member checks and peer debriefing entail some careful thought on the part of the researchers, who need to consider who to check with and how and when to do it. Researchers should establish criteria for whom they will include in member checks and peer debriefings and give a rationale for why they choose those individuals. They should also map out a strategy for conducting these two processes. The researcher should engage in an extended discussion with a peer of findings, conclusions, analysis, and hypotheses. The peer should pose searching questions to help the researcher confront his or her own values and to guide next steps in the study. Also, researchers may encounter contradictions or denials in the process of member checks and peer debriefings, so they need to give additional thought as to how to handle such situations. What if there are disagreements or an adversarial relationship between the researchers and participants or the stakeholder is not trustworthy?

Bhattacharya (2007) describes a situation in which the research participant indicated no desire to read the research notes or reports. (I have also had students tell me similar stories.) She described her response to this challenge:

> When I asked Neerada how she would feel if her mother or grandmother read about what she told me, my intent was not only to conduct member checks but also to identify nuggets of re-presentation. What stories did she want to tell without affecting her dignity? Perhaps, her mother or her grandmother will never read any of my work, but my obligation to her dignity kept me hounding mercilessly for stories that can/cannot be re-presented. Because my knowledge of Neerada's narratives extended beyond the scope of my role as a researcher, I questioned the ethics of re-presentation of information that transgressed the boundaries of researcher/researched and entered that of sisterhood and friendship. Grounded in transnational feminism, I was critically concerned about the contested space of collaborative participation and imposing a self-serving expectation on Neerada, especially when she trusted me. On one hand, my academic training implored me to verify the

> information, and the meaning I was making of it, and invite the participant to author her stories. On the other hand, without Neerada's engaged participation, I had to ask what secrets I wanted to reveal about Neerada and the production of her everyday life experiences. Knowing that missed and misunderstandings are always already contingent on the readers' dialogical interaction with the re-presentation, my writing became the hybrid space of contested loyalties to various academic and cultural gatekeepers. (p. 1105)

Negative Case Analysis. Working hypotheses can be revised based on the discovery of cases that do not fit. However, it should not be expected that all cases will fit the appropriate categories. Guba and Lincoln (1989) state that when a "reasonable" number of cases fit, negative case analysis provides confidence in the hypothesis that is being proposed. For example, suppose a researcher sees a pattern emerging that suggests that a top-down approach to a total-inclusion program creates resistance in the school staff (Mertens, 1992). The researcher could seek additional data for negative case analysis from a school that used a bottom-up approach to total inclusion. If resistance was identified in that setting as well, the researcher would need to revise the emerging hypothesis that administration style *alone* creates resistance. It may be one of many factors that contribute to resistance to change.

Progressive Subjectivity. Because researchers are the instruments in qualitative research, they need to monitor their own developing constructions and document the process of change from the beginning of the study until it ends. Researchers can share this statement of beliefs with the peer debriefer so that the peer can challenge the researcher who either does not keep an open mind or who is unaware of his or her own biases. Many researchers use journaling as a method to record their thoughts and feelings throughout the study. They can then use this both in conversation with peer debriefers and/or as data in the analysis phase of the study to provide insights into how they changed their understandings as the study progressed. This concept is extended in the transformative criteria of critical reflexivity and positionality.

Triangulation. Triangulation involves checking information that has been collected from different sources or methods for consistency of evidence across sources of data. For example, multiple methods such as interviews, observation, and document review can be used, and information can be sought from multiple sources using the same method (e.g., interviews with different groups, such as program administrators, service providers, service recipients, and people who are eligible to receive services but are not currently doing so). Guba and Lincoln (1989) no longer support this notion of triangulation because it implies that it is possible (or desirable) to find consistency across sources, which contradicts the notion of multiple realities discussed earlier in this chapter. They say that triangulation can still be used to check on factual data (e.g., how many children are in a program), but they recommend the use of member checks for other types of data. The researcher should be sure to explore rival explanations and to determine the convergence (or nonconvergence) of data from multiple sources in terms of supporting causal inferences. Freeman et al. (2007) also suggest using multiple researchers, multiple methods of data collection, and multiple theoretical analyses to improve validity associated with research-based claims.

Fetherston and Kelly (2007) provide an example of triangulation in their study of peace education: "We triangulated . . . our data, drawing from quantitative and qualitative sources: (a) marks, attendance, and demographic characteristics; (b) pre- and post-anonymous surveys of the cohort (82 registered students in the course); (c) pre- and post-interviews of a randomly selected group of 16 from the cohort; (d) analysis of student portfolios (71); and (e) our own field notes, memos, meeting records, e-mails of our observations and experiences of the class, interactions with students, and so on." (p. 266)

Transferability: Thick Description and Multiple Cases

Guba and Lincoln (1989) identify transferability as the qualitative parallel to external validity in postpositivist research. Recall that in the postpositivist paradigm, external validity enables generalization of findings based on the assumption that the sample used in the study is representative of the population. As this criterion is not applicable in qualitative research, Lincoln and Guba (1985) discussed the term "transferability" as the parallel concept that enables readers of the research to make judgments based on similarities and differences when comparing the research situation to their own. In qualitative research, the burden of transferability is on the reader to determine the degree of similarity between the study site and the receiving context. The researcher's responsibility is to provide sufficient detail to enable the reader to make such a judgment. Extensive and careful description of the time, place, context, and culture is known as "thick description." The term was coined by Geertz (1973) to capture the need for qualitative researchers to provide sufficient details about the context so that readers would be able to understand the complexity of the research setting and participants. This thick description enables readers to make judgments about the applicability of the research findings to their own situations.

For example, Mertens (1990) studied the reasons that referrals were increasing to a special school that served several school districts in a rural area. She provided an in-depth description of the community in which the special school was located as well as of the sending and receiving schools by means of demographic and observational data. She observed in all the schools and provided a description of the physical setup of the classrooms and the processes of instruction that were used. Thus, readers could determine how similar their own conditions were to those reported by Mertens. A thick description of the context was important because the rural nature of the community had an impact on understanding the reasons for the increased referrals (e.g., in terms of ability to attract and retain qualified special education staff and inability to hire personnel to serve the needs of students with low-incidence disabilities in sparsely populated areas).

Yin (2009) suggests that use of multiple cases can strengthen the external validity of the results. He also notes that the relationship between the case study and extant theories can lead to decisions about generalization from case study research.

Dependability

Guba and Lincoln (1989) identified dependability as the qualitative parallel to reliability. Reliability means stability over time in the postpositivist paradigm. In the constructivist paradigm, change is expected, but it should be tracked and publicly inspectable. A dependability audit can be conducted to attest to the quality and appropriateness of the inquiry process. Yin (2003) describes this process in case study research as maintaining a case study protocol that details each step in the research process.

For example, Mertens (1991) began a study of ways to encourage gifted deaf adolescents to enter science careers with a focus on instructional strategies used in science classes. However, emerging patterns in the data suggested the importance of examining administrative practices that facilitated the acquisition of competent interpreters or teachers and staff who were deaf. This change of focus is acceptable and to be expected in qualitative research, but it should be documented.

Confirmability

Guba and Lincoln (1989) identified confirmability as the qualitative parallel to objectivity. Objectivity means that the influence of the researcher's judgment is minimized. Confirmability means that the data and their interpretation are not figments of the researcher's imagination. Qualitative data can be tracked to their source, and the logic that is used to interpret the data should be made explicit. Guba and Lincoln recommend a confirmability audit to attest to the fact that the data can be traced to original sources and that the process of synthesizing data to reach conclusions can be confirmed. Yin (2009) refers to this as providing a "chain of evidence." The confirmability audit can be conducted in conjunction with the dependability audit. Thus, a special education researcher's peers can review field notes, interview transcripts, and so on and determine if the conclusions are supported by the data.

Transformative Criteria

Transformative criteria for quality in qualitative research are situated in concerns for social justice and human rights (Mertens, 2009). Scholars in the field describe several sets of criteria that are commensurate with this position. For example, Kirkhart (2005) describes multicultural validity and defines it as "correctness or authenticity of understandings across multiple, intersecting cultural contexts" (p. 22). I presented her five justifications for this type of validity in Chapter 1. Lincoln (1995, 2009) and Lincoln and Guba (2000) described authenticity as a type of validity that refers to providing a balanced and fair view of all perspectives in the research study and they included the following criteria:

Fairness. Fairness answers the question: To what extent are different constructions and their underlying value structures solicited and honored in the process? To be fair, the researcher must identify the respondents and how information about their constructions was obtained. Conflicts and value differences should be displayed. There should also be open negotiation of the recommendations and agenda for future actions. Total-inclusion research can be judged to be fair if the variety of viewpoints, both for and against (and the conditions under which inclusion would be supported), are included in the report (Keller, Karp, & Carlson , 1993; Mertens, 1992).

Ontological Authenticity. This is the degree to which the individual's or group's conscious experience of the world became more informed or sophisticated. This can be determined based on member checks with respondents or by means of an audit trail that documents changes in individuals' constructions throughout the process. In the study of increased referrals to a special school, respondents came to understand the discrepancy between policy and practice with regard to referral of students with disabilities to special schools (Mertens, 1990). The policy said that students with disabilities should be educated as much as possible with general education students and that, as a last resort, *before* referral to a special school, they should be provided with educational services in a separate, special education classroom in their home school. Local school staff did not support use of the special education classroom because they perceived it as stigmatizing for the student to go to a separate classroom. They preferred to refer a student to the special school when they had exhausted attempts to integrate a student with a disability in a general education classroom.

Community. Research takes place within and affects a community (Lincoln, 1995). The researcher should be able to know the community well enough to link the research results to positive action within that community. The researcher needs to demonstrate that a method of study was used that allowed the researcher to develop a sense of trust and mutuality with the participants in the study (Lincoln, 1995).

Attention to Voice. Lincoln (1995) cites the question that bell hooks (1990) has asked in her writing, Who speaks for whom? Who speaks for those who do not have access to the academy? The researcher must seek out those who are silent and must involve those who are marginalized.

Positionality or Standpoint Epistemology/Critical Reflexivity. Lincoln (1995) describes the inherent characteristic of all research as being representative of the position or standpoint of the author. Therefore, researchers should acknowledge that all texts are incomplete and represent specific positions in terms of sexuality, ethnicity, and so on. Texts cannot claim to contain all universal truth because all knowledge is contextual; therefore, the researcher must acknowledge the context of the research. The researcher must be able to enter into a high-quality awareness to understand the psychological state of others to uncover dialectical relationships (Lincoln, 1995). The researcher needs to have a heightened self-awareness for personal transformation and critical subjectivity.

Reciprocity/Sharing the Perquisites of Privilege. Researchers should give thought to what they give back to communities as a result of their research experiences. In some cases, members of the community may enhance their abilities to conduct research. In others, they may find the results useful to seek funding for or revision of important programs in their communities. Researchers should also be prepared to share the royalties of books or other publications that result from the research. Lincoln (1995) says, "We owe a debt to the persons whose lives we portray."

Catalytic Authenticity. This is the extent to which action is stimulated by the inquiry process. Techniques for determining the catalytic effect of research include respondent testimony and examination of actions reported in follow-up studies. The final activity of a project to improve access to court systems for people who are deaf and hard of hearing involved the participants in the development of a plans to improve access in their court systems in each state (Mertens, 2000). The planning groups included judges, members of their staff, and deaf people or advocates for deaf people. The researcher followed up a year later with the participants to review their plan and determine what changes they implemented. The follow-up data indicated that changes were made such as providing bench books for all judges to inform them about ways to appropriately support and accommodate deaf and hard-of-hearing people in their courtrooms. In addition, several of the deaf participants brought lawsuits against the court systems to improve access. While this was not a specific objective of the study, it does indicate that the project served to stimulate action to improve court access.

Praxis or Social Change

Transformative criteria also raise questions about the use of the research findings for the purpose of social change, and thus extend the concept of catalytic authenticity (Mertens, 2009; Mertens, Holmes, & Harris, 2009). Cho and Trent (2006) describe this as transformational validity, emphasizing the need for the researcher to engage in deep self-reflection in order to understand the social conditions and implications for bringing change to that setting. Another important implication for transformative criteria of validity is the extent to which resultant changes are prompted by the research findings (Ginsberg & Mertens, 2009). The application of such criteria is of course problematic for a number of reasons, not the least of which is determination of who has power to make changes and how that power can be challenged or redistributed in the interests of social justice. Cho and Trent discuss the challenges associated with this version of validity for praxis or social change purposes:

> A key aspect of the praxis/social change purpose of qualitative research lies in the relationship between researcher and researched. Change efforts become integral parts of the research design. In order for authentic change to occur, collaborative relationships between researcher and researched should be manifested during (and after) the research process. Authority, power, or privilege deployed, both implicitly and explicitly, from the side of the researcher needs to be deconstructed if not discarded entirely if the researcher hopes to make a realistic difference in either schools or society. (pp. 331–332)
>
> Validity as a process in the praxis/social change purpose involves inquiry with and on behalf of participants. Validity claims in this purpose are determined in part by the extent to which collaboratively involved participants are co-researchers in the research process. The warranted validity, of course, will be at risk if the relationship between researcher and researched is unequal, exploitative, or not taken seriously. To this end, major validity criteria that should be relationally and collaboratively adopted in this purpose are: (1) member checks as reflexive; (2) critical reflexivity of self; and (3) redefinition of the status quo. Member checks as reflexive refers to the constant backward and forward confirmation between the researcher and the participants under study in regard to re/constructions of constructions of the participants. Reflexive member checking seeks to illuminate a better representation of the lived experience of the participants being studied. Critical reflexivity of self should be played out in a way that challenges the researcher to be able to come across something unknown as they move on. In other words, the researcher should openly express how his or her own subjectivity has progressively been challenged and thus transformed as he or she collaboratively interacts with his or her participants. Lastly, in regard to the major outcome of the report/account, participants should be able to differently perceive and impact the world in which they live. (p. 333)

In her closing remarks at the annual meeting of the American Educational Research Association, Lincoln (1995) envisioned a different set of criteria for judging the quality of research from what is currently used in most academic settings. She said, "Try to imagine an academic world in which judgments about promotion, tenure, and merit pay were made on the basis of the extent of our involvement with research participants, rather than on our presumed distance."

Questions for Critically Analyzing Qualitative Research

1. Did the researcher maintain sufficient involvement at the site to overcome distortions, uncover people's constructions, and understand the context's culture and thus avoid premature closure?

2. Did the researcher use peer debriefing and member checks? Did the researcher prepare a statement of beliefs and share those with the peer debriefer?

3. Did the researcher use negative case analysis?

4. Did the researcher use triangulation?

5. Did the researcher provide sufficient thick description?

6. Did the researcher do a dependability audit?

7. Did the researcher do a confirmability audit?

8. Did the researcher display conflicts and value differences?

9. Did the individuals and groups become more informed or sophisticated about their experiences?

10. Did the researcher establish links with the community that indicated that a level of trust had been established?

11. Did the researcher seek out those who are silent and marginalized?

12. Was the researcher critically reflexive?

13. Were arrangements made to give back to the community and to share the perquisites of privilege?

14. Did the evaluation stimulate action? How did the research process and outcomes enhance social justice and human rights?

Extending Your Thinking: Quality of Qualitative Research

1. Given the following research problem (or one from an existing research study using qualitative methods), explain what the researchers could do to improve the quality of their study. Structure your answer using the following categories:

a. Credibility

b. Transferability

(Continued)

(Continued)

c. Dependability
d. Confirmability
e. Authenticity

Example: Pull-out programs (e.g., resource rooms or remedial classes) have been criticized for segregating low-achieving students, providing them with a fragmented curriculum, and allowing regular classroom teachers to avoid responsibility for meeting all the students' needs. Pull-in programs have been proposed as one alternative in which the special education or remedial teacher provides instruction in the regular classroom. One study used observations of two pull-in programs to obtain information about implementation, instructional context, and variability among classrooms implementing a pull-in approach. Three pull-out programs taught by the same special and remedial education teachers served as comparison groups (Geilheiser & Meyers, 1992).

2. Select two qualitative studies from the literature. Compare the authors' handling of the following dimensions:

a. Motivation for conducting the research
b. Data collection strategies
c. Credibility building/validity
d. Ethics

3. Answer these questions:

a. How and why do these texts differ? How do they relate to the theoretical readings you are currently doing?
b. Do you think the authors are justified in their methods or presentations? Why? Why not?
c. How will these readings help you make decisions about your own professional work in the field?
d. What do you think are the most important standards to use in comparing these two works?[5]

Summary of Chapter 8: Qualitative Methods

Researchers from different paradigmatic perspectives choose to use qualitative methods for different reasons. Constructivists use qualitative methods in order to explore the social construction of reality. Transformative researchers use qualitative methods to capture the lived experiences of those who are marginalized or the systemic oppression dynamics in society. Pragmatists use qualitative methods if they think that their research question justifies the use of such methods. Overall, qualitative methods allow a researcher to get a richer and more complex picture of the phenomenon under study than do quantitative methods. The most common methods of data collection associated with qualitative research include interviews, observations, and reviews of documents or other artifacts. Strategies for conducting phone and personal interviews were discussed in this chapter. Other data collection strategies for qualitative research are discussed in Chapter 12.

Notes

1. When qualitative methods are used within the postpositivist paradigm, typically, the researcher establishes predetermined, static questions to guide the research, converts the qualitative data to frequency counts, and so on. However, I focus on the use of qualitative methods within the constructivist/transformative traditions because of the unique criteria for judging quality associated with such research.

2. The intent of this example is to illustrate how behavioral observations can be used in a qualitative study to provide evidence of attitudinal change. Persons interested in further details about the study (such as the number and characteristics of the participants in the study and the pervasiveness of the attitude changes) are referred to Mertens et al. (1995).

In This Chapter

- A rationale for the importance of historical research in education and psychology is discussed.
- Types of historical research are identified: topical, biographical, autobiographical, oral history, and the narrative study of lives.
- Three sources of historical data are identified: documents, artifacts, and interviews.
- Steps in conducting historical research are described:

  1. Determining appropriate topics for historical research and sources that are helpful in the identification of such problems.
  2. Conducting the literature review, with particular attention to the preliminary and secondary sources most helpful for historical research.
  3. Identifying historical data, including documents, artifacts, and people to interview.
  4. Evaluating the quality of historical sources.

- Special considerations for conducting oral history, biographical, and autobiographical research are discussed.
- Questions for evaluating historical and narrative research are provided.

> Many of the modern social professions were formed or radically restructured during the Progressive Era (1890–1920). This is true for education in general and the associated profession of vocational guidance in particular. The foundations of these professions, and particularly their ideological underpinnings are, however, not always well understood. . . . In spite of the extensive concern for equality and personal development on the part of progressive educators, professions were often formed and developed in accord with principles that would have the effect of limiting opportunities and access to the occupational structure for the working classes, immigrant groups, people of color, and women. (Sherman, 1993, pp. 197–198)

Sherman conducted a historical study of vocational choice and examined implications for vocational guidance in today's schools. A summary of this study is presented in Sample Study 9.1.

9

History and Narrative Study of Lives

Importance of Historical and Narrative Research

Some people's view of history is that it is as dry as dust; others view it as a fiery debate. How can one area have such a diverse reputation? The controversy arises because of questions such as, whose history should children study? What has our experience been in America (or in other countries)? Who owns history? Nash (1995) identifies these as the questions that contributed to the "fiery debate" as the National Standards for History were being developed. The National Standards for History were developed through a broad-based national consensus-building process that worked toward reaching agreement on the larger purposes of history in the school curriculum and on the more specific history understandings and thinking processes that all students should have an equal opportunity to acquire over 12 years of precollegiate education (Crabtree & Nash, 1994).[1] Kammen (2008) comments that the National History Standards continue to be viewed as controversial:

> What took place between 1994 and 1996 was far more than a tempest in a teapot—it caused an entire nation to consider and reconsider how its history should be taught and understood in order to be meaningful and valued. It has not, unfortunately, put to rest the meaning and use of "historical interpretation" and "revisionism" as pejorative words in the minds of many politicians. Nor has it diminished their anxiety about the public's access to revealing information. At the Senate confirmation hearings held in 1997 for George Tenet to become the new director of the CIA, he was asked about the long-delayed declassification and release of historical documents. His symptomatic response fudged: "It's dangerous to look back over your shoulder." (p. 56)

Sample Study 9.1

Summary of a Historical Research Study

Research Problem: Contradictory perspectives of occupational choice or selection arise between the viewpoints that individuals are free to choose an occupation and that occupational choice is strongly influenced by issues of gender, race, ethnicity, and class.

Research Questions: What were the forces that influenced the development of the field of vocational guidance and the notion of vocational choice such that individuals are prepared differentially based on class, gender, and ethnicity, while still maintaining the illusion of equal and free choice? What does vocational choice mean in current psychological or vocational guidance practice?

Method: Historical documents from the Progressive Era were reviewed that related to education, growth of industrial capitalism, and the methods of production, from the 1890s through World War I. Records of business associations, such as the National Association of Manufacturers and the National Society for the Promotion of Industrial Education, were analyzed. The contribution of one individual, Frank Parsons, was examined in terms of his influence on defining the profession of vocational guidance through reliance on matching an individual's skills and attributes with specific occupations, within appropriate social roles as defined at the time.

Results: Public schooling and vocational guidance were viewed as a way to sort workers into occupations that were appropriate for the new industrial order. A two-tiered system of education was established: a liberal arts program for future managers and industrial subjects for those slated to be manual workers.

Discussion: Critics and reformers expressed concern about the development of a permanent working class. Current vocational guidance continues to rely on individual assessments of abilities, interests, and values and matching those to industrial requirements, without consideration of the ways in which class, race, ethnicity, or gender affect options.

SOURCE: Based on Sherman (1993).

Within the discipline of history, concerns arose about the lack of representation of oppressed groups in historical accounts, much as they have in other approaches to research. Scholars who took on the revision of history to represent those voices that had been traditionally overlooked created a movement in history known as *new social history*. Historians experienced what has been termed the *linguistic turn* in their discipline. "In the field of history the term *linguistic turn* denotes the historical analysis of representation as opposed to the pursuit of a discernible, retrievable historical 'reality'" (Canning, 1994, p. 369). The linguistic turn is manifest in cultural history[2] based on the French philosophers Derrida and Foucault. The pendulum swung further when historians also felt the presence of postmodernism and poststructuralists who criticized the foundation of history as a discipline, based on a position that holds that "history is an elaborate fiction produced by the human imagination: the past existed once, but we can never know it now, so we essentially make it up" (MacRaild, 2008, p. 115). MacRaild describes an evolving scholarship in history that is multifaceted with some scholars who are deeply entrenched in revisionist history, others in postmodernism, and some who are seeking a way to conduct historical research that is inclusive of historical record and reflects awareness of the influence of the historian conducting the study.[3]

As suggested in the introductory quotation to this chapter, educators and psychologists have not always appreciated the value of historical research. (In fact, one reviewer of my original outline for this book suggested that I leave out the chapter on historical research because she never teaches it anyway.) However, I have included this chapter for three reasons:

1. Educators and psychologists who do not know history cannot fully understand the present and are in a less advantageous position to address the future.

2. The mood within the historical community closely parallels the changes arising in educational and psychological researchers who are examining the implications of the transformative paradigm for their work.

3. Scholars who write about the lives of oppressed people emphasize the importance of an understanding of the historical, cultural, social, and economic conditions surrounding an event.

G. Tuchman (1994) makes the case that "adequate social science includes a theoretical use of historical information. Any social phenomenon must be understood in its historical context" (p. 306). Reinharz (1992) notes that historical research was especially important for feminists because it draws women out of obscurity and repairs the historical record in which women are largely absent. Indigenous scholars throughout the world and representatives from African American and Latino communities in the United States emphasize that understanding history is a critical element for the conduct of ethical research in their communities (Chilisa, 2005; Cram, 2009; Denzin, Lincoln, & Smith, 2008; LaFrance & Crazy Bull, 2009; Mertens, 2009; Mertens, Holmes, & Harris, 2009).

Stanfield (1994) identified the following elements for an indigenous-ethnic model for research:

1. It should be based on *oral communication* because so many non-Western cultures within and outside industrial nation-states are oral-communication based.

2. It should be *grounded in holistic* (not fragmented or dichotomized) *notions of human beings* because many non-Westerners view the social, the emotional, and the spiritual as integral parts of a whole person linked to a physical environment.

3. The methodology should incorporate the use of *historical documents, participant observation,* and *oral history* to allow people of color to articulate holistic explanations about how they construct reality.

He argues that the historical perspective is necessary to develop a logic of inquiry that is grounded in the indigenous experiences of people of color.

Types of Historical and Narrative Research

One way to categorize historical and narrative research is based on what is studied. For example, topical research focuses on a specific event or phenomenon, such as the history of vocational choice or vocational guidance. Biographical research concerns the life story of an individual other than the narrator-interviewee. Autobiographical history is the life story of the narrator-interviewee. Oral history is an interdisciplinary development involving education, anthropology, history, folklore, biographical literature, psychology, sociology, and ethnography (Yow, 2005). The Oral History Association (2008) provides this definition:

> Oral history is a field of study and a method of gathering, preserving and interpreting the voices and memories of people, communities, and participants in

past events. Oral history is both the oldest type of historical inquiry, predating the written word, and one of the most modern, initiated with tape recorders in the 1940s and now using 21st-century digital technologies.

Scholars who conduct oral history research are concerned with the making of meaning and power relationships in the interview situation. Oral history can include taped memoirs, typewritten transcripts, and a research method that involves in-depth interviewing. Different terms are used to describe oral history: *life history, self-report, personal narrative, life story, oral biography, memoir, testament, testimonio, in-depth interview, recorded memoir, recorded narrative, taped memoirs,* and *life review.* Yow (2005) characterizes oral history as involving an interviewer who inspires narrators to begin the act of remembering, jogs their memories, and records and presents the narrators' words through recorded in-depth interviews. In oral history, the researcher conducts in-depth interviews to determine how things got to be the way they are.[4] The focus is on the *past.*

When the same method is used within a research study that is *present-centered,* it is termed the *narrative study of lives.* A third genre with a strong relationship to narrative studies is *autobiographical, autoethnography,* or *self-study* (see Chapter 8 for additional discussion of autoethnography). Ellis and Bochner (2000) provide a definition of autoethnography/autobiographical research (see Box 9.1). Josselson (1993) describes the development of this approach as follows: "Listening to people talk in their own terms about what had been significant in their lives seemed to us far more valuable than studying preconceived psychometric scales or contrived experiments" (p. ix). She described a strong relationship between oral history and this present-centered use of in-depth interviews; therefore, I have chosen to include this approach in this chapter on historical research methods. The approach has been used by clinical psychologists to study pathological cases, the psychobiography of exemplary and ordinary people, and developmental experiences through the life span.

Box 9.1 Definition of Autoethnography/Autobiography Research

Autoethnography is an autobiographical genre of writing and research that displays multiple layers of consciousness, connecting the personal to the cultural. Back and forth autoethnographers gaze, first through an ethnographic wide-angle lens, focusing outward on social and cultural aspects of their personal experience; then, they look inward, exposing a vulnerable self that is moved by and may move through, refract, and resist cultural interpretation. . . . As they zoom backward and forward, inward and outward, distinctions between the personal and cultural become blurred, sometimes beyond distinct recognition. Usually written in the first-person voice, autoethnographic texts appear in a variety of forms—short stories, poetry, fiction, novels, photographic essays, personal essays, journals, fragmented and layered writing, and social science prose.

—Ellis and Bochner, 2000, p. 739

Sources of Data

To collect data, historical researchers do not go out and design experiments and test the effects of an independent variable on a dependent variable. Their data sources are already in existence and the events have already occurred. Therefore, their data sources include documents, artifacts, and oral stories collected by means of in-depth interviews. Historians do not conduct qualitative research only, because they can use quantitative data sources as well. For example, quantitative data from the census can be used to provide a general context for a period in history. A researcher might examine wages, literacy, education levels, and so on (G. Tuchman, 1994).

V. M. MacDonald (1995) provided a good example of the combination of qualitative and quantitative approaches in her study of Southern teachers before and after the Civil War. To provide a general picture of teacher characteristics during this era, she used a data set of 10,000 teachers randomly sampled from the federal censuses for 1860, 1880, 1900, and 1910. (She notes that the data were gathered at the Harvard Graduate School of Education under the direction of the principal investigators Joel Perlmann and Bob Margo, and the sampling methods are described in an article by Perlmann and Margo, 1989, in *Historical Methods.*)

V. M. MacDonald's (1995) qualitative data came from such sources as diaries, letters, reminiscences, school reports from Black and non-Black schools, newspapers, and contemporary journal articles. This combination of methods allowed her to tell the teachers' stories within the broader social and economic fabric of schooling and society.

So, how do you do historical-narrative research? How do you find the sources of data mentioned here? Read on.

Steps in Conducting Historical-Narrative Research

In some ways, almost all research studies start as historical research studies because the act of conducting a literature review involves locating and synthesizing information that is already known about a topic. In this sense, historical research is a comfortable and familiar process. However, there are unique twists and turns when the focus of the research is specifically on the historical events and life stories, and these are not familiar territory for most people in education and psychology. The study of how to do historical research is termed *historiography,* and several good texts are available to approach this in general, as well as specific, contexts. Box 9.2 lists a number of historiographic texts that the serious scholar can consult; additional resources are available at the Web site of the American History Association (www.historians.org/index.cfm).

Box 9.2 Historiographic Texts and Resources

General Texts

Barzun, J., & Graff, H. F. (2003). *The modern researcher* (6th ed.). Boston: Houghton Mifflin.

Breisach, E. (2003). *On the future of history: The postmodernist challenge and its aftermath.* Chicago: University of Chicago Press.

Burke, P. (2001). *New perspectives on historical writing* (2nd ed.). University Park: Pennsylvania State University Press.

Tierney, W. G. (2000). Undaunted courage: Life history and the postmodern challenge. In N. K. Denzin & Y. S. Lincoln (Eds.), *Handbook of qualitative research* (2nd ed., pp. 537–553). Thousand Oaks, CA: Sage.

Tosh, J. (2002). *The pursuit of history* (3rd ed.). New York: Longman.

(Continued)

Box 9.2 (Continued)

Feminist/Ethnic/Gay/Lesbian Historiography

Abernathy, D. (2003). *Partners to history: Martin Luther King, Jr., Ralph David Abernathy, and the Civil Rights Movement*. New York: Crown.
Abrahams, P. (2001). *The Black experience in the 20th century*. Bloomington: Indiana University Press.
D'Emilio, J. (2002). *The world turned: Essays on gay history, politics, and culture*. Durham, NC: Duke University Press.
Kessler-Harris, A. (2001). *In pursuit of equity: Women, men, and the quest for economic citizenship in 20th century America*. Oxford, UK: Oxford University Press.
Norton, M. B., & Alexander, R. M. (2003). *Major problems in American women's history: Documents and essays*. Boston: D. C. Heath.

Oral History and Narrative

Beverley, J. (2005). Testimonio, subalternity, and narrative authority. In N. K. Denzin & Y. S. Lincoln (Eds.), *The SAGE handbook of qualitative research* (3rd ed., pp. 547–558). Thousand Oaks, CA: Sage.
Dickson, D. S., Heyler, D., Reilly, L. G., & Romano, S. (2006). *The Oral History Project: Connecting students to their community. Grades 4–8*. Portsmouth, NH : Heinemann.
Elliott, J. (2005). *Narrative in social research*. London: Sage.
Jones, S. J. (2005). Authoethnography: Making the personal political. In N. K. Denzin & Y. S. Lincoln (Eds.), *The SAGE handbook of qualitative research* (3rd ed., pp. 763–793). Thousand Oaks, CA: Sage.
Riessman, C. K. (2008). *Narrative methods for the human sciences*. Thousand Oaks, CA: Sage.
Ritchie, D. A. (2003). *Doing oral history* (2nd ed.). Oxford, UK: Oxford University Press.
Yow, V. R. (2005). *Recording oral history: A guide for the humanities and social sciences* (2nd ed.). Walnut Creek, CA: AltaMira Press.

Step 1: Define the Problem

Problems appropriate to historical research can be identified through many of the same steps that other research problems are identified. You can be perplexed by current practices or social problems and desire to have a historical understanding of how the conditions developed. For example, the issues of racial, ethnic, gender, or disability-based discrimination all have historical roots, whether your interest is in effective teaching or testing methods or in some other aspect of education and psychology. New facts can be discovered that require a reexamination of old data or a reinterpretation of events using a different theoretical framework. Examples of historical-narrative research topics include the following:

1. *Topical Historical Research:* What were the forces that influenced the development of the field of vocational guidance and the notion of vocational choice such that individuals are prepared differentially based on class, gender, and ethnicity, while still maintaining the illusion of equal and free choice (Sherman, 1993)?

2. *Topical Historical Research:* What were the origins of the entrance of Black and White Southern women into the teaching profession before and after the Civil War (V. M. MacDonald, 1995)?

3. *Topical Historical Research:* How was race constructed and reconstructed between the late 19th century and the 1940s, and what are the implications of that reconstruction for classroom teaching (Banks, 1995)?

4. *Topical Historical Research.* What does education for all mean in international inclusive education policy for individuals with disabilities (Peters, 2007)?

5. *Cross-Cultural Historical Research:* Over the last half century, how culturally sensitive has psychological research published in English-language journals been with regard to the Arabic-speaking world (Zebian, Alamuddin, Maalouf, & Chatila, 2007)?

6. *Narrative Study of Lives:* How do adolescent girls understand themselves and their relationships, and how do their understandings change and develop over time (A. G. Rogers, Brown, & Tappan, 1994)?

7. *Oral History:* What are the lives of lower-income women like, from birth through old age (Buss, 1985)?

8. *Oral History:* What were the experiences of first responders to the hurricane and flooding of August/September 2005 in New Orleans in terms of scale of suffering during the crisis, societal response afterwards, and the extent to which these efforts succeeded or failed (Cave, 2008)?

9. *Autobiographical History:* How did a West Indian slave overcome psychological trauma, physical torture, and hardship? How did legal, economic, and social shackles affect her life? And how did she shape her environment to exercise some control over her future (M. Ferguson, 1993)?

10. *Biographical History:* What were the experiences of Margaret Wise Brown in teaching writing to children at Bank Street (Marcus, 1993)?

Journals as Sources of Research Problems

As with other types of research, you can often find a research problem by reviewing journals and focusing on the "additional research is needed" section of the articles. Box 9.3 provides a partial listing of journals that publish information that might be helpful for a scholar interested in pursuing the formulation of a research problem from a historical-narrative perspective.

Box 9.3 Useful Journals of Historical-Narrative Research

American Historical Review

The Annals of the American Academy of Political and Social Science

Canadian Journal of History

Colonial Latin American Historical Review

Comparative Studies in Society and History

Ethnohistory

Feminist Studies

(Continued)

Box 9.3 (Continued)

Gender & History

History of Education

History of Psychology

Immigrants & Minorities

International Journal of African Historical Studies

Journal of American History

Journal of Interdisciplinary History

Journal of Negro Education

Oral History Review

Psychoanalysis and History

Radical History Review

Signs: Journal of Women in Culture and Society

Electronic Resources

Currently, the range of historical Web sites combines a variety of functions:

- Professional organizations in history offer a multitude of resources, ranging from research reports, gateways to historical databases, and lists of recommended readings and electronic resources. See, for example, the American History Association (www.historians.org/) and the Oral History Association (www.oralhistory.org/).

- Archival collections of primary source materials, such as text, audio, video, graphics, or photos: for example, the Library of Congress American Memory project (http://memory.loc.gov/) or the archives at the U.S. Holocaust Memorial Museum (www.ushmm.org/research/collections/).

- Gateways providing access to collections of other sites organized around selected themes: For example, History Matters is a site that contains many primary historical materials as well as guidance for teaching history (http://historymatters.gmu.edu/), the American Social History Project offers a variety of materials related to U.S. history (www.ashp.cuny.edu/index.html), and the Digital History project (www.digitalhistory.uh.edu/) includes annotated primary sources on slavery, and United States, Mexican American, and Native American history.

- Thematic collections focusing on a specific historical event, individual, or theme: for example, Without Sanctuary, a Web site depicting the history of lynching in America (www.withoutsanctuary.org/), or a site on Women and Social Movements in the United States 1600–2000 (http://asp6new.alexanderstreet.com/was2/was2.index.map.aspx).

- The Best of History Web Sites is a portal with over 1,000 annotated links to history Web sites, as well as links to K–12 history lesson plans and history teacher guides (www.besthistorysites.net/).

"Mucking About" in an Archive or Contacting Professional Organizations

Sometimes, historical researchers do not start with a specific problem in mind. A historian might hear about new opportunities to have access to archival materials (e.g., the Nixon White House tapes or records concerning the Nazi's activities during World War II) and decide that it would be interesting to explore what is in the materials. By reading materials in an archive, a researchable question may emerge. As mentioned in Chapter 3, professional associations can also provide valuable guidance in seeking a research topic. In the case of historical research, you should be aware of the American Historical Association and the Oral History Association.

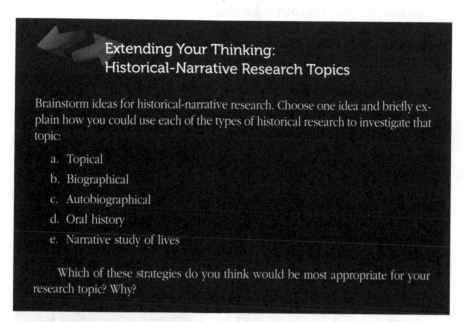

Extending Your Thinking: Historical-Narrative Research Topics

Brainstorm ideas for historical-narrative research. Choose one idea and briefly explain how you could use each of the types of historical research to investigate that topic:

a. Topical
b. Biographical
c. Autobiographical
d. Oral history
e. Narrative study of lives

Which of these strategies do you think would be most appropriate for your research topic? Why?

Step 2: Conduct the Literature Review

You should conduct a review of the literature with two goals. First, you should do background reading to find out what has been published about your topic already. As you struggle to define your research topic, it is important to remember to set limits in terms of geographic region and the time period covered. Local studies and state studies are valid and important parts of historical research, and delimiting a study can be an important step in designing a study that is doable.

Second, review literature that is actually the historical data that you seek to analyze (e.g., diaries, letters, etc.). To begin your search, you need to know which preliminary sources (databases) will yield information of a historical nature on your topic. You also need to distinguish between primary and secondary sources of information within a historical context.

In historical research, Purvis (1994) suggests the following distinction:

> Although the dividing line between a "primary" and a "secondary" source is somewhat arbitrary, the former is usually regarded as a text that came into being during the period of the past that is being researched while the latter is usually seen as a text that is produced much later than the events being studied, offering an interpretation and conversion of the primary data into an account that may be consulted by others. (p. 168)

Preliminary Sources

You should plan to conduct searches in the standard databases for education and psychology, such as ERIC and PsycINFO. In addition, you should search databases such as Historical Abstracts (covers the world, except for the United States) and American History and Life. Bibliographic indexes can be particularly helpful for locating literature of a historical nature. As the volume of resources available on the Web increases, researchers are more commonly searching for bibliographic information through electronic means. Bibliographic services are also available through the American Historical Association (AHA) in Washington, D.C., and the Association for the Bibliography of History in Alexandria, Virginia. The AHA publishes a directory of federal historical programs and activities that describes historical programs in many departments of the federal government, as well as lists hundreds of organizations with resources for history researchers. The volume includes many electronic resources as well and is available from the AHA.

If you are specifically interested in biography, the *Biography Index* could be useful (www.hwwilson.com/databases/bioind.htm). This is a reference that was previously published quarterly and contained biographical material that appeared in journals and books. However, it is currently available online and has citations from 1984 to the present. The *Dictionary of American Biography* (American Council of Learned Societies, 1927–1994) is available in both print and electronic format. The print version consists of 20 volumes of biographies of famous Americans; the electronic version started in 1997 and is now called the American National Biography Online (www.anb.org/qa.html). Harvard University Press published *Notable American Women* (Sicherman & Green, 1980), which contains the biographies of 163 20th-century women in diverse fields.

Extending Your Thinking: Types of Historical-Narrative Research

1. Through a search of the literature, identify one research study for each type of historical-narrative research strategy. Explain your basis for categorizing each study. For each study do the following:
   a. Identify the research problem.
   b. Identify the data collection methods that were used.
   c. Describe the organizing framework for the findings.
   d. Summarize the main findings.
   e. Use the questions for critical analysis at the end of this chapter to critically analyze each study.

2. Choose one topic for a historical-narrative research study. Conduct a literature review to identify at least three secondary sources that discuss your topic. Formulate a researchable historical-narrative question for your topic based on your literature review. Identify sources that you would search for primary data on that topic.

Step 3: Identify Sources of Historical Facts

Assuming that you have formulated your research questions and done the background reading about your problem, you are now ready to move on to the identification of the primary historical data themselves. As you recall, these include artifacts and documents and in-depth interviews.

Documents and Artifacts

Documents and artifacts can include personal and institutional documents as well as physical objects, such as textbooks, clothes, tools, desks, toys, and weapons, from that historical period. The personal and institutional documents include such items as personal and business correspondence, financial statements, photographs, diaries, manuscript drafts, institutional artifacts, and other unpublished materials. Published archival records include such things as official proceedings of an organization, vital statistics, and official institutional histories (Stanfield, 1993b). Published information also includes censuses, official reports, congressional records, and newspapers. Unpublished archival materials can be found in households, corporations, and private academic and independent research organizations and associations. Public settings include government agencies and repositories, public libraries, public academic institutions, and independent research universities.

The biases in archival materials have been pointed out by a number of historical scholars (B. T. Anderson, 1993; Reinharz, 1992; Stanfield, 1993b). Stanfield noted that history written based on this elite bias also reflects the bias of the affluent. Even history written about ordinary people was written from the archives of the affluent class, based on the assumption that ordinary people rarely if ever kept records. However, Blassingame (1972, cited in Stanfield, 1993b) identified voluminous slave autobiographies that have been overlooked (the existence of which had been ignored) by slavery historians for years; in addition, electronic databases have been compiled and made accessible on the topic of slavery as noted previously in this chapter. In conducting a study of Black women in college, Gasman (2007) found that diaries, letters, autobiographies, and oral histories were available to researchers, but few people had chosen to ask questions pertaining to Black women and gender relations; hence, these primary sources were underutilized. Ordinary people do keep records, such as personal letters, photo albums, diaries, church records, household bills, and neighborhood newspapers.

Many of the materials related to race and ethnicity and gender are found in private households and libraries because poor people and people of color do not often take their records to local university archives, and the university archives are more interested in famous people's records. A space problem forces archives to be selective, and they generally prefer to house the documents of famous people, not ordinary people (Stanfield, 1993b).

Thus, Stanfield (1993b) recommends seeking out private sources of historical documents when researching the lives of "ordinary people." And when using official archives, keep an open mind. Recognize that history and biography are value-laden activities. Know the literature well to compare what historians have written and what is actually in the archives. Identify gaps and presentations of complex individuals and issues in unidimensional ways. Often, actual review of archival materials results in quite different pictures of individuals and events than is presented in extant historical writings.

Finding Information in Archives

University libraries are a good source of information in that they typically contain collections of rare books, letters, periodicals, personal papers, and so forth. State and local libraries and archives are also accessible for historical research. Local historical societies, state historical societies, and museums can provide a great deal of information. Bair (2007) provides an extensive list of archives that are available in the Washington, D.C., area, and many of these resources are also available online.

A number of annotated lists of archives and electronic resources can be helpful in identifying the location of archived information. For example, the National Historical Publications and Records Commission (NHPRC), a statutory body affiliated with the National Archives and Records Administration, supports a wide range of activities to preserve, publish, and encourage the use of documentary sources relating to the history of the United States. Their Web site (www.archives.gov/nhprc/) or the Web site for the National Archives (www.archives.gov/) provides access to millions of historical records that are maintained by the federal government.

Of course, you can go directly to the National Archives, the branch of the U.S. government that preserves and makes available for reference and research the permanently valuable records of the U.S. government. Besides well-known documents such as the Declaration of Independence and the Constitution, the National Archives includes about 9 billion textual documents, 7.2 million maps, charts, and architectural drawings, 20 million still photographs, 365,000 reels of motion picture film, and 173,000 video and sound recordings—all created by federal government agencies since the creation of the nation. They are steadily increasing the archiving of electronic resources and making those available to the public. The National Archives and Records Administration operates 14 records centers, 12 regional archives, and 8 presidential libraries in 17 states. A full listing of their auxiliary locations is available at their Web site. The National Archives also opened a center in College Park, Maryland, that provides researchers with access to electronic records—motion picture, sound, and video records through state-of-the-art technology. Specific collections available include the Nixon Presidential materials, the John F. Kennedy Assassination Records Collection, and the Berlin Documents Center microfilm. Box 9.4 displays the records V. M. MacDonald (1995) used from the National Archives in a study of Black and White teachers before the Civil War. Through these materials, V. M. MacDonald was able to establish the mood of the Southern elite about who should teach the "Negro" children.

Box 9.4 National Archive Resources Example

First Semi-Annual Report of the Superintendent of Schools of the Freedmen's Bureau, January 1, 1866. Bureau of Refugees, Freedmen, and Abandoned Lands (BRFAL), Record Group 105 (On microfilm). Washington, DC: National Archives.

Letter to John Alvord. (1867, January 1). In the *Third Semi-Annual Report of the Superintendent of Schools.* Bureau of Refugees, Freedmen, and Abandoned Lands (BRFAL), Record Group 105 (On microfilm). Washington, DC: National Archives.

The Library of Congress (www.loc.gov/) compiles the *National Union Catalog,* a register of all books published since 1454 that are held in more than 1,100 North American libraries. Until 1993, the *National Union Catalog* was published in book form, so libraries may have the older editions in their collections. The *National Union Catalog* is now available online and can be accessed at www.loc.gov/coll/nucmc/. There are also other union catalogs that record the location of books in foreign languages, such as Slavic, Hebrew, Japanese, and Chinese.

The Library of Congress also offers assistance in locating source materials in libraries in the United States and throughout the world. It publishes, for a small fee, bibliographies, guides, and selected lists of materials on a variety of subjects. Through the Library of Congress's National Library Service for the Blind and Physically Handicapped (www.loc.gov/nls/) and a network of cooperating regional libraries, the Library of Congress can supply books and magazines recorded on disk or tape with playback equipment at no cost. The Library of Congress also has an online catalog on the World Wide Web that can be accessed at http://catalog.loc.gov/.

The National Endowment for the Humanities (www.neh.gov/) has an initiative called "We the People" that provides funding for projects related to American history and culture.

Another national resource is the National Museum of American History at the Smithsonian Institution (http://americanhistory.si.edu/). Of particular interest to historical researchers is their Web-based project on history and culture (www.si.edu/history_and_culture/). The museum also provides scholars with access to a collection of rare books relating to science and technology in its Dibner Library of the History of Science and Technology (www.sil.si.edu/libraries/Dibner/index.cfm).

The Genealogical Library of the Daughters of the American Revolution (DAR; www.dar.org/library/default.cfm) contains over 65,000 books and pamphlets and more than 30,000 manuscripts, much of it available in no other library and almost all of it out of print. The types of material available here are compiled genealogies; state, county, and local histories; published rosters of Revolutionary War soldiers and patriots; abstracts of some Revolutionary War pension files; published vital records; cemetery inscriptions of various county records (e.g., marriages, etc.); published archives of some of the 13 original states; federal census schedules (1850–1880, all states) and federal mortality schedules (a few states); and genealogical periodicals. Regretfully, finances do not permit staff members to do research in person or by mail. Another important source for genealogical information is contained in the Mormons' database in Salt Lake City, Utah.[5]

Copies of documents produced by other government agencies can be obtained by contacting the agency directly through the Freedom of Information Act. G. Tuchman (1994) suggests calling the agency that has the document and inquiring about the specifics for a document request to that agency under the Freedom of Information Act, because (as you might expect) each agency has some specific requirements. You will save time by finding out exactly what is needed by that agency, and each agency does have an office that handles such requests.

Accessing Historical Materials

Historical materials can be accessed in a variety of formats. Some can be obtained online or in CD-ROM format, others on microfiche, and still others need to be copied in print form. Some cannot be copied, and so you would need to take notes on the contents of those documents. It is important to establish what is available and possible with your source of information. Stanfield (1993b) emphasized the importance of knowing the legalities of literary heir rights. Even in documents found in private households, the researcher should develop a contractual agreement to protect the rights of access to and use of the materials. In institutions, the archivist usually supplies a contract on behalf of the literary heirs. Typically, access is easier if the researcher can demonstrate an understanding of the literature related to the problem under investigation. Citations can be made in letters to the heirs or archivists. Once a letter has been written, the researcher should follow up with a phone call and make an appointment to discuss the written contract regarding rights of access and use.

Using Archives

In an archive, typically, a register of materials is available that lists what is in the archive. Stanfield (1993b) recommends a careful review of this register, accompanied by an examination of sample files to get a better feel for the materials included. When historians use archives, they record bin, drawer, and call numbers, as well as date and publisher (G. Tuchman, 1994). It is important to follow the style of historians in recording your sources of information in case you have to return to the source. You will find it easier to reexamine the evidence if you have included the bin, drawer, and call numbers.[6]

Extending Your Thinking: Historical Resources

Choose a document from a federal agency that you would like to read related to a historical or current issue. Contact the agency and determine its procedures for obtaining the document through the Freedom of Information Act. Follow through on your request.

Interviewing: Oral Histories and Narrative Studies of Lives

The process of doing oral history includes the collection of memories and personal commentaries of historical significance through recorded interviews (Ritchie, 2003). Ritchie describes the process of inquiry for oral history as follows:

> An oral history interview generally consists of a well-prepared interviewer questioning an interviewee and recording their exchange in audio or video format. Recordings of the interview are transcribed, summarized, or indexed and then placed in a library or archives. These interviews may be used for research or excerpted in a publication, radio or video documentary, museum exhibition, dramatization or other form of public presentation. Recordings, transcripts, catalogs, photographs and related documentary materials can also be posted on the Internet. Oral history does not include random taping, such as President Richard Nixon's surreptitious recording of his White House conversations, nor does it refer to recorded speeches, wiretapping, personal diaries on tape, or other sound recordings that lack the dialogue between interviewer and interviewee. (p. 19)

Yow (2005) recognizes that oral history can provide answers to questions that are not available through other means. For example, oral history permits the questioning of witnesses, and thus description and interpretation comes from a witness of the event rather than through the researcher's efforts. This is not meant to imply that the researcher does not influence the results or that oral history speaks for itself in its entirety. The researcher influences the results of oral history studies by determining which questions to ask and by selection and editing decisions in reporting results.

However, oral history can provide greater insights into the reasons for actions than might otherwise be recorded without an understanding of the motivation for the action. In addition, oral history provides access to information that is not written down (either because of the nature of the events themselves or because of the characteristics of the people involved). People might be more inclined to discuss disagreements and controversies than to create a written record of such events. Life histories in the past have tended to represent only the well-to-do, but oral history makes it possible to record life histories for all socioeconomic levels of the population. Through in-depth interviewing, it is possible to reveal informal, unwritten rules. Reinharz (1992) notes that oral history is especially important for powerless groups, because their information is less likely to be included in written records.

Both Yow (2005) and Reinharz (1992) caution researchers about the limitations of oral history. The tendency in oral history is to focus on the individual, personal experience and less on the institutional, national, or international trends that were operating during a person's lifetime. Although it is important to use oral history to break silences, readers must also be aware of sociopolitical problems that are broader than an individual's experience. A second limitation is that oral histories are done with people who *survive*. Therefore, even though oral histories can be done with older, relatively powerless people, they cannot be done with the *most* vulnerable—those who did not survive or who are too weak or discouraged to tell their stories. Therefore, in conducting and reading oral histories, the reader should ask how the passage of time and self-selectivity has affected the sample of narrators available.

To overcome the possible bias of obtaining statements only from the most confident and articulate people, Yow (2005) recommends this:

> Bear with the inarticulate: Try to get them to talk when you know that they have been directly involved in the event you are studying. In your own sample, you will know the individuals you must seek out, no matter how laconic they may be. But if they refuse to talk except in monosyllables and your good interviewing techniques are of no avail, do not be discouraged. Knowing that you have done your best to interview this key witness, turn to the next narrator and try to get the information from other witnesses and written records. (p. 83)

Ritchie (2003) identifies another caution associated with doing oral history work that might be of particular interest to psychologists related to the fallibility of human memory. He suggests that oral history researchers keep in mind that people tend to remember events that had importance for them personally and to forget those activities that were more mundane or routine. The human memory does not work like a camera; rather, memory is selective and constructed by the person. Thus, it should not be surprising that no two individuals will give the exact same account of an event, especially when that event occurred many years in the past.

Assuming that you have gone through the previously outlined steps of identifying a topic and reading everything that has been published on that topic, how do you access data for an oral history study? Well, of course, you need people to interview and a list of topics (an interview guide) to use to guide the conversation. Yow (2005) suggests that you start with names from the published and unpublished documents that you have reviewed. Find out addresses for these individuals through their university affiliations or directory assistance if you have geographic locations for the people. Electronic searchers on the Web are also a powerful resource for finding people. Send a letter to the individuals and explain the general nature of your project. Ask about their willingness to talk with you further. Include your phone number in case they have any questions, but follow up with a phone call to determine their willingness to cooperate with you. These first contacts should not be to obtain substantive data about your topic; rather, they are informal interviews to determine the person's willingness to participate and to get ideas for additional actions on your part. Yow suggests asking questions such as these:

- If you were writing this study what would you include?
- Whom would you recommend that I interview?

- If you were writing this history, what would you consider important?
- Who was present at the event?
- Who was influential in making this event happen?
- Who was affected by this?

The sampling techniques commonly used in oral histories are the same as those for most qualitative research studies: snowball sampling, purposive sampling, universal sampling, and saturation. These strategies are discussed in detail in Chapter 11. I have included one excerpt from an oral history project to give you the flavor of sampling within the context of this approach to research. The researchers conducted a study of child workers in a mill village before World War I:

> For the mill village project, my co-researchers and I visited the ministers of the two churches and asked who the oldest members were. We wrote to these members. In addition, we put an advertisement in the local newspaper but got a poor response; nevertheless, other researchers have had better luck with this method. . . . I sought out every person mentioned to me as a worker in the mill early in the century. . . . At that point, the narrators were in their 70s and 80s, and I contacted all living persons who had been part of that history and still resided in that town. The number was so small that it was feasible to contact all survivors. In fact, the narrators finally numbered 30 men and women who were able and willing to talk to us. (Yow, 2005, p. 80)

A tentative list of narrators can then be drawn up and a letter prepared to introduce yourself and your study to those people you desire to interview. Yow says that the initial contact is almost always better done through a letter, with a follow-up phone call. She does recognize that some people might distrust anything in print or resist such an invitation. In such circumstances, it would be to your advantage to identify someone they trust to explain the project to them as a first method of contact. Keeping index cards with each person's name, address, and so on as well as his or her response to your contacts will be useful.

You should prioritize the names on your list for interviewing. Ritchie (2003) suggests starting with the oldest and most significant individuals. Begin with a few well-conducted, in-depth interviews. Once you have fully processed them, interview younger or secondary individuals.

According to the *Oral History Evaluation Guidelines* (Oral History Association, 2000), interviewees must be informed of the purpose, procedures, and potential use of the oral history project, and then they should be asked to sign a legal release permitting use of the data collected within the specified conditions. A sample legal release form can be found in Ritchie's (2003) *Doing Oral History.* The interviewee maintains the right to refuse to discuss certain subjects, to seal portions of the interview, or to choose to remain anonymous. The interviewee should also be made aware of any arrangements that the researcher has made to deposit the interviews in a repository such as an archive or library for use by other researchers. The responsibility for making data available through preservation in archives in historical research contrasts with the situation in education and psychology in which the data are more typically viewed as belonging to the individual researcher. Because of the importance of conducting research in an ethical manner, researchers interested in using the oral history approach should become familiar with the full text of the *Oral History Evaluation Guidelines* and *Oral History and the Law* (Neuenschwander, 1993).[7]

The actual process of conducting the interview is roughly parallel to that outlined in Chapter 8, so I will not repeat that here.

Step 4: Synthesize and Evaluate Historical Data

General Historical Documents

Once you have identified a list of references that you think might be relevant to your research problem, G. Tuchman (1994) suggests that you try to determine if the scholarship meets acceptable standards. One way to determine the acceptability of a source is to check how frequently that source is cited. This can be done by using a citation index such as the *Social Science Citation Index* or the *Arts and the Humanities Citation Index*.

In theory, the more times your source is cited, the greater contribution that source has made to the literature. However, G. Tuchman (1994) notes two caveats to this test: First, some sources may be frequently cited because other authors believe they are wrong and thus cite them as a classic example of a common misinterpretation. Second, few citations may result from a highly specialized topic. Thus, Tuchman suggests asking yourself four questions to establish a source's utility for you:

1. Why is the author making this argument?
2. Do other scholars dispute this argument?
3. Why were these particular materials chosen but not others?
4. Do the author's questions suggest other issues relevant to the project at hand?

To answer these questions, Tuchman suggests that you read book reviews of the work in scholarly journals of the time. You can use the Social Science Citation Index to locate reviews. Purvis (1994) warns that even book reviewers who wrote at the time of the book's publication can have biases that need to be explored before accepting their word as a final assessment of a document's worth.

Historical Materials in General

Stanfield (1993b) raises the issues of validity and reliability in his discussion of the quality of historical data. He defined validity in this context as the adequacy of the collected data for making theoretical statements that are isomorphic with empirical reality. In other words, what are the relationships between constructs that can be stated and supported by empirical evidence? Reliability asks, Can this be replicated under similar empirical conditions? Researchers need to be mindful of the ways in which a social setting can potentially limit what or who he or she sees. Stanfield depicts internal validity problems in the form of dilemmas for researchers:

- The single-case dilemma arises when one personal letter or diary entry suggests an event but no additional evidence can be found to corroborate that event.
- The historical-fame dilemma arises when a person becomes aware at some point of his or her historical fame and becomes more guarded in the content of printed documents produced.
- A dilemma arises over destroyed and forged documents. What was destroyed? Why?
- Researchers can be misled into overgeneralizing characteristics evidenced at one point in life without recognizing that people change as they get older.

External validity questions can be resolved by checking with other sources. Triangulation can be used to check with other sources, or consistency can be sought within a source.

G. Tuchman (1994) also suggests that the researcher ask questions of materials that have been archived:

- Who saved the materials and why?
- Who sorted them and how?
- What was the nature of the organizational system for filing?

Notes Specific to Personal Documents

Diaries, journals, and letters are examples of personal documents often used in historical research. Historical researchers caution that these must be read and interpreted in light of the conditions of the day. G. Tuchman (1994) suggests that researchers interrogate personal documents with such questions as the following:

- What could be written?
- How could it be expressed?
- Who would be reading it at the time?
- What were the characteristics of the writer?
- How should you view what was written in terms of its social location?

G. Tuchman indicates that it was common practice for teachers to read students' journals, thus influencing what students would be willing to write and how they would write it.

Purvis (1994) identifies a similar source of bias in letters written by women in prison during the Suffragette Movement. The prisoners were encouraged to write letters so that they could maintain connections with respectable friends. All the letters were read by prison authorities and censored if they found any of the material objectionable. Consequently, one might be a bit skeptical when the women's censored letters said that all was well, especially when those that were smuggled out of prison painted a very different picture. In addition, a number of women purposely wrote their letters with the intention of getting them published on the outside. The leaders of the movement tended to write such letters, including praise for their supporters and suggesting further direction for political activities.

Notes on Oral History and the Narrative Study of Lives

Oral histories are sometimes criticized because they represent retrospective evidence; that is, the witness is recalling events that happened a long time ago. To determine the worth of evidence from oral history, Yow (2005) suggests bearing in mind research about how memory functions:

> Beginning in their 40s and continuing through the rest of their lives, people reminisce. Memories of childhood, adolescence and early adulthood may be more easily recalled than those from middle and late years. If the event or situation was significant to the individual, it will likely be remembered in some detail, especially its associated feelings. However, the interpretation may reflect current circumstances and needs. (p. 21)

Recognizing the faults of human memory, researchers should be concerned with two aspects of the data: consistency in the testimony (reliability) and accuracy in relating factual information (validity). The researcher can check out inconsistencies within the testimony by asking for clarification from the narrator. Accuracy can be checked by consulting other sources and comparing accounts. The quality of the evidence provided by a witness can be determined by asking the following questions:

- What motive did the witness have for saying this?
- For whom was the interview transcript intended?
- How informed was this witness about the event?
- What prior assumptions did the witness bring to the observation?
- What kinds of details were omitted?

Oral historians need to be concerned about the amount of involvement the interviewer has in the interview process and in presenting the results. (This point was raised by scholars in oral history, but it actually applies to any type of historical writing.) Some interviewers use only very open-ended probes, such as "Tell me about your childhood," in an effort to avoid biasing the responses of the narrator. Others use a more direct approach, inquiring specifically about areas that might not be brought up otherwise. In writing oral histories, some authors use only the words of the narrators; others include their own questions and probes as part of the text, and still others add contextual and interpretive information as bridges between narrator comments. A variety of styles can be used. Reinharz (1992) comments as follows:

> In my view, feminist oral historians need not silence themselves to let other women be heard. The refusal to analyze transcripts does not produce a kind of purity in which women speak for themselves in an unmediated way. After all, the oral historian already had a role in producing the oral history and preparing it for publication. Since any involvement at all by the oral historian is a de facto interpretation, feminist researchers should be interested in providing an analysis so that the reader has a sense of the perspective used. (pp. 137–138)

MacRaild (2008) notes the ethical tension inherent in oral history research and the search for historical truth. He raises questions about the ethics of asking the person to give testimony that resurfaces feelings that were painful so many years ago and the desire to understand reasons for past events. Wolgemuth and Donohue (2006) and Stanfield (2006) argue for a transformative purpose in historical research. Stanfield says this purpose is to

> bring about healing, reconciliation, and restoration between the researcher and the researched. This is what I call the *restorative justice functions* of qualitative methodological techniques such as ethnography, oral history, case studies, social experiments, media analysis, and archival methods. When we think about restorative justice, what usually comes to mind are those instances in which the researcher's agenda uses a methodology to confirm a theory involving the mistreatment of a powerless population. . . . The researcher might also use a practical methodology to transform prolonged experiences of inter-group conflict in an institution, community or society into a peace-building experience. In recent years, the conflict resolution literature has begun to make way for the conflict

> transformation concerns of restorative justice researcher practitioners. Snapshots from ethnography and oral histories presented by the researcher practitioner who serves as the facilitator or convener of such reconciliation processes offer grounded theory senses of how such peace-building processes are structured and carried out. . . . The kind of restorative ethnographic qualitative methods I am referring to are those that structure a process in which everyone, including the researcher or the researcher practitioner, experiences the steps required for restorative justice (Volf, 1996) in order to promote a healing process. The goal is not to understand or to explain but to heal, to restore. Understanding and explanation are important aspects of the restoration process but they are midwives that provide opportunity structures for the clarity of consciousness and awareness of those who are transforming. They allow people to verbally and non-verbally make sense of their newly found voices, confessions, apologies, reconciliations and restorations. In this sense, understanding and explaining help people move away from lives amputated by dehumanizing others to new lives of interconnections not based on dehumanizing social markings such as race, gender, disability, class or religious affiliation. Explanation becomes the articulation of hope for a much better life restored through our humanization of others and therefore our own rehumanization. (p. 725)

Notes on Biographical Research

Biographies are life histories that contain more than a listing of chronological events in a person's life and more than just anecdotal stories about that person. Biographies should help the reader understand the way the individual sees (or saw) herself or himself—"the inner struggles and motivation, the way psychological makeup influenced the subject's interpersonal relationships, the interpretation the subject gave to life's events" (Yow, 2005, p. 220).

Biographies generally attempt to unite an individual story with the tenor of the times in which a person lived. Barbara Tuchman's (1978) *A Distant Mirror* provides one example in which the history of the 14th century in Europe is told largely through the biography of a single individual, Enguerrand de Coucy VII. Tuchman explains her rationale for choosing this individual:

> The fifty years that followed the Black Death of 1348–50 are the core of what seems to me a coherent historical period extending approximately from 1300 to 1450 plus a few years. To narrow the focus to a manageable area, I have chosen a particular person's life as the vehicle of my narrative. . . . The person in question is not a king or queen, because everything about such persons is *ipso facto* exceptional, . . . not a commoner, because commoners' lives in most cases did not take the wide range that I wanted . . . nor a woman, because any medieval woman whose life was adequately documented would be atypical. (p. xvi)

B. W. Tuchman (1978) provides insights into the difficulty of doing biographical research in her discussion of contradictions with regard to dates, numbers, and hard facts. During the Middle Ages, there was no standard calendar, thus confusing not only contemporary writers but also the people who lived during that time. Writers of the time tended to exaggerate the numbers of people in armies, battles, plagues, and so forth, because they viewed the use of numbers as a literary device with which they could amaze their readers. Discrepancies of supposed facts were the result of oral transmission of information or the misreading of available documents. Tuchman views contradictions as part of life and thus not merely a matter of conflicting evidence. She also recognizes that historians' prejudices and points of view influence the selection of materials reported in historical documents.

Some biographies are based on oral histories. When this is the case, it is important to get an agreement with the person as to the nature, duration, and control of the work. Writing a biography often involves extensive interviewing that could stretch over years. Establish a tentative work schedule that indicates the time and place and the nature of questions. Get a written contract with the individual that specifies access to other information and editorial rights to the final manuscript. In addition, it is important to point out that you are not going to include only positive things about the person. A biography that creates a "plaster saint" of an individual lacks credibility. It is important to be sensitive to the individual's feelings and to family members. When in doubt about the effect of including controversial information, seek advice from a trusted informant.

Yow (2005) suggests starting the interview process with some general questions:

- What are the most important events in your life?
- Which persons were significant in your life?
- Who knew you well? Shared your joys and sorrows?
- Are there letters, photographs, or newspaper clippings that would be useful?

Biographers for women should be aware of specific challenges presented because of the social influences of gender in a historical context. In *Notable American Women* (Sicherman & Green, 1980), a historical text of women's biographies, the authors stated that they were unable to include all the background information about each woman that they wanted. Even information about birth dates was often unattainable. Reinharz (1994) explores a number of reasons for this difficulty:

1. Women's lives were not viewed as significant; therefore, careful records were not kept.

2. Women were less likely to hold public offices; therefore, information about their lives would be less likely to be included in public records.

3. Many famous women, such as Elizabeth Cady Stanton and Alice Fletcher, have destroyed their primary documents.

4. Name changing is common for women, primarily due to marriage, but also many women used pseudonyms to disguise their gender for their public writing.

Despite these challenges, Reinharz suggests that writing feminist biographies is a rewarding experience for the writer and for readers, because it represents one way to add to our knowledge of the past and our understanding of the present.

Notes on Autobiographical/Self-Study Research

Scholarly advances in autoethnography (see Chapter 8) have increased attention to the broader research approach of autobiography. Autobiographical research has blossomed partly because of the scholarship mentioned in Chapter 8 about autoethnography.

Autobiographical researchers are faced with what might seem to be some obvious problems from the start related to the significance and credibility of their work (Bullough & Pinnegar, 2001). A researcher who chooses to conduct a self-study may ask questions that are of great personal relevance, but do not have significance for a wider audience. Feldman (2003) acknowledged that a research question for a self-study should transcend the purely personal and have significance at a broader level. However, he felt the most pressing issue was the challenge of establishing validity for a self-study. He stated,

> Issues of validity are important because when we engage in reflective processes that focus on ourselves (as in the construction of autobiographical narratives), we cannot be sure of the accuracy of what we see. That is because when we reflect, we do not know if what we see in the mirror is accurate or the distorted view provided by a funhouse mirror. (p. 27)

Feldman (2003) suggested the following procedures to increase the validity of self-study research:

- A clear and detailed description of the method used to collect data needs to be provided, including explicit criteria to determine what counts as data in this work.
- A clear and detailed description of how the researcher constructed the representation from the data (i.e., if an artistic representation is used, how were the data transformed to that end?).
- Triangulation should be extended beyond multiple sources of data to include explanations of multiple ways to represent the same self-study with a rationale as to why one type of representation was chosen over another. Multiple representations increase the credibility of the study.
- Evidence needs to be provided on the value of the changes that result from the self-study. For example, if a self-study is done by a person who prepares teachers, how has that researcher's way of being a teacher or a teacher educator changed?

Ellis and Bochner (2000) describe a somewhat different perspective when asked about how to judge the merits of an autoethnography. They write,

> I think it's the same judgment we make about any author or any character. Is the work honest or dishonest? Does the author take the measure of herself, her limitations, her confusion, ambivalence, mixed feelings? Do you gain a sense of emotional reliability? Do you sense a passage through emotional epiphany to some communicated truth, no resolution per se, but some transformation from an old self to a new one (Rhett, 1997)? Does the story enable you to understand and feel the experience it seeks to convey? There is complexity, multiplicity, uncertainty, desire. (p. 749)

Validity of self-study research can be increased by making the methods more transparent as well as by subjecting the researcher's own representation to critique based on its value for communicating an experience in a compelling way. Taylor (2008) adds that memoirs in the form of autobiographies have been useful for feminists to contest dominant narratives and to recast and reclaim gender stereotypes, as well as to further the feminist movement's goals.

Extending Your Thinking: Oral History and Biographical Studies

1. Role play the following scenarios:
   a. You want to conduct an oral history project on a specific topic. Role play your introductory interview with a prospective narrator.
   b. You want to conduct a biographical study. Role play your interaction with that person—assuming that he or she is still alive. How would you convince him or her that you are the right person to write a biography and that his or her biography is worth telling (should that person not think so)?
   c. You come across one piece of information in a letter suggesting that an important person you are researching stole votes to get passage of a crucial piece of legislation. You cannot find any other written record to corroborate the letter. Role play an interaction with a trusted confidant, discussing your appropriate action in this situation.

2. Kirby (2008) notes the potentially positive outcomes when oral history is combined with phenomenology (a qualitative approach, although some would argue it is a philosophy rather than a research approach; see more discussion of this in Chapter 8). Kirby cites the principles from phenomenology that have relevance for oral history as subjectivity and intersubjectivity of knowledge, time consciousness, and memory (i.e., history happens in the past; historical research looks back at past events from the perspective of the present and consequences of past actions), and value of openness to experience (i.e., researchers must avoid preconceived expectations about what they will find). Review the description of phenomenology in Chapter 8; discuss how you could apply this approach or philosophy in oral history research.

Questions for Critically Analyzing Historical-Narrative Research

Yow (2005) provides a comprehensive list of questions for evaluating oral history research studies. Many of these questions parallel those found in earlier chapters concerning clarity of purpose of the study and so on. Consequently, the questions presented here focus on the historical aspect of the study rather than on the introduction, literature review, interview process, or ethics with the narrator (that last topic is discussed in Chapter 12). Although the following list is a partial adaptation of Yow's questions, readers interested in conducting oral history studies are referred to Yow's complete list of criteria in *Recording Oral History*. Readers should also be aware of the American Historical Association's *Statement on Standards of Professional Conduct* (2005) (www.historians.org/PUBS/Free/ProfessionalStandards.cfm) and the Oral History Association's (2000) evaluation guidelines (www.oralhistory.org/network/mw/index.php/Evaluation_Guide).

The following questions can be used to assist you in critically evaluating historical-narrative research:

1. To what extent does the study add fresh information, fill gaps in the existing record, and/or provide fresh insights and perspectives?

2. To what extent is the information reliable and valid?

3. Is it eyewitness or hearsay evidence?

4. How well and in what manner does it meet internal and external tests of corroboration and explication of contradictions?

5. What is the relationship between information obtained from primary sources (e.g., interviews, letters, diaries, etc.) and existing documentation and historiography?

6. Are the scope, volume, and representativeness of the data used appropriate and sufficient to the purpose? If interviews were used, is there enough testimony to validate the evidence without passing the point of diminishing returns?

For oral history-narrative studies, the following questions can be used to guide you:[8]

7. In what ways did the interviewing conditions contribute to or distract from the quality of the data? For example, was proper concern given to the narrator's health, memory, mental alertness, ability to communicate, and so on? How were disruptions, interruptions, equipment problems, and extraneous participants handled?

8. Did the interviewer do the following?
   a. Thoroughly explore pertinent lines of thought.
   b. Make an effort to identify sources of information.
   c. Employ critical challenges when needed.
   d. Allow biases to interfere with or influence the responses of the interviewee.

Summary of Chapter 9: History and Narrative Study of Lives

Historical and narrative research can be based on a topic of study (e.g., educational experiences of deaf African American students during the Civil Rights era), life stories of individuals (biographies) or life stories of the narrator (autobiography), and autoethnography, which shifts the focus between the individual telling the story and multiple social and cultural layers. Historical research focuses on the past; narrative research focuses on the present. Data can be collected from archives, artifacts, and interviews (oral histories). Specific issues of ethics, authenticity, and comprehensiveness arise in the use of materials from the past that were created without regard to the current researcher's purposes. Historical and narrative research has an important role in making visible the context that surrounds present challenges that are encountered in education and psychology.

Notes

1. The National Standards for History were reviewed, revised, and published in 1996; they are available online at www.sscnet.ucla.edu/nchs/standards/. Readers interested in research on teaching history are referred to Stearns, Seixas, and Wineburg (2000) and Arthur and Phillips (2000).

2. For further reading in cultural history, see Chartier (1988).

3. For an interesting read on the history of historical research, I refer you to Geoff Eley, (2005). *A Crooked Line: From Cultural History to the History of Society,* Ann Arbor, University of Michigan Press.

4. This is not meant to imply that historians rely only on oral data. They avail themselves of information from other sources as well.

5. Contact the Historical Department, Church of Jesus Christ of the Latter-day Saints, 50 East North Temple, Salt Lake City, Utah, 84150.

6. Historians tend to use *The Chicago Manual of Style* (University of Chicago Press, 2003) rather than the *Publication Manual of the American Psychological Association* (2001), which is widely used in education and psychology.

7. Both of these documents are available from the Oral History Association, P.O. Box 3968, Albuquerque, New Mexico 87290–3968. For those who are interested in conducting oral history as a classroom project, the Oral History Association has a guide for teachers who want to use oral history as a teaching tool with their students (Lanham & Mehaffy, 1988).

8. The reader is referred to the *Oral History Evaluation Guidelines* (Oral History Association, 2000) for a more comprehensive listing.

In This Chapter

- Mixed methods research is defined, and typical characteristics are discussed.
- The importance of mixed methods in educational and psychological research is explored.
- The philosophical assumptions of this approach are explained, along with the methodological implications of those assumptions.
- Specific designs for mixed methods research are presented, along with examples of these approaches.
- Questions for critically analyzing mixed methods research are provided.

The Early Childhood Research Institute on Inclusion (ECRII) chose mixed methods to investigate the ecological system of inclusion for children with disabilities in preschool programs (Li, Marquart, & Zercher, 2000). They wanted answers to a number of questions, such as, what are the goals that families, teachers, program administrators, and policymakers have for inclusion? What are their multiple definitions and ways of implementing inclusion? What are the barriers to and facilitators of inclusion in various settings? The researchers used mixed methods to gain a broader perspective and deeper understanding of different levels of the systems and interactions than they could obtain through a single method of research.

10

Mixed Methods Research

Two sample studies that used mixed methods are included in Chapter 1. Berliner et al.'s (2008) study, summarized in Sample Study 1.5, illustrates research that used mixed methods within the pragmatic paradigm. Ward's (2002) study of the effects of a violence prevention program at high schools in the state of Massachusetts, in Sample Study 1.4, is an evaluation study that used mixed methods in the transformative paradigm. The vocabulary and methodological designs and their implications are discussed in this chapter.

Definition and Characteristics[1]

Mixed methods designs include both qualitative and quantitative features in the design, data collection, and analysis (Teddlie & Tashakkori, 2009). In the first issue of *Journal of Mixed Methods Research,* Tashakkori and Creswell (2007, p. 4) define mixed methods as "research in which the investigator collects and analyzes data, integrates the findings, and draws inferences using both qualitative and quantitative approaches or methods in a single study or program of inquiry." Hence, mixed methods can refer to the use of both quantitative and qualitative methods to answer research questions in a single study, as well as those studies that are part of a larger research program and are designed as complementary to provide information related to several research questions, each answered with a different methodological approach. While mixed methods have an intuitive appeal, they also demand that the researcher be expert in both approaches to research, or work with a team that has such expertise. There are issues related to the design of studies, as well as to ensuring the quality of a mixed methods approach that is explored in this chapter.

Teddlie and Tashakkori (2003) described the following characteristics as those of a truly mixed approach methodology:

- It would incorporate multiple approaches in all stages of the study (i.e., problem identification, data collection, data analysis, and final inference).
- It would include a transformation of the data and their analysis through another approach (e.g., content analysis of qualitative data followed by a quantitative analysis of the same data after they had been quantitized).

The intent may be to seek a common understanding through triangulating data from multiple methods, or to use multiple lenses simultaneously to achieve alternative perspectives that are not reduced to a single understanding.

J. C. Greene and Caracelli (2003) suggest that many researchers do not adhere to the full complement of characteristics that are listed by Teddlie and Tashakkori (2003). Rather, social researchers mix methods to a varying degree at various points in their research and still call their work mixed methods research. Researchers can insert multiple mixed options into their work at various points in the research process, including the definition of purpose, overall design, methods, sampling, data recording, analysis, and interpretation.

Importance in Educational and Psychological Research

Mixed methods have particular value when a researcher is trying to solve a problem that is present in a complex educational or social context (Teddlie & Tashakkori, 2009). Because mixed methods designs incorporate techniques from both the quantitative and qualitative research traditions, they can be used to answer questions that could not be answered in any other way. Many researchers have used mixed methods because it seemed intuitively obvious to them that this would enrich their ability to draw conclusions about the problem under study. J. Morse (2003) describes the advantages to using mixed methods this way:

> By combining and increasing the number of research strategies used within a particular project, we are able to broaden the dimensions and hence the scope of our project. By using more than one method within a research study, we are able to obtain a more complete picture of human behavior and experience. Thus, we are better able to hasten our understanding and achieve our research goals more quickly. (p. 189)

I. Newman, Ridenour, Newman, and DeMarco (2003) suggest that, when the purpose of the research is complex, it is necessary to have multiple questions, which frequently necessitates the use of mixed methods. Mixed methods have the potential to contribute to addressing multiple purposes and thus to meeting the needs of multiple audiences for the results.

ECRII conducted a multiphase study of the ecological systems of inclusion that used mixed methods (Li et al., 2000). The researchers described the need for and advantages of this approach as follows:

> This study was designed to answer key questions about the goals that families, teachers, program administrators, and policy makers have for inclusion; multiple definitions and ways of implementing inclusion; and barriers to and facilitators of inclusion in various settings. In order to understand the complex nature of the social ecology in inclusive programs, ECRII researchers used a mixed-method design for data collection and analysis. The multiple methods and measures provided a broader perspective and deeper understanding of different levels of the ecological systems and the interactions among different levels than could be achieved by a single-method design. (p. 117)

Feuer, Towne, and Shavelson (2002) support the legislatively mandated randomized field trials described in Chapter 4 of this book, while at the same time they recognize a need for multiple methods. They wrote,

> When properly applied, quantitative and qualitative research tools can both be employed rigorously and together often can support stronger scientific inferences than when either is employed in isolation. Again, the key to progress lies in the capacity and willingness of investigators from these different perspectives to constructively engage each other's differing perspectives around the common goal of advancing understanding. (p. 8)

Extending Your Thinking: Mixed Methods Advantages and Disadvantages

1. In your opinion, what are the advantages and disadvantages of using mixed methods in psychological or educational research?

2. Talk to potential users of research information or think of yourself as a consumer. What are the strengths and weaknesses of a mixed methods approach?

Philosophical Assumptions: Pragmatism, Mixing Paradigms, and Transformation

Based on a review of social research that claimed to use mixed methods, J. C. Greene and Caracelli (2003) concluded that inquiry decisions are rarely, if ever, consciously rooted in philosophical assumptions or beliefs. Rather, researchers based their choice of mixed methods on the nature of the phenomena being investigated, the contexts in which the study is conducted, or the funding agencies' requirements. Nevertheless, they did not conclude that paradigms and their associated philosophical assumptions were irrelevant—merely unexamined. They further suggested that by attending too little to philosophical ideas and traditions, many mixed method inquirers are insufficiently reflective and their practice insufficiently unproblematized. Examining the philosophical assumptions underlying research, mixed methods or not, can offer a better understanding of the complex social world in which educators and psychologists operate. (See a list of options concerning the relationship between paradigmatic stance and choice of mixed methods in Box 10.1.)

Box 10.1 Possible Reactions to Paradigms

- *Incompatibility Thesis*—Mixed methods are impossible due to the incompatibility of the paradigms underlying the methods.
- *Complementary Strengths*—Adhere to the tenets of rigor as defined within each paradigm.
- *Multiple Paradigms Drive Mixed Methods*—Mixed methods can be approached from a pragmatic or transformative paradigm.
- *Dialectical Pragmatism*—The research question is the dictator of method; qualitative and quantitative methods are taken seriously and results of both methods are synthesized for each study.
- *Transformative Mixed Methods*—Mixed methods enhance the ability of researchers to capture the complexity of issues of human rights and social transformation.
- *Dialectical Thesis*—All paradigms have something to offer; research will advance through the deliberate and critical dialogues that occur among scholars who situate themselves in different paradigms (J. C. Greene, 2007).
- *A-Paradigmatic*—Ignore philosophical assumptions (at your own risk).

SOURCES: J.C. Greene (2007); Mertens (2009); Teddlie & Tashakkori (2009).

Teddlie and Tashakkori (2009) propose the use of pragmatism as one philosophical orientation to guide mixed methods researchers. Simply put, pragmatists consider the research question to be more important than either the method they use or the worldview that is supposed to underlie the method. These researchers use the criterion "what works?" to determine which method to use to answer a specific research question. Thus the pragmatic orientation rejects the either/or mentality suggested by a choice between the postpositive and the constructivist paradigms. Here is how Teddlie and Tashakkori (2009) describe the pragmatic researcher:

> Pragmatists decide what they want to study based on what is important within their personal value systems. They then study the topic in a way that is congruent with their value system, including units of analysis and variables that they feel are most likely to yield interesting responses.... This description of pragmatists'

> behaviors is consistent with the way that many researchers actually conduct their studies, especially research that has important social consequences. (pp. 90–91)

This pragmatic basis can be contrasted with that of the transformative paradigm in which the emphasis is on the inclusion of values and viewpoints, especially of marginalized groups, as the driving force for all aspects of the research. Mertens (2009) and House and Howe (1999) question the notion of the centrality of the researcher's values in the pragmatic paradigm. They raise questions in terms of which values, whose values, and the role of the researcher within the context of values. While Teddlie and Tashakkori (2009) claim that practicality should serve as the value basis for a researcher's choices, researchers within the transformative paradigm would ask, practical for what? As House and Howe (1999) write,

> Something could be practical for bad ends. Using practicality as the primary criterion means evaluators (researchers) may serve whatever ends clients or policy makers endorse. Evaluation (research) should be premised on higher social goals than being useful to those in power. (p. 36)

Mertens (2009) and Creswell (2009) noted that a mixed methods design could also fit within a transformative framework if it was designed to reflect, in both perspective and outcomes, a dedication to social change at levels ranging from the personal to the political. Furthermore, they contend that it is possible to conduct almost any mixed methods study with a transformative or advocacy purpose.

Extending Your Thinking: Paradigms and Mixed Methods

What are the philosophical assumptions that underlie the mixed methods approach? How can you integrate the assumptions of the three major paradigms (postpositivist, interpretive/constructivist, and transformative) to guide your thinking in the use of mixed methods? What are the assumptions of the pragmatic paradigm and their implications for special education research?

Mixed Methods Design Options

The specific mixed methods approaches are defined by the ordering of the application of the quantitative and qualitative methods (simultaneously or sequentially), as well as at what point the mixing of methods occurs. Qualitative and quantitative data collection can occur in *parallel form* or *sequential form*.

- *Parallel form:* Concurrent mixed methods/model designs in which two types of data are collected and analyzed.

- *Sequential form:* One type of data provides a basis for collection of another type of data.

Creswell (2009) uses these two basic design types to organize possible variations in mixed methods designs, although he uses the term concurrent in place of parallel. I agree with Teddlie and Tashakkori (2009) that parallel is a more inclusive term than concurrent because the latter term implies the two methods must be used at the same time, rather than the inference from the term "parallel," which is that they occur in proximity to each other. Creswell describes possible twists, such as parallel (concurrent) designs that are explanatory (qualitative data are collected after quantitative data to try to explain the quantitative results) or exploratory (qualitative data collection is followed by quantitative data collection to explore a phenomenon), and sequential designs that are triangulated (use of both quantitative and qualitative data to see if there is convergence in findings), or embedded (one type of data plays a dominant role while the other type of data plays a supportive role).

Mixed methods can also involve the conversion of qualitative data to a quantitative form or vice versa; Teddlie and Tashakkori (2009) call this a conversion design. They also add another design called multilevel design in which quantitative data are collected at one level of an organization (e.g., student level) and qualitative data are collected at another level (e.g., administrator level). The mixed methods community also talks about designation of approaches as dominant or less dominant (or supportive), depending on the extent to which the overall study uses either quantitative or qualitative approaches—to the same extent or one or the other to a greater or lesser extent (Creswell, 2009; J. Morse, 2003; Teddlie & Tashakkori, 2009).

As I believe that paradigmatic stances are the beginning point for decision making in research, I separate the main design options into the two paradigms that are salient in the mixed methods research community: pragmatic and transformative. Table 10.1 provides a summary of four design options for a mixed methods approach.[2] Types of mixed methods designs are further elaborated in the next section.

Pragmatic Parallel Mixed Methods Design

The pragmatic parallel mixed methods design is one in which qualitative and quantitative data are collected and analyzed to answer a single study's research questions (Onwuegbuzie & Teddlie, 2002). The final inferences are based on both data analysis results. The two types of data are collected independently at the same time or with a short time lag. (If the research is designed with two relatively independent phases, one with qualitative questions and data collection and analysis techniques and the other with quantitative questions and data collection and analysis techniques, then Creswell (2009) calls this an *embedded design*. The inferences made on the basis of the results of each strand are pulled together to form meta-inferences at the end of the study.)

Li et al. (2000) provide a detailed example of a pragmatic parallel mixed methods design in their study of preschool inclusion. They planned an ecological systems study that consisted of a case study at each of 16 inclusion programs to provide an in-depth analysis of inclusion in the programs. They wanted to determine barriers to and facilitators of inclusion, as well as describe idiosyncratic issues. Quantitative and qualitative data were collected and analyzed concurrently.

The quantitative data were collected using six 30-minute observations of each child using an ecobehavioral observational system called the Code for Active Student Participation and Engagement Revised (CASPER II; W. H. Brown, Favazza, & Odom, 1995), a peer rating sociometric assessment (Asher, Singleton, Tinsley, & Hymel, 1979), and the Battelle Developmental Inventory (Newborg, Stock, Wnek, Guidubaldi, & Svinicki, 1988).

Table 10.1 Mixed Methods Design Options and Examples

	Philosophical Paradigm	
Temporal Relation	***Pragmatic***	***Transformative***
Parallel	Characteristics: Both qualitative and quantitative data are collected to answer the research question(s) Two types of data collected simultaneously or with small time lag Example: The ecological systems of inclusion in early childhood programs (Li et al., 2000) 16 case studies involving quantitative behavioral observation system, peer rating sociometric assessment, qualitative participant observations, and open-ended interviews	Characteristics: Uses mixed methods to promote change at any level, personal to political Deliberately seeks underrepresented populations Gives primacy to value-based and action-oriented dimensions Example: Shared Reading Project (SRP) for deaf children (Delk & Weidekamp, 2001; Mertens, Delk, & Weidekamp, 2003) Designed to meet the needs of traditionally underserved deaf and hard-of-hearing students: the SRP involved members of diverse ethnocultural groups, those with secondary disabilities, people in rural areas, and people from homes where English is not the primary language Used quantitative surveys, reading logs, qualitative interviews, and deaf interviewers conducted interviews of deaf tutors
Sequential	Characteristics: One type of data provides a basis for collection of another type of data It answers one type of question by collecting and analyzing two types of data Inferences are based on the analysis of both types of data Example: High school dropout study (Berliner et al., 2008) Analysis of quantitative dropout and reenrollment data, followed by semi-structured interviews with staff and students	Characteristics: Same as parallel transformative in terms of goals and focus on underrepresented populations and values, except one type of data provides a basis for collection of another type of data Other methodological characteristics are the same as sequential pragmatic designs Example: Parent experiences with their young deaf or hard-of-hearing child (Meadow-Orlans, Mertens, & Sass-Lehrer, 2003) National quantitative survey, followed by in-depth phone interviews with targeted groups and focus groups with ethnic/racial minority families

The qualitative data included participant observations that occurred in each preschool inclusion program two to three times a week for 6 to 16 weeks. The observers wrote field notes that included descriptions of the physical environment, classroom participants, activities, and interactions among participants. Observations lasted between 1 and 5 hours.

In addition, open-ended interviews were conducted with professionals, administrators, and family members. Teachers and family members also completed a Friendship Survey (Buyse, 1993). Moreover, observers who used the CASPER II observation system were asked to write post-CASPER notes following each session in which they identified the type of interaction that most represented the child's behavior during the 30-minute observation.

Each data set was analyzed according to appropriate analytic techniques (e.g., frequency tabulations were used to produce graphs for each child for each category of behavior observed using the CASPER II system). Child case summaries and vignettes were written for each child using thematic coding of the qualitative data. Thus, the results from each data set could be compared to increase the explanatory value of the findings. For example, the peer rating data indicated that one child was very sociable. The observation data provided a vignette describing the nature of her behavior to illustrate how this characteristic was manifested by that child.

Pragmatic Sequential Mixed Methods Design

In the pragmatic sequential mixed methods design, one type of data (e.g., quantitative) provides a basis for the collection of another type of data (e.g., qualitative; Creswell, 2009; Onwuegbuzie & Teddlie, 2002; Teddlie & Tashakkori, 2009). It answers one type of question by collecting and analyzing two types of data. Inferences are based on the analysis of both types of data. A sequential design is one in which the conclusions that are made on the basis of the first strand lead to formulation of questions, data collection, and data analysis for the next strand. The final inferences are based on the results of both strands of the study. In some cases, the second strand/phase of the study is used to confirm or disconfirm the inferences of the first strand or to provide further explanation for unexpected findings in the first strand. This approach can be used to generate hypotheses to be explored in more depth, or to develop surveys that use correct language for the population.

Berliner et al. (2008) provide an example of a sequential mixed methods design in their study of high school dropouts. The researchers had access to a longitudinal student-level database that contained information about the date that dropouts left school and if they reenrolled in the same district. They used data from a cohort of students who started high school in 2001/02 and were expected to graduate in the 2005/06 school year. They conducted quantitative statistical analyses on dates of withdrawal and return, graduation rates, student courses, and demographic characteristics, as well as their reasons for dropping out. The quantitative data revealed that dropping out is not necessarily a permanent decision. While only 45% of the students graduated within the expected four years, of those who did drop out, almost one third of the students reenrolled during the five years of the study and 18% of those graduated from high school in 2005/06. (Twenty percent of the students transferred to other school districts and researchers did not have access to their school outcomes.) The authors describe their sequential mixed methods design as follows: "Drawing on the preliminary analysis of the district dataset, interviews were conducted to clarify, affirm, or challenge the study findings and to explore state and district policies and practices that affect reenrollment and students' experiences dropping out and reenrolling in San Bernardino City Unified School District high schools. In fall 2007, interview data were collected from 20 district contacts during a weeklong, in-person site visit" (Berliner et al., 2008, p. ii).

Christ (2007, p. 228) provides another example of sequential design that began with a longitudinal quantitative survey of the supports needed by college students with disabilities. The researcher compared the results of a national survey that was conducted in 1999 and 2001 to see if changes occurred over this two-year period. The results were used to raise additional questions, frame criteria for purposeful selection of postsecondary institutions, and guide development of interview questions at the selected sites. Christ then conducted semistructured interviews at three postsecondary sites that were considered by experts in the field to be exemplary. The resulting data were analyzed to determine critical themes related to effectively supporting college students with disabilities. These data were then used as a basis for designing a third stage of the study: an intensive case study of a single institution that was facing a severe budget cut.

Transformative Parallel Mixed Methods Design

The transformative parallel mixed methods design is based on the use of both quantitative and qualitative methods in a study that has a goal of social change at levels ranging from the personal to the political (Mertens, 2009). The design gives primacy to the value-based and action-oriented dimensions of different inquiry traditions (J. C. Greene, 2007).

The Shared Reading Project (SRP) provides an example of a transformative mixed methods design that used parallel qualitative and quantitative data collection and analysis strategies (Delk & Weidekamp, 2001; Mertens, Delk, & Weidekamp, 2003). The SRP is designed to provide hearing parents and caregivers with visually based strategies to read books to their deaf and hard-of-hearing children from birth through age eight. The SRP was designed to meet the needs of five groups of traditionally underserved deaf and hard-of-hearing students, including members of diverse ethnocultural groups, those who have secondary disabilities, people who live in rural areas, people who come from homes in which a spoken language other than English is used, and/or people who are lower-achieving academically. Tutors, most of whom are deaf, visited the families in their homes to teach them signing and reading strategies and answer their questions about the process of teaching their children to read.

The SRP collected both quantitative and qualitative data to address multiple evaluation questions. The quantitative measures included closed-ended surveys and logs that the families kept that indicated such things as the demographic characteristics and the number of times families used the books that the tutors brought them between visits. The qualitative data were collected through in-person, on-site interviews with the families, tutors, and site coordinators. Foreign language interpreters were used in homes where the spoken language was other than English. Deaf interviewers conducted the interviews with the deaf tutors, which were videotaped and then transcribed. Participants were asked to describe such things as their role in the project, their emotional experiences during the project, and successes and challenges.

The quantitative and qualitative data were analyzed with a specific attempt to identify the impact of the project on the traditionally underserved groups. Quantitative data indicated that 104 of the 116 children belonged to at least one of the traditionally underserved groups. The quantitative and qualitative data were disaggregated in the analysis in order to provide a picture of the unique successes and challenges faced by members of these groups in teaching their deaf and hard-of-hearing children to read. Because the focus was on traditionally underserved groups, the results were shared with the people in their communities to determine lessons learned and options for additional action. Because of the demonstrable results in terms of improved literacy, several of the sites have moved to institutionalize the SRP, incorporating it into their regular school program. In some sites, the skill of the deaf tutors has been increasingly recognized and they have been given responsibilities to work in the classrooms as well as at the students' homes. One site has made a decision to expand the program to include Hmong and Latino families of children enrolled in the school.

Transformative Sequential Mixed Methods Design

The transformative sequential mixed methods approach shares the transformative goal described in the previous section, as well as the methodological sequencing of the pragmatic sequential option (Mertens, 2009).

Meadow-Orlans et al. (2003) provide an example of a transformative sequential mixed methods design in their study of parents' experiences with their young deaf and hard-of-hearing children. The study proceeded in three phases: first, a quantitative national survey; then, individual parent interviews; and, third, focus group interviews. The initial phase of the study was designed not only to provide a broad picture of parents' early experiences, but also to investigate differences in experiences based on such characteristics as race or ethnicity, parent hearing status, presence of additional disabilities beyond hearing loss, level of parent education, and the socioeconomic status of the family. The National Parent Project survey was designed to obtain information directly from families by eliciting descriptions of their experiences, evaluations of effectiveness of services, and recommendations for improvement. Parents provided important insights throughout the project from the design of the survey and interview protocol to the analyses and implications of the findings.

The quantitative data analysis indicated great diversity in the characteristics of the families and their responses to the survey questions. For example, one third of the participating parents had children with a disability in addition to a hearing loss, and many of these families encountered difficulties obtaining needed services. Overall, families generally expressed satisfaction with the services their children received; however, some families, particularly non-White families, were less satisfied with their services.

These findings led to the qualitative portion of the study, which used in-depth telephone interviews and a purposive sampling strategy to investigate in more depth the experiences of families with children with co-occurring disabilities, parents who were deaf or hard of hearing, parents of children with cochlear implants, and families of color. In the final phase, three focus groups of parents were conducted in large urban areas with the intention of expanding the number of Hispanic and African American families represented in the sample. In replying to very open-ended questions, participants provided insights into their experiences, feelings, and concerns during the time of suspicion and confirmation of their child's hearing loss; discussed the people or services that were most helpful and needs that were not addressed by early intervention services; described their communication decision-making process; and offered the advice they had for professionals and for other parents.

The data were analyzed and reported within the larger national context, while still preserving the subgroup analyses of traditionally underrepresented groups. Special attention was given to interrogating bodies of knowledge that have become institutionalized as established concepts and practices that were determined by groups that traditionally have power in our society. Banks (2000) suggests that the groups in power (generally professionals) largely determine for those with less power (parents) what are the accepted practices. These "cultural facts" are accepted without challenge until the voices of individuals affected have the opportunity to articulate their experiences and express their perspectives. Thus the parents' comments served as a basis to give insights not only to other parents who might be starting down the road of life with their deaf or hard-of-hearing child, but also to professionals who serve this population.

Extending Your Thinking: Mixed Methods Design Options

Explain the main design options for mixed methods research. Give an example of how each of these could be applied in educational and psychological research.

Select a research problem in education or psychology. Find a research study that uses a mixed methods approach. Use the questions for critically analyzing mixed methods research to identify its strengths and weaknesses. What improvements would you suggest for that study?

Questions for Critically Analyzing Mixed Methods Research

Teddlie and Tashakkori (2009) suggest that there is a unique character to mixed methods that transcends a simplistic combination of methods. Therefore, they suggest the term *inference quality* to refer to issues that would be termed internal validity in quantitative terms or trustworthiness in qualitative terms. J. C. Greene (2007) also discusses this concept as warranting the quality of inferences in mixed methods research. Based on the dialectical stance with regard to mixed methods research, she offers the following considerations for quality:

- Focuses on the available data support for the inferences, using data of multiple and diverse kinds;
- Could include criteria or stances from different methodological traditions;
- Considers warrants for inquiry inferences a matter of persuasive argument, in addition to a matter of fulfilling established criteria; and
- Attends to the nature and extent of the better understanding that is reached with this mixed methods design. (p. 169)

Table 10.2 provides a framework for considering criteria to determine quality in mixed methods research.

Table 10.2 Rigor: Criteria for Judging Quality in Quantitative, Qualitative, and Mixed Methods Research

Quantitative	*Qualitative*	*Mixed Method/Model*
Internal validity • History • Maturation • Testing; instrumentation • Statistical regression • Differential selection • Experimental mortality • Experimental treatment diffusion External validity • Sufficient description of treatment • Interference of multiple treatments • Treatment validity • Denial of treatment • Population/ sample issues • Contextual/ cultural factors Reliability • Evidence of reliable measures • Language/culture • Trained observers • Accommodations for disabled Objectivity • Distance from the subjects	Credibility (parallels internal validity) • Prolonged, substantial engagement • Persistent observation • Peer debriefing • Progressive subjectivity • Member checks • Triangulation Transferability (parallels external validity) • Thick description • Multiple cases Dependability (parallels reliability) • Dependability audit Confirmability (parallels objectivity) • Confirmability audit Authenticity • Fairness • Ontological authenticity • Catalytic authenticity Transformative • Positionality or standpoint • Attention to voice • Critical reflexivity • Reciprocity, sharing perquisites	• What are the multiple purposes and questions that justify the use of a mixed method design? • Has the researcher matched the purposes and questions to appropriate methods? • To what extent has the researcher adhered to the criteria that define quality for the quantitative portion of the study? • To what extent has the researcher adhered to the criteria that define quality for the qualitative portion of the study? • How has the researcher addressed the tension between potentially conflicting demands of paradigms in the design and implementation of the study? • Has the researcher appropriately acknowledged the limitations associated with data that were collected to supplement the main data collection of the study? • How has the researcher integrated the results from the mixed methods? If necessary, how has the researcher explained conflicting findings that resulted from different methods? • What evidence is there that the researcher developed the design to be responsive to the practical and cultural needs of specific subgroups on the basis of such dimensions as disability, culture, language, reading levels, gender, class, and race/ethnicity?

One approach to critically analyzing a mixed methods study would be to use the criteria that are presented in previous chapters on specific quantitative methods for the quantitative portion of the study and those in the chapters on qualitative methods for the qualitative portion. This is not a bad strategy and could be a useful way to assess the quality of the individual parts of the study. J. Morse (2003) suggests that researchers begin their critique of the quality of a mixed methods design by looking at the integrity of the methods as they are derived from the assumptions of each paradigm. So, using the questions in the appropriate methodology chapter to critically analyze the methods for particular approaches in a project is appropriate.

However, tensions can arise because conflicting demands can be present when more than one paradigm is operationalized (J. Morse, 2003). For example, if the researcher is working inductively within the qualitative part of the study, the sample is small and purposively selected, and therefore would not meet the criteria for a quantitative sample that needs to be larger and have been randomly selected. Morse contends that if a quantitative component is being sought, then a separate, randomized sample must be added for that portion. Small samples do raise issues of potential bias. Morse also raised the issue related to the use of a qualitative or quantitative data collection method to supplement the findings from the main study. For example, a quantitative study might include one or two focus groups to add a qualitative dimension to the main study. The researcher in such circumstances needs to acknowledge the limitations of the qualitative data, in that they cannot stand alone. They are only intelligible and interpretable when they are linked to the data from the main quantitative part of the study.

When looking at the conclusions of a mixed methods design, it is possible that the results from both methods will agree with each other and thus confirm the conclusions reached. It is also possible that they will not agree with each other. Then, the researcher must explore plausible explanations for the disagreement. It may be due to the difference in approach or because of changes in the context over time that could influence performance on the dependent measures.

The selection of different methods in a study may be necessary to accommodate differences based on disability, culture, language, reading or writing levels, gender, class, and race or ethnicity for specific subgroups in a population (Mertens, 2009). Practically, individuals with different types of disabilities may be better able to provide accurate information about themselves if a qualitative or quantitative method is used. For example, in the Delk and Weidekamp (2001) study, telephone surveys were not appropriate for deaf individuals without adequate English writing skills. Other human dimensions, such as race or ethnicity, also need to be considered in the design of a study. As Stanfield (1999) noted, an atmosphere of distrust has developed between researchers and many members of racial or ethnic minority communities because of historical events such as the Tuskegee experiments, in which Black men with syphilis were left untreated so that researchers could study the progress of the disease. Mixed methods may be necessary to provide an opportunity to build a sense of trust between the researcher and the community. A researcher could define the problem to be studied through a qualitative phase of interacting with members of the community, using observation and interviewing. If trust can be developed, then it might be appropriate to introduce a quantitative phase to the project.

These issues and concerns then give rise to the following questions that can be used to critically analyze mixed methods research studies:

1. What are the multiple purposes and questions that justify the use of a mixed methods design?

2. Has the researcher matched the purposes and questions to appropriate methods?

3. To what extent has the researcher adhered to the criteria that define quality for the quantitative portion of the study?

4. To what extent has the researcher adhered to the criteria that define quality for the qualitative portion of the study?

5. How has the researcher addressed the tension between potentially conflicting demands of paradigms in the design and implementation of the study?

6. Has the researcher appropriately acknowledged the limitations associated with data that were collected to supplement the main data collection of the study?

7. How has the researcher integrated the results from the mixed methods? If necessary, how has the researcher explained conflicting findings that resulted from different methods?

8. What evidence is there that the researcher developed the design to be responsive to the practical and cultural needs of specific subgroups on the basis of such dimensions as disability, culture, language, reading levels, gender, class, and race or ethnicity?

Extending Your Thinking: Rigor in Mixed Methods Research

Design a study using a mixed methods design. Explain how your design respects the integrity of the qualitative and quantitative methods. Explain how you would address the criteria implicit in the questions for critically analyzing mixed methods research.

Using one or more of the studies from the quantitative or qualitative chapters, rethink the study using mixed methods. How would the study change? What would you gain? What would you lose?

Summary of Chapter 10: Mixed Methods Research

In some ways, mixed methods is not a new way of doing research, as many researchers have engaged in the collection of both quantitative and qualitative data. However, the research community now reflects an increased interest in mixed methods and how to explore more systematically the advantages and disadvantages of their use. Both pragmatic and transformative paradigms are used as a basis for this exploration and to examine those elements of mixed methods studies that make them unique as compared to studies that use a single method. Designs for mixed methods include consideration of the temporal relation between the use of each type of method (quantitative and qualitative) and the philosophical belief systems that underlie the research decisions. Criteria for critically analyzing the strengths and weaknesses of mixed methods research include the criteria for the individual approaches (e.g., case studies or surveys), as well as consideration of the rationale for and implementation of the mixed methods themselves.

Notes

1. Multiple methods studies are considered those that use more than one method, but the methods chosen are singularly either quantitative or qualitative. Teddlie and Tashakkori (2009) label this monomethod multi-strand research.

2. In Teddlie and Tashakkori (2003), several typologies of mixed methods designs are presented in the various chapters. They note that the formal field of mixed methods research is in its adolescence and therefore it is to be expected that various typologies would be present in the literature. Main points of definition appear to be the temporal relation between the quantitative and qualitative data collections (parallel vs. sequential), the philosophical paradigm underlying the work (e.g., pragmatic or transformative), the priority given to either qualitative or quantitative approaches (Creswell [2003] had described this as dominant, subdominant relations), and the purpose of the research (confirmatory or exploratory). If design options were presented for each possible combination of these dimensions, then there would be a large number of possible designs for mixed methods. For the sake of parsimony, I elected to include four major categories for the major types of mixed methods designs.

In This Chapter

- The viewpoints of researchers who work within the postpositivist, constructivist, and transformative paradigms are contrasted in relation to sampling strategies and generalizability.
- External validity is introduced as a critical concept in sampling decisions.
- Challenges in the definition of specific populations are described in terms of conceptual and operational definitions, identifying a person's racial or ethnic status, identifying persons with a disability, heterogeneity within populations, and cultural issues.
- Strategies for designing and selecting samples are provided, including probability-based, theoretical-purposive, and convenience sampling. Sampling is also discussed for complex designs such as those using hierarchical linear modeling.
- Sampling bias, access issues, and sample size are discussed.
- Ethical standards for the protection of study participants are described in terms of an institutional review board's requirements.
- Questions to guide critical analysis of sampling definition, selection, and ethics are provided.

> Transformative research implies a philosophy that research should confront and act against the causes of injustice and violence, which can be caused not only by that which is researched but also by the process of research itself. Individuals involved in research can be disenfranchised in a few ways: (1) by the hidden power arrangements uncovered by the research process, (2) by the actions of unscrupulous (and even well-intentioned) researchers, but also (3) by researchers' failure to expose those arrangements once they become aware of them. Hidden power arrangements are maintained by secrets of those who might be victimized by them (because they fear retaliation).... [Researchers] contribute to this disenfranchisement if it prevents the exposure of hidden power arrangements. (Baez, 2002, pp. 51–52)

11

Sampling

Definition, Selection, and Ethics

Sampling Strategies: Alternative Paradigms

The decisions that a researcher makes regarding from whom data will be collected, who is included, how they are included, and what is done to conceal or reveal identities in research constitute the topics addressed in this chapter on sampling. As can be seen in the opening quotation, these decisions are complex and not unproblematic. In a simple sense, sampling refers to the method used to select a given number of people (or things) from a population. The strategy for selecting your sample influences the quality of your data and the inferences that you can make from it. The issues surrounding from whom you collect data are what sampling is all about. Within all approaches to research, researchers use sampling for very practical reasons. In most research studies, it is simply not feasible to collect data from every individual in a setting or population.

Sampling is one area in which great divergence can be witnessed when comparing the various research paradigms. In general, researchers who function within the postpositivist paradigm see the ideal sampling strategy as some form of probability sampling. Henry (1990) describes probability sampling as follows:

> Probability samples are selected in such a way that every member of the population actually has a possibility of being included in the sample. . . . Probability samples can be rigorously analyzed to determine possible bias and likely error. There is no such advantage for nonprobability samples. (p. 17)

Researchers within the constructivist paradigm tend to use a theoretical or purposive approach to sampling. Their sampling activities begin with an identification of groups, settings, and individuals where (and for whom) the processes being studied are most likely to occur (Denzin & Lincoln, 2000). As J. M. Morse (1994) explains,

> Data collection and sampling are dictated by and become directed entirely toward the emergent model. The researcher seeks indices of saturation, such as repetition in the information obtained and confirmation of previously collected data. Using theoretical sampling, he or she looks for negative cases to enrich the emergent model and to explain all variations and diverse patterns. (p. 230)

Researchers within the transformative paradigm could choose either a probability or theoretical-purposive approach to sampling, depending on their choice of quantitative, qualitative, or methods. However, they would function with a distinctive consciousness of representing the populations that have traditionally been underrepresented in research.

Despite the contrasting views of sampling evidenced within the various paradigms, issues of common concern exist. All sampling decisions must be made within the constraints of ethics and feasibility. Although randomized probability samples are set forth as the ideal in the postpositivist paradigm, they are not commonly used in educational and psychological research. Thus, in practice, the postpositivist and constructivist paradigms are more similar than different in that both use nonrandom samples. Sometimes, the use of convenience samples (discussed at greater length later in this chapter) means that less care is taken by those in both of these paradigms. All researchers should make conscious choices in the design of their samples rather than accepting whatever sample presents itself as most convenient.

External Validity (Generalizability) or Transferability

As you will recall from Chapter 4, *external validity* refers to the ability of the researcher (and user of the research results) to extend the findings of a particular study beyond the specific individuals and setting in which that study occurred. Within the postpositivist paradigm, the external validity depends on the design and execution of the sampling strategy. Henry (1990) talks about *generalizability* in terms of the *target population,* which he defines as the group to whom we want to generalize findings.

In the constructivist paradigm, every instance of a case or process is viewed as both an exemplar of a general class of phenomena and particular and unique in its own way (Denzin & Lincoln, 2000). The researcher's task is to provide sufficient thick description about the case so that the readers can understand the contextual variables operating in that setting (Lincoln & Guba, 2000). The burden of generalizability then lies with the readers, who are assumed to be able to generalize subjectively from the case in question to their own personal experiences (Stake, 2000). Lincoln and Guba (2000) label this type of generalizability *transferability.*

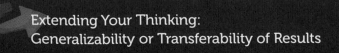

Extending Your Thinking: Generalizability or Transferability of Results

What is your opinion of a researcher's ability to generalize results? Is it possible? If so, under what conditions? What do you think of the alternative concept of transferability?

Defining the Population and Sample

Research constructs, such as *racial* or *ethnic minority* or *deaf student,* can be defined in two ways. Conceptual definitions are those that use other constructs to explain the meaning, and operational definitions are those that specify how the construct will be measured. Researchers often begin their work with a conceptual idea of the group of people they want to study, such as working mothers, drug abusers, students with disabilities, and so on. Through a review of the literature, they formulate a formal, conceptual definition of the group they want to study. For example, the target population might be first-grade students in the United States.

An operational definition of the population in the postpositivist paradigm is called the *experimentally accessible population,* defined as the list of people who fit the conceptual definition. For example, the experimentally accessible population might be all the first-grade students in your school district whose names are entered into the district's database. You would next need to obtain a list of all the students in that school district. This would be called your *sampling frame.* Examples of sampling frames include (a) the student enrollment, (b) a list of clients who receive services at a clinic, (c) professional association membership directories, or (d) city phone directories. The researcher should ask if the lists are complete and up-to-date and who has been left off the list. For example, lists of clients at a community mental health clinic eliminate those who need services but have not sought them. Telephone directories eliminate people who do not have telephone service, as well as those with unlisted or newly assigned numbers, and most directories do not list people's cell, or mobile, phone numbers. In the postpositivist view, generalizability is in part a function of the match between the conceptual and operational definitions of the sample. If the lists are not accurate, systematic error can occur because of differences between the true population and the study population (Henry, 1990). When the accessible population represents the target population, this establishes *population validity.*

The researcher must also acknowledge that the intended sample might differ from the obtained sample. The issue of response rate was addressed in Chapter 6 on survey research, along with strategies such as follow-up of nonrespondents and comparison of respondents and nonrespondents on key variables. The size and effect of nonresponse or attrition should be reported and explained in all approaches to research to address the effect of people not responding, choosing not to participate, being inaccessible, or dropping out of the study. This effect represents a threat to the internal and external validity (or credibility and transferability) of the study. You may recall the related discussion of this issue in the section on experimental mortality in Chapter 4 and the discussion of credibility and transferability in Chapter 8. A researcher can use statistical processes (described in Chapter 13) to identify the plausibility of fit between the obtained sample and the group from which it was drawn when the design of the study permits it.

Identification of Sample Members

It might seem easy to know who is a member of your sample and who is not; however, complexities arise because of the ambiguity or inadequacy of the categories typically used by researchers. Examples of errors in identification of sample members can readily be found in research with racial and ethnic minorities and persons with disabilities. Two examples are presented here, and the reader is referred to Chapter 5 on causal comparative and correlational research to review additional complexities associated with this issue.

Identification of Race and Ethnicity in Populations

Investigators who examine racial or ethnic groups and differences between such groups frequently do so without a clear sense of what race or ethnicity means in a research context (Blum, 2008). Researchers who use categorization and assume homogeneity of condition are avoiding the complexities of participants' experiences and social locations. Selection of samples on the basis of race should be done with attention to within-group variation and to the influence of particular contexts. Race as a biogenetic variable should not serve as a proxy variable for actual causal variables, such as poverty, unemployment, or family structure.

Heterogeneity has been recognized as a factor that contributes to difficulty in classifying people as African American or Latino (Massey, Zambrana, & Bell, 1995; Stanfield, 1993a). In reference to African American populations, Stanfield (1993a) writes,

> Identity questions—such as "What is a white person?" or "What is a Black person?"—become problematic when one considers the extensiveness of ethnic mixing that has occurred in the United States in reciprocal acculturation and cultural assimilation processes, if not in miscegenation experiences. (p. 21)

Thus, Stanfield recognizes that many people are not pure racially. In addition, some African American people have skin color that is light enough to "pass" for White.

Race is sometimes used as a substitute for ethnicity, which is usually defined in terms of a common origin or culture resulting from shared activities and identity based on some mixture of language, religion, race, and ancestry (C. D. Lee, 2003). Lee suggests that the profoundly contextual nature of race and ethnicity must be taken into account in the study of ethnic and race relations. Blum (2008) makes clear that use of broad categories of race can hide important differences in communities; using labels such as African American and Asian American ignores important differences based on ethnicity. Initial immigration status and social capital among different Asian immigrant groups result in stark differences in terms of advantages and positions in current racial and ethnic stratifications. For example, Hmong and Cambodians are generally less successful in American society than Asians from the southern or eastern parts of Asia. Ethnic plurality is visible in the Black community in terms of people who were brought to America during the times of slavery and those who have come more recently from Africa or the Caribbean.

In Massey et al.'s (1995) exploration of the meaning of the term *Latino,* they concluded that Latino does not exist apart from classifications created by the federal statisticians to provide data on people of Mexican, Cuban, Puerto Rican, Dominican, Colombian, Salvadoran, and other extractions. Also, *Hispanic* is a label that has been used to include all those who can trace their origins to an area originally colonized by Spain. These two labels obscure important national diversity within this population. The varied origins and immigration histories of groups termed Latino must be considered in the definition of the samples, or, the writers warn, the research is not likely to be productive.

The American Psychological Association Joint Task Force of Divisions 17 and 45's *Guidelines on Multicultural Education, Training, Research, Practice, and Organizational Change for Psychologists* (2002) and the Council of National Psychological Associations for the Advancement of Ethnic Minority Interests' *Guidelines for Research in Ethnic Minority Communities, 2000* (2000) provide detailed insights into working with four of the major racial/ethnic minority groups in the United States: Asian American/Pacific Islander populations, persons of African descent, Hispanics, and American Indians (see Box 11.1). (Although American Indians make up less than 1% of the national population, there are more than 500 federally recognized American Indian tribes in the United States, plus another 200 that are petitioning for recognition [Potter, 2003a].) Each recognized tribe has its own government and court system.

Box 11.1 Heterogeneity in Racial/Ethnic Minority and Immigrant Communities

The American Psychological Association (APA) developed guidelines for cultural competence in conducting research. Because of the unique salience of race/ethnicity for diversity-related issues in the United States, they developed guidelines for four specific racial ethnic groups: Asian American/Pacific Islander populations, persons of African descent, Hispanics, and American Indian participants (APA, 2002). The APA used race/ethnicity as the organizing framework; however, they also recognized the need to be aware of other dimensions of diversity. They had as a guiding principle the following:

> Recognition of the ways in which the intersection of racial and ethnic group membership with other dimensions of identity (e.g., gender, age, sexual orientation, disability, religion/spiritual orientation, educational attainment/experiences, and socioeconomic status) enhances the understanding and treatment of all people. (APA, 2002, p. 19)

They included the following narrative in their discussion:

> As an agent of prosocial change, the culturally competent psychologist carries the responsibility of combating the damaging effects of racism, prejudice, bias, and oppression in all their forms, including all of the methods we use to understand the populations we serve. . . . A consistent theme . . . relates to the interpretation and dissemination of research findings that are meaningful and relevant to each of the four populations and that reflect an inherent understanding of the racial, cultural, and sociopolitical context within which they exist. (APA, 2002, p. 1)

Stake and Rizvi (2009) and Banks (2008) discuss the effects of globalization in terms of complicating our understandings of who belongs in which groups and what the implications are for appropriate inclusion in research for immigrant groups particularly. The majority of immigrants coming to the United States are from Asia, Latin America, the West Indies, and Africa. With national boundaries eroding, people cross boundaries more frequently than ever before, resulting in questions about citizenship and nationality. In addition, political instability and factors such as war, violence, drought, or famine have led to millions of refugees who are essentially stateless. Researchers need to be aware of the status of immigrant and refugee groups in their communities and implications for how they sample in their studies. For example, the University of Michigan's Center for Arab American Studies (www.casl.umd.umich.edu/caas/) conducts studies that illuminate much of the diversity in that community. Kien Lee's work in immigrant communities provides guidance in working with immigrants to the United States from a variety of countries, including China, India, El Salvador, and Vietnam. See Box 11.2 for additional information about these sources.

Box 11.2 Working With Immigrant Communities (http://ctb.ku.edu/tools/)

Hampton, C., & Lee, K. (2003). *Strategies and activities for reducing racial prejudice and racism*. Community Tool Box [Online]. Available at http://ctb.ku.edu/tools/sub_section_main_1173.htm

Lee, K. (2003a). *Building inclusive communities*. Community Tool Box [Online]. Available at http://ctb.ku.edu/tools//sub_section_main_1880.htm

Lee, K. (2003b). *Creating opportunities for members of groups to identify their similarities, differences, and assets*. Community Tool Box [Online]. Available at http://ctb.ku.edu/tools/sub_section_main_1175.htm

Lee, K. (2003c). *Transforming conflicts in diverse communities*. Community Tool Box [Online]. Available at http://ctb.ku.edu/ar/tablecontents/sub_section_main_1845.htm

Lee, K. (2003d). *Understanding culture, social organization, and leadership to enhance engagement*. Community Tool Box [Online]. Available at http://ctb.ku.edu/tools/sub_section_main_1879.htm

People With Disabilities

As you will recall from Chapter 6, the federal legislation Individuals With Disabilities Education Act (IDEA, 2001; Public Law 108-446, Section 602), reauthorized in 2004, defines the following categories of disabilities:

- Mental retardation
- Hearing impairments
- Speech or language impairments
- Visual impairments
- Serious emotional disturbance
- Orthopedic impairments
- Other health impairments
- Specific learning disabilities
- Multiple disabilities
- Deaf-blindness
- Autism
- Traumatic brain injury
- Developmental delays

Mertens and McLaughlin (2004) present an operational and conceptual definition for each of these disability categories. The conceptual definitions can be found in the IDEA. The translation of these conceptual definitions into operational definitions is fraught with difficulty. You can imagine the diversity of individuals who would be included in a category such as serious emotional disturbance, which is defined in the federal legislation as individuals who are unable to build or maintain satisfactory interpersonal relationships, exhibit inappropriate types of behaviors or feelings, have a generally pervasive mood of unhappiness or depression, or have been diagnosed with schizophrenia. Psychologists have struggled for years with finding ways to accurately classify people with such characteristics.

A second example of issues that complicate categorizing individuals with disabilities can be seen in the federal definition and procedures for identification for people with learning disabilities displayed in Box 11.3. The definition indicates eight areas in which the learning disability can be manifest. This list alone demonstrates the heterogeneity that is masked when participants in studies are simply labeled "learning disabled." Even within one skill area, such as reading, there are several potential reasons that a student would display difficulty in that area (e.g., letter identification, word attack, comprehension). Then, there are the complications that arise in moving from this conceptual definition to the operational definition, that is, how are people identified as having a learning disability? And, how reliable and valid are the measures used to establish that a student has a learning disability (E. Johnson, Mellard, & Byrd, 2005)? Many researchers in the area of learning disabilities identify their participants through school records of Individual Education Plans; they do not do independent assessments to determine the validity of those labels. However, Aaron, Malatesha Joshi, Gooden, and Bentum (2008) conclude that many children are not identified as having a learning disability, yet they exhibit similar skill deficits as those who are so labeled, further complicating comparisons between groups. The National Dissemination Center for Children With Disabilities (www.nichcy.org) published a series of pamphlets on the identification of children with learning disabilities that are geared to professionals and parents (Hozella, 2007).

Box 11.3 Federal Definition of Specific Learning Disability and Identification Procedures

The following conceptual definition of learning disability is included in the IDEA legislation:

> "Specific learning disability" means a disorder in one or more of the basic psychological processes involved in understanding or in using language, spoken or written, that may manifest itself in an imperfect ability to listen, think, speak, read, write, spell, or to do mathematical calculations. Such term includes such as perceptual disabilities, brain injury, minimal brain dysfunction, dyslexia, and developmental aphasia. . . . Such term does not include a learning problem that is primarily the result of visual, hearing, or motor disabilities, of mental retardation, of emotional disturbance, or of environmental, cultural, or economic disadvantage. (34 CFR 300.7[c][10])

The federal government addressed the issue of an operational definition of learning disability as a determination made by the child's teachers and an individual qualified to do individualized diagnostic assessment such as a school psychologist, based on:

- The child does not achieve adequately for the child's age or to meet state-approved grade-level standards in one or more of the following areas, when provided with learning experiences and instruction appropriate for the child's age or state-approved grade-level standards:
  - Oral expression.
  - Listening comprehension.
  - Written expression.
  - Basic reading skills.
  - Reading fluency skills.
  - Reading comprehension.
  - Mathematics calculation.
  - Mathematics problem solving.

(Continued)

Box 11.3 (Continued)

- The child does not make sufficient progress to meet age or State-approved grade-level standards in one or more of the areas identified in 34 CFR 300.309(a)(1) when using a process based on the child's response to scientific, research-based intervention; or the child exhibits a pattern of strengths and weaknesses in performance, achievement, or both, relative to age, State-approved grade-level standards, or intellectual development, that is determined by the group to be relevant to the identification of a specific learning disability, using appropriate assessments, consistent with 34 CFR 300.304 and 300.305; and the group determines that its findings under 34 CFR 300.309(a)(1) and (2) are not primarily the result of:
    - A visual, hearing, or motor disability;
    - Mental retardation;
    - Emotional disturbance;
    - Cultural factors;
    - Environmental or economic disadvantage; or
    - Limited English proficiency.

To ensure that underachievement in a child suspected of having a specific learning disability is not due to lack of appropriate instruction in reading or math, the group must consider, as part of the evaluation described in 34 CFR 300.304 through 300.306:

- Data that demonstrate that prior to, or as a part of, the referral process, the child was provided appropriate instruction in regular education settings, delivered by qualified personnel; and

- Data-based documentation of repeated assessments of achievement at reasonable intervals, reflecting formal assessment of student progress during instruction, which was provided to the child's parents.

SOURCES: 34 CFR 300.309; 20 U.S.C. 1221e-3, 1401(30), 1414(b)(6).

Cultural issues also come into play in the definition of people with disabilities. For example, people who are deaf use a capital D in writing the word *Deaf* when a person is considered to be culturally Deaf (Harris, Holmes, & Mertens, 2009). This designation as culturally Deaf is made less on the basis of one's level of hearing loss and more on the basis of one's identification with the Deaf community and use of American Sign Language.

Sampling Strategies

As mentioned previously, the strategy chosen for selecting samples varies based on the logistics, ethics, and paradigm of the researcher. An important strategy for choosing a sample is to determine the dimensions of diversity that are important to that particular study. An example is provided in Box 5.1. Questions for reflection about salient dimensions of diversity in sampling for focus groups are included in Box 11.4.

Box 11.4 Dimensions of Diversity: Questions for Reflection on Sampling Strategy in Focus Group Research

Box 5.1 describes the sampling strategy used by Mertens (2000) in her study of deaf and hard-of-hearing people in the court system. The following are questions for reflection about salient aspects of that strategy:

1. What sampling strategies are appropriate to provide a fair picture of the diversity within important target populations? What are the dimensions of diversity that are important in gender groups? How can one address the myth of homogeneity in selected cultural groups, for example, all women are the same, all deaf people are the same, and so on?

2. What is the importance of considering such a concept in the context in which you do research/evaluation?

Extending Your Thinking: Dimensions of Diversity

How do you think researchers can address the issues of heterogeneity within different populations? Find examples of research studies with women, ethnic minorities, and people with disabilities. How did the researchers address heterogeneity in their studies? What suggestions do you have for improving the way this issue is addressed?

Henry (1990) divides sampling strategies into probabilistic and nonprobabilistic. Persons working in the interpretive paradigm rarely use the term *nonprobabilistic,* preferring the terms *theoretical* or *purposive* to describe their sampling strategies (J. M. Morse, 1994). A third category of sampling that is often used, but not endorsed by proponents of any of the major paradigms, is *convenience sampling.*

Probability-Based Sampling

Henry (1990) and Conley and Fink (1992) make a case for the use of probability-based sampling because mathematically it is possible to analyze the possible bias and likely error. *Sampling error* is defined as the difference between the sample and the population, and can be estimated for random samples. *Random samples* are those in which every member of the population has a known, nonzero probability of being included in the sample. *Random* means that the selection of each unit is independent of the selection of any other unit. Random selection can be done in a variety of ways, including using a lottery procedure drawing well-mixed numbers, extracting a set of numbers from a list of random numbers, or producing a computer-generated list of random numbers. If the sample has been drawn in such a way that makes it probable that the sample is approximately the same as the population on the variables to be studied, it is deemed to be *representative* of the population. Researchers can choose from several strategies for probability-based sampling. Five examples are presented here:

Simple Random Sampling

Simple random sampling means that each member of the population has an equal and independent chance of being selected. The researcher can choose a simple random sample by assigning a number to every member of the population, using a table of random numbers, randomly selecting a row or column in that table, and taking all the numbers that correspond to the sampling units in that row or column. Or the researcher could put all the names in a hat and pull them out at random. Computers could also be used to generate a random list of numbers that corresponds to the numbers of the members of the population.

This sampling strategy requires a complete list of the population. Its advantages are the simplicity of the process and its compatibility with the assumptions of many statistical tests (described further in Chapter 13). Disadvantages are that a complete list of the population might not be available or that the subpopulations of interest might not be equally represented in the population. In telephone survey research in which a complete listing of the population is not available, the researcher can use a different type of simple random sampling known as random digit dialing (RDD). RDD involves the generation of random telephone numbers that are then used to contact people for interviews. This eliminates the problems of out-of-date directories and unlisted numbers. If the target population is households in a given geographic area, the researcher can obtain a list of the residential exchanges for that area, thus eliminating wasted calls to business establishments.

Systematic Sampling

For systematic sampling, the researcher will take every *n*th name off the population list. The procedure involves estimating the needed sample size and dividing the number of names on the list by the estimated sample size. For example, if you had a population of 1,000 and you estimated that you needed a sample size of 100, you would divide 1,000 by 100 and determine that you need to choose every 10th name on the population list. You then randomly pick a place to start on the list that is less than *n* and take every 10th name past your starting point.

The advantage of this sampling strategy is that you do not need to have an exact list of all the sampling units. It is sufficient to have knowledge of how many people (or things) are in the accessible population and to have a physical representation for each person in that group. For example, a researcher could sample files or invoices in this manner. Henry (1990) notes that the systematic sampling strategy can be used to accomplish de facto stratified sampling. Stratified sampling is discussed next, but the basic concept is sampling from previously established groups (e.g., different hospitals or schools). If the files or invoices are arranged by group, the systematic sampling strategy can result in de facto stratification by group (i.e., in this example, location of services).

One caution should be noted in the use of systematic sampling. If the files or invoices are arranged in a specific pattern, that could result in choosing a biased sample. For example, if the files are kept in alphabetical order by year and the number *n* results in choosing only individuals or cases whose last names begin with the letter A, this could be biasing.

Stratified Sampling

This type of sampling is used when there are subgroups (or *strata*) of different sizes that you wish to investigate. For example, if you want to study gender differences in a special education population, you need to stratify on the basis of gender, because boys are known to be more frequently represented in special education than girls. The researcher then needs to decide if he or she will sample each subpopulation proportionately or disproportionately to its representation in the population.

- *Proportional stratified sampling* means that the sampling fraction is the same for each stratum. Thus, the sample size for each stratum will be different when using this strategy. This type of stratification will result in greater precision and reduction of the sampling error, especially when the variance between or among the stratified groups is large. The disadvantage of this approach is that information must be available on the stratifying variable for every member of the accessible population.

- *Disproportional stratified sampling* is used when there are big differences in the sizes of the subgroups, as mentioned previously in gender differences in special education. Disproportional sampling requires the use of different fractions of each subgroup, and thus requires the use of weighting in the analysis of results to adjust for the selection bias. The advantage of disproportional sampling is that the variability is reduced within the smaller subgroup by having a larger number of observations for the group. The major disadvantage of this strategy is that weights must be used in the subsequent analyses; however, most statistical programs are set up to use weights in the calculation of population estimates and standard errors.

Cluster Sampling

Cluster sampling is used with naturally occurring groups of individuals—for example, city blocks or classrooms in a school. The researcher would randomly choose the city blocks and then attempt to study all (or a random sample of) the households in those blocks. This approach is useful when a full listing of individuals in the population is not available but a listing of clusters is. For example, individual schools maintain a list of students by grade, but no state or national list is kept. Cluster sampling is also useful when site visits are needed to collect data; the researcher can save time and money by collecting data at a limited number of sites.

The disadvantage of cluster sampling is apparent in the analysis phase of the research. In the calculations of sampling error, the number used for the sample size is the number of clusters, and the mean for each cluster replaces the sample mean. This reduction in sample size results in a larger standard error and thus less precision in estimates of effect.

Multistage Sampling

This method consists of a combination of sampling strategies. For example, the researcher could use cluster sampling to randomly select classrooms and then use simple random sampling to select a sample within each classroom. The calculations of statistics for multistage sampling become quite complex, and the reader is referred to Henry's (1990) discussion of this topic. Henry does note that too few strata would yield unreliable extremes of the sampling variable. Hess (1985) suggests that roughly between 30 and 50 strata work well for multistage samples using regression analysis.

Complex Sampling Designs in Quantitative Research

Spybrook, Raudenbush, Liu, Congdon, and Martinez (2008) discuss sampling issues involved in complex designs such as cluster randomized trials, multisite randomized trials, multisite cluster randomized trials, cluster randomized trials with treatment at level three, trials with repeated measures, and cluster randomized trials with repeated measures. The sampling issues arise because these research approaches involve the assignment of groups, rather than individuals, to experimental and control conditions. This complicates sampling issues because the *n* of the clusters may be quite small and hence limit the ability of the researcher to demonstrate sufficient power in the analysis phase of the study. However, Spybrook and colleagues developed a sophisticated analytic procedure that accommodates the small cluster sizes while still allowing larger sample sizes within the clusters to be tested appropriately. The statistical procedures involved in such designs exceed the scope of this text; hence, readers are referred to Spybrook et al. (2008) and other sources such as Mertler and Vannatta (2005).

Examples of Sampling in Quantitative Studies

Researchers in education and psychology face many challenges in trying to use probability-based sampling strategies. Even in Borman et al.'s (2007) study of Success for All reading program that is summarized in Chapter 1, they were constrained by the need to obtain agreement from schools to participate. They could not select randomly from the group of schools that agreed to the conditions of the study because it was already a relatively small group. Probability-based sampling is generally easier to do with survey research when a list of people in the population is available. For example, Nardo, Custodero, Persellin, and Fox (2006) used the National Association for the Education of Young Children's digital database of 8,000 names of programs that had fully accredited centers for their study of the musical practices, musical preparation of teachers, and music education needs of early childhood professionals in the United States. They gave the list to a university-based research center and asked them to prepare a randomized clustered sample of 1,000 early childhood centers. The clusters were based on the state in which the programs were located, and the number of centers chosen was proportional to the number of centers in each state.

Henry, Gordon, and Rickman (2006) conducted an evaluation study of early childhood education in the state of Georgia in which they were able to randomly select 4-year olds receiving early education services either through Head Start (a federal program) or in a Georgia Pre-K program (a state program). They first established strata based on the number of 4-year olds living in each county. Counties were randomly selected from each stratum. Then, sites within the counties were randomly selected from both Head Start and Pre-K programs and five children were randomly selected from each classroom. This resulted in a list of 98 pre-K and Head Start sites, all of which agreed to participate in the study (which the authors acknowledge is "amazing" [p. 83]). The researchers then asked for parental permission; 75% or more of parents in most sites consented, resulting in a Head Start sample size of 134. Data were not collected for 20 of these 134 students because students moved out of state, withdrew from the program, or lacked available baseline data. From the 353 pre-K children, the researchers ended up with 201 students who matched those enrolled in Head Start in terms of eligibility to be considered for that program based on poverty indicators. Clearly, thoughtful strategies are needed in applying random sampling principles in research in education and psychology.

Purposeful or Theoretical Sampling

As mentioned previously, researchers working within the constructivist paradigm typically select their samples with the goal of identifying information-rich cases that will allow them to study a case in-depth. Although the goal is not generalization from a sample to the population, it is important that the researcher make clear the sampling strategy and its associated logic to the reader. M. Q. Patton (2002) identifies the following sampling strategies that can be used with qualitative methods:

Extreme or Deviant Cases

The criterion for selection of cases might be to choose individuals or sites that are unusual or special in some way. For example, the researcher might choose to study a school with a low record of violence compared with one that has a high record of violence. The researcher might choose to study highly successful programs and compare them with programs that have failed. Study of extreme cases might yield information that would be relevant to improving more "typical" cases. The researcher makes the assumption that studying the unusual will illuminate the ordinary. The criterion for selection then becomes the researcher's and users' beliefs about which cases they could learn the most from. Psychologists have used this sampling strategy to study deviant behaviors in specific extreme cases.

Intensity Sampling

Intensity sampling is somewhat similar to the extreme-case strategy, except there is less emphasis on extreme. The researcher wants to identify sites or individuals in which the phenomenon of interest is strongly represented. Critics of the extreme- or deviant-case strategy might suggest that the cases are so unusual that it distorts the situation beyond applicability to typical cases. Thus, the researcher would look for rich cases that are not necessarily extreme. Intensity sampling requires knowledge on the part of the researcher as to which sites or individuals meet the specified criterion. This knowledge can be gained by exploratory fieldwork.

Maximum-Variation Sampling

Sites or individuals can be chosen based on the criterion of maximizing variation within the sample. For example, the researcher can identify sites located in isolated rural areas, urban centers, and suburban neighborhoods to study the effect of total inclusion of students with disabilities. The results would indicate what is unique about each situation (e.g., ability to attract and retain qualified personnel) as well as what is common across these diverse settings (e.g., increase in interaction between students with and without disabilities).

Homogeneous Sampling

In contrast to maximum variation sampling, homogeneous sampling involves identification of cases or individuals that are strongly homogeneous. In using this strategy, the researcher seeks to describe the experiences of subgroups of people who share similar characteristics. For example, parents of deaf children aged 6 through 7 represent a group of parents who have had similar experiences with preschool services for deaf children. Homogeneous sampling is the recommended strategy for focus group studies. Researchers who use focus groups have found that groups made up of heterogeneous people often result in representatives of the "dominant" group monopolizing the focus group discussion. For example, combining parents of children with disabilities in the same focus group with program administrators could result in the parents' feeling intimidated.

Typical-Case Sampling

If the researcher's goal is to describe a typical case in which a program has been implemented, this is the sampling strategy of choice. Typical cases can be identified by recommendations of knowledgeable individuals or by review of extant demographic or programmatic data that suggest that this case is indeed average.

Stratified Purposeful Sampling

This is a combination of sampling strategies such that subgroups are chosen based on specified criteria, and a sample of cases is then selected within those strata. For example, the cases might be divided into highly successful, average, and failing schools, and the specific cases can be selected from each subgroup.

Critical-Case Sampling

M. Q. Patton (2002) describes critical cases as those that can make a point quite dramatically or are, for some reason, particularly important in the scheme of things. A clue to the existence of a critical case is a statement to the effect that "if it's true of this one case, it's likely to be true of all other cases" (p. 243). For example, if total inclusion is planned for children with disabilities, the researcher might identify a community in which the parents are highly satisfied with the education of their children in a separate school for children with disabilities. If a program of inclusion can be deemed to be successful in that community, it suggests that it would be possible to see that program succeed in other communities in which the parents are not so satisfied with the separate education of their children with disabilities.

Snowball or Chain Sampling

Snowball sampling is used to help the researcher find out who has the information that is important to the study. The researcher starts with key informants who are viewed as knowledgeable about the program or community. The researcher asks the key informants to recommend other people to whom he or she should talk based on their knowledge of who should know a lot about the program in question. Although the researcher starts with a relatively short list of informants, the list grows (like a snowball) as names are added through the referral of informants.

Criterion Sampling

The researcher must set up a criterion and then identify cases that meet that criterion. For example, a huge increase in referrals from a regular elementary school to a special residential school for students with disabilities might lead the researcher to set up a criterion of "cases that have been referred to the special school within the last 6 months." Thus, the researcher could determine reasons for the sudden increase in referrals (e.g., did a staff member recently leave the regular elementary school? Did the special school recently obtain staff with expertise that it did not previously have?).

Theory-Based or Operational Construct Sampling

Sometimes, a researcher will start a study with the desire to study the meaning of a theoretical construct such as creativity or anxiety. Such a theoretical construct must be operationally defined (as discussed previously in regard to the experimentally accessible population). If a researcher operationalizes the theoretical construct of anxiety in terms of social stresses that create anxiety, sample selection might focus on individuals who "theoretically" should exemplify that construct. This might be a group of people who have recently become unemployed or homeless.

Confirming and Disconfirming Cases

You will recall that in the grounded theory approach (discussed in Chapter 8 on qualitative methods), the researcher is interested in emerging theory that is always being tested against data that are systematically collected. The "constant comparative method" requires the researcher to seek verification for hypotheses that emerge throughout the study. The application of the criterion to seek negative cases suggests that the researcher should consciously sample cases that fit (*confirming*) and do not fit (*disconfirming*) the theory that is emerging.

Opportunistic Sampling

When working within the constructivist paradigm, researchers seldom establish the final definition and selection of sample members prior to the beginning of the study. When opportunities present themselves to the researcher during the course of the study, the researcher should make a decision on the spot as to the relevance of the activity or individual in terms of the emerging theory. Thus, opportunistic sampling involves decisions made regarding sampling during the course of the study.

Purposeful Random Sampling

In qualitative research, samples tend to be relatively small because of the depth of information that is sought from each site or individual. Nevertheless, random sampling strategies can be used to choose those who will be included in a very small sample. For example, in a study of sexual abuse at a residential school for deaf students, I randomly selected the students to be interviewed (Mertens, 1996). The result was not a statistically representative sample but a purposeful random sampling that could be defended on the grounds that the cases that were selected were not based on recommendations of administrators at the school who might have handpicked a group of students who would put the school in a "good light."

Sampling Politically Important Cases

The rationale for sampling politically important cases rests on the perceived credibility of the study by the persons expected to use the results. For example, if a program has been implemented in a number of regions, a random sample might (by chance) omit the region in which the legislator who controls funds for the program resides. It would be politically expedient for the legislator to have information that came directly from that region. Therefore, the researcher might choose purposively to include that region in the sample to increase the perceived usefulness of the study results. Henry (1990) agrees that "sampling for studies where the results are to be used in the political environment may require an additional layer of concern for political credibility beyond scientific concerns for validity" (p. 15).

Case Study Sampling

Stake (2005) provides direction in his comments regarding choosing the sample for case study research that depend on the purpose of the case study, as well as on logistics, likely receptiveness, and available resources. He identifies three approaches to case study, each of which calls for different sampling strategies.

1. Intrinsic case studies are conducted when a particular case is of specific interest such that the case is in essence already decided before the research begins. This is often the case in evaluation of specific programs or in biographical research. With this type of study, generalization is less important than achieving a thorough understanding of that particular case.

2. Instrumental case studies are undertaken to gain an understanding of a phenomenon with the goal of enhancing ability to generalize to other cases, for example, improving race relations. Stake writes,

> The researcher examines various interests in the phenomenon, selecting a case of some typicality but leaning toward those cases that seem to offer *opportunity to learn*. My choice would be to choose the case from which we feel we can learn the most. That may mean taking the one most accessible or the one we spend the most time with. Potential for learning is a different and sometimes superior criterion to representativeness. Sometimes it is better to learn a lot from an atypical case than a little from a seemingly typical case. (Stake, 2005, p. 451)

3. Collective case study (also known as multiple case study) is an approach in which several cases are selected to study because of a desire to understand the phenomenon in a broader context. "They are chosen because it is believed that understanding them will lead to better understanding, and perhaps better theorizing, about a still larger collection of cases" (Stake, 2005, p. 446). It is possible that a researcher will not know all the cases until the study is underway and new issues arise that suggest that other cases are necessary.

For each of these three types of case studies, sampling decisions still need to be made with regard to persons, specific locations, events, timing, subgroups, and dimensions.

Examples of Qualitative Research Sampling

In her discussion of oral history, Yow (1994) describes using a variety of sampling strategies. In a study of child workers in a mill village before World War I, she asked the ministers of the two village churches who the oldest members were. In a study of a World War II industrial town, she read the company newsletter to identify names and then checked the city directory to see who still lived there. Using the names of a few superintendents and workers identified by this means, she used snowball sampling, asking those initially identified to name employees who still lived in the vicinity and were well enough to participate. Then Yow and her colleagues asked those employees who they thought the researchers should talk with. This provided the researchers with a tentative list of narrators (people to interview). They then made decisions as to who to interview based on which narrators were involved in pivotal events and who had lived in the community longest.

Yow (1994) adapted the stratified sampling design discussed under quantitative sampling strategies in her study of a psychiatric hospital. She wanted to interview narrators at every level in the workforce: grounds workers, housekeepers, maintenance people, psychiatrists, mental health workers, social workers, nurses, occupational therapists, cooks, carpenters, the administrative director, and members of the board of trustees. She combined this stratified approach with purposive sampling by deliberately seeking a variety of opinions on controversial topics and a variety of levels of allegiance to the formal organization. She interviewed people who no longer worked in the hospital, people who were for and against the union, people known to be favored by the administration, and those reported to be dissatisfied with the way things were going. Yow's complex sampling strategy contrasts with that of Schneider et al.'s (2004) study of schizophrenia in which the participants were chosen because they were members of a support group that met regularly in the geographic area close to the university.

Convenience Sampling

Convenience sampling means that the persons participating in the study were chosen because they were readily available (Henry, 1990; M. Q. Patton, 2002). Although this might be the least desirable sampling strategy, it is probably the most commonly used. Much psychological research has been conducted using undergraduate students in psychology classes because they are available. When such a convenience sample is used, the researcher must acknowledge the limitations of the sample and not attempt to generalize the results beyond the given population pool. The cost of convenience sampling is illustrated in the following example:

> When Ann Landers, the advice columnist, asked people to write in and answer the question, "If you had it to do over again, would you have children?" 70% of the nearly 10,000 respondents said that they would not have children if they could make the choice to be a parent again. However, when a statistically designed opinion poll on the same issue a few months later was conducted, it was reported that 91% of parents said that they would have children again! (D. Moore & McCabe, 1993, p. 248)

It appears that parents who were unhappy about having been parents were much more likely to volunteer their views than parents who were happy being parents. (The "happy" parents were probably either too busy to respond, or they don't read Ann Landers because they don't need any advice.)

It should be noted, however, that because of ethical concerns, all samples are in the end volunteers. In addition, reality constraints such as access and cost must be considered in all sampling decisions. Luanna Ross's (1992) description of her sampling strategy in a study of Native American women in prison exemplifies the constraints sometimes encountered and how this researcher worked around them (see Box 11.5).

Box 11.5 Example of Constraints in Sampling Procedures

A series of constraints were encountered during the initial phase of sample selection. I originally planned on using a snowball technique, starting with my cousin and spinning off from there. After my first interview, which was with my cousin, the treatment specialist presented me with a list of incarcerated mothers, Indian and white, whom she thought I should interview. I wondered who she left off the list and why, and I felt too intimidated to suggest a different technique. Also, she said that I would not be allowed, for my own safety, to interview dangerous offenders with the exception of one woman because the treatment specialist thought she would "be interesting." I took the list and started interviewing women from my reservation whom I had known for several decades.

Next, feeling constrained by the situation, I followed the treatment specialist's instructions and went down the list of women. After several weeks, however, I became familiar with women in the halls and would request that the guards send them to me to be interviewed, although they

(Continued)

Box 11.5 (Continued)

were not on the list. For example, one young pregnant woman seemed appealing given her age and pregnancy; and, from other prisoners, I heard about and then interviewed an Indian woman who was confined in an isolation cell in the general population building. When the staff discovered this, nothing was said and I continued the process. Thus, I purposefully chose women I wanted to interview. I knew that I wanted a sample that would elicit data regarding variations: for instance, different races, mothers with children of various ages, and prisoners confined in different units.

—Ross, 1992, pp. 79–80

Mixed Methods Sampling

Mixed methods researchers cannot escape the complexities in sampling for either quantitative or qualitative research; rather their challenges are magnified by having both sets of issues plus the complexity of mixed methods to deal with. For example, K. M T. Collins, Onwuegbuzie, and Jiao (2007) raise the question, "Is it appropriate to triangulate, expand, compare, or consolidate quantitative data originating from a large, random sample with qualitative data arising from a small purposive sample?" (p. 269). Mixed methods researchers identify several sampling strategies that are unique to mixed methods research (K. M. T. Collins et al., 2007; B. Johnson & Christensen, 2008; Teddlie & Tashakkori, 2009; Teddlie & Yu, 2007). Recall from Chapter 10 that mixed methods research designs can be parallel (different methods used at the same time) or sequential (different methods used one after the other). These design options influence the sampling strategies for mixed methods, which include

- identical sampling (same people in qualitative and quantitative samples),
- parallel sampling (different people in the quantitative and qualitative samples, but both from the same population, e.g., school children in a district),
- nested sampling (a subset of those in one method of the study are chosen to be in the other part of the study), and
- multilevel sampling (different people from different populations are chosen for the different approaches of the study).

In a mixed methods study conducted by a team of deaf researchers and myself (Mertens, Holmes, Harris, & Brandt, 2007), we used a sequential nested sampling/multilevel sampling strategy. We started with a qualitative phase in which we had a subsample of graduates from a program to prepare teachers for students who are deaf and have additional disabilities. Following that data collection and analysis, we sent a quantitative survey to all the graduates of the program (nested sampling). Subsequently, we conducted qualitative interviews with the staff and faculty from the university and the cooperating schools (multilevel sampling).

In the pragmatic sequential mixed methods study summarized as Sample Study 1.5, Berliner et al. (2008) used a convenience sample for the quantitative portion of their study that consisted of data from 3,856 students. They then conducted interviews to clarify, affirm, or challenge the study findings and to explore state and district policies and practices that affect reenrollment and students' experiences dropping out and reenrolling in San Bernardino City Unified School District high schools. In fall 2007 interview data were collected from 20 district contacts during a weeklong, in-person site visit. . . . The assistant superintendent identified seven district administrators to be interviewed based on their professional roles and knowledge of dropout and reenrollment issues. . . . The five principals of the district's traditional high schools and the two principals of the district's continuation schools were then interviewed about school perspectives on reenrolling dropouts. . . . The principals then identified dropouts who reenrolled in district schools for the student interview sample. Six students, each from different high schools, were interviewed about their dropout and reenrollment experiences. . . . They then interviewed district administrators, principals, and students. (p. 19)

Extending Your Thinking: Sampling Strategies

- Using some of the research studies you previously identified through literature searches, read through the sections on sample selection and participant characteristics. Try to identify the different types of sampling discussed in this chapter. Justify your choice of a "label" for the type of sampling used in the studies, based on evidence presented in the article. Be sure to look at studies that exemplify the four major paradigms discussed in this book.
- Select a research problem of your own (or in a group in your class). Discuss how you could use the different sampling strategies described in this chapter. Provide examples for all of the different types of probability-based, theoretical-purposive, and convenience sampling strategies. What is the effect of the sampling strategy on the way you view your research problem? Do you find yourself modifying the research problem to accommodate the different sampling requirements?

Sampling Bias

Henry (1990) identifies three sources of bias related to sampling design:

1. *Nonsampling bias,* which includes systematic error due to differences among the true population and the study population and measurement error (discussed in the next chapter)
2. *Sampling bias,* which includes systematic error from sampling approaches that over-represent a portion of the study population
3. *Sampling variability,* which is related to sample size and sample homogeneity

Henry (1990) criticizes nonprobability-based sampling strategies primarily on the basis of sampling bias that might occur:

> Because of the subjective nature of the selection process, nonprobability samples add uncertainty when the sample is used to represent the population as a whole. Confounding variables can influence the study results. The accuracy and precision of statements about the population can only be determined by subjective judgment. The selection procedure does not provide rules or methods for inferring sample results to the population, in contrast to probability sampling. . . . Therefore, there is a risk that the findings are not valid because of bias in the selection process. (p. 24)

In the constructivist spirit, Guba and Lincoln (1989) reject the notion that it is possible to reach a generalizable conclusion because of a particular sampling strategy. They argue that research and evaluation results are limited by context and time and that "one cannot determine that this curriculum (as an example) will fit into and work in a given setting without trying it in that setting" (p. 61). They continue with their views on sampling within this paradigmatic framework:

> First, respondents who will enter into the hermeneutic process must be selected. But such sampling is not carried out for the sake of drawing a group that is representative of some population to which the findings are to be generalized. Nor is the sample selected in ways that satisfy statistical requirements of randomness. The sample is selected to serve a different purpose; hence the term "purposive sampling" is used to describe the process. . . . For the constructivist, maximum variation sampling that provides the *broadest scope of information* (the broadest base for achieving local understanding) is the sampling mode of choice. (pp. 177–178)

Guba and Lincoln describe a sampling process that is not preordained but allowed to evolve with the emergence of issues in the research.

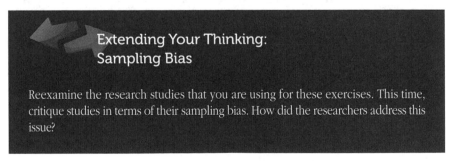

Extending Your Thinking: Sampling Bias

Reexamine the research studies that you are using for these exercises. This time, critique studies in terms of their sampling bias. How did the researchers address this issue?

Access Issues

Accessibility to a sample or population is an important factor to consider when making decisions about sampling designs. For some populations, such as illegal drug users or homeless people, it might not be possible to obtain a complete listing of the members of the population, thus making it difficult to use the probability-based sampling strategies (Hedrick et al., 1993; Henry, 1990). The likelihood of a population's being accessible or willing to respond to mail or phone surveys should also be considered. The populations just mentioned might not be accessible by these means because of residential transience, for financial reasons, or lack of trust of people outside their communities.

Access to different communities can be more or less challenging. Kien Lee (2004) conducted research on civic participation in immigrant communities in the United States. She pursued this work partially because of expressed difficulties on the part of other researchers regarding getting members of these communities to engage in research or evaluation projects, whether this was because of a distrust of government based on past experiences in the home country, or wariness of revealing personal information to an outsider, or language barriers that inhibited effective communication. Lee reported that she was able to identify organizations that were viewed as having credibility in the various communities, such as faith-based organizations, regional or hometown associations, professional associations for members of their cultural group, cultural and benevolent associations, advocacy groups, and refugee resettlement services that served as points of entry into the communities (see Box 11.2).

Access in Educational Settings

Maruyama and Deno (1992) address the issues involved in accessing samples in educational settings. They recognized that it can be a long process to finally reach agreement with the appropriate persons who can authorize the research and who will participate in the research itself as sample members. Identification of the appropriate persons who have the power to grant access is a complex issue in itself. The appropriate point of entry depends partially on the scope of the study that you plan. If you are interested in using only a few classrooms, you might start with teachers to determine their willingness to support your request to administrators. On the other hand, school-level research might start at the principal level and district-level research with the superintendent. Whichever level you start with should be viewed as only a starting point, because each school district has specific procedures for requesting access to its students and staff for research purposes. Early contacts can be helpful to ascertain procedures, test the waters, and cultivate advocates for your later, more formal requests.

Researchers should be aware of complications from real life that can present obstacles to sampling as it is ideally conceived. For example, some educators might resist participating in research because they view research as a risky operation that can produce results that will damage their reputations. Also, some schools receive requests for a variety of different research projects, and thus the effect of the treatment you design might be compromised because of interactions with another experimental treatment. Staff changes or district reorganizations can result in schools pulling out of projects after you think you have your sample defined.

Assuming that you can reach agreement on particular schools or classrooms, you must obtain consent from the individuals (students or parents or staff members) who will be asked to provide data in the study. This issue is discussed further in the section of this chapter on ethics. However, it does have implications for the type of sampling design that is feasible.

School systems will rarely allow a researcher to take all student participants and randomly assign them to conditions. It is not that school systems are mean-spirited; they have the students' best interests at heart. For example, teachers will often recommend a student with disabilities when they feel that the student is ready to enter a mainstream environment and the environment has been suitably adapted for the student's special needs. Randomly selecting students for assignment to mainstream classrooms could result in educationally unsound and ethically indefensible decisions.

More frequently, researchers need to adjust their sampling plans to allow for working with intact groups—for example, administering a treatment to an entire class of students. This, of course, presents challenges related to differential selection as a threat to internal validity in quasi-experimental designs, which were discussed in Chapter 4, and has implications for statistical analysis, discussed in Chapter 13.

Researchers who wish to use stratified sampling should also be aware of the complexities of subdividing the sample on the basis of gender, race or ethnicity, disability, or ability levels within a school setting. First, there are the logistical and ethical obstacles to using stratification. It might not be feasible, educationally sound, or ethical to divide students by demographic categories as would be called for in a stratified sampling design. Second, there are definitional problems in that schools might not use the same definition to "label" students as you have in mind. Also, if you are using more than one site, definitions might vary by site.

Mertens and McLaughlin (2004) describe issues that complicate sampling with special education populations. First, the researcher needs to be aware of the heterogeneity within any special education category and variables that might be uniquely associated with any particular group of people with disabilities. For example, in the area of deafness, characteristics that are important include things such as when the person became deaf, whether the parents are hearing or deaf, and what the person's language is (signed vs. spoken; American Sign Language vs. cued speech). Second, some disability conditions occur with a low frequency, and thus sampling becomes problematic because of the low incidence of individuals within any one setting. This has implications for variability across contexts as well as for adequate sample size. Sample size then has implications for sampling bias and error. Third, researchers commonly seek comparison groups to include in their samples. Selecting an appropriate comparison group for special education populations can be tricky. DeStefano and Wagner (1991) discuss the following options:

1. *Selecting individuals from the general population.* It is important to remember that people with disabilities differ from nondisabled peers in important ways; for example, the disabled population contains more males, African Americans, urban dwellers, people with lower incomes, and single-parent households (Marder & Cox, 1990).

2. *Comparisons across disability categories.* You should be aware of the heterogeneity within categories, as well as variations on variables, such as IQ, between categories.

3. *Cross-unit comparisons that involve the comparison of students with disabilities in one school or school district with students in another school or school district.* Of course, contextual variation is a problem here.

4. *Longitudinal studies that allow comparisons with one group at two or more points in time.* Variation in results could be attributable to historical factors (as discussed in Chapter 4 regarding threats to internal validity).

Access to Records

Although much of the discussion of sampling has implied that the sample consists of people, I do not want to ignore a source of data that is frequently used in educational and psychological research—extant records. The researcher needs to be concerned with the accessibility of the records for research purposes. Hedrick et al. (1993) suggest that researchers sample the desired records on a pilot basis to ensure that the records contain the information required for the study and that they are appropriately organized for the research study. For example, records might be kept only at a local level and not centralized at any one location, making data collection problematic. In addition, the records may or may not contain all the information that the researcher needs for the study.

The researcher must also be able to demonstrate how the confidentiality of the records will be protected. In most organizations, the records contain the names of the clients or students, and thus the organization might not be willing to provide the researcher access to the records themselves. The researcher can then consider the feasibility and appropriateness of alternative means of achieving access to the archival information, such as asking the agency to provide the records with identifying information deleted, asking if an employee of the agency could be paid to code the information from the records without names, or determining if it is possible to obtain a computer printout with codes in place of personal identification information.

Sample Size

The optimum sample size is directly related to the type of research you are undertaking. For different types of research, rules of thumb can be used to determine the appropriate sample size. It should be noted that there are some research methodologists who feel that rules of thumb are never appropriate as a basis for making sample size decisions (e.g., Krathwohl, 2009). Nevertheless, I present these as guides to new researchers who need some kind of ballpark feel for sample sizes.[1] In some cases, your sample size will be determined by very practical constraints, such as how many people are participating in a program or are in a classroom. (This is often, but not always, the case in evaluation studies.) When you are conducting quantitative experimental research and you have the freedom to choose a sample size, there are formulas that can guide you in those decisions. So, let us take a look at sample size from these different perspectives: rules of thumb and formulaic determination.

Rules of Thumb

Quantitative Research Rules of Thumb

Using power analysis formulas, Onwuegbuzie, Jiao, and Bostick (2004) calculated the size of samples needed for correlational, causal comparative, and experimental research in order to find a "medium (using J. Cohen's [1988] criteria, one-tailed and/or two-tailed statistically significant relationship or difference with .80 power at the 5% level of significance" (K. M. T. Collins et al., 2007, p. 273). The recommended sample sizes for multiple regression and survey research come from Borg and Gall (1989).

Type of Research	*Recommended Sample Size*
Correlational	64 participants for one-tailed hypotheses; 82 participants for two-tailed hypothesis[a]
Multiple regression	At least 15 observations per variable[b]
Survey	100 observations for each major subgroup; 20 to 50 for minor subgroups[b]
Causal comparative	51 participants per group for one-tailed hypotheses; 64 for two-tailed hypotheses[a]
Experimental or quasi-experimental	21 participants per group for one-tailed testing[a]

a. Onwuegbuzie et al. (2004).

b. Borg & Gall (1989).

A more complex rule-of-thumb table can be found in J. Cohen (1992). He provides suggested sample sizes for eight different statistical tests (e.g., *t* test, correlation, chi-square) based on small, medium, and large effect sizes at power = 0.80,[2] for a = 0.01, 0.05, and 0.10. Further explanation of these concepts is presented in a subsequent section of this chapter.

Qualitative Research Rules of Thumb

The sample size decisions are a bit more dynamic in qualitative research than in quantitative research in that the number of observations is not determined in the former type of research prior to data collection. Rather, a researcher makes a decision as to the adequacy of the observations on the basis of having identified the salient issues and finding that the themes and examples are repeating instead of extending. Thus, sample size is integrally related to length of time in the field. Nevertheless, rules of thumb for sample sizes in qualitative research can give you an estimate of the number of observations needed for different kinds of qualitative research. I return to the types of research discussed in Chapter 8 for the suggestions listed below:

Type of Research	*Recommended Sample Size*
Ethnography	Approximately 30 to 50 interviews[a]
Case studies	Can be only 1 case or can be multiple cases
Phenomenology	Approximately 6 participants[a]
Grounded theory	Approximately 30 to 50 interviews[a]
Participative inquiry	Small working team; whole communities for meetings; samples for surveys (see quantitative rules of thumb)
Clinical research	Can focus in-depth on 1 client; can include more
Focus groups	6 to 9 people per group; 4 groups for each major audience[b]

a. The suggested sample sizes for ethnography, phenomenology, and grounded theory are from J. M. Morse's (1994) example of a comparison of strategies in the conduct of a hypothetical project.

b. Krueger (2000).

Qualitative researchers are often challenged by the question: How do you know you have enough data? How do you know when it is time to stop? Stake (2005) acknowledges that sometimes the researcher stops collecting data when their time and money run out, especially in program evaluation studies. Researchers need to plan carefully to ensure that they maximize the time and money available to them in order to do the best study within the constraints of the context. Charmaz's (2006) advice reflects a perspective that is less bound by these constraints and is more situated in the concept of "saturation." She suggests that researchers (in grounded theory specifically) call a halt when "gathering fresh data no longer sparks new theoretical insights, nor reveals new properties of your core theoretical categories" (p. 113).

Formulaic Determinations of Sample Size

Lipsey (1990) and J. Cohen (1988) have written excellent texts that describe the logic and procedure for selection of sample size when the researcher is conducting a quantitative study of treatment effectiveness. Lipsey (1990) frames his discussion around the concept of *design sensitivity,* which he defines as follows: "Design sensitivity . . . results in data that are likely to yield statistical significance if, in fact, the treatment under investigation is effective" (p. 10). In other words, how big does your sample have to be to obtain statistically significant results, if the treatment is indeed effective? He continues, "Sensitivity refers to the likelihood that an effect, if present, will be detected" (p. 12).

So what does sample size have to do with detecting statistically significant differences? Our ability to detect statistically significant differences is determined in part by the amount of variability in our dependent measure within the sample:

Less variability = greater sensitivity

More variability = less sensitivity

And sample size has a direct relationship with variability:

Larger sample sizes = less variability

Smaller sample sizes = more variability

If you put the logic of these two statements together, you realize that it is easier to obtain statistical significance if you have a larger sample. However, there is one sticking point:

Larger samples = more costly

Smaller samples = less costly

So, as a researcher, you want to know what is the smallest sample you can use that will take into account the variability in the dependent measure and still be *sensitive* enough to detect a statistically significant difference, if there is one.

Another important concept that enters the discussion of sample size calculation is the *power* of a statistical test, defined as its ability to detect deviations from the null hypothesis (D. Moore & McCabe, 2003). Lipsey (1990) defines *power* as "the probability that statistical significance will be attained *given* that there really is a treatment effect" (p. 20). Thus, power in one sense is the quantification of the sensitivity. Sensitivity or power in statistical language is described in terms of probability of finding a difference when there really is one there. I digress for a moment to explain a few terms to finish the explanation of statistical power.

If we claim that we *do* have a real difference, but we really *do not,* this is called a *Type I error.* Usually, researchers establish a level of Type I error that they are willing to live with, and this is called an *alpha level* (α). For example, if researchers are willing to live with a .05 probability that they might say there is a statistically significant difference when there is not, they have established an *alpha* level of .05. If we claim that we *do not* have a real difference, but we really *do,* this is a *Type II error* (or *beta* or β). Perhaps a graphic display will help:

Your Claim	*Statistically Significant?*	*Type of Error*
Really	Really not	
Yes, a difference	X	Type I (alpha)
No difference	X	Type II (beta)

All this explanation was necessary because the *power of a statistical test* can be defined as 1 – b (Krathwohl, 2009).

There are also tables you can use to estimate sample sizes that are based on the establishment of your acceptable *alpha level* and the estimated effect size you expect to find between the treatment and comparison groups. (The effect size is the difference between the two group means in terms of their common standard deviation.) Lipsey (1990) presents such a table for studies that involve experimental and control group comparisons; Shaver (1992) provides a similar table for correlational research; and, as previously mentioned, J. Cohen (1992) provides a more comprehensive table of sample sizes for eight different statistical procedures.

Because this section has the title "Formulaic Determinations of Sample Size," you are probably wondering where the formulas are. I am going to provide you with one formula to give an idea of how the formulas work. However, you should be aware of a number of caveats in regard to the use of such a formula. D. Moore and McCabe (2003) identify the following assumptions that underlie the use of simplistic formulas such as the one presented here:

1. The data must be from a simple random sample. If data are not from a simple random sample, the researcher must be able to plausibly think of the data as independent observations from a population.

2. The formula is not correct for any sampling designs that are more complex than a simple random sample.

3. There are no correct methods for data that are haphazardly collected with bias of unknown size.

4. Outliers can have a large effect on the confidence interval; therefore, extreme values should be corrected or removed before conducting the analysis.

5. Small sample sizes and nonnormality in the population can change the confidence level.

Given those caveats, Borg and Gall (1989) present the following formula for estimating the size of sample needed:

$$N = \frac{2s^2 \times 4t^2}{D}$$

where

N = number of people needed in each group

s = standard deviation of your dependent variable

t = t test value needed to get your desired *alpha* level

D = estimated difference between experimental and control groups

You may be wondering, where do I get the standard deviation or effect size without having already done the research? Good question. You could rely on estimates of s and D that are available from previous research reported in the literature, or you could conduct pilot work to obtain your own estimates. Lipsey (1990) also suggests the possibility of establishing an acceptable effect size based on discussions with program leaders to determine what would be a meaningful result. The *t* test value can be obtained from a table in any statistics book once you have established your desired *alpha* level.

You may also be wondering what to do in case your sampling strategy does not fit all of the caveats presented previously. In actuality, the preferred method for calculating estimated sample size is to use any of the various statistical programs that are now available for estimating power or sample size. These allow you to personalize the estimation process to your exact needs as well as to play with the estimates of sample size to weigh the differential effects on precision and cost.

You should be aware of the important implications of this discussion of sample size. As Lipsey (1990) and Hedrick et al. (1993) point out, much educational and psychological research is doomed to failure before any data are collected because of insufficient power to detect the effects of an intervention. Hedrick et al. also point out that increasing sample size is not the only route to increasing statistical power. Other alternatives include improving the delivery of the treatment, selecting other statistical tests, or raising the *alpha* level. Mark and Gamble (2009) discuss ethical implications of power analysis for sample size estimate in that the number of participants needed to observe the effect of interest determines how many people will be exposed to an uncertain treatment or denied access to a beneficial treatment. If power analysis is not conducted, then "more participants than needed may have been exposed to a less effective treatment (or there may have been too few participants to observe the effect of interest, reducing the potential benefit of the study). Power analyses have become relatively commonplace, reducing the magnitude of risk" (p. 205). Of course, sample size is also influenced by the willingness of the chosen people to participate in the study. The determination of conditions under which people are recruited and informed about the research leads to questions of ethics, our next topic.

Extending Your Thinking: Sample Size

- Compare a number of studies' sample sizes. What justification do the researchers provide for their choice of sample size?
- Think of a simplistic experimental design that would have two groups and allow simple random sampling. Using numbers available in published literature, use the preceding formula for calculating sample size. Calculate the sample size needed for different levels of confidence in the results.
- Identify a computer program that allows you to conduct a power analysis of different sample sizes.
- Play with the program with a hypothetical example or use a published research study to determine what the effect of having had a different sample size would have been.

Ethics and Protection of Study Participants

A useful insight derived from postmodern scholars is encapsulated in Clegg and Slife's (2009) description of the relationship between research methodology and ethics. They write,

> One of the primary lessons of a postmodern approach to research ethics is that every research activity is an exercise in research ethics, every research question is a moral dilemma, and every research decision is an instantiation of values. In short, postmodernism does not permit the distinction between research methods and research ethics. (Clegg & Slife, 2009, p. 24)

As Clegg and Slife make clear, ethics is not something that happens at the stage of sampling; it needs to guide the entire process of planning, conducting, and using research. However, there are specific implications for ethical behavior related to the protection of people who participate in the studies. For that reason, information about ethical review boards is included in this chapter. Most novice researchers encounter serious questions about the ethics of their planned research within the context of their institutions' institutional review boards (IRB) or human subjects committees. An IRB is a committee mandated by the National Research Act, Public Law 93-348. Every university or other organization that conducts biomedical or behavioral research involving human subjects is required to have an IRB if federal funding is used for research involving human subjects. The federal regulations are included in Title 45 of the Code of Federal Regulations, Part 46. You can obtain a copy of these regulations from any university's research office, a reference librarian, or from the Office for Protection from Research Risk in the National Institutes of Health (NIH, located in Bethesda, Maryland). Information is available on the Web on IRB requirements in many locations. You can read the Belmont Report at www.hhs.gov/ohrp/humansubjects/guidance/belmont.htm, and the NIH Web site that addresses human subject approval processes and institutional review at http://ohsr.od.nih.gov/cbt. It is possible to complete an NIH certificate as a part of your training program via the Web.

You should always contact your own institution's IRB to find out its policies and procedures early in your research planning process. Sometimes, review by the IRB can occur in stages if you are planning to conduct pilot work or obtain funding from an external agency. In any case, you should be prepared to submit your research proposal in the appropriate format to the IRB well in advance of the time that you actually plan to start data collection. The IRB committee members need time to read and discuss your proposal, and they might have questions that will require some revision of your planned procedures. Lead time, an open mind, and a cooperative attitude help.

IRBs need to approve all research that is conducted that involves human subjects (with a few exceptions that will be discussed soon). If you are planning to conduct pilot testing as a part of your study, you should contact your IRB to determine its policy with regard to that. Sieber (1992) found that, generally, IRBs do not review proposals for pilot testing if it just involves fine-tuning an instrument or a research procedure. However, they do review pilot testing that is conducted as an exploratory study to determine if additional research is necessary. Because pilot testing is an important part of many surveys and qualitative studies, it is important that you are aware of this requirement.

Certain exemptions to IRB approval are relevant to research conducted with school children. Even if you think your research might fall into one of the exempt categories, you should contact your IRB because most institutions still require an abbreviated review to establish the legitimacy of the exemption. Possible exemptions include the following:

1. Research that is conducted in established or commonly accepted educational settings, involving normal education practices, such as instructional strategies or classroom management techniques

2. Research that involves the use of educational tests if unique identifiers are not attached to the test results

An interesting development occurred with regard to IRB approval and oral history proposals for research. The Office for Human Research Protections, the federal office that oversees human volunteers in research, decided that oral history interviews generally do not fall under the government's definition of research and therefore do not need to be regulated by IRBs. Their rationale was that the federal definition of research that involves human subjects has as its goal a systematic investigation designed to develop or contribute to generalizable knowledge. Because oral history is done to study a particular past, rather than to identify generalizable principles, it does not fit the federal definition of research that requires human subject protection. At the time of this writing, the decision covers only researchers financed by the Department of Health and Human Services. Updates on this situation and its broader impact could be found at the Web sites for the Office for Human Research Protections, the American Historical Association, and the Oral History Association (Brainard, 2003). The Department of Health and Human Services now includes this language that provides expedited review status for various types of social science research:

> Research on individual or group characteristics or behavior (including, but not limited to, research on perception, cognition, motivation, identity, language, communication, cultural beliefs or practices, and social behavior) or research employing survey, interview, oral history, focus group, program evaluation, human factors evaluation, or quality assurance methodologies. (Note: Some research in this category may be exempt from the HHS regulations for the protection of human subjects. 45 CFR 46.101(b)(2) and (b)(3). This listing refers only to research that is not exempt.) (U. S. Department of Health and Human Services, 2007)

You need to give the IRB a research protocol that may be a summary of your actual proposal with specific ethical issues addressed in greater detail. For the exact specifications at your institution, again, check with your IRB. For a general sense of what the IRB might want to see in a research protocol, see Box 11.6 for a checklist. The first three items on the protocol checklist parallel closely what you would put into your research proposal itself, although the IRB usually asks for a shorter version. Items 4 through 10 on the checklist really zero in on the issues specific to ethical practice in research. You will notice that Item 10 concerns a consent form that you should have your study participants sign. Box 11.7 shows a sample consent form. NOTE: Check with your institution's ethical review board. Some institutions have a standard form for the informed consent that you are required to use.

Box 11.6 Checklist for Research Protocol

1. Cover Page, including

   Name and department of the principal investigator (PI)

   The PI's faculty rank or student status

   The PI's home and office phone number and address

   The project title

   The type of research (e.g., faculty research, externally funded project, student-directed research)

(Continued)

Box 11.6 (Continued)

Intended project starting and ending dates

The PI's qualifications in a paragraph or two (or in an attached *curriculum vitae* or within the description of the methodology)

Signature of the PI

If PI is a student, signature of the adviser[a]

2. A description of the research

   The purpose of the research and the hypotheses

   The literature review (in a summary form)

   The research method, design, and mode of analysis

   A realistic statement of the value of the research (specifically addressing what value it will have for the participants and their community, the research institution, the funder, or science)

   The location of the research (e.g., the exact laboratory, community, institution), why that setting was chosen, and how the researcher happens to have access to it

   Duration of time for the project and how that time frame relates to the project (e.g., in terms of the school calendar, etc.)

3. A description of the research participants

   Demographic characteristics: for example, ethnic background, sex, age, and state of health

   Rationale for the choice of this population

   Source from which the research participants will be obtained

   A statement of the selection criteria

   If vulnerable populations are included (e.g., children, mentally disabled, drug abusers), the rationale for their use should be stated

   If the participants are coming from an institutional setting (e.g., school, clinic, hospital, club), written permission of the person in charge must be attached to the protocol

   The expected number of participants should be provided

4. A discussion of the possible risks

   Inconveniences or discomforts, especially to the participants, and an estimate of the likelihood and magnitude of harm

   What will be done to allay each actual risk or unwarranted worry

   Any alternative methods that were considered and why they were rejected

   A justification if unique identifiers will be collected

5. Discussion of inducements and benefits to the research participants and others

6. Freedom of research participants to withdraw at any time with no adverse consequences

7. Source and amount of compensation in the event of injury (if any, although this is not usually offered to participants in educational and psychological research studies)

8. Analysis of risks and benefits (and a description of how the benefits will substantially outweigh the risks)

9. The informed consent procedure should be described

   How, where, and by whom the informed consent will be negotiated

   How debriefing will be conducted

   Procedures for obtaining children's consent and parental or guardian permission for the research

   The actual consent form should be attached to your protocol

   If oral consent is planned, provide a description of the information that will be presented

   Attach a copy of the information to be used in debriefing

10. A copy of the consent form itself should be attached. It should include the following:

    An explanation of the research purpose, duration, and procedures; if deception is to be used, the researcher should explain that not all of the details can be provided at this time but that a full explanation will be given later

    A description of any foreseeable risk or discomfort

    A description of alternative ways people can obtain the services (e.g., educational intervention or counseling) if they choose not to participate in the research

    A description of how confidentiality or anonymity will be ensured

    A statement as to whether compensation or treatment for harm or injury is available (if the research involves more than minimal risk)

    The name of a person to contact for answers to additional questions

    A statement that participation is voluntary, that refusal will not result in any penalty, and that the person is free to withdraw at any time[b]

11. Any additional attachments (e.g., letters of permission, interview or survey questions, materials to be presented to the participants, tests, or other items connected with the research)

    a. If the research is student-directed research, include the name of the faculty adviser and indicate if the research is for a thesis or dissertation or for a course requirement (include course number and faculty name).

    b. The person must be given a copy of the consent form.

SOURCE: Adapted from Sieber (1992).

Box 11.7 Sample Informed Consent Form

Project Title:	Support Services for Parents of Children Who Are Deaf or Hard of Hearing
Principal Investigator:	Kathryn Meadow-Orlans, Senior Research Scientist, Center for Studies in Education and Human Development, Gallaudet University, Washington, DC 20002-3695
Phone:	(202) 651-XXXX (V or TDD)
E-mail:	KMEADOWORLAN@XXXXX.XXXXX

Thank you for volunteering to participate in a group interview as a follow-up to the Gallaudet National Survey for Parents. Your signature on this consent form shows that you have been informed about the conditions, risks, and safeguards of this project.

1. Your participation is voluntary. You can withdraw from the study at any time, for any reason, without penalty.
2. There is no more than minimal risk to individuals who participate in this research, and complete confidentiality is ensured. Your name will not be used. Instead, you will be given a code number in order to guarantee your anonymity. The typed transcript of the interview will show this code number rather than your name. Your comments will be entered on a computer, and any identifying information will be changed for any written reports. Only the project investigators and their research assistants will have access to the transcript.
3. Questions about risk to you because of participation in this study may be addressed to the researcher at the phone number or e-mail listed at the top of this page or to Dr. Carolyn Corbett, Chairperson, Gallaudet University Institutional Review Board for Protection of Human Subjects (IRB) at (202) 651-XXXX (V or TDD).
4. To cover possible incidental expenses that you might have related to your participation, you will be paid an honorarium of $50. In addition, you have our deep appreciation. We believe that this study will help to improve support services for parents and for children who are deaf and hard of hearing.

I have read the information provided and agree to participate in the interview for parents.

Signature Date

Please print name

Marginalized Populations and Informed Consent

Informed Consent and Children. Vargas and Montoya (2009) address ethical concerns of doing research with children. Parents are usually the people who have legal authority to give permission for research participation for their children under the age of 18. However, ethical practice calls for getting "assent" from the child by explaining the study to the young person in language that is understandable to them and getting their agreement to participate. In addition, certain circumstances might arise in which it is potentially not in the child's interest to have their parents' know about their participation (e.g., if the child is lesbian or gay and has not "outed" themselves to their parents). In such a situation, another adult can take responsibility for signing the informed consent as a legal representative for the child. Vargas and Montoya also discuss issues related to cultural complexity and differences in parental expectations that need to be considered when conducting research with children.

Informed Consent and Older People. Szala-Meneok (2009) explains that older people may need special care in terms of ascertaining if they consent to participate in research. Such people may sign a consent form when they are lucid and might experience subsequent development of dementia. In this circumstance, is the informed consent still valid? Szala-Meneok suggests that researchers who work with older people periodically revisit the consent agreement throughout the process of the study. If signs of dementia emerge, then the researcher can ask a significant other to reaffirm the consent in the interest of ethical practice.

Informed Consent and People With Mental Illness. People with mental illness vary in terms of their abilities to provide informed consent. In New York, researchers are barred from conducting experiments with mentally ill patients in the state's psychiatric hospital without first obtaining their informed consent. This raises a conflict: How can people be declared involuntarily mentally incompetent (which is the basis for placement in the state psychiatric hospital) and execute legal documents subjecting themselves to experiments? Several approaches have been recommended, such as use of advance directives that are signed by the person when their symptoms do not impair their ability to give consent, and use of monitors such as family members, advocates, or surrogates who can safeguard the person's interests. Ethical responsibility includes monitoring participants closely to determine any negative effects of the research, such as an increase in symptom severity. The researcher then needs to make a decision about making other treatments available as needed, defining appropriate criteria for withdrawal from the study, and building in "back-up" clinical care options for participants who must leave the study (American Psychiatric Association, 2006).

Indigenous and Postcolonial Peoples and Research Ethics. Indigenous and postcolonial peoples contribute critically important insights into ethics, not only for research in their own communities, but also as a way of understanding broader ethical issues in the surrounding world. LaFrance and Crazy Bull (2009), Cram (2009), Chilisa (2009), and Quigley (2006) provide thoughtful descriptions of the ethical review process in American Indian, Maori, and African communities. Researchers interested in working in such communities will find sophisticated review process grounded in cultural heritage and values.

Confidentiality and Anonymity

Two terms used in the ethical review for the protection of research participants need additional clarification:

- *Confidentiality* means that the privacy of individuals will be protected in that the data they provide will be handled and reported in such a way that they cannot be associated with them personally.

- *Anonymity* means that no uniquely identifying information is attached to the data, and thus no one, not even the researcher, can trace the data back to the individual providing them.

Confidentiality and anonymity promises can sometimes be more problematic than anticipated. See the case described in Box 11.8 for an example of an unanticipated complication. In addition, transformative researchers suggest that the expectation of confidentiality or anonymity that represents the status quo in research may be misguided. Baez (2002) makes the case that confidentiality protects secrecy and thus hinders transformative political action. "Transformative political action requires that researchers and respondents consider themselves involved in a process of exposing and resisting hegemonic power arrangements, but such action is thwarted by secrecy and the methods used to protect it" (p. 35). Baez does not recommend discarding confidentiality entirely; rather he recommends that researchers critically question what confidentiality allows to be hidden or revealed during the entire process of the research. This illustrates the tensions inherent in the need to protect individuals who have experienced discrimination and oppression by not reporting or altering the details to protect their identity with the need to reveal specific examples of such behaviors in the name of accuracy of results as well as to further social transformation and justice. Researchers need to be cognizant of the repercussions of revealing the identity of persons who provide data.

Several other scholars write about the complexity of confidentiality, for example:

- Ntseane (2009) conducted a study of poverty reduction in Africa based on data collected from women who owned businesses. The women told Ntseane that they wanted their names used because they were proud of the work they were doing and felt that if she could name people in her writing who wrote articles about economic development, surely it would be insulting to them not to use their names as they were the ones who had succeeded in the struggles of business in Africa.

- Dodd (2009) discussed the real dangers of revealing the identities of youth who are lesbian, gay, bisexual, transsexual, or queer who had not revealed this to their parents, teachers, or others in the outside community.

- Brabeck and Brabeck (2009) collected data from Spanish-speaking women who were abused by their spouses. Some of the women wanted their names used in the written reports; the researchers counseled them against that based on the need to protect the women from further abuse.

- J. A. King, Nielsen, and Colby (2004) wrestled with the question of revealing identities when the study they conducted indicated that an incompetent manager was responsible for the failure of a program.

Each of these examples highlights the tension between the assumptions that guide ethical review boards in terms of the necessity for and feasibility of maintaining confidentiality or anonymity, as well as providing insights into the dynamics of maintaining an ethical stance throughout the research process. Bhattacharya (2007) proposed modifications to IRB guidelines that would acknowledge the fluid nature of consenting and ways the researcher could be responsive to potential departures from the traditional form that is signed at the beginning of a study. She acknowledges that researchers may not be able to anticipate all the ethical dilemmas that will present during a study. If a participant does not fully understand the implications of revealing details about their lives, alternative means might be used to elicit the degree of revelation that is safe and comfortable. For example, Bhattacharya (2007) asked her respondent if all the things revealed in the data were things she would feel comfortable if her mother or grandmother knew about her. Another possibility is to require consent at the time of publication or by asking the participants to coauthor reports of the research. These strategies of course introduce additional challenges for researchers, who may feel that their integrity is being sacrificed to protect the participants.

Box 11.8 Protection of Human Participants and the Law

Sheldon Zink is an ethnographer who conducted a study in a hospital on the experiences of a patient who received an experimental heart transplant. After conducting the study for 18 months, the patient died. The family sued the hospital and various others involved in the patient's care. The lawyers issued a subpoena for Zink's field notes. Zink refused to turn over her notes because she had promised confidentiality to the participants in the study. Five lawyers told Zink that she would have to choose between turning over her notes and going to jail because the confidentiality of an ethnographer's notes is not protected by law the way a lawyer's or physician's records are. The American Anthropological Association's code of ethics says that anthropologists must do everything in their power to protect their subjects, including maintaining confidentiality and anonymity. However, it also adds that it should be made clear to informants that such anonymity may be compromised unintentionally. As in Zink's case, the law, as it is currently written, requires researchers to release their notes or go to jail.

SOURCE: R. Wilson (2003).

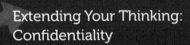

Extending Your Thinking: Confidentiality

Using pseudonyms or fictionalizing details are two ways that researchers deal with confidentiality issues. However, this may not be sufficient protection for the participants as witnessed in an experience I had at a professional meeting in which a researcher reported a study in which the participant was described in an unflattering way (to put it mildly). The researcher said that she had made a previous presentation on this study in another venue, and one person in the audience told her afterward that she knew who the participant was and assured the researcher that she had been very accurate in her portrayal of the woman in question. The researcher had not used the

(Continued)

(Continued)

name of the participant; however, she revealed sufficient details about the participant that the audience member was able to identify her. I wondered if the participant knew how she was being portrayed and if she had agreed to the use of her data in that way. The researcher told me that she had not shared her analysis of the data with the participant and that she did not see a need to do so because the participant had signed an informed consent letter. What are your thoughts about the ethics of reporting the information in this study? What responsibility does the researcher have after the informed consent is signed?

As discussed in the section on access to records earlier in this chapter, it is sometimes possible to obtain data within the context of anonymity by having someone other than the researcher draw the sample and delete unique identifying information. Sieber (1992) also suggests the possibility of having a respondent in a mail survey return the questionnaire *and* mail a separate postcard with his or her name on it. Thus, the researcher would be able to check off those who had responded and to send a second mailing to those who had not.

However, in many instances, this is not feasible, and the researcher must arrange to respect the privacy and confidentiality of the individuals in the research study. This can be done by coding the data obtained and keeping a separate file with the code linked to unique identifying information. The separate file can then be destroyed once the necessary data collection has been completed.

Federal legal requirements concerning confidentiality include the following:

1. The Buckley Amendment, which prohibits access to children's school records without parental consent
2. The Hatch Act, which prohibits asking children questions about religion, sex, or family life without parental permission
3. The National Research Act, which requires parental permission for research on children

There are two circumstances in which the IRB can choose *not* to require parental permission:

1. If the research involves only minimal risk (i.e., no greater risk than in everyday life), parental permission can be waived.

2. If the parent cannot be counted on to act in the best interests of the child, parental permission can be waived. This circumstance usually involves parents who have been abusive or neglectful.

As a part of the confidentiality issue, the research participants should also be informed that the researcher is required by law to inform the appropriate authorities if they learn of any behaviors that might be injurious to the participants themselves or that cause reasonable suspicion that a child, elder, or dependent adult has been abused. In Ross's (1995) study of Native American women in prison, for example, she told her participants that she was required to report to the warden if they revealed involvement in illicit activities, such as drug usage or escape plans.

Extending Your Thinking: Ethical Review Boards

Contact your institution's IRB. Review its requirements in terms of review of proposals and format of prospectus. Write a sample research prospectus that you think would satisfy your institution's IRB. (A smaller bite of the same apple: Write an informed consent form that you could use for a sample study. Variations on a theme: Write the informed consent form for an adult, for a parent of a child, for an adult with limited mental abilities.)

Deception in Research Studies

The American Psychological Association (2002) recognizes that deception and invasion of privacy must be given serious consideration in research planning. Deception is an ethical problem that has been debated in the research community for many years. The justification put forward for the use of deception is usually that the results of the study would be compromised without it because people would alter their behavior if they knew what the researcher was really investigating. Most professional associations' ethical guidelines for psychologists and educators prohibit the use of deception unless it can be justified and the effect of the deception "undone" after the study is completed. The undoing of deception is supposed to be accomplished by the following means:

1. *Debriefing* the research participants after the research study; this means that the researcher explains the real purpose and use of the research.

2. *Dehoaxing* the research participants, in which the researcher demonstrates the device that was used to deceive the participants. The researcher's responsibility is to attempt to allay a sense of generalized mistrust in educational and psychological research.

3. Guarding the *privacy and confidentiality* of the research participants.

4. Obtaining *fully informed consent.*

Years ago, Guba and Lincoln (1989) maintained that the allowance of deception in research settings was one of the main failings of the postpositivist paradigm. They point out that the professional associations' codes of ethics that focus on harm are inadequate to guard against the harm that results from discovering that you have been duped and objectified. Such harm includes "the loss of dignity, the loss of individual agency and autonomy, and the loss of self-esteem" (p. 121). They point out the contradiction in using deception to serve the search for "truth" through science. The requirement for fully informed consent and use of deception also creates a contradiction for the researcher: How can people give their fully informed consent to participate in a research study if they do not know what the real purpose of the research is?

Lincoln (2009), Lincoln and Denzin (2005), and Christians (2005) argue that deception cannot be a part of the constructivist paradigm because the goal is to collect and debate the various multiple constructions of the different constituencies affected by an issue. Nevertheless, researchers functioning within the constructivist paradigm are not immune to ethical challenges. The following excerpt provides one example of an ethical dilemma that arose during a study conducted within the parameters of the constructivist paradigm.

Gary Fine and Kent Sandstrom (1988) describe the following situation in their study of White, preadolescent boys:

> One day I was driving some boys home, we passed some young Blacks riding bicycles in that almost entirely White suburb. One boy leaned out the car window and shouted at the "jungle bunnies" to "go back where you came from." The ethical problem was what to do or say in reaction to this (and similar) behaviors. In this instance (and others), I offered no direct criticism, although a few times when the situation was appropriate, I reminded the boys of the past prejudices against their own ethnic groups [Irish American]. (pp. 55–56)

Fine comments that he made the judgment not to react to these racist comments because he wanted the children to continue to trust him. This raises other ethical issues in terms of how far researchers should go to engender the trust of their informants. Fine and Sandstrom raise the questions: Should you smoke a joint? Join in a gang fight? Commit a crime?

By being present and tolerant of drug use, racist behavior, and so on, is one supporting that behavior? G. Fine and Sandstrom (1988) comment that "one must wonder whether the researcher who 'enables' drug dependency or who permits crimes to occur is really acting in accord with the presumption of 'doing no harm'" (p. 68). For another ethical dilemma, see Box 11.9 on playing the card game "Asshole" with abused and at-risk youth.

Box 11.9 Ethical Dilemma Related to Playing a Card Game With Abused and At-Risk Youth

Donna Podems (2004) designed her dissertation combining action research and feminist approaches to understand a donor-funded program in South Africa. Abused youth participated in wilderness programs designed to build their self-esteem and self-confidence. The program used experiential learning techniques, with a heavy focus on games. She provides the following description of her experience:

> I had met with the staff individually and explained the research and each staff signed a consent form promising them confidentiality, among other standard practices. About three months into my research, one male staff member suggested that we play a card game called "Asshole." Not being a card player, I did not know this game. They explained the game in that the person who got rid of their cards first was the president, then vice-president, then assistant to the asshole, then asshole. The loser has to do what everyone says, which can be getting drinks to something unmentionable.
>
> I asked another card player, who is my best friend, how he felt after this game. He admitted rather sheepishly, that he was "relieved" and felt "glee" that I was the asshole for most of the game, because it meant that he was not. Playing the game with me, he watched me grow more and more upset, yet he, and the others, let the game continue.
>
> Having played this game with the Program staff, I was horrified at their apparent joy at my distress. Even though they saw that I was upset, they wanted to continue the game.

I had a horrible thought: was this game played with emotionally and physically abused kids? I questioned staff members and each staff member that I spoke with said yes, the staff played it with emotionally and physically abused kids, just not officially; they played it "all the time" after dinner in "open" or "rest" hours. Most staff that I interviewed even said that the person in the asshole position usually became upset but explained that was because they were a poor sport. The staff members defended the use of this game and chided me for my feelings.

This was my first of many experiences with a program where what the staff said they believed (we care about people) and were about (growing/healing people) and what they actually believed and did were two different things. I was left with the following dilemma: I accessed the fact that this game was played with emotionally abused and at-risk youth through confidential interviews, yet it greatly disturbed me that this game might be negatively affecting youth. Should I tell the director, or was I bound by confidentiality?

Extending Your Thinking: Ethics and Deception in Research

The question of whether or not researchers should be allowed to use deception in their research has been hotly debated in the research community and in the wider society. Sieber (1992) summarizes her stance as follows:

> I can only hope that I have brought all readers to recognize two things: (a) Some important forms of behavior vanish under obvious scrutiny; concealment or deception is sometimes necessary in research, and (b) the more objectionable forms of deception are unnecessary. (p. 70)

What is your opinion? Should deception be allowed in research? If so, under what conditions? What do you think of the conditions permitted by the various professional associations cited in this chapter (e.g., with debriefing, dehoaxing, informed consent)?

Questions for Critically Analyzing Sampling Strategies

All of these questions might not be equally important for research conducted within the different paradigms. For example, an affirmative answer to the question about generalizability or transferability might not be as important to a researcher in the interpretive or transformative paradigms. Nevertheless, an answer to the question is still possible and informative.

1. What is the population of interest? How was the sample chosen—probability, purposeful, convenience sampling? What are the strengths and weaknesses of the sampling strategy?

2. What are the characteristics of the sample? To whom can you generalize or transfer the results? Is adequate information given about the characteristics of the sample?

3. How large is the population? How large is the sample? What is the effect of the sample size on the interpretation of the data?

4. Is the sample selected related to the target population?

5. Who dropped out during the research? Were they different from those who completed the study?

6. In qualitative research, was thick description used to portray the sample?

7. In qualitative research, what is the effect of using purposive sampling on the transferability to other situations?

8. Are female participants excluded, even when the research question affects both sexes? Are male subjects excluded, even when the research affects both sexes?

9. Does the researcher report the sample composition by gender and other background characteristics, such as race or ethnicity and class?

10. How does the researcher deal with the heterogeneity of the population? Are reified stereotypes avoided and adequate opportunities provided to differentiate effects within race/gender/disability group by other pertinent characteristics (e.g., economic level)?

11. Did the researcher objectify the human beings who participated in the research study?[3]

12. Did the researcher know the community well enough to make recommendations that will be found to be truly useful for community members?

13. Did the researcher adequately acknowledge the limitations of the research in terms of contextual factors that affect its generalizability or transferability?

14. Whose voices were represented in the research study? Who spoke for those who do not have access to the researchers? Did the researchers seek out those who are silent? To what extent are alternative voices heard?

15. If deception was used in the research, did the researcher consider the following issues (adapted from Sieber, 1992):

   a. Could participant observation, interviews, or a simulation method have been used to produce valid and informative results?
   b. Could the people have been told in advance that deception would occur so they could then consent to waive their right to be informed?
   c. How are the privacy and confidentiality of the participants ensured?
   d. If you are studying bad behavior, have the people agreed to participate in the study? Can you run a pilot group in which you honestly inform people of the type of behavior you are studying and determine if they would agree to participate?

e. If studying bad behavior, is the behavior induced? How strongly?
f. How will debriefing, dehoaxing, and desensitizing (removing any undesirable emotional consequences of the research) be handled?
g. Is the study important enough and well designed enough to justify deception?

Extending Your Thinking: Critically Analyzing Sampling in Research

Identify research studies that exemplify different paradigms and different methods. Use the questions for critical analysis to thoroughly critique their sampling section and ethical integrity.

Summary of Chapter 11: Sampling

Different paradigmatic stances are used to raise questions about appropriate sampling strategies. For example, in postpositivist quantitative research, probability-based sampling strategies raise questions concerning the generalizability of the results. With the constructivist paradigm, purposeful sampling raises questions about the transferability of results. The transformative paradigm provides an opportunity to ask questions about issues of power and respect for those who are included or excluded from participation in research. All researchers share concerns about ethics and have ethical review boards, professional codes of ethics, and cultural awareness to guide them in proper sampling procedures. In the next chapter, we move to the collection of data from the people who have been chosen as participants in our research studies.

Notes

1. I am in good company: J. Cohen (1992) also published a rule-of-thumb guide for researchers who might find the formulaic approach too complicated. His guide is much more comprehensive than that presented here and could actually serve as a basis for decisions about sample size.

2. J. Cohen (1992) chose power = .80, because smaller values would incur too great a risk of Type II error; larger values might lead to excessive cost in trying to select a larger sample.

3. Items 11 through 14 are adapted from Lincoln (1995).

In This Chapter

- Operationalizing concepts is explained as the basis for making decisions about data collection.
- Specific topics related to quantitative measures are discussed:
  - Standardized and nonstandardized testing
  - Norm-referenced and criterion-referenced testing
  - Individual and group tests, speed and power tests
  - Performance and portfolio assessment (including rubrics)
  - Curriculum-based assessment
  - Secondary sources of data
- Selection and development of data collection instruments are described in terms of the following:
  - Sources of previously developed instruments
  - Steps in the development of your own instrument
- Qualitative approaches to data collection are described:
  - Observations
  - Interviews (individual and focus groups)
  - Records and document review
  - Participatory data collection strategies
  - Visual data
- Mixed methods issues related to data collection are explored.
- Standards for judging the quality of data collection are discussed from the vantage point of various paradigms:
  - Reliability and dependability
  - Validity and credibility
  - Objectivity and confirmability
  - Avoidance of bias based on dimensions of diversity such as gender, race and ethnicity, or disability
  - Contributions to quality from universal design
- Questions for critically analyzing data collection in research are provided.

Did deaf and hearing students increase their interactions with each other as a result of being included in the same classroom? Did the social interaction skills of all the students change as a result of training in how to work together? What concerns did the teachers and parents of the students express related to the inclusion of deaf and hearing students in the same classroom? What communication problems arose? How were these resolved? What was the cost of the intervention? What changes in school achievement were observed at the end of the school year?

The common theme of all of these questions is the need for information. We acquire information about people and things through collecting data. Data collection is the vehicle through which researchers answer their research questions and defend their conclusions and recommendations based on the findings from the research. The collection of data allows researchers to anchor what they wish to discuss in the empirical world.

12

Data Collection

In education and psychology, data are often collected to make decisions about individuals regarding diagnoses, treatment, or school placement. Data collection for individual decision making is sometimes called *psychological* or *educational assessment*. Although much of what you know about psychological and educational assessment will transfer into the research setting, you should be aware that the use of data for such decisions differs from the use made for research purposes.

Options for data collection in research include tests, surveys, checklists, observations, records and document reviews, and interviews (personal and telephone). (See Table 12.1 for a comparison of options with their associated purposes, advantages, and disadvantages.) Hedrick et al. (1993) divided the information sources into primary—people (surveys and interviews), observation of events, physical documents (products such as student portfolios), and assessments (tests)—and secondary—administrative records, prior research studies, extant databases (e.g., the National Assessment of Educational Progress), and various forms of documentary evidence (e.g., evaluation reports). I first address conceptual and procedural issues for quantitative and qualitative data collection strategies, and then describe standards for judging the quality of data collection in research from various paradigmatic perspectives.

Operationalizing Concepts

The purpose of data collection is to learn something about people or things. The focus is on the particular attribute or quality of the person or setting. For example, adolescents' tendency for risky behavior is a subjective concept that needs to be operationalized in order to study it. Lane, Parks, Kalberg, and Carter (2007) were interested in measuring

Table 12.1 Overview of Methods to Collect Information

Method	*Overall Purpose*	*Advantages*	*Challenges*
Questionnaires, surveys, checklists	When you need to quickly and/or easily get lots of information from people in a nonthreatening way	Can complete anonymously Inexpensive to administer Easy to compare and analyze Administer to many people Can get lots of data Many sample questionnaires already exist	Might not get careful feedback Wording can bias client's responses Are impersonal In surveys, may need sampling expert Doesn't get full story
Interviews	When you want to fully understand someone's impressions or experiences, or learn more about their answers to questionnaires	Get full range and depth of information Develops relationship with client Can be flexible with client	Can take much time Can be hard to analyze and compare Can be costly Interviewer can bias client's responses
Documentation review	When you want an impression of how a program operates without interrupting the program. Comes from a review of applications, finances, memos, minutes, etc.	Get comprehensive and historical information Doesn't interrupt program or client's routine in program Information already exists Few biases about information	Often takes much time Info may be incomplete Need to be quite clear about what looking for Not flexible means to get data; data restricted to what already exists
Observation	To gather accurate information about how a program actually operates, particularly about processes	View operations of a program as they are actually occurring Can adapt to events as they occur	Can be difficult to interpret seen behaviors Can be complex to categorize observations Can influence behaviors of program participants Can be expensive
Focus groups	To explore a topic in depth through group discussion (e.g., about reactions to an experience or suggestion, understanding common complaints, etc.); useful in evaluation and marketing	Quickly and reliably get common impressions Can be efficient way to get much range and depth of information in short time Can convey key information about programs	Can be hard to analyze responses Need good facilitator for safety and closure Difficult to schedule a large number of people together
Case studies	To fully understand or depict a client's experiences in a program and to conduct comprehensive examination through cross-comparison of cases	Fully depicts client's experience in program input, process, and results Powerful means to portray program to outsiders	Usually quite time-consuming to collect, organize, and describe Represents depth of information, rather than breadth

SOURCE: McNamara (2008).

adolescents' tendency for risky behaviors as a beginning step toward identifying students with whom to take preventative steps. This measurement challenge is of interest to psychologists and educators alike, because it has relevance for individuals' psychological, behavioral, and academic experiences. Lane et al. recognized the need for a conceptual model that would include the complex dimensions associated with risky behavior. The model rests on the assumption that teachers can identify students at risk or potentially at risk by rating them on the following behaviors: stealing; lying, cheating, sneaking; and exhibiting behavior problems; peer rejection; low achievement; negative attitude; and aggressive behavior.

In the initial stages of planning data collection, the challenge to the researcher is twofold: First, the attributes of interest must be identified; second, a decision must be made about how to collect data about those attributes. Building on the work that you did during your review of the literature, you should have formulated research questions or hypotheses that can guide you in the identification and operationalizing of the attributes. How can the researcher decide what to include in data collection? Previous experiences with the research topic are an important preliminary guide. The literature review is the central information base for identifying what attributes to include and how to collect data about them. The process of determining what to collect data about and how to do it is often referred to as *operationalizing*. That is, through these steps, the researcher identifies the strategies that will make it possible to test the concepts and theories posed through the research question.

In Lane et al.'s (2007) study of screening for risky behavior in adolescents, they operationalized the concept through data collection with the Student Risk Screening Scale (SRSS; Drummond, 1994). This instrument was originally developed for use in Grades K–6, and Lane et al. wanted to establish its validity and reliability for middle school students.

> The 1-page instrument provides a place to list·all students in the first column, with 7 items listed across the top row: steals; lies, cheats, sneaks; behavior problems; peer rejection; low achievement; negative attitude; and aggressive behavior. In this study, homeroom teachers rated each student on the 7 items using a 4-point Likert-type scale (0 = *never,* 1 = *occasionally,* 2 = *sometimes,* 3 = *frequently).* Teachers completed the SRSS for all of the students in their class in approximately 15 min. Total scores were used to classify students into three levels of risk: low (0–3), moderate (4–8), and high (9–21). (pp. 212–213)

Texts and other resources related to educational and psychological measurement are listed in Box 12.1.

Box 12.1 Educational and Psychological Measurement Resources

General Measurement Texts

Bartram, D., & Hambleton, R. (Eds.). (2005). *Computer-based testing and the Internet: Issues and advances*. St. Paul, MN: Assessment Systems Corporation.

Brennan, R. L. (Ed.). (2006). *Educational measurement* (4th ed.). Westport, CT: National Council on Measurement in Education and American Council on Education.

Hogan, T. P. (2005). *Educational assessment.* Indianapolis: IN: Jossey-Bass.

(Continued)

Box 12.1 (Continued)

Lopez, S. J., & Snyder, C. R. (2003). *Positive psychological assessment: A handbook of models and measures.* Washington, DC: American Psychological Association.
McIntire, S. A., & Miller, L. A. (2006). *Foundations of psychological testing* (2nd ed.). Thousand Oaks, CA: Sage.
Merrell, K. W. (2007). *Behavioral, social and emotional assessment of children and adolescents.* New York: Routledge.
Reynolds, C. R., & Kamphaus, R. W. (Eds.). (2003). *Handbook of psychological and educational assessment of children: Intelligence, aptitude, and achievement.* New York: Guilford.
Wright, R. J. (2007). *Educational assessment.* Thousand Oaks, CA: Sage.

Measurement and Culture

Abedi, J., Leon, S., & Kao, J. C. (2008). *Examining differential item functioning in reading assessments with students with disabilities.* Los Angeles, CA: National Center for Research on Evaluation, Standards, and Student Testing.
Ekstrom, R. B., & Smith, D. K. (2002). *Assessing individuals with disabilities in educational, employment, and counseling settings.* Washington, DC: American Psychological Association.
Gopaul-McNicol, S. A., & Armour-Thomas, E. (2002). *Assessment and culture: Psychological tests with minority populations.* San Diego: Academic Press.
Hambleton, R. K., Merenda, P. F., & Spielberger, C. D. (2005). *Adapting educational and psychological tests for cross-cultural assessment.* St. Paul, MN: Assessment Systems Corporation.
Joint Committee on Testing Practices. (2004). *Code of fair testing practices in education.* Washington, DC: American Psychological Association.
Nahari, S. G., Lopez, E. C., & Esquivel, G. B. (2007). *Multicultural handbook of school psychology: An interdisciplinary perspective.* New York: Routledge.
National Task Force on Equity in Testing Deaf and Hard of Hearing Individuals. (2008). Gallaudet University. Accessed October 21, 2008, from http://gri.gallaudet.edu/TestEquity/index.html
Thurlow, M., Quenemoen, R., Altman, J., & Cuthbert, M. (2008). *Trends in the participation and performance of students with disabilities* (Technical Report 50). Minneapolis: University of Minnesota, National Center on Educational Outcomes.
Wolf, M. K., Herman, J. L., Kim, J., Abedi, J., Leon, S., Griffin, N., et al. (2008). *Providing validity evidence to improve the assessment of English Language Learners.* Los Angeles: National Center for Research on Evaluation, Standards, and Student Testing.

Measurement Journals

Applied Measurement in Education

Applied Psychological Measurement

Educational and Psychological Measurement

Educational Research Quarterly

Journal of Psychoeducational Assessment

Multivariate Behavioral Research

Web Sites

Association of Test Publishers
http://www.testpublishers.org

The Consortium for Equity on Standards and Testing
http://www.bc.edu/research/csteep/CTESTWEB/start.html

Educational Testing Service
http://www.ets.org

FairTest: The National Center for Fair and Open Testing
http://www.fairtest.org

National Center for Research on Evaluation, Standards & Student Testing
http://www.cse.ucla.edu

National Council on Measurement in Education
http://www.ncme.org/about/index.cfm

Quantitative Measurement Topics

A researcher needs to decide whether to (a) use a measurement instrument that is commercially available or one developed by other researchers, (b) adapt an existing instrument, or (c) create a new one to meet the needs of the proposed research. In quantitative research, your decision will be clearer if you understand some of the common terms used in describing different types of measurement instruments displayed in Table 12.2.

Questions arise about the use of standardized tests as exemplified by this comment from Solórzano (2008, p. 282):

> But are standardized tests valid for the various audiences for which they are being used? Or, for the decisions that policy makers are advocating? Standardized tests are usually associated with high stakes assessments because they generally go through several iterations to ensure that they are well constructed. The assumption is that they are valid, reliable, and fair, and results can be compared across student populations from various school districts.

These issues are discussed later in this chapter in the section on determining the quality of data collection instruments for research purposes.

Performance and Portfolio Assessment

Performance assessment is a process for collecting information through systematic observation in order to make decisions about an individual. Performance assessment

Table 12.2 Types of Quantitative Measurement Instruments

Type	*Description*	*Examples*
Standardized Tests	Uniform directions for administering and scoring; rigorous development	
Norm-referenced test	A well-defined, previously tested group (the norm group) participated in the standardization of the test. Respondents are compared to the norm group via norm tables in the form of statistical values such as percentiles. Caution: Check representation of groups on the basis of race, ethnicity, gender, and specific types and severity of disabilities.	SAT, GRE, IQ; Minnesota Multi-Phasic Personality Inventory
Criterion-referenced test	The test is designed to address the content or domain of the attribute being tested. The concept of criterion is applied when the researcher identifies a particular level of performance that test takers should reach as a result of being exposed to a particular intervention. Curriculum-based tools are a type of criterion-referenced test that is being more commonly used as states align their standards, curriculum, and assessment. Salvia, Ysseldyke and Bolt (2007) defined *curriculum-based tools* as "assessment methodologies that are used to collect and evaluate student achievement data in order to monitor student progress" (p. 636).	Brigance Inventory of Early Development-II High/Scope Child Observation Record for Infants and Toddlers (Rous, McCormick, Gooden, & Townley, 2007)
Nonstandardized Tests	Limited purpose and application	Teacher- or researcher-made test
Individual tests	Test administered on an individual basis with only the administrator and the participant.	Wechsler intelligence tests
Group tests	Test administered in a group. Caution: Students with disabilities or those who are not a part of the dominant culture or language group may not fare as well on group tests.	SAT, GRE, MMPI; most academic achievement tests
Power tests	Items may be fairly difficult but a liberal time frame is allowed. Respondents are encouraged to skip problems they do not know and answer all the ones they do know.	Wechsler Intelligence Scale for Children (WISC) subtests: Block Design and Picture Completion
Speed tests	Administration requires a prespecified relatively short response time. Respondents are instructed to try not to make mistakes, but to answer as many items as possible in a limited time. Caution: Students with disabilities or those who are not a part of the dominant culture or language group may not fare as well on speed tests.	Name as many letters of the alphabet as you can in a short time period; WISC subtests: Coding and Symbol Search

relies on the use of multiple types of assessments, not a single test or measurement device, and assessment occurs across time. The primary vehicle for assessment is the direct observation of performance in the form of behavior and products. Performance assessment is an essential element of alternative assessment, and the portfolio is the vehicle through which performance assessment information is stored (Roeber, 2002).

Roeber (2002) defined portfolios as purposeful and systematic collections of student work that are evaluated and measured against predetermined scoring criteria. The information contained in the portfolios may serve as measures of the dependent variable in a research study and include collections of participant work representing a selection of the participant's performance, such as written assignments, videotapes, or solutions to math problems. Many states and school divisions use portfolios as an alternative to standardized assessment. There are challenges to using portfolios in research and evaluation studies because of the subjective nature of the collection and scoring of the information found in the portfolio. Salvia and Ysseldyke (2000, cited in S. J. Thompson. Quenemon, Thurlow, & Cuthbert, 2001) suggest that the following issues need to be considered:

- How the content will be selected for inclusion in the portfolio
- What quality of work will be included—best versus typical
- Whether students should participate in selecting the work that will be included
- How much information is required to get a true score
- How reliability and validity of the information will be determined

One method for scoring the information in portfolios is to use a rubric. According to Solomon (2002), a rubric is an assessment tool for verbally describing and scaling levels of student achievement as represented, for example, by products found in a portfolio. The rubric presents a gradation of performance from *poor* to *excellent* or *above standard, at standard,* or *below standard,* and a scale value for each gradation (1 = *poor,* 5 = *excellent*) represents the score.

While there are several types of rubrics, the developmental rubric is the most useful because the score provides a gauge for where the participant is on a continuum and allows the researcher to make comparisons that are both criterion referenced (where the participant is with respect to his or her performance) and normative (where the participant is relative to other participants). Two excerpts from a rubric for evaluating a lesson plan are set forth in Tables 12.3 and 12.4. Column one of the rubric gives the first of eight components of an effective lesson. The last four columns, with numbers 1, 2, 3, or 4, offer progressive descriptors for continuous improvement of a lesson. The lesson being evaluated could be given an individual score for each component, or the average of the eight components could be presented. Tips to developing rubrics and a sample rubric are found in Box 12.2 and at the Web site www.4teachers.org with instructions and examples of rubrics in their tool RubiStar (http://rubistar.4teachers.org/index.php). Another Web site with rubric examples is Teachnology (www.teach-nology.com/web_tools/rubrics/general/).

Table 12.3 Sample Rubric for Evaluating a Lesson Plan

Components	*1 No Evidence*	*2 Some Evidence*	*3 Evidence*	*4 Strong Evidence*
Concepts/ Concept Statement	No evidence of concept statement(s). Concept statement(s) do not relate to Ohio Proficiency Test outcomes (OPT) and/or the Ohio Competency Based Model (OCBM)	Concept statement(s) demonstrates relationship to OPT outcomes and/or the OCBM	Concept statement(s) clearly defines the focus of the lesson plan and the relation to OPT outcomes and/ or the OCBM	Concept statement(s) clearly defines the focus of the lesson plan and shows the interrelationship among concepts and relation to OPT outcomes and/or the OCBM

SOURCE: www.uc.edu/certitest/rubric/rubric.htm

Table 12.4 Sample Rubric for Evaluating Art in the Form of Mural

MURAL	*Novice*	*Apprentice*	*Veteran*	*Master*
Accurate detail and depth	Incorrect or few facts, hardly any detail (1–3 pts.)	Some facts are accurate; some detail (4–6 pts.)	Substantial amount of facts, good amount of detail (7–9 pts.)	Exceptional amount of facts, vivid descriptions (10–12 pts.)
Clear focus	Vague and unclear (1–2 pts.)	Some focus, but not organized enough (3–4 pts.)	Well organized and clearly presented (5–6 pts.)	Highly organized and easy to follow (7–8 pts.)
Design	Little to no layout and design (1–3 pts.)	Simple design, but layout could be more organized (4–6 pts.)	Attractive and invites the viewer (7–9 pts.)	Exceptional design and outstanding visual appeal (10–12 pts.)

SOURCE: Adapted from www.rubrics4teachers.com.

Box 12.2 Tips on Developing Rubrics

- Decide whether the rubric addresses the most important aspects of student performance.
- Decide whether or not the rubric addresses the instructional outcome(s) to be measured.
- Decide whether the rubric includes anything extraneous. If so, change the rubric or use a different one.
- Don't pay too much attention to the rubric's stated grade level. It may be usable at other grades with little or no modification.
- See if a rubric from a different subject area can be adapted to fit your needs. Reading rubrics can often be used to assess listening, writing rubrics may be adapted to assess speaking, and fine arts rubrics can sometimes be applied to several different art forms.
- Make sure the rubric is clear.
- Try the rubric out on some actual samples of student work.
- See if you and your colleagues can usually arrive at consensus about what scores to assign a piece of student work.

SOURCE: Stix, A. (1997). *Creating rubrics through negotiable contracting and assessment.* U.S. Department of Education. (ERIC No. TM027246).

Computers and Assessment

Despite the incredible ubiquity of technology, Baker (2007) asserts that technology-enhanced tests "have not yet stepped up to early expectations. In large-scale testing, they serve efficiency without capitalizing on their potential to leverage better design and higher fidelity experience (e.g., simulations), provide instant scoring of open-ended responses, or exploit students' ease with technology. They have been stuck in the useful but limited domain of computer-adaptive tests" (p. 311). Baker lists a number of innovations that are possible because of technology that can improve assessment such as computer-scoring of open-ended questions, optical scanning of students' written work that can be scored on the computer, speech recognition software advances, use of computer games and virtual worlds as assessment venues, and knowledge-bases attached to assessments to aid in scoring tests. Wang, Jiao, Young, Brooks, and Olson's (2008) comparison of computer-based testing and paper-and-pencil testing in K–12 reading assessments indicated that the results were influenced by computer practice and the computer algorithm (whether the test was administered linearly or with computerized adaptive testing).

Secondary Data Sources

Secondary sources of data can be found, for example, in sources such as administrative records and previous research studies. Analysis of existing documents is discussed in a subsequent section of this chapter on qualitative data collection methods. However, there are several quantitative databases that researchers should know about. Several examples were mentioned in Chapter 6 of this text on survey research. Other examples include the National Assessment of Educational Progress (NAEP), the High School and Beyond Longitudinal Studies, and the National Longitudinal Transition Study of Special Education Students.

Such databases can provide a wealth of information; however, they should be used with appropriate caution. Some national databases do not allow for disaggregation by variables such as race, gender, or type of disability. In others, certain categories of persons have actually been excluded. Prior to 2002, NAEP excluded students with disabilities; however, with the passage of No Child Left Behind, they changed their policy. Currently, NAEP offers accommodations to all students who need them to demonstrate their knowledge and ability, and thus no longer has nonaccommodated samples. They provide limited reports based on learner outcomes by type of disabilities.

Selection and Development of Quantitative Instruments

Now that you have a basic understanding of the language of psychometrics, measurement, and data collection, you are in a position to decide on the best method for collecting your data. (Qualitative data collection methods are discussed later in this chapter.) In this section, I address the sources and criteria for choosing to use an existing instrument for quantitative research.

Identifying an Instrument: Sources of Information

In your literature review, you may have come across a measurement instrument that was used in previous research that seems just right for your purposes. If so, that is great!

It will give you a place to start to determine if that is, indeed, the appropriate instrument for you. I will first explain sources of information about tests and other data collection instruments, and then I will discuss criteria for the selection of existing instruments. Your first source of information about possible data collection instruments for your own research is the literature review. If you have not zeroed in on a particular instrument through your initial searching, now is the time to go back to the databases described in Chapter 3 and conduct a more focused search to determine what instruments have been used to measure your constructs of interest.

In addition, other sources, listed here, have been created specifically to make your search for a data collection instrument easier and more thorough. Box 12.3 displays a list of sources for finding tests and other data collection instruments that are already available.

Box 12.3 Resources for Tests and Other Measurement Instruments

The Seventeenth Mental Measurement Yearbook (Geisinger, Spies, Carlson, & Plake, 2007). The *Mental Measurement Yearbook (MMY*; available from the Buros Institute for Mental Measurements Web site at www.unl.edu/buros) contains descriptive information on hundreds of tests in many major categories. Each new yearbook contains information about tests that have been published or revised since the last edition or that have generated 20 or more references since the last *MMY*. The information about each test in the *MMY* is quite extensive, including the title, group for which the test is intended, its acronym, available subscale scores, criticism of the test, whether it is for individuals or groups, how many forms are available, its cost, the author and publisher, and references on construction, validity, use, and limitations. In addition, test reviews are printed that are written specifically for the *MMY*.

Tests in Print, also from the Buros Institute for Mental Measurements, is a volume that is published annually. *Tests in Print (TIP)* serves as a supplemental source of information to the *MMY* in that it contains a comprehensive bibliography of all tests that appeared in preceding *MMYs*. However, *TIP* is not limited to tests that have been published, revised, or generated 20 or more references since the last *MMY*. Rather, it contains information about any test that is *in print and available for purchase or use*. There is also a search engine available at the Buros center's Web site (www.unl.edu/buros) with information on tests and testing called Test Reviews Online. The **Test Locator** is a gateway to various sources of information on tests; its Web sites include http://ericae.net, http://buros.unl.edu/buros/jsp/search.jsp, and www.ets.org/testcoll.

PRO-ED Inc. publishes tests and test critiques of standardized tests in the areas of speech-language pathology, special education and rehabilitation, psychology and counseling, occupational and physical therapy, and early childhood. They offer tests and published critiques of tests at their Web site at www.proedinc.com/.

The **American Psychological Association** (APA) provides information on locating both published and unpublished tests at their Web site at www.apa.org/science/faq-findtests.html. They have sections on finding information on particular tests, purchasing tests, and the proper use of tests. The information about unpublished tests includes a link to the Directory of Unpublished Experimental Measures, a volume that is updated periodically and contains information about tests that are not commercially available.

ETS Test Collection. The Educational Testing Service (ETS) Test Collection database contains records on over 25,000 tests and research instruments. ETS provides a wide range of means to access information about tests. It maintains a test collection that contains over 17,000 tests and other measurement devices from the United States and a few other countries (Canada, England, and Australia). The test collection is accessible to any qualified person, based on publishers' restrictions. The ETS publishes over 500 annotated test bibliographies in specific subject areas, available for a modest fee. The bibliographies include the following information about each test: title, author, publication date, target population, publisher or source, and an annotation indicating the purpose of the instrument. The test collection file is now available as a publicly searchable database on the World Wide Web. The test collection provides current information on available published and unpublished tests and related activities. The online database (Test Link) uses ERIC descriptors and can be searched using the same search strategies used to access ERIC. For more information, contact ETS at (609)734-5689 in Princeton, NJ, or go to their Web site. Their URL is www.ets.org/testcoll.

PsycINFO is the database developed by Educational Resources Information Center (ERIC) of the American Institutes for Research that indexes research published in the educational and psychological literature (http://search.ebscohost.com/login.aspx). The ERIC Clearinghouse on Tests, Measurement, and Evaluation (ERIC/TM) maintains a database that reviews tests in education (www.eric.edu.gov/).

The Test Publisher. If you feel fairly certain that you want to use a particular measurement instrument, you can request a copy directly from the publisher. Most instruments come with a manual that explains administration procedures and other background information about the test. You should be cautious about using the test manual as your sole source of information about a test, because it may not present information that is critical of the test. Always be sure to check multiple sources for information about any instrument that you decide to use.

Advice for Selecting an Instrument

Based on advice from the Joint Committee on Testing Practices (2004), I provide the following list to help you in selecting your data collection instrument:

1. Define the purpose for testing, the content and skills to be tested, and the intended test takers. Select and use the most appropriate test based on a thorough review of available information.

2. What are the variables that the test measures? What subscales are included in the test?

3. Review and select tests based on the appropriateness of test content, skills tested, and content coverage for the intended purpose of testing.

4. Review materials provided by test developers and select tests for which clear, accurate, and complete information is provided. What is the format of the instrument? How much time is needed for administration? To what extent do these features promote or restrict accuracy of assessment for the people in the proposed research? How much time is required for scoring? Are alternate or short forms available? What is the cost of the

instrument? Can it be scored by hand? Or computer? Can you do it yourself or do you have to send it to the test developer?

5. Select tests through a process that includes persons with appropriate knowledge, skills, and training.

6. Evaluate evidence of the technical quality of the test provided by the test developer and any independent reviewers (e.g., what evidence is reported as to its reliability, norm group representation, validity, type of administration?).

7. Evaluate representative samples of test questions or practice tests, directions, answer sheets, manuals, and score reports before selecting a test. What type of training is needed for administering, scoring, and interpreting the test?

8. Evaluate procedures and materials used by test developers, as well as the resulting test, to ensure that potentially offensive content or language is avoided. Does the instrument satisfy concerns about language and culture in terms of avoiding bias on the basis of gender, race or ethnicity, and disability?

9. Select tests with appropriately modified forms or administration procedures for test takers with disabilities who need special accommodations.

10. Evaluate the available evidence on the performance of test takers of diverse subgroups. Determine to the extent feasible which performance differences may have been caused by factors unrelated to the skills being assessed.

If modifications are needed in an available instrument, Thurlow, Ysseldyke, and Silverstein (1993) suggest that the researcher ask the following questions:

1. If accommodation is made on the basis of a specific characteristic (e.g., a disability), how should eligibility for accommodation be determined?

2. What type of modifications should be allowed?

3. Do scores achieved under nonstandard conditions have the same meaning?

4. If there is a difference in performance levels between standard and nonstandard administrations, are these due to actual differences in the construct being measured, or are they artifacts of modifications of the testing process?

Researchers can use pilot tests to determine the impact of modifications of existing instruments.

Developing a Data Collection Instrument

Development of a data collection instrument is a complex and time-consuming task. After an exhaustive search of the literature, you may determine that no existing instrument will measure exactly the construct in which you are interested. Thus, you will find it necessary to develop your own data collection instrument. The steps outlined here give you a rough guide to this complex process. If you really intend to get involved in instrument development, you should check on other sources that provide more detail, such as the texts listed in Box 12.1.

The following steps are adapted from DeVellis (2003). Similar steps can be found in most test and measurement texts. These steps relate to the measurement of a construct, such as optimism or anxiety. If you are interested in collecting information from a general survey instrument, review the steps for constructing a questionnaire in Chapter 6. In this section, I use the development of the Assessment Individual Motives-Questionnaire (AIM-Q; Bernard, Mills, Swenson, & Walsh, 2008) as an example of the instrument development process.

Step 1: Define the Objective of Your Instrument

What is the specific purpose of the proposed measurement instrument? What information do you want on what attribute? As an example, have you ever wondered what motivates people? Do you listen to news reports, observe student or client behaviors, or look at your own children and wonder, why did they do that? Bernard et al. (2008) wondered about individuals' motivations and they set out to develop an instrument that would provide a multidimensional approach to measuring individual differences of 15 human motives. They were working within an evolutionary psychological theoretical framework, which holds that "motivated behavior is purposeful behavior. Purposeful behavior is neither random nor simply reflexive. Purposeful behavior solves challenges to survival posed by what evolutionary psychologists call the 'Environments of Evolutionary Adaptedness' (EEA)" (p. 17). They wanted an instrument that would be useful to applied psychologists in the areas of forensic, clinical, health, and educational psychology, as well as being capable of testing the theory of evolutionary psychology about motivation.

Step 2: Identify the Intended Respondents and Make Format Decisions

The relevance of the criterion centers on the persons for whom the measurement is intended. Factors related to the administration of the instrument should be considered, such as amount of time required to complete it, reading level, format for items, response option formats, and test setting. Format options include true-false, matching, multiple choice, sentence completion, ranking items, Likert-type scales, and open-ended essay-type questions. Examples of several of these formats can be found in Chapter 6. You are probably familiar with most of these formats simply by virtue of having been a student and taking tests yourself. However, being able to recognize an item type and being able to write good, high-quality items are two entirely different matters. You should review one of the measurement texts cited earlier for rules for item construction of the different types.

The Likert-type scale is a type that you may well have responded to on instruments rating the quality of your instruction in your university courses, but you may not recognize the name itself. Quite simply, this is the type of item that makes a statement, such as the following:

"My emotional problems interfere with my usual daily activities."

You would then indicate the strength of your agreement or disagreement with that statement on a 4- or 5-point scale that might look like this: 1 = *strongly agree,* 2 = *moderately agree,* 3 = *neutral,* 4 = *moderately disagree,* 5 = *strongly disagree.* This is the type of item that Bernard et al. (2008) used in AIM-Q; they had a paper-and-pencil version and online Web version. The intended respondents for the AIM-Q are adults from diverse backgrounds and ages, although the researchers acknowledge that the majority of the people in the development process were university students.

Step 3. Review Existing Measures

You already reviewed existing measures to decide that you needed to create your own. However, methods for formatting and administering the measure as well as for determining its reliability and validity can be identified from the developmental work conducted by other researchers. Bernard et al. (2008) use their extensive review of literature on motivation to derive a list of 15 motives, each related to a social domain. "They are as follows: (a) Self-Protection Domain—Aggression, Curiosity, Health, Play, and Safety; (b) Mating Domain—Sex and the "status motives" of Appearance, Material, Mental, and Physical; (c) Relationship Maintenance/Parental Care Domain—Affection; (d) Coalition Formation Domain—Altruism and Conscience; and (e) Mimetic Domain—Legacy and Meaning" (p. 18).

Step 4. Develop an Item Pool

There are many avenues open to the researcher in preparing draft items for the new measurement device. Some may be adopted or adapted from current measures. Others might be developed using experts or program staff responsible for the program being studied. Four psychologists from different areas (social, behavioral, evolutionary, and clinical psychology) and six advanced undergraduate psychology students developed items for the AIM-Q (Bernard et al., 2008). The item writing process is described as follows:

> A first attempt at item writing produced 300 items (20 per scale). The items were then randomized and the same writers independently identified each of the 300 items with one of the 15 motives according to their operational definitions. Agreement of 80% or better for motive assignment was achieved for 190 items. Some of the items with poorer interrater agreement were rewritten, and some entirely new items were added to the pool. A total of 306 surviving, edited, and new items were randomized and the same writers again independently sorted all of them onto one of the 15 motive scales. The 12 items with the highest rate of agreement (ranging from 80% to 100%) for each scale were selected for further analysis. (p. 18)

Sensitivity to Multicultural Concerns

The most important advice about collecting data in diverse, multicultural contexts is to ensure that members of the targeted community are included in the review process of the constructs, procedures, and instruments (Bravo, 2003, p. 232). Concerns about multicultural issues in the construction of data collection instruments have been addressed in the following resources:

- *Handbook of Multicultural Counseling,* Second Edition (Ponterotto, Casas, Suzuki, & Alexander, 2001).
- *Guidelines on Multicultural Education, Training, Research, Practice, and Organizational Change for Psychologists* (APA, Joint Task Force of Divisions 17 and 45, 2002).
- *Guidelines for Research in Ethnic Minority Communities, 2000* (Council of National Psychological Associations, 2000; available at www.apa.org/pi/oema/programs/cnpaaemi_pubs.html).
- Interagency Advisory Panel on Research Ethics (2003; available at www.pre.ethics.gc.ca).

Covert (1977) suggests that you should take some time to think of an appropriate title for your data collection instrument. This is the first thing that the respondent will read, so you want it to be motivating and conceptually consistent with the content of the instrument. Following the title, you might want to include a short, introductory paragraph explaining the purpose of the instrument and its intended use. (This information is sometimes more extensively described in a cover letter.) The introductory statement can be used to explain how you got the person's name or why he or she was selected, as well as to provide assurances of confidentiality or anonymity. Obviously, the introductory paragraph (and all statements on the instrument) should be written in language that is understandable to the intended respondents.

Directions for how to complete the instrument should be included next. These could be as simple as, "Circle the appropriate response." If a separate answer sheet is used, more complex instructions may be necessary. It is also possible to start with general directions and then supply more specific directions for individual parts as appropriate. As mentioned in Chapter 6, it is important to tell the respondent who to give or send the instrument to after completion.

Step 5. Prepare and Pilot Test the Prototype

After the item pool has been developed, the researcher will assemble the first draft of the instrument. To develop a good instrument, you need to go through a number of pilot tests. At first, it is recommended that the developer ask other professionals knowledgeable about the attribute and its measurement in the targeted sample to review the prototype. These experts will be looking for content validity in addition to relevance for the target population.

After revisions have been made as a result of the first review, the prototype can be tried out on a small sample of the intended respondents. Typically, this is done by the researcher under expected administration procedures to get a general idea of the quality of the information as well as any problems in administration and scoring. The researcher should provide a means for the members of the pilot group to give feedback on the instrument in terms of items that might need additional clarification. This can be done after they complete the instrument through written comments, some type of modified focus group format, or both.

The final pilot test should be conducted with a large enough sample to enable the researcher to gather reliability and validity information. If the instrument depends on the use of interviewers, observers, or document reviewers, the researcher must collect interrater and intrarater reliability indices at this time.

Bernard et al. (2008) went through a three-year development process during which they conducted eight pilot tests in order to refine items and establish reliability and validity for their instrument.

Step 6. Conduct an Item Analysis and Revise the Measure

The answers to each item should be reviewed to determine if a pattern suggests ambiguity or bias in the item. The final revisions of the instrument can then be made. The researcher should be careful to document all the pilot test procedures and revisions in the instrument so that these can be presented in the research report as evidence of the quality of the measurement.

Advice for Administering Data Collection Instruments

The Joint Committee on Testing Practices (2004, p. 7) provides the following advice on administering instruments for data collection:

1. Follow established procedures for administering tests in a standardized manner.

2. Provide and document appropriate procedures for test takers with disabilities who need special accommodations or those with diverse linguistic backgrounds. Some accommodations may be required by law or regulation.

3. Provide test takers with an opportunity to become familiar with test question formats and any materials or equipment that may be used during testing.

4. Protect the security of test materials, including respecting copyrights and eliminating opportunities for test takers to obtain scores by fraudulent means.

5. If test scoring is the responsibility of the test user, provide adequate training to scorers and ensure and monitor the accuracy of the scoring process.

6. Correct errors that affect the interpretation of the scores, and communicate the corrected results promptly.

7. Develop and implement procedures for ensuring the confidentiality of scores.

Extending Your Thinking: Instrument Development

Identify an attribute that you might want to investigate in a research study. Following the steps for instrument development in this chapter, develop a draft instrument to measure the intended attribute. Try it out on a small group of appropriate respondents.

Qualitative Data Collection Methods

As discussed in Chapter 8, the researcher is the instrument in qualitative research studies. In other words, instead of using a test or questionnaire to collect data, the researcher is the instrument that collects data by observing, interviewing, examining records, documents, and other artifacts in the research setting, or using some combination of these methods. Many issues related to the role of the researcher as instrument are discussed in Chapter 8. In this chapter, I focus on the three main qualitative data collection methods: observation; interview; and document, records, and artifacts review. There is an additional section on participatory and visual data collection approaches.

Observation

Qualitative observations differ based on the specific approach and purpose of the study, as well as the beliefs of the researcher and the demands of those being observed.

Hesse-Biber and Leavy (2006) list possible researcher roles as complete observer, observer-as-participant, participant-as-observer, and complete participant. I have experienced these roles in my various research activities.

- *Complete observer.* In my early work in vocational education, I was asked to play a complete observer role in a study of transition to work for high school age youth. I entered the situation and attempted to become "invisible." Of course, my initial appearance at work sites caused some reaction from the people being observed; however, I assured them that I was going to blend into the background and take notes. Eventually, they tired of trying to engage me in conversation and proceeded with their regular activities. In my more recent work on teacher preparation for students who are deaf and have additional disabilities, the team observed a reflective seminar for graduates of the program without participating in any of the discussions.

- *Observer-as-participant.* In the beginning of my work with a program for gifted deaf adolescents in marine biology, I observed in settings in which it was possible for me to contribute by discussing activities with the teachers and young people, while my primary role was to take notes on what was happening.

- *Participant-as-observer.* During the marine science project, my role sometimes shifted to participant as observer. For example, when we were at the shoreline and the students had nets in which they were collecting sea creatures, the students needed an interpreter to communicate with the hearing teacher. The students were divided into small groups, and the certified interpreters could not be in all places at once. Hence, I served as interpreter as I helped pull the nets from the water with the students. Obviously, note taking in this setting was limited to retrospective writing after returning to the dryer parts of the area. Cocks (2008) also used this approach in her study of the peer culture of children with learning difficulties. She was unable to take notes during her observations because she chose to participate in the small group activities with the children in order to enhance the quality of the data collected.

- *Complete participant.* This approach to observation is more common in action research in which a person who is an employee of an agency or a community member undertakes the qualitative data collection. It can also appear when community members are invited to join the research as co-researchers. When I was employed (for a short time) as an evaluator for a private corporation that employed a large sales force, I was required to take the same training that the sales force took as part of my work as an evaluator. I attended all the training sessions and completed all the activities, capping off my "complete participant" role by demonstrating what I had learned about salesmanship through a presentation "selling" the importance of understanding principles of developmental psychology for teachers in training. I guess I was already mentally moving on to my next career at Gallaudet University.

So, then, what do observers observe? M. Q. Patton (2002) suggests the following list as ideas for an observer to attend to.

1. *Program Setting.* The physical environment within which the program takes place should be described in sufficient detail to permit the reader to visualize the setting. Avoid interpretive adjectives unless they represent quotations from the participants (e.g., comfortable, beautiful, and stimulating are interpretive); colors, measurements, and purpose are less interpretive (e.g., "a blue room with a green chalkboard at one end measuring 40' by 25'" or "a library with the walls lined with books"). Describe the way the walls look in the room, the amount of space available, how the space is used, the nature

of the lighting, how people are organized in the space, and the interpretive reactions of program participants to the physical setting. If I am entering a new setting for observation, I often take the first few minutes to sketch out a picture of the room, furniture, salient objects, and persons. I will sometimes label people as S1, S2, S3, or T (teacher). Once I have finished my drawing, usually the people in the room have started to forget that I am there. Then I continue my observations.

2. *Human and Social Environment.* Look for ways in which people organize themselves into groups and subgroups. Watch patterns of interaction, frequency of interaction, direction of communication patterns (from staff to participants and participants to staff), and changes in these patterns. Note characteristics of people in the different groups (male and female group interactions, different background characteristics, racial and ethnicity differences, and different ages). Try to detect decision-making patterns: Who makes decisions about the activities that take place? To what extent are decisions made openly so that participants are aware of the decision-making process? How are decisions by staff presented to the full group? How are decisions communicated?

3. *Program Activities and Participant Behaviors.* What do people do in the program? How do they experience the program? What is it like to be a participant in the program? What would one see if one were watching the program in progress?

Find a unit of activity—for example, a class session, mealtime, or meeting. A comprehensive description of an activity includes the following:

At the beginning,

How is the activity introduced or begun?

Who is present at the beginning?

What exactly was said at the beginning?

How did participants respond or react to what was said?

In the middle,

Who is involved?

What is being said by staff?

What are participants doing?

What is being said by participants?

What are the variations in how participants are engaging in the activity being observed?

How does it feel to be engaged in this activity? (Observer records own feelings.)

In the end,

What are the signals that the activity unit is ending?

Who is present at the time?

What is said?

How do participants react to the ending of the activity?

How is completion of this unit of activity related to the other program activities and future plans?

4. *Informal Interactions and Unplanned Activities.* Simply continue to gather descriptive information about what people do and, in particular, what people are saying to each other. Data include things such as the following:

"None of the participants talk about a session when it is over."

"Everyone splits in a different direction when a session is over."

> "People talk about personal interests and share gossip that has nothing to do with the program."
>
> "Learning occurs in unstructured moments through personal interactions."

Observe body language and nonverbal cues.

5. *Attend to the Native Language of the Program Participants.* Part of the observer's task is to learn the native language of the program—that is, the literal meanings, connotations, and symbolism. The field notes of the observer should include the exact language used by the participants to describe their experiences so that patterns of word usage can emerge.

6. *Nonverbal Communication.* In many settings, nonverbal communication includes patterns established for the participants to get the attention of or otherwise approach another person. Fidgeting, moving about, or trying to get comfortable can communicate things about attention to and concentration on group processes. Dress, expression of affection, physical spacing, and arrangements are nonverbal cues.

7. *Unobtrusive Measures.* These include physical clues about program activities—for example, "wear" spots on the floor, dusty equipment, and areas used a lot or a little.

8. *Observing What Does Not Happen.* If the program goals, implementation design, or proposal suggest that certain things ought to happen or are expected to happen, it is appropriate for the observer to note that those things did not happen. When your basic experience with a program suggests that the absence of some particular activity or factor is noteworthy, be sure to note what did not happen.

Box 12.4 provides an example of an observational strategy used for data collection in a study of peer culture for children with learning disabilities.

Box 12.4 Observational Strategy Example

Generally the observations occurred in 6-week blocks at intervals throughout a 12-month period. Each 6-week block comprised 2 observations each week—1 at each setting—thus resulting in 12 observations per block. The intention was to observe the settings through the seasons and festive holidays such as Christmas and Easter. By the completion of field notes there were 48 recorded visits, which represented 195 hours of observation. The length of each observation varied according to the planned activity of the day, the day of the week and whether or not it was school holidays. School term weekday observations were from 4.00 pm until 6.30 pm in one setting, and 4.00 pm until 8.30 pm in the other. This difference reflects the times children attended each of the settings. During the holidays and at weekends the observations were from 10.00 am until 4.00 pm in both settings. The aim was to organize my attendance at the settings to reflect the times children attended in order to purposely avoid arriving at the same time as staff and other adults.

—Cocks, 2008, p. 169

Interviewing: Individual and Focus Group

Although observation allows collection of data through the researcher's direct contact in the setting, not all researchers have the opportunity or inclination to conduct extensive observations. However, qualitative researchers almost always include interviewing as an important method of data collection. Interviews can be structured or unstructured, in person or via electronic means, in group or with an individual. (Recall that phone interviewing was discussed in Chapter 6 on survey research.) Typically, interviews in a qualitative study are done with an unstructured or minimally structured format. Interviewing can be conducted as a part of participant observation or even as a casual conversation. Researchers sometimes start with very broad questions and then allow other questions to emerge as the researcher is sensitized to the meanings that the participants bring to the situation. As the study evolves, interviewing can become more or less structured or formal.

Interviews can be conducted individually or in a group. The *focus group* approach was described in Chapter 8. Although focus groups have been used extensively in market research, they can also be used in needs sensing for training and service programs, for instrument review, and for many other research purposes. Because the focus group is a guided discussion, the facilitator usually has a list of five to seven questions to ask during a 1.5- to 2-hour session. The questions are used in a semistructured way to ensure coverage of important issues yet allow for flexibility in responding to group-initiated concerns. One of the benefits of focus group research is the additional insight gained from the interaction of ideas among the group participants.

The characteristics of questions for focus group interviews have been delineated by Krueger (2003) and Krueger and Casey (2000) as follows:

1. Usually, focus group interviews include fewer than 10 questions and often around 5 or 6 total.

2. Focus group interviews use open-ended questions. So instead of asking, "Does your child play at the playground?" ask, "Where does your child usually play?"

3. Avoid using "why" questions. These questions can set off a defensive reaction by the respondent. Modify the question, such as "What prompted you to want to participate in the program?"

4. Carefully develop the questions. Brainstorming sessions with colleagues or audience members is one way to generate questions. Many questions can be generated this way, and then priorities can be established to determine critical questions.

5. Establish the context for questions so participants are ready to respond. Provide enough information in each question so that the participants understand what you are asking for.

6. Questions should be arranged in a logical order, sometimes from general to specific.

Box 12.5 provides examples of focus group questions from counseling and community education focus group studies. The role of the focus group facilitator is a challenging one. He or she needs to be able to control the interview process so that all participants can express themselves, one or a few people do not dominate the discussion, more introverted people are encouraged to speak, and all important topics are covered.

Box 12.5 Sample Focus Group Questions

Sessions and Yanos (1987) conducted focus group interviews to determine desirable characteristics of a counseling agency. They asked such questions as these:

1. What qualities would one look for in a counselor?

2. What types of office setting would be preferable for the provision of counseling services?

3. If a person were seeking counseling, what days or hours would be most desirable?

4. What sort of services would be most desired—individual counseling, group counseling, or family counseling?

5. What other factors should be considered in providing a counseling service to persons living, say, in the eastern suburbs of a particular city?

Krueger (1988) also presents many excellent examples of focus group questions. The following illustrates a focus group question that could be used to develop a strategic plan for community education:

> I'd like each of you to take a few moments and fill out this list. [Pass out page.] I've listed several categories of problems or issues that may affect you and others in your community. The categories include the following: work and business, family, leisure, community, and environment. Take a moment and jot down what you think to be the most important issues in each of these categories. . . . Which of the issues that you mentioned on your list could be solved or lessened by education or information? (p. 70)

When conducting interviews with individuals, Hesse-Biber (2007) identifies a continuum of types of interviews from formal to informal, with varying degrees of structure. Generally speaking, qualitative researchers tend to favor semistructured or unstructured individual interview formats. (See Box 12.6 for McCracken's [1988] views on the necessity of having a questionnaire for long interviews.) Researchers sometimes start with more informal interviewing strategies to establish a relationship with the participant. Using very general open-ended questions allows the respondent's concerns and interests to surface, providing a broader lens for the researcher's gaze. Sample questions might be: "How did you come to be in this position?" "What is it like to work here?" A more structured approach to an interview means that the researcher develops an interview guide with topics, issues, or questions that they intend to cover during the interview. The researcher is open to following leads from the respondent to determine the ordering of questions and the use of probes to further explore relevant points.

Feminists have endorsed the idea that interviewers should be cognizant of power differences between the interviewer and the participants (Hesse-Biber, 2007). The focus is on trying to uncover knowledge about women's lives that reflects the diversity of experiences as well as illuminates hidden aspects of their lives related to social justice. Hesse-Biber explains that what is essential for qualitative interviewing to reflect a feminist perspective is the type of questions that are asked and the relationship between the researcher and the respondent: "Research that gets at *an understanding of women's lives and those of other oppressed groups,* research that promotes *social justice and social change,* and research that is mindful of the *researcher-researched relationship* and the *power and authority* imbued in the researcher's role are some of the issues that engage the feminist researcher" (p. 117). To this end, she recommends in-depth interviewing as an appropriate data collection strategy to reach understanding of women's lived experiences.

Interviewing *people with disabilities* can present challenges because of the abilities or communication needs of the respondents. For example, P. M. Ferguson (1992) did a case study of autistic students in which he conducted interviews with adults who had various connections to autistic individuals at the school, including regular and special education teachers, administrators, and support staff. He commented, "Because of the limited verbal skills of the students in Mel's class, I did not conduct formal interviews with any of them. I did have short, informal conversations with the students when I was there doing observations" (p. 166).

Box 12.6 Using a Questionnaire in Interviewing

> The use of a questionnaire is sometimes regarded as a discretionary matter in qualitative research interviews. But, for the purposes of the long qualitative interview, it is indispensable. . . . The questionnaire has several functions. Its first responsibility is to ensure that the investigator covers all the terrain in the same order for each respondent (preserving in a rough way the conversational context of each interview). The second function is the care and scheduling of the prompts necessary to manufacture distance. . . . The third function of the questionnaire is that it establishes channels for the direction and scope of discourse. The really open-ended interview is an ever-expanding realm of possibility in which the generative power of language is unleashed to potentially chaotic effect. The fourth function of the questionnaire is that it allows the investigator to give all his or her attention to the informant's testimony. . . . It is important to emphasize that the use of the questionnaire does not preempt the 'open-ended' nature of the qualitative interview. Within each of the questions, the opportunity for exploratory, unstructured responses remains. . . . The interviewer must be able to take full advantage of the contingency of the interview and pursue any opportunity that may present itself. In sum, the questionnaire that is used to order data and free the interviewer must not be allowed to destroy the elements of freedom and variability within the interview.
>
> —McCracken, 1988, pp. 24–25

In some circumstances, researchers choose to record their interviews via audio or video technology for later transcription. In other circumstances, researchers must record their interviews in notes on the spot because of logistical reasons. When Mertens (1991) interviewed gifted deaf adolescents at the marine science summer camp, she found that it was necessary to train herself to take notes while watching the respondent in order to not miss any of their signs. She found that she could accommodate to this situation by using a clipboard that was tilted enough for her to see with her peripheral vision that the writing was going onto the right part of the page. She also paused between questions to finish writing each response and then spent time immediately after each interview filling in any holes that had been created by this interview process. As mentioned in Chapter 6, ethical concerns direct that researchers explicitly turn control of the interview over to the person being interviewed. *Turning over control* means allowing the person to end the interview at any time, choose not to answer specific questions, raise issues that the researcher did not bring up, and have the opportunity to review his or her comments before they are made part of the official record for the research data.

Document and Records Review

All organizations leave trails composed of documents and records that trace their history and current status. Documents and records include not only the typical paper products, such as memos, reports, and plans, but also computer files, tapes (audio and video), and other artifacts. The qualitative researcher can turn to these documents and records to get the necessary background of the situation and insights into the dynamics of everyday functioning. The researcher cannot be in all places at all times; therefore, documents and records give the researcher access to information that would otherwise be unavailable. In special education research, documents that might be important include report cards, special education files, discipline records, Individual Education Plans (IEPs), IEP meeting minutes, curriculum materials, and test scores. Access to records and documents needs to be negotiated up front. You should be sensitive to the types of records and documents that might be associated with a particular setting.

Lincoln and Guba (1985) distinguish between documents and records as follows:

Type	*Purpose*	*Examples*
Records	Prepared for official reasons	Marriage certificates Driving licenses Bank statements File records
Documents	Prepared for personal reasons	Diaries Memos Letters Field notes

Charmaz (2007) also makes a distinction between elicited and extant texts. Elicited documents are those that the researcher asks the participants to create as part of the data collection process (such as keeping diaries, journals, or logs of behavior). Extant texts, for example those listed by Lincoln and Guba (1985), require that the researcher be aware of the need to temper their use with an understanding of the time, context, and intended use for which the materials were created. As noted in Chapter 9, particularly with historical research, it may not be possible to interact with the people who produced the materials. The researcher then faces the challenge of how to interpret the meaning of such materials. Hodder (1994) suggests that the qualitative researcher use the same rules of thumb that guide other types of qualitative data and ask such questions as, "How does what is said fit into more general understanding?" (p. 398). Then examine patterns and inconsistencies in the evidence. When the authors or users are still alive, the researcher can conduct "member checks" to determine various perspectives for the interpretation of the data.

Participatory Data Collection Strategies

Participatory data collection strategies tend to fit more comfortably into the qualitative approaches, although not all qualitative approaches are participatory. In participatory approaches to data collection, the stakeholders are responsible for collecting and analyzing information, as well as for generating recommendations for actions based on the interpretation of the results. The researcher's role is more to support and facilitate the process (Kemmis & McTaggart, 2005; World Bank Group, 2003). There are many different participatory tools and strategies. Box 12.7, on Web resources for participatory data collection, provides you with a list of such resources. Four participatory methodologies are discussed here:

Participatory Rural Appraisal

The name of this approach—*participatory rural appraisal* (PRA)—is a bit misleading as it is not limited to use in rural areas. PRA includes a number of different techniques, all of which are based on some version of semistructured interviewing, that are aimed at sharing learning between local people and outsiders. During the interviews, a variety of diagrammatic techniques are commonly used, such as mapping techniques, ranking exercises, and trend analysis. The diagrams are used to stimulate discussion and are not necessarily drawn on computer screens or paper. They can be drawn on the ground with sticks, stones, seeds, or other local materials (and can be transferred to print later if appropriate).

Box 12.7 Web Resources for Participatory Data Collection

http://www.eldis.org/	Institute of Development Studies (IDS): Eldis is a gateway to information sources on participatory monitoring and evaluation.
http://www.worldbank.org/	The World Bank Participation Thematic Team promotes methods and approaches that encourage the involvement of various stakeholders, especially the poor, in development initiatives that affect them.
http://www.worldbank.org/wbi/sourcebook/sbhome.htm	The World Bank Participation Sourcebook (1996) lists methods and tools helpful in participatory rural appraisals.
http://www.undp.org/eo/documents/who.htm	This site provides the United Nations Development Program's *Who Are the Question-Makers? A Participatory Evaluation Handbook* (1997).

Mapping Techniques. Mapping as a PRA activity can take various forms, such as (a) historical maps that depict the changes that have occurred in a community; (b) social maps that illustrate the makeup of the community, including characteristics associated with access to resources, school attendance, or involvement in community activities; (c) personal maps that are drawn by individuals that can show the different sections of the community (such as men vs. women or rich vs. poor), in terms of places that are important to them or ways the community could be improved; or (d) institutional maps that can represent the different groups and organizations within a community as well as their relationships and opportunities for participation in decision making.

Ranking Exercises. Exercises can be done to rank such things as problems, preferences, or wealth. Problem ranking involves asking participants to list six or so main problems with a particular project and then asking them to rank them in order of importance. Problems can be written on cards and participants can be asked to identify "which is the bigger problem" when holding the cards two at a time. Preference ranking is sometimes done by asking participants to list items and their criteria for determining their preference for the items. A matrix is then constructed with the items along the horizontal axis and the criteria on the vertical axis. Each item can be ranked individually and then discrepancies can be explored in groups. Wealth ranking involves the identification of different wealth groups in a community. This can be started as an individual ranking effort using card sorting and followed by focus groups.

Trend Analysis. PRA researchers have undertaken trend analysis using such things as seasonal calendars and daily activity charts. Calendars can be used to indicate periods of high or low activity. Appropriate seasonal variables can be included depending on the purpose of the research, such as rainfall, crop sequences, labor demand, availability of paid employment, incidence of human diseases, and so on. Such calendars can indicate whether project-related activities generate sources of income or food when they are really needed. Daily activity charts provide a graphic way for individuals to depict how they spend their day. This also allows for comparisons between men and women, those who are employed versus not employed, and so on. This individual activity record can also show the busiest times of the day or year and so can be useful in monitoring changes in the time use of the participants.

Beneficiary Assessment

A beneficiary assessment (BA) is conducted to determine the perceptions of the beneficiaries regarding a project or policy. Participants are asked about their use of a service, satisfaction with that service, and ideas for changes that might be needed. Typically, three methods of data collection are used in BA: semistructured interviews, focus group discussions, and participant observation.

Self-Esteem, Associative Strength, Resourcefulness, Action Planning, and Responsibility (SARAR)

SARAR is an acronym that takes its name from the five attributes and capacities that are considered the minimum essentials for participation to be a dynamic and self-sustaining process (World Bank, 1996). The *creative* techniques that can be used in a SARAR include mapping and nonserial posters to encourage participants to reflect on their lives and experiences. Nonserial posters involve the use of poster-sized pictures that depict dramatic human situations that are fairly ambiguous in nature. The participants are asked to put in order a limited number (usually four) of the pictures to tell a story about an issue of concern to them.

Investigative techniques such as a pocket chart can also be used. The pocket chart is a matrix made of pockets that are labeled by simple drawings. Participants vote by putting counters in the pockets to indicate their situation or preference. A three-pile sorting activity is an *analytic* technique that can allow participants to either show knowledge (pictures depicting good/bad/ambiguous hygienic practices) or identify who they think is responsible for solving a problem (e.g., responsibility of the household/local government/both together).

Gender analysis is a technique that gives insights into differentiated impact on the access to and control of domestic and community resources. The technique uses three large drawings of a man, a woman, and a couple, as well as a set of cards showing different resources and possessions owned by people in the community, such as cattle, food, water pots. Participants then assign the resources to the man, woman, or couple, depending on who works with particular physical and community resources and who owns or makes decisions about them.

Several *planning* techniques can be used in SARAR, including

- "Story with a gap," in which one picture depicts "before" and the second "after," and participants are encouraged to discuss the steps needed to reach the situation in the "after" picture
- Force-field analysis, in which a "before" and "after" scenario is used and the participants are encouraged to identify what factors will facilitate/inhibit the achievement of the desired picture

Appreciative Inquiry

A final participatory data collection strategy comes from the field of organizational development. *Appreciative inquiry* (AI) looks at organizational issues, challenges, and concerns by focusing on what is working particularly well in an organization (Coghlan, Preskill, & Catsambas, 2003). Instead of focusing on problems and possible solutions, AI asks participants to envision what it might be like if their organization functioned in an optimal manner more of the time. AI typically has a four-step process (Watkins & Mohr, 2001):

1. AI begins with a *Discovery Phase,* in which participants interview each other, sharing their peak experiences in the organization with another individual and then with the group. The results of this initial activity can be used to structure another interview protocol that focuses on priority areas.
2. The *Dream Phase* asks participants to envision themselves and their organization working at their best.
3. In the *Design Phase,* participants use their dreams to propose strategies, processes, and systems that will help create and support positive change.
4. In the *Destiny Phase,* participants begin the implementation of the identified strategies from the Dream and Design Phases. They monitor their progress and engage in new dialogue and additional AI as necessary.

In Preskill and Coghlan's (2004) edited volume on AI, they provide a number of detailed examples. McNamee (2004) reports on her use of AI with an evaluation of a schoolwide curriculum reform project that occurred in a highly contentious climate.

She asked such questions as, "Have you heard or experienced conversations within the school—at any level—related to how your department operates and envisions itself that have been especially constructive? What do you think made these conversations constructive?" (p. 27).

A second example of AI was based on an evaluation of a Family Rehabilitation Center (FRC) in Sri Lanka in an environment of civil war that had resulted in much trauma (Jacobsgaard, 2004). Jacobsgaard asked such questions as the following:

- What excites you the most about working for FRC?
- Tell us about a time when clients responded really positively to FRC's work.
- Tell us about situations when you [FRC] have been most successful in prevention of torture and violence.

Such stimulating questions resulted in data that supported how the FRC had found ways of achieving its objectives even when it did not provide the services as prescribed in the original project document.

Participatory data collection strategies are not without their challenges. (AI is often criticized for focusing only on the positive to the neglect of problem areas. AI advocates respond that issues and concerns are addressed; however, they surface in a context of constructive action for a positive future, building on strengths.) The researcher must fulfill the role of educator to prepare the participants to engage in the processes. All of these strategies can be used in conjunction with more formal surveys or more extensive collection of observational data. The key to success is to be flexible and innovative and willing to adapt to the local circumstances.

Visual Data

Voithofer (2005) extends thinking about data collection as it relates to technological innovations and includes production and reception that are occurring

> through the convergence of text, video, film, animation, audio, photographs, and 2D and 3D graphics that are combined (i.e., authored, linked), stored (i.e., organized, manually and automatically indexed), and presented (i.e., searched, retrieved, and displayed through a graphical interface or metaphor) on some form of video monitor (e.g., personal computer, laptop, personal digital assistant, cellular phone) and that are transferred over distributed wired and wireless electronic networks. Although access to computer hardware and software resources and levels of technical skill vary among scholars, Internet-connected devices represent an increasingly taken-for-granted tool for researchers. Whether for gleaning data and reference sources from the Internet; communicating with collaborators and participants; processing statistical data; collecting, coding, and synthesizing qualitative data; writing research interpretations; or authoring data summaries in multiple media, the computer is a primary tool for many education [and psychology] researchers. (p. 4)

This is an area that continues to advance and with that advance, additional research questions arise.

Newton (2009) and Farough (2006) examine issues involved in the collection of visual data, including photographs and videos, especially as it relates to privacy issues. They discuss ways to disguise the people in the photos by making sure that the photo is devoid of any information that would make it possible to identify specifically the geographic location or identity of the individual, or refraining from publishing pictures until many years after they were taken so the persons in the pictures are no longer in the same situation. However, these strategies do not serve to protect against all unethical uses of visual data. Additional measures can be taken by including the participants in collecting and interpreting the visual data.

Mixed Methods and Data Collection

As mentioned in Chapter 10 on mixed methods, researchers make choices about the type and sequence of data collected. Different designs reflect different data collection strategies, such as collecting quantitative data first to use as a basis for collecting more in-depth qualitative data. Meadow-Orlans et al. (2003) used this strategy in their nationwide study of parents' experiences with their deaf or hard-of-hearing children. Christ (2007) also used this strategy in a national study of disability support coordinators, using first a quantitative survey to reveal trends and to establish criteria for selecting exemplary programs that provided services to college-level students with disabilities. The quantitative data were also used to guide the construction of key semistructured interview questions used to collect data for the qualitative cross-case analysis at the three selected sites.

Data collection strategy decisions in mixed methods research should be guided by the purpose of the research and the paradigmatic belief systems of the research team (J. C. Greene, 2007). Onwuegbuzie and Johnson (2006) note that the strength of mixing data collection methods is that one can capitalize on the strengths of one method over another for a particular purpose. Greene discusses the need for additional research into the mixing of data collection methods when she writes:

> Not enough is known about methodological strengths and weaknesses, propensities and biases. And these are not only technical concerns, as in social desirability biases in survey response or overestimates of pre-post gains due to regression to the mean. These are also contextual and political concerns, as in the varying credibility of some forms of data among different audiences for social inquiry and the differential capacity of different methods to meaningfully capture and represent the interests and perspectives of different members of a social context. (p. 120)

Mixed methods research is fertile ground for research on the implications of different data collection choices.

Extending Your Thinking: Data Collection: Quantitative and/or Qualitative?

- Select a specific research question, either one from your own research proposal or one from published literature. Brainstorm ideas for data collection strategies for both quantitative and qualitative techniques. Which would be most appropriate for your question? On what basis did you make that decision?
- Identify attributes of people that might be the focus of research (such as gender, race and ethnicity, or disability) and describe how the impact of each attribute on data collection strategies might be investigated.

Standards for Judging Quality of Data Collection

The way that the researcher chooses to operationalize the attributes is crucial in that this determines the inferences that can be made from the data. Beyond conceptual relevance and appropriateness, the researcher needs to consider the quality of the data collection strategy. The researcher must establish indicators that provide evidence that the information generated in the research is trustworthy and believable. Three standards have emerged from the postpositivist paradigm for judging the quality of quantitative research measurement: reliability, validity, and objectivity. The parallel criteria from the constructivist paradigm collection of qualitative data are dependability, credibility, and confirmability (Guba & Lincoln, 1989). The qualitative community has expressed concern about the use of parallel criteria because they seem to situate quality of qualitative data too closely to the postpositivist paradigm (Whittemore, Chase, & Mandle, 2001). As discussed in Chapter 8, additional criteria for judging quality have been proposed that are seen as more aligned with the philosophical beliefs that underlie the constructivist paradigm (Charmaz, 2006; Corbin & Strauss, 2008). The criteria for qualitative data quality are discussed only briefly in this chapter because they were discussed in more depth in Chapter 8. Although both qualitative and quantitative researchers have traditionally expressed concern for avoidance of bias based on gender, race and ethnicity, sexual orientation, or disability, in the transformative paradigm, bias related to these sources is explicitly recognized as a central tenet of research. Therefore, this category of quality for data collection is discussed within that context. You can use the outline of the standards for judging quality of data collection in research presented in Box 12.8 to guide you through this section of this chapter.

Box 12.8 Standards for Judging Quality of Data Collection

Reliability-Dependability

Postpositivist: Reliability

Repeated measures

- Coefficient of stability (test-retest)
- Alternate-form coefficient (parallel forms)

Internal consistency

- Kuder-Richardson formulas
- Cronbach's coefficient

Reliability with observers

- Interrater reliability
- Intrarater reliability

Constructivist:

- Dependability

(Continued)

Box 12.8 (Continued)

Validity-Credibility

Postpositivist: Validity

- Construct validity
- Content validity
- Predictive validity
- Concurrent validity
- Consequential validity

Constructivist:

- Credibility

Objectivity-Confirmability

Postpositivist: Objectivity

Constructivist: Confirmability

Transformative Paradigm: Avoidance of Bias

- Feminist issues
- People with disabilities
- Racial, ethnic, and language minorities

Postpositivist: Reliability

To be useful, data collection instruments must be consistent. When we measure a particular attribute, we are concerned about the accurate estimate of the target attribute. If you measured students' ability to handle interpersonal conflict one day and, without additional instruction or intervention, gave them the same instrument the next day, you would expect that their scores on the instrument would be about the same. The ability to handle interpersonal conflict, like most attributes, does not vary across time without some intervention. In this example, if the students' scores changed, their performance must have been influenced by something other than their ability to handle interpersonal conflicts. These other influences cause error; the extent to which measurement instruments are free from error indicates their reliability. The more reliable the measurement, the better the researcher can arrive at a true estimate of the attribute that the instrument purports to measure.

The purpose of measurement is to get an accurate estimate of a particular attribute. Accuracy is achieved by minimizing sources of error as much as possible and obtaining an estimate of how much error remains. Two types of error can influence performance on a measurement instrument: systematic and unsystematic. Systematic errors inflate or deflate performance in a fixed way and thus do not affect a measure's reliability. (They do, however, affect validity.) In the previous example, additional instruction on how to handle interpersonal conflicts could be thought of as a systematic influence on performance. The effect of a systematic error on performance is constant and therefore can be predicted.

Unsystematic errors, however, are a concern for researchers. These vary at random from situation to situation and therefore cannot be predicted. Unsystematic errors are produced by factors that fall into three categories:

Those within the person being measured (e.g., motivation or alertness)

The conditions of the administration of the measurement (e.g., providing different instructions, changing the environment, or allowing more time)

Changes in the measurement instrument or tasks (e.g., changes in the items on the instrument or the behaviors being sampled)

Typically, reliability is calculated using a statistic that compares performances by the same individuals at different times or on different parts of the instrument. The reliability coefficient is interpreted much like a correlation coefficient. As you will recall from Chapter 5, correlation coefficients range from 0.00 to +/- 1.00, with 1.00 indicating perfect reliability, which is rarely accomplished for any measure. The closer to 1.00, the more reliable the instrument. Most reliability coefficients range from .75 to .95. The important thing to remember is that anything less than 1.00 indicates the presence of error. The researcher's task is to identify the potential sources of such error and make them public.

How is reliability determined? Researchers can use several approaches to determine the reliability of a particular data collection instrument. Two of the most common approaches involve the use of repeated measures (e.g., test-retest and parallel forms) and calculation of internal consistency (e.g., Kuder-Richardson formulas or coefficient alpha). If observational data are collected within a quantitative study, the consistency between observers and within an observer must be addressed. For a more thorough review of reliability concepts, the reader is referred to Bruce Thompson's (2003) *Score Reliability: Contemporary Thinking on Reliability Issues*.

Before I explain the specific ways to determine the reliability of a data collection instrument, it is important for you to know that the reliability reported in the test manual or published literature does not follow the test or instrument. Reliability should be calculated after every use. You may well find that your obtained reliability will be lower than the published ones because of differences in groups, settings, and so on. This caveat should also be kept in mind for validity claims.

Repeated Measures Reliability

Two types of repeated measures reliability are the coefficient of stability and the alternate-form coefficient.

Coefficient of Stability (Test-Retest). This technique for determining reliability involves administering a test to a group of individuals, waiting a period of time, and then administering the same test to the same individuals a second time. The second administration can occur immediately or after a time delay. Scores from both administrations are compared to determine the consistency of response. One of the drawbacks of this approach is the potential for practice effects or remembering items across administrations of the test. For example, Lane et al. (2007) calculated three test-retest correlations for three time periods: 14, 34, and 20 weeks. Their results revealed reliabilities of .66, .56, and .80, respectively.

Alternate-Form Coefficient (Parallel Forms). If practice effects are a concern, the researcher might choose the alternate or parallel-forms approach. In this case, an *equivalent form* of the test is used in the second administration. In addition to eliminating the practice effect, this approach enables the researcher to determine the degree to which performance might be influenced by new items. Of course, the major concern with the parallel-forms reliability check is the degree to which the tests are equivalent. For example, researchers used the Word Recognition Placement subtest of the Comprehensive Inventory of Basic Skills (CIBS-R; Brigance, 1999) to identify students in need of further testing for consideration of special education placement (VanDerHeyden, Witt, & Barnett, 2005). They reported an alternate form correlation of .94; hence they concluded that the test was reliable.

Internal Consistency

The method of internal consistency can be used with only one administration of an instrument. It is appropriate for use when the instrument has been designed to measure a particular attribute that is expected to manifest a high degree of internal consistency. Several statistical procedures can be used; however, the most frequently used are Cronbach's coefficient alpha and various Kuder-Richardson formulas (e.g., KR-20 and KR-21). These formulas can be used to compare responses within one administration of an instrument to determine its internal consistency. Most statistical packages for computer applications will calculate a reliability coefficient such as those named here. In the Lane et al. (2007) study, teachers rated the entire student body at three time points—fall (n = 500), winter (n = 451), and summer (n = 474)—during the 2005–2006 academic year; corresponding values for Cronbach's alpha were .78, .85, and .85. The researchers concluded the screening device was reliable.

Reliability With Observers

Interrater Reliability. In studies that use quantitative data that are collected through observation, the researcher needs to be concerned with the reliability between two independent observers or raters (thus the term *interrater reliability*). The degree of interrater reliability can be expressed either as a reliability coefficient calculated between two sets of observations collected by independent observers or it can be expressed as a simple percentage of agreement between the two observational data sets.

Intrarater Reliability. Intrarater reliability is similar to interrater reliability, except that the comparisons are made between two data collection efforts by the *same observer* (thus *intrarater reliability*). The calculations are the same: either a reliability coefficient or a percentage of agreement.

Constructivist: Dependability

As you will recall in Chapter 8, Guba and Lincoln (1989) identify dependability as the interpretive paradigm's parallel standard for reliability. Within this paradigm, change is expected, and therefore the postpositivist notion of stability is not appropriate. However, the researcher who works within this paradigm does have a responsibility to track the change and provide a publicly documentable record of the change process. The quality of the data collection can be determined by means of a dependability audit in which the change process can be inspected to attest to the quality and appropriateness of the inquiry process.

Moss (1995) raises questions about the traditional psychometric approach to establishing reliability in the context of exploring what the constructivist paradigm of research could offer to educators and psychologists interested in the quality of measurement.

She describes the traditional method of determining reliability as "operationalized by examining consistency, quantitatively defined, among independent observations or sets of observations that are intended as interchangeable—consistency among independent evaluations or readings of a performance, consistency among performances in response to independent tasks, and so on" (p. 6). This reliance on quantification of consistency across independent observations requires a significant level of standardization. Moss sees such privileging of standardization as problematic and proposes this alternative to reliability grounded in the constructivist paradigm:

> A hermeneutic approach to assessment would involve holistic, integrative interpretations of collected performances that seek to understand the whole in light of its parts, that privilege readers who are most knowledgeable about the context in which the assessment occurs, and that ground those interpretations not only in the textual and contextual evidence available, but also in a rational debate among the community of interpreters. Here, the interpretations might be warranted by criteria like a reader's extensive knowledge of the learning context; multiple and varied sources of evidence; an ethic of disciplined, collaborative inquiry that encourages challenges and revision to initial interpretations; and the transparency of the trail of evidence leading to the interpretations, which allows users to evaluate the conclusions for themselves. (p. 7)

These criteria have been mentioned by several scholars in the field of qualitative methods and seem to stand the test of time (Charmaz, 2006; Corbin & Strauss, 2008).

Postpositivist: A Unified Concept of Validity

The appropriateness of a data collection instrument is only partially determined by its reliability or dependability. A second category of quality is validity of the meaning of scores derived from the data collection instrument. The conventional definition of the validity of an instrument is the extent to which it measures what it was intended to measure. In practice, however, the validity of an instrument is assessed in relation to the extent to which evidence can be generated that supports the claim that the instrument measures attributes targeted in the proposed research. Citing Messick's work in validity (1995, 1996), the *Standards for Educational and Psychological Testing* (American Educational Research Association [AERA], American Psychological Association, & National Council on Measurement in Education, 1999) explain that validity is a unitary concept that measures the degree to which all the accumulated evidence supports the intended interpretation of test scores for the proposed purpose. Therefore, it is critical to determine the stated purposes of the test or assessment instruments and align those purposes with the intended use in the research study.

Even though Messick wrote of the unified concept of validity in the mid-1990s and the *Standards* were published in 1999, scholars who have reexamined the concept of validity more recently affirm the unified concept, but also acknowledge the need for different forms of evidence to support validity claims. Sireci (2007, p. 477) writes,

> My reading of the validity literature over the years has led me to the following conclusions regarding fundamental aspects of validity:
>
> - Validity is not a property of a test. Rather, it refers to the use of a test for a particular purpose.

- To evaluate the utility and appropriateness of a test for a particular purpose requires multiple sources of evidence.
- If the use of a test is to be defensible for a particular purpose, sufficient evidence must be put forward to defend the use of the test for that purpose.
- Evaluating test validity is not a static, one-time event; it is a continuous process.

Messick (1995) broadly defines validity as "nothing less than an evaluative summary of both the evidence for and the actual—as well as potential—consequences of score interpretation and use" (p. 742). An overarching concern related to validity is the extent to which the instrument measures the attributes it was intended to measure rather than bias due to gender, race and ethnicity, class, disability, or other cultural factors. To be valid, testing must be nondiscriminatory; that is, tests and procedures used to evaluate a person's characteristics, knowledge, or attributes must be free of bias both in the way they are administered and in the content of the items on the test. Messick (1995) identifies two major threats to construct validity:

1. Construct underrepresentation, in which the assessment is too narrow and fails to include important dimensions or facets of the construct

2. Construct-irrelevant variance, in which the assessment is too broad and contains excess variance because of intrusion of other constructs. Construct-irrelevant variance can artificially lower scores for individuals with limited reading skills or limited English skills when undue reading comprehension is required in a test of subject matter knowledge (e.g., on a knowledge test in science). Or scores can be artificially inflated on a test of reading comprehension for a group that has greater familiarity with the subject matter.

Messick (1996) explains that a test could not be considered valid if adverse social consequences were attributable to construct underrepresentation or construct-irrelevant variance. Messick includes appraisal of the social consequences of testing, including an awareness of the intended and unintended outcomes of test interpretation and use, as an aspect of construct validity. Because of the central importance of this issue and the advances that have been made in understanding this threat to validity in data collection, the standard of quality related to avoidance of bias is discussed as a separate topic in this chapter.

Sources of Evidence for Construct Validity

The principal method of establishing validity involves "the appraisal of theoretically expected patterns of relationships among item scores or between test scores and other measures" (Messick, 1995, p. 743). It is important to remember that validity is a unified concept and that multiple sources of evidence are needed to support the meaning of scores. According to Messick (1995), validity cannot rely on any one form of evidence; however, it is not necessary to have every form of evidence explained here:

> What is required is a compelling argument that the available evidence justifies the test interpretation and use, even though some pertinent evidence had to be forgone. Hence, validity becomes a unified concept, and the unifying force is the meaningfulness or trustworthy interpretability of the test scores and their action implications, namely construct validity. (p. 744)

Researchers interested in measuring a hypothetical construct, such as intelligence, anxiety, creativity, or the like, need to explicate the theoretical model that underlies the constructs. Controversy frequently surrounds the establishment of construct validity in measurement because of cultural differences that can result in different performances. For example, with tests of intelligence, researchers need to be sensitive to the extent to which they are measuring intelligence, not language or cultural differences, or opportunities to learn specific information or practice certain skills.

One way to establish construct validity involves identifying a group of people who theoretically should perform differently from other groups on the task on the basis of a pre-identified trait. For example, if I had created a test of anxiety level, I could establish two or three groups that I would predict (on the basis of theory) would perform differently on that task. The three groups might be (a) college students on vacation on a Caribbean island, (b) people who had been hospitalized because of an anxiety-related condition, and (c) students in a research methodology course. I would predict that the students on vacation would score very low on the anxiety measure and that the hospitalized patients would score very high. I just would not know what to do with the research students, so I would probably drop them from the sample. If those who were on vacation did score low on the instrument and those in the hospital scored high, I would say the instrument has construct validity.

Construct validity can also be established by correlation with other tests that have been validated as measuring the attribute of interest or by means of factor analysis to support the structure of the attribute as it has been designed by the researcher. For example, Lane et al. (2007) correlated the results of the screening test with ratings by teachers on a second instrument: Strengths and Difficulties Questionnaire (Goodman, 2001) and reported statistically significant positive correlations for the overall score of .66 and subtest correlations between .41 and .55. Such a positive correlation is called convergent validation. Borsboom (2005) cautions that correlations between tests do not in and of themselves reveal validity because what it really *means* for a test to measure a psychological attribute is simply the following: "The primary objective of validation research is not to establish that the correlations go in the right directions, but to offer a theoretical explanation of the processes that lead up to the measurement outcomes" (p. 163).

Content Validity

If the purpose of the research is to evaluate achievement of a specific body of knowledge, the researcher needs to be concerned with content validity. The researcher needs to be certain that the test covers the appropriate content. For example, if you were studying research methodology and you entered the classroom on test day and found a test on underwater photography, you would probably complain that that was not covered in the course. You would be right to say that the test was not content-valid for that purpose.

To establish content validity, you need to review the items or tasks in the measurement instrument to determine the degree to which they represent the sample of the behavior domain of interest in the research study. Sometimes, it is helpful to build a specifications matrix that lists the items and the content area domains covered by each item. The higher the degree of overlap, the better the representation of the behavioral domain, the higher the content validity. Content validity is often established using content experts to make judgments following a process based on alignment methodology (Webb, Alt, Ely, Cormier, & Vesperman, 2005). Content validity is especially important in studies that purport to compare two (or more) different curricula, teaching strategies, or school placements. If all the students are taking the same test but all the students were not exposed to the same information, then the test is not equally content valid for all the groups.

Predictive Validity[1]

Sometimes, a researcher wants to use a test score to predict some future behavior. In other words, I want to obtain a measure of some attribute today and then be able to estimate the likelihood that a person will perform some specific behavior later. For example, academic institutions want to know who will succeed in specific programs prior to admission. Therefore, tests such as the Graduate Record Examination (GRE) or the Medical Schools Admissions Test (MCAT) are used by universities to predict who will be successful in their programs. Predictive validity is also important for tests that purport to measure intelligence in infants or preschoolers, school readiness tests for slightly older children, and aptitude tests for any age group.

Although time-consuming, the typical approach to establishing the predictive validity of a measurement instrument is to administer the test, wait until the predicted behavior occurs, and correlate measures of this behavior with the student's performance on the original test. As the time between the administration of the test and the opportunity to observe the predicted behavior increases, the more likely the researcher would be better off using an established instrument.

As a researcher, you should be aware of a number of variables that can constrict the value of a predictive validity coefficient. In most complex human behaviors, a variety of variables influence performance. To establish the predictive validity of a test such as the GRE, university officials would have to (theoretically speaking) allow all applicants to enter regardless of their score on the GRE. Then, they would have to wait to obtain the final grade point average (GPA) for all the entrants. They could then calculate a correlation between the GRE score and the final GPA to determine the predictive validity of the GRE. Of course, this approach is fraught with problems. Here are just a few:

- Universities try to be selective as to whom they admit, so they are not likely to admit everyone regardless of GRE scores.
- Typically, universities use more than one criterion for selecting students, so GRE scores are not the only basis for selection.
- The students who are accepted probably represent a restricted range on the predictive variable (i.e., the students with the higher GRE scores would be accepted).
- Students who actually complete the program will also represent a restricted range of values on the criterion variable (i.e., the GPA) because, generally, graduate students can make only As or Bs. If they get Cs or worse, they would be on probation or suspended.
- Many personal factors influence a student's performance in graduate school, such as motivation, economic conditions, and family responsibilities.

Thus, as a researcher, you should be sensitive to the range of values possible for the predictive and criterion variables, as well as to the other variables that might influence performance on the criterion variables.

Concurrent Validity

Concurrent validity is conceptually similar to predictive validity, except your interest is in using a test or other measurement instrument to gauge a person's current behavior, interests, personality characteristics, or knowledge. In other words, the interest is in the relationship between a test score and *current* behavior or attributes. This type of validity can also be established in a method similar to predictive validity, except that the researcher does not have to wait any specific period of time to obtain the measure on the criterion variable. This type of validity is appropriate for such characteristics as personality traits or work attitudes.

For example, if I want to determine respondents' ability to handle interpersonal conflicts, I could give them a test and then either simulate or observe their performance in a natural setting that involved interpersonal conflict. I could then calculate a correlation coefficient between the two measures to obtain the concurrent validity value. Sometimes, researchers will identify an instrument that has already established concurrent validity for measuring a particular trait. They will then administer the new instrument along with the older instrument and calculate a correlation between the two scores. If the correlation is high, the new instrument is said to have concurrent validity.

In the Lane et al. (2007) study, the researchers used concurrent validity to justify using a shorter version of a measurement instrument that was designed to identify the students who might engage in risky behaviors. They compared an instrument that took 15 minutes for the teachers to complete with another that took an hour. They also compared students who were rated as highly likely and least likely to engage in risky behaviors on indicators such as referrals for disciplinary problems in school, thus establishing concurrent validity.

Consequential Validity

Consequential validity refers to the social consequences of test interpretation and use. Messick (1995) cautions that this type of validity should not be viewed in isolation as a separate type of validity because it is integrally connected with construct validity. The researcher needs to identify evidence of negative and positive, intended and unintended, outcomes of test interpretation and use:

> A major concern in practice is to distinguish adverse consequences that stem from valid descriptions of individual and group differences from adverse consequences that derive from sources of test invalidity such as construct underrepresentation and construct-irrelevant variance. The latter adverse consequences of test invalidity present measurement problems that need to be investigated in the validation process, whereas the former consequences of valid assessment represent problems of social policy. (p. 744)
>
> The researcher must ensure that low scores do not occur because the assessment is missing something relevant to the focal construct that, if present, would have permitted the affected persons to display their competence. Moreover, low scores should not occur because the measurement contains something irrelevant that interferes with the affected persons' demonstration of competence. (p. 746)

Serci (2007) identifies the following areas for additional research in terms of furthering our understandings of the meaning of validity:

- evaluating the comparability of different versions of a standardized assessment (e.g., test accommodations for individuals with disabilities, translated versions of tests),

- the role of test-curriculum framework alignment in educational accountability systems,

- the different roles of stakeholder groups in the evaluation of testing consequences, and

• how specific statistical procedures (e.g., differential item functioning) and research designs (e.g., comparison of instructed and noninstructed groups of students) fit into . . . sources of validity evidence. (p. 481)

Constructivist: Credibility

Guba and Lincoln (1989) identify credibility as the interpretive parallel to validity. The rationale that supports this criterion is the question, is there a correspondence between the way the respondents actually perceive social constructs and the way the researcher portrays their viewpoints? The following research strategies can enhance credibility (see Chapter 7 for more details):

- Prolonged and substantial engagement
- Persistent observation
- Peer debriefing
- Negative case analysis
- Progressive subjectivity
- Member checks
- Triangulation

By these means, the researcher can increase the credibility of the results of a qualitative study.

Postpositivist: Objectivity

In quantitative studies, objectivity refers to how much the measurement instrument is open to influence by the beliefs and biases of the individuals who administer, score, or interpret it. Objectivity is determined by the amount of judgment that is called for in these three processes. More objective measures consist of short-answer, multiple-choice, and true-false format options. Less objective measures include essay tests, although these can be made more objective by establishing criteria for scoring the responses. Standardized tests are often described as very objective because the instructions are read verbatim from the test manual; the manual tells the amount of time allowed and acceptable answers to students' questions; and answers are scored objectively with an answer key.

In some research situations, objectivity is deliberately sacrificed to allow the respondents a wider range of possible responses. Objectivity in projective tests can be exchanged for the value of having expert judgment involved in the administration, scoring, and interpretation of the test results. In cases such as this, it is important to know that the persons who are responsible for the test processes have received the necessary training in the administration, scoring, and interpretation of the tests. You should ask, what are the researchers' qualifications? What steps were taken to reduce bias? Was it possible to use "blind" testers (i.e., people who were unaware of the experimental condition of the respondent administrated the test)?

When the measurement instrument is a person who serves as an interviewer, observer, or reviewer of documents, the concern arises as to the objectivity of the person as instrument. Then you might ask, are these data independent of the person doing the observations? Would another person come to the same conclusions? Would the observer have seen things the same way at a later date? These are issues that are addressed in the interpretive paradigm.

Constructivist: Confirmability

Just as postpositivists seek to minimize the influence of the observer's judgment, the interpretive researcher seeks to confirm that the data and their interpretation are not figments of the researcher's imagination (Guba & Lincoln, 1989). A confirmability audit can be used to trace the data to their original sources and to confirm the process of synthesizing data to reach conclusions using a chain of evidence. Qualitative researchers generally agree that having a strict definition of standards of quality is not possible and that different approaches require different criteria for making such judgments. As Sparkes (2001, p. 550) writes,

> A multitude of criteria for judging both the process and products of qualitative research will continue to emerge, and these will need to be debated along the way. It would be recognized that there can be no canonical approach to qualitative inquiry, no recipes or rigid formulas, as different validation procedures or sets of criteria may be better suited to some situations, forms of representation, and desires for legitimating than others. As such, the terrains on which judgments get made are continually shifting and characterized by openness rather than stability and closure. It is in this situation of flux that the qualitative . . . research community must grapple with the criteria issue and learn to judge a variety of approaches in different but appropriate ways.

Transformative Paradigm: Avoidance of Bias

All researchers, in all paradigms, must be sensitive to avoiding bias in data collection that results from differences in gender, race or ethnicity, sexual orientation, religion, disability, or socioeconomic status. As you read previously, psychometricians include assessment of the social consequences of test interpretation and use as a part of construct validity. Messick (1995, p. 748) addresses the issue as follows:

> Some measurement specialists argue that adding value implications and social consequences to the validity framework unduly burdens the concept. However, it is simply not the case that values are being *added* to validity in this unified view. Rather, values are intrinsic to the meaning and outcomes of the testing and have always been. As opposed to adding values to validity as an adjunct or supplement, the unified view instead exposes the inherent value aspects of score meaning and outcome to open examination and debate as an integral part of the validation process (Messick, 1989). This makes explicit what has been latent all along, namely, that validity judgments *are* value judgments.

Moss (1995) also reminds us that, "If interpretations are warranted through critical dialogue, then the question of who participates in the dialogue becomes an issue of power" (p. 9). She criticizes the traditional psychometric approach because it "silences the voices of those who are most knowledgeable about the context and most directly affected by the results" (p. 10).

Because this is the central concern of the transformative paradigm, I describe specific examples of ways that data collection has been insensitive on these criteria and ways that it can be made to be more sensitive. My examples derive from writings about data collection from the perspectives of feminists, people with disabilities, and racial and ethnic minorities (African American, American Indian, and Latino American).

Feminist Issues in Data Collection. Eichler (1991) identifies a number of issues related to data collection that provide evidence of sexist bias in the collection of research data. Problems that researchers should avoid include the following:

1. Research instruments validated for one sex that are used for both sexes

2. Questions that use sexist language

3. Studies that do not take into account the fact that male and female researchers may elicit different responses from respondents

4. Questions premised on the notion of sex-inappropriate behavior, traits, or attributes

5. Research instruments that stress sex differences with the effect of minimizing the existence and importance of sex similarities

6. Gender insensitivity demonstrated by people being asked about the behaviors, traits, or attributes of members of the other sex and then by such information being treated as fact rather than opinion

Lewin and Wild (1991) examined the impact of the feminist critique on tests, assessment, and methodology through an analysis of changes in psychological, vocational, and educational tests. They note,

> Tests that classify respondents on the basis of their similarity to people who are located in highly sex-stereotyped settings, such as the occupational world, risk reproducing patterns of past discrimination. It is easier for the feminist critique to call attention to a few blatantly sexist individual items on a scale than to get fundamental changes of familiar measures. (p. 585)

Lewin and Wild (1991) compared the impact on testing in two different contexts: the Strong-Campbell Interest Inventory (successful) and the Minnesota Multiphasic Personality Inventory (MMPI; not successful). The story of these two tests provides some insight into the issues that feminists raise about testing and measurement.

When the Strong Vocational Interest Blank was first published, women with interests in "typical male occupations" were compared with men in that occupational area. As a result of feminist critique, the test was revised so that women could be compared not only with men but also with other women who were in that occupation. The 1987 revised form, called the Strong-Campbell Interest Inventory, included sex-merged forms and an updated reference group. In that edition, only 5 of the 207 occupations lacked adequate samples of both genders (i.e., female agribusiness managers and male dental assistants, dental hygienists, home economics teachers, and secretaries).

Continuing problems with the MMPI illustrate that changes are still needed in psychological testing to avoid bias based on gender. One of the MMPI scales is called "Masculinity-Femininity" (Mf). The femininity score was originally validated in 1956 on a criterion group of 13 gay men. Yes, the scale that was supposed to assess the femininity of heterosexual women was based on a small number of gay men. When the test was revised in 1990, a new normative, nationally representative sample of the U.S. population was drawn; however, the Mf scores were not validated against any criterion whatsoever. The test manual describes various characteristics associated with high and low scorers on the Mf scale; however, it does not provide any validity data (concurrent or construct) to support the claims. Butcher (1989) states that although the manual uses characterizations, such as that males who score highly on the feminine scale are likely to be "sensitive, aesthetic, passive," and possibly have "low heterosexual drive," while low-scoring males are viewed as "aggressive, crude, adventurous, reckless, practical, and having narrow interests," no evidence is offered. Females who score highly "masculine" are seen as "rough, aggressive, self-confident, unemotional, and insensitive," whereas low-scoring (i.e., "feminine") women are seen as "passive, yielding, complaining, fault-finding, idealistic, and sensitive" (cited in Lewin & Wild, 1991, p. 586).

Lewin and Wild (1991) conclude that the MMPI Mf scale is ambiguous and open to bias and potential discrimination based on inappropriate use of it in contexts such as personnel hiring. They suggest that the scale should be dropped until such time as the developers can provide clear evidence of what they are measuring. Constantinople (2005) wonders whether it is appropriate to try to measure masculinity-femininity as a *uni*-dimensional attribute on a bipolar scale. Are masculinity and femininity opposite ends of a continuum? Is it appropriate to assume that because men and women answer items differently that this is an indication of "normal" tendencies?

The *Standards for Educational and Psychological Testing* (AERA et al., 1999) is divided into three major sections. The first part discusses general concerns related to testing, the second addresses fairness in testing and test use, and the third includes specific testing application standards. One of the standards that is particularly germane to issues of fairness and gender and other dimensions of diversity is Standard 7.3, which states,

> When credible research reports that differential item functioning exists across age, gender, racial/ethnic, cultural, disability, or linguistic groups in the population of test takers in the content domain measured by the test, test developers should conduct appropriate studies when feasible. Such research should seek to detect and eliminate aspects of test design, content, and format that might bias test scores for particular groups. (p. 81)

People With Disabilities: Issues in Data Collection. The influence of the theoretical framework on the types of questions asked of people with disabilities is described in Chapter 3. You will recall that questions can be framed to suggest that the problem is "in" the individual with the disability or to suggest that the problem is "in" the societal response to the individual's needs. Issues of validity and reliability arise in this population for a variety of reasons due to the heterogeneity of disabilities and the implications for performance on tests. "Standardization as a solution risks reducing the integrity of the assessment results when the methods do not match the population being assessed and how that population demonstrates competence in the academic domains" (Quenemoen, 2008 p. v). One of the major concerns that remain is the validity of the test under the accommodation conditions—does the score accurately reflect the students' understanding of the construct being measured, rather than the influence of their disability?

Research and evaluation studies addressing issues related to special education often are confronted with the challenge of collecting information from participants who for various reasons cannot respond to typical assessment processes. These include persons whose disability prevents them from responding. For example, a person with a visual impairment or individuals with limited English or low literacy skills may not be able to take a written assessment. In addition, the age of the participant may preclude his or her involvement in the traditional assessment process. For example, researchers working with young children may have to engage the assistance of the child's parents. A very helpful resource for adapting research and evaluation strategies for hard-to-reach participants was developed by the Children, Youth and Families Education and Research Network (www.cyfernet.org).

Mertens and McLaughlin (2004) provide a summary of the types of accommodations that have been investigated for data collection with people with disabilities. Commonly identified accommodations include[2]

- the use of Braille, magnifying glass, audiocassette tapes/digital audio, and large print for tests; oral reading of the text; large-type answer sheets; raised-line drawings, three-dimensional models, physical objects, talking calculators, and Braille computers
- changing the test environment
- flexible time arrangements (e.g., unlimited time or taking the test over several sessions to alleviate fatigue)
- signing instructions (e.g., the National Task Force on Equity in Testing Deaf and Hard of Hearing Individuals at Gallaudet University provides additional guidance for testing with individuals who are deaf or hard of hearing at http://gri.gallaudet.edu/TestEquity/index.html)

The *Standards for Educational and Psychological Testing* (AERA et al., 1999; hereafter called the 1999 *Standards*) should be consulted by the special education researcher or evaluator who plans to make accommodations in the test or testing conditions. The 1999 *Standards* include six strategies for test accommodation: (a) modification of presentation format, including the use of Braille or large-print booklets for visually impaired examinees or the use of written or signed test directions for hearing-impaired examinees; (b) modification of response format, including providing a scribe to mark answers or allowing the use of a computer to record responses; (c) modification of timing, including extended testing time or frequent breaks; (d) modification of test setting, including individual administration and altering lighting or other physical test setting conditions; (e) using only parts of a test, which is more relevant to clinical settings; and (f) using alternate assessments. The 1999 *Standards* also include 12 standards specifically applicable when testing individuals with disabilities.

The 1999 *Standards* cite examples when test accommodations may be inappropriate. The test taker's disability may be directly relevant to the characteristic being measured in the assessment. For example, if the assessment was aimed at identifying a particular set of skills relevant to succeeding on an employment task, it would be inappropriate to mask the interaction of disability and task competence through modifications. A second, and perhaps obvious, challenge to the appropriateness of modification occurs when the purpose of the assessment is to identify a specific disability. Finally, the 1999 Standards caution that, as noted by Fuchs and Fuchs (1999), there are occasions when the test does not need to be modified—no gain would be observed.

The No Child Left Behind Act includes a mandate for aligning assessments with curriculum standards, as well as for testing all children, whatever their disabilities. Hence, work on alternative assessment strategies have been developed through the National Alternate Assessment Center (www.naacpartners.org), the National Center for the Improvement of Educational Assessment (www.nciea.org), and the National Center on Educational Outcomes (www.nceo.info) in the form of performance assessments, checklists, and portfolio assessment. Along with work on the development of alternative assessments has come a call for approaching test development using the principles of universal design. "Rather than having to retrofit existing assessments to include these students (through the use of large numbers of accommodations or a variety of alternative assessments), new assessments can be designed and developed from the beginning to allow participation of the widest possible range of students, in a way that results in valid inferences about performance for all students who participate in the assessment" (S. J. Thompson, Johnstone, & Thurlow, 2002).[3]

Universal design began with a movement within the field of architecture to design spaces that are accessible to everyone. The Center for Universal Design (Waloszek, 2007, p. 1) defined universal design as "the design of products and environments to be usable by all people, to the greatest extent possible, without the need for adaptation or specialized design." This movement has expanded and now has a significant presence in the domains of education and psychology in terms of the development of instruction and assessment that is accessible to everyone. The Center for Applied Special Technology (2008) developed guidelines for universal design (see Box 12.9) that are based on the following three principles:

Principle I. Provide Multiple Means of Representation (the "what" of learning). Students differ in the ways that they perceive and comprehend information that is presented to them. For example, those with sensory disabilities (e.g., blindness or deafness), learning disabilities (e.g., dyslexia), language or cultural differences, and so forth may all require different ways of approaching content. Others may simply grasp information better through visual or auditory means rather than printed text. In reality, there is no one means of representation that will be optimal for all students; providing options in representation is essential

Principle II: Provide Multiple Means of Action and Expression (the "how" of learning). Students differ in the ways that they can navigate a learning environment and express what they know. For example, individuals with significant motor disabilities (e.g., cerebral palsy), those who struggle with strategic and organizational abilities (executive function disorders, ADHD), those who have language barriers, and so forth approach learning tasks very differently and will demonstrate their mastery very differently. Some may be able to express themselves well in writing text but not oral speech, and vice versa. In reality, there is no one means of expression that will be optimal for all students; providing options for expression is essential

Principle III: Provide Multiple Means of Engagement (the "why" of learning). Students differ markedly in the ways in which they can be engaged or motivated to learn. Some students are highly engaged by spontaneity and novelty while other are disengaged, even frightened, by those aspects, preferring strict routine. In reality, there is no one means of representation that will be optimal for all students; providing multiple options for engagement is essential

Box 12.9 Guidelines for Universal Design

Representation

1. **Provide options for perception**
   - Options that customize the display of information
   - Options that provide alternatives for auditory Information
   - Options that provide alternatives for visual information

2. **Provide options for language and symbols**
   - Options that define vocabulary and symbols
   - Options that clarify syntax and structure
   - Options for decoding text or mathematical notation
   - Options that promote cross-linguistic understanding
   - Options that illustrate key concepts non-linguistically

3. **Provide options for comprehension**
   - Options that provide or activate background knowledge
   - Options that highlight critical features, big ideas, and relationships
   - Options that guide information processing
   - Options that support memory and transfer

Expression

4. **Provide options for physical action**
   - Options in the mode of physical response
   - Options in the means of navigation
   - Options for accessing tools and assistive technologies

5. **Provide options for expressive skills and fluency**
   - Options in the media for communication
   - Options in the tools for composition and problem solving
   - Options in the scaffolds for practice and performance

6. **Provide options for executive functions**
   - Options that guide effective goal-setting
   - Options that support planning and strategy development
   - Options that facilitate managing information and resources
   - Options that enhance capacity for monitoring progress

Engagement

7. **Provide options for recruiting interest**
   - Options that increase individual choice and autonomy
   - Options that enhance relevance, value, and authenticity
   - Options that reduce threats and distractions

8. **Provide options for sustaining effort and persistence**
   - Options that heighten salience of goals and objectives
   - Options that vary levels of challenge and support
   - Options that foster collaboration and communication
   - Options that increase mastery-oriented feedback

9. **Provide options for self-regulation**
   - Options that guide personal goal-setting and expectations
   - Options that scaffold coping skills and strategies
   - Options that develop self-assessment and reflection

CAST (2008). *Universal design for learning guidelines version 1.0.* Wakefield, MA: Author.

These principles and guidelines were developed from the perspective of developing instruction and assessment tools; however, they have applicability in the context of developing and using data collection instruments for research and evaluation. CAST recognizes that the guidelines are a beginning point and they welcome researchers to provide feedback on their use so that they can be improved and updated as needed. The guidelines were developed not only for use with people with disabilities, but also for people whose home language is not English and/or who are disenfranchised by the dominant culture.

Racial, Ethnic, and Language Minorities: Issues in Data Collection. National data that illustrate the ongoing academic disparities of the racial, ethnic, and language minority groups and White students reveal that students from these groups score well below the national achievement average (DeVoe & Darling-Churchill, 2008). The use of standardized tests in particular has raised cause for concern about bias against members of racial and ethnic minority groups. Lewis, Hancock, James, & Larke (2008) analyzed the impact of NCLB legislation on the reading and math achievement of African American K–12 students. The researchers concluded, among other things, that the policies enacted under NCLB had no impact on achievement, because 88% (reading) and 87% (math) of the students scored at "basic" and "below basic" levels at Grade 4. Stated differently, given the slow rate of change, during the first 5 years of NCLB, "it will take another 45 years for all African American students in the eighth grade to achieve 'At Proficient' levels in reading and math This is in comparison to 60% (reading) and 53% (math) of White students at Grade 4 who reached the 'At Proficient' category" (Lewis et al., 2008, p. 130).

Paradoxically, the very legislation that mandates high standards and academic achievement for all students appears to undermine and shortchange African American learners (Lewis et al., 2008, p. 139). This dilemma exemplifies how access to educational institutions does not secure the ability to marshal these resources to remedy the legacy of social-structural inequality in American education. Lewis et al. (2008) argue that the results of these standardized tests are not valid indicators of the abilities of African American (and by inference, other minority racial and ethnic groups who are not part of the dominant culture); rather, they are a reflection of racism as a factor in African American underachievement. Racism is an elaborate process . . . which maintains racial categorizations and ideologies as the method for determining which group receives the best and least of society's resources. "Several hypotheses for the causations of the Black-White achievement gap accuse the African American family's culture or deficient family and community practices. These theories have muffled the voices of a few scholars who still insist that racism is an overlooked and systemic variable whose lingering consequences are manifested in the achievement outcomes for today's African American students." (Lewis et al., 2008, p. 128) Ladson-Billings (2006) asserts that the achievement "gap" between Blacks and Whites, Latinos and Whites, and new immigrants and Whites needs to be understood in historical, economic, and sociopolitical terms that recognize the legacy of discrimination and oppression. Given this line of thinking, it seems that the identification of researchable topics, development of interventions, and data collection need to be set in a wider social and cultural context.

Specific problems related to the use of standardized tests with racial and ethnic minorities have been identified by a number of authors. The following list is a synthesis of issues mentioned by J. M. Patton (1993) and Suzuki and Kugler (1995).

1. *Test Content.* Inclusion of items that reflect White, middle-class values and noninclusion of items and procedures that reflect various racial and ethnic minority groups.

2. *Examinee Readiness, Motivation, and Response Set.* Most middle-class children have been socialized to accept the cultural values that achievement is an individual accomplishment and that such accomplishment should be publicly displayed (J. E. Davis, 1992). However, many non-middle-class children and children from other cultures do not share those values. Thus, many children have no clear idea of what testing is when

they encounter it for the first time in school, nor have they grown up in environments in which children are asked to give information to adults. Davis (1992) uses as an example many American Indian cultures that socialize children through nonverbal communication, emphasizing visual and spatial memory, visual and motor skills, and sequential visual memory over verbal skills. Many of these cultures also emphasize sharing and working together. The tests that these children encounter in school focus on verbal skills and force children to work alone. Because of the patterns of teaching in Navajo society, many Navajo children encountering a test for the first time see it literally as a game, not as an evaluation tool (McShane, 1989).[4]

3. *Standardization Level.* Racial and ethnic groups are often underrepresented in standardization samples. National norms more commonly reflect predominantly White, middle-class samples, for which results may be inappropriately applied to minorities.

4. *Examiner Bias and Language Differences.* Noninclusion of individuals knowledgeable of and sensitive to language and cultural differences can result in bias in the results. The test administrator can misjudge, stereotype, or intimidate the respondent because of difficulties in verbal and nonverbal communication.

5. *Reliability and Validity Issues.* Because tests are developed with specific populations, the reliability and validity for racial and ethnic minority groups may be questionable. Tests may actually measure different attributes when used with individuals from different cultures (construct validity), and the predictive validity may be inaccurate in comparison to White, middle-class individuals.

6. *Societal Inequities.* Because of histories of oppression and discrimination, members of racial and ethnic minority groups are already at a disadvantage in educational and vocational achievement. Thus, discrepancies between groups may reflect systemic problems rather than deficits inherent in the individuals providing the data.

Suzuki and Kugler (1995) suggest the following issues in the use of intellectual and personality instruments with different racial and ethnic groups:

1. *Conceptual Equivalence.* The researcher needs to check that the concepts being measured have the same meaning across and within different cultural groups (called concept equivalence).

2. *Demographic and Environmental Variables.* Demographic and environmental variables, such as language, socioeconomic status, educational level, acculturation status, and region of the country, must be taken into consideration. Be aware of the multiplicity of factors that can influence performance, such as poverty, educational failure, malnutrition, and other health-related concerns.

3. *Racial Identity and Level of Acculturation.* Knowing how the people in your research study perceive their own racial identities can be important, because it may affect the impact of cultural influences such as the nature and configuration of symptoms, the way in which problems are reported, strategies of problem solving, attributions regarding the origin of the presenting concerns, and appropriate interventions. Some individuals of different racial and ethnic groups may adhere strongly to the beliefs and values of the dominant White culture to the exclusion of their own racial identity. Others may value their own culture to the exclusion of the dominant culture. Information regarding identity

development and acculturation may be obtained through interviews or standardized measures.

Use of Translated Measures. Ægisdóttir, Gerstein, and Çinarbaş (2008) note that sometimes the cultures are so different that new measures that are culturally responsive need to be developed, thus limiting comparisons that can be made across cultures. For cultures that are not so dissimilar, researchers need to consider a number of factors for translation of instruments. Translated materials can be helpful; however, they should be used cautiously. As Temple and Young (2004) note, the process of translation involves much more than knowing vocabulary and providing word-for-word translations. Rather, issues of cultural awareness and power relations are important in terms of who decides which translation is an accurate representation. Anderman and Rogers's (2003) *Translation Today* is an edited volume that addresses many of the challenges associated with translation of instruments for data collection in education and psychology. The problem of concept equivalence must be addressed, because psychological constructs may not have such a direct translation in another culture. The researcher should also check to see if the format is acceptable to people in that culture and that validity and reliability are established for the different cultural group. You should also investigate the method of translation that was used to be sure that a back translation yields similar concepts. Ægisdóttir et al. (2007) recommend factor analyzing results on instruments that are used with different cultural groups to determine if the underlying structure of the concepts in different groups is the same.

For example, Pearce et al. (2003) conducted a study of spousal abuse against pregnant women in Puerto Rico. They hired a bilingual and bicultural translator who had lived in Puerto Rico who was familiar with the content of the instruments because of work experience in an agency serving individuals who experienced intimate partner violence. Once the translator had a draft version of the instrument prepared, a panel of five bilingual and bicultural experts who spoke Puerto Rican Spanish as their first language compared the original version with the translated version and provided feedback on words and concepts. Then, a second bilingual, bicultural translator "back translated" the instrument from Puerto Rican Spanish to the original language. The results of this process were given to the original translator to reconcile who should make decisions about wording changes. The researchers pilot tested the instrument with women of Puerto Rican heritage who could speak and write English and Spanish fluently. The women completed both the English and Spanish versions and made notes about any differences and mailed these to the researchers. The bicultural, bilingual translator reviewed these results, consulted with another expert in the area, and determined the wording for the final version.

Extending Your Thinking: Translation in Data Collection

Temple and Young (2004) raise these questions that researchers should consider when reading or conducting research where more than one language is used:

- What language was used in data collection?
- At what stage were the interviews [data] translated and transcribed?

(Continued)

(Continued)

- What translation and transcription issues were there?
- What are the implications of power and language dominance in the translation process?
- How are decisions made with regard to which language is used for which purpose?
- How did the researchers address the interpreters' level of familiarity with the topic and cultural group?

Look for research studies that involve more than one language. What information do the researchers provide with regard to Temple and Young's questions? How does this influence your critical assessment of the quality of the research?

Questions for Critically Analyzing Data Collection

Methodological Validity

1. *Face validity*. Do the items on the measurement instrument appear relevant to the life experiences of persons in a particular cultural context?

2. *Content validity*. Do the measurement items or tools have content relevance?

3. *Criterion-related validity*. Have the measures selected been validated against external criteria that are themselves culturally relevant?

4. *Construct validity*. Are the constructs that are used developed within an appropriate cultural context?

5. *Generalization*. Have threats to generalization of causal connections been considered in terms of connections across persons and settings, nonidentical treatments, and other measures of effects?

6. What evidence is provided of the quality of the data collection instruments in terms of the following:

   a. Reliability or dependability?

   b. Validity or credibility?

   c. Objectivity or confirmability?

   d. Freedom from bias based on gender, race and ethnicity, or disability?

7. Are the procedures used by the test developers to establish reliability, validity, objectivity, and fairness appropriate for the intended use of the proposed data collection techniques? Was the research instrument developed and validated with representatives of both sexes and of diverse ethnic and disability groups?

8. Is the proposed data collection tool appropriate for the people and conditions of the proposed research?

9. Given the research questions of the proposed research, when and from whom is it best to collect information?

10. Does the instrument contain language that is biased based on gender, race and ethnicity, class, or disability?

11. If observers are used, what are the observers' qualifications? What steps were taken to reduce bias? Was it possible or reasonable to use "blind" observers? Are the data independent of the person doing the observations? Should they be? What is the influence of the nature of the person doing the observations? Is this discussed? Would another person come to the same conclusions? What unique insights and sensitivities can or does the observer claim? Would the observer have seen things the same way at a later date?

12. Were instruments explored for gender bias? For example, were instruments used for both sexes that had only been validated for one sex? Did questions use sexist language? Was consideration given to the sex of the test administrator? Were questions premised on the notion of sex-inappropriate behavior, traits, or attributes? Did the research instruments stress sex differences with the effect of minimizing the existence and importance of sex similarities? Was information about one sex obtained by asking people of the other sex about their behaviors, traits, or attributes and then treating such information as fact rather than opinion?

13. In terms of race and ethnicity biases, were the data collection instruments screened so that the test content reflected various racial and ethnic minority groups? Was consideration given to cultural differences in terms of examinee readiness, motivation, and response set? Were racial and ethnic groups appropriately represented in the standardization group? Were examiner bias and language differences considered? Was reliability and validity established for racial and ethnic minority groups? Were systemic problems that might lead to differences in performance considered? Did the researcher check on the conceptual equivalence of the items for the different cultural groups? Was the researcher aware of the level of acculturation for members of minority racial and ethnic groups? Were translated measures used appropriately? Did the researcher investigate the dominant language for the respondents?

14. If the instrument is to be or was used with people with disabilities, was the accommodation made on the basis of a specific disability? How was eligibility determined for the accommodation? What type of modification was or should be allowed? Do the scores achieved under the nonstandard conditions have the same meaning? If there is a difference in performance levels between standard and nonstandard administrations, are these due to actual differences in the construct being measured, or are they artifacts of modifications of the testing process?

15. Did the researcher consider his or her own prejudices and biases that might affect data collection? If a research team was used, how sensitive were team members to cultural issues? Was training provided to people in dealing with people who are culturally different from themselves?

16. Were the various different cultural groups involved in planning, implementing, and reviewing the data collection instruments? In the results?

17. Were multicultural issues addressed openly at all stages of the research process?

18. In observational research, was it possible or reasonable to use multiple observers or teams, diverse in age, gender, or ethnicity? Were observational findings cross-checked with other researchers? Were negative cases sought out to test emergent propositions? Were the research setting and findings described in such a way that the reader can "see" and "feel" what it was like there? Was reliability addressed by making observations in various settings, at various times of the day, days of the week, and months of the year?

Extending Your Thinking: Critical Analysis of Data Collection

1. Identify several of the main journals in education and psychology. Examine their instructions to potential authors to see what the journal editors require in the way of evidence of measurement reliability, validity, objectivity, and lack of bias based on gender, ethnicity or race, and disability. Compare these instructions with those found in journals that specialize in publishing research about multicultural, gender, or disability issues mentioned in Chapter 2 of this text. Do you see any differences in the instructions related to this issue? Locate a commercially developed measure and review the manual to determine how the developers have treated the concepts of reliability, validity, objectivity, and bias based on gender, ethnicity or race, class, and disability. Compare the information available in the test manual with that from an independent source, such as the *MMY* or *TIP*.

2. Review the same test and determine to what extent you think it is appropriate for males and females, people of different racial and ethnic backgrounds, people who speak languages other than English, and people with different types of disabilities. What kinds of accommodations would be needed to administer the instrument to people with different types of disabilities? What would be the impact of those accommodations? What could you do to determine the answer to these questions?

3. Identify several research articles that provide descriptions of their data collection strategies (of course, they all should have such sections). Using the questions for critical analysis provided in this chapter, analyze the strengths and weaknesses of the data collection sections of the research articles. Be sure to look at examples of both qualitative and quantitative research studies.

4. Using the research proposal that you have been developing as you move through this text (assuming that you are developing one), write out the data collection plan for your study. Be sure to include information about how you will ensure the quality of the data that you propose to collect.

Summary of Chapter 12: Data Collection

Data collection is a complex and important part of the research process. Researchers can sometimes find data collection measures that were used in previous studies that they can use. However, if none are available, then they need to undertake the development of a unique instrument. Criteria for data collection quality differ depending on the paradigm from which the research is conducted. For example, postpositivists are concerned with reliability, validity, and objectivity. Constructivists are concerned with confirmability, credibility, and transferability. Transformative researchers raise questions that specifically focus on biases based on issues of power that might enter into the data collection decisions, particularly with reference to women, people of color, and people with disabilities. Once the data are collected, the researcher is ready to move on to data analysis, the subject of the next chapter.

Notes

1. Predictive validity and concurrent validity are sometimes combined into one category called *criterion validity*.

2. Many sources provide guidance on acceptable accommodations. See for example the National Assessment of Educational Progress's table of acceptable accommodations (available at http://nces.ed.gov/nationsreportcard/about/inclusion.asp#accom_table).

3. Peter A. Beddow, Ryan J. Kettler, & Stephen N. Elliott (2008) developed the Test Accessibility and Modification Inventory (TAMI) for the purpose of modifying existing measures to improve their accessibility (available at http://peabody.vanderbilt.edu/tami.xml).

4. For additional information about testing and assessment with American Indian populations, see Mckinley, Brayboy, Castagno, & Maughan (2007) and Sternberg (2008).

In This Chapter

- Common types of statistics used for quantitative data analysis are defined, along with methods for choosing among them.
- Interpretation issues relevant to quantitative data analysis are discussed, including randomization, sample size, statistical versus practical significance, cultural bias, generalizability, and options for reporting quantitative results, such as effect sizes and variance accounted for, replication, use of nonparametric statistics, exploration of competing explanations, recognition of a study's limitations, and a principled discovery strategy.
- Statistical synthesis (i.e., meta-analysis) as a literature review method is explained.
- Options for qualitative analysis are described, along with selected computer programs that are available.
- Interpretation issues related to qualitative data analysis are discussed, including use of triangulated data, audits, cultural bias, and generalization of results.
- Mixed methods analysis and interpretation issues are addressed.
- Development of a management plan for conducting a research study is described as a tool to be included in the research proposal.
- Writing research reports is described in terms of dissertation and thesis requirements, alternative reporting formats (including performance), and publication issues.
- Strategies are discussed for improving the probability of the utilization of your research results.

Beware of testing too many hypotheses; the more you torture the data, the more likely they are to confess, but confession obtained under duress may not be admissible in the court of scientific opinion.

—Stigler, 1987, p. 148 (cited in Mark & Gamble, 2009, p. 210)

My personal view is that p-values should be relegated to the scrap heap and not considered by those who wish to think and act coherently.

—Lindley, 1999, p. 75

13

Data Analysis, Interpretation, and Use

By reading and studying this book, you have moved through the steps of preparing a research proposal or critiquing a research study to the point of data analysis. If you are preparing a research proposal, your next step is to describe the data analysis strategies that you plan to use. In most research proposals, this section is followed by a management plan that specifies what tasks you will complete within a specified time frame and what resources will be required to complete the research project. Then, you would be in a position to complete the research study itself and to write up the results. Thus, the organizing framework for this chapter is designed to take you through the data analysis decisions, the design of a management plan, and ideas concerning writing research. If your goal is to critique research (rather than conduct it yourself), you will find guidelines that will help you identify the strengths and weaknesses of this portion of a research study.

A final section addresses the utilization of research results. Although this section appears at the end of this text, ideas to enhance utilization have been integrated throughout the descriptions of the research planning process in this text. If you wait until after the research is finished to consider utilization, chances are that your research could become a "dust catcher" on someone's shelf. That would not be a happy ending after all your work, so it is important to build in strategies for utilization during your planning process.

Quantitative Analysis Strategies

Will struggling first-grade language-minority readers who receive tutoring make greater gains in their reading achievement than struggling readers who do not receive tutoring but are enrolled in the same schools (Ehri, Dreyer, Flugman, & Gross, 2007)? How do experiences of discrimination relate to levels of engagement in school for African American youth (Smalls, White, Chavous, & Sellers, 2007)? These are the types of questions for which researchers use quantitative research methods to investigate. Brief descriptions of two studies that explored answers to these questions are provided in Box 13.1. The analytic and interpretive strategies used in these studies are used as examples of the various concepts described in this section of the chapter.

Box 13.1 Brief Descriptions of Two Quantitative Studies

Study 1: Reading Rescue: An Effective Tutoring Intervention Model for Language-Minority Students Who Are Struggling in First Grade (Ehri, Dreyer, Flugman, & Gross, 2007)

The researchers wanted to test the effectiveness of Reading Rescue, a tutoring program in which school staff provide tutoring to first-grade students in phonological awareness, systematic phonics, vocabulary, fluency, and reading comprehension. They compared students in the Reading Rescue condition with students who had a small group intervention, as well as a control group that had neither intervention. The majority of the tutored students reached average reading levels, whereas the majority in both control groups did not.

Study 2: Racial Ideological Beliefs and Racial Discrimination Experiences as Predictors of Academic Engagement Among African American Adolescents (Smalls, White, Chavous, & Sellers, 2007)

These researchers studied the relationship between African American adolescents' experiences with discrimination and their academic engagement outcomes. Experience with discrimination was measured by rating 17 experiences (e.g., having your ideas ignored, being insulted) using a scale from 0 = *never* to 5 = *once a week or more*) and how bothered they were by the discrimination experience (with scores ranging from 0 = *has never happened* to 5 = *bothers me extremely*). A composite score was created by multiplying respondents' ratings of the frequency of each event with their ratings of how much the event bothered them and then averaging across the product scores for the 17 events to create a composite racial discrimination score.

Negative school behaviors were measured by a response scale ranging from 1 = *never* to 6 = *more than 20 times* with four negative school behaviors: (a) skipped a class without a valid excuse; (b) got into a fight at school; (c) been sent to the principal's office for doing something wrong; and (d) cheated on tests or exams. Using hierarchical linear regression analysis, the researchers concluded that students who experienced higher levels of racial discrimination also reported more negative school behaviors.

Commonly Used Quantitative Data Analysis Techniques

It is not possible to explain all the different types of statistics, the derivation of their formulas, and their appropriate uses in this chapter. The reader is referred to general statistics books for more specific information on this topic (see, e.g., Gelman & Hill, 2007; Holcomb, 2006; Stevens, 2002; Urdan, 2005). First, I define and give examples of some of the more commonly used quantitative data analysis techniques. Then, I provide you with a model to aid you in making decisions about the most appropriate data analysis techniques. Finally, I discuss issues related to the interpretation of quantitative data analysis results.

Statistics can be thought of as being descriptive (i.e., they describe characteristics of your sample), correlational (i.e., they describe the strength and direction of relationships), and inferential (i.e., they allow you to make group comparisons). Box 13.2 provides definitions of the most commonly used descriptive, correlational, and inferential statistics.

Box 13.2 Definitions of Commonly Used Statistics

Descriptive Statistics: Statistics whose function it is to describe or indicate several characteristics common to the entire sample. Descriptive statistics summarize data on a single variable (e.g., mean, median, mode, standard deviation).

Measures of Central Tendency

Mean: The mean is a summary of a set of numbers in terms of centrality; it is what we commonly think of as the arithmetic average. In graphic terms, it is the point in a distribution around which the sum of deviations (from the mean point) is zero. It is calculated by adding up all the scores and dividing by the number of scores. It is usually designated by an X with a bar over it ($\bar{X}$) or the capital letter *M*.

Median: The median is the midpoint in a distribution of scores. This is a measure of central tendency that is equidistant from low to high; the median is the point at which the same number of scores lies on one side of that point as on the other.

Mode: The mode is a measure of central tendency that is the most frequently occurring score in the distribution.

Measures of Variability

Range: The range is a measure of variability that indicates the total extension of the data; for example, the numbers range from 1 to 10. It gives the idea of the outer limits of the distribution and is unstable with extreme scores.

Standard Deviation: The standard deviation is the measure of variability, that is, the sum of the deviations from the mean squared. It is a useful statistic for interpreting the meaning of a score and for use in more sophisticated statistical analyses. The standard deviation and mean are often reported together in research tables because the standard deviation is an indication of how adequate the mean is as a summary statistic for a set of data.

Variance: The variance is the standard deviation squared and is a statistic used in more sophisticated analyses.

(Continued)

Box 13.2 (Continued)

Correlational Statistics: Statistics whose function it is to describe the strength and direction of a relationship between two or more variables.

Simple Correlation Coefficient: The simple correlation coefficient describes the strength and direction of a relationship between two variables. It is designated by the lowercase letter *r.*

Coefficient of Determination: This statistic is the correlation coefficient squared. It depicts the amount of variance that is accounted for by the explanatory variable in the response variable.

Multiple Regression: If the researcher has several independent (predictor) variables, multiple regression can be used to indicate the amount of variance that all of the predictor variables explain.[1]

Inferential Statistics: Statistics are used to determine whether sample scores differ significantly from each other or from population values. Inferential statistics are used to compare differences between groups.

Parametric Statistics: Statistical techniques used for group comparison when the characteristic of interest (e.g., achievement) is normally distributed in the population, randomization is used in sample selection (see Chapter 11) and/or assignment (see Chapter 4), and the interval or ratio-level of measurement is used (e.g., many test scores).

t tests: Inferential statistical tests are used when you have two groups to compare. If the groups are independent (i.e., different people are in each group), the *t* test for independent samples is used. If two sets of scores are available for the same people (or matched groups), the *t* test for correlated samples is used.

ANOVA: The *analysis of variance* is used when you have more than two groups to compare or when you have more than one independent variable.

ANCOVA: The *analysis of covariance* is similar to the ANOVA, except that it allows you to control for the influence of an independent variable (often some background characteristic) that may vary between your groups before the treatment is introduced.

MANOVA: The *multivariate analysis of variance* is used in the same circumstances as ANOVA, except that you have more than one dependent variable.

Structural Equation Modeling. SEM is used to test complex theoretical models or confirm factor structures of psychological instruments. It can assess relationships among both manifest (observed) and latent (underlying theoretical constructs) variables. For further information, see Chan, Lee, Lee, Kubota, and Allen (2007).

Nonparametric Statistics: Statistical techniques used when the assumption of normality cannot be met, with small samples sizes, and with ordinal (rank) or nominal (categorical) data.

Chi-Square: Used with nominal level data to test the statistical independence of two variables.

Wilcoxon Matched Pairs Signed-Ranks Test: Used with two related samples and ordinal level data.

Mann-Whitney U Test: Used with two independent samples and ordinal level data.

Friedman Two-Way Analysis of Variance: Used with more than two related samples and ordinal level data.

Kruskal-Wallis One-Way Analysis of Variance: Used with more than two independent samples and ordinal-level data.

Descriptive Statistics

Researchers commonly report means and standard deviations for the descriptive statistics portion of their report. The usual format is to first state the mean and then show the standard deviation in parentheses immediately following the mean. Ehri et al. (2007) measured students' reading comprehension using a scale of the Gates-MacGinitie Reading Tests (4th ed.; MacGinitie, MacGinitie, Maria, & Dreyer, 2000). The results were: experimental group: a mean of 43.5 with a standard deviation of 12.9; for the control group 1: 37.8 (13.8), and for control group 2, 35.3 (11.2). Sample size is usually indicated by the letter "*n*" and in this case, the sample sizes for the three groups were 62, 60, and 60, respectively. In the Smalls et al. (2007) study, they reported descriptive statistics as follows: "With regard to primary predictor variables, we found that participants on average reported experiencing racial discrimination infrequently ($M = 1.65$, $SD = 1.05$ on a scale of 1 to 5). However, only 3.6% of participants reported experiencing none of the racial discrimination events over the past year" (p. 314). In this study, they use the letter *M* to indicate the mean and *SD* for standard deviation.

Correlational Statistics

Smalls et al. (2007) wanted to test the strength of the relationship between their predictor variables and school outcomes. They reported simple correlation coefficients between the variables: "Higher racial discrimination scores were related to . . . more [self-reported] negative school behaviors ($r = .12$, $p < .05$)" (p. 315). The letter *r* is used to stand for the correlation coefficient statistic. They also chose to use a hierarchical linear regression technique[2] that allowed them to test the relationship of blocks of predictor variables in the same statistical analysis. They used three blocks of predictor variables: background (e.g., gender), racial identity variables, and racial discrimination. They reported that experiencing more racial discrimination related to more self-reported negative behaviors at school (beta = .13, $SE = .01$, $p < .01$; F (14, 390) = 2.18, $p < .008$). The researchers also report that the model accounts for 13% of the variance in negative school behaviors. In English, this parenthetical expression would be read: Beta equals .13, standard error equals .01, and significance level of *p* is less than .01 for the racial discrimination variable alone. The *F* value is a test of the statistical significance of the full model of prediction of negative school behaviors. In English, this reads: *F* equals 2.18 with 14 and 390 degrees of freedom, and a significance level of *p* less than .008.

Beta is a standardized regression coefficient obtained by multiplying the regression coefficient by the ratio of the standard deviation of the explanatory variable to the standard deviation of the response variable. Thus, a standardized regression coefficient is one that would result if the explanatory and response variables had been converted to standard z scores prior to the regression analysis. This standardization is done to make the size of beta weights from regression analysis easier to compare for the various explanatory variables.

Researchers use the symbol R^2 to indicate the proportion of variation in the response variable (in this case negative school behaviors) explained by the explanatory variable (in this case experience with racial discrimination) in this multiple regression. F is the statistic used to determine the statistical significance of this result. That is, is the contribution of the explanatory variable to the prediction of the response variable statistically significant? And p is the level of statistical significance associated with F. (Statistical significance is explained in the next section.)

Degrees of freedom indicate the appropriate degrees of freedom for determining the significance of the reported F statistic. F distributions are a family of distributions with two parameters—the degrees of freedom in the numerator of the F statistic (based on the number of predictor variables or groups) and those associated with the denominator (based on the sample size). If you know the number of explanatory variables and the sample size, the computer program will calculate the appropriate degrees of freedom and will use the appropriate sampling distribution to determine the level of statistical significance.

Based on these results, Smalls et al. (2007) conclude that experiences of racial discrimination may increase students' disenfranchisement with school. They suggest a need to make issues of discrimination and oppression more visible so that students can potentially avoid being caught in a negative spiral. They hypothesize that if students are taught to recognize oppression and to understand it in terms of a shared history with other minority groups, then they may be able to develop effective strategies for resistance.

Statistical Significance

B. Thompson defines statistical significance testing in terms of the calculated probability *(p)* with possible values between .00 and 1.00 of the sample statistics, given the sample size, and assuming the sample was derived from a population in which the null hypothesis (H_0) is exactly true (2002a). The null hypothesis is the statement that the groups in the experiment do not differ from one another or that there is no statistically significant relationship between two or more variables. Several important concepts are included in that description: Statistical testing is probability based, sample size influences statistical significance, the sample should be representative of the population, and the probability that is calculated reflects the probability that the null hypothesis can be rejected. A test of statistical significance indicates if researchers can accept or reject the null hypothesis and the level of confidence they could have in their decision. When you read in a research report that the results were significant at the .05 level (usually depicted as $p < .05$), the researcher is telling you that there is a 5% chance that he or she rejected a null hypothesis that was true. In other words, there is a 5% chance that the researcher made a mistake and said there is a statistically significant difference (or relationship) when there really is not. This is called a Type I error. (The converse of this is a Type II error; that is, the researcher fails to reject a false hypothesis.) In the Smalls et al. (2007) study, the researchers rejected the null hypothesis that there is no relationship between experiences of discrimination and negative school outcomes. Their hierarchical linear regression results produced a statistical significance level of .008. Thus, the researchers rejected the null hypothesis that no statistically significant relationship existed between experiences of discrimination and self-reported negative school behaviors.

The concept of statistical significance is not unproblematic (B. Thompson, 2002b). The APA's Board of Scientific Affairs appointed a Task Force on Statistical Inference to make recommendations regarding a possible ban of the use of statistical significance testing. In 1999, the task force issued a recommendation against a ban; however, they did recommend a number of reforms of contemporary analytic practice (Wilkinson & APA Task Force on Statistical Inference, 1999). Issues associated with the decision to use a test of statistical significance are discussed in two subsequent sections of this chapter: Interpretation Issues in Quantitative Analysis and Options for Reporting Statistical Results.

Inferential Statistics

The definition of ANOVA in Box 13.2 is a bit oversimplified. If researchers have one independent variable with more than two levels (e.g., three approaches to reading instruction), then they would use ANOVA. However, if the researchers had more than one independent variable (e.g., two types of test administration and presence or absence of a learning disability), then they would need to conduct a factorial ANOVA. For example, Elbaum (2007) wanted to know if students would improve their performance on mathematics tests if someone read the test to them as compared to standard test administration. She also wanted to know if students with and without learning disabilities would differ in their performance with different administration conditions. Before Elbaum proceeded with the test of the main research question, she wanted to confirm that middle school and high school students did not differ from each other, so she conducted a t test that resulted in no statistically significant differences for either students with LD, $t\ (386) = -1.07$, $p = .28$, or students without disabilities, $t\ (235) = 0.44$, $p = .66$ (p. 224). Therefore, she progressed to testing the effects that were of primary interest. She had two independent variables: type of administration and disability status. Therefore, Elbaum's study is an example a 2x2 factorial design that was analyzed using a factorial ANOVA. The factorial ANOVA allows you to test for main effects (i.e., is there a significant effect for each of the independent variables?) and for interaction effects.

This design can be depicted as follows:

A

B

A x B

where

A means administration by read-aloud or standard administration procedures

B means a student has a learning disability or does not have one

A x B is the interaction of the two variables

Elbaum's (2007) results indicated that math scores were significantly higher by disability status ($F\ (1623) = 275.56$, $p < .001$), where students without a learning disability scored higher than those with a disability. There was also a statistically significant difference by the type of administration ($F(1623) = 86.21$, $p < .001$). The read-aloud administration resulted in higher scores than the standard administration condition.

Before drawing conclusions, it was important to also test if there were any interaction effects of the variables (i.e., did the independent variables vary systematically with each other?). In this study, the researcher also reported a significant interaction between disability and test condition (F (1623) = 13.87, p = < .001). The researcher concluded, "Overall, students without disabilities benefited more from the read-aloud accommodation than did students with LD" (Elbaum, 2007, p. 224). Interpretation of interaction effects is made far easier by graphing the disaggregated results, as can be seen in Figure 13.1.

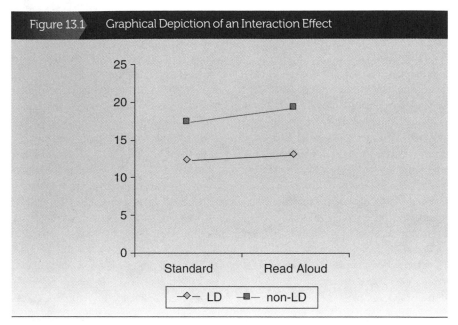

Figure 13.1 Graphical Depiction of an Interaction Effect

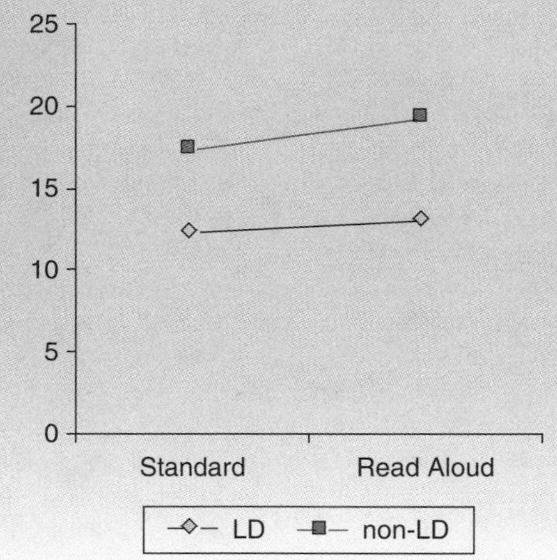

SOURCE: Elbaum (2007).

The graphical display makes it clear that the people in the read-aloud group uniformly scored higher on their math tests. However, students without disabilities not only started with higher scores, but they also improved their scores more than the students with learning disabilities did under the read-aloud condition.

Variations on ANOVA

ANCOVA. It is also possible to have another type of "independent" variable—one that is not of central interest for the researcher but that needs to be measured and accounted for in the analysis. This type of variable is called a *covariate*. It might be entry-level test scores or socioeconomic indicators for two different groups. In this case, the researcher would use an analysis of covariance (ANCOVA). In the Ehri et al. (2007) study, the researchers needed to use this statistical technique because they were interested in determining the statistical significance of group differences in reading, while controlling for entry-level reading ability. Therefore, they conducted an analysis of covariance (ANCOVA) that held the pretest scores constant for the three groups, and then tested for group differences. The results revealed an F value of 7.05, $p < .001$, indicating that a statistically significant difference was found in comparing the three groups. (To find out which groups had scores that were statistically different from each other, read the section below on post hoc analysis.)

MANOVA. If you have included more than one dependent measure in your design, you may need to use a multivariate analysis of variance (MANOVA). If you are getting into this level of complexity in your analysis, you definitely need to refer to a statistics book.

Post Hoc Analysis

Once you have completed an analysis, such as a three-way ANOVA or a MANOVA, you need to determine where the significant effects are. This can be done using multiple-comparison *t* tests or other post hoc procedures, such as Tukey's, Scheffe's, or Bonferroni post hoc tests. Such post hoc tests allow you to focus on which of several variables exhibit the main effect demonstrated by your initial analysis. Ehri et al. (2007) did a post hoc analysis (Bonferroni post hoc pairwise comparisons), which showed that tutored students significantly outperformed both the control groups (small group intervention and no intervention groups), who did not differ from each other.

Choice of Statistic

Before explaining in detail the decision strategy for choosing a statistical procedure, I wish to digress for a moment to describe one concept on which the basis for choosing a statistical procedure rests—the *scale of measurement*. As a researcher you need to ask, what is the scale of measurement for the data for both the independent and dependent variables?

Scale of Measurement

The four scales of measurement are defined and examples of each are provided in Table 13.1. The scale of measurement is important because it determines which type of statistical procedure is appropriate. As you will see later, this has an influence on deciding between parametric or nonparametric statistics as well as on the appropriate choice of correlation coefficient.

Table 13.1 Scales of Measurement

Scale of Measurement	*Definition*	*Example*
Nominal	Categorical data	Color: red, green, blue Label: male, female
Ordinal	Ranked data organized according to increasing or decreasing presence of a characteristic	Tallest to shortest Sweetest to sourest Heaviest to lightest
Interval	Equal intervals, but zero is arbitrary	Temperature
Ratio	Equal intervals, and zero is defined as meaning the absence of the characteristic	Weight, age, IQ, many personality and educational tests

The choice of a statistical procedure is outlined in Table 13.2. Your choice will depend on the following factors:

1. Your research question, which can be descriptive, concerns the extent of relationships between variables, determines significance of group differences, makes predictions of group membership, or examines the structure of variables
2. The type of groups that you have (i.e., independent, dependent, repeated measures, matched groups, randomized blocks, or mixed groups)
3. The number of independent and dependent variables you have
4. The scale of measurement
5. Your ability to satisfy the assumptions underlying the use of parametric statistics

Each type of research question leads you to a different statistical choice; thus, this is the most important starting point for your decisions.

Before jumping into complex statistical analysis, it is important to really understand what your data look like. Statisticians recommend that you always graph your data before you start conducting analyses. This will help you in several respects. First, you will be closer to your data and know them better in terms of what they are capable of telling you. Second, they will help you determine if you have met the appropriate assumptions required for different types of analyses. Third, you will be able to see if you have any "outliers"—that is, values for variables that are very different from the general group response on your measure.

Table 13.2 can be used as a flowchart to think logically through your statistical choices. For example, in the Smalls et al. (2007) study, the researchers first wanted to know to what extent the students in their study experienced racial discrimination. This portion of their study is descriptive; therefore, they could go to the first section in Table 13.2 to identify their statistical options. Their scale of measurement is assumed to be interval, so they determined that the mean was the appropriate measure of central tendency and the standard deviation was useful to describe variability in the data.

Smalls et al. (2007) had an additional research question: What was the relationship between their experiences of discrimination and students' reports of negative behaviors? Therefore, they could go to the second section in Table 13.2, because their research question was one of relationships. They have several blocks of predictor variables (background, e.g., gender, racial identity variables, and racial discrimination), with interval data, so they chose to conduct hierarchical linear regression analysis.

Assumptions for Parametric Statistics

As mentioned in Table 13.2, it is important for you to be aware of the assumptions that underlie the use of parametric statistics. These include (a) normal distribution of the characteristic of interest in the population, (b) randomization for sample selection or group assignment (experimental vs. control), and (c) an interval or ratio level of measurement. The assumption that the population is normal rules out outliers in your data, so the presence of outliers shows that this assumption is not valid. Also, if the distribution of the characteristic in the population is skewed (i.e., bunched up at one end of the continuum or the other), the assumption of normality is not met. In the case of skewed distribution, it may be possible to transform the data to approximate a normal distribution using a logarithmic transformation (Gay et al., 2009). If the assumptions cannot be met, you need to consider alternative data analysis strategies. That is where the choice of nonparametric statistics becomes attractive (sometimes called distribution-free inference procedures).[3]

Table 13.2 Choice of a Statistical Procedure

Research question: Descriptive	
For interval or ratio data:	Mean, median, or mode, and variance
For ordinal data:	Median
For nominal data:	Mode
Research question: Relationship	
For two variables	
For interval or ratio data:	Pearson product-moment coefficient of correlation
For ordinal data:	Spearman rank order coefficient of correlation or Kendall rank correlation
For interval and nominal or ordinal data:	Point biserial
For interval and artificial dichotomy on an ordinal scale (dichotomy is artificial because there is an underlying continuous distribution):	Biserial
For nominal data:	Contingency coefficient
For more than two variables	
For interval or ratio data:	Multiple regression analysis
For ordinal data:[a]	Kendall partial rank correlation
For nominal data:	Discriminant analysis
Research question: Group differences	
For two variables	
For related samples	
For interval or ratio data:	*t* test for correlated samples[b]
For ordinal data:	Wilcoxon matched-pairs signed-ranks test
For nominal data:	McNemar test for the significance of changes
For independent samples	
For interval or ratio data:	*t* test for independent samples
For ordinal data:	Mann-Whitney U test or Kolmogorov-Smirnov two-sample test
For nominal data:	Chi-square test
For more than two variables	
For related samples	
For interval or ratio data:	Repeated measures ANOVA
For ordinal data:	Friedman two-way analysis of variance
For nominal data:	Cochran Q test
For independent samples	
For interval or ratio data:	ANOVA
For ordinal data:	Kruskal-Wallis one-way ANOVA
For nominal data:	Chi-square test for *k* independent samples
Research question: Prediction of group membership	
For all data:	Discriminant function[c]
Research question: Structure of variables	
For interval or ratio data:	Factor analysis

a. Ordinal and nominal data can be used in multiple regression equations through a process called "dummying-up" a variable. Refer to one of the statistical texts cited at the beginning of this chapter for more details on this procedure.

b. All *t* tests and variations on ANOVA require that the data satisfy the assumptions for parametric statistical procedures.

c. Discriminant functions can be one-way, hierarchical, or factorial depending on the number of independent and dependent variables.

Interpretation Issues in Quantitative Analysis

A number of challenges are presented for quantitative researchers for the interpretation of the results of their data analysis:

1. The influence of (or lack of) randomization on statistical choices and interpretation of results
2. The analytic implications of using intact groups
3. The influence of sample size on achieving statistical significance
4. Statistical versus practical significance
5. Issues related to cultural bias
6. Variables related to generalizability

Following a discussion of these challenges, I present options for responding to some of them, such as reporting effect sizes and amount of variance accounted for, the use of confidence intervals, replication, use of nonparametric statistics, exploration of competing explanations, recognition of a study's limitations, and principled discovery strategies (Mark, 2009).

Randomization

Early statisticians (e.g., R. A. Fisher [1890–1962] and William Sealy Gosset [1876–1937], inventor of the statistical test called "Student's t") based their work on the assumption that randomization is a necessary condition for the use of typical tests of parametric statistics. Randomness can be achieved by either random sampling or random assignment to conditions. Random sampling has to do with how the participants were chosen from the population (see Chapter 11). Random assignment has to do with how participants were assigned to levels of the independent variable so that variability between groups is statistically evened out (see Chapter 4). Random sampling is a very difficult condition to meet in most educational and psychological research, and random assignment is not always possible.

You might recall the difficult time that Borman et al. (2007) had recruiting schools to be in their study, thus making it impossible to select schools or students at random. They were able to assign schools that volunteered to either the experimental or control conditions, but not assign individual students. A second example, from the Ehri et al. (2007) study, illustrates similar challenges. The researchers started with five schools in a district. They could not randomly select the students, as they wanted to select students based on test scores and to match students based on demographic characteristics. They then wanted to assign matched pairs of students randomly to the experimental and control groups. In four of the five schools, the administrators assigned one group of the intended participants to a third group that received a small group intervention. The researchers were able to randomly assign the remaining students to one of the three groups. In the Elbaum (2007) study of test administration procedures, she was not able to randomly select the students from the population, but she was able to randomly assign the treatment conditions by classrooms (not by individual student).

In many situations, it is not possible for ethical or practical reasons to assign people randomly, and it may not be possible to randomly select individuals from a larger population. Much research in education and psychology is done with available populations, and therefore the use of parametric statistics is questionable. If intact classes are used, the class becomes the unit of analysis, thus necessitating either having a large number of classes involved in the research to conduct meaningful statistical analysis or the use of more sophisticated statistical strategies (Schochet, 2008). In studies with intact classes or groups, researchers can choose to use a regression analysis rather than ANOVA. In regression analysis, there is no need to create small groups based on collapsing scores on variables. Thus, this approach can provide a more desirable option because it would not require expanding the sample size.

Sample Size

Sample size is a basic influence on statistical significance (Hubbard & Lindsay, 2008). Virtually any study can have statistically significant results if a large enough sample size is used. For example, with a standard deviation of 10 and a sample size of 20, a difference of 9.4 between two independent means is necessary for statistical significance at the .05 level in a nondirectional test. However, if the sample size is 100, a difference of only 4.0 is required, and with a sample size of 1,000, a difference of only 1.2 is required (Shaver, 1992). An overly large sample size can result in obtaining statistical significance, even though the results may have little practical significance (see the next paragraph for further elaboration of this idea). When researchers are working with low-incidence populations, as commonly happens in special education research, the small sample size itself might prevent the researcher from obtaining statistical significance. Small sample sizes also have implications for the researcher's ability to disaggregate results by characteristics, such as gender, race or ethnicity, or type of disability. In such cases, the researcher needs to plan a sample of sufficient size to make the disaggregation meaningful. With power analysis (discussed in Chapter 11), a researcher can determine the size of sample needed in order to obtain a statistically significant result.

Statistical Versus Practical Significance

The influence of the size of the sample on the ease or difficulty of finding statistical significance brings up the issue of statistical versus practical significance (B. Thompson, 2002a). Simply because it is easier to obtain statistical significance with larger samples, researchers need to be sensitive to the practical significance of their results. For example, statistical significance may be obtained in a study that compares two drug abuse treatment interventions. In examining the size of the difference, the data may indicate that there is only two days longer abstinence for the experimental group. Thus, the researcher needs to be aware of the practical significance of the results, particularly if there are big differences in the costs of the two programs. Is it worth changing to a much more expensive program to keep someone off drugs for two additional days?

Ziliak and McCloskey (2007) use a simple comparison to illustrate the difference between statistical and practical significance:

> Crossing frantically a busy street to save your child from certain death is a good gamble. Crossing frantically to get another mustard packet for your hot dog is not. The size of the potential loss if you don't hurry to save your child is larger, most will agree, than the potential loss if you don't get the mustard. [Researchers] look only for a probability of success in the crossing—the existence of a probability of success better than .99 or .95 or .90, and this within the restricted frame of sampling—ignoring in any spiritual or financial currency the value of the prize and the expected cost of pursuing it. In the life and human sciences a majority of scientists look at the world with what we have dubbed "the sizeless stare of statistical significance." (p. vii)

Cultural Bias

As discussed in Chapter 11 on sampling, use of a label to indicate race when investigating the effects of various social programs can do an injustice in terms of who is included in the study as well as how the results are interpreted and used. Ladson-Billings (2006) and Bledsoe (2008) address the injustices when stereotypic beliefs based on skin color or other phenotypic characteristics serve as a basis for cultural bias in the research process, including the analysis, interpretation, and use of data. Rather than relying on an overly simplistic category such as race for an explanatory variable to categorize people uncritically and assume homogeneity in their conditions, they argue that researchers need to address the complexity of participants' experiences and social locations. Random selection and assignment cannot make up for cultural bias. Bledsoe (2008) cites an example of this lack of cultural sensitivity in her research on social programs designed to provide prenatal care and prevent and treat obesity in African American communities. She discovered that the program providers made assumptions about the reasons African Americans did not get prenatal services or participate in obesity treatment and prevention programs that were in conflict with the pervasive beliefs of members of the community or that were unrealistic given the conditions in their surrounding environments.

However, researchers who critically examine race as a distinct cultural pattern realize that interpretations must be tied to the socioeconomic and environmental context. Thus policy and program decisions based on this perspective can be more responsive to the social and cultural settings of programs. This brings us full circle from the perspectives discussed in Chapter 1. If the researcher starts from a deficit view of the minority population, the interpretation of the data will focus on the dysfunctions found within that community. If the researcher starts with a transformative perspective, the researcher will attempt to identify the broader cultural context within which the population functions. For example, African Americans are at greater risk than other populations for living in poverty. These circumstances are important because of the relationship between poverty and oppressive social experiences. Rather than focusing on the "deficit" of being raised in a single-parent household, researchers need to understand the notion of extended family and its particular importance for African American children. They also need to understand the contextual information about the experiences and characteristics of racial communities concerning the environments in which children live that make them less likely to be in a position to be in a position of privilege with regard to access to social and educational opportunities.

Generalizability

As mentioned in previous chapters, external validity is defined in terms of the generalizability of the results of one particular research study to a broader population. Randomized sampling strategies are supposed to ensure that the results can be generalized back to the population from which the sample was drawn. Randomized sampling is not always possible, and therefore researchers need to be careful in the generalizations they make based on their results. When working with racial and ethnic minority groups or people with disabilities, generalizations about group differences are often put forward without much attention to within-group variation and the influence of particular contexts. Bledsoe (2008) describes this problem within the African American community in that many social prevention programs have been conceived from dominant middle-class perspectives, and many of these programs have been implemented in African American communities.

Although researchers sometimes acknowledge that culturally specific approaches are needed, there have been few serious efforts to design and evaluate programs based on culturally diverse perspectives. A notable exception is the work of Hood et al. (2005) in culturally responsive evaluations. When researchers use inappropriate measurement strategies with minority groups, they can erroneously reach conclusions that the programs are or are not effective. The people who are hurt by such inappropriate conclusions are those who have the least power. The following comments by J. E. Davis (1992) summarize the problems with reliance on statistical outcomes without proper sensitivity to contextual variables:

> Data-analytical techniques should not completely replace informed program analysis based on knowledge obtained in the context of program participants' lives and experience. An enormous amount of information about the location and contexts of programs is missing from the discussion of programs' causal claims. Often, knowledge of a program's clientele and the program's appropriateness for its environment is needed to advance thinking about the program's causal assertions. Unfortunately for African Americans and other U.S. racial minorities, this information is, at best, partially known but discarded or, at worst, not known or even cared about. This is not to say that experimental and quasi-experimental studies are not useful for program evaluation; to the contrary. These methods are very powerful in revealing program effects, but results must be examined more carefully, and with sensitivity to diverse populations.
>
> A comparative analytical approach works from the assumption that because African Americans are homogeneous in their condition and experience, programs are homogeneous in their effects. There is relatively little information about the many sources of variation within the Black population. African Americans are the largest racial minority in this country, but much within-group variation and in-depth understanding will be completely lost with traditional race-comparative analysis in program evaluation. (p. 63)

Options for Reporting Statistical Results

The APA task force recommendations concerning reform in the use of tests of statistical significance included reporting effect sizes, confidence intervals, and using graphics (B. Thompson, 2002b; Wilkinson & APA Task Force on Statistical Inference, 1999). These were not entirely new recommendations, as researchers have offered a number of options in the past for reporting statistical results of quantitative research that include effect sizes, percentage of variance accounted for, and examining within- and between-group differences.

Effect Size. For studies that have experimental and control groups, Schochet (2008, p. 64) provides the following explanation of effect size: Effect size is calculated as a percentage of the standard deviation of the outcome measures (also known as Cohen's *d*), to facilitate the comparison of findings across outcomes that are measured on different scales (J. Cohen, 1988). An effect size is a way of representing the size of a treatment's effect in standardized units that then allows for comparisons across studies that might use different outcome measures. An effect size can be calculated to capture the difference between the means for experimental and control groups, calculating the distance between the two group means in terms of their common standard deviation (H. M. Cooper, 1989). Thus an effect size of 0.5 means that the two means are separated by one half of a standard deviation. This is a way of describing how well the average student or client who received the treatment performed relative to the average student or client who did not receive the treatment. For example, if an experimental group of persons with behavioral problems received a drug treatment and the control group received a placebo, an effect size of 0.8 would indicate that the experimental group's mean was 0.8 standard deviation above the control group.

An increasing number of journals in education and psychology are now requiring that researchers include effect size in their submissions. In relation to effect size reporting, Wilkinson and the APA Task Force on Statistical Inference (1999, p. 599) wrote, "Always provide some effect-size estimate when reporting a *p* value" and emphasized that "reporting and interpreting effect sizes in the context of previously reported effects is essential to good research." Later in this chapter, I describe how to use effect sizes for meta-analysis—that is, a statistical synthesis of previously conducted research.

B. Thompson (2002a) warns against a blind interpretation of effect size based on magnitude and suggests that the judgment of significance rests with the researcher's, user's, and reviewer's personal value systems; the research questions posed; societal concerns; and the design of a particular study. For more detailed information on effect size, the reader is referred to Hubbard and Lindsay (2008) and Grissom and Kim (2005).

Confidence Intervals. Confidence intervals are used to indicate the degree of confidence that the data reflect the population mean or some other population parameter (B. Thompson, 2002b). Confidence intervals are frequently seen in mainstream media in prediction of election outcomes in the form of a percentage of people who agree or disagree on a candidate, plus or minus a certain percentage to indicate the range of values and the level of confidence that the range includes the population parameter. Because of sampling error, researchers expect the mean to vary somewhat from sample to sample. Most commonly used statistical software packages will compute confidence intervals. APA's manual states, "Because confidence intervals combine information on location and precision and can often be directly used to infer significance levels, they are, in general, the best reporting strategy. The use of confidence intervals is therefore strongly recommended" (APA, 2001, p. 22).

Correlational Research and Variance Accounted For. Lewin and Wild (1991) contrast two ways that researchers could report information about the amount of variance accounted for in a correlational study:

> If we read that a sample of men score "significantly higher at the .01 level" than do women on some scale or test, the implication is quite different from that of a report that reads, "Sex differences, although significant at the .01 level, account for only 3% of the variance on this scale. A combined index of the level of training on three skills: X, Y, and Z, plus months of experience in two settings: P and Q, jointly accounts for 73% of the variance in scale scores." (p. 584)

They note that both of these statements could well be accurate descriptions of exactly the same research study. However, the conclusions that would be drawn from each statement might differ markedly. The first statement suggests that women do not do as well as men. The second description indicates that training and experience are very important, whereas the impact of gender is trivial.

J. E. Davis (1992) suggests that reporting differences between identified racial groups is overemphasized and suggested that more attention be given to important variations within racial groups. For example, differences between urban and rural African American families could account for much of what appears to be cross-race difference. He also recommended having members of racial and ethnic groups review the research results before they are disseminated to help detect bias and inaccuracies.

Replication

When the data do not meet the assumptions necessary for reaching conclusions about statistical significance, Carver (1992) recommends that researchers replicate the study's results as the best replacement for information about statistical significance. Building replication into research helps eliminate chance or sampling error as a threat to the internal validity of the results. This also emphasizes the importance of the literature review, discussed in Chapter 3, as a means of providing support for the generalizability of the results. However, Mark (2009, p. 210) notes that replication is not always or even often a viable option:

> The false confession problem also would be solved if the experimenter could snoop in the data from one study and then, if an important finding emerges (e.g., a program benefits one subgroup and harms another), see if the pattern replicates in another study. Unfortunately, options for replication are limited in many areas of applied social research. For example, some program evaluations take years and cost millions of dollars; so replication is an infeasible strategy relative to the timeline for decision making.

Use of Nonparametric Statistics

Nonparametric statistics provide an alternative for researchers when their data do not meet the basic assumptions of normality and randomization, they have small samples, or they use data of an ordinal or nominal nature.

Competing Explanations

No matter what design, paradigm, or type of data collected, researchers always need to consider competing explanations. (In the postpositivist paradigm, these are called threats to internal and external validity.) Such competing explanations become critical when it is time to interpret the results. Recall from Chapter 4 that Borman et al. (2007) discussed numerous possible competing explanations, such as the overall willingness of a school's leaders and teachers to accept a systemwide change in their approach to reading instruction.

In Elbaum's (2007) study of test administration conditions with students with and without learning disabilities, she explored a number of competing explanations for why students without learning disability benefited more from the read-aloud condition than did the students with learning disabilities. She hypothesized that the read-aloud strategy did not address a specific disability-related characteristic of students with learning disabilities. (There is no "magic bullet" called read-aloud test administration that will bring about equal performance on math tests for these two groups of students.) She explored the possibility that reading aloud benefits both types of students because of several factors: Students who are poor readers will benefit with this approach even if they are not identified with a learning disability. Many of the students in their nondisabled group were poor readers: "95% of students with LD were failing the high-stakes high school reading assessment, so were two-thirds of the students without an identified disability. These students, although not formally identified as having a reading disability, would clearly be defined as poor or very poor readers by the state's yardstick" (Elbaum, 2007, p. 225). She offered another competing explanation for the reason that nondisabled students benefited more from the read-aloud condition: "This finding would lend further support to the idea that providing access to test items by removing reading ability as a barrier will differentially improve the performance of students who have a higher level of skill in the content area being tested" (p. 227). And finally, she hypothesized that the read-aloud condition might make it possible for students to stay on task better than standard administrations do.

Recognizing Limitations

As should be clear by now, it is not possible to design and conduct the "perfect" research study in education or psychology. Therefore, it is incumbent on the researcher to recognize and discuss the limitations of a study. For example, Elbaum (2007) recognized the limitations of her study because the read-aloud condition could be confounded by the pacing of the reading or the staying on task dimension. Also, she did not have individual reading scores for the students that she could use to test their hypotheses about the effect of reading ability on math performance. An important limitation that she did not discuss is that a read-aloud strategy does not address a specific disability-related characteristic of students with learning disabilities. What does the read-aloud strategy address? What strategies of teaching, learning, and assessment would address the specific disability-related characteristics of the students?

Principled Discovery

Mark and Gamble (2009) propose that a strategy called principled discovery offers promise for addressing many of the challenges associated with statistical significance testing. "In short, the idea is to complement traditional analyses of experimental and quasi-experimental research with iterative analysis procedures, involving both data and conceptual analysis. The goal is to discover complexities, such as unpredicted differential effects across subgroups, while not being misled by chance" (p. 210). Remember that statistics are probability-based and that conducting multiple analyses with the same data set increases the chance of finding something significant. "Principled discovery has been offered as a way to try to discover more from the data while not being misled by false confessions" (p. 210). Mark and Gamble suggest that principled discovery begins with testing a prior hypothesis, such as the new treatment will result in improved performance as compared to the old treatment.

> The principled discovery that follows involves two primary stages (which may further iterate).
>
> In the first stage, the researcher carries out exploratory analyses. For example, an experimental program evaluator might examine whether the program has differential effects by looking for interaction effects using one after another of the variables on which participants have been measured (e.g., gender, race, age, family composition). A wide variety of statistical techniques can be used for the exploratory analyses of this first stage of principled discovery (Mark, 2003; Mark et al., 1998).
>
> If the Stage 1, exploratory analyses result in an interesting (and unpredicted) finding (and if replication in another study is infeasible), then in the second stage of principled discovery the researcher would seek one or another form of independent (or quasi-independent) confirmation of the discovery. In many

> instances, this will involve other tests that can be carried out within the same data set (although data might be drawn from other data sets, or new data might be collected after Stage 1). For example, if a gender effect is discovered in an educational intervention, this might lead to a more specific prediction that boys and girls will differ more after transition to middle school than before. As this example illustrates, Stage 2 of principled discovery includes conceptual analysis as well as data analysis. That is, the second stage of principled discovery will generally require an interpretation of the finding from the Stage 1 exploration. (Mark & Gamble, 2009, pp. 210–211)

Mark and Gamble (2009) explain that this two-stage process protects against tortured data confessing falsely because if the effect observed in Stage 1 is purely due to chance, then there is no expectation that it will occur again in Stage 2.

> For example, if a gender effect from Stage 1 had arisen solely due to chance, it would be unlikely that the size of the gender difference would be affected by the transition to middle school. Principled discovery has considerable potential for enhancing emergent discovery in quasi-experimental (and experimental) research, while reducing the likelihood of being misled by chance findings. Despite its potential benefits, important practical limits will often apply to principled discovery. These include the possibility that in some studies data elements will not be available for the second stage of principled discovery, as well as the likelihood that statistical power may be inadequate for some contrasts (Mark, 2009). Despite such limits, principled discovery appears to be an approach that can help address some of the practical and ethical objections to randomized and quasi-experimental studies of the effects of interventions in a complex world. (Mark & Gamble, 2009, p. 211)

Extending Your Thinking: Statistical Analysis

1. How can sample size influence statistical significance? Why is this particularly important in special education research?

2. Why is randomization an important consideration in the choice of a statistical test? Why is this particularly important for research that uses small, heterogeneous, or culturally diverse samples?

3. What can a researcher do when the basic assumptions for parametric inferential statistics are not met?

Special Application: Statistical Synthesis as Literature Review

Statistical syntheses are appropriate for experimental, quasi-experimental, causal comparative, and correlational research. However, even within these types, constraints apply. A statistical summary is not appropriate as a way of explaining the historical course of events; a narrative approach is needed for that purpose. Meta-analyses cannot in and of themselves take into account the heterogeneity of studies in terms of samples, diversity, and quality of methods, as such aggregation can obscure important differences.

Meta-Analysis

Meta-analysis is one statistical approach to research synthesis that uses additional analyses to aggregate the findings of studies and reach conclusions about the overall effect of an independent variable. Meta-analysis is a quantitative synthesis of the existing research that uses effect sizes as a way to standardize outcomes and facilitate comparisons across studies. Using primary source information from the literature, the meta-analyst establishes empirical evidence to increase understandings about a particular theory. In meta-analysis, the researcher addresses studies that have attempted to establish a causal relationship between some intervention and an outcome based on a review of available literature.

Wang et al. (2008) conducted a meta-analysis to determine the effect of using computer-based testing (CBT) as compared to paper-and-pencil testing (PPT) in reading. They described their literature search process in detail and explained their inclusion and exclusion rules (see Chapter 3 for more about these topics). Each study had to meet the following inclusion criteria:

- The study had to be conducted between 1980 and 2005.
- The samples of study had to be drawn from the K–12 student population, and the within-group sample size had to be larger than 25.
- The study should have quantitative outcome measures (mean and standard deviation) of one of student achievement, aptitude, or ability of reading on both CBT and PPT.
- The study should have the design to compare the scores from both CBT and PPT.
- The test language in the study must be English because the major target population (U.S. K–12 students) in this report uses English. (p. 11)

Wang et al. (2008) calculated the effect size for each study in their sample. For studies that use means to compare an experimental and control group, the effect size is defined as the distance between the two group means in terms of their common standard deviation (H. M. Cooper, 1989).[4] It is calculated as follows:

$$d = \frac{M_1 - M_2}{s}$$

where

M_1 = the mean or average for one group (e.g., experimental group)

M_2 = the mean or average for the other group (e.g., control group)

s = the within-group standard deviation (measure of variability within groups)

d = the effect size or the difference between the two means

Thus, an effect size of 0.5 means that the two means are separated by half a standard deviation. This is a way of describing how well the average student who received the treatment performed relative to the average student who did not receive the treatment. For example, if an experimental group of students with behavioral problems received a drug treatment and the control group received a placebo, an effect size of 0.8 would indicate that the experimental group's mean was 0.8 standard deviation above the control group.

Once the effect size for each study has been computed, an average effect size is calculated by combining the *d* for each study. For example, Wang et al.'s (2008) meta-analysis of computer-based testing compared to paper-and-pencil testing resulted in an effect size of −.004 with a 95% confidence interval of [−.031, .023], which is not statistically significant at the alpha level of .01 ($p = .782$). Thus, the researchers concluded that examinees' performance on paper-and-pencil tests was not significantly better than their performance on computer-based tests.

Interpretation of effect sizes is not clear-cut. J. Cohen (1988) proposes the following (somewhat arbitrary) guideline:

0.20 is small

0.50 is medium

0.80 is large

B. Thompson (2002b) argues that researchers should not use these benchmarks as rigid judgments about the significance of an effect size. Rather, he recommends that researchers present their effect sizes within the context of other studies to illustrate how replicable or stable the effect sizes are in a given area of inquiry. "The overly rigid use of fixed benchmarks for small, medium, and large effects fails to consider the possibility that small, replicable effects involving important outcomes can be noteworthy, or that large effects involving trivial outcomes may not be particularly noteworthy" (p. 30).

There are many pros and cons for deciding to use meta-analysis. It does offer a systematic and objective method of aggregating the results of a large number of studies on a specific topic. On the other hand, this approach suffers from the same threats faced in other research efforts—the exhaustive nature of the retrieval process and the diversity of research quality in the studies selected.

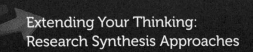

Extending Your Thinking: Research Synthesis Approaches

What are the advantages and disadvantages of selecting either a narrative or statistical option for synthesizing research results? Discuss in terms of (a) quality of research studies used to reach conclusions, (b) the size of differences between groups, and (c) the limitations of meta-analysis. (Is the concept of a meta-analysis clear to you?)

Qualitative Analytic Strategies

As mentioned before, but repeated here for emphasis, data analysis in qualitative studies is an ongoing process. It does not occur only at the end of the study as is typical in most quantitative studies. The fact that the topic is explored in depth here is simply an artifact of the way the human brain works. It is not possible to learn about everything all at once. So realize that analysis in qualitative studies designed within the ethnographic or phenomenological traditions is *recursive;* findings are generated and systematically built as successive pieces of data are gathered (Bogdan & Biklen, 2003; M. Q. Patton, 2002; Wolcott, 2001).

Qualitative data analysis has sometimes been portrayed as a somewhat mysterious process in which the findings gradually "emerge" from the data through some type of mystical relationship between the researcher and the sources of data. Anyone who has conducted in-depth qualitative analysis will testify that a considerable amount of work occurs during the data collection and analysis phases of a qualitative study.

Several analytic strategies can be used in qualitative data analysis, including grounded theory, narrative, and discourse analysis. In addition, Miles and Huberman (1994) prepared a sourcebook that can be used to guide the novice researcher through the process of qualitative data analysis that involves data reduction through the use of various kinds of matrices. Researchers can also choose to analyze data the old-fashioned way (cut and paste pieces of paper) or using one of the many computer-based analysis programs that have grown in popularity over the years. More details about these options are presented later in this chapter.

Steps in Qualitative Data Analysis

Hesse-Biber and Leavy (2006) provide a step-by-step description of data analysis strategies for qualitative data, despite their acknowledgement that undertaking such a task sets up an oxymoronic condition in that qualitative data analysis in essence defies a step-by-step approach. Yet, as mere mortals, we are faced with the task of starting somewhere; thus, we begin by taking a look at our data as it is collected.

Step 1. Preparing the data for analysis.

This step assumes that the researcher has been reviewing and reflecting on the data as it is collected. How this is done depends to some degree on the type of data collected and the method of collecting and recording the data. For example, if the researcher used video or audio taping, then questions arise about the transcription of the data: Should all the data be transcribed? If not, how are decisions made about which parts should be transcribed and which should not? How will the researcher handle nonverbal behaviors or elements of the interviews such as laughter or pauses, emotions, gestures? Should the researchers themselves do the transcription? Hesse-Biber and Leavy argue that the process of transcription should be undertaken by the researcher because this is part of the data analysis process engendered by interacting with the data in an intensive and intimate way. As the questions raised in this paragraph illustrate, transcription is not a transparent process. Researchers bring their own point of view to the process, including noting multiple meanings that lie in what might appear to be simple utterances. They write,

> Transcribing research data is interactive and engages the reader in the process of deep listening, analysis, and interpretation. Transcription is not a passive act, but instead provides the researcher with a valuable opportunity to actively engage with his or her research material right from the beginning of data collection. It also ensures that early on, the researcher is aware of his or her own impact on the data gathering process and he or she has an opportunity to connect with this data in a grounded manner that provides for the possibility of enhancing the trustworthiness and validity of his or her data gathering techniques. (p. 347)

While this higher level of thinking is happening, researchers should also take care of practical considerations, such as being sure their notes and files of data are well labeled and organized to facilitate data analysis processes and accurate reporting of the results.

Steps 2 and 3. Data exploration phase and data reduction phase.

These two phases are synergistic: As you explore your data, you will be thinking of ways to reduce it to a manageable size that can be used for reporting. Exploring means reading and thinking and making notes about your thoughts (called "memoing" by the qualitative research community). Memos can take the form of questions about meanings, graphic depictions of how you think data relate to each other, or important quotes that you want to be sure you don't lose track of during the analysis process. The data reduction occurs as you select parts of the data for coding, that is, assigning a label to excerpts of data that conceptually "hang together." Box 13.3 contains an example of codes used in a study, along with an excerpt from the codebook. The first few lines of this example provide the information about the source of the data. The comments on the side are the codes used to identify portions of text that exemplify relevant concepts.

Box 13.3 Codes and Codebook Excerpts

Field Notes by Donna Mertens, evaluator Project Success Teachers Reflective Seminar May 11, 2007, 9AM–noon

Facilitator (F) introduced the evaluation team and their purpose.

F: Divide into pairs and discuss your life experiences. Then we'll come back together and each of you will describe one "WOW" experience and one challenging experience.

Observation: the 2 current students did not interact; F talked with one teacher. Four African Americans teachers; 6 white female teachers; 1 white female grad students.

WOW and challenges:

T5: My students are under 5 years old and they come with zero language and their behavior is awful. They can't sit for even a minute. Kids come with temper tantrums and running out of the school building. I have to teach these kids language; I see them start to learn to behave and interact with others. My biggest challenge is seeing three kids run out of school at the same time. Which one do I run after? One kid got into the storm drain. I'm only one teacher and I have an assistant, but that means there is still one kid we can't chase after at the same time as the other two. DivBhvr

T7: I had my kids write a letter to their teachers to express their appreciation. That was a WOW experience. WOW Challenge—I don't like to be negative. My real challenge is that I feel kind of isolated because of being in a separate building—other teachers don't even know who I am. Iso

T6: I had a student from a Spanish speaking country. He struggled to pick up ASL. Once he starting picking it up, he was very quick. I noticed this student is now asking for more challenge; he participated in his IEP meetings. Now he is going to general education classes; I can't remember any kids from special ed going to general ed before. ESL, ASL, DivComm

Challenge: I feel teachers in the mainstream resist our students, especially students with multiple disabilities.

T8: I teach students who are mainstreamed for 2 or 3 classes; the school sees my students as being very low, but my students want to know things. Low

(Continued)

Box 13.3 (Continued)

T3: My WOW and challenge are really the same thing. When I graduated, I thought I was ready to teach. Then the principal gave me my list of students and my classroom and just washed his hands of me. You're on your own. The principal did not require me to submit weekly plans like other teachers because he thought I'd only be teaching sign language. But I told him, I'm here to really teach. We (my students and I) were not invited to field day or assemblies. That first year really hit me—what a challenge and a WOW at the same time. So I changed schools and this one is definitely better. Now I'm in a school where people believe that deaf students can learn.

Low, ChgScSys, NoSup

T4: I have 6 students in my classroom. There are no other teachers there to help me. My class has kids who use 3 different methods of communication: sign, oral, and cued speech. I tried to explain in sign, but the other kids don't understand. I was always saying: what should I do? I have a co-teacher in the afternoon, but she doesn't really support me. So I told her I needed her to really help me. So she works with one kid who got a cochlear implant. He can say his name now, but nothing else.

DivComm

Codebook Excerpts:

ASL—American Sign Language

ESL—English as a Second Language

ChgScSys—Changed school systems

DivBhvr—Diverse Behavior—Teachers' experience challenges because of diverse student behavior. Includes behavioral issues.

DivComm—Diverse communication modes—combination of communication modes in classroom—sign, oral, CI, cued speech.

Iso—Teacher feels isolated.

Low—Low expectations for students.

NoSup—No support system.

WOW—Something wonderful that happened to the teachers.

SOURCE: Mertens, Holmes, Harris, & Brandt (2007).

Charmaz (2007) provides a detailed description of coding strategies that she developed within the grounded theory method of data analysis that involves two phases: initial coding and focused coding. (Grounded theory is not the only analytic strategy for qualitative data; however it does reflect many of the characteristics of qualitative data analysis that are common across other approaches. Corbin and Strauss (2008) use the terms open coding and axial coding instead of Charmaz's initial and focused coding. See Box 13.4 for brief descriptions of two other data analysis approaches: narrative and discourse analysis.) In the initial coding phase, the researcher codes individual words, lines, segments, and incidents. The focused coding phase involves testing the initial codes against the more extensive body of data to determine how resilient the codes are in the bigger picture that emerges from the analysis. The development of codes can be used to form the analytic framework needed for theory construction.

Box 13.4 Narrative and Discourse Analysis Approaches

Narrative Analysis

Narrative analysis focuses on the stories, whether they are told verbally or in text or performance formats (Bingley, Thomas, Brown, Reeve, & Payne, 2008; Leavy, 2009). The researcher tries to identify the content, structure, and form of life stories based on the available data. This might take the form of a biography or autobiography, a timeline of important life events, or an exploration of the meaning of life events within a broader sociocultural context. Narratives can be analyzed as separate voices to reveal diversity of perspectives of an issue. As a researcher approaches narrative analysis, it is important to consider whose story will be told and how the person's story will be represented. Arts-based researchers (Leavy, 2009) have contributed to the analytic processes in narrative analysis and extended this to include analysis of such genres as poetry, music, dance, and the visual arts.

Gubrium and Holstein (2009) note that a distinct characteristic of narrative analysis is that it draws on literary devices such as "topics, plots, themes, beginnings, middles, ends, and other border features that are assumed to be the defining characteristics of stories" (p. 226). The stories are of importance; the way the stories are told are of importance, as are the wider societal context and past and future events. They write, "To capture the richness of narrative reality, analysis needs to focus on both the circumstantial variety and the agentic flexibility of stories, not just on the structure of the accounts themselves" (p. 228).

Discourse Analysis

Discourse analysis focuses on understanding the meaning of participants' language. Huygens (2002) offers such questions as the following to guide discourse analysis: "What are the participants actually saying?" and "Why did they choose to say it this way?" The researcher is trying to read between the lines to determine deeper meanings to such qualities of language as colloquialisms, images, rules of turn taking. The researcher is interested in "how the story is told, what identities, activities, relationships, and shared meanings are created through language" (Starks & Trinidad, 2007, p. 1383). The basic analytic process involves examining three dimensions (Fairclough, 2003):

- analysis of the text, which involves the study of language structures such as use of verbs; use of statement, questions, or declarations; and the thematic structure,
- the analysis of discursive practice, which involves how people produce, interpret, disseminate, and consume text, and
- the analysis of sociocultural practice, which involves issues of power in the discourse context and its implications in wider society.

R. Rogers, Malancharuvil, Mosley, Hui, and Joseph (2005) provide a review of critical discourse analysis in educational research based on the major databases and journals in the field. They provide numerous examples of the application of critical discourse analysis in research in education and psychology.

Charmaz (2006) gives this advice for the initial coding phase:

- Remain open
- Stay close to the data
- Keep your codes simple and precise
- Construct short codes
- Preserve actions
- Compare data with data
- Move quickly through the data (p. 49)

From my experience, I would add, involve team and community members in the coding when appropriate; discuss differences in interpretation and use of the codes (Mertens, 2009). Allow the codes to emerge and be revised as necessary, especially in the early stages of coding. Explore differences in interpretations; this can be an opportunity for surprising discoveries. Make a codebook that includes brief descriptions of each code. Having such a codebook facilitates the employment of a constant comparative method of analysis. Corbin and Strauss (2008) provide this definition of constant comparative analysis:

> Comparing incident against incident for similarities and differences. Incidents that are found to be conceptually similar to previously coded incidents are given the same conceptual label and put under the same code. Each new incident that is coded under a code adds to the general properties and dimensions of that code, elaborating it and bringing in variation. (p. 195)

This is the bridge to the focused phase of coding that Charmaz (2006) describes: "Focused coding means using the most significant and/or frequent earlier codes to sift through large amounts of data. Focused coding requires decisions about which initial codes make the most analytic sense to categorize your data incisively and completely" (p. 57). If a researcher is using a grounded theory approach, the focused coding will lead to identifying relations among the coding categories and organizing them into a theoretical framework. You validate the hypothesized relationships with the data available to you and fill in categories that need further refinement and development. This step is integrative and relational; however, Corbin and Strauss (2008) note that the analysis that occurs at this stage of the study is done at a higher, more abstract level. During this phase of analysis, the researcher identifies the core category or story line, and then relates the subsidiary categories to the core through a model. (Corbin and Strauss use the term *paradigm;* however, I use the term *model,* because paradigm has a different meaning in this book.[5]) The model includes an explication of the conditions, context, strategies, and consequences identified in the coding phase. You then validate your theory by grounding it in the data; if necessary, you seek additional data to test the theory.

The coding example shown previously in this chapter of the study of teachers who work with students who are deaf and have an additional disability illustrates how the transformative lens was brought into the analysis to support the focused coding phase (Mertens et al., 2007). We were able to see connections between social justice issues in teacher preparation and support in early years of teaching based on the challenges that new teachers faced in terms of being marginalized at their schools (manifest by low expectations from administrators and exclusion from mainstream school activities) and a need to fully address language diversity (e.g., home languages other than English; use of a variety of languages and communication modes such as American Sign Language, speaking English while using ASL signs, and cued speech; use of a variety of assistive listening technologies such as cochlear implants and hearing aids.) If all students have a right to an education, how can colleges of education prepare teachers who can respond appropriately to these educational challenges?

Using Computers in Qualitative Analysis

Because qualitative studies tend to result in mountains of data (literally), many researchers have turned to computerized systems for storing, analyzing, and retrieving information. Presently, a large number of computer programs are available (e.g., ATLAS/ti, The Ethnograph, HyperRESEARCH, and NVivo), and this is an area in which rapid changes are occurring. Hence, I will not recommend any particular software, but refer you to a Web site that I have found to be useful called Computer Assisted Qualitative Data Analysis where you will find analyses of various programs, as well as breaking news in this area (http://caqdas.soc.surrey.ac.uk/). One of the features of computer-based coding is that codes can be generated "in vivo," that is, codes can be generated by highlighting specific text in the file.

Before making a decision about which software program to use, you should review the resources cited in this chapter (as well as any more recent developments in this rapidly changing field). You need to pick a system that is compatible with your hardware as well as with your research purposes. One caution: No matter how attractive the software, nothing should separate you from active involvement with your data. Qualitative data analysis is really about *you* thinking about your data and hypothesizing possible relationships and meanings. A computer can be an important aid in this process, but you should not let it become a means of separating you from the process of knowing what your data have to say.

Interpretation Issues in Qualitative Data Analysis

Triangulating Data

Triangulation, as it was discussed in Chapter 8, involves the use of multiple methods and multiple data sources to support the strength of interpretations and conclusions in qualitative research. As Guba and Lincoln (1989) note, triangulation should not be used to gloss over legitimate differences in interpretations of data; this is an inaccurate interpretation of the meaning of triangulation. Such diversity should be preserved in the report so that the "voices" of the least empowered are not lost. L. Richardson and St. Pierre (2005) suggest that a better metaphor for this concept is crystallization; Mertens (2009) suggested the metaphor of a prism. The crystal and the prism metaphors suggest multifaceted sources of data that are brought to bear on the interpretation of findings.

Audits

Two types of audits were described in Chapter 8: the dependability audit and the confirmability audit. Through the use of these two strategies, the researcher can document the changes that occurred during the research and the supporting data for interpretations and conclusions. The process of memoing discussed previously in the coding section has been noted to contribute to a researcher's ability to make visible the decision-making trail that occurred during the course of the study (Birks, Chapman, & Francis, 2008). Memos can serve as an audit trail to document the progression of the study, as well as changes that occurred and the context for those changes.

Questions to guide an audit for reviewing qualitative studies were suggested by Schwandt and Halpern (1988, cited in Miles & Huberman, 1994). The questions are as follows:

1. Are findings grounded in the data? (Is sampling appropriate? Are data weighted correctly?)

2. Are inferences logical (Are analytic strategies applied correctly? Are alternative explanations accounted for?)

3. Is the category structure appropriate?

4. Can inquiry decisions and methodological shifts be justified? (Were sampling decisions linked to working hypotheses?)

5. What is the degree of researcher bias (premature closure, unexplored data in field notes, lack of search for negative cases, feelings of empathy)?

6. What strategies were used for increasing credibility (second readers, feedback to informants, peer review, adequate time in the field)? (p. 439)

Cultural Bias

The comments included in the section on cultural bias for quantitative research are equally appropriate when analyzing and interpreting qualitative research. The opportunity to see things from your own cultural bias is recognized as a potential problem in qualitative research. Many of the safeguards discussed in Chapter 8 are useful for minimizing this source of bias or for recognizing the influence of the researcher's own framework. You should begin by describing your own values and cultural framework for the reader. Then you should keep a journal or log of how your perspectives change through the study. Discussing your progress with a peer debriefer can enhance your ability to detect when your cultural lens is becoming problematic. Conducting member checks with participants who are members of the culture under study can help you see where divergence in viewpoints may be based on culturally different interpretations.

Generalization/Transferability

Differences of opinion exist in the qualitative research community with regard to claims that can be made about the generalizability of the findings. Recall that generalizability is a concept that is rooted in the postpositivist paradigm and technically refers to the ability to generalize results of research conducted with a sample to a population that the sample represents. In qualitative research, Guba and Lincoln (1989) proposed that the concept of transferability would be more appropriate. With this approach, the burden of proof for generalizability lies with the reader, and the researcher is responsible for providing the thick description that allows the reader to make a judgment about the applicability of the research to another setting. Stake (2005) offers the opinion that case studies can be conducted with no intention to generalize to other situations; these cases are studied because of intrinsic interest in that case. He also recognizes that case studies are sometimes undertaken to be able to describe a typical situation so the case provides an opportunity to learn that may provide insight into other similar situations, or multiple case studies might be undertaken to demonstrate the range of commonality and diversity of a phenomenon. Aggregating across cases must be done cautiously and without loss of the uniqueness in the context of each case.

Ruddin (2006) extends this argument in asserting that it is false to think that a case study cannot grant useful information about the broader class. Rather, the strength of a case study is that it captures "reality" in greater detail and thus allows for both the analysis of a greater number of variables and for generalization from the concrete, practical, and context-dependent knowledge created in the investigation. He further explains, "We avoid the problem of trying to generalize inductively from single cases by not confusing case inference with statistical inference. Case study reasoning would be seen as a strong form of hypothetico-deductive theorizing, not as a weak form of statistical inference" (p. 800).

Member Checks

As mentioned in Chapter 8, member checks can be used during the process of data collection. They have a place at the stages of data analysis and writing as well. Darbyshire et al. (2005) note that repetitive use of member checks at different phases of the study provide a method of increasing validity. They cite the work of Dockett and Perry (2003), who used member checking in a photo essay project. The children in the study were asked to discuss written and photographic portrayals of the findings. They were able to suggest additions and deletions in order to tell the story the way they thought it should be told.

Analytic and Interpretive Issues in Mixed Methods

Analytic and interpretive issues in mixed methods research are influenced by the researcher's paradigm and the design of the study. If a sequential design is used, it is more likely that the data analysis of one type of data will precede that of the other type, with little consequence for integrating the two types of data. However, it is possible that researchers might want to use the data from both types of data collection to inform their conclusions, and this would be especially true in concurrent mixed methods designs. Hence, discussion of analytic and interpretive issues here focus on the nexus at which the two types of data actually meet and are intended to have an interactive relationship with the intention of seeing how they might inform each other.[6] This is the strategy used in the study of parents and their deaf children (see Chapter 10, Meadow-Orlans et al., 2003). A national survey resulted in quantitative data that were disaggregated to determine characteristics of parents associated with different levels of satisfaction with early intervention services. These data were used to identify subgroups of parents from whom qualitative data would be collected by means of in-depth interviews or focus groups. In the final analysis and interpretation phase of the study, the quantitative data were used to provide a picture of each subgroup of parents, while the qualitative data provided a richer explanation of their experiences with their young deaf or hard-of-hearing child.

Jang, McDougall, Pollon, Herbert, and Russell (2008) provide reflections on mixed methods data analysis in their study of successful schools that had high percentages of immigrant students and were in economically distressed areas. They used a concurrent mixed methods design,

> composed of qualitative approaches using interviews with teachers and principals and focus groups with students and parents, and a quantitative survey of principals and teachers. This concurrent mixed methods design was to serve the complementarity function in that the general description of school improvement from the survey was enriched, elaborated, and clarified with contextually specific accounts of school success from interviews involving multiple perspectives. (p. 226)

Jang et al. (2008) used traditional quantitative statistical analysis techniques to perform a factor analysis on the quantitative survey data. They also engaged in traditional qualitative analysis strategies of developing codes and checking the coding process with a team of researchers. However, they went much further with their data analysis to integrate the quantitative and qualitative data. They "qualitized" the factors that were identified by the factor analysis and compared the associated concepts with the themes that had emerged from the qualitative data. They then merged the themes from the two types of data and used the new set of themes as an organizing framework to categorize the items from the survey according to which theme they represented. They then conducted quantitative analysis of the subgroups of survey items to see how the participants responded in this thematic context. They also conducted these analyses for each school to see what differentiated one school from another. They were able to see the commonality of themes that emerged across the various schools that provide an explanatory basis for the school's success. They also identified a factor that was different among schools that exhibited higher or lower levels of success—parental involvement. Using the data from the re-analyzed survey data and the comments made by participants about parental involvement, the researchers were able to provide specific recommendations to improve parental involvement in the less-successful schools.

Remember Berliner et al.'s (2008) mixed methods study of policies and practices to improve high school graduation for dropouts? They investigated the quantitative patterns in reenrollment and subsequent graduation from high school. In addition, their qualitative data analysis provided them with insights as to why students reenroll (e.g., it is hard for a high school dropout to get a job). They also identified factors that challenge school districts when trying to reenroll dropouts. Demand at alternative high schools exceeds capacity, yet traditional high schools do not offer the interventions needed to support reenrollees. State funds were tied to enrollment and attendance rates; dropouts even with reenrollment result in fewer state dollars. This is complicated by the requirements for specific tests and other curriculum requirements needed for graduation. The combination of the quantitative results that support the effects of reenrollment in the long term with the identification of challenges from the policies in place at the state and district levels provides a basis for recommendations for improving graduation rates for this population of students.

A Research Plan: The Management Plan and Budget

A research plan is needed to outline the steps that must be taken to complete the research study within a specific time frame and to identify the resources needed to accomplish this complex task. The research plan consists of two parts: the management plan and budget. Together, these can be used to guide you as you conduct your research and to monitor your progress.

The Management Plan

To develop a management plan, you need to analyze the major steps in the research process—for example, the literature review, design of the study, implementation of the study, and analysis and report of the study. Then, for each major step, you should list the substeps that you need to accomplish to conduct your research. A sample management plan is presented in Table 13.3. You can use the management plan to monitor your progress and to make any midcourse corrections that might be necessary. In addition, it can serve as a trail that documents your actions, which would allow researchers to audit your work, including any divergences from the original plan and the reasons for those changes. Particularly in qualitative research, the divergences are important because they are expected to occur. Thus, you are able to establish a trail of evidence for decisions that influenced the direction of the project and to support any conclusions you reached based on the research outcomes.

Table 13.3 Sample Management Plan for Research Proposal

Research Function	*Subtasks*	*Person Responsible*	*Start Date*	*End Date*
1. Literature review	1.1 Identify key terms 1.2 Identify databases 1.3 Conduct electronic search 1.4 Conduct hand search of journals 1.5 Contact experts in the field, etc.	Research director	September 2009	November 2009
2. Instrument development	etc.[a]	Research director	November 2009	December 2009
3. Data collection	etc.	Research director	January 2010	March 2010
4. Data analysis	etc.	Research director	March 2010	April 2010
5. Reporting	etc.	Research director	April 2010	May 2010

a. You will be clearer about the other subtasks needed after you complete your literature review.

If you are involved in a large-scale research project, it might be helpful to divide the work that will be done by people (defined in terms of positions—e.g., project director, research assistant) and identify the amount of time that each person will devote to the various activities. Such a person-loading chart can help with budgeting and justification for funding requests.

The Research Budget

Many dissertations and theses are written with very little or even no external funding. However, it is common for institutions to offer small grants to support such research or even for advanced students to seek outside funding. A sample budget sheet is presented in Table 13.4. General budget categories include personnel and nonpersonnel items. Under personnel, you should list all the people who will be involved in the research process, the amount of time each will be expected to work, and the rate at which each will be paid. Typical nonpersonnel items include travel, materials, supplies, equipment, communication expenses (telephone, postage), and copying. If you plan to pay people who participate in your research, that should be included in your budget as well. If you are seeking funds from an external source, you will need to include *indirect costs*. This is typically a percentage of the overall amount requested that your institution will expect to receive to cover such costs as maintaining the building in which you have an office, the heat, the water, and other indirect costs of supporting you as you conduct your research.

The budget can be arranged by research activities, to indicate which categories or activities require varying proportions of the funds. Arranging the budget this way makes it possible to show the impact of budget cuts on the research activities themselves. For example, if funds are budgeted for a follow-up of nonrespondents and this amount is cut from the budget, it would have deleterious effects on the quality of the research.

Table 13.4 Sample Budget

Personnel Research Director (9 months @ $2,000/month)	$18,000[a]
Nonpersonnel Travel (2 trips @ $1,000/trip)	$ 2,000[b]
Communication Costs	
Postage (100 surveys @ $ 0.44)	$ 44.00
Second mailing (80 surveys @ $0.44)	$ 35.20
Third follow-up (50 surveys @ $0.44)	$ 22.00
Telephone (30 calls to nonrespondents @ $10)	$300.00
Copying (5 pages x 230 surveys @ $0.10/page)	$115.00
Total	**$20,516.20**

a. Most institutional small grant programs disallow you paying yourself to complete your dissertation or thesis research. However, you might be able to obtain funds to support a research assistant to help with the copying, mailing, coding, or entry of data.

b. Typically, a budget would require specific justification for travel expenditure in terms of the cost of an airline ticket, hotel room, meals (sometimes calculated as a per diem), and so on.

Writing Research Reports

Typically, researchers think of writing up their research in a fairly standard format for reporting results and providing a documentation of their methods and interpretations. This section will provide guidance on such writing. Alternatives to presentation of results in a written report will also be presented in terms of performance as a means of reporting research results.

Writing Reports

The benchmark style manual for writing educational and psychological research reports is the *Publication Manual of the American Psychological Association* (APA, 2001). Guidance in writing is available at APA's Web site (www.apastyle.org/). In some disciplines (e.g., history), other style manuals may be recommended, such as *The Chicago*

Manual of Style (2003) or Turabian's (1996) *A Manual for Writers of Term Papers, Theses, and Dissertations*. The APA also publishes a number of references on nondiscriminatory use of language, available from their publications office located in Washington, D.C., or online at www.apastyle.org/styletips.html. They have style types for removing bias in the use of language for the following topics: people with disabilities, racial or ethnic minority groups, and sexuality. Other professional organizations publish similar sets of guidelines, such as the American Educational Research Association (AERA; www.area.net), also located in Washington, D.C.

Students should check with their university regarding local style requirements. Individuals who wish to publish their research should check with prospective publishers for their requirements. Journals generally tend to include publication requirements in the front or back of each issue.

Dissertations and Theses

Most dissertations and theses consist of the same first three chapters:

Chapter 1: Introduction

Chapter 2: Literature Review

Chapter 3: Methodology

Quantitative dissertations and theses typically have two additional chapters:

Chapter 4: Results

Chapter 5: Discussion and Conclusions

Meloy (2001) found that qualitative dissertations tended to have different formats for the final chapters, such as chapters on emergent analyses, individual case study reports, and conclusions and implications. An outline for writing dissertation and thesis proposals for different paradigms is provided in the Appendix.

Before you start writing, you should determine if your institution has a formal style manual. In addition, ask questions to determine the general practices at your school:

1. What is the acceptable number of chapters in a dissertation or thesis? What flexibility exists for alternative formats?

2. How much control do students, faculty members, and the graduate school have in determining the appearance and style of the dissertation or thesis? Which decisions, if any, are negotiable?

3. Do you write in the first-person or third-person voice? Do you use past, present, or future tense?

4. What are the local guidelines and requirements for selecting a committee? How many committee members must you have? What is the recommended or acceptable role for the committee members?

5. How supportive is the environment at your university or college for postpositivist, constructivist, or transformative research?

Reporting Format Options

Although you may have been working in the mind-set of producing a dissertation or thesis, you will want to be cognizant of alternative reporting formats for your academic research, as well as for your future research studies. Researchers have a wide range of options available to them for reporting their research: for example, presentations at professional meetings, journal articles, and technical reports. Typically, a research report includes an introduction (with a literature review) and sections for method, results, and discussion. The exact structure differs depending on the type of research (quantitative or qualitative), the audience, and purpose of the report. Research reports can have multiple uses for different audiences; thus, alternative reporting formats should be considered for dissemination.

In both quantitative and qualitative studies, the researcher should tie the results back to the purpose for the study and to the literature in the discussion section of the report. Furthermore, findings should be based on data, and caution should be exercised in recommendations for practice. Limitations of the work should be recognized.

Quantitative Reports

In the quantitative report format, results are typically reported by the use of tables and graphs. Researchers also tend to write in a detached style, avoiding the use of the first-person pronoun and employing the passive voice. Although qualitative reports can use tables and graphs, they typically present results in a more narrative style and include more personal revelations about the author (L. Richardson & St. Pierre, 2005).

M. A. Moore (1991) identifies problems in writing the results of quantitative data analyses. She explains three problems commonly related to the use of the term *significant* in such reports. First, writers frequently use the term significant without the appropriate accompanying modifier term—for example, *statistically*—in the description of the results. The reader cannot infer that the term significant implies statistical significance. However, without that modifying term, the intended meaning of significance is not clear in this context. Second, writers sometimes assume that the use of the term *statistically significant* means that the results are important or meaningful. As mentioned in the section on the difference between statistical and practical significance, you know that having statistical significance does not necessarily equate with being important. Third, writers sometimes talk about *approaching significance.* This is not appropriate language in a research report. Results are either statistically significant or not; they do not approach (or avoid) significance.

In B. Thompson's (2007) analysis of common errors found in quantitative dissertations, he also notes this problem with language that describes statistical significance: Writers will sometimes interpret significance tests as if they were effect sizes (e.g., results were highly significant or results approached statistical significance). In addition, he notes the following common errors:

1. When the sample size is small and the effect size is large, the results are often underinterpreted. (As you will recall, it is harder to get statistical significance with a small sample, so if a large effect size is found under these conditions, it should be noted.) If the sample size is large and effect sizes are modest, the results can be overinterpreted.

2. Researchers sometimes use many univariate tests of statistical significance when a multivariate test would be more appropriate. The probability of making a Type I error is increased when multiple univariate tests are applied to one data set.

3. Researchers sometimes convert continuous (ratio or interval) data to categorical (nominal) data to conduct a chi-square or some type of ANOVA. Thompson points out that much variance is lost by this conversion and suggests that researchers ask themselves whether a regression analysis might be more appropriate as a way of preserving the variance in the data.

4. ANCOVA is sometimes employed to provide statistical control when random assignment was not performed with the expectation that the statistical adjustments will magically make groups equivalent. However, when the data cannot satisfy the underlying assumption of homogeneity of regression, it is not appropriate to use ANCOVA. The assumption states that the relationship between the covariate and the dependent variable is equivalent in all experimental groups; for example, children in a treatment group learn at the same rate as children in the control group. If the relationship between the dependent variable and the covariate is different under different treatments, the ANCOVA should not be used. The effect of not satisfying the homogeneity of regression assumption can be to suppress evidence of program effects.

5. Researchers who use regression analysis should apply the regression equation to a fresh sample of data to see how well it does predict values on the criterion variable (replication and validation).

6. Researchers should always report the psychometric integrity of the measures they use.

Qualitative Reports

For qualitative reports, the reader looks for deep and valid descriptions and for well-grounded hypotheses and theories that emerge from a wide variety of data gathered over an extended period of time. The researcher should also seek contextual meaning; that is, he or she should attempt to understand the social and cultural context of the situation in which the statements are made and the behaviors exhibited. This includes a description of relevant contextual variables, such as home, community, history, educational background, physical arrangements, emotional climate, and rules. It should also include a statement that makes clear the positionality of the researcher as the instrument. Borum (2006) positions herself as an African American Womanist and offers this self-description in her writing:

> I am an "inside" member of the African American community and have lived in African American communities most of my life. I not only am intellectually aware of cultural nuances but also live the cultural nuances found in African American culture and experiences. Therefore, I will explicate the following: I am single (never married) and have never given birth, thus, I have no biological children—both decisions are by choice. However, I have worked with families and their deaf children in school and home settings for more than 10 years. I received my BA in psychology with minors in biology and philosophy from Mundelein Women's College in Chicago. I received my MSW with a concentration in deafness from Gallaudet University, and I am fluent in American Sign Language. I received my PhD from Howard University, a *Research I* Historically Black University where my dissertation topic was African American families with deaf children. (p. 343)

Writing up qualitative research has emerged as an area of controversy partially reflected in the struggle of how to present qualitative data based on whose *voice* is represented in the written report. McGee-Brown (1994) struggled with the implications for representing different voices in research in a way that would be meaningful for those who would be affected by the results. She notes that participants' constructions of meaning in social context often vary radically from the researcher's constructions because of different histories or experiences. She says that such variations do not discourage her from conducting and reporting research of a qualitative nature. Indeed, she views the variations as an impetus to seek the most accurate understanding possible of what is happening in contexts from as many perspectives as possible. She suggests that structural change is necessary to create formats for data dissemination that include all voices meaningfully in the discourse. Researchers need to establish mechanisms for speaking with the people for whom the research is conducted. For example, in education, researchers need to communicate about the research with students, teachers, and administrators. Currently, there is little value attached to such discourse, because a researcher is rewarded for publication in scholarly journals and presentations at professional meetings that the students, teachers, and administrators typically do not attend.

M. Fine et al. (2000) offer the following questions for researchers to ask themselves as a way of gauging their responsiveness to the voices of the participants:

- Have you worked to understand your contribution to the materials/narrations provided and those silenced?
- Have you worked to explain to readers the position from which informants speak?
- Have you worked to recast the person(s) whom the informant chooses to "blame" or credit for social justice or injustice (be it a social worker, the informant's mother, black men)? (p. 127)

Freeman et al. (2007) also raise questions for qualitative research writers because of the close connection between the researchers and participants, as well as because of concerns about representation. They offer the following guiding questions:

- How can we best listen to, work with, and represent the people our work is intended to serve?
- Do authors of research reports reveal themselves as their own best critics?
- Do they discuss the limits and uncertainties of their work?
- How forthright are they about competing interpretations and explanations for the patterns they claim? (p. 30)

These researchers offer advice on how to answer these questions, such as demonstrating the relationship between the data and claims by giving sufficient data to support each claim. This can be accomplished by inclusion of extensive quotations or by making data available to others. The extent to which a researcher chooses to allow others to have access to the data is based on a complex set of considerations. For example, should a researcher make video data or interview and field notes available on the Web for others to see? Oral historians have tended to make their data available in this way. However, other approaches to research offer confidentiality to their participants, hence suggesting that such a strategy would violate ethical principles. Members of indigenous groups have expressed concerns about having data about themselves displayed in public forums because of a legacy of distrust with dominant cultures.

Organizing Qualitative Writing. Qualitative researchers often end up with a mountain of data that needs to be reduced to some manageable form so that others will be able and willing to read it. At a minimum, McDuffie and Scruggs (2008) suggest that the writer include a description of research methods, including how the data were coded, along with a rationale for what was and was not included in the research. They should also include reflections on possible researcher bias and provide references to related research.

Wolcott (1994) suggests the following possibilities for organizing the presentation of the results:

- Events can be presented in *chronological order,* as they occurred in the data collection setting.
- Events can be presented in the order in which the *narrators* revealed them to the researcher.
- The researcher can write using *progressive focusing;* that is, the researcher can describe a broad context and then progressively focus in on the details of the particular case.
- You can report events as a *day-in-the-life* description of what life is like for people in that setting.
- You can focus on one or two *critical or key events.*
- You can introduce the main *characters* and then tell the story, revealing the *plot* as in a stage play.
- The main *groups* in the setting can be described along with the way they *interact* with each other.
- You can use an *analytic framework* (described earlier in the chapter in the section on grounded theory analysis strategies) to organize the writing.
- You can tell the *story several different ways,* from the viewpoint of different actors in the setting. Wolf (1992) used such a strategy in her book *A Thrice Told Tale,* in which she reports the same field study as a work of fiction, in the form of field notes, and as a self-reflexive account.
- You can present the research problem as a *mystery* to be solved, and then bring the pieces of data into the story as a way of solving the mystery.

Performance as Research Reporting. In the later 1980s and early 1990s, sociologists began to turn their ethnographic notes into performances with the goal of presenting their results in a more engaging manner and thus encouraging social action to follow the presentation (McCall, 2000). Such an approach means that the ethnographer (researcher) needs to write a script and then cast and/or perform the scripted materials. Cho and Trent (2006) describe the benefits of ethnographic performance as, "'Readers . . . move through the re-created experience with the performer' (Denzin, 2000, p. 950) to be able to differently perceive the world in which we live and to actively engage themselves in this world" (Cho & Trent, 2006, p. 332). The goal is to bring about transformation by looking at the "taken for granted" in new and unexpected ways.

Mienczakowski (2000) provides an example of the use of performance to report the results of an ethnographic study in the form of theater with transformative intentions. He used the experiences of the health consumer community representing schizophrenic psychosis and institutionalized detoxification processes as a way of communicating to groups of health and student communities. He terms the medium *ethnographically derived theater,* because the meanings and explanations of the performances are negotiated with audiences in forum discussion at the close of each performance. Thus, the potential is created to share insights and negotiate explanations with an eye to provoking change among those who play an active part in the construction of health services.

Multiple forms of performance have been developed in the qualitative research community. *The SAGE Handbook of Qualitative Research* (Denzin & Lincoln, 2005) includes chapters on performance in the same genre as Mienczakowski's (2000) staged production (Finley, 2005), as well as chapters on poetry (Brady, 2005; Stewart, 2005), and visual arts (Harper, 2005). In addition, Leavy's (2009) book on arts-based methods in research offers a similarly wide range of possible performance genres. Borum (2006) used poetic prose as a method of qualitative reporting in her work with African American women with deaf daughters (see Box 13.5). She interspersed poetic lines with excerpts from her interview data to create a written report that exemplified the strength and resilience she found in these mothers and daughters.

Box 13.5 Poetic Prose as Qualitative Reporting

She loves struggle—

If I do what God tells me to do, things will work out. Even if I have hard times, I have hard times gloriously. I enjoy my hard times. I can praise Him when I'm doing good, or not doing good. Abundance or nothing, I'm alright with Him. I don't have any problems saying I don't have. My Father is rich and I know He won't let me suffer and I just move on. . . . It gets rough sometimes because it is so hard because I'm in this thing by myself, but I'm not, it just seems like it.

It has been very challenging. I welcome the challenge. I love it.

She loves Spirit—

And I started walking and God told me all the things He would do for her if I stayed with her. It will be rough but He will take care of me and her, and I will be able to handle anything that came against me. God said, "I'll do anything but fail!"

And, God—definitely. Without Him, where would we be? I give Him all the praise. He has been my strength, and I believe through Him my child will prosper . . .

The first few days were stressful. I had a lot of support, Bible study group, my faith was very strong, and a lot of prayers were all very helpful. I got strength from God.

She loves to love—

I find that this young woman gives me another dimension. I try and I love all these children, but she's special to me. I actually think she would be special even if she weren't deaf . . . and I love learning with her. I love helping her. I love the fact that I can see in her eyes that I have improved in my signing and I know that makes her proud of me. I love the fact that I can communicate with her now and that she likes being with me and likes telling me things and comes to me and talks to me.

—Borum, 2006, p. 346

Clarity in Writing

Clarity of writing seems, at first glance, to be an essential characteristic of a research report, especially one that purports to be directed at political change—a goal toward which transformative researchers strive. As obvious as this criterion might seem, it is not uncontested in the scholarly world. Lather (1995) was criticized because her published writings, which feature complex language and a complicated writing style, are not considered to be easily accessible to many audiences. In her own defense, and as a point to be made more broadly about language, she warns that simple, clear writing might disguise the complexity of an issue. She says, "Sometimes we need a density that fits the thoughts being expressed" (p. 4). She raises some provocative questions:

> What would it mean to position language as revealing or productive of new spaces, practices, and values? What might be the value of encouraging a plurality of theoretical discourses and forms of writing in a way that refuses the binary between so-called "plain speaking" and complex writing? What are the power issues involved in assumptions of clear language as a mobilizing strategy? What are the responsibilities of a reader in the face of correspondence theories of truth and transparent theories of language? What is the violence of clarity, its non-innocence? (p. 4)

Lather (1995) contends that writing that the reader is able to understand is accomplished at the cost of filtering the information to minimize demands on the reader. To make use of a text, a reader needs to see it as an opportunity to wrestle with ideas, become reflective, read it again, and come up with a personal understanding.

Extending Your Thinking: Clarity in Writing

Reread the preceding passage in which Lather (1995) contests the "innocence" of clear, simplistic writing. She further explains her own way of writing as follows:

> Across the sweep of post-humanist theory, I find confirmations of and challenges and directions to my efforts. I am on to something, inchoate as it often is, turning to the theory that helps me articulate the investments and effectivities of what I have wrought, reading both the affirmations of my efforts and the critiques of it in a way that lets me keep on keeping on, stubbornly holding on to the rhythms of the unfoldings of a book that is as much writing me as the other way around. This exploration of possibilities in the face of limit questions marks my desire to "trouble" the dualism between calls for accessibility and the assumption that academic "High Theory" is a sort of masturbatory activity aimed at a privileged few that can have no "real" effect in the material world. (p. 12)

What is your view of the dichotomy set up (and rejected) by Lather in this passage: accessibility versus "High Theory"? What do you think Lather means when she says that simple, clear writing is not "innocent"? Can you think of examples of things you have struggled to read and then found that you gained new, deeper, and different understandings with rereading?

Representation. Qualitative researchers participated in a panel discussion about issues related to writing their research reports at the International Congress on Qualitative Inquiry in 2007 and published a transcript of their remarks (Ellis et al., 2008). They raised an important ethical issue in the form of a question: "What happens when the people in your study don't see what you wrote about them until after it is published and they are angry when they see how they are described?" This question goes beyond the ethical principles used by ethical review boards and centers on the more relational aspects of research writing.

Ellis (2007) described the tensions she felt in her work in wanting to be friends with the people in the community, yet also wanting to build her career in academia. The people told her things that you tell a friend about relationships, dating, and scandals; but a friend would not reveal such secrets. She admitted that "Writing; I failed to consider sufficiently how my blunt disclosures in print might affect the lives of the people about whom I wrote. Instead I cared about how committee members reacted to my dissertation and whether my manuscript would be published as a book" (p. 10). When she returned to the community, she was faced with people who were angry about what she had written about them, and she said this experience motivated her to conduct her research in a different and more egalitarian and participative way. She gives this sage advice to people who inquire as to how to present results in an ethical manner:

> I tell them our studies should lead to positive change and make the world a better place. "Strive to leave the communities, participants, and yourselves better off at the end of the research than they were at the beginning," I say. "In the best of all worlds, all of those involved in our studies will feel better. But sometimes they won't; you won't." I tell them that most important to me is that they not negatively affect their lives and relationships, hurt themselves, or others in their world. I tell them to hold relational concerns as high as research. I tell them when possible to research from an ethic of care. That's the best we can do. (Ellis, 2007, p. 26)

Utilization of the Research Results

Utilization of research results is more likely to occur when the researcher integrates strategies to enhance utilization into the research proposal. As mentioned in Chapter 2, the first edition of the *Standards for Program Evaluation* (Joint Committee on Standards for Educational Evaluation, 2009) listed utilization as the first, and most important, criterion for judging the quality of an investigative effort. Although their focus was on investigations for evaluation purposes, the importance of utilization of research in education and psychology should not be overlooked. The following strategies have been identified to enhance utilization of research:

1. Identification and involvement of appropriate audiences for the proposed research, including representation of those who would be most likely to benefit from, or be hurt by, the research.

2. Frequent and appropriate methods of communication with the intended users of the research, including targeting reports to appropriate audiences.

3. Provision of reports that clearly describe the theoretical framework for the study, the procedures, and the rules for interpretation of the data.

4. Reaching intended users of the research through a variety of dissemination modes, with presentation of the research results in a timely manner, such that the information can be used for decision making.

Types of utilization of research and evaluation findings range from sharing results with participants to determine next steps to publication in scholarly journals to serving as a basis for social action at the policy level. Rosenstein's (2000) work on an evaluation project involving Arab and Jewish elementary schools in Jerusalem offers one example of the use of video-based data to stimulate thinking about next steps in this war-torn area (see Box 13.6). The program used folklore in the form of traditional activities, such as doll-making, pickle-making, and games, as a basis for joint learning experiences in matched Arab and Jewish schools in Israel (Traditional Creativity Through the Schools Project operated by The Center for Creativity in Education and Cultural Heritage, Jerusalem[7]). Later in the project, selections of the video footage were used as a way of reporting back findings and allowing the participants to both interpret what they were seeing as well as to draw inferences about next steps in the program.

Box 13.6 Utilization of Evaluation Study Results Using Video-Based Images

Before actually viewing the videotape, the stakeholders discussed "what had happened" during the event. The discussion was hypothetical and there was no development. It did not lead to self-generated knowledge, but rather, reiterated preconceived notions. The general feeling as expressed by one of the mothers was "They (the boys) are simply not interested in the program or in communicating."

In the post viewing session, however, the participants questioned this "given." "Perhaps, they do want to make friends?" "Look, they *are* interacting!" This uncertainty concerning the "fact" enabled them to reflect on the event, to examine the issues more deeply, entering into a discussion of kinds of interaction and which kind they wanted as a suitable goal for the program. . . . There was a consensus concerning "what happened" as confirmed by the video, and the interpretations followed. Each interpretation added to the general development of the discussion. From their exclamations during the viewing, "There is a connection. You can see it," it was clear that there was a discrepancy between what they thought had occurred and what they saw on the screen. Their surprise, "It seems that something is happening" sparked their reflection: "How can we use that connection and build it into a more meaningful relationship?" This reflection in turn generated the ensuing productive discussion. "For my part, if the children learn from this that they are all people, with interests and preferences, then, that's enough for me."

—Rosenstein, 2000, pp. 386–387

Writing for Publication

Journals vary in what they are looking for and will find acceptable for publication. Inside the front or back covers of most journals, you will find a publication policy statement. Typically, the journal editors prepare a statement that describes the type of articles that they want to publish. Some journals specialize in theoretical work, others focus on empirical research studies, and some publish a combination of both. You generally find a description of the content that the editors view as being appropriate for that journal as well. You can sort of guess what that description will say by the title of the journal; however, it is good to review the statement, as well as a sampling of the articles that have been recently published in that source.

When you submit a manuscript for consideration to a journal, if it is a refereed journal, the editors will send the manuscript to several reviewers. The reviewers are given a checklist that allows them to make suggestions about your manuscript:

- That it be published as is (if you receive such a letter, save it, frame it, and hang it on the wall)
- That it be published with minor changes
- That it be revised and resubmitted for another review
- That it be rejected as inappropriate for that journal

Reviewers are typically given a set of criteria for justifying their ratings of various aspects of the manuscript. Usually, they will be asked to rate such things as the following:

- The clarity of the problem
- The logical progression of ideas
- The significance of the issues raised (for the readers of that journal, specifically)
- The appropriateness of the research design for that problem
- The appropriateness of the conclusions based on the data analysis
- The readability of the text
- Appropriateness of tone (not overly emotional)
- Need for additional editing
- Appropriateness of references (in terms of quantity, quality, inclusion of important studies, and timeliness)

If you are thinking about publishing your research as a book, you should do some research on publishers to see who is publishing books on similar topics. This is important not just to determine potential interest on the part of the publisher, but also to assess the publisher's ability to market the book to appropriate audiences for you. When you have identified one or a few potential publishers, it is appropriate to contact them and ask for their prospectus guidelines. Although publishers vary somewhat, they typically have an outline that delineates the type of information they need about your intended book to make a decision about their desire to publish it for you. Some publishers will request a sample chapter, whereas others will be satisfied with a detailed outline. Your prospectus is usually sent out to reviewers by the publisher who then uses their comments as a basis for deciding to accept or reject your book proposal.

Use for Social Change

Many researchers believe that their responsibility is limited to the creation of knowledge. Hence, once the data are collected, analyzed, and reported their job is essentially finished. However, researchers who place themselves in the transformative paradigm hold a fundamental belief that directs them to facilitate the use of their research findings for social action. This, of course, is not an unproblematic stance. For example, how can researchers be held responsible for the use of their findings (Ginsberg & Mertens,

2009)? What happens if the members of the community do not have the means to use the research themselves for social change? Does the responsibility then revert back to the researchers? There are no simple answers to these questions. However, there are resources that have been developed that offer strategies for increasing the probability that research results will be used for social actions focused on increased social justice. In particular, The California Endowment (Guthrie, Louie, David, & Foster, 2005), a foundation that supports equity in access to health services, and a grassroots organization, the Work Group on Health Promotion and Community Development at the University of Kansas in Lawrence, developed community-based toolboxes that lead the reader through a step-by-step process to use research findings for social change. Both organizations have made their resources available for free on the Web (www.calendow.org and http://ctb.ku.edu).

Use of Research in the Courts. Ancheta (2006) reviews the many times that research data have been used in the courts to demonstrate disparities in education and the consequent need for increased constitutional protection for racial and ethnic minorities, women, immigrants, and other subordinated groups. This intersection of research and court personnel is complicated by the dissimilarities between these two cultures in terms of language, expertise, and standards of evidence. Ancheta asks, "How should education researchers move forward in the coming years, particularly when educational inequality remains a pressing problem in American society and educational policies designed to foster racial integration and diversity continue to be challenged in the courts?" (p. 29). He notes that the future will bring additional questions that educational and psychological researchers need to consider such as how the racial diversity in student bodies, teachers, and faculty constitutes a compelling state interest, and whether training minority professionals will lead to improved educational and life experiences for members of their own community. Ancheta recognizes that the courts play a different role than policymakers in education and social policies; however, they do have a part to play in bringing to light the need for revision in public policies that allow problems of segregation and inequality to continue.

Use of Research: Final Reflection. Ferdinand, Pearson, Rowe, and Worthington (2007) revisit the tension created between different purposes of research in their discussion of what the researcher's responsibility is if corruption is discovered as part of the research findings. They note that for researchers who accept the purpose of research as creating knowledge, then there is no need to worry about revealing corruption. Speaking from a transformative stance, they write,

> critical researchers have an ethical responsibility to expose unjust or unethical exploitative, oppressive or illegal practices. The point is not just to understand the world we live in; the point is to change it. (p. 532)
>
> Rapport and ethics: builds up trust and reduces 'reactivity,' and thus helps the researchers to capture social reality, in whatever setting, as it really is. But is this not a mild form of deceit and exploitation? We argue that research activism brings about greater awareness of the issues and concerns of people going about their daily lives. The real danger of codes of ethics lies in their potential to silence those voices that do not fit with the current dominant view of ethical research standards and behaviour. If we are complicit in this silencing, as researchers, we are behaving unethically. (p. 540)

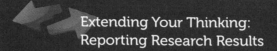

Extending Your Thinking: Reporting Research Results

1. Elijah Anderson (1990) conducted research in a run-down neighborhood of poor and working-class Blacks. In an article in *The Chronicle of Higher Education,* Anderson was described as feeling frustration at the way various groups interpret and use his work (Coughlin, 1994). The following passage appeared in the article:

> Lingering racism and lack of jobs, he insists repeatedly, almost like a mantra, are at the root of the ghetto's chaos and despair.
>
> So it is a particular frustration to Mr. Anderson that conservative pundits and others have seized on his work, reading it as evidence for the necessity of cracking down on crime and reforming the welfare system. . . ."Conservatives, liberals, whoever, pick pieces of it to make their points," he [Anderson] says. "My job is to describe and represent and analyze in such a way that people who have no experience in that setting can learn something." (p. A9)

Critically analyze Anderson's description of the role of the researcher in terms of representation, interpretation, and utilization of research.

2. McGee-Brown (1994) addresses the need to bring researchers and practitioners closer together in the following comments:

> Once educators are directly involved in the research process, then natural interactive discourse among educational researchers in higher education and public school will take place. We will not have to try to discover formats through which voices of all participants emerge, nor will we have to structure presentation formats which encourage interaction. Educational researchers who participate in AERA are hungry for discourse. Teachers are no less hungry for that dialogue in research which will make the culture of schooling not only more effective for student learning, but more tolerable as a culture for them and their students. The stress of multiple competing responsibilities among teachers is at a peak. Can we ask them to take on yet another one, research, without providing them the resources and knowledge they need to accomplish it? Can we afford to continue to exclude them from the discourse by suggesting that they share their own research among themselves in journals and meetings where they talk to each other as we talk to each other through our professional channels? It is time for the two discourses to meet. (p. 5)

What kinds of changes are necessary to bring about a true discourse between researchers and practitioners? McGee-Brown's comments were made within the context of educational research. What are the parallel issues for researchers in psychology? What can be done to make research more "usable" for practitioners? What responsibility do researchers have for interacting with the people who will be affected by the research results?

Questions for Critically Analyzing Data Analysis and Interpretation

Quantitative Research

The reader is referred to the general statistical texts referenced at the beginning of this chapter for further explanations of the statistical terms and concepts used in these questions.

1. What types of statistical analysis were used? Were they appropriate to the level of measurement, hypotheses, and the design of the study? What alpha level was used to determine statistical significance?

2. Is there statistical significance? What was the effect size?

3. Does the researcher interpret significance tests correctly (i.e., avoid saying the results were highly significant or approached significance)?[8]

4. When the sample size is small and the effect size large, are the results underinterpreted? Or if the sample size is large and effect size modest, are the results overinterpreted?

5. Are many univariate tests of significance used when a multivariate test would be more appropriate?

6. Are basic assumptions for parametric, inferential statistics met (i.e., normal distribution, level of measurement, and randomization)?

Qualitative Research

1. Did regularities emerge from the data such that addition of new information would not change the results?

2. Was there corroboration between the reported results and people's perceptions? Was triangulation used? Were differences of opinions made explicit?

3. Was an audit used to determine the fairness of the research process and the accuracy of the product in terms of internal coherence and support by data?

4. Was peer debriefing used? Outside referees? Negative case analysis? Member checks?

5. Is the report long and rambling, thus making the findings unclear to the reader?

6. Was the correct conclusion missed by premature closure, resulting in superficial or wrong interpretations?

7. Did the researcher provide sufficient description?

Interpretation Issues

1. How do you account for the results? What are the competing explanations and how did the authors deal with them? What competing explanations can you think of other than those the author discussed?

2. How would the results be influenced if applied to different types of people (e.g., rural or urban)?

3. What were the processes that caused the outcomes?

4. What conclusions and interpretations are made? Are they appropriate to the sample, type of study, duration of the study, and findings? Does the author over- or undergeneralize the results?

5. Is enough information given so that an independent researcher could replicate the study?

6. Does the researcher relate the results to the hypotheses, objectives, and other literature?

7. Does the researcher overconclude? Are the conclusions supported by the results?

8. What extraneous variables might have affected the outcomes of this study? Does the author mention them? What were the controls? Were they sufficient?

9. Did the author acknowledge the limitations of the study?

Extending Your Thinking: Critically Analyzing Data Analysis and Interpretation

1. Answer the questions for critically analyzing data analysis and interpretation in quantitative research for a study that you identified in your literature search.

2. What is the basis for judging the quality of data analysis and interpretation in qualitative research?

3. Answer the questions for critically analyzing data analysis and interpretation in qualitative research for a study that you identified in your literature search.

Summary of Chapter 13: Data Analysis, Interpretation, and Use

Data analysis strategies for quantitative data are generally statistical in nature and the choice of the appropriate statistic is based on the purpose of the research, the design of the study, and the characteristics of the data themselves. Qualitative data analysis can be started even before the interview or observation notes are collected. Researchers can begin writing their thoughts and feelings in a journaling format and use that as part of the data analysis. Qualitative data generally consist of words, but can also include visual items such as artifacts, video, and pictures. Interpretation of both types of data requires sensitivity to cultural issues. Strategies for use of research findings range from publication in scholarly formats (including dissertations or theses) to serving as a basis for social action.

Notes

1. More complex correlational statistics are explained in Chapter 5 as part of the causal comparative and correlational approaches to research.

2. The experimental study summarized in Sample Study 1.1 also used a hierarchical linear regression statistical analysis. This allowed Borman et al. (2007) to test the effects of both school-level and student-level effects. This approach used school-level pretest scores as a covariate before achievement scores were compared.

3. It should be noted that the choice of an analytic strategy is not without controversy. Carver (1992) and Shaver (1992) contend that researchers who cannot satisfy the assumptions for parametric statistics must use alternative analytic strategies. In practice, many researchers assume that the parametric statistics are robust—that is, the assumptions can be violated without serious consequences.

4. Wang et al. (2008) provide several pages of formulas to calculate effect sizes that are used when the study has a small sample or when the size of samples varies greatly from study to study. I reserve the use of the term paradigm for one's overarching view of the world, including one's philosophical assumptions about the nature and truth of knowledge.

6. J. C. Greene (2007) discusses various strategies for importing data of one type into a software program of another type to enable the researcher to conduct analyses that include both types of data. Bazeley (2006) describes software programs that allow for data importation of qualitative or quantitative data to facilitate this type of analysis. Greene (2007) also mentions data conversion (i.e., qualitative data is converted to numbers) as another data analytic strategy used in mixed methods research.

7. The Center for Creativity in Education and Cultural Heritage is directed by Dr. Simon Lichman, 20 Koreh HaDorot, Jerusalem, 93387.

8. Items 3 through 6 were adapted from B. Thompson (1988).

Appendix

Writing the Research Proposal

Getting the Research Idea

Many students reading this document will already have some idea of what they want to study for their research. However, several sources of research ideas (for students who are still searching for the right topic) include your personal experience, reading in the professional literature, discussions with professors or students, and current issues in your field.

Research Concept Paper

Before proceeding with a full proposal, you should start with a research concept paper that is used for discussion purposes with the professor. This provides a basis for further development of the proposal itself. The purpose is to describe the research idea, present a brief commentary on the literature, and propose an appropriate methodology to conduct the inquiry.

Formal Research Proposal

The formal research proposal is begun after the professor approves the research concept or topic. Typically, the formal research proposal is written in the future tense and includes the specific information that will form the basis of the first three chapters of your dissertation.

Educational and psychological researchers are engaged in a paradigm debate that influences decisions about approaches to research. A paradigm is a worldview that includes certain philosophical assumptions about the nature of ethics, reality, knowledge, and systematic inquiry (i.e., axiology, ontology, epistemology, and methodology). The four major paradigms that are currently being discussed in the research community include postpositivism, constructivism, transformative, and pragmatic. The assumptions associated with these paradigms are discussed in Chapter 1. As is made clear throughout this text, a researcher's paradigmatic stance has implications for choices of method. For example, postpositivism typically employs a preordinate, quantitative design, which means that the researcher establishes the research questions prior to data collection (research questions are "preordained").

The constructivist paradigm is typically associated with qualitative research designs that are described as contextual, inclusive, involved, and emergent. In the constructivist paradigm, an emergent, qualitative design means that the research questions are allowed to emerge from the data as the study progresses.

The transformative paradigm represents a third worldview that explicitly addresses the issues of oppression, power, and politics in research. Feminists, ethnic minorities, and persons with disabilities are among those who have written about the philosophical assumptions and methodological implications of this paradigm. Methodologically, this paradigm leads to decisions about method based on an understanding of cultural norms and power issues. Mixed methods designs are often used by researchers whose belief systems align with this paradigm.

The pragmatic paradigm serves as the philosophical basis for mixed methods designs that place primary focus on allowing the nature of the research questions to drive decisions about methods. Researchers who hold that some research questions are better answered by quantitative, qualitative, or both types of data tend to align themselves with the pragmatic paradigm.

It is beyond the scope of these guidelines to explore the underlying axioms of each paradigm; however, researchers should be familiar with the paradigm debate, read and reflect on this topic, and establish their own worldview as it affects their research activities.

The researcher's worldview influences the nature of the research questions and proposed methodology. These three elements (i.e., worldview, research questions, and proposed methodology) place you in one of the major research paradigms discussed in the professional literature concerning the researcher's philosophical orientation. Currently, the postpositivist paradigm is most closely associated with quantitative methods and the constructivist paradigm is associated with qualitative methods. In the transformative paradigm, scholars generally include qualitative methods; often, they also include the use of quantitative methods. Pragmatic researchers commonly used mixed methods designs. You should not confuse paradigm with method. You may choose to use a design that mixes both quantitative and qualitative data collection; however, the study will reflect one philosophical orientation by the philosophical assumptions that guide the research.

You should place yourself within one of the major paradigms for your research based on the correspondence with your worldview and the assumptions associated with each paradigm. The suggestions that follow describe the three chapters that make up the proposal (i.e., problem statement, literature review, and methodology).

Proposal Considerations

Chapter 1: Problem Statement

A. Area of Study. This provides a general introduction to the area of study. It briefly outlines the problem to be investigated, the purpose of the study, and significance of the problem and the justification for investigating it. If you are proposing to use qualitative methods, you should recognize the evolving nature of the problem statement and acknowledge that this is just a beginning point for the study.

B. *Definition of Terms.* Important terms and concepts should be defined. If you are proposing a qualitative study, initial definitions for important terms and concepts should be included, while recognizing that these will change as the study proceeds.

C. *Paradigm and Assumptions.* You should discuss your choice of the paradigm for the proposed study and explain the philosophical assumptions that make that paradigm choice appropriate.

Chapter 2: Literature Review

A. *History.* Chapter 2 in the proposal provides a review of the historical background and the theory relevant to the major questions of the research.

B. *Current Literature.* A review of current relevant literature should be included. To exhibit adequate mastery of the literature, both supporting and opposing views should be presented. Emphasis should be placed on critically analyzing the strengths and weaknesses of previous research.

C. *Research Problem.* The literature review should build to the description of the research problem described in Chapter 3 of this text and the research questions described in Chapter 3 of the dissertation. If you are proposing qualitative research, acknowledge that the study may uncover other areas of literature that will need to be explored as the study progresses.

Chapter 3: Methodology

A. *Research Questions and Hypothesis.* For quantitative research, you should present major and minor research questions that emanate from the literature review. These questions should be translated into researchable hypotheses when the design requires the use of such. For qualitative research, you should present the initial questions and objectives that will focus the study. A qualitative study usually focuses on a specific phenomenon (e.g., rules for classroom interaction) that emanates from the inadequacies of current theory and research. The precise nature of the questions to be researched evolves in the process of collecting and analyzing data. The initial questions may be vague, but stating the questions is important because they frame the procedures for collecting and analyzing data. The questions should follow from the theoretical and research background and should guide the design of the study. If mixed methods are proposed, then the researcher should clearly indicate the questions associated with quantitative, qualitative, or both types of data.

B. *Research Design.* The research design should be described. Many available references discuss research design; therefore, that information will not be repeated here. For quantitative research, you may conduct research using a variety of approaches, such as experimental, survey, and comparative data analysis. Basic assumptions of the selected designs must be addressed. If you are using an experimental or quasi-experimental design, inclusion of a schematic drawing of the design is appropriate. For qualitative research, many different design options are available to a student who works in the emergent, qualitative tradition. You should describe the design that will be used, such as ethnography or phenomenology. This will communicate to the reader whether the emphasis will be on cultural issues or individual, subjective experiences. You should present a rationale for the design of choice in terms of the research problems identified. For mixed methods, the design options are presented in Chapter 10 of this text. You should justify your choice of the mixed methods design and support your arguments with a rationale for the contribution of using a mixed methods design to the quality of the study.

C. *Sample.* For quantitative research, you should describe the general characteristics of the population from which data will be collected. In addition, the sampling technique must be fully described, as well as the rationale for the method used for selecting the sample. Choice of sample size should be defended. For qualitative research, you should discuss the criteria for the selection of the participants and the setting of the study. Qualitative studies typically occur in natural settings and all individuals in the settings are considered as participants. You should describe the method that will be used to identify those participants who will serve as a subsample to provide in-depth information. For mixed methods design, explain clearly both the quantitative and qualitative sampling strategies and provide a justification for each.

   All research involving human beings, no matter where those people are located (on or off campus), must be reviewed by the university's institutional review board (IRB). This is necessary prior to conducting any research. (Even research that will ultimately be ruled exempt from IRB approval must be reviewed by an IRB.) The current members of the board and procedures for submitting a research proposal are generally available from the institution's/university's Web site. Approval for the study should occur after the proposal is accepted by the committee and before beginning to collect any data.

D. *Measures.* For quantitative research, you should describe the variables that will be measured and delineate how they will be operationalized. You must address the issues of reliability and validity in measurement. In many studies, pilot testing of the instrument and procedures is necessary. For qualitative research, the researcher is the data collection instrument in the collection of much of the data. Therefore, the researchers must describe themselves in terms of closeness to the topic, values, and the like. In mixed methods studies, follow the recommendations for both quantitative and qualitative instrumentation.

E. *Data Collection Procedures.* For quantitative research, you should describe the procedures by which the data will be collected (e.g., survey, test, observation, etc.; administered by mail, researcher, collaborating teacher, etc.). For qualitative research, you should describe the design for the data collection, including a clear description of the procedures that will be used. The researcher's role should be described in terms of the degree of participation in which the researcher will engage. Supplemental methods of data collection, such as videotapes, audiotapes, diary notes, or journal entries should be described. The time period for data collection should be identified. You should acknowledge that data collection and analysis overlap in qualitative studies and should reflect on possible changes in the type of data or the focus, time, or strategies used in the study. You should address the qualitative parallels to reliability and validity in measurement as they are explicated in the literature, including credibility, transferability, dependability, and confirmability, and describe the methodological strategies that will be used to ensure that high-quality data are collected. Mixed methods studies should address both the quantitative and qualitative data collection strategies and support their choice based on a rationale for using mixed methods in the study.

F. *Pilot Testing*. In many studies, pilot testing of the instrument and procedures is necessary. This is especially important in qualitative studies, because pilot studies are often necessary in qualitative studies to help provide a framework and research questions. You should describe the pilot study procedures and results as well as insights from the pilot study that will affect the research itself.

G. *Data Analysis Procedures*. For quantitative research, the data analysis section should describe how you plan to handle the data in terms of processing of data, data coding and entry, and accuracy checks. In addition, you should provide information on which statistical procedures will be used for each research question. For qualitative research, data analysis strategies should be described. If triangulation is planned, you should explain the multiple sources of data and the conditions under which corroboration of evidence will be sought. Mixed methods studies should explain how the two types of data will be integrated.

H. *Limitations of the Study*. Anticipated limitations of the study should be explained. For example, limitations may arise because of the nature of the available sample or instruments. You should explore the limitations and any strategies that will be used to minimize their impact. Implications for conducting and generalizing the study should be discussed.

I. *Timelines*. You should include a proposed timeline that clearly depicts the approximate time in which each research activity will be completed (e.g., instrument selected or developed, pilot test conducted, etc.).

Recommended Proposal Document Format

Sequencing Layout of Proposal

Title page

Abstract

Table of contents

List of tables (if any)

List of illustrations (if any)

Chapter 1: Statement of the problem

Chapter 2: Review of the literature

Chapter 3: Methodology

Appendixes

References

References

Aaron, P. G., Malatesha Joshi, R., Gooden, R., & Bentum, K. E. (2008). Diagnosis and treatment of reading disabilities based on the component model of reading: An alternative to the discrepancy model of LD. *The Journal of Learning Disabilities, 41*(1), 67–84.

Abedi, J., Leon, S., & Kao, J. C. (2008). *Examining differential item functioning in reading assessments with students with disabilities.* Los Angeles, CA: National Center for Research on Evaluation, Standards, and Student Testing.

Abernathy, D. (2003). *Partners to history: Martin Luther King, Jr., Ralph David Abernathy, and the civil rights movement.* New York: Crown.

Abma, T. A. (2006). The practice and politics of responsive evaluation. *American Journal of Evaluation, 27,* 31–43.

Abrahams, P. (2001). *The Black experience in the 20th century.* Bloomington: Indiana University Press.

Achenbach, T. M. (1991). *Manual for the Child Behavior Checklist: 4–18 and 1991 profile.* Burlington: University of Vermont, Department of Psychiatry.

Ægisdóttir, S., Gerstein, L. H., Çinarbaş, C. D. (2008). Methodological issues in cross-cultural counseling research: Equivalence, bias and translations. *The Counseling Psychologist, 36,* 188–219.

Agar, M. H. (1996). *Language shock: Understanding the culture of conversation.* New York: HarperCollins.

Airasian, P. W., & Gay, L. R. (2003). *Educational research: Competencies for analysis and application* (7th ed.). Upper Saddle River, NJ: Prentice Hall.

Alcoff, L., & Potter, E. (1993). Introduction: When feminisms intersect epistemology. In L. Alcoff & E. Potter (Eds.), *Feminist epistemologies* (pp. 1–14). New York: Routledge.

Alkin, M. C. (Ed.). (2004). *Evaluation roots: Tracing theorists' views and influences.* Thousand Oaks, CA: Sage.

Alkin, M. C. (2007, November). *Evaluation roots revisited.* Presentation at the annual meeting of the American Evaluation Association, Baltimore, MD.

Altschuld, J., & Witkin, B. R. (2000). *From needs assessment to action: Transforming needs into solution strategies.* Thousand Oaks, CA: Sage.

American Anthropological Association. (1998, May 17). *AAA statement on "race."* Retrieved October 29, 2003, from http://www.aaanet.org/stmts/racepp.htm

American Association for Public Opinion Research. (2008). *Standard definitions: Final dispositions of case codes and outcome rates for surveys* (5th ed.). Lenexa, KS: Author.

American Association for Public Opinion Research. (2008). *Standards and best practices.* Available online at http://www.aapor.org/bestpractices

American Association for the Advancement of Science. (1989). *Science for all Americans.* New York: Oxford University Press.

American Council of Learned Societies (Ed.). (1927–1994). *Dictionary of American biography* (Vols. 1–20, Suppl. 1–7, & Index Guide). New York: Scribner.

American Educational Research Association. (2003). *Resolution on the essential elements of scientifically-based research.* Retrieved September 24, 2008, from http://www.eval.org/doeaera.htm

American Educational Research Association. (2004). *Publishing educational research: Guidelines and tips.* Available online at http://aera.net/uploadedFiles/Journals_and_Publications/Journals/pubtip.pdf

American Educational Research Association, American Psychological Association, & National Council on Measurement in Education. (1999). *Standards for educational and psychological testing.* Washington, DC: American Educational Research Association.

American Evaluation Association. (2003). Response to U. S. Department of Education Notice of proposed priority, *Federal Register* RIN 1890-ZA00, November 4, 2003. "Scientifically Based Evaluation Methods" http://www.eval.org/doestatement.htm Accessed June 18, 2009.

American Evaluation Association. (2004). *Guiding principles for evaluators.* Retrieved April 30, 2009, from http://www.eval.org/Publications/GuidingPrinciples.asp

American Historical Association. (2005). *Statement on standards of professional conduct.* Washington, DC: Author.

American Psychiatric Association Task Force on Research Ethics. (2006). Ethical principles and practices for research involving human participants with mental illness. *Psychiatric Services, 57,* 552–557. (DOI: 10.1176/appi.ps.57.4.552)

American Psychological Association. (2001). *Publication manual of the American Psychological Association* (5th ed.). Washington, DC: Author.

American Psychological Association. (2002). *Ethical principles of psychologists and code of conduct.* Washington, DC: Author. Retrieved April 30, 2009, from http://www.apa.org/ethics/code2002.html

American Psychological Association Joint Task Force of Divisions 17 and 45. (2002). *Guidelines on multicultural education, training, research, practice, and organizational change for psychologists.* Washington, DC: Author.

Ancheta, A. N. (2006). Civil rights, education research, and the courts. *Educational Researcher,* 35, 26–29.

Anderman, G., & Rogers, M. (Eds.). (2003). *Translation today: Trends and perspectives.* Buffalo, NY: Multilingual Matters.

Anderson, B. T. (1993). Minority females in the science pipeline: Activities to enhance readiness, recruitment, and retention. *Initiatives, 55*(3), 31–38.

Anderson, E. (1990). *Streetwise: Race, class, and change in an urban community.* Chicago: University of Chicago Press.

Anderson, L. (2006). Analytic autoethnography. *Journal of Contemporary Ethnography, 35*(4), 373–395.

Anderson, M. L. (1993). Studying across differences: Race, class, and gender in qualitative research. In J. H. Stanfield & R. M. Dennis (Eds.), *Race and ethnicity in research methods* (pp. 39–52). Newbury Park, CA: Sage.

Anyon, J. (2005). *Radical possibilities: Public policy, urban education, and a new social movement.* New York: Routledge Falmer.

Arthur, J., & Phillips, R. (Eds.). (2000). *Issues in history teaching.* London: Routledge.

Asher, S. R., Singleton, L. C., Tinsley, B. R., & Hymel, S. (1979). A reliable socio-metric measure for preschool children. *Developmental Psychology, 15,* 443–444.

Aspinwall, L. G., & Staudinger, U. M. (2003). *A psychology of human strengths: Fundamental questions and future directions for a positive psychology.* Washington, DC: American Psychological Association.

Atkinson, P., & Hammersley, M. (1994). Ethnography and participant observation. In N. K. Denzin & Y. S. Lincoln (Eds.), *Handbook of qualitative research* (pp. 248–261). Thousand Oaks, CA: Sage.

Au, W. (2007). High-stakes testing and curricular control: A qualitative metasynthesis. *Educational Researcher, 36*(5), 258–267.

Baez, B. (2002). Confidentiality in qualitative research: Reflections on secrets, power and agency. *Qualitative Research, 2*(1), 35–58.

Bailey, D. B., Jr., Bruder, M. B., Hebbeler, K., Carta, J., Defosset, M., Greenwood, C., et al. (2006). Recommended outcomes for families of young children with disabilities. *Journal of Early Intervention, 28,* 227–251.

Bair, B. (2007, October). Research repositories in Washington, D. C. *Perspectives.* Retrieved April 19, 2009, from http://www.historians.org/perspectives/issues/2007/0710/0710ann5.cfm

Baker, E. L. (2007). 2007 Presidential address: The end(s) of testing. *Educational Researcher, 36,* 309–317.

Balch, G., & Mertens, D. M. (1999). Focus group design and group dynamics: Lessons from deaf and hard of hearing participants. *American Journal of Evaluation, 20*(2), 265–277.

Ball, A. (Ed.). (2006). *With more deliberate speed: Achieving equity and excellence in education.* (NSSE 2006 Yearbook: National Society for the Study of Education.) Malden, MA: Blackwell.

Bamberger, M., Rugh, J., & Mabry, L. (2006). *Real World Evaluation.* Thousand Oaks, CA: Sage.

Banks, J. A. (1995). Multicultural education: Historical development, dimensions, and practice. In J. A. Banks & C. A. McGee-Banks (Eds.), *Handbook of research on multicultural education* (pp. 3–24). New York: Macmillan.

Banks, J. A. (2000). The social construction of difference and the quest for educational equality. In R. S. Bradt (Ed.), *Education in a new era* (pp. 21–45). Alexandria, VA: Association for Supervision and Curriculum Development.

Banks, J. A. (2008). Diversity, group identity, and citizenship education in a global age. *Educational Researcher, 37,* 129–139. (DOI: 10.3102/0013189X08317501)

Banks, J. A., & McGee-Banks, C. A. (Eds.). (2003). *Handbook of research on multicultural education* (2nd ed.). San Francisco: Jossey-Bass.

Barnett, D. W., Daly, E. J., III, Jones, K. M., & Lentz, F. E., Jr. (2004). Response to intervention: Empirically based special service decisions from single-case designs of increasing and decreasing intensity. *The Journal of Special Education, 38,* 66–79.

Bartram, D., & Hambleton, R. (Eds.). (2005). *Computer-based testing and the Internet: Issues and advances.* St. Paul, MN: Assessment Systems Corporation.

Barzun, J., & Graff, H. F. (2003). *The modern researcher* (6th ed.). Boston: Houghton Mifflin.

Bassett, R., Beagan, B. L., Ristovski-Slijepcevic, S., & Chapman, G. E. (2008). Tough teens: The methodological challenges of interviewing teenagers as research participants. *Journal of Adolescent Research, 23,* 119–131.

Batsche, G., Elliot, J., Graden, J. L., Grimes, J., Kovaleski, J. F., Prasse, D., et al. (2005). *Response to intervention: Policy considerations and implementation.* Alexandria, VA: National Association of State Directors of Special Education.

Battiste, M. (Ed.). (2000). *Reclaiming indigenous voice and vision.* Vancouver: University of British Columbia Press.

Bazeley, P. (2006). The contribution of computer software to integrating qualitative and quantitative data analyses. *Research in the Schools, 13*(1), 64–74.

Beddow, P., Kettler, R. J. & Elliott, S. N. (2008). Test accessibility and modification inventory. http://peabody.vanderbilt.edu/tami.xml. Accessed June 18, 2009.

Beebe, T. J., Davern, M. E., McAlpine, D. D., Call, K. T., & Rockwood, T. H. (2005). Increasing response rates in a survey of Medicaid enrollees: The effect of a prepaid monetary incentive and mixed-modes (mail and telephone). *Medical Care, 43,* 411–414.

Begg, C. B. (1994). Publication bias. In H. M. Cooper & L. V. Hedges (Eds.), *The handbook of research synthesis* (pp. 399–410). New York: Russell Sage.

Beins, B. (1993, Fall). Examples of spuriousness. *Teaching Methods, 2,* 3.

Berberich, D. A. (1998). Posttraumatic stress disorder: Gender and cross-cultural clinical issues. *Psychotherapy in Private Practice, 17,* 29–41.

Berliner, B., Barrat, V. X., Fong, A. B., & Shirk, P. B. (2008). *Reenrollment of high school dropouts in a large, urban school district.* (Issues & Answers Report, REL 2008–N0.056). Washington, DC: U.S. Department of Education, Institute of Education Sciences, National Center for Education Evaluation and Regional Assistance, Regional Educational Laboratory West. Retrieved January 29, 2009, from http://ies.ed.gov/ncee/edlabs.

Bernard, L. C., Mills, M., Swenson, L., & Walsh, R. P. (2008). Measuring motivation multidimensionally: Development of the assessment of individual motives—questionnaire (AIM-Q). *Assessment, 15,* 16–35.

Betts, J., Pickart, M., & Heistad, D. (2009). Construct and predictive validity evidence for curriculum-based measures of early literacy and numeracy skills in kindergarten. *Journal of Psychoeducational Assessment, 27,* 83–95.

Beverley, J. (2005). Testimonio, subalternity, and narrative authority. In N. K. Denzin & Y. S. Lincoln (Eds.), *The SAGE handbook of qualitative research* (3rd ed., pp. 547–558). Thousand Oaks, CA: Sage.

Bhattacharya, K. (2007). Consenting to the consent form: What are the fixed and fluid understandings between the researcher and the researched? *Qualitative Inquiry, 13,* 1095–1115.

Bickman, L. (1999). Practice makes perfect and other myths about mental health services. *American Psychologist, 54*(11), 965–978.

Bickman, L., Lambert, E. W., Andrade, A. R., & Penaloza, R. V. (2000). The Fort Bragg continuum of care for children and adolescents: Mental health outcomes over 5 years. *Journal of Consulting and Clinical Psychology, 68*(4), 710–716.

Bickman, L., Lambert, E. W., Karver, M. S., & Andrade, A. R. (1998). Two low-cost measures of child and adolescent functioning for services research. *Evaluation and Program Planning, 21,* 263–275.

Billingsley, B. S. (2004). Special education teacher retention and attrition: A critical analysis of the research literature. *Journal of Special Education, 38,* 39–55.

Bingley, A. F., Thomas, C., Brown, J., Reeve, J., & Payne, S. (2008). Developing narrative research in supportive and palliative care: The focus on illness narratives. *Palliative Medicine, 22,* 653–658.

Birks, M., Chapman, Y., & Francis, K. (2008). Memoing in qualitative research: Probing data and processes. *Journal of Research in Nursing, 13,* 68–75.

Bisol, C. A., Sperb, T. M., & Moreno-Black, G. (2008). Focus groups with deaf and hearing youths in Brazil: Improving a questionnaire on sexual behavior and HIV/AIDS. *Qualitative Health Research, 18,* 565–578.

Black, P. A., & Glickman, N. S. (2006) Demographics, psychiatric diagnoses, and other characteristics of North American deaf and hard-of-hearing inpatients. *Journal of Deaf Studies and Deaf Education, 11*(3), 303–321.

Blackorby, J., Knokey, A. M., Wagner, M., Levine, P., Schiller, E., & Sumi, C. (2007). What makes a difference? Influences on outcomes for students with disabilities. Washington, DC: U.S. Department of Education, Office of Special Education Programs (Contract Number ED-00-CO-0017).

Blanchett, W. J. (2006). Disproportionate representation of African American students in special education: Acknowledging the role of White privilege and racism. *Educational Researcher, 35,* 24–28.

Bledsoe, K. (2008, November). *Transformative mixed methods.* Presentation at the 2008 annual meeting of the American Evaluation Association, Denver, CO.

Bledsoe, K., & Graham, J. A. (2005). Using multiple evaluation approaches in program evaluation. *American Journal of Evaluation, 26*(3), 302–319.

Bloch, M. (2004). A discourse that disciplines, governs, and regulates: The National Research Council's report on scientific research in education [Electronic version]. *Qualitative Inquiry, 10,* 96–110. (DOI: 10.1177/1077800403259482)

Blum, L. (2008). White privilege: A mild critique. *Theory and Research in Education, 6*(3), 309–321. (DOI: 10.1177/1477878508095586)

Bock, M. A. (2007). A social-behavioral learning strategy intervention for a child with Asperger syndrome: Brief report. *Remedial and Special Education, 28,* 258–265.

Bogdan, R. C., & Biklen, S. K. (2003). *Qualitative research for education* (4th ed.). Boston: Allyn & Bacon.

Boote, D. N., & Beile, P. (2005, August/September). Scholars before researchers: On the centrality of the dissertation literature review in research preparation. *Educational Researcher, 34*(6), 3–15.

Borg, W. R., & Gall, M. D. (1989). *Educational research.* White Plains, NY: Longman.

Borman, G. D., Slavin, R. E., Cheung, A., Chamberlain, A. M., Madden, N. A., & Chambers, B. (2005). Success for All: First-year results from the national randomized field trial. *Educational Evaluation and Policy Analysis, 27,* 1–22.

Borman, G. D., Slavin, R. E., Cheung, A. C. K., Chamberlain, A. M., Madden, N. A., & Chambers, B. (2007). Final reading outcomes of the national randomized field trial of Success for All. *American Educational Research Journal, 44,* 701–731.

Borsboom, D. (2005). *Measuring the mind: Conceptual issues in contemporary psychometrics*. Cambridge, UK: Cambridge University Press.

Borum, V. (2006). Reading and writing Womanist poetic prose: African American mothers with deaf daughters. *Qualitative Inquiry, 12,* 340–352.

Bowker, A. (1993). *Sisters in the blood*. Newton, MA: Women's Educational Equity Act Equity Resource Center.

Boykin, L. L. (1950). Differentials in Negro education. *Journal of Educational Research, 43*(7), 533–540.

Brabeck, M. (2000). *Practicing feminist ethics in psychology*. Washington, DC: American Psychological Association.

Brabeck, M. M., & Brabeck, K. M. (2009). Feminist perspectives on research ethics. In D. M. Mertens & P. E. Ginsberg (Eds.), *Handbook of social research ethics* (pp. 39–53). Thousand Oaks, CA: Sage.

Bracht, H. G., & Glass, V. G. (1968). The external validity of experiments. *Journal of the American Educational Research Association, 5*(4), 437–474.

Brady, I. (2005). Poetics for a planet: Discourse on some problems of being-in-place. In N. K. Denzin & Y. S. Lincoln (Eds.), *The SAGE handbook of qualitative research* (3rd ed., pp. 979–1026). Thousand Oaks, CA: Sage.

Brainard, J. (2003, October 21). Federal agency says oral history is not subject to rules on human research volunteers. *The Chronicle of Higher Education*. Retrieved October 21, 2003, from http://chronicle.com/daily/2003/10/2003102101n.htm

Braverman, M. T. (1996). Sources of survey error: Implications for evaluation studies. In M. T. Braverman & J. K. Slater (Eds.), *Advances in survey research* (New Directions for Program Evaluation, No. 70, pp. 17–28). San Francisco: Jossey-Bass.

Bravo, M. (2001). Instrument development: Cultural adaptations for ethnic minority research. In J. G. Ponterotto, J. M. Casas, L. A. Suzuki, & C. M. Alexander (Eds.), *Handbook of multicultural counseling* (2nd ed., pp. 220–236). Thousand Oaks, CA: Sage.

Bravo, M. (2003). Instrument development: Cultural adaptations for ethnic minority research. In G. Bernal, J. E. Trimble, A. K. Burlew, & F. T. L. Leong (Eds.), *Handbook of racial & ethnic minority psychology* (pp. 220–236). Thousand Oaks, CA: Sage.

Breaugh, J. A., & Arnold, J. (2007). Controlling nuisance variables by using a matched-groups design. *Organizational Research Methods, 10*(3), 523–541. (DOI: 10.1177/1094428106292895)

Breisach, E. (2003). *On the future of history: The postmodernist challenge and its aftermath*. Chicago: University of Chicago Press.

Brennan, R. L. (Ed.). (2006). *Educational measurement* (4th ed.). Westport, CT: National Council on Measurement in Education and American Council on Education.

Brigance, A. (1999). *Comprehensive Inventory of Basic Skills-Revised*. North Billerica, MA: Curriculum Associates.

Brinkerhoff, R. O., Brethower, D. M., Hluchyji, T., & Nowakowski, J. R. (1983). *Program evaluation*. Hingham, MA: Kluwer Boston.

Broad, K. L., & Joos, K. E. (2004). Online inquiry of public selves: Methodological considerations. *Qualitative Inquiry, 10,* 923–946.

Brossart, D. F., Parker, R. I., Olson, E. A., & Mahadevan, L. (2006). The relationship between visual analysis and five statistical analyses in a simple AB single-case research design. *Behavior Modification, 30,* 531–563.

Brown, A. (1944). An evaluation of the accredited secondary schools for Negroes in the South. *Journal of Negro Education, 13*(4), 488–498.

Brown, J. H., D'Emidio-Caston, M., & Benard, B. (2001). *Resilience education*. Thousand Oaks, CA: Corwin.

Brown, W. H., Favazza, P. C., & Odom, S. L. (1995). *Code for Active Student Participation and Engagement Revised (CASPER II): A training manual for observers*. Unpublished observer training manual, Vanderbilt University, Early Childhood Research Institute on Inclusion.

Bruce, C. S. (2001). Interpreting the scope of their literature reviews: Significant differences in research students' concerns. *New Library World, 102*(4), 158–166.

Buch, E. D., & Staller, K. M. (2007). The feminist practice of ethnography. In S. N. Hesse-Biber & P. L. Leavy (Eds.), *Feminist research practice* (pp. 187–222). Thousand Oaks, CA: Sage.

Bullough, R., & Pinnegar, S. (2001). Guidelines for quality in autobiographical forms of self-study. *Educational Researcher, 30*(3), 13–22.

Burke, P. (2001). *New perspectives on historical writing* (2nd ed.). University Park: Pennsylvania State University Press.

Burnard, P. (2008). A phenomenological study of music teachers' approaches to inclusive education practices among disaffected youth. *Research Studies in Music Education, 30*(1), 59–75.

Burns, G. (1984). *Dr. Burns' prescription for happiness.* New York: Putnam.

Bursztyn, A. (2006). *Praeger handbook of special education.* Westport, CT: Greenwood.

Busk, P. L., & Marscuilo, L. A. (1992). Statistical analysis in single-case research: Issues, procedures, and recommendations, with applications to multiple behaviors. In T. R. Kratochill & J. R. Levin (Eds.), *Single-case research design and analysis* (pp. 159–182). Hillsdale, NJ: Lawrence Erlbaum.

Buss, F. (1985). *Dignity: Lower income women tell of their lives and struggles.* Ann Arbor: University of Michigan Press.

Butcher, J. E. (1989). Adolescent girls' sex role development: Relationship with sports participation, self-esteem, and age at menarche. *Sex Roles, 20*(9–10), 575–593.

Buyse, V. (1993). Friendships of preschoolers with disabilities in community settings. *Journal of Early Intervention, 17,* 380–395.

Caldwell, C. H., Guthrie, B. J., & Jackson, J. S. (2006). Identity development, discrimination, and psychological well-being among African American and Caribbean Black adolescents. In A. J. Schulz & L. Mullings (Eds.), *Gender, race, class & health: Intersectional approaches* (pp. 163–191). San Francisco: Jossey-Bass.

Campbell, D. T. (1975). Degrees of freedom and the case study. *Comparative Political Studies, 8,* 178–193.

Campbell, D. T., & Stanley, J. C. (1963). Experimental and quasi-experimental designs for research on teaching. In N. L. Gage (Ed.), *Handbook of research on teaching* (pp. 171–246). Chicago: Rand McNally.

Campbell, D. T., & Stanley, J. C. (1966). *Experimental and quasi-experimental designs for research.* Skokie, IL: Rand McNally.

Campbell, P. B. (1988). *Rethinking research: Challenges for new and not so new researchers.* Groton, CT: Author.

Campbell, P. B. (1989). *The hidden discriminator: Sex and race bias in educational research.* Newton, MA: Women's Educational Equity Act Equity Resource Center.

Canning, K. (1994, Winter). Feminist history after the linguistic turn: Historicizing discourse and experience. *Signs: Journal of Women in Culture and Society, 19*(2), 368–404.

Caplan, J. B., & Caplan, P. J. (2005). The perseverative search for sex differences in mathematics abilities. In A. M. Gallagher & J. C. Kaufman (Eds.), *Gender differences in mathematics: An integrative psychological approach.* Cambridge, UK: Cambridge University Press.

Carver, R. P. (1992, April). *The case against statistical significance testing, revisited.* Paper presented at the annual meeting of the American Educational Research Association, San Francisco.

Cave, M. (2008). Through hell and high water: New Orleans, August 29–September 15, 2005. *The Oral History Review, 35*(1), 1–10.

Center for Applied Special Technology (CAST). (2008). *Universal design for learning guidelines version 1.0.* Wakefield, MA: Author.

Chan, F., Lee, G. K., Lee, E., Kubota, C., & Allen, C. A. (2007). Structural equation modeling in rehabilitation counseling research. *Rehabilitation Counseling Bulletin, 51,* 44–57.

Chapman, T. K. (2007). Interrogating classroom relationships and events: Using portraiture and critical race theory in education research. *Educational Researcher, 36,* 156–162.

Charmaz, K. (2006). *Constructing grounded theory.* Thousand Oaks, CA: Sage.

Charmaz, K. (2007). Grounded theory. In G. Ritzer (Ed.), *Blackwell encyclopedia of sociology.* Oxford, UK: Blackwell.

Chartier, R. (1988). *Cultural history.* Ithaca, NY: Cornell University Press.

Chen, H. T. (1990a). Issues in constructing program theory. In L. Bickman (Ed.), *Advances in program theory* (New Directions for Evaluation, No. 47, pp. 7–18). San Francisco: Jossey-Bass.

Chen, H. T. (1990b). *Theory-driven evaluations*. Newbury Park, CA: Sage.
Chen, H. T. (1994). Current trends and future directions in program evaluation. *Evaluation Practice, 15*(3), 229–238.
Chen, H. T., & Rossi, P. H. (1992). *Using theory to improve program and policy evaluation*. Westport, CT: Greenwood.
The Chicago manual of style (15th ed.). (2003). Chicago: University of Chicago Press.
Chilisa, B. (2005). Educational research within postcolonial Africa: A critique of HIV/AIDS research in Botswana. *International Journal of Qualitative Studies in Education, 18,* 659–684.
Chilisa, B. (2009). Indigenous African-centered ethics: Contesting and complementing dominant models. In D. M. Mertens & P. E. Ginsberg (Eds.), *Handbook of social research ethics* (pp. 407–425). Thousand Oaks, CA: Sage.
Cho, J., & Trent, A. (2006). Validity in qualitative research revisited. *Qualitative Research, 6,* 319–340.
Christ, T. W. (2007). A recursive approach to mixed methods research in a longitudinal study of postsecondary education disability support services. *Journal of Mixed Methods Research, 1,* 226–241.
Christensen, H. P. (2004). Children's participation in ethnographic research: Issues of power and representation. *Children and Society, 18,* 165–176.
Christian, L. M., & Dillman, D. A. (2004). The influence of graphical and symbolic language manipulations on responses to self-administered questions. *Public Opinion Quarterly, 68*(1), 58–81.
Christians, C. G. (2005). Ethics and politics in qualitative research. In N. K. Denzin & Y. S. Lincoln (Eds.), *The SAGE handbook of qualitative research* (3rd ed., pp. 139–164). Thousand Oaks, CA: Sage.
Clegg, J. W., & Slife, B. D. (2009). Research ethics in the postmodern context. In D. M. Mertens & P. E. Ginsberg (Eds.), *The handbook of social research ethics* (pp. 23–38). Thousand Oaks, CA: Sage.
Cocks, A. (2008). Researching the lives of disabled children: The process of participant observation in seeking inclusivity. *Qualitative Social Work, 7,* 163–180.
Coghlan, A. T., Preskill, H., & Catsambas, T. T. (2003). An overview of appreciative inquiry in evaluation. In H. Preskill & A. T. Coghlan (Eds.), *Using appreciative inquiry in evaluation* (New Directions for Evaluation, No. 100, pp. 5–22). San Francisco: Jossey-Bass.
Cohen, C. (2006). *The Black youth project: The youth culture survey methodology report.* Chicago: University of Chicago, National Opinion Research Center.
Cohen, J. (1988). *Statistical power analysis for the behavioral sciences.* Hillsdale, NJ: Lawrence Erlbaum.
Cohen, J. (1992). A power primer. *Psychological Bulletin, 112*(1), 155–159.
Coll, C. G., Akerman, A., & Cicchetti, D. (2000). Cultural influences on developmental processes and outcomes: Implications for the study of development and psychopathology. *Development & Psychopathology, 12,* 333–356.
Collins, K. M. T., Onwuegbuzie, A. J., & Jiao, Q. G. (2007). A mixed methods investigation of mixed methods sampling designs in social and health science research. *Journal of Mixed Methods Research, 1,* 267–294. (DOI: 10.1177/1558689807299526)
Collins, P. H. (2000). *Black feminist thought: Knowledge, consciousness and the politics of empowerment.* New York: Routledge.
Comas-Diaz, L. (2000). An ethnopolitical approach to working with people of color. *American Psychologist, 55,* 1319–1325.
Conley, H., & Fink, L. (1992). *Using statistical sampling*. Washington, DC: U.S. General Accounting Office.
Conroy, M. A., Asmus, J. M., Sellers, J. A., & Ladwig, C. N. (2005). The use of an antecedent-based intervention to decrease stereotypic behavior in a general education classroom: A case study. *Focus on Autism Other Developmental Disabilities, 20,* 209–221.
Conroy, M. A., Stichter, J. P., Daunic, A., & Haydon, T. (2008). Classroom-based research in the field of emotional and behavioral disorders: Methodological issues and future research directions. *The Journal of Special Education, 41,* 209–222.
Constantinople, A. (2005). Masculinity-femininity: An exception to a famous dictum? *Feminism & Psychology, 15*(4), 385–407.

Converse, P. D., Wolfe, E. W., Huang, X., & Oswald, F. L. (2008). Response rates for mixed-mode surveys using mail and e-mail/Web. *American Journal of Evaluation, 29,* 99–107. (Originally published online Jan. 8, 2008)

Cook, C., Heath, F., & Thompson, R. (2000). A meta-analysis of response rates in Web or Internet-based surveys. *Educational and Psychological Measurement, 60,* 821–836.

Cook, T. D., & Campbell, D. T. (1979). *Quasi-experimentation: Design and analysis issues for field settings.* Chicago: Rand McNally.

Cooper, H. M. (1989). *Integrating research.* Newbury Park, CA: Sage.

Cooper, H. M., & Hedges, L. V. (1994). Potentials and limitations of research synthesis. In H. M. Cooper & L. V. Hedges (Eds.), *The handbook of research synthesis* (pp. 521–530). New York: Russell Sage.

Cooper, R. (2000). Preparing students of the new millennium. *Journal of Negro Education, 68*(1), 1–3.

Corbin, J., & Strauss, A. (2008). *Basics of qualitative research* (3rd ed.). Thousand Oaks, CA: Sage.

Coughlin, E. K. (1994, September 21). Mean streets are a scholar's lab. *The Chronicle of Higher Education,* pp. A8–A9, A14.

Coulter, D. L., Weins, J. R., & Fenstermacher, G. D. (Eds.). (2008). *Why do we educate? Renewing the conversation.* Malden, MA: Blackwell.

Council of National Psychological Associations for the Advancement of Ethnic Minority Interests. (2000). *Guidelines for research in ethnic minority communities, 2000.* Washington, DC: American Psychological Association. Retrieved May 26, 2004, from http://www.apa.org/pi/oema/guidelinesremc.pdf

Couper, M. P. (2005). Technology trends in survey data collection. *Social Science Computer Review, 23,* 486–501.

Cousins, J. B., & Earl, L. (Eds.). (1995). *Participatory evaluation in education.* London: Falmer.

Covert, R. W. (1977). *Guidelines and criteria for constructing questionnaires.* Unpublished manuscript, University of Virginia, Charlottesville.

Crabtree, C., & Nash, G. B. (1994). *National standards for history for grades K–4: Expanding children's world in time and space.* Los Angeles: University of California, National Center for History. (ERIC Document Reproduction Service No. ED375075)

Cram, F. (2009). Maintaining indigenous voices. In D. M. Mertens & P. E. Ginsberg (Eds.), *Handbook of social research ethics* (pp. 308–322). Thousand Oaks, CA: Sage.

Cram, F., Ormond, A., & Carter, L. (2004). *Researching our relations: Reflections on ethics and marginalization.* Paper presented at the Kamehameha Schools 2004 Research Conference on Hawaiian Well-being, Kea'au, HI. Retrieved September 15, 2006, from www.ksbe.edu/pase/pdf/KSResearchConference/2004presentations.

Creswell, J. W. (2003). *Research design* (2nd ed.). Thousand Oaks, CA: Sage.

Creswell, J. W. (2009). Research design: Qualitative, quantitative, and mixed methods approaches (3rd ed.). Thousand Oaks, CA: Sage.

Cronbach, L. J., Ambron, S. R., Dornbusch, S. M., Hess, R., Hornik, R. C., & Phillips, D. C., et al. (1980). *Toward reform of program evaluation.* San Francisco: Jossey-Bass.

Crotty, M. (1998). *The foundations of social research.* Thousand Oaks, CA: Sage.

Crowe, T. V. (2003). Using focus groups to create culturally appropriate HIV prevention material for the deaf community. *Qualitative Social Work, 2,* 289–308.

Dang, A., & Vianney, C. (2007). *Living in the margins: A national survey of lesbian, gay, bisexual and transgender Asian and Pacific Islander Americans.* New York: National Gay and Lesbian Task Force Policy Institute.

Darbyshire, P., MacDougall, C., & Schiller, W. (2005). Multiple methods in qualitative research with children: More insight or just more? *Qualitative Research, 5,* 417–436.

Davies, R. (2004). Scale, complexity and the representation of theories of change. *Evaluation, 10,* 101–121.

Dávila, N. G. (2001). *Escolios a un texto implicito.* Bogota, Colombia: Villegas Editores.

Davis, C. S., & Ellis, C. (2008). Performing as a moral act: Ethical dimensions of the ethnography of performance. *Text and Performance Quarterly, 5*(2), 1–13.

Davis, J. E. (1992). Reconsidering the use of race as an explanatory variable in program evaluation. In A. Madison (Ed.), *Minority issues in program evaluation* (New Directions for Evaluation, No. 53, pp. 55–68). San Francisco: Jossey-Bass.

de Leeuw, E. D. (2005). To mix or not to mix data collection modes in surveys. *Journal of Official Statistics, 21*(2), 233–255.

Delgado, R. (Ed.). (1995). *Critical race theory: The cutting edge*. Philadelphia: Temple University Press.

Delgado, R., & Stefancic, J. (2001). *Critical race theory: An introduction*. New York: New York University Press.

Delgado Bernal, D. (2002). Critical race theory, Latino critical theory, and critical raced-gendered epistemologies: Recognizing students of color as holders and creators of knowledge. *Qualitative Inquiry, 8,* 105–126.

Delk, L., & Weidekamp, L. (2001). *Shared Reading Project evaluation: Expanding to new settings, 1997–1999*. Sharing Results Series. Washington, DC: Gallaudet University, Laurent Clerc National Deaf Education Center.

D'Emilio, J. (2002). *The world turned: Essays on gay history, politics, and culture*. Durham, NC: Duke University Press.

Denscombe, M. (2008). The length of responses to open-ended questions: A comparison of online paper questionnaires in terms of a mode effect. *Social Science Computer Review, 26*(3), 359–368. (Originally published online Dec 10, 2007; DOI: 10.1177/0894439307309671)

Denzin, N. K. (2003). *Performance ethnography: Critical pedagogy and the politics of culture*. Thousand Oaks, CA: Sage.

Denzin, N. K., & Lincoln, Y. S. (1994). *Handbook of qualitative research*. Thousand Oaks, CA: Sage.

Denzin, N. K., & Lincoln, Y. S. (Eds.). (2000). *Handbook of qualitative research* (2nd ed.). Thousand Oaks, CA: Sage.

Denzin, N. K., & Lincoln, Y. S. (Eds.). (2005). *The SAGE handbook of qualitative research* (3rd ed.). Thousand Oaks, CA: Sage.

Denzin, N. K., Lincoln, Y. S., & Smith, L. (2008). *Handbook of postcolonial and indigenous research*. Thousand Oaks, CA: Sage.

Derrida, J. (1981). *Positions*. Baltimore: Johns Hopkins University Press.

Desimone, L. M. (2006). Consider the source: Response differences among teachers, principals, and districts on survey questions about their education policy environment. *Educational Policy, 20*(4), 640–676.

DeStefano, L., & Wagner, M. (1991). *Outcome assessment in special education: Lessons learned*. Menlo Park, CA: SRI International.

DeVellis, R. F. (2003). *Scale development: Theory and applications* (2nd ed.). Applied Social Research Methods Series, Vol. 26. London: Sage.

DeVoe, J. F., & Darling-Churchill, K. E. (2008). *Status and trends in the education of American Indians and Alaska Natives: 2008*. Washington, DC: U.S. Department of Education, National Institute of Education Sciences. (NCES 2008084)

Dickson, D. S., Heyler, D., Reilly, L. G., & Romano, S. (2006). *The Oral History Project: Connecting students to their community: Grades 4–8*. Portsmouth, NH: Heinemann.

Dickson-Swift, V., James, E. L., Kippen, S., & Liamputtong, P. (2007). Doing sensitive research: What challenges do qualitative researchers face? *Qualitative Research, 7,* 327–353.

Dillman, D. A. (2007). *Mail and Internet surveys: The tailored design method* (2nd ed., 2007 update). Hoboken, NJ: John Wiley.

Dillman, D. A., & Christian, L. M. (2005). Survey mode as a source of instability in responses across surveys. *Field Methods, 17*(1), 30–52.

Dockett, S., & Perry, B. (2003). Children's views and children's voices in starting school. *Australian Journal of Early Childhood, 28*(1), 12–17.

Dodd, S. (2009). LGBTQ: Protecting vulnerable subjects in all studies. In D. M. Mertens & P. E. Ginsberg (Eds.), *The handbook of social research ethics* (pp. 474–488). Thousand Oaks, CA: Sage.

Dodson, L., Piatelli, D., & Schmalzbauer, L. (2007). Researching inequality through interpretive collaborations: Shifting power and the unspoken contract. *Qualitative Inquiry, 13,* 821–834.

Doe, T. (1996, June). *Doing participatory action research.* Paper presented at the annual meeting of the Society for Disability Studies, Washington, DC.

Donaldson, S. I. (2007). *Program theory-driven evaluation science.* Mahwah, NJ: Lawrence Erlbaum.

Donaldson, S. I., & Lipsey, M. W. (2006). Roles for theory in contemporary evaluation practice: Developing practical knowledge. In I. F. Shaw, J. C. Greene, & M. M. Mark (Eds.), *The SAGE handbook of evaluation* (pp. 56–75). London: Sage.

Drummond, T. (1994). *The student risk screening scale (SRSS).* Grants Pass, OR: Josephine County Mental Health Program.

Easterbrooks, S. R., & Stoner, M. (2006). Using a visual tool to increase adjectives in the written language of students who are deaf or hard of hearing. *Communication Disorders Quarterly, 27,* 95–109.

Echevarria, J. (1995). Interactive reading instruction: A comparison of provincial and distal effects of instructional conversations. *Exceptional Children, 61,* 535–552.

Edgington, E. S. (1992). Nonparametric tests for single-case experiments. In T. R. Kratochwill & J. R. Levin (Eds.), *Single-case research design and analysis* (pp. 133–157). Hillsdale, NJ: Lawrence Erlbaum.

Edno, T., Joh, T., & Yu, H. C. (2003). *Voices from the field: Health and evaluation leaders on multicultural evaluation.* Oakland, CA: Social Policy Research Associates.

Ehri, L. C., Dreyer, L. G., Flugman, B., & Gross, A. (2007). Reading Rescue: An effective tutoring intervention model for language-minority students who are struggling in first grade. *American Educational Research Journal, 44*(2), 414–448.

Eichelberger, R. T. (1989). *Disciplined inquiry: Understanding and doing educational research.* New York: Longman.

Eichler, M. (1991). *Nonsexist research methods.* New York: Routledge.

Ekstrom, R. B., & Smith, D. K. (2002). *Assessing individuals with disabilities in educational employment, and counseling settings.* Washington, DC: American Psychological Association.

Elbaum, B. (2007). Effects of an oral testing accommodation on the mathematics performance of secondary students with and without learning disabilities. *The Journal of Special Education, 40*(4), 218–229. (DOI: 10.1177/00224669070400040301)

Eley, G. (2005). *A crooked line: From cultural history to the history of society.* Ann Arbor: University of Michigan Press.

Elliott, J. (2005). *Narrative in social research.* London: Sage.

Ellis, C. (2007). Telling secrets, revealing lives: Relational ethics in research with intimate others. *Qualitative Inquiry, 13,* 3–29.

Ellis, C., & Bochner, A. P. (2000). Autoethnography, personal narrative, reflexivity: Researchers as subject. In N. K. Denzin & Y. S. Lincoln (Eds.), *Handbook of qualitative research* (2nd ed., pp. 733–768). Thousand Oaks, CA: Sage.

Ellis, C., Bochner, A., Denzin, N., Lincoln, Y., Morse, J., Pelias, R., & Richardson, L. (2008). Talking and thinking about qualitative research. *Qualitative Inquiry, 14,* 254–284.

Erickson, F., & Gutierrez, K. (2002). Culture, rigor, and science in educational research. *Educational Researcher, 31*(8), 21–24.

Erickson, W., & Lee, C. (2008). *2007 Disability status report: United States.* Ithaca, NY: Cornell University Rehabilitation Research and Training Center on Disability Demographics and Statistics.

Errante, A. (2001). But sometimes you're not part of the story: Oral histories and ways of remembering and telling. *Educational Researcher, 29*(2), 16–27.

Evers, A., Anderson, N., & Voskuijl, O. (Eds.). (2005). *The Blackwell handbook of personnel selection.* Oxford, UK: Blackwell.

Fairclough, N. (2003). *Analyzing discourse: Textual analysis for social research.* New York: Routledge.

Farough, S. D. (2006). Believing is seeing: The matrix of vision and White masculinities. *Journal of Contemporary Ethnography, 35*, 51–83.

Feldman, A. (2003). Validity and quality in self-study. *Educational Researcher, 32*(3), 26–28.

Ferdinand, J., Pearson, G., Rowe, M., & Worthington, F. (2007). A different kind of ethics. *Ethnography, 8*(4), 519–543.

Ferguson, M. (1993). *The history of Mary Prince: A West Indian slave, related by herself.* Ann Arbor: University of Michigan Press.

Ferguson, P. M. (1992). The puzzle of inclusion: A case study of autistic students in the life of one high school. In P. M. Ferguson, D. L. Ferguson, & S. J. Taylor (Eds.), *Interpreting disability: A qualitative reader.* New York: Teachers College Press.

Fetherston, B., & Kelly, R. (2007). Conflict resolution and transformative pedagogy: A grounded theory research project on learning in higher education. *Journal of Transformative Education, 5*, 262–285.

Fetner, T., & Kush, K. (2008). Gay-straight alliances in high schools: Social predictors of early adoption. *Youth Society, 40*, 114–130.

Fetterman, D. M. (2001). *Foundations of empowerment evaluation*. Thousand Oaks, CA: Sage.

Fetterman, D. M. (2009). Empowerment evaluation: By the people and for the people. *Evaltalk.* Retrieved February 2, 2009, from http://homepage.mac.com/profdavidf/.

Fetterman, D. M., & Wandersman, A. (2004). *Empowerment evaluation principles in practice*. New York: Guilford.

Fetterman, D., & Wandersman, A. (2007). Empowerment evaluation: Yesterday, today, and tomorrow. *American Journal of Evaluation, 28*, 179–198.

Feuer, M. J., Towne, L., & Shavelson, R. J. (2002). Scientific culture and educational research. *Educational Researcher, 31*(8), 4–14.

Fidell, L. S. (1970). Empirical verification of sex discrimination in hiring practices in psychology. *American Psychologist, 25*, 1094–1097.

Fine, G., & Sandstrom, K. L. (1988). *Knowing children: Participant observation with minors.* Newbury Park, CA: Sage.

Fine, M. (1992). Passions, politics, and power: Feminist research possibilities. In M. Fine (Ed.), *Disruptive voices* (pp. 205–232). Ann Arbor: University of Michigan Press.

Fine, M. (1994). Working the hyphens: Reinventing self and other in qualitative research. In N. K. Denzin & Y. S. Lincoln (Eds.), *Handbook of qualitative research* (pp. 70–82). Thousand Oaks, CA: Sage.

Fine, M., & Gordon, S. M. (1992). Feminist transformation of/despite psychology. In M. Fine (Ed.), *Disruptive voices* (pp. 1–25). Ann Arbor: University of Michigan Press.

Fine, M., Weis, L., Pruit, L. P., & Burns, A. (Eds.). (2004). *Off white: Readings on power, privilege, and resistance* (2nd ed.). New York: Routledge.

Fine, M., Weis, L., Weseen, S., & Wong, L. (2000). For whom: Qualitative research, representations, and social responsibilities. In N. K. Denzin & Y. S. Lincoln (Eds.), *Handbook of qualitative research* (2nd ed., pp. 107–131). Thousand Oaks, CA: Sage.

Finley, S. (2005). Arts-based inquiry: Performing revolutionary pedagogy. In N. K. Denzin & Y. S. Lincoln (Eds.), *The SAGE handbook of qualitative research* (3rd ed., pp. 651–680). Thousand Oaks, CA: Sage.

Fisher, C. B. (2003). *Decoding the ethics code: A practical guide for psychologists.* Thousand Oaks, CA: Sage.

Fitzpatrick, J., & Bledsoe, K. (2007). Evaluation of the Fun with Books program: An interview with Katrina Bledsoe. *American Journal of Evaluation, 28*, 522–535.

Fitzpatrick, J. L., Sanders, J. R., & Worthen, B. R. (2004). *Program evaluation* (3rd ed.). Boston, MA: Pearson.

Flores, K. S. (2007). *Youth participatory evaluation: Strategies for engaging young people.* San Francisco: Jossey-Bass.

Foley, D., & Valenzuela, A. (2005). Critical ethnography: The politics of collaboration. In N. K. Denzin & Y. S. Lincoln (Eds.), *The SAGE handbook of qualitative research* (3rd ed., pp. 217–234. Thousand Oaks, CA: Sage.

Fontes, L. A. (1998). Ethics in family violence research: Multicultural issues, family relations. *Interdisciplinary Journal of Applied Family Studies, 47,* 53–61.
Foster, S. (1993a, August). *Ethnographic interviews in disability studies: The case of research with people who are deaf.* Paper presented at the annual meeting of the American Sociological Association, Miami, FL.
Foster, S. (1993b, April). *Outsider in the deaf world: Reflections of an ethnographic researcher.* Paper presented at the annual meeting of the American Educational Research Association, Atlanta, GA.
Foucault, M. (1980). *Power/knowledge: Selected interviews and other writings.* Brighton, UK: Harvester Press.
Fournier, D. M. (2005). Evaluation. In S. Mathison (Ed.), *Encyclopedia of evaluation* (pp. 139–140). Thousand Oaks, CA: Sage.
Fowler, F. J., Jr. (2008). *Survey research methods* (4th ed.). Thousand Oaks, CA: Sage.
Free Appropriate Public Education. (2008). *Dictionary of terms used in special education.* Retrieved November 24, 2008, from http://www.fapeonline.org/terms.htm
Freeman, M., deMarrais, K., Preissle, J., Roulston, K., & St. Pierre, E. A. (2007). Standards of evidence in qualitative research: An incitement to discourse. *Educational Researcher, 36,* 25–32.
Freeman, M., & Mathison, S. (2008). *Researching children's experiences.* New York: Guilford.
Freire, P. (1971). *Pedagogy of the oppressed.* New York: Hender & Hender.
Fuchs, L. S., & Fuchs, D. (1999). Fair and unfair testing accommodations. *School Administrator, 56*(10), 24–27.
Furumoto, L. (1980). Mary Whiton Calkins (1863–1930). *Psychology of Women Quarterly, 5,* 55–68.
Gadsden, V. L. (2008). The arts and education: Knowledge generation, pedagogy, and the discourse of learning [Electronic version]. *Review of Research in Education, 32,* 29–61. (DOI: 10.3102/0091732X07309691)
Gaiber-Matlin, S., & Haskell-Hoehl, M. (2007, June). Reauthorizing No Child Left Behind. *Monitor on Psychology, 38*(6), 72.
Gall, M. D., Gall, J. P., & Borg, W. R. (2003). *Educational research: An introduction.* New York: Allyn & Bacon.
Gall, M. D., Gall, J. P., & Borg, W. R. (2007). *Educational research: An introduction* (8th ed.). Cranberry, NJ: Merrill.
Gasman, M. (2007). Swept under the rug? A historiography of gender and Black colleges. *American Educational Resource Journal, 44,* 760–805.
Gay, L. R., Mills, G., & Airasian, P. (2009). *Educational research: Competencies for analysis and applications* (9th ed.). Cranberry, NJ: Merrill.
Gaynor, S. T., & Harris, A. (2008). Single-participant assessment of treatment mediators: Strategy description and examples from a behavioral intervention for depressed adolescents. *Behavior Modification, 32,* 372–402.
Geertz, C. (1973). *The interpretation of cultures: Selected essays.* New York: Basic Books.
Geilheiser, L. M., & Meyers, J. (1992, April). *Pull-in and pull-out programs: A comparative case study.* Paper presented at the annual meeting of the American Educational Research Association, San Francisco.
Geisinger, K., Spies, R. A., Carlson, J. F., & Plake, B. S. (Eds.). (2007). *The seventeenth mental measurements yearbook.* Lincoln, NE: Buros Institute for Mental Measurements.
Gelman, A., & Hill, J. (2007). *Data analysis using regression and multilevel/hierarchical models.* New York: Cambridge University Press.
Gentlewarrior, S., Martin-Jearld, A., Skok, A., & Sweetser, K. (2008). Culturally competent feminist social work: Listening to diverse people. *Affilia, 23,* 210–222. (Originally published online May 27, 2008)
Gerich, J., & Lehner, R. (2006). Video computer-assisted self-administered interviews for deaf respondents. *Field Methods, 18*(3), 267–283.
Gill, C. (1999). Invisible ubiquity: The surprising relevance of disability issues in evaluation. *American Journal of Evaluation, 29*(2), 279–287.
Gilligan, C. (1982). *In a different voice: Psychological theory and women's development.* Cambridge, MA: Harvard University Press.

Ginsberg, P. E., & Mertens, D. M. (2009). Frontiers in social research ethics: Fertile ground for evolution. In D. M. Mertens & P. E. Ginsberg (Eds.), *Handbook of social research ethics* (pp. 580–613). Thousand Oaks, CA: Sage.

Glasser, H. M., & Smith, J. P., III. (2008). On the vague meaning of "gender" in education research: The problem, its sources, and recommendations for practice. *Educational Researcher, 37,* 343–350.

Goldberg-Dey, J., & Hill, C. (2007). *Behind the pay gap.* Washington, DC: American Association of University Women Educational Foundation.

Gonzalez, J. E., & Uhing, B. M. (2008). Home literacy environments and young Hispanic children's English and Spanish oral language: A communality analysis. *Journal of Early Intervention, 30,* 116–139.

Goodman, R. (2001). Psychometric properties of the Strengths and Difficulties Questionnaire (SDQ). *Journal of the American Academy of Child and Adolescent Psychiatry, 40,* 1337–1345.

Gopaul-McNicol, S. A., & Armour-Thomas, E. (2002). *Assessment and culture: Psychological tests with minority populations.* San Diego: Academic Press.

Gordon, B. M. (1995). Knowledge construction, competing critical theories, and education. In J. Banks & C. A. McGee-Banks (Eds.), *Handbook of research on multicultural education* (pp. 184–202). New York: Macmillan.

Graves, K. N., Frabutt, J. M., & Shelton, T. L. (2007). Factors associated with mental health and juvenile justice involvement among children with severe emotional disturbance. *Youth Violence and Juvenile Justice, 5,* 147–167.

Greene, B. (2000). African American lesbian and bisexual women. *Journal of Social Issues, 56,* 239–249.

Greene, J. C. (2000). Understanding social programs through evaluation. In N. K. Denzin & Y. S. Lincoln (Eds.), *Handbook of qualitative research* (2nd ed., pp. 981–999). Thousand Oaks, CA: Sage.

Greene, J. C. (2006). Evaluation, democracy, and social change. In I. F. Shaw, J. C. Greene, & M. M. Mark (Eds.), *The SAGE handbook of evaluation* (pp. 118–140). London: Sage.

Greene, J. C. (2007). *Mixed methods in social inquiry.* San Francisco: Jossey-Bass.

Greene, J. C., & Abma, T. A. (Eds.). (2001). *Responsive evaluation* (New Directions for Evaluation, No. 92). San Francisco: Jossey-Bass.

Greene, J. C., & Caracelli, V. J. (2003). Making paradigmatic sense of mixed-method practice. In A. Tashakkori & C. Teddlie (Eds.), *Handbook of mixed methods in social & behavioral research* (pp. 91–110). Thousand Oaks, CA: Sage.

Grissom, R. J., & Kim, J. J. (2005). *Effect sizes for research.* Clinton, NJ: Routledge.

Groves, R. M., Couper, M. P., Presser, S., Singer, E., Tourangeau, R., Acosta, G. P., & Nelson, L. (2006). Experiments in producing nonresponse bias. *Public Opinion Quarterly, 70*(5), 720–736.

Guba, E. G., & Lincoln, Y. S. (1989). *Fourth generation evaluation.* Newbury Park, CA: Sage.

Guba, E. G., & Lincoln, Y. S. (1994). Competing paradigms in qualitative research. In N. K. Denzin & Y. S. Lincoln (Eds.), *Handbook of qualitative research* (pp. 105–117). Thousand Oaks, CA: Sage.

Guba, E. G., & Lincoln, Y. S. (2005). Paradigmatic controversies, contradictions, and emerging confluences. In N. K. Denzin & Y. S. Lincoln (Eds.), *The SAGE handbook of qualitative research* (3rd ed., pp. 191–216). Thousand Oaks, CA: Sage.

Gubrium, J. F., & Holstein, J. A. (2000). Analyzing interpretive performance. In N. K. Denzin & Y. S. Lincoln (Eds.), *Handbook of qualitative research* (2nd ed., pp. 487–508). Thousand Oaks, CA: Sage.

Gubrium, J. F., & Holstein, J. A. (2009). *Analyzing narrative reality.* Thousand Oaks, CA: Sage.

Gudiño, O. G., Lau, A. S., Yeh, M., McCabe, K. M., & Hough, R. L. (2009). Understanding racial/ethnic disparities in youth mental health services: Do disparities vary by problem type? *Journal of Emotional and Behavioral Disorders, 17,* 3–16.

Guthrie, K., Louie, J., David, T., & Foster, C. C. (2005). *The challenge of assessing policy and advocacy activities: Strategies for a prospective evaluation approach.* Los Angeles: The California Endowment.

Hackett, E. (2008). Gender as mere difference. *Men and Masculinities, 11*(2), 211–218.

Hadley, R. G., & Mitchell, L. K. (1995). *Counseling research and program evaluation.* Pacific Grove, CA: Brooks/Cole.

Hambleton, R. K., Merenda, P. F., & Spielberger, C. D. (2005). *Adapting educational and psychological tests for cross-cultural assessment.* St. Paul, MN: Assessment Systems Corporation.

Hammersley, M. (2006). Ethnography: Problems and prospects. *Ethnography and Education, 1*(1), 3–14.

Hampton, C., & Lee, K. (2003). *Strategies and activities for reducing racial prejudice and racism. Community Tool Box* [Online]. Retrieved January 13, 2003, from http://ctb.ku.edu/tools/sub_section_main_1173.htm

Hann, J., Todd, P., & Van der Klaauw, W. (2001). Identification and estimation of treatment effects with a regression-discontinuity design. *Econometrica, 69,* 200–209.

Haraway, D. (1988). Situated knowledge: The science question in feminism and the privilege of partial perspective. *Feminist Studies, 14*(3), 575–599.

Harding, R., & Peel, E. (2007). Surveying sexualities: Internet research with non-heterosexuals. *Feminism Psychology, 17,* 277–285.

Harding, S. (1987). Is there a feminist method? In S. Harding (Ed.), *Feminism and methodology* (pp. 1–15). Bloomington: Indiana University Press.

Harding, S. (1993). Rethinking standpoint epistemology: What is "strong objectivity"? In L. Alcoff & E. Potter (Eds.), *Feminist epistemologies* (pp. 49–82). New York: Routledge.

Harper, D. (2005). What's new visually? In N. K. Denzin & Y. S. Lincoln (Eds.), *The SAGE handbook of qualitative research* (3rd ed., pp. 747–762). Thousand Oaks, CA: Sage.

Harris, R., Holmes, H., & Mertens, D. M. (2009). Research ethics in sign language communities. *Sign Language Studies, 9*(2), 104–131.

Harry, B., Klingner, J. K., & Hart, J. (2005). African American families under fire: Ethnographic views of family strengths. *Remedial and Special Education, 26,* 101–112.

Hart, C. (1999). *Doing a literature review: Releasing the social science research imagination.* London: Sage.

Hartsock, N. (1983). The feminist standpoint: Developing the ground for specifically feminist historical materialism. In S. Harding & M. B. Hintikka (Eds.), *Discovering reality* (pp. 283–310). Amsterdam: D. Reidel.

Hartsock, N. (1985). *Money, sex and power: Towards a feminist historical materialism.* Boston: Northeastern University Press.

Hawken, L. S., Vincent, C. G., & Schumann, J. (2008). Response to intervention for social behavior: Challenges and opportunities. *Journal of Emotional and Behavioral Disorders, 16,* 213–225.

Hedrick, T. E., Bickman, L., & Rog, D. (1993). *Applied research design: A practical guide.* Newbury Park, CA: Sage.

Henry, G. T. (1990). *Practical sampling.* Newbury Park, CA: Sage.

Henry, G. T. (1996). Does the public have a role in evaluation? In M. T. Braverman & J. K. Slater (Eds.), *Advances in survey research* (New Directions for Evaluation, No. 70, pp. 3–16). San Francisco: Jossey-Bass.

Henry, G. T., Gordon, C. S., & Rickman, D. K. (2006). Early education policy alternatives: Comparing quality and outcomes of Head Start and state prekindergarten. *Educational Evaluation and Policy Analysis, 28,* 77–99.

Hess, I. (1985). *Sampling for social research surveys 1947–1980.* Ann Arbor: University of Michigan Press.

Hesse-Biber, S., & Leavy, P. (2006). *The practice of qualitative research.* Thousand Oaks, CA: Sage.

Hesse-Biber, S. N. (2007). The practice of feminist in-depth interviewing. In S. N. Hesse-Biber & P. L. Leavy (Eds.), *Feminist research practice* (pp. 111–148). Thousand Oaks, CA: Sage.

Hilliard, A. G. (1978). *The future of follow-through.* Washington, DC: ERIC. (ERIC Document Reproduction Service No. ED255284)

Hilliard, A. G. (1983). IQ and the courts: Larry P. v. Wilson Riles and PASE v. Hannon. *Journal of Black Psychology, 10*(1), 1–18.

Hilliard, A. G. (1984). Democracy in evaluation: The evolution of an art—science in context. In P. Hosford (Ed.), *What we know about teaching* (pp. 113–138). Charlottesville: Virginia Association for Supervision and Curriculum.

Hilliard, A. G. (1989). Kemetic (Egyptian) historical revision: Implications for crosscultural evaluation and research in education. *Evaluation Practice, 10*(2), 7–23.

Hilliard, A. G. (1992). The pitfalls and promises of special education practice. *Exceptional Children, 59*(2), 168–172.

Hilliard, A. G. (1996). Either a paradigm shift or no mental measurement: The nonscience and nonsense of *The Bell Curve. Cultural Diversity and Mental Health Journal, 2*(1), 1–20.

Hilliard, A. G. (1997). Language, culture, and the assessment of African American children. In A. Lin Goodwin (Ed.), *Assessment for equity and inclusion: Embracing all our children* (pp. 229–240). New York: Routledge.

Hilliard, A. G. (2000). *The state of African education.* Paper presented at the annual meeting of the American Educational Research Association, New Orleans, LA.

Hilliard, A. G. (2007). *Shaping research for global African educational excellence: It is now or never.* Paper presented at the annual meeting of the American Educational Research Association, Chicago.

Hodder, I. (1994). The interpretation of documents and material culture. In N. K. Denzin & Y. S. Lincoln (Eds.), *Handbook of qualitative research* (pp. 393–402). Thousand Oaks, CA: Sage.

Hodgkin, S. (2008). Telling it all: A story of women's social capital using a mixed methods approach. *Journal of Mixed Methods Research, 2,* 296–316.

Hogan, T. P. (2005). *Educational assessment.* Indianapolis: IN: Jossey-Bass.

Holcomb, Z. C. (2006). *SPSS Basics: Techniques for a first course in statistics.* Glendale, CA: Pyrczak.

Hood, S., & Hopson, R. K. (2008). Evaluation roots reconsidered: Asa Hilliard, a fallen hero in the "Nobody Knows My Name" project, and African educational excellence. *Review of Educational Research, 78,* 410–426.

Hood, S., Hopson, R. K., & Frierson, H. T. (Eds.). (2005). *The role of culture and cultural context: A mandate for inclusion, the discovery of truth and understanding in evaluative theory and practice.* Charlotte, NC: Information Age.

hooks, b. (1990). *Yearning: Race, gender, and cultural politics.* Boston: South End.

Hopson, R. K., & Hood, S. (2005). An untold story in evaluation roots: Reid E. Jackson and his contributions towards culturally responsive evaluation at 3/4 century. In S. Hood, R. K. Hopson, & H. T. Frierson (Eds.), *The role of culture and cultural context: A mandate for inclusion, the discovery of truth and understanding in evaluative theory and practice* (pp. 85–102). Charlotte, NC: Information Age.

House, E. R. (1993). *Professional evaluation: Social impact and political consequences.* Newbury Park, CA: Sage.

House, E. R., & Howe, K. R. (1999). *Values in evaluation and social research.* Thousand Oaks, CA: Sage.

House, E. R., & Howe, K. R. (2000). Deliberative democratic evaluation. In K. E. Ryan and L. DeStefano (Eds.), *Evaluation as a democratic process: Promoting inclusion, dialogue, and deliberation* (New Directions for Evaluation, No. 85, pp. 3–12). San Francisco: Jossey-Bass.

Howe, K. R., & MacGillivary, H. (2009). Social research attuned to deliberative democracy. In D. M. Mertens & P. E. Ginsberg (Eds.), *The handbook of social research ethics* (pp. 565–579). Thousand Oaks, CA Sage.

Hozella, P. (2007). *Identification of children with specific learning disabilities.* Washington, DC: National Dissemination Center for Children With Disabilities.

Hubbard, R., & Lindsay, R. M. (2008). Why *P* values are not a useful measure of evidence in statistical significance testing. *Theory and Psychology, 18*(1), 69–88. (DOI: 10.1177/0959354307086923)

Huygens, I. (2002, June). Journeys away from dominance: Dissonance, struggle, and right relationships—the journey to accepting indigenous authority. Paper presented at the eighth biennial conference of the Society for Community Research and Action, Atlanta, GA.

Hyde, J. A., & Lindberg, S. M. (2007). Facts and assumptions about the nature of gender differences and the implications for gender equity. In S. S. Klein, B. Richardson, D. A. Grayson, L. H. Fox, C. Kramarae, D. S. Pollard, & C. A. Dwyer (Eds.), *Handbook for achieving gender equity through education* (2nd ed., pp. 19–32). Mahwah, NJ: Lawrence Erlbaum.

Interagency Advisory Panel on Research Ethics. (2003). *Tri-council policy statement: Ethical conduct for research involving humans.* Retrieved December 22, 2003, from http://www.pre.ethics.gc.ca.

Internet World Stats. (2008). Retrieved November 24, 2008, from http://www.internetworldstats.com/.

Jackson, R. E. (1940a). An evaluation of educational opportunities for the Negro adolescent in Alabama I. *Journal of Negro Education, 9*(1), 59–72.

Jackson, R. E. (1940b). An evaluation of educational opportunities for the Negro adolescent in Alabama II. *Journal of Negro Education, 9*(2), 200–207.

Jackson-Triche, M. E., Sullivan, J. G., Wells, K. B., Rogers, W., Camp, P., & Mazel, R. (2000). Depression and health-related quality of life in ethnic minorities seeking care in general medical settings. *Journal of Affective Disorders, 58,* 89–97.

Jacobsgaard, M. (2004). Using appreciative inquiry to evaluate project activities of a nongovernmental organization supporting victims of trauma in Sri Lanka. In H. Preskill & A. T. Coghlan (Eds.), *Using appreciative inquiry in evaluation* (New Directions for Evaluation, No. 100, pp. 53–62). San Francisco: Jossey-Bass.

James, S., & Busia, A. (1993). *Theorizing black feminisms.* New York: Routledge.

Jang, E. E., McDougall, D. E., Pollon, D., Herbert, M., & Russell, P. (2008). Integrative mixed methods data analytic strategies in research on school success in challenging circumstances. *Journal of Mixed Methods Research, 2,* 221–247.

Jennings, B., & Callahan, D. (1983, February). Social sciences and the policy-making process. *Hastings Center Report,* 3–8.

Johnson, B., & Christensen, J. (2008). *Educational research* (3rd ed.). Thousand Oaks, CA: Sage.

Johnson, B., & Onwuegbuzie, A. (2004). Mixed methods research: A research paradigm whose time has come. *Educational Researcher, 33*(7), 14–26.

Johnson, E., Mellard, D. F., & Byrd, S. E. (2005). Alternative models of learning disabilities identification: Considerations and initials conclusions. *Journal of Learning Disabilities, 38*(6), 569–572. (DOI: 10.1177/00222194050380061401)

Johnson, J. W., McDonnell, J., Holzwarth, V. N., & Hunter, K. (2008). The efficacy of embedded instruction for students with developmental disabilities enrolled in general education classes. *Journal of Positive Behavior Interventions, 6,* 214–227.

Joint Committee on Standards for Educational Evaluation. (2008). *The personnel evaluation standards* (2nd ed.). Thousand Oaks, CA: Sage.

Joint Committee on Standards for Educational Evaluation. (2009). *The program evaluation standards: How to assess evaluations of educational programs* (3rd ed.). Thousand Oaks, CA: Sage.

Joint Committee on Testing Practices. (2004). *Code of fair testing practices in education.* Washington, DC: National Council on Measurement in Education.

Jones, J. H. (1992). *Bad blood: The Tuskegee syphilis experiment* (Rev. ed.). New York: Free Press.

Jones, S. J. (2005). Authoethnography: Making the personal political. In N. K. Denzin & Y. S. Lincoln (Eds.), *The SAGE handbook of qualitative research* (3rd ed., pp. 763–793). Thousand Oaks, CA: Sage.

Josselson, R. (1993). A narrative introduction. In R. Josselson & R. Lieblich (Eds.), *The narrative study of lives* (Vol. 1, pp. ix–xv). Newbury Park, CA: Sage.

Kammen, M. (2008). The American past politicized: Uses and misuses of history. *The Annals of the American Academy of Political and Social Science, 617,* 42–57.

Keller, C., Karp, J., & Carlson, H. L. (1993, April). *The community and school contexts for the integration of students with disabilities in general education.* Paper presented at the annual meeting of the American Educational Research Association, Atlanta, GA.

Kellogg Foundation, W. K. (1998). *W. K. Kellogg Foundation evaluation handbook.* Retrieved April 30, 2009, from http://www.wkkf.org/default.aspx?tabid=1174&NID=331&Year=&Issue=15&LanguageID=0&dg1454pi=6

Kelly, G. J., Luke, A., & Green, J. (2008). What counts as knowledge in educational settings: Disciplinary knowledge, assessment, and curriculum. *Review of Research in Education, 32*(1), vii.

Kelly, L., Burton, S., & Regan, L. (1994). Researching women's lives or studying women's oppression? Reflections on what constitutes feminist research. In M. Maynard & J. Purvis (Eds.), *Researching women's lives from a feminist perspective* (pp. 27–48). Bristol, PA: Taylor & Francis.

Kemmis, S., & McTaggart, R. (2005). Participatory action research: Communicative action and the public sphere. In N. K. Denzin & Y. S. Lincoln (Eds.), *The SAGE handbook of qualitative research* (3rd ed., pp. 559–604). Thousand Oaks, CA: Sage.

Kessler-Harris, A. (2001). *In pursuit of equity: Women, men, and the quest for economic citizenship in 20th century America*. Oxford, UK: Oxford University Press.

King, J. A., Nielsen, J. E., & Colby, J. (2004). Lessons for culturally competent evaluation from the study of a multicultural initiative. In M. Thompson Robinson, R. Hopson, & S. SenGupta (Eds.), *In search of cultural competence in evaluation* (New Directions for Evaluation, No. 102, pp. 67–79). San Francisco: Jossey-Bass.

King, J. E. (2005). A transformative vision of Black education for human freedom. In J. E. King (Ed.), *Black education: A transformative research and action agenda for the new century* (pp. 3–17). Washington, DC: American Educational Research Association.

Kirby, R. K. (2008). Phenomenology and the problems of oral history. *The Oral History Review, 35*(1), 22–38.

Kirkhart, K. E. (1995). Seeking multicultural validity: A postcard from the road. *Evaluation Practice, 16*(1), 1–12.

Kirkhart, K. (2005). Through a cultural lens: Reflections on validity and theory in evaluation. In S. Hood, R. K. Hopson, & H. T. Frierson (Eds.), *The role of culture and cultural contest* (pp. 21–38.) Charlotte, NC: Information Age.

Kitayama, S., & Cohen, D. (Eds.). (2007). *Handbook of cultural psychology*. New York: Guilford.

Klein, S. (2007). *Handbook for achieving gender equity through education* (2nd ed.). Mahwah, NJ: Lawrence Erlbaum.

Kolar, T., & Kolar, I. (2008). What respondents really expect from researchers. *Evaluation Review, 32*, 363–391.

Koretz, D. M. (2008). *Measuring up: What educational testing really tells us*. Cambridge, MA: Harvard College.

Koro-Ljungberg, M. (2008). Positivity in qualitative research: Examples from the organized field of postmodern/poststructuralism. *Qualitative Research, 8*(2), 217–236.

Krathwohl, D. R. (2009). *Methods of educational and social science research* (3rd ed.). White Plains, NY: Longman.

Kratochwill, T. R. (1992). Single-case research design and analysis: An overview. In T. R. Kratochwill & J. R. Levin (Eds.), *Single-case research design and analysis* (pp. 1–12). Hillsdale, NJ: Lawrence Erlbaum.

Krueger, R. A. (1988). *Developing questions for focus groups*. Thousand Oaks, CA: Sage.

Krueger, R. A. (2000). *Focus groups: A practical guide for applied research* (3rd ed.). Thousand Oaks, CA: Sage.

Krueger, R. A. (2003). *Focus group interviewing*. Retrieved December 22, 2003, from http://www.tc.umn.edu/~rkrueger/focus.html

Krueger, R. A., & Casey, M. A. (2000). *Focus groups: A practical guide for applied research*. Thousand Oaks, CA: Sage.

Kuhn, T. (1996). *The structure of scientific revolutions*. Chicago: University of Chicago Press. (Original work published 1962)

Ladson-Billings, G. (2000). Racialized discourses and ethnic epistemologies. In N. K. Denzin & Y. S. Lincoln (Eds.), *Handbook of qualitative research* (2nd ed., pp. 257–278). Thousand Oaks, CA: Sage.

Ladson-Billings, G. (2006). Introduction. In G. Ladson-Billings & W. F. Tate (Eds.), *Education research in the public interest* (pp. 1–15). New York: Teachers College Press.

Ladson-Billings, G., & Donnor, J. (2005). The moral activist role of critical race theory scholarship. In N. K. Denzin & Y. S. Lincoln (Eds.), *The SAGE handbook of qualitative research* (3rd ed., pp. 279–301). Thousand Oaks, CA: Sage.

LaFrance, J., & Crazy Bull, C. (2009). Researching ourselves back to life: Taking control of the research agenda in Indian Country. In D. M. Mertens & P. E. Ginsberg (Eds.), *Handbook of social research ethics* (pp. 135–149). Thousand Oaks, CA: Sage.

LaFromboise, T. (1988). American Indian mental health policy. *American Psychologist, 43,* 388–397.

Lane, K. L., Parks, R. J., Kalberg, J. R., & Carter, E. W. (2007). Systematic screening at the middle school level: Score reliability and validity of the student risk screening scale. *Journal of Emotional and Behavioral Disorders, 15,* 209–222.

Lanham, B. A., & Mehaffy, G. L. (1988). *Oral history in the secondary school classroom.* Los Angeles: Oral History Association.

Lannie, A. L., & McCurdy, B. L. (2007). Preventing disruptive behavior in the urban classroom: Effects of the good behavior on student and teacher behavior. *Education and Treatment of Children, 30*(1), 85–98.

Larwin, K. H., & Larwin, D. A. (2008). Decreasing excessive media usage while increasing physical activity: A single-subject research study. *Behavior Modification, 32,* 938–956.

Lather, P. (1992). Critical frames in educational research: Feminist and post-structural perspectives. *Theory and Practice, 31*(2), 1–13.

Lather, P. (1995, April). *Troubling clarity: The politics of accessible language.* Paper presented at the annual meeting of the American Educational Research Association, San Francisco.

Lather, P. (2004). This IS your father's paradigm: Government intrusion and the case of qualitative research in education. *Qualitative Inquiry, 10*(1), 15–34.

Lather, P. (2007). *Getting lost: Feminist efforts toward a double(d) science.* Albany: State University of New York Press.

Lawrence-Lightfoot, S. (2005). Reflections on portraiture: A dialogue between art and science. *Qualitative Inquiry, 11*(2), 3–15.

Leavy, P. (2009). *Method meets art.* New York: Guilford.

Lechago, S. A., & Carr, J. E. (2008). Recommendations for reporting independent variables in outcome studies of early and intensive behavioral intervention for autism. *Behavior Modification, 32,* 489–503.

Lee, C. D. (2003). Why we need to re-think race and ethnicity in educational research. *Educational Researcher, 32*(5), 3–5.

Lee, C. D. (2008). The centrality of culture to the scientific study of learning and development: How an ecological framework in education research facilitates civic responsibility (Wallace Foundation Distinguished Lecture). *Educational Researcher, 37,* 267–279.

Lee, K. (2003a). Building inclusive communities. *Community Tool Box* [Online]. Retrieved January 13, 2003, from http://ctb.ku.edu/tools//sub_section_main_1880.htm

Lee, K. (2003b). Creating opportunities for members of groups to identify their similarities, differences, and assets. *Community Tool Box* [Online]. Retrieved January 13, 2003, from http://ctb.ku.edu/tools/sub_section_main_1175.htm

Lee, K. (2003c). Transforming conflicts in diverse communities. *Community Tool Box* [Online]. Retrieved January 13, 2003, from http://ctb.ku.edu/ar/tablecontents/sub_section_main_1845.htm

Lee, K. (2003d). Understanding culture, social organization, and leadership to enhance engagement. *Community Tool Box* [Online]. Retrieved January 13, 2003, from http://ctb.ku.edu/tools/sub_section_main_1879.htm

Lee, K. (2004). *The meaning and practice of civic participation among four immigrant communities.* Unpublished doctoral dissertation, Union Institute, Cincinnati, OH.

Lee, O. (2005). Science education with English Language Learners: Synthesis and research agenda. *Review of Educational Research, 75,* 491–530.

Lehtonen, M. (2006). Deliberative democracy, participation, and OECD peer reviews of environmental policies. *American Journal of Evaluation, 27,* 185–200.

Levin, J. R. (1992). Single-case research design and analysis: Comments and concerns. In T. R. Kratochwill & J. R. Levin (Eds.), *Single-case research design and analysis* (pp. 213–222). Hillsdale, NJ: Lawrence Erlbaum.

Lewin, M., & Wild, C. L. (1991). The impact of the feminist critique on tests, assessment, and methodology. *Psychology of Women Quarterly, 15,* 581–596.

Lewis, C., Hancock, S., James, M., & Larke, P. (2008). African American students and No Child Left Behind legislation: Progression or digression in educational attainment? *Multicultural Learning & Teaching, 43,* 127–153.

Li, S., Marquart, J. M., & Zercher, C. (2000). Conceptual issues and analytic strategies in mixed-method studies of preschool inclusion. *Journal of Early Intervention, 23*(2), 116–132.

Lillis, T. (2008). Ethnography as method, methodology, and "deep theorizing": Closing the gap between text and context in academic writing research. *Written Communication, 25,* 353–388.

Lincoln, Y. S. (1995, April). *Standards for qualitative research.* Paper presented at the annual meeting of the American Educational Research Association, San Francisco.

Lincoln, Y. S. (2009). Ethical practices in qualitative research. In D. M. Mertens & P. E. Ginsberg (Eds.), *The handbook of social research ethics* (pp. 150–169). Thousand Oaks, CA: Sage.

Lincoln, Y. S., & Denzin, N. K. (2000). The seventh moment: Out of the past. In N. K. Denzin & Y. S. Lincoln (Eds.), *Handbook of qualitative research* (2nd ed., pp. 1047–1065). Thousand Oaks, CA: Sage.

Lincoln, Y. S., & Denzin, N. K. (2005). Epilogue: The eighth and ninth moments—qualitative research in/and the fractured future. In N. K. Denzin & Y. S. Lincoln (Eds.), *The SAGE handbook of qualitative research* (3rd ed., pp. 1115–1126). Thousand Oaks, CA: Sage.

Lincoln, Y. S., & Guba, E. G. (1985). *Naturalistic inquiry.* Beverly Hills, CA: Sage.

Lincoln, Y. S., & Guba, E. G. (2000). Paradigmatic controversies, contradictions, and emerging confluences. In N. K. Denzin & Y. S. Lincoln (Eds.), *Handbook of qualitative research* (2nd ed., pp. 163–188). Thousand Oaks, CA: Sage.

Lindley, D. V. (1999). Comment on Bayarri and Berger. In J. M. Bernardo, J. O. Berger, A. P. Dawid, & A. F. M. Smith (Eds.), *Bayesian statistics* (Vol. 6, p. 75). Oxford, UK: Clarendon.

Lipsey, M. K. (1990). *Design sensitivity.* Newbury Park, CA: Sage.

Locke, L. F., Spirduso, W. W., & Silverman, S. J. (1993). *Proposals that work.* Newbury Park, CA: Sage.

Lopez, G. I., Figueroa, M., Connor, S. E., & Maliski, S. L. (2008). Translation barriers in conducting qualitative research with Spanish speakers. *Qualitative Health Research, 18,* 1729–1737.

Lopez, S., & Mertens, D. M. (1993, April). *Integrating the feminist perspective in educational research classes.* Paper presented at the annual meeting of the American Educational Research Association, Atlanta, GA.

Lopez, S. J., & Snyder, C. R. (2003). *Positive psychological assessment: A handbook of models and measures.* Washington, DC: American Psychological Association.

Luiselli, J. K., & Diament, C. (Eds.). (2002). *Behavior psychology in the schools: Innovations in evaluation, support and consultation.* New York: Haworth.

MacDonald, B., & Kushner, S. (2005). Democratic evaluation. In S. Mathison (Ed.), *Encyclopedia of evaluation* (pp. 108–113). Thousand Oaks, CA: Sage.

MacDonald, V. M. (1995, April). *Portraits in black and white: A micro and macro view of Southern teachers before and after the Civil War.* Paper presented at the annual meeting of the American Educational Research Association, San Francisco.

MacGinitie, W., MacGinitie, R., Maria, K., & Dreyer, L. (2002). *Gates-MacGinitie Reading Tests, 4th Edition: Technical Report.* Itasca, IL: Riverside.

Macias, R. F. (1993). Language and ethnic classification of language minorities: Chicano and Latino students in the 1990s. *Hispanic Journal of Behavioral Sciences, 75*(2), 230–257.

MacRaild, D. M. (2008). The moloch of details? Cycles of criticism and the meaning of history now. *Journal of Contemporary History, 43,* 113–125.

Madison, D. S. (2005). *Critical ethnography: Method, ethics, and performance.* Thousand Oaks, CA: Sage.

Madriz, E. (2000). Focus groups in feminist research. In N. K. Denzin & Y. S. Lincoln (Eds.), *Handbook of qualitative research* (2nd ed., pp. 835–850). Thousand Oaks, CA: Sage.

Marcus, L. S. (1993). The here and now comes of age: Margaret Wise Brown, Lucy Sprague Mitchell, and the early days of writing for children at Bank Street. In F. Pignatelli & S. W. Pflaum (Eds.), *Celebrating diverse voices* (pp. 177–196). Thousand Oaks, CA: Corwin.

Marder, C., & Cox, R. (1990). More than a label: Characteristics of youth with disabilities. In M. Wagner, L. Newman, & D. L. Shaver (Eds.), *Young people with disabilities: How are they doing? A comprehensive report from Wave 1 of the National Longitudinal Transition Study of Special Education.* Menlo Park, CA: SRI International.

Mark, M. M. (2009). Credible evidence: Changing the terms of the debate. In S. Donaldson, T. C. Christie, & M. M. Mark (Eds.), *What counts as credible evidence in applied research and evaluation?* (pp. 214–238). Thousand Oaks, CA: Sage.

Mark, M. M., & Gamble, C. (2009). Experiments, quasi-experiments and ethics. In D. M. Mertens & P. E. Ginsberg (Eds.), *Handbook of social research ethics* (pp. 198–213). Thousand Oaks, CA: Sage.

Mark, M. M., Greene, J. C., & Shaw, I. E. (2005). The evaluation of policies, programs, and practices. In I. F. Shaw, J. C. Greene, & M. M. Mark (Eds.), *The SAGE handbook of evaluation* (pp. 33–55). Thousand Oaks, CA: Sage.

Mark, M. M., Henry, G. T., & Julnes, G. W. (1998). A realist theory of evaluation practice. In G. T. Henry, G. W. Julnes, & M. M. Mark (Eds.), *Realist evaluation: An emerging theory in support of practice* (pp. 3–32). San Francisco: Jossey-Bass.

Mark, M. M., & Reichardt, C. S. (2009). Quasi-experimentation. In L. Bickman & D. Rog (Eds.), *Handbook of applied social research methods* (2nd ed., pp. 182–213). Thousand Oaks, CA: Sage.

Marshall, C., & Rossman, G. B. (2006). *Designing qualitative research* (4th ed.). Thousand Oaks, CA: Sage.

Martusewicz, R. A., & Reynolds, W. M. (1994). Introduction: Turning the study of education inside/out. In R. A. Martusewicz & W. M. Reynolds (Eds.), *Inside out: Contemporary critical perspectives in education.* New York: St. Martin's.

Maruyama, G., & Deno, S. (1992). *Research in educational settings.* Newbury Park, CA: Sage.

Massey, D. S., Zambrana, R. E., & Bell, S. A. (1995). Contemporary issues in Latino families: Future directions for research, policy, and practice. In R. E. Zambrana (Ed.), *Understanding Latino families* (pp. 190–192). Thousand Oaks, CA: Sage.

Mastropieri, M. A., Scruggs, T. E., Graetz, J., Norland, J., Gardizi, W., & Mcduffie, K. (2005, May). Case studies in co-teaching in the content areas: Successes, failures, and challenges. *Intervention in School and Clinic, 40,* 260–270.

Mathison, S. (Ed.). (2005). *Encyclopedia of evaluation.* Thousand Oaks, CA: Sage.

Mathison, S. (2008). What is the difference between evaluation and research—and why do we care? In N. L. Smith & P. R. Brandon (Eds.), *Fundamental issues in evaluation* (pp. 183–196). New York: Guilford.

Mathison, S. (2009). Public good and private interest in educational evaluation. In W. Ayers (Ed.), *Handbook of social justice in education* (pp. 5–14). New York: Routledge.

Matson, J. L., & LoVullo, S. V. (2008). A review of behavioral treatments for self-injurious behaviors of persons with autism spectrum disorders. *Behavior Modification, 32,* 61–76.

Matt, G. E., & Cook, T. D. (1994). Threats to the validity of research synthesis. In H. Cooper & L. V. Hedges (Eds.), *The handbook of research synthesis* (pp. 503–520). New York: Russell Sage.

Maxcy, S. J. (2003). Pragmatic threads in mixed methods research in the social sciences: The search for multiple modes of inquiry and the end of the philosophy of formalism. In A. Tashakkori & C. Teddlie (Eds.), *Handbook of mixed methods in social & behavioral research* (pp. 51–90). Thousand Oaks, CA: Sage.

Maxwell, J. A. (2004). Casual explanation, qualitative research, and scientific inquiry in education. *Educational Researcher, 33*(1), 3–11.

Mayo, C. (2007, March). Queering foundations: Queer and Lesbian, Gay, Bisexual, and Transgender educational research. *Review of Research in Education, 31,* 78–94. (DOI: 10.3102/0091732X06298013)

McCall, M. M. (2000). Performance ethnography: A brief history and some advice. In N. K. Denzin & Y. S. Lincoln (Eds.), *Handbook of qualitative research* (2nd ed., pp. 421–433). Thousand Oaks, CA: Sage.

McClelland, S. I., & Fine, M. (2008). Research embedded science: Critical analysis of abstinence-only evaluation research. *Cultural Studies <=> Cultural Methodologies, 8,* 50–81.

McCracken, G. (1988). *The long interview.* Qualitative Research Methods Series (Vol. 13). Newbury Park, CA: Sage.

McCreanor, T., Tipene-Leach, D., & Abel, S. (2004). The SIDS careworkers study: Perceptions of Maori SIDS families. *New Zealand Journal of Social Policy, 23,* 154–166.

McCreanor, T., Watson, P., & Denny, S. (2006). "Just accept us how we are more": Experiences of young Pakeha with their families in Aotearoa New Zealand. *Social Policy Journal of New Zealand, 27,* 156–170.

McDermott, K. A. (2007). Expanding the moral community or blaming the victim? The politics of state education accountability policy. *American Educational Resource Journal, 44,* 77–111.

McDuffie, K. A., & Scruggs, T. E. (2008). The contributions of qualitative research to discussions of evidence-based practice in special education. *Intervention in School and Clinic, 44,* 91–97.

McGee-Brown, M. J. (1994, April). *Accuracy in data collection, representation, and presentation: Towards an ethics of educational research.* Paper presented at the annual meeting of the American Educational Research Association, New Orleans, LA.

McIntire, S. A., & Miller, L. A. (2006). *Foundations of psychological testing* (2nd ed.). Thousand Oaks, CA: Sage.

McKay, R. B., Breslow, M. J., Sangster, R. L., Gabbard, S. M., Reynolds, R. W., Nakamoto, J. M., & Tarnai, J. (1996). Translating survey questionnaires: Lessons learned. In M. T. Braverman & J. K. Slater (Eds.), *Advances in survey research* (New Directions for Evaluation, No. 70, pp. 93–104). San Francisco: Jossey-Bass.

McKee, N. (1992). Lexical and semantic pitfalls in the use of survey interviews: An example from the Texas-Mexico border. *Hispanic Journal of Behavioral Sciences, 14*(3), 353–362.

Mckinley, B., Brayboy, J., Castagno, A., & Maughan, E. (2007). Equality and justice for all? Examining race in education scholarship. *Review of Research in Education, 31,* 159–194. (DOI: 10.3102/0091732X07300046159)

McLaughlin, J. A., & Jordan, G. B. (1999). Logic models: A tool for telling your program's performance story. *Evaluation and Program Planning, 22,* 65–72.

McNamara, C. (2008). Basic guide to program evaluation. Minneapolis, MN: Authenticity Consulting. Retrieved April 25, 2009, from http://www.mapnp.org/library/evaluatn/fnl_eval.htm#anchor1665834

McNamee, S. (2004). Appreciative evaluation within a conflicted educational context. In H. Preskill & A. T. Coghlan (Eds.), *Using appreciative inquiry in evaluation* (New Directions for Evaluation, No. 100, pp. 23–40). San Francisco: Jossey-Bass.

McShane, D. (1989, April). *Testing American Natives and Alaskan Natives.* Paper presented at Native American Hearing of the National Commission on Testing and Public Policy, Albuquerque, NM.

Meadow, K. P. (1967). The effects of early manual communication and family climate on the deaf child's development. Unpublished docotoral dissertation, University of California, Berkeley.

Meadow-Orlans, K., Mertens, D. M., & Sass-Lehrer, M. (2003). *Parents and their deaf children: The early years.* Washington, DC: Gallaudet Press.

Medved, C. E., Morrison, K., Dearing, J. E., Larson, R. S., Cline, G., & Brummans, B. H. (2001). Tensions in community health improvement initiatives: Communication and collaboration in a managed care environment. *Journal of Applied Communication Research, 29,* 137–151.

Mellor, J. M, Rapoport, R. B., & Maliniak, D. (2008). The impact of child obesity on active parental consent in school-based survey research on healthy eating and physical activity. *Evaluation Review, 32*(3), 298–312.

Meloy, J. M. (2001). *Writing the qualitative dissertation* (2nd ed.). Hillsdale, NJ: Lawrence Erlbaum.

Merrell, K. W. (2007). *Behavioral, social and emotional assessment of children and adolescents.* New York: Routledge.

Mertens, D. M. (1990). Practical evidence of the feasibility of the utilization-focused approach to evaluation. *Studies in Educational Evaluation, 16,* 181–194.

Mertens, D. M. (1991). Instructional factors related to hearing impaired adolescents' interest in science. *Science Education, 75*(4), 429–441.

Mertens, D. M. (1992, November). *Increasing utilization through a collaborative model of evaluation in an international setting: Holding hands across the culture gap*. Paper presented at the annual meeting of the American Evaluation Association, Seattle, WA.

Mertens, D. M. (1995). Identify and respect differences among participants in evaluation studies. In W. Shadish, D. Newman, M. A. Scheirer, & C. Wye (Eds.), *The American Evaluation Association's guiding principles* (pp. 91–98). San Francisco: Jossey-Bass.

Mertens, D. M. (1996). Breaking the silence about sexual abuse of deaf youth. *American Annals of the Deaf, 141*(5), 352–358.

Mertens, D. M. (2000). Deaf and hard of hearing people in court: Using an emancipatory perspective to determine their needs. In C. Truman, D. M. Mertens, & B. Humphries (Eds.), *Research and inequality* (pp. 111–125). London: Taylor & Francis.

Mertens, D. M. (2003). The inclusive view of evaluation: Visions for the new millennium. In S. I. Donaldson & M. Scriven (Eds.), *Evaluating social programs and problems: Visions for the new millennium* (pp. 91–107). Hillsdale, NJ: Lawrence Erlbaum.

Mertens, D. M. (2005). *Research and evaluation in education and psychology: Integrating diversity with quantitative, qualitative, and mixed methods* (2nd ed.). Thousand Oaks, CA: Sage.

Mertens, D. M. (2009). *Transformative research and evaluation*. New York: Guilford.

Mertens, D. M., Berkeley, T. R., & Lopez, S. (1995). Using participatory evaluation in an international context. In J. B. Cousins & L. M. Earl (Eds.), *Participatory evaluation in education* (pp. 140–156). Washington, DC: Falmer.

Mertens, D. M., Delk, L., & Weidekamp, L. (2003). Evaluation of early intervention programs. In B. Bodner-Johnson & M. Sass-Lehrer (Eds.), *The young deaf or hard of hearing child: A family-centered approach to early education* (pp. 187–220). Baltimore: Brookes.

Mertens, D. M., Farley, J., Madison, A., & Singleton, P. (1994). Diverse voices in evaluation practice: Feminists, minorities, and persons with disabilities. *Evaluation Practice, 15*(2), 123–129.

Mertens, D. M., Foster, J., & Heimlich, J. E. (2008). M or F?: Gender, identity and the transformative research paradigm. *Museums and Social Issues, 3*(1), 81–92.

Mertens, D. M., & Ginsberg, P. E. (Eds.). (2009). *The handbook of social research ethics* (pp. 521–536). Thousand Oaks, CA: Sage.

Mertens, D. M., Holmes, H., & Harris, R. (2009). Transformative research and ethics. In D. M. Mertens & P. E. Ginsberg (Eds.), *Handbook of social research ethics* (pp. 85–102). Thousand Oaks, CA: Sage.

Mertens, D. M., Holmes, H., Harris, R., & Brandt, S. (2007). *Project SUCCESS: Summative evaluation report*. Washington, DC: Gallaudet University.

Mertens, D. M., & McLaughlin, J. (2004). *Research and evaluation methods in special education*. Thousand Oaks, CA: Corwin.

Mertle, C. A., & Vannatta, R. A. (2005). *Advanced and multivariate statistical methods* (3rd ed.). Glendale, CA: Pyrczak.

Messick, S. (1989). Meaning and values in test validation. *Education Researcher, 18*(2), 5–11.

Messick, S. (1995). Validity of psychological assessment. *American Psychologist, 50,* 741–749.

Messick, S. (1996). Validity of performance assessment. In G. Philips, (Ed.), *Technical issues in large-scale performance assessment*. Washington, DC: National Center for Educational Statistics.

Mienczakowski, J. (2000). People like us: Ethnography in the form of theatre with emancipatory intentions. In C. Truman, D. M. Mertens, & B. Humphries (Eds.), *Research and inequality* (pp. 126–142). London: Taylor & Francis.

Miles, M. B., & Huberman, A. M. (1994). *Qualitative data analysis* (2nd ed.). Thousand Oaks, CA: Sage.

Miller, R. L., & Campbell, R. (2007). Taking stock again results in the same conclusions: A reply to Fetterman and Wandersman's defense of empowerment evaluation. *American Journal of Evaluation, 28,* 579–581.

Miller, W. L., & Crabtree, B. F. (2005). Clinical research. In N. K. Denzin & Y. S. Lincoln (Eds.), *The SAGE handbook of qualitative research* (3rd ed., pp. 605–640). Thousand Oaks, CA: Sage.

Minneapolis Public Schools. (2004). *Minneapolis kindergarten assessment*. Minneapolis, MN: Minneapolis Public School Research, Evaluation & Assessment Division.

Mio, J. S., & Iwamasa, G. (1993). To do or not to do: That is the question for White cross-cultural researchers. *The Counseling Psychologist, 21*(2), 197–212.

Moewaka Barnes, H., McCreanor, T., Edwards, S., & Borell, B. (2009). Epistemological domination: Social science research ethics in Aotearoa. In D. M. Mertens & P. E. Ginsberg (Eds.), *Handbook of social research ethics* (pp. 442–457). Thousand Oaks, CA: Sage.

Moore, D., & McCabe, D. (1993). *Introduction to the practice of statistics* (2nd ed.). New York: Freeman.

Moore, D., & McCabe, D. (2003). *Introduction to the practice of statistics* (4th ed.). New York: Freeman.

Moore, M. A. (1991, April). *The place of significance testing in contemporary social sciences.* Paper presented at the annual meeting of the American Educational Research Association, Chicago. (ERIC Document Reproduction Service No. ED333036)

Morgan, D. L. (2007). Paradigms lost and pragmatism regained: Methodological implications of combining qualitative and quantitative methods. *Journal of Mixed Methods Research, 1,* 48–76.

Morgan, D. L., & Morgan, R. K. (2009). *Single-case research methods for the behavioral and health sciences.* Thousand Oaks, CA: Sage.

Morse, J. (2003). Principles of mixed- and multi-method research design. In A. Tashakkori & C. Teddlie (Eds.), *Handbook of mixed methods in social & behavioral research* (pp. 189–208). Thousand Oaks, CA: Sage.

Morse, J. M. (1994). Designing funded qualitative research. In N. K. Denzin & Y. S. Lincoln (Eds.), *Handbook of qualitative research* (pp. 220–235). Thousand Oaks, CA: Sage.

Morse, J. M. (2003). A review committee's guide for evaluating qualitative proposals. *Qualitative Health Research, 13,* 833–851.

Mosley-Howard, G. S., & Burgan, E. C. (2000). Relationships and contemporary experiences of the African American family: An ethnographic case study. *Journal of Black Studies, 30,* 428–452.

Moss, P. A. (1995). Can there be validity without reliability? *Educational Researcher, 23*(2), 5–12.

Moss, P. A. (Ed.). (2007). *Evidence and decision making.* Malden, MA: Blackwell.

Mottier, V. (2004). Pragmatism and feminist theory. *European Journal of Social Theory, 7*(3), 323–335.

Nahari, S. G., Lopez, E. C., & Esquivel, G. B. (2007). *Multicultural handbook of school psychology: An interdisciplinary perspective.* New York: Routledge.

Naples, N. A. (2003). *Feminism and method: Ethnography, discourse analysis, and activist research.* New York: Routledge.

Nardo, R. L., Custodero, L. A., Persellin, D. C., & Fox, D. B. (2006). Looking back, looking forward: A report on early childhood music education in accredited American preschools. *Journal of Research in Music Education, 54,* 278–292.

Nash, G. B. (1995, April 21). The history children should study. *The Chronicle of Higher Education,* p. A60.

National Commission for the Protection of Human Subjects of Biomedical and Behavioral Research. (1978). *The Belmont Report: Ethical principles and guidelines for the protection of human subjects of research* (DHEW Publication No. OS 78–0012). Washington, DC: Government Printing Office.

National Education Association. (2003). Response to No Child Left Behind. Letter to Secretary of Education Rod Paige,WashingtonDC: Author. December 3, 2003. http://www.eval.org/doe.nearesponse.pdf Accessed June 18, 2009.

National Research Council. (2002). *Scientific research in education.* Committee on Scientific Principles for Education Research. R. J. Shavelson & L. Towne (Eds), Center for Education. Division of Behavioral and Social Sciences and Education. Washington, DC: National Academy Press.

National Science Foundation. (2002). *User-friendly handbook for mixed-methods evaluations.* Retrieved April 13, 2004, from http://www.nsf.gov

National Survey on Drug Use and Health. (2005). *Frequently asked questions.* Retrieved November 24, 2008, from the NSDUH homepage at https://nsduhweb.rti.org/

National Task Force on Equity in Testing Deaf and Hard of Hearing Individuals. (2008). Gallaudet University. Accessed October 21, 2008, from http://gri.gallaudet.edu/TestEquity/index.html

Neuenschwander, J. A. (1993). *Oral history and the law* (Rev. ed., Pamphlet Series No. 1). Albuquerque, NM: Oral History Association.

Newborg, J., Stock, J. R., Wnek, L., Guidubaldi, J., & Svinicki, J. (1988). *Battelle Developmental Inventory.* Allen, TX: DLM.

Newman, I., Ridenour, C. S., Newman, C., & DeMarco, G. M. (2003). A typology of research purposes and its relationship to mixed methods. In A. Tashakkori & C. Teddlie (Eds.), *Handbook of mixed methods in social & behavioral research* (pp. 167–188). Thousand Oaks, CA: Sage.

Newman, L. (2008, June 10–12). Postsecondary school enrollment and experiences of youth with disabilities: A national perspective. Presentation at the Institute of Education Sciences Third Annual Research Conference, Washington, DC.

Newton, J. H. (2009). Visual reprsenation of people and information: Translating lives into numbers, words, and images as research data. In D. M. Mertens & P. E. Ginsberg (Eds.), *Handbook of social research ethics* (pp. 353–372). Thousand Oaks, CA: Sage.

No Child Left Behind Act of 2001, Pub. L. No. 107-110, Title IX, Part A, A7 9101(37). Available at http://www.harborhouselaw.com/articles/nclb.reading.research.htm

Noddings, N. (2003). *Caring: A feminine approach to ethics and moral education* (2nd ed.). Berkeley: University of California Press.

Northwest Evaluation Association. (2003). *Technical manual for the NWEA Measures of Academic Progress and Achievement Level Tests.* Portland, OR: Northwest Evaluation Association.

Norton, M. B., & Alexander, R. M. (2003). *Major problems in American women's history: Documents and essays.* Boston: D. C. Heath.

Ntseane, P. G. (2009). The ethics of the researcher-subject relationship: Experiences from the field. In D. M. Mertens & P. E. Ginsberg (Eds.), *Handbook of social research ethics* (pp. 295–307). Thousand Oaks, CA: Sage.

O'Connor, C., Lewis, A., & Mueller, J. (2007). Researching "Black" educational experiences and outcomes: Theoretical and methodological considerations. *Educational Researcher, 36,* 541–552.

Ogawa, R. T., & Malen, B. (1991). Towards rigor in reviews of multivocal literatures: Applying the exploratory case study method. *Review of Educational Research, 61*(3), 265–286.

Okie, S. (2000, November 24). Health officials debate ethics of placebo use. *The Washington Post,* p. A3.

Olesen, V. (2005). Early millennial feminist qualitative research: Challenges and contours. In N. K. Denzin & Y. S. Lincoln (Eds.), *The SAGE handbook of qualitative research* (3rd ed., pp. 235–278). Thousand Oaks, CA: Sage.

Olesen, V. L. (2000). Feminisms and qualitative research at and into the millennium. In N. K. Denzin & Y. S. Lincoln (Eds.), *Handbook of qualitative research* (2nd ed., pp. 215–256). Thousand Oaks, CA: Sage.

Oliver, M. (1992). Changing the social relations of research production? *Disability, Handicap & Society, 7*(2), 101–114.

Onwuegbuzie, A., & Teddlie, C. (2002). A framework for analyzing data in mixed methods research. In A. Tashakkori & C. Teddlie (Eds.), *Handbook of mixed methods in social and behavioral research* (pp. 351–384). Thousand Oaks, CA: Sage.

Onwuegbuzie, A. J., Jiao, Q. G., & Bostick, S. L. (2004). *Library anxiety: Theory, research, and applications.* Lanham, MD: Scarecrow Press.

Onwuegbuzie, A. J., & Johnson, R. B. (2006). The validity issue in mixed research. *Research in the Schools, 13*(1), 48–63.

Oral History Association. (2000). *Oral history evaluation guidelines.* Retrieved December 12, 2008, from http://www.oralhistory.org/network/mw/index.php/Evaluation_Guide

Oral History Association. (2008). *Oral history.* Retrieved December 12, 2008, from http://www.oralhistory.org/do-oral-history/

Oreck, B. (2004). The artistic and professional development of teachers: A study of teachers' attitudes toward and use of the arts in teaching. *Journal of Teacher Education, 55,* 55–69.

Owano, A., & Jones, C. (1995, March). *Participatory evaluation handbook: A resource for resident evaluators.* Paper presented at the Washington Evaluator's Conference, Washington, DC.

Parker, L. (2007, March). Difference, diversity, and distinctiveness in education and learning [Electronic Version]. *Review of Research in Education,* 31, xi–xv. (DOI: 10.3102/0091732X07300546)

Patton, J. M. (1993). Psychoeducational assessment of gifted and talented African Americans. In J. H. Stanfield II & R. M. Dennis (Eds.), *Race and ethnicity in research methods* (pp. 198–216). Newbury Park, CA: Sage.

Patton, M. Q. (1987). Evaluation's political inherency: Practical implications for design and use. In D. J. Palumbo (Ed.), *The politics of program theory* (pp. 100–145). Newbury Park, CA: Sage.
Patton, M. Q. (1991). Towards utility in reviews in multivocal literatures. *Review of Educational Research, 61*(3), 287–292.
Patton, M. Q. (1994). Developmental evaluation. *Evaluation Practice, 15*(3), 311–320.
Patton, M. Q. (2002). *Qualitative research & evaluation methods* (2nd ed.). Thousand Oaks, CA: Sage.
Patton, M. Q. (2008). *Utilization-focused evaluation* (4th ed.). Thousand Oaks, CA: Sage.
Pearce, C. W., Hawkins, J. W., Kearney, M., Peyton, C. E., Dwyer, J., Haggerty, L. A., et al. (2003). Translation of domestic violence instruments for use in research. *Violence Against Women, 9*(7), 859–878.
Perlmann, J., & Margo, R. (1989). Who were America's teachers? Toward a social history and a data archive. *Historical Methods, 22*(2), 68–73.
Peters, S. J. (2007). "Education for all?": A historical analysis of international inclusive education policy and individuals with disabilities. *Journal of Disability Policy Studies, 18,* 98–108.
Podems, D. (2004). *A monitoring and evaluation intervention for donor-funded NPOs in the developing world: A case study.* Unpublished doctoral dissertation, Union Institute, Cincinnati, OH.
Pollard, D. S. (1992, February). Toward a pluralistic perspective on equity. *Women's Education Equity Act Publishing Center Digest,* pp. 1–2, 7.
Ponterotto, J. G., Casas, J. M., Suzuki, L. A., & Alexander, C. M. (Eds.). (2001). *Handbook of racial/ethnic minority counseling research* (2nd ed.). Thousand Oaks, CA: Sage.
Potter, W. (2003a). American Indians seek a voice in affirmative-action debate. *The Chronicle of Higher Education.* Retrieved June 6, 2003, from http://chronicle.com/free/v49/i39/39a02201.htm
Potter, W. (2003b, June 6). Many Hispanic students live in states that already ban affirmative action. *The Chronicle of Higher Education.* Retrieved June 6, 2003, from http://chronicle.com/free/v49/i39/39a02101.htm
Preskill, H. (2008). Evaluation's second act: A spotlight on learning. *American Journal of Evaluation, 29,* 127–138.
Preskill, H., & Boyle, S. (2007, November). *Evaluation capacity building unplugged.* Think tank session presented at the American Evaluation Association annual conference, Baltimore, MD.
Preskill, H., & Coghlan, A. T. (Eds.). (2004). *Using appreciative inquiry in evaluation* (New Directions for Evaluation, No. 100). San Francisco: Jossey-Bass.
Preskill, H., & Torres, R. T. (1999). *Evaluative inquiry for learning in organizations.* Thousand Oaks, CA: Sage.
Purvis, J. (1994). Doing feminist women's history: Researching the lives of women in the Suffragette Movement in Edwardian England. In M. Maynard & J. Purvis (Eds.), *Researching women's lives from a feminist perspective* (pp. 166–189). London: Taylor & Francis.
Quenemoen, R. (2008). *A brief history of alternate assessments based on alternate achievement standards.* Minneapolis: University of Minnesota, National Center on Educational Outcomes.
Quigley, D. (2006). Perspective: A review of improved ethical practices in environmental and public health research: Case examples from native communities. *Health Education Behavior, 33,* 130–147.
Quintana, S. M., Troyano, N., & Taylor, G. (2001). Cultural validity and inherent challenges in quantitative methods for multicultural research. In J. G. Ponterotto, J. M. Casas, L. A. Suzuki, & C. M. Alexander (Eds.), *Handbook of multicultural counseling* (2nd ed., pp. 604–630). Thousand Oaks, CA: Sage.
Ramazanoglu, C., & Holland, J. (2002). *Feminist methodology.* Thousand Oaks, CA: Sage.
Reason, P. (1994). Three approaches to participative inquiry. In N. K. Denzin & Y. S. Lincoln (Eds.), *Handbook of qualitative research* (pp. 324–339). Thousand Oaks, CA: Sage.
Reason, P., & Bradbury, H. (2006). *Handbook of action research.* London: Sage.
Reichardt, C. S., & Rallis, S. F. (1994). Qualitative and quantitative inquiries are not incompatible: A call for a new partnership. In C. S. Reichardt & S. F. Rallis (Eds.), *The qualitative/quantitative debate* (New Directions for Program Evaluation, No. 61, pp. 85–91). San Francisco: Jossey-Bass.
Reinharz, S. (1992). *Feminist methods in social research.* New York: Oxford University Press.

Reinharz, S. (1994). Feminist biography: The pains, the joys, the dilemmas. In A. Lieblich & R. Josselson (Eds.), *Exploring identity and gender* (The Narrative Study of Lives, Vol. 2, pp. 37–82). Thousand Oaks, CA: Sage.

Reynolds, C. R., & Kamphaus, R. W. (Eds.). (2003). *Handbook of psychological and educational assessment of children: Intelligence, aptitude, and achievement*. New York: Guilford.

Rhett, K. (1997). *Survival stories: Memories of crisis*. Garden City, NY: Doubleday.

Richardson, L. (2000). Writing: A method of inquiry. In N. K. Denzin & Y. S. Lincoln (Eds.), *Handbook of qualitative research* (2nd ed., pp. 923–948). Thousand Oaks, CA: Sage.

Richardson L., & St. Pierre, E. A. (2005). Writing: A method of inquiry. In N. K. Denzin & Y. S. Lincoln (Eds.), *The SAGE handbook of qualitative research* (3rd ed., pp. 959–978). Thousand Oaks, CA: Sage.

Richardson, V. (Ed.). (2001). *Handbook of research on teaching*. Washington, DC: American Educational Research Association.

Riessman, C. K. (2008). *Narrative methods for the human sciences*. Thousand Oaks, CA: Sage.

Ritchie, D. (2003). *Doing oral history* (2nd ed.). Oxford, UK: Oxford University Press.

Roeber, E. (2002). *Setting standards on alternate assessments* (NCEO Synthesis Report 42). Minneapolis: University of Minnesota, National Center on Educational Outcomes. Retrieved February 2, 2009, from http://education.umn.edu/NCEO/OnlinePubs/Synthesis42.html

Roethlisberger, F. J., & Dickson, W. J. (1939). *Management and the worker*. Cambridge, MA: Harvard University Press.

Rogers, A. G., Brown, L. M., & Tappan, M. B. (1994). Interpreting loss in ego development in girls: Regression or resistance? In A. Lieblich & R. Josselson (Eds.), *Exploring identity and gender: Vol. 2. The narrative study of lives* (pp. 1–36). Thousand Oaks, CA: Sage.

Rogers, P. J., & Williams, B. (2006). Evaluation for practice improvement and organizational learning. In I. F. Shaw, J. C. Greene, & M. M. Mark (Eds.), *The SAGE handbook of evaluation* (pp. 76–97). London: Sage.

Rogers, R., Malancharuvil-Berkes, E., Mosley, M., Hui, D., & Joseph, G. O. (2005). Critical discourse analysis in education: A review of the literature. *Review of Educational Research, 75,* 365–416.

Rosenstein, B. (2000). Video use for program evaluation, a conceptual perspective. *Studies in Educational Evaluation, 26,* 373–394.

Ross, L. (1992). *Mothers behind bars: A comparative study of the experiences of imprisoned American Indian and White women*. Unpublished doctoral dissertation, University of Oregon, Eugene.

Ross, L. (1995, June). *Imprisoned Native American women and denial of culture*. Paper presented at the annual meeting of the Sociologists for Women in Society, Washington, DC.

Rossi, P. H., Freeman, H. E., & Lipsey, M. W. (2003). *Evaluation: A systematic approach* (7th ed.). Thousand Oaks, CA: Sage.

Rous, B., McCormick, K., Gooden, C., & Townley, K. F. (2007, January). Kentucky's early childhood continuous assessment and accountability system: Local decisions and state supports. *Topics in Early Childhood Special Education, 27,* 19–33.

Ruddin, L. P. (2006, August). You can generalize stupid! Social scientists, Bent Flyvbjerg, and case study methodology. *Qualitative Inquiry, 12,* 797–812.

Salvia, J., Ysseldyke, J. E., & Bolt, S. B. (2007). *Assessment in special and inclusive education* (10th ed.). Boston: Houghlin Mifflin.

Sampson, H., Bloor, M., & Fincham, B. (2008). A price worth paying? Considering the 'cost' of reflexive research methods and the influence of feminist ways of 'doing.' *Sociology, 42*(5), 919–933.

Sanday, P. R. (2008, December). Packing and unpacking gender. *Men and Masculinities, 11*(2), 206–210.

Sands, R. G., & Nuccio, K. (1992). Postmodern feminist theory and social work. *Social Work, 37*(6), 489–494.

Sansosti, F. J., & Powell-Smith, K. A. (2006, January). Using social stories to improve the social behavior of children with Asperger syndrome. *Journal of Positive Behavior Interventions, 8,* 43–57.

Sansosti, F. J., & Powell-Smith, K. A. (2008, July). Using computer-presented social stories and video models to increase the social communication skills of children with high-functioning autism spectrum disorders *Journal of Positive Behavior Interventions, 10,* 162–178.

Schirmer, B. R., & McGough, S. M. (2005). Teaching reading to children who are deaf: Do the conclusions of the National Reading Panel apply? *Review of Educational Research, 75*(1), 83–117.

Schneider, B., Scissons, H., Arney, L., Benson, G., Derry, J., Lucas, K., et al. (2004, April). Communication between people with schizophrenia and their medical professionals: A participatory research project. *Qualitative Health Research, 14*(4), 562–577.

Schochet, P. Z. (2008, March). Statistical power for random assignment in evaluations of education programs. *Journal of Educational and Behavioral Statistics, 33*(1), 62–87. (DOI: 10.3102/1076998607302714)

Schwandt, T. A. (2000). Three epistemological stances for qualitative inquiry: Interpretivism, hermeneutics, and social constructionism. In N. K. Denzin & Y. S. Lincoln (Eds.), *Handbook of qualitative research* (2nd ed., pp. 189–214). Thousand Oaks, CA: Sage.

Schwandt, T. A. (2001). A postscript on thinking about dialogue. *Evaluation, 7*(2), 264–276.

Scott-Jones, D. (1993, April). *Ethical issues in reporting and referring in research with minority and low-income populations.* Paper presented at the biennial meeting of the Society for Research in Child Development, New Orleans, LA.

Scriven, M. (1967). The methodology of evaluation. *AERA Monograph Series in Curriculum Evaluation, 1,* 39–83.

Scriven, M. (1991). *Evaluation thesaurus* (4th ed.). Newbury Park, CA: Sage.

Scriven, M. (2003). Evaluation in the new millennium: The transdisciplinary vision. In S. I. Donaldson & M. Scriven (Eds.), *Evaluating social programs and problems* (pp. 19–42). Mahwah, NJ: Lawrence Erlbaum.

Scriven, M. (2005). Empowerment evaluation principles in practice. *American Journal of Evaluation, 26,* 415–417.

Scriven, M. (2009, January 6). *Merit of the evaluand.* Message posted to EvalTalk, the American Evaluation Association discussion list, available at http://www.aime.ua.edu/archives/evaltalk.html

Seelman, K. D. (2000). *The new paradigm on disability: Research issues and approaches.* Washington, DC: National Institute for Disability and Rehabilitative Research.

Seigart, D., & Brisolara, S. (Eds.). (2002). *Feminist evaluation: Explorations and experiences* (New Directions for Evaluation, No. 96). San Francisco: Jossey-Bass.

Seligman, M. E. P., & Csikszentmihalyi, M. (2000). Positive psychology: An introduction. *American Psychologist, 55,* 5–14.

Sessions, J. T., & Yanos, J. H. (1987, November). *Desirable characteristics of a counseling agency.* Paper presented at the annual meeting of the American Evaluation Association, Boston.

Shadish, W. R. (1994). Need-based evaluation: Good evaluation and what you need to know about it. *Evaluation Practice, 15*(3), 347–358.

Shadish, W. R., Cook, T. D., & Campbell, D. T. (2002). *Experimental and quasi-experimental designs for generalized causal inference.* New York: Houghton Mifflin.

Shadish, W. R., Jr., Cook, T. D., & Leviton, L. C. (1991). *Foundations of program evaluation.* Newbury Park, CA: Sage.

Shakeshaft, C., Campbell, P., & Karp, K. (1992). Sexism and racism in educational research. In M. C. Alkin (Ed.), *Encyclopedia of educational research* (6th ed., Vol. 4, pp. 1210–1216). New York: Macmillan.

Shaver, J. P. (1992, April). *What statistical significance testing is, and what it is not.* Paper presented at the annual meeting of the American Educational Research Association, San Francisco.

Shaw, I. F., Greene, J. C., & Mark, M. M. (Eds.). (2006). *The SAGE handbook of evaluation.* Thousand Oaks, CA: Sage.

Sherman, P. R. (1993). What do you want to be when you grow up? The ideology of vocational choice. In F. Pignatelli & S. W. Pflaum (Eds.), *Celebrating diverse voices* (pp. 197–220). Thousand Oaks, CA: Corwin.

Shih, T.-H., & Fan, X. (2008, August). Comparing response rates from Web and mail surveys: A meta-analysis. *Field Methods, 20*(3), 249–271.

Shipman, S., MacColl, G. S., Vaurio, E., & Chennareddy, V. (1995). *Program evaluation: Improving the flow of information to the Congress* (Report to the ranking minority members, Committee on Labor and Human Resources, U. S. Senate). Washington, DC: U.S. General Accounting Office.

Sicherman, B., & Green, C. H. (1980). *Notable American women: The modern period.* Cambridge, MA: Harvard University Press.

Sieber, J. E. (1992). *Planning ethically responsible research.* Newbury Park, CA: Sage.

Sieber, J. E. (1998). *Understanding the perspective or culture of research subjects and other stakeholders.* Hayward: California State University.

Sielbeck-Bowen, K. A., Brisolara, A., Seigart, D., Tischler, C., & Whitmore, E. (2002). Exploring feminist evaluation: The ground from which we rise. In D. Seigart & S. Brisolara (Eds.), *Feminist evaluation: Explorations and experiences* (New Directions for Evaluation, No. 96, pp. 3–8). San Francisco: Jossey-Bass.

Sireci, S. G. (2007). On validity theory and test validation. *Educational Researcher 36,* 477–481.

Sirotnik, K. A., & Oakes, J. (1990). Evaluation as critical inquiry: School improvement as a case in point. In K. A. Sirotnik (Ed.), *Evaluation and social justice* (New Directions for Evaluation, No. 45, pp. 37–60). San Francisco: Jossey-Bass.

Slavin, R. E. (2002). Evidence-based education policies: Transforming educational practice and research. *Educational Researchers, 31*(7), 15–22.

Smalls, C., White, R., Chavous, T., & Sellers, R. (2007). Racial ideological beliefs and racial discrimination experiences as predictors of academic engagement among African American adolescents. *Journal of Black Psychology, 33*(3), 299–330.

Smedley, A. (2007, March 14–17). The history of the idea of race ... and why it matters. Paper presented at the conference, Race, Human Variation and Disease: Consensus and Frontiers, American Anthropological Association (AAA) and Ford Foundation, Warrenton, VA. Retrieved October 30, 2008, from http://www.understandingrace.org/resources/papers_activity.html

Smith, D. E. (1987). *The everyday world as problematic.* Boston: Northeastern University Press.

Smith, L. T. (2005). On tricky ground: Researching the native in the age of uncertainty. In N. K. Denzin & Y. S. Lincoln (Eds.), *The SAGE handbook of qualitative research* (3rd ed., pp. 85–108). Thousand Oaks, CA: Sage.

Smith, M. (1994). Enhancing the quality of survey data on violence against women: A feminist approach. *Gender & Society, 8*(1), 109–127.

Smith, N. L. (2007). Empowerment evaluation as evaluation ideology. *American Journal of Evaluation, 28*(2), 169–178.

Smolin, L., Lawless, K., & Burbules, N. C. (Eds.). (2007). *Information and communication technologies: Considerations of current practice for teachers and teacher educators.* Malden, MA: Blackwell.

Solomon, P. G. (2002). *The assessment bridge: Positive ways to link tests to learning, standards, and curriculum improvement.* Thousand Oaks, CA: Corwin.

Solórzano, R. W. (2008). High stakes testing: Issues, implications, and remedies for English Language Learners. *Review of Educational Research, 78,* 260–329.

Southeast Kansas Education Service Center. (2008). *Fairfax County youth survey.* Girard, KS: Author.

Sparkes, A. C. (2001, July). Qualitative health researchers will agree about validity. *Qualitative Health Research, 11,* 538–552.

Spry, T. (2007, July). *Peforming autoethnography.* Paper presented at the Mixed Methods Conference, Homerton School of Health Sciences, Cambridge, UK.

Spybrook, J., Raudenbush, S. W., Liu, X. F., Congdon, R., & Martinez, A. (2008). Optimal design for longitudinal and multi-level research: Documentation for the "Optimal Design" software. Ann Arbor: University of Michigan.

Stake, R. E. (1983). The case study method in social inquiry. In G. F. Madaus, M. Scriven, & D. L. Stufflebeam (Eds.), *Evaluation models* (pp. 279–286). Boston: Kluwer-Nijhoff.

Stake, R. E. (2000). Case studies. In N. K. Denzin & Y. S. Lincoln (Eds.), *Handbook of qualitative research* (2nd ed., pp. 435–454). Thousand Oaks, CA: Sage.

Stake, R. E. (2004). *Standards-based & responsive evaluation.* Thousand Oaks, CA: Sage.

Stake, R. E. (2005). Qualitative case studies. In N. K. Denzin & Y. S. Lincoln (Eds.), *The SAGE handbook of qualitative research* (3rd ed., pp. 443–466). Thousand Oaks, CA: Sage.

Stake, R. E. (2006). *Multiple case study analysis.* New York: Guilford.

Stake, R., & Rizvi, F. (2009). Research ethics in transnational spaces. In D. M. Mertens & P. E. Ginsberg (Eds.), *The handbook of social research ethics* (pp. 521–536). Thousand Oaks, CA: Sage.

Stanfield, J. H., II. (1993a). Epistemological considerations. In J. H. Stanfield II & R. M. Dennis (Eds.), *Race and ethnicity in research methods* (pp. 16–36). Newbury Park, CA: Sage.

Stanfield, J. H., II. (1993b). In the archives. In J. H. Stanfield II & R. M. Dennis (Eds.), *Race and ethnicity in research methods* (pp. 273–283). Newbury Park, CA: Sage.

Stanfield, J. H., II. (1994). Ethnic modeling in qualitative research. In N. K. Denzin & Y. S. Lincoln (Eds.), *Handbook of qualitative research* (pp. 175–188). Thousand Oaks, CA: Sage.

Stanfield, J. H., II. (1999). Slipping through the front door: Relevant social scientific evaluation in the people-of-color century. *American Journal of Evaluation, 20,* 415–432.

Stanfield, J. H., II. (2006). The possible restorative justice functions of qualitative research. *International Journal of Qualitative Studies in Education, 19*(6), 723–727.

Stanfield, J. H., II, & Dennis, R. M. (Eds.). (1993). *Race and ethnicity in research methods.* Newbury Park, CA: Sage.

Starks, H., & Trinidad, S. B. (2007). Choose your method: A comparison of phenomenology, discourse analysis, and grounded theory. *Qualitative Health Research, 17,* 1372–1380.

Steady, F. C. (1993). Women and collective action. In S. M. James & A. P. A. Busia (Eds.), *Theorizing black feminisms* (pp. 90–101). London: Routledge.

Stearns, P. N., Seixas, P., & Wineburg, S. (Eds.). (2000). *Knowing, teaching, and learning history: National and international perspectives.* New York: New York University Press.

Steinbugler, A. C., Press, J. E., & Dias, J. J. (2006). Gender, race, and affirmative action: Operationalizing intersectionality in survey research. *Gender & Society, 20,* 805–825.

Stern, M. J. (2008). The use of client-side paradata in analyzing the effects of visual layout on changing responses in Web surveys. *Field Methods, 20,* 377–398.

Sternberg, R. (2008). Applying psychological theories to educational practice. *American Educational Research Journal, 45,* 150–165.

Stevens, J. P. (2002). *Applied multivariate statistics for the social sciences* (4th ed.). Hillsdale, NJ: Lawrence Erlbaum.

Stewart, K. (2005). Cultural poesis: The generativity of emergent things. In N. K. Denzin & Y. S. Lincoln (Eds.), *The SAGE handbook of qualitative research* (3rd ed., pp. 1027–1042). Thousand Oaks, CA: Sage.

Stix, A. (1997). *Creating rubrics through negotiable contracting and assessment.* Washington, DC: U.S. Department of Education. (ERIC Document Reproduction Service No. TM027246)

Stockdill, S. H., Duhon-Sells, R. M., Olsen, R. A., & Patton, M. Q. (1992). Voices in the design and evaluation of a multicultural education program: A developmental approach. In A. M. Madison (Ed.), *Minority issues in program evaluation* (New Directions for Program Evaluation, No. 53, pp. 17–34). San Francisco: Jossey-Bass.

Storey, K., & Horner, R. H. (1991). An evaluative review of social validation research involving persons with handicaps. *Journal of Special Education, 25*(3), 352–401.

St. Pierre, E. (2000). Poststructural feminism in education: An overview. *International Journal of Qualitative Studies in Education, 13*(5): 477–515.

St. Pierre, E. (2002). Comment: "Science" rejects postmodernism. *Educational Researcher, 31*(8), 25–27.

St. Pierre, E. A. (2006). Scientifically based research in education: Epistemology and ethics. *Adult Education Quarterly, 56*(4), 239–266.

Strauss, A., & Corbin, J. (1994). Grounded theory methodology: An overview. In N. K. Denzin & Y. S. Lincoln (Eds.), *Handbook of qualitative research* (pp. 273–285). Thousand Oaks, CA: Sage.

Stronge, J. H., & Tucker, P. D. (Eds.). (2003). *Handbook on teacher evaluation: Assessing and improving performance*. Larchmont, NY: Eye on Education.

Stufflebeam, D. L. (1983). The CIPP model for program evaluation. In G. F. Madaus, M. Scriven, & D. L. Stufflebeam (Eds.), *Evaluation models* (pp. 117–142). Boston: Kluwer-Nijhoff.

Stufflebeam, D. L., Madaus, G. F., & Kellaghan, T. (2000). *Evaluation models: Viewpoints on educational and human services evaluation*. Boston: Kluwer.

Stufflebeam, D. L., & Shinkfield, A. J. (2007). *Evaluation theory, models, and applications*. San Francisco: Jossey-Bass.

Sue, S. (1999). Science, ethnicity, and bias: Where have we gone wrong? *American Psychologist, 54,* 1070–1077.

Sullivan, M. (2009). Philosophy, ethics and the disability community. In D. M. Mertens & P. E. Ginsberg (Eds.), *The handbook of social research ethics* (pp. 69–84). Thousand Oaks, CA: Sage.

Sullivan, P. M. (1992). The effects of psychotherapy on behavior problems of sexually abused deaf children. *Child Abuse and Neglect: The International Journal, 16*(2), 297–307.

Sulzer-Azaroff, B., Fleming, R., Tupa, M., Bass, R., & Hamad, C. (2008). Choosing objectives for a distance learning behavioral intervention in autism curriculum. *Focus on Autism and Other Developmental Disabilities, 23,* 29–36.

Suzuki, L. A., & Kugler, J. F. (1995). Intelligence and personality assessment: Multicultural perspectives. In J. G. Ponterotto, J. M. Casas, L. A. Suzuki, & C. M. Alexander (Eds.), *Handbook of multicultural counseling* (pp. 493–515). Thousand Oaks, CA: Sage.

Szala-Meneok, K. (2009). Ethical research with older adults. In D. M. Mertens & P. E. Ginsberg (Eds.), *Handbook of social research ethics* (pp. 507–518). Thousand Oaks, CA: Sage.

Szarkowski, A. (2002). *Positive aspects of parenting a deaf child.* Unpublished doctoral dissertation, Gallaudet University, Washington, DC.

Tashakkori, A., & Creswell, J. W. (2007). Editorial: The new era of mixed methods. *Journal of Mixed Methods Research, 1,* 3–7.

Tashakkori, A., & Teddlie, C. (1998). *Mixed methodology*. Thousand Oaks, CA: Sage.

Tashakkori, A., & Teddlie, C. (Eds.). (2003). *Handbook of mixed methods in social & behavioral research*. Thousand Oaks, CA: Sage.

Tate, W. F. (1997). Critical race theory and education: History, theory, and implications. In M. W. Apple (Ed.), *Review of research in education* (Vol. 22, pp. 191–243). Washington, DC: American Educational Research Association.

Taylor, J. (2008). The problem of women's sociality in contemporary North American feminist memoir. *Gender & Society, 22,* 705–727.

Teddlie, C., & Tashakkori, A. (2003). Major issues and controversies in the use of mixed methods in the social and behavioral sciences. In A. Tashakkori & C. Teddlie (Eds.), *Handbook of mixed methods in social & behavioral research* (pp. 3–50). Thousand Oaks, CA: Sage.

Teddlie, C., & Tashakkori, A. (2009). *Foundations of mixed methods research*. Thousand Oaks, CA: Sage.

Teddlie, C., & Yu, F. (2007). Mixed methods sampling: A typology with examples. *Journal of Mixed Methods Research, 1,* 77–100.

Tedlock, B. (2005). The observation of participation and the emergence of public ethnography. In N. K. Denzin & Y. S. Lincoln (Eds.), *The SAGE handbook of qualitative research* (3rd ed., pp. 467–482). Thousand Oaks, CA: Sage.

Temple, B., & Young, A. (2004). Qualitative research and translation dilemmas. *Qualitative Research, 4*(2), 161–178.

Thomas, V. G. (2004). Building a contextually responsive evaluation framework: Lessons from working with urban school interventions. In V. G. Thomas & F. I. Stevens (Eds.), *Co-constructing a contextually responsive evaluation framework: The talent development model of reform* (New Directions for Evaluation, No. 101, pp. 3–24). San Francisco: Jossey-Bass.

Thomas, V. G., & Stevens, F. I. (Eds.). (2004). *Co-constructing a contextually responsive evaluation framework: The talent development model of reform* (New Directions for Evaluation, No. 101). San Francisco: Jossey-Bass.

Thompson, B. (1988, January). *Common methodology mistakes in dissertations: Improving dissertation quality*. Paper presented at the annual meeting of the Mid-South Education Research Association, Louisville, KY.

Thompson, B. (2002a). "Statistical," "practical," and "clinical": How many kinds of significance do counselors need to consider? *Journal of Counseling and Development, 80,* 64–71.

Thompson, B. (2002b). What future quantitative social science research could look like: Confidence intervals for effect size. *Educational Researcher, 31*(3), 25–32.

Thompson, B. (2003). *Score reliability: Contemporary thinking on reliability issues*. Thousand Oaks, CA: Sage.

Thompson, B. (2007). Computing and interpreting effect sizes, confidence intervals, and confidence intervals for effect sizes. In J. Osborne (Ed.), *Best practices in quantitative methods*. Thousand Oaks, CA: Sage.

Thompson, S., Blount, A., & Thurlow, M. L. (2002). *A summary of research on the effects of test accommodations: 1999–2001* (Technical Report 34). Minneapolis: University of Minnesota, National Center on Educational Outcomes.

Thompson, S. J., Johnstone, C. J., & Thurlow, M. L. (2002). Universal design applied to large scale assessments (NCEO Synthesis Report 44). Minneapolis: University of Minnesota, National Center on Educational Outcomes.

Thompson, S. J., Quenemoen, R. F., Thurlow, M. L., & Ysseldyke, J. E. (2001). *Alternate assessments for students with disabilities*. Thousand Oaks, CA: Corwin.

Thompson-Robinson, M., Hopson, R., & SenGupta, S. (Eds.). (2004). *In search of cultural competence in evaluation: Toward principles and practice* (New Directions for Evaluation, No. 102). San Francisco: Jossey-Bass.

Thurlow, M., Quenemoen, R., Altman, J., & Cuthbert, M. (2008). *Trends in the participation and performance of students with disabilities* (Technical Report 50). Minneapolis: University of Minnesota, National Center on Educational Outcomes.

Thurlow, M. L., Ysseldyke, J. E., & Silverstein, B. (1993). *Testing accommodations for students with disabilities*. Minneapolis: University of Minnesota, National Center on Educational Outcomes.

Tierney, W. G. (2000). Undaunted courage: Life history and the postmodern challenge. In N. K. Denzin & Y. S. Lincoln (Eds.), *Handbook of qualitative research* (2nd ed., pp. 537–553). Thousand Oaks, CA: Sage.

Tillman, L. C. (2006). Researching and writing from an African-American perspective: Reflective notes on three research studies. *International Journal of Qualitative Studies in Education, 19*(3), 265–287.

Torres Campos, C. M. (2008, April). *Promoting academic success among ethnically-diverse adolescents: Longitudinal research on the role of mentors and social support*. Paper presented at the annual conference of the Society for Research in Child Development, Denver, CO.

Tosh, J. (2002). *The pursuit of history* (3rd ed.). New York: Longman.

Trenholm, C., Devaney, B., Fortson, K., Quay, L., Wheeler, J., & Clark, M. (2007). *Impacts of four abstinence education programs*. Princeton, NJ: Mathematica Policy Research Institute. Retrieved February 2, 2009, from http://www.mathematica-mpr.com/abstinencereport.asp.

Trochim, W. M. (2006). The research methods knowledge base (2nd ed.). Ithaca, NY: Author. Retrieved April 30, 2009 from http://www.socialresearchmethods.net/kb/.

Tuchman, B. W. (1978). *A distant mirror: The calamitous 14th century*. New York: Knopf.

Tuchman, G. (1994). Historical social science: Methodologies, methods, and meanings. In N. K. Denzin & Y. S. Lincoln (Eds.), *Handbook of qualitative research* (pp. 306–323). Thousand Oaks, CA: Sage.

Turabian, K. L. (1996). *A manual for writers of term papers, theses, and dissertations* (6th ed.). Chicago: University of Chicago Press.

Turque, B. (2008, Novermber 9). Overhauling D.C. school overcome by violence. *The Washington Post,* p. C01.

Unger, R. K. (1979) Toward a redefinition of sex and gender. *American Psychologist, 34,* 1085–1094.

United Nations Development Programme. (1997). *Who are the question-makers? A participatory evaluation handbook.* OESP Handbook Series. New York: Office of Evaluation and Strategic Planning. Retrieved January 12, 2003, from http://www.undp.org/eo/documents/who.htm

United Nations Development Programme. (2002). *Handbook on monitoring and evaluating for results.* New York: Author.

Urdan, T. C. (2005). *Statistics in plain English* (2nd ed.). Mahwah, NJ: Lawrence Erlbaum.

U.S. Census Bureau. (2001). *Census 2000 shows America's diversity.* Washington, DC: Author. CB01-CN.61.

U.S. Department of Education. (2003). *Identifying and implementing educational practices supported by rigorous evidence: A user friendly guide.* Available at http://www.ed.gov/rschstat/research/pubs/rigorousevid/index.html

U.S. Department of Education, Office of Special Education and Rehabilitative Services. (2002). *A new era: Revitalizing special education for children and their families.* Washington, DC: Author.

U.S. Department of Health and Human Services. (2007). Categories of research that may be reviewed by the institutional review board (IRB). Available online from http://www.hhs.gov/ohrp/humansubjects/guidance/expedited98.htm

VanDerHeyden, A. M., Witt, J. C., & Barnett, D. W. (2005). The emergence and possible futures of response to intervention. *Journal of Psychoeducational Assessment, 23,* 339–361.

Vargas, L. A., & Montoya, M. E. (2009). Involving minors in research: Ethics and law within multicultural settings. In D. M. Mertens & P. E. Ginsberg (Eds.), *Handbook of social research ethics* (pp. 489–506). Thousand Oaks, CA: Sage.

Villegas, A. M. (1991). *Culturally responsive pedagogy for the 1990s and beyond.* Princeton, NJ: Educational Testing Service.

Voithofer, R. (2005, December). Designing new media education research: The materiality of data, representation, and dissemination. *Educational Researcher, 34,* 3–14.

Wagner, M., Newman, L., Cameto, R., Levine, P., & Marder, C. (2007). *Perceptions and expectations of youth with disabilities: A special topic report from the National Longitudinal Transition Study-2 (NLTS2).* (NCSER 2007–3006). Menlo Park, CA: SRI International.

Wallerstein, N., & Martinez, L. (1994). Empowerment evaluation: A case study of an adolescent substance abuse prevention program in New Mexico. *Evaluation Practice, 15*(2), 131–138.

Waloszek, G. (2007). *Universal design.* Retrieved April 25, 2009, from the Center for Universal Design at http://www.design.ncsu.edu/cud/.

Wandersman, A., Snell-Johns, J., Lentz, B., Fetterman, D., Keener, D. C., Livet, M., et al. (2005). The principles of empowerment evaluation. In D. M. Fetterman & A. Wandersman (Eds.), *Empowerment evaluation principles in practice* (pp. 27–41). New York: Guilford.

Wang, S., Jiao, H., Young, M. J., Brooks, T., & Olson, J. (2008, February). Comparability of computer-based and paper-and-pencil testing in K–12 reading assessments: A meta-analysis of testing mode effects. *Educational and Psychological Measurement, 68,* 5–24.

Ward, K. J. (2002). Reflections on a job done: Well? In D. Seigart & S. Brisolara (Eds.), *Feminist evaluation: Explorations and experiences* (pp. 41–56). San Francisco: Jossey-Bass.

Warren, C. A. B. (1988). *Gender issues in field research.* Newbury Park, CA: Sage.

Watkins, J. M., & Mohr, B. J. (2001). *Appreciative inquiry.* San Francisco: Jossey-Bass.

Webb, N. L., Alt, M., Ely, R., Cormier, M., & Vesperman, B. (2005). *The WEB alignment tool: Development, refinement, and dissemination.* Washington, DC: Council of Chief State School Officers.

Weiss, C. H. (1987). Where politics and evaluation research meet. In D. J. Palumbo (Ed.), *The politics of program evaluation* (pp. 47–70). Newbury Park, CA: Sage.

Whitmore, E. (1996). *Ideology in evaluation.* Unpublished manuscript.

Whitmore, E. (Ed.). (1998). *Understanding and practicing participatory evaluation* (New Directions for Evaluation, No. 80). San Francisco: Jossey-Bass.

Whittemore, R., Chase, S. K., & Mandle, C. L. (2001). Validity in qualitative research. *Qualitative Health Research, 11,* 522–537.

Wilkerson, J. R., & Lang, W. S. (2007). *Assessing teacher dispositions.* Thousand Oaks, CA: Corwin.

Wilkinson, L., & American Psychological Association Task Force on Statistical Inference. (1999). Statistical methods in psychology journals: Guidelines and explanations. *American Psychologist, 54,* 594–604.

Williamson, C. E. (2002). Transition of deaf and hard of hearing adolescents to four-year post secondary programs. Unpublished doctoral dissertation, Gallaudet University, Washington, DC.

Wilson, A. T. (2001). Development assistance from American organizations to deaf communities in the developing world: A qualitative study in Jamaica. Unpublished doctoral dissertation, Gallaudet University, Washington, DC.

Wilson, R. (2003, May 16). When should a scholar's notes be confidential? *The Chronicle of Higher Education.* Retrieved May 16, 2003, from http://chronicle.com/weekly/v49/i36/36a01001.htm

Witte, K., & Morrison, K. (1995). Intercultural and cross-cultural health communication: Understanding people and motivating healthy behaviors. In R. L. Wiseman (Ed.), *Intercultural communication theory* (pp. 216–246). Thousand Oaks, CA: Sage.

Wittrock, M. C. (1986). Students' thought processes. In M. C. Wittrock (Ed.), *Handbook of research on teaching* (pp. 297–314). New York: Macmillan.

Wnek, A. C., Klein, G., & Bracken, B. A. (2008). Professional development issues for school psychologists: What's hot and what's not in the United States. *School Psychology International, 29,* 145–160.

Wolcott, H. F. (1994). *Transforming qualitative data.* Thousand Oaks, CA: Sage.

Wolcott, H. F. (2001). *Writing up qualitative research* (2nd ed.). Thousand Oaks, CA: Sage.

Wolf, M. (1992). *A thrice-told tale: Feminism, postmodernism, and ethnographic responsibility.* Stanford, CA: Stanford University Press.

Wolf, M. K., Herman, J. L., Kim, J., Abedi, J., Leon, S., Griffin, N., et al. (2008). *Providing validity evidence to improve the assessment of English Language Learners.* Los Angeles: National Center for Research on Evaluation, Standards, and Student Testing.

Wolgemuth, J. R., & Donohue, R. (2006). Toward an inquiry of discomfort: Guiding transformation in "emancipatory" narrative research. *Qualitative Inquiry, 12,* 1012–1039.

Wood, S. J., Murdock, J. Y., & Cronin, M. E. (2002). Self-monitoring and at-risk middle school students. *Behavior Modification, 26*(5), 605–626.

World Bank Group. (1996). *Data collection methods.* Retrieved April 25, 2009, from http://www.worldbank.org/poverty/impact/methods/datacoll.htm

Wright, R. J. (2007). *Educational assessment.* Thousand Oaks, CA: Sage.

Wu, A. W. (2000). Quality-of-life assessment in clinical research: Application in diverse populations. *Medical Care, 38,* II130–II135.

Yancey, A. K., Jordan, A., Bradford, J., Voas, J., Eller, T. J., Buzzard, M., et al. (2003, April). Engaging high-risk populations in community-level fitness promotion: ROCK! *Richmond Health Promotion Practice, 4*(2), 180–188.

Yin, R. K. (2003). *Case study research: Design and methods* (3rd ed.). Thousand Oaks, CA: Sage.

Yin, R. K. (2009). *Case study research: Designs and methods* (4th ed.). Thousand Oaks, CA: Sage.

Youm, H.-K. (2007). Processes used by music, visual arts, media, and first-grade classroom teachers for developing and implementing an integrated curriculum: A case study. *Update: Applications of Research in Music Education, 26,* 41–52.

Yow, V. R. (1994). *Recording oral history: A practical guide for social scientists.* Thousand Oaks, CA: Sage.

Yow, V. R. (2005). *Recording oral history: A guide for the humanities and social sciences* (2nd ed.). Walnut Creek, CA: AltaMira Press.

Zebian, S., Alamuddin, R., Maalouf, M., & Chatila, Y. (2007). Developing an appropriate psychology through culturally sensitive research practices in the Arabic-speaking world: A content analysis of psychological research published between 1950 and 2004. *Journal of Cross-Cultural Psychology, 38,* 91–122.

Zhang, D., & Katsiyannis, A. (2002). Minority representation in special education: A persistent challenge. *Remedial and Special Education, 23,* 180–187.

Ziliak, S. T., & McCloskey, D. N. (2007). *The cult of statistical significance: How the standard error costs us jobs, justice, and lives.* Ann Arbor: University of Michigan Press.

Zurbriggen, E. L., & Sherman, A. M. (2007). Reconsidering 'sex' and 'gender': Two steps forward, one step back. *Feminism & Psychology, 17*(4), 475–480.

Author Index

Subject Index